GENUINE MULTICULTURALISM

Genuine Multiculturalism

The Tragedy and Comedy of Diversity

CECIL FOSTER

McGill-Queen's University Press
Montreal & Kingston · London · Ithaca

131847

© McGill-Queen's University Press 2014

ISBN 978-0-7735-4255-6 (cloth)
ISBN 978-0-7735-4256-3 (paper)
ISBN 978-0-7735-8943-8 (ePDF)
ISBN 978-0-7735-8944-5 (ePUB)

Legal deposit first quarter 2014
Bibliothèque nationale du Québec

Printed in Canada on acid-free paper that is 100% ancient forest free
(100% post-consumer recycled), processed chlorine free

This book has been published with the help of a grant from the Canadian
Federation for the Humanities and Social Sciences, through the Awards to
Scholarly Publications Program, using funds provided by the Social Sciences
and Humanities Research Council of Canada.

McGill-Queen's University Press acknowledges the support of the Canada
Council for the Arts for our publishing program. We also acknowledge the
financial support of the Government of Canada through the Canada Book
Fund for our publishing activities.

Library and Archives Canada Cataloguing in Publication

Foster, Cecil, 1954–, author
Genuine multiculturalism: the tragedy and comedy of diversity / Cecil
Foster.

Includes bibliographical references and index.
Issued in print and electronic formats.
ISBN 978-0-7735-4255-6 (bound). – ISBN 978-0-7735-4256-3 (pbk.). –
ISBN 978-0-7735-8943-8 (ePDF). – ISBN 978-0-7735-8944-5 (ePUB)

1. Multiculturalism – Canada. I. Title.

FC105.M8F68 2013   305.800971   C2013-906752-3
                                                C2013-906753-1

This book was typeset by Interscript in 10.5/13 Sabon.

Contents

Preface   ix

Introduction: The Tragedy of Living, the Comedy of Trying   3

PART ONE   NATURAL DIFFERENCES AND SOCIAL EQUALITY

1   Genuine Multiculturalism   49
2   Dramatis personae   64

PART TWO   PRACTICES AGAINST SOCIAL DIVERSITY

3   A Hegelian – Christian Model   97
4   Multiculturalism in the Americas   133
5   Canada's Second Covenant: The Charter of Rights   170
6   When Tragedy Becomes Comedy   192
7   The Legacy of the US Civil War   217
8   Canada: Forging a Single Consciousness   237
9   Citizenship with Difference: The CBC and I   258
10   Crisis 2001: Not Enough People!   277
11   Massey and Culture: From Bi to Multi   299

PART THREE   ACCEPTING DIVERSITY, PROMOTING
SOCIAL EQUALITY

12   Tyranny v. Freedom: Strauss v. Kojève   329
13   Rawls and Trudeau's Just Society   357
14   Rethinking the CBC and Me: From Tragedy to Comedy   373
15   Tragedy: The Comedic Folk Saviour   398

Notes   435
Index   479

Preface

APPROACH OF THE STUDY

I set up this study as a search for social justice in Western societies now grappling with diversity in multiple forms. The task is how to produce initially a mechanical sense of sameness in the face of countless differences in the ways citizens of the modern state are *naturally* human and social beings. At the end of the process should be a transformation that is a reconciliation, rather than the wiping out, of these differences: of moving from a mechanistic solidarity to a fraternity of thick relationships that might even be considered as organic and as on a par with those perceived as harmonious in any discussion about the natural folk, their land, and their state. This is analogous to starting life as a tragedy and moving to a comedy, where ideally everyone receives what she or he knows that he or she deserves in life. Or at least they agree to act as if there is justice. The primary site for this examination is Canada: the so-called first postmodern nation-state but also the first country to declare itself officially multicultural. The implicit meaning is that Canada wants to emphasize the multiple differences that make up the Canadian identity and way of life. What then are this Canadian identity and way of life? Why – they are still evolving. Canada as a final stage for the acting out of what people agree on as socially just is still under construction, the final act in this drama not yet complete. The alternative to this inventiveness on the fly, which Canada has obviously rejected, has been to search historically for a single conformist model that assimilates all differences into a single identity or a peculiar set of cultural practices that a few impose on the many. For too many people, such an existence has been merely tragic. Historically, such a model led the search for social justice into a dead end and despair resulting from realizing that even the way back is not an option.

With this approach I am hoping to make an important intervention in a generations-old argument on whose voice matters in debating what Canada is, what Canada as a whole or in parts is good for, what its future should be, and, very important, which folks are deciding on that future. Currently, observers often present this discussion as either a debate on power relations between two nationalisms that have long dominated Canada, namely the French and the English, about how any domination should continue or ease between the two groups, or a very separate debate on justice for the aboriginal/indigenous people of the part of Turtle Island now called "Canada." I am offering an intervention for another group – those whom Canada routinely calls "immigrants," even when they are full citizens but who are not aboriginal, even if for some of them there is little or no difference in the low social statuses they share with indigenous Canadians. Yet they are citizens; unlike the First Nations, they come from elsewhere and applied for and received supposedly full membership in the existing state, which now claims them as citizens.

Yet they retain the ascribed identity of immigrant as Canadian sociologist Peter Li suggests in *Destination Canada: Immigration Debates and Issues*, primarily because they are not of European ethnicities and racialized as white, and they are not indigenous.[1] This is a group fast achieving "numbers that matter." According to Statistics Canada in 2006, "the proportion of Canada's population who were born outside the country reached its highest level in 75 years. The census enumerated 6,186,950 foreign-born in Canada in 2006. They represented virtually one in five (19.8%) of the total population, the highest proportion since 1931."[2] This says nothing of the offspring of those whom Canada still identifies as immigrant or as visible minorities, the term I use most in this volume.

Continuation of current immigration patterns, along with the aging of the Canadian-born population, suggests this group will keep increasing its share of the citizenry. It will continue to shape Canada. Indeed, its voting federalist in the second Quebec referendum on sovereignty in 1995 saved Confederation by the slimmest of majorities – 50.58 per cent no to 49.42 per cent yes. Its support remains essential for any reformulations that will take place in Quebec or Canada as a whole.

With this intervention, I argue that the indigenous/aboriginal peoples and those stigmatized as new Canadians or immigrants are ultimately the groups that will drive Canada towards becoming a just society. I see this achievement as the rationalization of a genuine multiculturalism deriving ultimately from the demise of the dominant nationalisms of French and English as the purported essences of an exclusively ethnoracially white mainstream of Canadian life. Canada must transcend the state or states that some in Quebec challenge to become its own independent state and become more inclusive. It is the two traditional ethnic nationalisms that have confronted each other for dominance and even exclusivity because they see themselves as founding peoples of Canada and/or Quebec, which in fact must die in their historic forms.[3] They should transfigure themselves into just another particular way of life in a diverse Canada (or even multi-ethnic Quebec) for genuine multiculturalism as social justice and civic liberalism to occur. Any alternative with exclusive ethnoracial nationalism would not be democratic and, hence, would not be socially just. Any retreat would be back to the beginning, to issues of natural justice that only the indigenous peoples of the Americas could justifiably determine. This would mean applying their rules of social justice, which were in place before what we now call "contact" led to Europeans' supplanting existing societies with their own and then trying to discover how to make these newer systems that we now inhabit socially just.

STRUCTURE OF THE BOOK

I lay out my case in three parts; each discusses both the theory of the ideals of multicultural and the living experience that is Canada: part I: Natural Differences and Social Equality, part II: Practices against Social Diversity, and part III: Accepting Diversity, Promoting Social Equality.

Part I consists of two chapters. Chapter 1 lays out the mythology on which genuine multiculturalism rests, as a quest for freedom and social justice, which we may as youngsters absorb in the form of fairy tales and stories of good and evil and of how good eventually will triumph and lead the way to social justice for all the people. These accounts present ideals of who is good and who is evil and of the types of characters that would make good citizens. We receive from them the archetypes of Bad John, Cinderella, Prince Charming, Snow White, Sleeping Beauty, and other ideal types in a society that challenges them and forces them to struggle, so that in the end they may "live happily ever after." Significant to these tales is the enduring notion that the state, as a producer as well as the collective of the people, is female and seemingly always virginal, like Snow White, and without agency, like Sleeping Beauty.

But the giver of life to the state, ironically – the real god – has traditionally, in Judaeo-Christian mythology and Eurocentric society, been male. This gendering of the state to favour patriarchy is the antithesis of genuine multiculturalism. In this analysis, I am arguing that these archetypes have outlasted their usefulness: genuine multiculturalism assumes no social archetypes – no intrinsic or essential characters. This argument anticipates the later discussion of the archetypal Bad John, which marginalized Western societies traditionally presentas a universal nature or essence. This is not, however, to propose the mythological Bad John as a universal norm of a new Western humanism, but to offer an example of the *manner* in which society socializes and pacifies such a *natural* character, rendering him a common, non-threatening citizen. The ideal, then, is a society without Bad Johns – and, for that matter, Prince Charmings – either in perception or in reality.

In chapter 2, I present these characters as dramatis personae in that tragedy that is social living and describe the components of tragedy and comedy. I suggest that genuine multiculturalism attacks many of the norms and archetypes that we inherit through socialization as representing what is good for the modern state. Some of these norms cause us to perceive persons first as beings that are different because of their gender, language, place of birth, race, religion, or sexuality and therefore inimical to prevailing common wisdom of how to achieve happiness in a plural society that is free. This is why a just society is one that undermines all social formations deriving from these differences, whether real or imaginary. It privileges a unity and sameness, even if we have to imagine this way of thinking about which groups make good citizens in order to create a fraternity of equals. Citizenship trumps any other social identity. In and of itself, it is the highest recognized identity in the culture. But if we must reject the standard modernist norms about who can be a good citizen, are there norms that offer us a guide as to how to achieve this just society?

Chapter 2 suggests norms that have developed pragmatically within the Western-modern ambit that might prove quite instructive. However, these efforts, because they seemed to challenge dominant practices in modernity, appeared marginal. Chapter 2 proposes that, in a true spirit of multiculturalism, we should move these practices from the margins to the mainstream. In effect, I am arguing that modernity has produced many more cultural archives than those that Eurocentric states value. Too often these other archives of how other groups have fared and survived are marginalized, and often even ignored, in what we now call "industrialized" and "developed" states primarily in the global North.

I point out that my socialization began in such a marginalized society, in the global South, specifically Barbados in the English-speaking Caribbean. I self-reflexively examine how my placement and positioning in an officially multicultural Canada help me to evaluate a deeper meaning of Canadian citizenship. Starting from a perspective of citizenship, I try to cut across arguments that seem intractable to fraternal living when we analyse them solely in terms of class, gender, religion, sexuality, and so on – all categories that I subsume in the universality of citizenship. Therefore in a society that we assume consists of the intrinsic and the extrinsic, archetypal Bad Johns and Prince Charmings, ancient Canadians and newcomers, there must be a social death, not only of the natures and archetypes but of the state itself. That is the only route from existential tragedy for a comedy of full fraternity.

Part II includes chapters 3–11. Chapter 3 offers a Hegelian explanation for multiculturalism as life and therefore as tragedy, as well as how Hegelian thought offers a form of reconciliation of differences deriving from the Christian mythology of death and resurrection as a means of transition from tragedy to comedy. In a previous work, I used a Hegelian phenomenology to examine what it means to be black – primarily ethnically and racially – in Western mythology and to be a black citizen in multicultural Canada.[4] That book situates a specific identity and culture, black and blackness, within a universal way of life that is Western in multicultural Canada. Even then, it suggests that gender differences within blackness challenge the homogenization of an ethno-racial identity and culture for all blacks in Canada. In chapter 3, I begin moving beyond black and blackness to examine the practicality of having a single, universal identity, as in citizenship. This is where the dominant social construction sees persons as particular and different rather than as all the same. The dominant way of life sees persons as first and foremost representatives of a specific nature or as a combination of essential characteristics that might undermine a new, socially constructed universal identity.

A Hegelian analysis allows for self-reflexivity: it is idealistically an examination by a Self, already aware of how it came to exist at a specific moment and time. This Self is trying to find out if it is indeed a universal in all aspects of ways of life; whether, idealistically, it is a person positioned not according to race, gender, sexuality, or any combination of social categories, but as typifying a universal self that is capable of achieving the happiness expected of citizens. Indeed, the implication of this analysis is that unless that self is fully a citizen, fully embedded in the culture, she or he would be unhappy. For if the culture does not identify her or him exclusively as a citizen, she or he can in a universal sense represent only some less socially important form of categorization.

Therefore an analysis relying solely on race, ethnicity, gender, sexuality, and the like will not explain citizenship as the all-encompassing measurement of complete social happiness. It would not allow us to move beyond the recognition of difference within us to the recognition of sameness and unity among us.

Significantly then, a self that is formatively Caribbean and male reflects on his placement and positioning in a wider self that is modern Canada. It is thereby attempting to illuminate the distinctive culture and identity Caribbean Canadian – a Caribbean self or being trying to understand how it can be universally Canadian; a universal being that is Canadian with acknowledged differences within its body trying to reflect on what it means to be one of them, Caribbean, and still, ultimately, fully a Canadian citizen.

As I suggested in *Blackness and Modernity*, Canada incorporates black and Caribbean females more fully than it does black and Caribbean males. Generally, experiences of black-Caribbean males and females are not the same. My social construction places me within a wider niche that is part of the Canadian universal and has the according limits and/or advantages. Even if I try to avoid it, in the particular, this analysis will be the perspective of a black male in a putative multicultural Canada. This too is symptomatic of tragedy – while we might try to arrive at a position and perspective that is universal, individual and particular experiences will inform it.

The arguments the reader encounters in this book are individualistic in that sense, but in the spirit of comedy I am hoping there will be some universal implications. To this end, I argue that this mythology presents a possible antidote to the unhappiness among and bad feelings between different ethnicities and racialized groups in the Americas because the societies grew from desires of fear and not love. I argue that this was in keeping with a model of colonization that Machiavelli made popular, in which its Prince was, ironically, not charming but actually a divisive colonizer.

Chapter 4 tells the story of multiculturalism as a political and sociological process immanent in the Americas, where the dominant societies were not for the primordial inhabitants but primarily for European settlers. These societies did not emerge organically from the land and its natural and primordial peoples – indeed, far from it. The chapter traces some of the developments historically that culminated in Canada's becoming the world's first officially multicultural country in 1971.

Chapter 5 examines Canadian multiculturalism as an unhappy consciousness, where policies and practices do not match, and where the search for an organic folk is elusive and even combative. At issue is the ontological status of official multiculturalism: is it a description of multi-ethnicities within a plural state or a diffusing of power and citizenship rights equally among everyone, regardless of ethnicity or racialization? Chapter 6 presents a theory of how comedy can emerge out of tragedy and looks at what insights such a narrative offers into how to overcome the unhappy consciousness that in Canada is multiculturalism. Chapter 7 argues that the tragic narrative of Canada – like that of all of North America – is a response to the American Civil War and the blood-soaked struggle of diremption over ideal forms of nation-state construction to determine which ethnic groups and racialized individuals should be citizens and which should remain on the margins. Chapter 8 looks at socio-philosophical arguments over how to settle such bouts of diremption so that Canadian society can become a single consciousness, even when facing deep differences. Chapters 9 and 10 look at how modern forms of immigration are producing a Canadian citizenship displaying diversity and ethnic difference. Using myself as an example, I show how the challenges of integration remain tragic for members of visible minorities and systematically marginalized groups, even while they are citizens. They can become trapped in a dominant discourse that aims to satisfy personal but selfish desires at the expense of the greater good.

Chapter 11 analyses Canada as a consciousness that is unhappy because it aims to be fully a liberal democracy, where citizens enjoy a multicultural citizenship that recognizes them as first of all liberal citizens with fundamental rights. However, it also ascribes these citizens with specific identities deriving from ethnic and racial categories – identities that can translate into statuses that deny the rights of social mobility towards achieving the statuses that are the ideals of liberal thinking. In this light, I examine Canadian multiculturalism as unavoidably a tragedy. I again return to the mythology underpinning construction of Western states and examine what it implies about creating if not something naturally organic, then at least fraternal and solidaristic among radically different members of a society.

Part III explores a potential way out of the unhappy consciousness of tragedy and offers the hope of life's eventually becoming a comedy. Chapter 12 begins by examining Canadian multiculturalism as tragic

because it assumes duelling ideals of state formation: a liberal, individu-
alist ideal and the idea of Canada as a confederation of putative homelands. It looks at a debate between arch-conservative Leo Strauss and
leftist Hegelian Alexandre Kojève on the issue of sovereignty in the
state – a continuation of a discussion dating back to ancient Greece and
the Bible. I use this chapter to reinforce the idea that Canadian society is
at heart a Christian tragedy and that any escape presumes a Christian
ritual of life-death-resurrection.

Chapter 13 examines duelling models of multiculturalism in Canada
that need reconciliation – one privileging individualism as a step to personal entrenchment in a strong, centralized federation, the other resulting from the world of *realpolitik* – a confederate approach to forming
a nation-state with provinces as the sovereign homelands of different
nations.

Chapter 14 discusses the rationalism inherent in Canadian multiculturalism as Prime Minister Pierre Trudeau propagated it in the 1970s
and the difficulties it encountered practically as it sought to move Canada
from an unhappy consciousness into a strong, unified country of citizens
as persons.

Chapter 15 allows us to consider reconciliation through genuine multiculturalism as an act of faith. This endeavour, I argue, places a heavy
onus on the traditional mediator in this Hegelian and biblical tragedy –
the Canadian state. Not only must the tragic actors die and seek renewal,
but the very stage on which they perform must change radically, props
and all, if the people as the intended folk are to move from a tragedy of
living and dying in the same moment to the hope of a comedy.

GENUINE MULTICULTURALISM

If I were two-faced, would I be wearing this one?
Abraham Lincoln

Introduction:
The Tragedy of Living, the Comedy of Trying

This book is about a way of life we call "multiculturalism," or rather about genuine multiculturalism, in its most idealistic yet pragmatic form. It is about nation building in what we now call "late modernity" or even "the postmodern," whose hallmarks supposedly include multicultural-ism itself. The beauty *of genuine multiculturalism* is that it assumes that nations and states are constructed mechanically, indeed pragmatically, in the moment, by the people, for the people, and of the people – that is, *citizens*.

But just imagining this process actually happening is pure idealism. People as persons or citizens and as social actors always come first. They antedate ethnic groups, nations, and ultimately confederations or unions that we call "states" and "countries." As persons, they are more than discrete individuals – at the extreme, libertarian beings with a minimum of socialization and culture, who see themselves organically and authen-tically as separate, socially distinct, and, undoubtedly, uncultured. As Aristotle argues, such an individual anthropologically "must be either a beast or a god: he is no part of a state."[1]

But persons are social and socialized beings: they have an ever-changing series of personalities like different masks that they wear or perform from behind as dramatis personae; their performances are in social and not hermit-like conditions, much like the ancient Roman ideal of a person having a specific identity and social position because of social responsibilities and rights.[2] And as each mask changes, something dies and something is born, tragedy and comedy all at the same time.

Persons are worthy of love and capable of love – of envelopment in a fraternity within which they find unity through full recognition as simul-taneously the loved and the lover. This is what dignifies them as human beings in general and as citizens of a particular social. Their biggest social commitment to one another is simply to love them, despite seemingly profound natural differences and orientations, to be the best fraternal lovers possible. This is how they perform good citizenry, by offering and receiving love as a never-ending series of attempts to overcome wilfully the separateness of abject individualism and to gain unity.

Too often, and for too long, many thinkers have standardized such ontological social beings sociologically and mythologically as man, European, and even heterosexual. But whatever the presumed ethnicity, gender, racialization, sexuality, social status – indeed, whatever attributes of personality a social setting normatively confers on them – these beings stand in need of citizenship. They start out socially as classical specimens of the tragic figure – as a seeming god in a state of nature that must die in society to become a member of it. But tragically, and this point is often overlooked, the society too must die to fully incorporate the new members, thereby becoming in spirit a new entity inclusive of all members old and new, all bearing the same equality.

This is death through transcendence – of changing wilfully so as to fulfil all the potential that idealistically is achievable only in the future and that we can only glimpse in the present. This is the death necessary for becoming socially more perfect, primarily by overcoming nature's diversities and differences. This is the death that must take place for people to experience social love and loving, on their way to becoming more socially perfect. It is like what the entire hemisphere of the Americas have become in this moment in theory, where daily living is now marked by rampant diversity within social unities. Collectively and separately these nation states are analogously a gallimaufry, that seemingly unappetizing dish that changes with the addition of every new ingredient, but still remains a ragout-type meal. On a hungry day, it does the job, even if the consumer cannot really stomach separately the various constituents; and in moments of carnival and lightheartedness, it can be nosh for fun times, drinking and gastronomical overindulgences.

This is the ideal of representatives of all humanity, with all its natural diversity and seeming social imperfection, living freely and peacefully in a fraternity of equals. Such would be the long-held dreams or slogans of the main revolutions, American, French, and Haitian, that launched modernity the era of freedom or living without the compulsory conformity that had traditionally produced power for a few people and social injustices for the many. The state, which political thinkers have traditionally presented as the ultimate in rationality – with its customs, laws, rituals, and social pecking order – can at best be rational for only so long before the never-ending need for greater freedoms unsettles it. Tragically, it must die many deaths in its evolution to what might only be a dream, that of living ever after as the most rational or socially just way for *all* humans to exist together free.

To this end, then, the discussion in this book is first and foremost about citizens. Citizenship is what renders meaningless stratification and socialization according to such categories as ethnicity, gender, language, place of birth, sexuality – indeed of all social categorizations other than citizenship itself. Whether society places and positions persons primarily in terms of a specific categorization (such as might be the case if it identifies them exclusively by ethnicity, gender, race, or any other of the categories that became so important to a modernist identity), or whether such persons possess an identity and social standing resulting from the intersecting of any of the main modernist categories of identity, citizenship negates all these prior social constructions. For citizenship is the ultimate in social construction and perfectibility, particularly in a genuinely multicultural setting. In a truly fraternal setting, which recognizes all members with rights of belonging and entitlements to the social capital of the state, the only categorization that matters is citizenship – the equalizer, and the hallmark, of equality and, in a multicultural setting, freedom. Holders of citizenship hold trump cards: in terms of a social identity, it is the only intrinsic marker.

To many readers, what I have described may seem counterintuitive and unnatural, especially in plural societies.[3] Perceptually, we define members of *The People* in terms of what we assume to be essential or intrinsic categories – such as those specific to ethnicity, gender, race, sexuality – or of traits and personalities that we imagine might flow from a mixing of these essences that were all previously bestowed by nature. Indeed, it has always been a challenge to modernist thinking how to place and position in modern society the *mixed*, whether ethnicities, genders, languages, races. Indeed, common sense has led us mythologically to be suspicious of all that *mixing* of assumed nature and essences. Common sense may tell us that such mixing undermines authenticity and trustworthiness and makes impure the intentions of those such intermingling produced. The acceptance of such myths has produced the flawed but well-intentioned and alienated tragic characters so prevalent in modernist literature, such recurring archetypes as Antigone, Oedipus,

Othello, or Prometheus, and in our constructions of ideal societies. Genuine multiculturalism subverts such common sense thinking and mythologies by asserting that, indeed, social mixing as a means of social perfectibility is not only natural but it is the ideal for modern living.

PLAYERS ON A STAGE

Based on fixed perceptions, we may start by identifying these potentially social characters as individuals whom we may slot into specific categories within a seemingly never-changing social order. Within a dominant culture, this is particularly true for people such as immigrants who are strangers and whose habits we may not know and may even find suspicious. We then treat them as typical of the entire group or category of which they are presumably members – as we presume we *ought* to treat them – rather than uniquely as individuals, far less persons.

The difference between personhood and individualism in this sense is one of positive belonging. It is an issue, I contend, of *fraternity*, or, as I argue, *full recognition* that can occur only through full citizenship. This determination, which observers base on group traits, is particularly evident vis-à-vis native ethnic groups that already exist prominently within states but that refuse assimilation into the dominant group or culture. These long-standing ethnic groups may even appear distinct and different within a wider union. They might even have social positioning with a sense of fraternity deriving from their own uniqueness. But this determination of social place and positioning occurs as well towards immigrants in their many guises – the many ways they emerge as cultural outsiders. The marks on their skin, the languages they speak, the clothes they wear, the religions they follow, all taken as signs of their arriving from a supposed state of nature – all markers that make *them* appear different from *us*, who seem already at home in the receiving civil society.

Such is the beginning of a living tragedy. Often, the curtains open on these players in social engagements, revealing them as transgressive; their very *natural* differences because of how they appear make them abnormal and deviant. Differences make them suspects, capable of going beyond acceptable boundaries and of knowing no limits. Prudence, perception really, tells the old-timers and members of the dominant cultures that this is how it should be – they should behave prudently, even if stereotypically: they should limit the social roles these cultural outsiders perform.

Objectively, the script is fairly predictable in the modern state. So are the expectations of the roles the transgressors would play and of the behaviour they would naturally exhibit and perform, for either the benefit or the disadvantage of the state. Judging solely by our perceptions, we may start such encounters by objectively ascribing statuses to people carrying the marks of differences on their bodies and in their cultures. This is how we may personalize these individuals who come among *us*, who may regard ourselves as the intrinsic essence and manifestation of the rational state: first, we strip them of any personality they carry, then, subjectively, we clothe them in one of our choosing. To this end, we categorize them according to some virtue we assume. Generally, we position them as extrinsic and even superficial to the state. Maybe someday they might transcend themselves, change their very nature, become as naturalized and harmonized in the state as are we the *authentic* citizens. They might become somewhat intrinsic, but perceptually, from our starting position, it will always be *somewhat*. Even the best of socialization cannot make them genuinely natural or authentic to their new state.

Instead of personalities capable of producing and performing any number of social roles as humanly possible, we restrict them to effectively wearing one or two masks in society. They might be workers only, and then expected to perform only lower-status jobs or those the more authentic members of society do not want. Or society may limit where they live, if they can vote, how they may worship, what religious icons they can wear or promote, and what languages they may use. Not only the compulsory wearing of very specific masks, but the limitations we may impose on them, constitutes the true nature of their social interactions. Society may prevent them from wearing and performing the full complement of masks and social roles of a genuine citizen. Thus it rebrands those who are not *authentically* any of us. These positions and placements are what it thinks would make these non-members a suitable fit. It then may expect them to conform to its expectations for their behaviour and to accept what it thinks makes them happy.

Such thinking goes this way: *we* are the subjects in the society and therefore the persons who legitimately belong; *they* are the objects for us perhaps to place and position in a society to which we, as subjects, feel they do not authentically belong. In this way, the perceptually true subjects position those objects, just as they would any other form of human or natural resources that the subjects have the right to deploy for the benefit primarily of those who really belong.

GENUINE MULTICULTURALISM

Genuine multiculturalism postulates that such placement and position-ing (such a priori expectations of inequality, no matter how people form and reason them) impose social conformity and are therefore both unreasonable and socially unacceptable in a free state. It challenges and even seeks to overthrow much of what society, perhaps unthinking, takes as the norm for good living socially. It says that much joy and good can arise in the mixing of identities to produce a citizenship that is univer-sally inclusive of all differences and diversity. These reasons alone are enough to make genuine multiculturalism postmodern.

Certainly if it is still just modern, it is ideally a self-reflexive modernity looking at itself and noticing its shortcomings in how it incorporates differences and diversities in its members. There is an implicit indict-ment here of the modernist attempt to situate members in terms of sec-ondary and extrinsic attributes instead of citizenship – the only category officially intrinsic and meaningful. Genuine multiculturalism implies that society's imposing conformity cannot produce happiness – not for people it perceives as objects having to conform; not for subjects imposing it; not for the state in which this drama is occurring. Genuine multiculturalism postulates that every citizen, having willingly left the presumed state of nature for social living, must by right have the oppor-tunity and ability to wear all the masks of social recognition citizens have traditionally worn; this is justice that is natural yet, most impor-tant, also social. Genuine multiculturalism argues that social justice at its best is love in its many forms, including the erotic and even licentious, but primarily fraternal. Love is the social antidote for overcoming sepa-ration, diversity, difference, and all other seeming notions of diremp-tions in humanity.

As individuals, people whom society marks as *different* want to be free subjects: they want social mobility and the recognition that offers achievable status. They want to share and benefit fully from all the posi-tions and placements available to any citizen, for that status signifies the attainment and possession of the highest statuses and prestige in the modern state, which embody desires and potential that people might associate more fully with some prevailing social identity, such as ethnic-ity, gender, race, religion, and sexuality.

What is the best use for these bundles, which would enhance and not threaten society? Citizenship is the only designation that should matters socially: it is the certification of socialization. More than that, even as immigrants, as ideal types, those who would take on the new social identity of citizens do not see them themselves as beings starting out without personality, even if that is the way others see them. Traditionally, immigrants struggle to maintain as much as possible of their previous personal culture and traits. They do not see themselves as arriving in a new land and culture without prior socialization of value. Neither do they dismiss all their prior socialization as meaningless in the new society. Indeed, they often argue that cultural hybridization can enrich the new society by allowing them to contribute the best of their primary socialization. As social actors on a new stage, they perform differently from the script society hands them; they act as if they are actually and authentically one of *us* – citizens aspiring to remake to their likeness themselves and the world around them, just as, they perceive, any other citizen would.

Practically, they want to escape the pigeonholes and inferior stratification into which *we* have categorized them and negatively placed them. At the same time, they want to place themselves positively in the pigeonhole or category of their own choosing – a placement they base on the personality they desire and on the social morality they brought with them as part of their socialization.

People whom society marks as different want to become persons by embedding themselves fully and meaningfully at the level of their choosing. They seek both continuity and discontinuity – keeping what they deem valuable from the old way of life, but letting go of whatever they choose of their previous socialization. They want to have a full sense of belonging to a new fraternity in a new land and culture; they want to feel they have the full entitlement to which this membership entitles them; romantically they may remain members of an old homeland that nature gave them. Even if as free individuals and social beings physically they have left this native land, they still want to believe they retain much of what nature gave to them. Such naturalness they associate with homeland and its socialization. But in a very practical sense, they want to become full and active members of the new grouping they have joined. Idealistically, they want to embed themselves fully in a new *homeland* that with their arrival must now reconstitute itself differently from what existed before primarily through the removal of any barriers to their full self-actualization. They desire two things at the same time: the first is the recognition that they can belong to a native land that is not now the stage for their social performances on a daily basis; the second is the fraternal recognition that comes with taking the identity, culture, and socialization of the new state. And this recognition should be as if they had no other primary socialization and association elsewhere: they expect the country they have chosen to treat them as if it is, indeed, their native land. For it is their homeland not by nature, but more important by choice: the land and people to which they have freely naturalized. It is where they choose freely to act out their humanity and become as socially perfectible as possible. They are seeking the individualistic freedom to differ from others in a single collective: they want recognition as different but yet as the same as all other members who like them are also freely building the homeland they share. And they also desire the mirror image of this recognition – social stratification that entitles all fraternal members of the society to the same levels of social justice because of the all-important equality of all members. But in the final analysis, they want the social makeover they have undertaken to trump the natural attributes associated with them when in the new setting they act or must perform social roles solely because of a universal membership in society. They want full recognition as importantly natural but also equally importantly as social.

Here I am reclaiming part of Isaiah Berlin's declaration: "The desire for recognition is a desire for something different (self-liberty but): for union, closer understanding, integration of interests, a life of common dependence and common sacrifice."[4] This comes with being a social actor in a fraternity to which one feels intrinsic belonging, namely, true citizenship, regardless of any other social identity or extrinsic category. Much discussion about multiculturalism, as I show below, emphasizes a one-sided definition of recognition, what I call "epistemic acknowledgment of difference" or statements attesting to the diversity of nature – the right to be unique among others. I contend that such a definition limits the radical democracy in multiculturalism and pigeonholes it politically and sociologically – it seems just another aspect of liberal pluralism with a primary focus on what makes us culturally different – and which aspects of this difference to tolerate and preserve – even when we live together in the same societies that are already perfectible social orders.

The aspect of recognition that we need to reclaim and emphasize is that which sees individuals as persons living in a society that is meaningful to them because they are part of and belong intrinsically to a social whole of equals and which have not yet reached perfectibility. The newcomers want socially meaningful roles. On this stage, they want both the natural justice that the state of nature had previously conferred on them and – in return for any rights they might freely give up for citizenship – all the rights and privileges of belonging to the new social. In this reincarnation, all social masks must be available to them for there to be justice.

Tragically, perception intervenes in practice: many types of newcomers do not receive, and often no one offers them, the social standing and recognition they desire. And because of their inferior statuses, society often perceives certain types of immigrants as lacking appropriate socialization, so that they appear not to possess sufficient social capital such as employment experience, language skills, and political understanding that normally would allow them to become successful citizens.

Again, none of the actors on either side of this perception line is happy socially. This unhappiness is one of the ironies of living in a plural federal state perceptually consisting seemingly of ethnic homelands elsewhere and presuming claims of unchangeable ascribed statuses flowing from historic rights of belonging for dominant groups of individuals in a new homeland. Often the dominant groups propose "accommodations"– 'reasonable' limits on the aspirations and achievements of the cultural outsiders, including newcomers and other people who are just *different*. This approach creates deeper contradictions. In a liberal democracy, such limits bring about the greatest of ironies – imposing on a citizen as a putative free individual a social position that confirms the acknowledged inequalities of those with certain group identities. Such accommodation merely attests to how dominant groups see some citizens as not as intrinsic to the state as those who dominate. Ironically, they challenge the universal equality of citizenship in practice.

And in a liberal society, are not citizens, by definition, free to follow the dictates of their heart over those of another? Are not all citizens free to follow the desires their socialization gives them? And if they attain their desires, would they not be more accepting of their placement and position, believing that realization of their desires has given them the status that society offered them and that they wanted? Opposing desires and perceptions seem to have collided in this scenario of seeking to accommodate *others*, who by receiving accommodation cannot by definition still have full choice and freedom, cannot be full citizens. Citizens want to be free, even if compatriots wish to accommodate them; society forbids restrictions on full members as anathema to full citizenship. Yet dominant groups may seek to restrict some members of society if accommodation of differences is to occur. This conflict of desires provides the material of much tragedy. Genuine multiculturalism tries to reconcile these conflicting desires under the ideal of a common citizenship that is indivisible: all citizens are persons for they are individuals, but they are also fully equals in a common society. How to create through socialization the same desires in *all* citizens – those who have been around for a long time and those who just arrived?

Since genuine multiculturalism starts with the ideal that all these beings, with their human differences, are subjects and citizens first, in practice it shifts the encounter to another stage, from activities in a state of nature to those of social construction. There is now no room for differentiation because of natural attributes, shapes, histories, and traits. All beings begin their social existence as new citizens who are all the same in that they are equally citizens.[5] But how do they behave or perform social roles? What is the dominant socialization, and what are the appropriate levels of social stratification? In an ironic twist, genuine multiculturalism says that there is no dominant socialization beyond what these new creatures are willing to accept in the new fraternity. This new social construction does not grandfather historically well-off groups as still dominant. This is one reason genuine multiculturalism is largely unattainable and remains in the transcendent as utopia that offers moral ideals of just social behaviour.

In effect, genuine multiculturalism checks the tyranny in us as the collective, dominant power that might claim authority to force accommodation on strangers for any number of reasons: length of residence or superiority of language, sexuality, or religion – whatever forms of racialization and stratification that, by creating social hierarchies, can reasonably support superior claims to rights and entitlements of power over those it categorizes as different. In this respect, these new creatures carry on their primordial cultures and primary socialization until a new way of life emerges organic and natural to the new fraternity. Here, subjects who are citizens decide who they are, what they do, what they can become. Genuine multiculturalism insists that in a society of equals, none of the erstwhile claims to superiority – especially those from nature, history, or culture – can be reasonable authority for dominance and superiority. Indeed, the biggest tyrant to check is the one speaking in the voice of an ethnic nationalism and acting to preserve an ethnoracial nationalism.

Instead, genuine multiculturalism calls on the historical archetypical slave, outsider, foreigner, immigrant, and asks her or him to self-identify as socially worthwhile – to stake a claim to equality. Under such idealism, social positioning and placement come solely on the basis of recognition flowing from fraternity of membership in the society. This community must change and remake itself by the sheer presence of this newcomer – theoretically, by *every* newcomer. In this sense, such an existence is tragic – for, like everything human, and therefore social, there is no guarantee of permanence, not even for the state. Fluidity and not permanent social orders are, indeed, the order of living. Everything social or human will – nay, must – die someday. Genuine multiculturalism defines how to live always in the shadows of social death, the loss of rationality as culture has defined it, for such is the human condition, but more so in a plural society.

Genuine multiculturalism does not start out viewing society as structurally and functionally perfect, with everything in place and with the people having to fit themselves into an existing structure. Rather, it argues that people as citizens make the structure and decide the functions. Structurally and functionally, the state dies from day to day. It also refashions itself daily according to the wishes of people whenever the people reconstitute themselves. It is constructionist – the people as the gods of the piece are constantly passing judgment on their handiwork, constantly making and remaking. Each time they find the state not to be in the image of these gods, the state dies and recreation of a new one begins.

What is normal to living socially is constant change. This process is mostly reconstruction: taking much from the past, including what is available in the present moment, and (re)producing it according to an ever-changing framework of desires. With each (re)creation, the actors intend the result to be the masterpiece that will make as much sense to future generations as to the creators. Chances are what emerges will not please all the creators, far less all members of future generations.

In the interim, until a lasting framework finally – if ever – crystallizes, the multicultural norm is that there are no lasting norms. In practice, the key material, or the constant throughout the various versions or constructions, is the *people* – the diversity of human capital the world over. This is the case of a country such as Canada, officially multicultural, but I contend also of every other state in the Americas. It is virtually the same for all countries dependent on immigrants – for those that genuinely want to make newcomers full citizens. Through globalism, these primordial differences and diversities come together in one place. They hope to produce a singular, indivisible nation that will survive the test of time: a single state where everyone, regardless of differences biological or cultural will be happy. Genuine multiculturalism envisions a society of persons, equally of immigrants and native members. As citizens they share a common intention to create a society that will be meaningful and acceptable to all the people now and in the future. This is the central desire of their common socialization and the basis for any acceptable stratification, for indisputable social justice.

MULTICULTURALISM AND MYTH

But these individual citizens are never happy either, because of the changes in and around them or because of the permanence implicit in the belief that they are living in the definitive, lasting framework, with unchangeable levels of stratifications. In practice, all the people never have things the way they want them. There is no lasting social justice. So some of them are disruptive and even deviant – becoming just like the stereotypical outsider that society deems and labels as unsociable and without appropriate socialization. Often, in a bid to make the world in their individual images, some of them tear down structures that might be generations old or as recent as yesterday. If the structure and functions do not fit, then they reject them. These individuals see this as the only way to make the society free, a liberal democracy where citizenship means universal equality and "the people" means all those individuals who have membership and entitlements of citizenship, regardless of the prevailing social stratification.

As long as society socializes individuals as citizens, then they have the right to be free of the types of social stratification that make some citizens superior and some inferior, particularly in those areas of political and economic life most central to good living. Some other citizens, however, reject immediate change and even full incorporation of newcomers. Too much change and too little permanence leave some old-timers unhappy, and if there is unhappiness in the state, then the state has not achieved its goal of giving its citizens a happy life. This never-ending unhappiness on all sides, even with contradictory causes, is the backbeat to the tragedy of living in a society.

Genuine multiculturalism as conciliation, as trying to bring disagreeing sides to a common happiness, thus supposes that societies evolve as moral communities in time, thereby making them simultaneously tragic and comic. It imagines society as having distinctly a past, a present, and a future – all part of an overarching narrative that makes a society socially just. But it argues that the present is always most important: it is always the point most crucial to survival. How do we ensure survival forever, a never-ending present?

In this final status, as in fairy tales, "they all live happily ever after," where what is in the present extends into the future. This is just as much an ending of the tragic experience, for one stage of life has ended and slipped into the past. But this moment is also one of re-creation – perhaps even of the beginnings of that masterpiece that will last for generations, if not forever. It is the second expectation, of the beginning of everlasting happiness, that makes the idea of disagreeing groups living together a comedy, for such agreement would be permanent only if time itself stops, or if survivability extends, if there are no new socially disruptive desires to contend with. And it is because of this dualism of expectations, often in conflict, that we can see genuine multiculturalism most clearly through its founding myths and on legends, the same way philosophers and social scientists have historically talked about fates and destinies – of ending tragic existences and of the enduring life of perpetual happiness and peace as social beings. The eminent mythologist Joseph Campbell reminds us: "*Myths*[,] that is to say, religious recitations conceived as symbolic of the play of Eternity in Time. These are rehearsed, not for diversion, but for the spiritual welfare of the individual or community. *Legends* also appear; i.e. reviews of a traditional history (or of episodes from such a history) so rendered as to permit mythological symbolism to inform human event and circumstances. Whereas myths present in pictorial form cosmogonic and ontological intuition, legends refer to the more immediate life and settling of the given society."[6]

Genuine multiculturalism is about telling tales of a coming time when tragedy will end; happiness and perpetual peace will reign in human affairs the same way as if gods had created a harmonious cosmology. But until that time, humans will continue to make imperfect societies. Societies will be places without social justice until humanity or the *people*, not gods, create genuine multiculturalism. Until then, human existence is, socially, a tragedy rich with the hopes that someday human existence will become a comedy. In very patriotic countries, or ones where dominant groups are happy with existing privileges, it is hard to tell people that their society is not already just short of perfection or that it is not the epitome of the best that imperfect human beings can produce. For them, theirs is already a country of social justice, where as best as is humanly possible tragedy has given way to comedy permanently. They do not like to be told different – and worse, they do not like legendary strangers undermining this belief or dominant myth.

Legendary Characters

A meaningful question then: how do we place, within what can be only a prototype of a cosmologically meaningful society, people to whom society ascribes statuses that are evocatively *legendary*? Do they enter and remain as heroes? Do they start out perceptually as unheroic, as what I describe in this book as the Bad Johns or the social misfits of folklore, and remain that way? Or do they achieve the designation of heroic as a new status because of their value or usefulness in the new society? Does this relabelling occur because of how willing they are to accept their beginner's status in relation to the dominant groups that already exist? And where does the social morality that determines dominance – and even acceptable levels of perfection – come from? What gives dominant groups the authority to determine, such as by approving and sanctioning the designations they impose on those I describe as mythological Prince Charmings, whose actions and performances they interpret as legendary? More important, who can decide whether indeed certain ontological beings, such as the *types* of strangers whom the social imaginary would later position as Bad Johns or Prince Charmings by nature or essences, are ever legendary or noble? Who can determine social justice and then assure social happiness from its attainment?

In this analysis, I argue that the underpinning mythology of social justice in Western societies is Christian and therefore has clear implications of what ought to be paths to fraternal love in a society constructed on ideals of justice for all. It is from there that ideals of social happiness arise even for countries that no longer have an official religion. The positions they confer on newcomers derive from the basic stories that explain society as a moral community in time but as moving towards an end-of-time moment when "they all live happily after." These myths and legends undergird ideals of who has full socialization. They decide suitable social strata for various legendary people in terms of status and prestige as citizens who seek happiness. These myths determine who is legendary – the heroes and villains of the piece that is the social setting. The heroes are those who will help produce or maintain a state of happiness; the villains, those who transgress and perceptually whose nature inclines them to produce unhappiness. For even though these prototypes of eventual citizens are of legendary figures coming out of seemingly the same state of nature, it is the socialization process that determines which character should live its social existence tragically in the guise of a Bad John and which should have the comedic mask of a Prince Charming. Genuine multiculturalism is always calling on us to challenge this determination process for hints of any perceptual biases in the process and to rid the system of them.

Genuine multiculturalism in a Western setting borrows from while subverting these fairy tales – and how the ideal states have evolved through time – the very model of how society should unfold across time. This model is the prototype for a model of social construction that allows societies to still claim fidelity to the dominant mythologies and ideal legendary figures. Campbell explains: "Through the vogues of literary history, the folk tale has survived. Told and retold, losing here a detail, gaining there a new hero, disintegrating gradually in outline, but re-created occasionally by some narrator of the folk, the little masterpiece transports into the living present a long inheritance of story-skill, coming down from the romancers of the Middle Ages, the strictly disciplined poets of the Celts, the professional story-men of Islam, the exquisite, fertile, brilliant fabulists of Hindu and Buddhist India ... If ever there was an art on which the whole community of mankind has worked – seasoned with the philosophy of the codger on the wharf and singing with the music of the spheres – it is the ageless tale."[7]

This model emphasizes change, which arises organically out of the folk or the common people, regardless of subsequent secondary categorization such as race, ethnicity, sexuality, gender and the like – change through death and rebirth, or re-creating. This is the death and rebirth so central to the tragic life in Christianity. Indeed, genuine multiculturalism is a postmodern tale of how individuals from around the world – in all their differences, diversities, and personalities, most of them, we are to believe, lacking in cultural sophistication – can survive happily and peacefully in the same place. It is how they can build a lasting narrative, or a socializing identity, about *themselves*, even if what *is* themselves – what is *the people* – changes constantly in time and space. They try to remain authentic to their dreams, their identities, and their purposes in life. Individually, they desire fulfilment of their various myths' promise of a time coming when "they all live happily ever after," when, legendary, they are all citizen heroes in a land their god has given to them, when they are all the personalities their individuality and their culture shape, inseparable from the rest of the folk. In their different ways, collectively they have a common desire and purpose, even if these attributes and traits came from different gods and cultures.

The resulting production also shows an organic culture that aspires to be rational, and thereby fair and reflective of the equal freedom of all members through the just recognition of all, evolving morally. This process must always include death and rebirth – converting differences into sameness, which splinters tragically into *acceptable* differences. Moments of seeming *natural* or organic rationalism give way to moments of irrationality and then, in all hope, a permanent moment of rationality. The comedy is the hope that the difference emanating from this splintering would be acceptable, desirable, even ethically manageable. Such a shattering would be *reasonable* or testable and verifiable by an internal logic organic to the dominant myth on social justice.

Genuine multiculturalism thus starts out as a tragedy. It is a battle for dominance and permanence, especially in creating societal norms and values that always reflect the spirit of the folk or the people. Intellectually, it is a struggle over how content must always be shaping form; it is a fight over how individuals or out-of-step minorities make room for themselves in a country that their god wants to be as much theirs as it is that of the dominant majorities or groups, of how they become simple folk just like everybody else. Those making room for themselves might be minority groups that society identifies or socially constructs as having a specific history, perspective, and even goals that are not quite compatible with those of the majority or the historically dominant.

But that is only a position with a social mask that society or inheritance *ascribes* – a point of departure, a new beginning – for the dominant mythology says that in a liberal Western society what matters most for legendary figures is status they *achieve*, what arrives as an end-of-time position, the wearing of the social masks of choice. Society must make room for them as equals, as both folk and an organic folk spirit. Genuine multiculturalism in a Western setting is living with the contradictions of liberal democracy – privileging the rights and protection of the individual or minority while reaching for a lasting mechanism that allows decisions and power to the majority, all as if the same desires wedded an indivisible folk that produced it. It constantly makes sure that minorities are by rights always somehow part of the majority or dominant groups that, without stratification, speak to and for the folk.

Ironically, these contradictions render genuine multiculturalism a comedy. For how to square them in real life? How can there be happiness or a seamless folk culture, especially where some members regard themselves as hieratically superior to the mere folk. How can there be perpetual peace and sameness in the midst of such diversity, difference, and constant conflict and change? How can there not be social inequality and the resulting democratic claim by the unequal for a better society, where socially different groups and individuals would be equal to any other citizen?

Genuine multiculturalism is thus, tragically, about existing collectively with inherent difference, but comedically, also about ignoring the tragedy of existence from moment to moment. It is ignoring the obvious – a willing false consciousness that can appear to rational minds only as comedic or even *schizophrenic,* a term observers often associate with multiculturalism. Considering the alternative, especially in a time and place where nothing is normal, schizophrenia might be the best, indeed only, *sane* and ethical way of surviving – and that too is the reality and pragmatism of genuine multiculturalism. For the people always have inherent fractures and factions – but then again, they are just the folk.

OLD WORLD AND NEW

For these reasons, it is hard to see a genuine multiculturalism fully taking hold in old countries, such as those in Europe, with dominant ethnic and religious groups that are already the folk. There we find countries that name and imagine past, present, and future communities for the benefit of a specific, seemingly primordial ethnicity. This group must, mythologically, always be dominant in the country that carries its name, otherwise there cannot be cosmological peace and happiness. A given ethnicity has mapped within the genes of its folk a perceived ethnic nationalism that is the group desity, its end-of-history arrival point when the group has overcome all human tragedies and can live happily ever after. Members of the dominant group are the only legendary heroes. Non-members are by definition the legendary villains, representative of the fates that would prevent the nation-state from achieving its promised mythological destiny of perpetual happiness and peace as befitting its particular fairy tale or folk story.

Anthony Smith argues this point to make the case that nations and nationalist fervour in old countries usually reach back for something that is almost primordial, indeed even folkish, around which to build their current identities. For, idealistically, such nationalists are imagining a nation-state in a time when the past, present, and the future are the same, comedically when time stops, especially in what is constituted as the people. "Modern political nationalisms cannot be understood without reference to these earlier ethnic ties and memories," Smith argues, "and, in some cases, to pre-modern ethnic identities and communities. I do not wish to assert that every modern nation must be founded on some antecedent ethnic ties, let alone a definite ethnic community; but many such nations have been and are based on these ties, including the first nations in the West – France, England, Castile, Holland, Sweden – and they acted as models and Pioneers of the idea of the 'nation' for others. And when we dig deeper, we shall find an ethnic component in many national communities since – whether the nation was formed slowly or was the outcome of a more concerted project of 'nation-building.'"[8]

Countries themselves start out with ascribed identities and positions that their nationalistic members, as members of a mythological and legendary folk, perceive. But if states are truly to express the will of the people, they must become like the people: they must become as *human* as the folk and strive to become the images of the people as the people imagine and desire for themselves. If the definition of this mythological people changes, such as by recognizing the presence of immigrants who are not traditional within a particular folk, so too would the notion of an "authentic" ethnic group as the founding peoples of the nation-state have to change. This is so because the *folk itself* has changed. With this change would come another, in the perception of those whom myth still deems to have the rights in perpetuity to be dominant and of those who have none.[9]

States, too, must flee the pigeonholes of their history for the pigeonholes they imagine as ideal for surviving the present in the hopes of establishing the ideals all their citizens imagine, as the quintessential folk, for the future. This is one way in which states can become or remain what I call "radically democratic." In this condition, social relations derive from social construction of equality for all members as persons, which recognizes them not only as abstract individuals with liberal rights but fully as human beings in a society that they make while in turn it is making them into persons or full citizens. Regardless of beginning ethnicity or racialization, everyone must have the authority as members of the folk to transform the state and to, as the saying goes, colonize their own futures for the citizens to inherit. The same is true of *any* citizen in any category of socialization, especially those categories that unreasonably constrain the authority of the governing members, such as disability, gender, language, religion, sexuality – all the categories that democracy historically has attacked as not consistent with full membership in the folk.

None of the modern states in the Americas can remotely lay claim to an existence reflecting Smith's ethnic symbolism. Instead these states are undoubtedly pure social construction, realizing some dominant group's imaginary community. To this end, genuine multiculturalism is most natural and organic to the Americas, a point I argue at length below; it is about how to create a folk – with all that is organic, natural, and unifying, as the term implies – when all that is available is a people notable more for differences and diversity.

For conceptually multiculturalism is a creature of the archetypal inorganic – of a colonial process in the Americas for the last five hundred years. Colonialism began the tragic experiences of trying to produce societies flowing from the nationalist fervour that Smith explains, of robbing much of humanity of their self-worth by denying them the ability to form desirable fraternal relationships in the countries where they lived. In tragic irony, the excluded were too much of the folk to receive fraternal membership in a higher form of the new folk inorganic to the land, those elites which these European colonies stratified as the real people. When this approach failed particularly in the Americas, as most visible in the US Civil War, multiculturalism emerged from attempts at compromise to replace a history of conflict with a story of eventual happiness for a people that, with time and socialization, has become as natural to the land as if it had been the original natural folk. Ironically, this meant a most tragic beginning: dismissing and even attempting to wipe out the very people with any authentic claim to natural belonging in the Americas, for the existing societies were never intended or constructed for their benefit or good.[10] This was the comedic phase of idealistically pretending that a bit of water in the wine is better for the eventual good of everyone. The alternatives to compromise so everyone can just get along is even more tragic – genocide, separation, segregation, reservations, and ultimately even internecine civil war between dominant forces. Sociologically, the alternative to this compromise is continuing marginalization of people whom the state stratifies as reasonably and systemically unequal because of such factors as race, ancestry, place of origin, colour, ethnic origin, citizenship, creed, sex, sexual orientation, age, marital status, family status, and disability – all those mainly non-white

people whom Canada defines as visible minorities primarily and ironically because of their *in*visibility from the corridors of power and "natural" identity as authentically Canadian.

LINCOLN AND TRUDEAU: TRAGIC FIGURES

At the heart of the remaining conflict in this drive towards the ideals
of genuine multiculturalism in Canada is the disagreement between
dominant groups over which of their imaginary futures and their ideals of social justice should dominate, which should be the national and
even universal ideal. Again we see tragedy resulting from a conflict of
desires. Genuine multiculturalism is radical democracy: it is about living, about surviving by all means collectively, if only to survive the
current moment that appears so morally unreal to the individuals and
groups. Multiculturalism is about clinging to humanity in the face of
unimaginable alternatives – physical death, annihilation, or social
abstraction of the individual and the groups in which the individual
seeks or claims membership.

Surviving, to the socially influential person, does not mean acquiescing, for such is not how radical democracy takes place; rather, it means
the opposite of acquiescence and passive conformity – fighting in the
hope of eventual victory. It means inclusion in the creative process that
is nation making, if only to shape the nation-state itself. This is so if only
to ensure adequate consideration for the values, positions, and goals of
the individual or group when, as part of the constant of its reconstructing, society decides democratically what to keep and what to change. It
means that living is akin to surviving in a marketplace, where everything
that matters in fairness to *all* citizens needs debating and then acceptance or rejection in the public sphere. More than that, what people
reject today they might very well accept tomorrow, so that even individual ideals they reject never die but are always seeking acceptance in
the next round of political bargaining.

In turn, this argument means that the public, like democracy itself, is
constantly attacking the next barrier of entrenched differences that produce social inequalities. And in the next round, any new citizen, including one who started out as immigrant or foreigner, has the equal and
democratic right to ask for changes to past structures and functions and
to ask for normalization of a range of foreign values and norms. Because
society no longer excludes such individuals, they must have full rights of
recognition – the right to act out full membership in the social. Even if

the newcomer does not get her or his way, democracy and equality of citizenship demand a fair hearing, serious consideration. By nature, genuine multiculturalism at its best is conflictive and apparently even anarchic and chaotic, for the only constant is change – especially as long as newcomers continue to join the debate. At least mythologically, society accommodates differences without enslavement; the ideal of freedom for everyone persists.

A key question is how we as citizens survive individually and collectively – how we can be at least liberal democrats in a land and time when, like change itself, difference and diversity are the norm. But to fully live our humanity, we have to be more than Adamic individuals; we must also be social beings, enjoying the fraternity of belonging in a community with others. We must be persons, just folks. That some members of the fraternity are different is the challenge for genuine multiculturalism as it tries to bring about a sociological and philosophical sameness that at best we can only imagine – it can only be spiritual or a social construct. How do we survive a tragedy of social alienation when there are no norms or moral authorities other than those that the sword, the gun, or the most recent psychological weapon imposed?

Even then, life remains tragic for those on either side of the weapon of conformity, for both confront death – death that is assimilation that goes all the way from enforcing cultural conformity to genocide and ethnic cleansing; death that is slavery or the social death of misrecognition or non-recognition, as Orlando Patterson and, before him, the early American suffragists testified;[11] death of the ideal that societies can be safe spaces for everyone. Death that is the permanence of what is not only undesirable but also enforceable without hopes of escape. Often the tragedy is that to avoid death, we have to substitute another's for our own. The death of the individual comes with the creation of the state. But unless the state changes constantly, the new life proffers a new death or slavery in social conformity and the slavery of ideals from another time and another people. How can we reconcile by becoming persons, citizens with a strong sense of belonging and entitlement but with free will, agency, and some rights to individuality?

Abraham Lincoln, US president 1861–5, reportedly said in the throes of the Civil War that he would do anything to preserve the union as an indivisible state. If achieving this end meant emancipating people in physical bondage, he would – and he did. He was simultaneously a mythological Bad John to those who disagreed and physically fought him and a Prince Charming for those who saw him as saviour of their Union. Hence he appeared to have two faces, the traditional mark of a tragic hero, someone embodying stability and permanence but also espousing change and transformations, someone who is a member of the folk but also not the folk.

The irony of it all is that even then Lincoln was trying to achieve the seemingly impossible. The state he was trying to preserve had already died. There *was* no common folk living in harmony and solidarity. In fact, there never had been, for the United States was ethnically a European institution and was, colonially, inorganic to the land. That state needed renewal and rebirth in the hope of perfection and becoming organic; it would for the rest of its life have to go through death and rebirth just about every generation.

While this union's physical shape might have been the same after the war as before, its spirit had died or undergone *metanoia*, the hollowing out of the physical structure through the death of the old spirit and the instilling of a new spirit or approach to life. While the state might appear indivisible, is it still not fragmentary in practices if not in intention? Metanoia is at one and the same time discontinuity and continuity, a cycle of beginnings and endings in the same moment, the return of the old with difference, newness whose lineage is the old.[12] In a moment of improvisation – what I call "the creativity of blackness" – it is death and rebirth, not entirely annihilating the old but rearranging it to take on a new manifestation that, tantalizingly, makes what emerges different. It is like Joseph Campbell's description of the evolution of myths and folktales.

In the lands that have written in blood the ideals of genuine multiculturalism as radical democracy with equal liberal citizenship, there is no greater tragic figure, no more ironic icon of an unhappy consciousness, than Honest Abe. He is the icon of the tragic figure trying to prevent one death but ending up with others, who in the midst of warding off all these deaths held up the candle of life. But he is also the figure who in a somewhat comedic guise still causes us to wince in laughter at the comedy of errors that bring us back seemingly to the same point every day: that of trying to reconcile conflicting desires no matter how hard we try for different outcomes. Even in the discontinuity of death there is continuity of the same. Even with the best of intentions and great goodwill, how can we not show two faces – the ultimate tragic and multicultural figure?

On the Canadian side, a similar tragic figure is Pierre Elliott Trudeau, prime minister 1968–79 and 1980–4, whom many observers consider the father of multiculturalism. He personifies the struggle to produce an indivisible Canadian state with equality of citizenship regardless of socialization. Whether friends or foes are describing him, one word seems to capture Trudeau: *contradiction*. Ron Graham, the editor and collaborator with Trudeau on a book about the leader's thoughts, comments: "For counterbalancing the strong provinces with a strong federal government, he was branded a centralist – even though he argued in favour of strengthening the provinces in the 1950s [before he sought political office] and gave them unprecedented resources in the 1970s. For counterbalancing the strong corporations with a strong state he was branded a socialist – even though he opposed the nationalization of Quebec's hydro companies in the 1960s and entrenched the rights and freedoms of individuals in the 1980s. His efforts to strengthen Canada vis-à-vis the United States were confused with ethnic nationalism he so adamantly opposed in both English-speaking Canada and French-speaking Quebec. His lifelong devotion to multiculturalism as a key to social tolerance, democratic pluralism, and individual fulfillment was twisted to appear like a ploy to undermine the two-nations theory of Confederation, a ruse to capture the immigrant vote, a sop to Western Canada's pioneering communities, and an argument for collective rights."[13]

Particularly in Quebec, certain circles loathed him as a betrayer, a turncoat, *un roi nègre*, and even the personification of illiberality for his willingness to use the state's power to crush minority aspirations. In this regard, he is the arch-foe of Quebec nationalism based on French ethnicity and racialization.[14]

If it is true that Trudeau's aim was to stamp out Quebec-French ethnic nationalism, he could attempt this only by burying its counterpart, the dominant anglophone Canadian state. Tragically, the only hope for a new Canada would come not from the preservation of either of the traditional ethnic nations in Canada – but from the death and rebirth of both as a single federal state. The process for achieving this was and is multiculturalism. In this regard, I argue that Trudeau learned valuable lessons from the kindred spirit Lincoln himself in promoting Canada as a unified but equally a multicultural country.

In this regard, all of us who believe that people of diversity can actually live in a society without physically destroying themselves and the society are as tragic and as comedic as Honest Abe. In the Americas, this is the continuing narrative of unhappy consciousness: seeking to bring to a happy ending the story of life itself, a story of the folk, of how in the face of routine differences and diversity we can make happiness organic. The epitome of this narrative is the American Civil War, with its struggle to end a social death. It is this common desire for sameness as equality and fraternity that fuels the hope – even the prayer – that the soldiers who died physically for the greater ideals of a new social life of full citizenship and democracy for everyone would not have done so in vain. Rather, even in personal death, they would live on spiritually for as long as such a state of freedom exists, for as long as equality of persons is the fulfilment of citizenship. This is the mythology of genuine multiculturalism – a myth of life as tragedy and possibly also as comedy.

AIMS, AUDIENCE, AND METHODS

This book seeks to examine multiculturalism analogously as a tragedy in both a political and a speculative sense. Here we talk about two distinct aspects of multiculturalism: state formation and liberal citizenship. The first involves, as I indicated above, creation and preservation of civic fraternity, patriotism, or national unity among individuals and groups representing the diversity and differences of humanity itself. These constitute the folk, and this discussion concerns how they socialize as such *naturally*. The second speaks to power and sovereignty – to absolutism of citizenship, vis-à-vis an individual's right to recognition or a group's claiming inviolable rights because of its identity and being – rights that the majority can never remove. This is an issue of stratification: how do members of the folk share in the happiness (or unhappiness) they all produce?

Unfortunately, much of today's discourse conflates these distinct aspects of multiculturalism. Critics thinking only about state formation may argue that multiculturalism means the creation of ethnic ghettoes and the fragmenting of the nation-state. They ignore the liberal spirit of multiculturalism that envisages a day of full liberty and equality, when in the same state individuals and minority groups will be full citizens, as free and as powerful as the majorities; as cultured persons, they would be sovereign too. Indeed, multiculturalism speaks to the age-old ideals of so many previous revolutions, which flowed from speculation about how humanity can create states assuming notions of sameness – ideals of freedom. But revolutionaries also speculated about the possibility of individuals remaining agents who are free and equal in the distribution of the powers and of the authority of sovereignty among citizens – free to achieve the stratification of choice. Official multiculturalism exhibits all the advantages and flaws of a democracy that is liberal.

In a practical sense, multiculturalism results from a desire by peoples and groups exhibiting different virtues – seemingly natural ways of life, attitudes, and abilities – to live together in peace as if they were all indivisible folks of the land. This wish results from attempts to reconcile two opposites – our need for love by others, including even those we may consider lesser beings, and our fear of enslavement or even destruction by people from whom we might otherwise expect fraternal love. These conflicting feelings shape our ways of thinking and our mythology in two types of stories – the tyrant and the prince. The ancient Greek tragedian Xenophon told of a hated ruler who wants to be loved by citizens and who has to end up dreaming of a world that reconciles love and tyranny. The fifteenth-century Italian Niccolò Machiavelli wrote *The Prince* about how to survive in a society that is really a place of war, where the individual must vigilantly fear all other people as threats.

Viewing multiculturalism as a conflict of desires that often appear unrequited, I explore its implications for critical approaches in politics, the social sciences, and the humanities. Fear and the need for fraternal love are the concerns of our daily lives, what decides whether we view our living through the rose-coloured glasses of a comedy or as unadorned and unvarnished before the naked eye as tragedy. Therefore I take a phenomenological approach, which should offer us a different way of looking at many things we take for granted in our social orders. I argue that genuine multiculturalism as the acting out of a Hegelian recognition heals and binds separate entities with conflicting desires into a unity of love. It fuses them collectively into a new being and culture with new desires and intentions now common – indeed organic – recognizing everyone as immanent to a new folk of the people. Through recognition, love triumphs over fear, loathing, and lamentations, leaving absolute love the only unrequited desire, for members of the union to create for themselves. This creation flows out of a public discourse in which all members, immigrant and native alike, enter as equals. Each person starts with her or his own cultural values and morality from prior socialization and offers what he or she considers to be good and valuable from them for adoption in the ethical order under construction.

In a philosophical sense, I want this analysis to be dialogical, one where questions about proof and acceptance of claims to knowledge bring answers that engender further questions. Therefore everything that society gives will be up for challenge – everything that starts from an a priori position, that common sense tells us should naturally be the way it is or appears. We will be hoping to find the aporias that are the foundation for differences and misunderstanding in social life. These aporias will take us back to each citizen's or minority group's social beginnings – to all their primordialism before the current round of social construction. At the same time, we would be witnesses at the death beds of what is old as well as at the birthing chambers of all that is new. This way, by viewing the aporias, we may discern why some things do not work out in society and how we may prevent unintended consequences of our well-intentioned actions.

All of this will lead, I hope, to some first principle that allows us to state our "truth" in a way that makes sense to someone else, especially to you, the reader. As Richard Zaner suggest in *The Way of Phenomenology*, this will be "no more nor less than philosophical criticism and grounding carried out to their fullest extent – to the foundation."[15] It is our search for the basic, for what we cannot further divide, so that we can arrive at the root causes and the foundational materials that produced the new state. We will also know what about these actors auditioning for roles of full citizens is disposable and even inessential. This analysis will focus on Canada, the place where official multiculturalism burst forth in human consciousness, a country that is still on a path to becoming the just society that is the end point of genuine multiculturalism.

I am hoping, as the Hegelian philosopher J.M. Bernstein states, to change the topic of conversation to one of civic belonging and embedding and away from ethnic national ownership and rights in the hope of bringing new insights and reflections to an old moral problem that seems intractable, particularly in an officially multicultural society such as Canada. How can multiculturalism succeed if newcomers are not willing to conform to "the liberal views" of Canada, for example? I hope we can rephrase that question to something about why multiculturalism is not working as we idealized and intended it. What do we need to change? How then do we obtain a pure heart, with citizens living in peace, order, and good government as Canada originally intended – in other words, in a just society? In theory, this form of social justice would bridge two seemingly conflicting divides: the fraternal recognition/socialization that offers all members the same identity as persons while allowing them to preserve their individualism and a form of social stratification that allows citizens to be equal and all members to have the same chances and opportunity to live in a society of their own making and desires.

To achieve this ideal would require in general the recognition of the law and the ethics of the sovereign that Canada is officially a multicultural country and that it is a liberal democracy. Law bases its citizenship on the equality of citizens, whether born in Canada or elsewhere. According to our various human rights bills and the Charter of Rights and Freedoms, this equality translates into freedom from discrimination because of ethnicity, language, place of birth, race, religion, and sexuality. It also guarantees the positive freedom of social mobility and various political and economic rights of self-determination and of achieved statuses.

Yet some people, invoking privilege or historical advantages, consider themselves the real Canadians; they do not accept the proclaimed law, intentions, and morality of the sovereign that guarantees *all* Canadians equality of social status and recognition. Those opposing this new general will are a law unto themselves, recognizing the sovereign wishes as external to them as the leading actors; as moral agents they follow a script they know will pilot them to happiness and peace. And as a law unto themselves, openly and overtly, they challenge the wishes of the sovereign as the authority of the folk – in effect, technically making criminals of perceived transgressors and certainly social deviants out of themselves. They refuse to accept the admonition by such thinkers as Rousseau that the sovereign, as the expression of the general will or national spirit, has a right to make members of the society free by demanding coercion and conformity to the prevailing spirit of the times. They are, in practice, becoming hardened lawbreakers by going against the expressed and official wishes of the sovereign or state. Yet they do not see themselves as naturally transgressive.

These opponents are tragic figures, refusing to give in to the limits that a higher authority imposes. The result is unhappiness from dividing citizens and potential citizens into two camps – people who fear and hate the new order because it does not take into account differences and diversity flowing from prior socialization and historical claims of entitlement, and people who can transcend differences and diversity to love and care for one another as fellow citizens simply because the new order promises to deliver what they desire most.

How can a free society that does not rely on coercion for social wellbeing stop some of its members from acting criminally by following their own laws and inclinations? How does it encourage holders of aberrant views to accept the laws of the sovereign as personally and organically theirs – not as that of an external and artificial legislation? How can the recalcitrant members accept the new manifestation of the general will when its dictates appear as something that does not flow naturally from inside them? Is there an ascribed unchangeable and natural Canadian of ancient lineage, because immigrants recognize themselves as change agents? The very act of immigrating is one of change, or a severe diremption, that shatters an organic nature. This is what separates people whom a particular state and culture initially socialized one way from the unquestioning love of their compatriots and culture. Diremption sets them adrift and places these seeming cultural castaways under the law of a different people and culture. The outsiders can only hope that eventually Canadians will love them as much as any other Canadian. This would be an achieved status. They can also hope that the new society will be one that treasures diversity. These new arrivals are tragic heroes who find themselves under a law not of their making. They also hope to ultimately find themselves in a comedy – one in which they feel love and acceptance, something that goes far beyond mere tolerance and even accommodation of their differences and diversity.

This is why, for me, the focus of change has to be on those who believe there is no need for change from within themselves. In status, the ascribed Canadian, like the ascribed outsider, must mythologically become the achieved-status Canadian. We focus on those members who behave and act as if they are already the legislator or the embodiment of the spirit of the sovereign, the embodiment of the folk, naturally or otherwise. They are probably firm in their perception of who the heroes and villains of the piece are. More than likely, they believe they know with certainty that those they legislate about and keep in check are separate and apart from them. But to their consternation, they must come to realize that the sovereign has a different view – indeed, the sovereign's favour might have shifted away from them and now resides with others whom they perceive to be less deserving. The sovereign might even oppose them. In effect, these recalcitrant old-timers in seeming positions of privilege are no different from the tragic hero who acts only narcissistically, out of self-love. They have withdrawn from a wider universal infinity that is the state to a loveless world of fear with tight boundaries and limits. They are the tragic heroes who find themselves in an environment where imposed limits and boundaries are the norms – except that this time, they are partially responsible for the limits, which are intrinsic to the formation of the society, even if it does not address their desires anymore.

By changing the gaze to examine tragedy and comedy in the generic sense, I hope that I can give this book some appeal to students of social science and the humanities, particularly students of literature, or at least those who combine the formal study of literature with cultural studies. By examining tragedy in the particular that is a Canadian setting, I hope we can highlight issues of morality and ethical relations that stem from a bold initiative by Canadians to carve out in Western civilization a place that really lives up to its ideals of egalitarianism and democracy as the epitome of living free – the fairytale ending: "and they all lived happily ever after."

And if we have not yet arrived in such a mythological place, this book might be instructive, helping us to understand why such unhappiness occurs, why this goal might always exceed our grasps, and why, ironically, that might be a good thing – why the goal as such should intentionally be no more than as civic citizens just trying to get along – to allow erstwhile foes to simply become just *players,* if not actually ones who love one another; to at least recognize that each must use the other and likewise be used for another's benefit, all for the glory first of society and only second, if ever, of the players: that is the story of the search for a genuineness that is organic to a life of tragedy.

In this respect, I trust this book will have some appeal in such areas as politics, political philosophy, social anthropology, critical sociology, cultural studies, literature, and communication – in short, in the many facets of our everyday lives.

A CONFESSION

Now for a confession as to why I am writing this book. I want to assert a Canadian claim for the conception and practice of official multiculturalism. Canadian theorists receive worldwide notice for their contribution to the discussion of how people can get along, particularly people of different backgrounds and supposedly different moral codes. I want to explain as clearly as possible the thinking that has produced an ideal of what I call "genuine multiculturalism," something that even Canadians are still trying to introduce into daily living. This practice aims for a radical, egalitarian form of democracy that restrains the tyranny of the state and of any majority. So it is a special type of democracy, but most basically assuming a common citizenship in which everyone is equal and an active participant in managing the country. This echoes a dream that

I have called elsewhere a society "where race does not matter."[16] To this end, this is an exercise in self-reflexivity, and in particular, an attempt by a writer who is ascriptively an outsider or an immigrant who is male and non-white from the South – specifically Barbadian – using his perspective and positioning to understand the lived reality of Canadian citizenship.

In a real sense, then, Canadian multiculturalism is ideology: a belief or even secular theology that as an act of faith suggests that there is a proper way to behave in the hope of getting out of life the optimum, or the greatest good. In that sense, it is a statist approach to good living, based on what ought to be a way of improving on what history has brought us. In this respect, as an ideology, it can be evaluated as a theory and its successes and failures ticked off and compared.

But multiculturalism in Canada is more than ideology and theory – it is a way of being, an existence, that has to be the point of departure in any analysis of who we are as a people, what we want, why we act the way we do, and how we happen to be the way we are. This is an existence that precedes anything we do in a state: we start out as if we are coming into the state or country from a state of nature that is by perception multicultural. This means, collectively, that diversity and differences permeate us in the new state. The people start out as a heteronymous entity or being – as arriving already dirempted and inorganic to all but a limited native land. There is no *natural* sameness in this human creature we call "Canada." There is no purity, no single type of human being, as nature created. Any attempt at imposing sameness starts out as an exercise in violence by imposing a specific essence or identicalness, and the state that results must by nature be exclusionary. This resulting sameness is slavery rather than freedom, for it imprisons those within and it imprisons those that cannot enter. There can be no equality or universal justice; otherwise the notion of sameness would be internally meaningless – it would mean that we are all the same yet we are all fundamentally different. Genuine multiculturalism shifts the argument not to contesting the superiority of inferiority of different ways of being but to solving the contradictions of sameness and diversity as I just outlined them.

This is the irony and contradiction of genuine multiculturalism: the sameness that we have must be both imaginary and a product of our social living. This happens in the way we see one another not so as to privilege our differences but so as to transcend the diversity. In our genuinely multicultural state, we take all the diversity that nature has given us, and we process it mentally: we change it in thought and expectations, and we create an equivalence among all the different parts. This equivalence is what we consider the humanity in all the different specimens we perceive, out of which we must create a single state that is by nature constitutively plural. We see ourselves not as how nature made us but as how our social living together, our histories and cultures, make us the same *type* of human. Genuine multiculturalism socially constructs a special type of folk – one that is unnatural but very sociable. Mythologically, the folk is the quintessence of the rational, which sublimates and homogenizes differences and diversities into a sameness. Individuals and societies are at one, where individuals are not only lawgivers but are at harmony with the law. In this rational state, everyone is free, as free as she or he wishes, knowing that his or her wishes are the same as those of the wider collective or state. Among the folk, he or she is fully a person, a rational individual who is part of a rational culture.

At the same time, genuine multiculturalism starts by recognizing that even in a civil state of laws, common aspirations, and make-believe equivalences, we are all different and we can be as different as we want to be. A major problem occurs in practice when an old, statist ideology of a seamless assimilation keeps intruding on our thinking. It forces us to keep searching for a state or country as a physical existence where there is no difference and where we are all seemingly copies of one another. In practice, this appears to us as the height of scepticism, where there is no reconciliation between what our cultural and ethical conditions tell us we should see and the reality of what we *actually* see. There is alienation, because the two do not add up. Ironically, we have to force ourselves, intentionally, as rational beings not to lapse into the expectations of this old, discredited model of assimilation – in effect, to see what we want to see and to believe that it is the reality. Instead of accepting that life is tragic, we tell ourselves we have arrived in a comedy. We force ourselves to be idealistic, and thus we eliminate the contradictions that would otherwise confront us and make a seemingly delusionary choice: we accept as true what we imagined over what our senses tell us is natural.

Genuine multiculturalism rejects physical and enforced assimilation in exchange for arriving at this comedic reality. This sea change occurs through a conversion that, as with any religion, derives from faith and from belief that in turn emerges from desire. This conversion calls for transcending what would otherwise appear natural and real. Genuine multiculturalism puts in place of a conversion, which other people mandate and prescribe, personal freedom and choice. It means choosing out of personal volition to accept a contradiction. One side says that any collection of human beings is as diverse and as shot through with differences as it consists of individuals and groups in the collective. The other attests that the same collective – because it is a collective – is by definition and in practice a unity, a universal, in which its many and different members share one essential characteristic: their humanity.

For Canadians, the highest expression of that common humanity is citizenship. Basic to this understanding is acceptance that the world starts out as multicultural. A new state comes into being out of what was there before. Within the boundaries of this state, the collective of citizenry will always possess diversity and differences. The citizenry is simply a part of the world now that now exists within boundaries of this state. Within this exclusive terrain, citizens act as if there is no diversity. They display the equivalence and identicalness of a common citizenship that speaks to the sameness of membership.

But there is a meaningful caveat: genuine multiculturalism argues that moments of rationality are rare and fleeting. Such is the tragedy. We are always in need of socialization – reminding – that we can, as an exercise in positive freedom, become rational and live in a fraternal harmony. And in accepting this tragic existence, genuine multiculturalism suggests that, as we strive for this folkishness or transcendental rationality, we devise laws and norms of socialization that are as rational as our history and culture have tested, that we change them when these laws and norms prove not to be rational or as rational as we thought or wish, and that, as we build mechanistically these ethical norms and ways, we live as if we have in fact reached that promised land of rationality, that we are the best social construction of a folk we can ever be, that we are in or nearing one of those rare moments of rationality – that we imagine life as a comedy rather than as the tragedy that it is most times.

It is for this reason, then, that multiculturalism in Canada has a much wider meaning than other liberal democratic countries commonly understand. This is true, for example, of the United States, where multiculturalism is primarily an ideology or a way of making sense of life. In this sense, multiculturalism in the main is a mechanism – a means to an end – whether through affirmative action to repair historical disadvantages or as a means to reshape institutions that have developed through a history of ethnic and racial assimilation. The initial damage occurred because the society held one type of American as the ideal and then forced every other type to adapt and conform to this norm of living. This type of analysis and practice results in tribalism and other forms of identity politics, all aiming to force the acceptance of diversity and difference as state policy and practice, as an antidote to historical racist practices. Typical of this thinking is the criticism of US multiculturalism by the educationalist John F. Welsh:

Racism defends and promotes the philosophy and practices of differentiating and separating people for the purpose of domination and subjugation based on race, ethnicity, and/or linguistic group. It elevates some groups above others. It argues that the allocation of social desiderata should be based on a racial or cultural identity. Multiculturalism particularizes by defending and promoting the philosophy and practice of differentiating and separating people for the purpose of subjugating them to the authority of political, cultural elites and educational elites, who are presumed to promote ideas and public policies oriented toward the emancipation of disadvantaged racial, cultural and linguistic groups ... Preferential practices have been effectively and appropriately criticized by a variety of political interests as a new form of discrimination. To the extent that multiculturalism promotes the differentiation and elevation of some groups at the expense of others, it is a form of tribalism and an enemy of human liberation. At the very minimum, this dimension of multiculturalism eschews discourse on the universal meaning of human liberation as far as individuals are concerned in favour of discourse that focuses on reinforcing boundaries that separate ethno-racial blocs.[17]

Welsh offers a way of studying a world that is still in the grip of diremption – where the unity has been shattered, and where there is no real love, solidarity, or recognition of the humanity in all human beings in the state. Life has become segmented and abstract. This is not genuine multiculturalism, which builds on love and unity and which is not exclusively a means or a mechanism to achieve some laudable ending. Rather, and significant, it is the very spirit and the desire for unity as the best way for humans to exist that fuels this need for oneness and sameness. At the same time, it recognizes that within this desired unity life can express itself in as many forms as life itself thinks necessary.

Life produced the spark or thought that led to the creation of a particular nation-state. This spirit or desire is the acting out of life itself: as a state of being in which diversity and differences are the norm or natural way of existing and, seemingly contradictorily, as a striving for a sameness of experience for all the diverse individuals and groups, producing a common existence from living together – from trying to get along. The nation-state that life demands cannot turn around without shattering life itself by walling off one part of life and keeping it as an unchanging flame behind the bars of the nation-state's physical boundaries or culture. The freedom of a unity with accepted diversity is the genuine multiculturalism that Canada has as a goal, and it lifts up, rather than wiping out, the differences and diversity that intuitively seem to be the opposite of what is unitary, seamless, and whole.

But there is a second reason for this book that goes with the first of reviewing how the Canadian experience spawned official multiculturalism as a modern identity and culture. Talk of multiculturalism is worldwide and often pejorative. I recall sitting on a panel in Lisbon in 2006 at a Metropolis Conference, which brings together academics, government officials, and public intellectuals from around the world to talk about immigration, immigrant settlement, and citizenship. On my panel were participants from Canada, Britain, and Australia, talking about multiculturalism. And it was while listening to some of the other panellists that I realized that multiculturalism does not have a precise meaning. In my remarks, I commented facetiously that maybe we Canadians should take out a trademark on the term and make sure that people use it correctly. For, in my estimation, "multiculturalism" in Britain and Australia might conceptually have been a good example of a special form of pluralism, but not the kind of pluralism that we in Canada call "multiculturalism." Britain and Australia start with the idea that there is an English nation and a special type of Australian and that everyone else has to assimilate or adapt to these dominant groups. This is not genuine multiculturalism. What is missing is some powerful sense of egalitarianism and that the society is still under construction and that all hands have equal influence in fashioning what is in the works.

So what is genuine multiculturalism? Ironically, in the last several years, some Canadians seem to be turning their backs on and even denying the remarkable multiculturalism they have developed at home, and instead to start talking about a universal type of multiculturalism along the lines of the European or even the American model. Fear rather than loving dominates these other lived experiences as the best ways to express the desire to be free. This is often an illiberal, conformist, accommodationist type of pluralism, where one or two supposedly "true" or intrinsic groups claim dominance over the entire land, its culture, and its history and demand by right the ability to deal with members who deviate from established norms. There is a norm of citizens, and some ethnic group is repository of it. Everything else has to assimilate to this norm. Everything else is relative to this storehouse. This thinking has led in Canada to the very divisive debate over "reasonable accommodation" of immigrants and visible minorities – an issue that one would believe would be a liberal absurdity if citizenship means anything in general, and if in particular it really means equality.

On top of this, there is much discussion in Europe and particularly, judging from what I see and hear on television, in the United States on immigration policy. In the United States, it seems that the country is under siege by foreigners. First, there are all those illegal immigrants storming the "broken" borders from both north and south, provoking endless discussion of what immigration is doing to the personality of the country. The changes are frightening to many people, and their impact seems to them to be nothing short of an attack on the entrenched, historically perceived nation-state. And this angst over the shift that is occurring seems to intensify with each report by the US Census Bureau, reinforcing the perception that the country is changing demographically. Most recent reports indicate, at the time of writing, that by 2040, the United States will no longer be a white people's country, at least demographically. "In a few decades," reported the *Miami Herald* on its website in the summer of 2008, "all Americans will be [members of] minorities. White non-Hispanics will drop below 50 percent of the population as early as 2042, according to U.S. Census Bureau projections to be released Thursday. That's about 10 years earlier than demographers previously had predicted, said Grayson Vincent, a demographer with the Census Bureau."[18]

This news caused an echo around the world. "According to the US census bureau," Britain's *Guardian* reported, on 14 August

the dominance of non-Hispanic white people, who today account for two-thirds of Americans, will be whittled away, falling steadily to less than half in 2042 and 46% by 2050. In the opposite trajectory, those who describe themselves as Hispanic, black, Asian and Native American will increase in proportion from about a third now to 54% by 2050. Such a rapid demographical shift is in tune with trends that have been seen for some time, but it is happening much faster than experts had predicted even four years ago. Demographers see it as among the most intensive changes of a country's racial and ethnic make-up in history, every bit as dramatic as the huge influx of Italian, Irish and east European immigrants that transformed the US in the early 20th century.

It seems that much of the anger in this discussion stems from recognition that most of the illegal immigration that lies at the heart of this debate is from Mexico and other Spanish-speaking countries. This unregulated influx is happening at a time of growing concern by dominant groups that they are likely to become minorities in the coming decades and may "lose control." Indeed, subsequently, most analyses of the 2012 results that saw re-election of the first African-American president reinforced this trend: the emergence of an alliance of non-traditional voters that can change the country. This coalition of mainly members of ethnic and racialized minorities, women, and members of the lesbian, bisexual, gay, and transsexual communities appears in opposition to a bloc of mainly white and male voters that traditionally dominated national politics. This analysis presents the sea change in voting patterns as the death and rebirth of the United States – as tragedy or comedy, depending on opposing perspectives.

An earlier article, in the influential *New York Times,* spoke to this fear that a tragic trend was emerging for defenders of the existing social order.

With the number of non-white Americans above 100 million for the first time, demographers are identifying an emerging racial generation gap. "That development may portend a nation split between an older, whiter electorate and a younger overall population that is more Hispanic, black and Asian and that presses sometimes competing agendas and priorities ... The Census Bureau estimated yesterday that from July 1, 2005, to July 1, 2006, the nation's minority population grew to 100.7 million from 98.3 million; this is about one in three of all Americans. The new figures also suggest that many states are growing more diverse as minorities disperse. As a result of immigration and higher birthrates among newcomers, the number of Hispanics grew by 3.4 percent nationwide and Asians by 3.2 percent. Meanwhile, the black population rose by 1.3 percent, and that of non-Hispanic whites by 0.3 percent. (The number of American Indians and Alaska Natives increased by 1 percent, and Native Hawaiians and Pacific Islanders by 1.7 percent.) More than 20 percent of children in the United States either are foreign-born or have a parent who was born abroad. Nearly half the children under age 5 are Hispanic, black or Asian.[19]

To some people, these kinds of changes are frightening. Typical is a commentary on Haaretz.com that looks at the changing demographic picture worldwide, one in which former minority groups challenge, even replace, traditional ethnic majorities – the victory of the powerless and even enslaved and accommodated. One of the biggest fears is what will happen when those old majority groups and were the standards for normality lose their status. As Yoav Orgad, a Harvard University researcher, asks, will the new majority of minorities be able to keep the rights that liberal states traditionally extend to minorities? Ironically, growing minorities seem to be liberalizing the United States! Orgard states:

This assumption becomes less self-evident in a world in which there is immigration of a scope that is unprecedented in history. The reference here is not merely to the huge number of migrants knocking on the doors of the developed world, but also to their character. They come from the Third World – Asia, Africa and the Middle East – to societies whose culture is different from theirs. Some of them create cultural enclaves and challenge local culture. The immigrants' objectives have also undergone change: Today most of these families are not migrating in search of temporary work; they seek permanent status.

And thus it happens that the majority feels the need to protect its own character. In the year 2035, for example, there is expected to be a Hispanic majority in Texas; the same thing is supposed to happen in 2040 in California. This population, most of which is Mexican, has a different way of life, language and education from the majority in those states, even in terms of its second generation. Even though these people do not challenge the right of existence of the American nation or its basic values, public discourse in the United States is full with demographic fears. Mexican immigration makes a huge economic contribution to the United States, but those who oppose it see it as a cultural danger to the nation's values.

Demographic fears in Europe are more significant. Within something like 20 years, a Muslim majority can be expected in Brussels – and this may happen just a few years later also in Amsterdam, Berlin, and Oslo. Immigration laws recently enacted in Europe are an expression of the demographic hysteria there. The federal state of

Baden-Wurttemberg in Germany recently introduced a questionnaire that examines immigrants' points of view with regard to culture, sport, women's rights, homosexuality and anti-Semitism. Holland demands a certain level of fluency in its language, and asks immigrants to sign a 'contract of integration' with the government. This week Britain launched a reform that includes demands for knowledge of English and for acceptance of British culture as a condition for immigration.[20]

Why any of this should be a reason for lament rather than celebration remains a mystery to me – unless there is the underlying assumption that the American melting pot or ethnic assimilation is not working and that there is a danger of the country's becoming more multicultural in practice, even if not only in official theory. As Orgad suggests, something wider is at issue here. It is what I describe in this book as concern about the existing way of life, about perhaps the very being of these countries that are multicultural demographically even if not officially: the difference between what they really are and how people perceive and understand them, how they make sense of themselves. "There is a common denominator," Orgad argues, "between the demographic fears of Europe, the U.S. and Israel: the connection between maintaining the culture of the majority and self-determination. In Europe they are afraid of the establishment of a Muslim state in the heart of the continent, and there have been expressions supporting this on the part of Muslim clerics in Holland. In the U.S., they are worried that Mexican migration will create territorial enclaves whose values are foreign to American culture, and there have been Mexican public figures who have expressed the wish to turn the community into a linguistic-cultural-national minority that is recognized by law."

Indeed, it looks as if Canada has already been there and done that, although the angst in some quarters remains just as strong. Canada struggled with the ideal of producing what in its time seemed the perfect country – a white man's paradise – but those intentions failed miserably. Now Canada, as an official multicultural entity, trying to survive, recognizes that the act of survival alone requires it to have no real intentions: it has no visions or ideals of becoming a perfect country. Such perfection can exist only in the transcendent, a thing of dreams. Canada is about the job of actually living, of taking what it has – all the various levels of perfection – and fashioning an existence out of them. Without intentions there can be no great designs, no end-of-history triumphs or *telos* or end points, no manifest destinies, and, effectively, no exclusive homeland for some privileged ethnic or racialized groups. Living is now without intentions. Life is messy: it is about different and diverse people having no bigger challenge than to get along together and in the process build something more *authentic* to their time and place, an achievement for which there is no guarantee and that would not count as a failure if it never achieved authenticity. For just to live together is to be inauthentic.

How Canada set out to deal with this particular development is a story worth sharing. And sharing this story might even help us in Canada to really come to terms with our own immigrant problems and the need to deepen and further enrich our multicultural mosaic.

Another form of besiegement for the United States and other Western countries also appears to be coming from foreigners and from those in other parts of the world with links to multiculturalism. Again fear dominates. This is the never-ending threat of terrorism from abroad and of radical jihadists and other Islamic fundamentalists at home in a country that is, in theory, not a Christian nation-state, although from practice this is hard to tell. For these are not the guises in which we expect the next Prince Charming to materialize out of the wilds. They are more in keeping with the image and purpose of a Machiavellian Prince than with one from common folk tales.

If the present brings a gospel, it is always bleak. It seems that the United States, for example, is like the eponymous protagonist of *Gulliver's Travels*, whom the Lilliputians have tied down: the culprits hail mostly from among its own citizens. It appears that the nation has forgotten how to dream of better times. In this sense, this story appears to be not a tragedy as much as a comedy – a resignation to having to live within limits that others impose. In effect, what we witness on our televisions, hear on our radios, and read in the printed press is the personality of a truly tragic figure of a president, regardless of party affiliation, caught in the web of good and evil and waging a seemingly interminable war to eradicate evil.

But history tells us, speculatively, that this will never happen: evil will simply shift its identity, shape, form, and even source, for moral laws are powerless to overcome evil and to conquer its source. This is so because often good and evil flow from the same source, and only later can someone evaluate whether specific actions met a standard of good or evil. Perhaps it is for these reasons that the Western world seems destined to fight a never-ending war on terrorism, for, in the end, who really knows who is a terrorist? And aren't even those we now consider to be good likely to become terrorists if circumstances change? Current determination of good and evil can be relative only to a specific moment, that of 11 September 2001 and the attacks of terrorists on New York's World Trade Center towers and the Pentagon. That day is not only the moment of a new creation but also that of a mythological Fall of biblical proportion, when humans supposedly acquired a new consciousness, when they ate from the tree of knowledge and realized that for the most part life is bitter and tragic. Such are the fruits of human bondage and the desire to be free, to return to a pre-creation moment when good and evil, as we now determine them, did not exist. As the Russian Christian philosopher Nikolai Berdyaev states, the irony of this kind of situation is that "the moral good has a bad origin and its bad origin pursues it like a curse," making this situation truly a tragedy.[21]

The image of tormented human beings eternally cast out from Eden and relentlessly, even if vainly, trying to revert to those more paradisiacal times remains with the president on whose watch the Fall occurred; he remains historically in our mind forever a tragic person. This is an image of humans in need of redemption, someone standing in the need of prayer to quote the old African-American spiritual: someone on whom is stuck the mask not of life but of death. In this regard, morality and personality seemed to inextricably intertwine, giving shape and form to each other.

Genuine multiculturalism is about hope and dreaming – and about creating a state or world in which, despite all their differences and diversity, people can get along and love and be loved. This is so because they have learned how to *want* to get along. They know no other way besides just getting along that could satisfy their desire for freedom. In this respect, multiculturalism is quintessentially American, especially in the wider sense where the geographic term applies to the entire hemisphere. Genuine multiculturalism grows from the practice of different and diverse people coming from around the world, joining others already in the Americas, and then establishing an ethical order different from anything elsewhere in the world. That the Americas are effective settler communities in the eyes of the dominant groups makes the region by definition multicultural; the people of the Americas, or any state in the region, are hybrids of different peoples and cultures. This gives the region a distinctive demographic and cultural identity.

This creation put into play for the settlers an ethical order consisting of different peoples, all with no prior claim to the Americas as fatherland or motherland, all with different values, abilities, and world views. All the individuals have in common is a desire to live in what each of them thinks is freedom. In this new setting, they fight among themselves to determine for which single group or combination of groups the constructed state or states will become a homeland. In this state, the initial desire for freedom comes into fruition. For the unlucky, the new reality stifles and suppresses that desire, even if it can never obliterate it from their hearts. Once this order is in place, its preservation and retention are justifiable on the same grounds as if the ethical order had sprung fully formed out of the land and the living experience, as in Europe.

There are always people existing in the state who have require accommodation because the dominant ethical order cannot satisfy or realize the desires they brought into the state. Often, the state has to give them a reason to accept a social order that appears to cherish them less than others. They have to abide by norms with underlying rules and values from a more homogeneous and demographically selective European experience. They have to trade in their ethnic authenticity for an easy living in a state whose institutional ideals and norms Europeans developed for themselves.

What attitude should such people have towards or expect from others: fear, or perhaps love, just like those who feel that society meets their desires? Similarly, what should society expect from the people it accommodates as their price for even partial membership? Should they fear the society and keep agitating to make it in their eyes more just and accepting of them, or should they show love even to those who do not fully reciprocate such affection and show fidelity to the existing order? Whether the individual or the collective exorcises the fear, we are dealing with a tragedy resulting from unacknowledged virtues and unmet desires. The alternative would be a comedy, even a utopia or the kind of thing that has enriched the dreams of ancient philosophers and modern-day idealists alike.

This is why central to this book is the telling of the story of the Bad John, who is a character out of the Americas. But the Bad John story is even more important for its archetypical characters that have no name. These are the females who are powerful figures behind the various masks. At times, they are really the characters with two faces – the mothers and the fathers – and at times, they are neither. They are just nameless persons on whom weight, production, and direction rest. Genuine multiculturalism occurs when a society, in a world where traditionally the only gender that matters is male, consists of all Bad Johns, none of them fitting the social norm, for this is a society without lasting norms and where values are always in flux.

As Prime Minister Pierre Trudeau argued, in multicultural Canada "we are all minorities," and the idea of an average Canadian to which all others must conform is an absurdity. The beauty and indeed challenge of living in such a relationship: conformity is not necessary. As Trudeau stated, the realization that often Canadians cannot even agree among themselves on what is Canadian is something worthy of celebration rather than of hand wringing. This lack of conformity is its opposite – *freedom* – and that, ultimately, is genuine multiculturalism. That is why there should be no melancholia: for who really misses conformity when the opposite is freedom? Indeed, not even a tyrant.

Still, there is a second way in which multiculturalism is American – at least philosophically and sociologically, for it is steeped in the uniquely American way of rationalizing what meaning there is in our world. Multiculturalism is effectively pragmatism: that culture and way of thinking that reject absolutes, such as definitive and never-changing notions of good and evil. Pragmatism tries to arrive at a livable compromise while putting off a final absolute decision until a future time. But then again, the country that presents itself to the world as truly American has long strayed from its pragmatic roots at home and abroad and has been dabbling in absolutes. This is why it shifted from a country that fought against colonialism to seeking to become a colonial power in the Middle East. This is why it has thumbed its nose at what it long led the world to accept as an institution of pragmatic politics, the United Nations.

The United Nations is the stage where, with a straight face and seemingly with no intended duplicity, sovereign nation-states can give up part of their sovereignty and still claim to be totally free and independent; where even the smallest and weakest nation-state can claim the same equality as the strongest superpower and largest entity; which can force the would-be great men and women of these states to climb down from seemingly tyrannical positions and conform to the desires of the weakest without losing face, by pleading that they are simply respecting the rules of the stage and the game – they are the protectors of law, order, procedure, and rationalism; the United Nations, as the platform for comedy and even self-delusional farce, the ultimate in inauthenticity and American pragmatism as a philosophy of life. Ironically, some

Canadians have seemed anxious to emulate the United States and to steer a course away from what Canada has pioneered in human relations. So, perhaps, this is a story of groping towards genuine multiculturalism that Canadians also need to hear, if only as a reminder of the distance we have come and how much further we still have to go to reach our ideal. So that, in the words of the African-American spirituals, "Now ain't the time for turning back nor for backsliding."

In a real sense, the issues that I have just raised speak to the questions of how we see the world and how we see ourselves in it, and this view forces us to confront a major attribute of multiculturalism: it is about power – not how to centralize and tyrannize power, but how to diffuse and share it, how to use it for the common good. Such is the way of tragedy and comedy. And, again, this is a story of any Bad John.

A FINAL CAVEAT

As I indicated above, this is an exercise in idealism. Indeed, readers may question if any discussion about multiculturalism can be other than idealistic. However, I recognize that some readers might be uneasy about this book's appeal to a Judaeo-Christian mythology to explain basic issues of socialization and stratification in supposedly secular societies that are liberal democracies. This is not an attempt to preach or seek converts to a specific religion. It is an effort to deconstruct much of the Western way of living, especially in the New World. Can anyone truly say that she or he can be fully Western and not celebrate Christmas, even carnival, Easter, or New Year's, in ways that are not socializing to a specific culture? Can anyone attend a sports event or political rally, salute the flag, or enjoy classics of literature, theatre, music, and film without participating, even if unintentionally, in this way of life? Can anyone participate in the normal rituals of social living – marriage, birthdays, divorce, schooling, attending court, and paying tax – without encountering ideals of justice and social living that spring from Christian sources and even motivation?

I argue that even when they claim to be secular, those societies build on Judaeo-Christian notions of justice. And I contend that to understand issues of justice that assume diversity and difference, it is necessary to understand the very foundations of justice. We should examine phenomenologically the basis for the structures societies have historically put in place to determine who is a citizen, who is entitled to justice. Such an examination can explain why, because of those structures, it is difficult to reconcile the competing claims for justice of people whom an implicit Christian mythology defines as different. Indeed, the story of liberal democracy and the freedom it brought to unequals or outsiders – people in that condition because of such categories as race, ethnicity, gender, sexuality, and disability – is a narrative of how those people had to first overcome arguments legitimizing these inequalities.

In traditional Western societies, as we can see in such seminal works as Thomas Hobbes's *Leviathan*, these points of view grew from an understanding of what a Christian God would demand of any social order, Hobbes's Christian Commonwealth. Similarly John Locke, a key thinker of state formation, argues that the aim of a civil state is simply to protect rights that God gives to individuals. For Locke, and in keeping with a Christian narrative, whether in a state of nature or in society, the ultimate appeal against an injustice is to God in heaven.[22] Put another way, the description of society as Christian is purely ontological and sociological rather than an ethical, political, or philosophically determining of ideals or advocated stances. It is an attempt to explain a specific social reality. Others may find much of Christianity in other Occidental religious myths and influences – perhaps suggesting that its diversity makes genuine multiculturalism naturally polytheistic.

If then the analysis in this book engages with the Christian mythology of social living, it is, I submit, a result of the legacy of contributions to the formulation of Canadian multiculturalism by Hegelians[23] – especially those of the Toronto School – and their fellow travellers who call themselves, philosophically, pragmatists, communitarians, and personalists.

PART ONE
Natural Differences and Social Equality

1

Genuine Multiculturalism

Repairing where he judg'd them prostrate fell
Before him reverent, and both confess'd
Humbly their faults, and pardon begg'd, with tears
Watering the ground, and with their sighs the Air
Frequenting, sent from hearts contrite, in sign
Of sorrow unfeign'd, and humiliation meek.

John Milton[1]

The destruction of the colonial world is no more and no less than
the abolition of one zone, its burial in the depths of the earth
or its expulsion from the country.

Franz Fanon[2]

In the dominant mythology of Western societies, the lesser beings in society often remind us of our total and most basic humanity.[3] It is the narrative of how those who do not have entitlement – whether from lack of education or money or through other forms of categorization as inferiors, as foreigners, women, or slaves – come to have a sense of belonging or full recognition; how, most important, they become sovereigns. For these are the "codgers," as Joseph Campbell describes them, even the lowest elements of the folk, who are so central to the production and development of Western myths and fairy tales. And, as he suggests, they are also the characters in the stories. French revolutionary Charles Fourier articulated these concerns some two hundred years ago: "Why does philosophy jest with these poor creatures by offering them the rights of sovereignty when they demand only the rights of servitude, and the right to work for the pleasure of the idle?"[4]

Our standard ideal of sovereignty or freedom is that of liberal democracy, with individuals possessing rights as inalienable possessions but living in a society or having fraternity with similar social democratic idealists. To me (and this is an argument I am offering), these socially inferior beings are mythologically the true human beings in their confrontation with death from moment to moment. They are capable of pushing the entrenched people to greater heights of humanness. In one of our dominant fairy tales, the true human is the unassuming Prince Charming, the outsider who must risk even his physical death to achieve his life's goal, he on whom a socially dead Snow White, Cinderella, or Sleeping Beauty awaits her revival to a new, more just life. In using myth and mythology, I want to build on what Campbell offers by referring to what Reinhold Niebuhr calls our "poetic metaphor" – the way we speak idealistically about ourselves and our cultures.[5] This is what the eminent Canadian cultural theorist Northrop Frye calls an "understanding," not in the common, literal sense as "the explicit meaning that a prose paraphrase would give, but [in] the integral meaning presented by its metaphors, images and symbols."[6] As the new citizens in a society, immigrants are most likely to reify the latest image of the state. They are generally the poor, the oppressed, the outcasts, and often those whom the entrenched members of society reject. Historically, this type of treatment, which we observe in their social inequalities, has given them a special prophetic role according to the primary religion or theodicy of Western society.

They are the very people on whose side, as American liberation theorist James Cone argues, the now-dominant Judaeo-Christian ideology places God. Since God is ultimately the chief rational idealist or equalizer in the entire cosmos and the figure in whose image the world is being made, this dynamic privileges the new citizen.[7] As we saw above in the Introduction, the dystopian or negative equalizer is of course physical death – that towards which all humanity heads. But it is also a thought with a long history of what universally is humanitarian, of who can become fully human and in our modern times fully a citizen. Hannah Arendt has reminded us that, traditionally, "A human being or *homo* in the original meaning of the word indicat[ed] someone outside the range of the law and the body politic of the citizen, as for instance a slave – but certainly a politically irrelevant being."[8] The quest was always how the inferiors were to become relevant, at least politically. We have come to associate political relevance with liberal rights.[9] And in the burgeoning thought on social justice, these lesser mortal are the ones whom such eminent theorists as John Rawls consider the benchmarks for testing the appropriateness of any action in a liberal society. Rawls defines true liberal justice as a situation where collective actions do not further disadvantage those who are the worst off in the state.[10]

These characteristics of liberal justice were in favour with the Liberal government of Pierre Elliott Trudeau, the founding father of a new Canada. It developed the notion of an officially multicultural nation – a liberal democracy aiming to become a just society, a communitarian or personalist paradise. Looking back on his government's actions after he left office, he stated,

> I was always concerned, for example, about the injustice done to people living in those parts of Canada where they couldn't make a living or where they had a standard of living that was far below the norm – it just wasn't fair. They didn't have the services from their governments, they didn't have the opportunity for investment …
> We tried to find the right tools … there were no easy solutions. But we did get some results. Jobs were created, the poverty rate lowered considerably; and the objective corresponded to my view of Canada that a citizen has a right to expect to lead a decent life in any part of the country. It was necessary in a country as vast and sparsely populated as Canada, and it was a matter of justice.[11]

Even without Trudeau's history, a speculative reading of Western mythology and traditions would suggest that new citizens are still the people on the right side of the force of history, looking to help create an ideal society that is good and free. The narrative of multiculturalism, then, starts as a quest for freedom, for social life, for individuals' recognition as full citizens.

These types of citizens are the ones whom political theory from antiquity to modern times has associated with fraternal love, which we see most clearly in the solidarity of the folk or the reverence for a fatherland or a mother tongue. They are the opposite, as political creatures, of the tyrant, whom people despise and fear in a social setting and who can only desire love while acting out a nature that subjects can only fear. Tyrants have power, often for life and particularly that of physical death over others, mostly the meek folk; they do not have moral authority, for they have no uncritical acceptance by the people. Theirs is a tragic existence, where their natural desires and propensities make the individual incapable of living within the settings that society demands. Facing this living reality, these individuals, in return for love and even care from cradle to grave, delude themselves into thinking that they live in a world of only love. This delusion makes their living comedic, for they base it on pretense. As tyrants, they have moral authority ontologically for they are liberal individuals. But what also makes them tragic is that they have no *real* power. Power without authority is hollow; authority without power is useless. The ideal social being possesses both. Real power means the ability to freely realize individual desires. Most tyrants, though possessing life-and-death power over others, are unhappy because in practice they have one and not the other, they cannot make even those who are lesser than they love them, so that they lack emotional and psychic fulfilment. They are unhappy consciousnesses who must endlessly search for meaning and relevance in life, especially in the areas that psychically matter most to them as social beings.

Symbolically, the state in which tyrants and their loved citizens live must appear natural to both characters – and therefore the state has two faces. It appears to be a tragedy because it must sympathize with people who want to break all limits and be free, but it also appears as a comedy to those who recognize that they would lose their way of life if they were truly free. Facing the demands from both sides for an authentic relation, the state ends up an unhappy consciousness, trying its darnedest to please both sides, and failing both spectacularly.

The state, too, lives a tragic experience, for it does not want this chasm between those who fear and those who love it: it wants love from all its children, er, citizens. All it really wants to do is to survive in a basic, animal sense by preserving itself while also meeting the human desires, dreams, and machinations of its citizens, every one of them. This is ironic, since it is the very opposite of the priorities individual citizens have for the state: mostly, they want their way, for the state to act in their individual narrow interest first.

As we saw above, Rawls argues that inequalities are permissible in a liberal society only if they do not further aggravate the situation of the poorest and least advantaged. In Trudeau's argument for official multiculturalism – an argument that he calls "Social Justice"[12] – we continue to hear echoes of Rawls's seminal *Theory of Justice*, which has become a Bible of sorts for liberal theorists and practitioners of social justice. This acknowledgment that there is a ground for good social behaviour makes the newcomer more of an *authentic* prototype of the ideal citizen than those who might passively claim, like any mythological Snow White, Cinderella, or Sleeping Beauty, an ancient legacy or vintage,[13] but whose likeness has not kept up with the state's changing ideal. And ironically, the old-timers are never the most recent image of the state, because those of so-called ancient lineage, of a specific essence, who might consider themselves *pure laine*, or of an unhyphenated nationality and patriotism, must present themselves as changeless.

By its very nature, the state, to survive across time, must be changeable and accommodating to just about any context or exigency. It must remain relevant. In contrast, the old-timers trap themselves in an ancient, outdated archetype of the state, compromising the state's current authenticity. This is the opposite of what we expect of the *Bildung* process, which outlines how individuals actually follow their dreams to fufil a destiny that we presume they impose on themselves, which is akin to Isaiah Berlin's epitomizing positive freedom as self-mastery;[14] for in its truest form mythologically, *Bildung* works best when individuals can see themselves in comparison to some higher desire. As the pragmatist George Herbert Mead suggests, there must be recognition – acceptance by an Other significant enough to matter.[15] More than that, there must exist some desire and a feeling of alienation such that his or her status no longer satisfies the individual, who aims for something different – often for a way of life that he or she perceives in people whom he or she considers the very opposite. "It is not enough," says the German philosopher Hans-Georg Gadamer, "to observe more closely, to study a tradition more thoroughly, if there is not already a receptivity to the 'otherness' of the work of art or of the past [that captures the differences]. That is what, following Hegel, we emphasized as the general characteristic of *Bildung*: keeping oneself open to what is other – to other, more universal points of view. It embraces a sense of proportion and distance in relation to itself, and hence consists in rising above itself universally. To distance oneself from oneself and from one's private purpose means to look at these in the way that others see them."[16]

If the old-timers are changeable, they lose all bragging rights and all legitimacy of special benefits and privileges, even by their own argument. In a sense, because they must always be changeless, they find themselves wielding a two-edged sword: on the outward thrust, it can maim and hurt other people; on the return, it can also hurt and maim them themselves. Society has to be adaptable to survive, and the main aim and goal of any society has to be its longevity rather than the maintenance of an old image, even that of the state's purported founders. Society has to concern itself about the present and the future – particularly how the present will contribute to *its* future. Society always has to be evolving, remoulding and reconstructing itself, to become less in the image of Nature and more in the image of all humanity – and not just a privileged faction thereof. Society must constantly reconstitute itself.

But analogously, as our fairy tale tells us, Snow White, sporting all her purity, must die so that she can receive a new spirit. The spark that occurs when the lips of the stranger touch hers – an act devoid of her own choice or volition, for she has become a dead body without any human desires – reverts to a level that is lower than the animal, for the animal can at least assist in the preservation of its own life.[17] Our Snow White (and particularly Sleeping Beauty) and her kingdom had simply returned to their most basic form: she had returned aporiatically to the point at which there can be no further diminution, to her virginal state as clump of clay under a glass, and her kingdom had returned to the state of nature of vines, trees, and thickets that require revivification to become human again. Children do not usually play among such thickets and thorns. Prince Charming has to risk life and limb to make it through the thickets and thorns, and then risk his health by offering the kiss that will produce his dearest desire as a beloved. In so doing, he takes the chance of catching whatever laid her low. This does not matter, as the mythology implies he will be the king and ruler of any future society, so not much ill can come to him in this act.

The state always has to find a way not only to make sure its youngsters not only play free of dangers and pain but to make sure that there are always more of them coming along. Rationally, the state's first acts always have to be in service to Prince Charming, to make sure he can deliver that kiss. More than that, if there is a real moral to this story, something that we hope to learn from this fairy tale, it is that ultimately Snow White or Sleeping Beauty herself has to agree with the state that, for the preservation of life, people must attend to human desires if there is to be justice – for the state, at least. The bringer of life has to receive a willing embrace and even internalization. It becomes Sleeping Beauty's task to teach, educate, and ultimately domesticate or socialize this archetypal desired immigrant, the one we have come to know as Prince Charming. The gender implications are quite tragic for the female – she must be willing to offer up her body or to remain dead to the social world.

As Jane Billinghurst argues in *Temptress: From the Original Bad Girls to Women on Top*, the Westernized story of the world as ideally gendered is an old one but still very much in vogue in modern society: "There has always been the pervasive feeling that men, the rational sex, impose order, whereas women, the emotional sex, subvert it. Men control nature, whereas women collude with it. When there is a general nervousness about where the civilized world is headed, storytellers remind men of women's connection with the world's naturally chaotic state. They tell tales of what happens when women tempt men from the straight and narrow."[18] Usually when women do not conform to this gendering, the mythology presents them as temptress. "She finds a victim and uses him to pursue a selfish plan. Such tales serve as an advance warning system: there's potential danger, but if men stick together, the situation should not get out of control. To underscore this point, the storytellers make sure that the wayward dame – along with the poor man she duped – gets her comeuppance in the end."[19] And as Billinghurst notes, "Men, the designated storytellers for most of history, are the keepers of temptress tales."[20]

THE SWORD OF ACCOMMODATION

Using the analogy of the swordsman, society as the sword is warring with the perceived fighter just as he is with the seeming foes. From the point of view of entrenched people, it is ironic whom the sword actually cuts, slices, or even destroys. Often it is the outsiders who feel the wrath of the sword: unless society ascribes them as Prince Charmings, it sees them as usurpers – they are the citizens that it must accommodate in inferior statuses and positions. But, as in the mythology of the Garden of Eden, a story replete with angels bearing flaming swords, the fall in human society tends to occur when those who feel they are greater than the common humans in society conspire against lower beings by seeking to place accommodations or social limits on them. For only a sovereign can impose accommodations on underlings, for they involve things it will not allow, whether through force, cultural ostracism, or some other form of violence. This is tantamount to telling Prince Charming where and how he can kiss the Sleeping Beauty or Snow White, as if the voice from the dead has the power to instruct the living and, by extension, the giver of new life.

Accommodation is the privileging of a narrow form of civic citizenship over all the other elements we associate with modern citizenship. These other factors include the political, which society now couples with democratic rights; the element of social welfare, which derives from the rights of all citizens to have the minimum daily requirements to keep body and soul together and to avoid falling into poverty; and recognition, whereby all citizens have the right to have an identity of their own that sets them apart from fellow citizens but does not negate the universal civic identity of the entire nation-state. Accommodation is privileging of a part over the whole and a way of limiting citizenship as an attempt to capture and recognize the universalism and oneness that is humanity. It prolongs modernity's quest for freedom by misguidedly aiming to shape a unique and discrete citizenship out of humanity. It does so by culling all those people it deems not worthy and by leaving them out of a state. Its hope is to maintain some vague ideal of civic and social authenticity. Effectively, this state is now no more than an ethnic nation with a supposedly distinct and uncontaminated culture. It assures accommodation only at the point of the sword or of some other weapon of conformity and social death.

Contrary to the aims of liberal democracies, accommodation is a perverse form of identity politics that aims to produce or maintain social inequalities. It is contrary to the idealism of creating a modern state that is free of rigid or ascribed social hierarchies, especially those that can be caste-like and derive from such factors as ability, ethnicity, gender, language, origin, race, and sexuality. If there is a group or individual that it must accommodate, then it must also be an accommodator, which legitimizes and recognizes a specific type of behaviour or particular classes of acts or non-acts as having met the level and quality it requires for validation as worthy of accommodation. The folktale of Sleeping Beauty, and similarly of Snow White or Cinderella, has no social meaning if it places Prince Charming in the shackles of accommodation; he must have the full rein of citizenship, not only that of a workman helping to produce the next generation.

Accommodation can follow only from the belief that there are two types of peoples, owners and others – all those who do not own – and that ownership translates into a sense of belonging and the exclusive rights of disposal. Such thinking in modern times is a residue from the discredited dreams of another era, dreams that imagined countries as homelands for specific and exclusive ethnic and cultural nations. In Canada, this thinking is a reminder that there are still rational idealists who believe that Canada is properly a "white man's country," even if it now has occupants who are other than white or ethnically European and Caucasian, but whom this thinking must naturally place and position appropriately through accommodation.

To this end, we may think of how the concept limits social mobility in a liberal democracy and how, in the history of the Americas, accommodation is central to placing and positioning specific groups of people as superior and inferior. For example, in *Caste and Class in a Southern Town* (1937), sociologist-psychologist John Dollard looked at how southern US states entrenched white supremacy and black inferiority following the Civil War. "Slavery was a means of keeping peace between the races from one point of view, but it had to be maintained ultimately by force, as indeed all societies do. The use of force was most apparent when counter-aggression on the part of those coerced was most obvious, in the case, for example, of slave revolt. It was true that force could be kept in the background and even greatly diminished, once the underdogs had acquired the habit of suppressing protest against the slave system and aggression had become blunted within the slave personality. This acceptance of frustrating circumstances without open resistance we call 'accommodation.'"[21] Accommodation, then, is traditionally the opposite to the ideal that "fundamental to all 'freedom' in our system is free disposition of one's own person, and the right to move where advantage seems to lead."[22] To be historically relevant, it must invoke the spectre of the Civil War and of civil rights battles as a meaningful solution to the social problems such as those that Dollard documented and that today could still under-privilege some unfortunate citizens.

Counter-intuitively, people who consider themselves the "salt of the earth," the son and daughters of the fatherland, the speakers of the one and only mother tongue, can damage society. They see themselves as battling for authenticity against the barbarians, the Bad Johns, the uncultured, the strangers, the immigrants, the refugees, the fifth columns and proverbial Trojan horses. In modern terms, they believe that they are fighting against all the Others – those whom, as agents of change, they deem initially and quite correctly to be a threat to the existing way of life, privileges, and ideals of social well-being. Seldom do these defenders of the traditional life appear to grasp the lessons of our fairy tales, especially the one about how our Snow White and particularly Sleeping Beauty, she of ancient lineage in the kingdom but now dead to the world, must await the outsider, he from another kingdom and time, to bring with him different values and virtues, to bring her the kiss of life so that they might live happily after. Ironically, as we saw above, Prince Charming might also be a Bad John. And just as important, the nation or state has historically been gendered as male in a way that suggests there could be no alternative way of gendering, a kind of thinking that genuine multiculturalism challenges.

But, historically, the genuineness and ideological purity of nationalism and patriotism evaporate not when the perceived lesser beings "corrupt" the presumably perfect society. Instead, the real damage – a snuffing out of the vibrancy and the life itself of the society occurs when old-timers, those with the greatest claim to cultural perfection and belonging, fail to realize that they are neither the preferred groups nor the sole ones to produce the future history of the society. Rather, it is the people whom they often view as inferior and as having virtually no real claim to belonging, legacy, absolute inheritance, and fidelity of race and ethnicity that really capture the humanity of the moment and are the new life force, especially in a society that depends on immigrants for continuing existence. Ironically, the outsiders add variety, spice, and even continuity to the existing way of life through their infusion of blood, both literally and figuratively. And they produce a transfiguration of sort: for once the society claims them as citizens, it deems that it has made them over in its own image, or its latest and most idealized likeness. But, as any mirror shows, the image must logically also be a true, reverse representation of what is in front of it, which suggests that what is there is also a true reflection of what is in the mirror. Genuine multiculturalism challenges these norms of a good life, and for this reason it gestures to the freedom of living in a normless society.

Such is the tragedy, for people claiming privileges and higher and even prior claims over every other citizen, especially for those who believe that their ethnicity is the determining factor in a nation-state. Or perhaps they believe that longevity, such as ancestry in the state, gives them a prior right to control and even to dictate what is in the state's best interest. And here we might think of any ethnic dispute around the world, of the struggle over the accommodation of minorities in plural societies, and of the placement and positioning of immigrants in societies where there is some ethnic or national collective that claims linguistic, economic, or even political advantages over newcomers. Tragedy tells us that the favours of the gods – and even the blessings thereof – are mythologically on the side of the seemingly culturally inferior beings: the ones who will give to their new land not only their body and its physical strength, in the form of their seeds and gonads, but also a new culture that is fully acceptable neither to the "founding" groups nor to those needing the outsiders for life itself. Indeed, it is a truism of life that nothing ever comes free of charge. Immigration as a major component of state formation and preservation is one of the finest examples of where this truism is, dare I say, true. As I stated earlier, indeed, Nature favours the Bad John – or it does initially.

To this end, there is another lesson of life for the learning: that the latest good is often fractured and heteronymous; seldom is it a unity in more than name, so that in this battle, and as the mirror teaches us, if good wins, so does evil. The result is a new or evolved state of existence that locks good, in its mutated form, and evil in a new relationship, both trying to act as if they are separate, independent, and autonomous of the other. The most recent moment is always one of compromised existence, with neither good nor evil fully having its way. If we are lucky, good has the upper hand and imposes its will, albeit temporarily. More than likely, this imposition also involves evil's agreeing to accept habitually the dictates and commands of good, but this takes place with the knowledge all around that evil will attempt to slip its bonds and take over at its first opportunity.

Under this covenant, neither evil nor good can sleep comfortably. This anticipation, with its attendant excitement, strategizing, and relationship dynamics, is life itself. A specific society has to mould new human good out of its old notions of good: Who belongs? Who has privilege? It contrasts these people against those whom it initially positioned as outsiders, who arguably do not belong. For the mythology to remain relevant and true, evil in its many personifications must contest and try God and the good.

Such, too, is the story of the tragedy of living in human society. Good and evil also change with direct intervention not by individual members but rather by the collective. For often what would become the new good – such as a will for life – requires collective imposition. This is most appropriate in a society where the state is sovereign, receiving its empowerment from all the people – in other words, a traditional democracy. But once the outsiders have merged with and extended old definitions of "the people" by becoming citizens, the state has no choice but to side with *all the people* – a group now inclusive of and sympathetic to the welfare and desires also of the once-outsiders rather than vis-à-vis just the previous groups, regardless of their prior dominance. This is particularly so if citizenship translates, at least in theory, into equality and where, idealistically, a citizen is a citizen is a citizen, with no meaningful differences among them. Even more, this should be the case when, as in liberal democracies, citizens are abstract holders of rights, each having the same number and types of rights, so that, as in Canada, the state cannot recognize any meaningful difference between a citizen born in Canada and one native to elsewhere. Those who were once dominant and even authentic representatives of the state are now, in the eyes of the evolving sovereign state, no more than fractions of the people. The state would have to conform with the new spirit of what it is to be *a people* or even *a nation*. This is so even if old-timers may see the state as now kowtowing to that ideal of a new, wider, and more universal definition of the people; even if they know the state is supporting the ideal of equal citizenship regardless of heritage and longevity in the land.

One of these ethical values guarantees Bad Johns equal possession of all that the society commonly produces and owns. This assurance is foundational or constitutional, in return for the outsiders' willingness to trade perceived absolute freedom for social membership. This is the gain that society promises from belonging and sharing a common identity or citizenship. Bad Johns do not have entitlement to a superior share or treatment, for that would be to treat them as if they were still absolutely free. Neither would they receive a smaller or inferior share, for that would not be an incentive for them not to declare open warfare on everyone else and resort to their old ways. Therefore, in a practical application, freedom *is* equality. Freedom, as we see it in equality of treatment, becomes the standard way of life. It becomes the culture, and any deviation from this equality in areas enjoying freedom would breach the state's founding principles.

This is the spirit that most of us intuitively believe makes the difference between life that is social and cultural and life that is purely random and left to open chance. In the former, there is still *time*, which is the way we measure change from one state to another. But we also want those changes to have coordination and a pattern, to conform to our notion of what is good and desirable. Therefore, we want society to direct and even manage and accommodate the changes. And for this to happen, we must assume that there is a manager and director of change, something cultural that determines the direction and extent for what is, effectively, change. That director and manager, that maker of culture, society, and history, is the *spirit*, often called the "spirit of the times."

One thing we have come to notice about this spirit is that in time it causes everything to die, even the freedom that would remain unattainable if it were to remain in the transcendent and beyond time and human interaction. The same is true of all those Aristotelian gods, Bad Johns, and Prince Charmings that are the gendered ideals of immigrants. If they want to become human and social, they too must be willing to die socially, to let go of what to the senses could only be an irrational world in favour of a rational one. This is the story of tragedy, for once the eternal and incorruptible enters time, involves itself in the human society that experiences change, even the once everlasting must die.

If the everlasting did not die, it would not be human and would therefore not be sharing fully in human life. This is one of the historic truths
about multiculturalism – the tragedy that the gods of the universe must
undergo so as to live in a new time that socialization makes rational.
This is equally true of those groups and individuals who hope to stall or
even prevent the changes that emerge when other ethnic or cultural
groups begin living in the same society. They want to maintain historical
stratification. It is equally tragic when we read the stories in the mainstream media about a father steeped in an old traditional or fundamental way of life who strangles the life literally out of a daughter or son, or
about a father or husband who refuses to allow a wife to live the new life
of a new society, trying to prevent changes in her way of life. It is tragic
on a human level, because it is a vain attempt to force others to live
within limits that someone else deems natural and who takes on the
form of a tyrant and, ultimately, even of a giver and taker of life.

The *natural* in society is change, which is the measurement of time.
Change means adopting the new and throwing off the old. This is why,
tragically, the old has to fall hardest to accommodate the new spirit. This
is why the state, as the sole sovereign capable of lasting in a given form
across time, must be receiving and even championing change. It has to
choose life to transcend the generations. This means it must constantly
reject the old and embrace the new, otherwise it would stifle and even
snub out life itself, for in time everything changes, and time occurs only
in human society. Human society is always in search of the new spirit,
even if this is a quest in vain for an evolving spirit that would put an end
to change. Ironically, even for the state, society, by trying to remain
changeless across time and generations, must be changeable.

The paradoxical unchanging change would be that of values, of what
the individual considers good and proper. It would be attitudinal, expressing itself in open-mindedness and willingness to appreciate difference
and change in the same spirit. The paradox would be to live in a time
that envelops change while existing in circumstances that effectively are
timeless and always current. We hope that newcomers would accept and
subscribe unthinkingly to the same values as all of us and that they would
show this change of heart by their unchanging respect for the laws of the
land, in the same way in which we allow for the supremacy not of individuals among us but of the rule of law. We hope they would have, ultimately, the same personality we all share. As twentieth-century Dutch
political philosopher Hugo Krabbe put it, we want them to join with us
in the creation of the modern state, a state in which that which knits us

together is a new spirit that could be either secular or religious, and sometimes both, as we saw above with Niebuhr and see below with Charles Taylor – a spirituality and love for one another that now resides in all members of the community.

Krabbe states,

> This spiritual nature is the source from which *real* forces and through which duties are aroused to living consciousness. These forces rule in the strictest sense of the word. Obedience can be freely rendered to these forces, for the very reason that they do proceed from the spiritual nature of mankind. The power which they are able to exert has its roots just in this, – that we voluntarily follow their guidance. Such a spiritual force permits law and right (*Recht*) to be born and continually permits them to be born anew. That which works in us as the instinct, the feeling, the sense of right, and which lives in our souls as an original force of nature, lies at the basis of that authority which compels us to live in a society. It is the foundation of the rulership which is inherent in the idea of the state.[23]

In the end, I am reaching for a definition of *spirit* that is similar to what Charles Taylor offers in *Multiculturalism: The Politics of Recognition* (or is it the politics of *love?*). "The notion of authenticity," he says, "develops out of a displacement of the moral accent in this idea. On the original view, the inner voice was important because it tells us what the right thing to do is. Being in touch with our moral feelings matters here, as a means to the end of acting rightly. What I'm calling the displacement of the moral accent comes about when being is touched with our feelings takes on independent and crucial moral significance. It comes to be something we have to attain if we are to be true and full human beings."[24] This spirit, then, as authenticity, is the genuine consciousness that emerges as the hybrid awareness and social conscience in a community. It is that desire and good will and the freedom to *act* according to morals that liberate the self or consciousness and whose actions or ethical behaviour make this self genuine and true to its ideals – to itself.

A new spirit or conscience would be abroad in the land, and all of us, native born and immigrant, equally would be carriers of it with love and the respect that goes before a compulsory, even hypocritical tolerance. For this to happen, there would need to be quite a few changes: a new spirit or ethical order for the state and more confidence about its future; a new attitude and even image for those old-timers claiming legacy and longevity as conditions of ownership of the state; a transformation in the newcomers who have changed radically into ideal specimens of what the state wants for its *future*, particularly *its* future citizens. With these changes would come hopes for a better life, if not for ever and ever, as in fairy tales, at least for today and possibly tomorrow, too.

In chapter 2, we return more fully to the idea of the Bad John and how, ironically, such a universal person is also in every player in society, in all of us. For within this dominant mythology, who other than the Bad John can be the embodiment of the new spirit of the times in all its revolutionary fervour for change? But to best trace out this ideal type – thereby speaking to the power of diversity and difference – we must place him in another world than that which Western thought usually projects as the norm of appropriate socialization and historical development.

2

Dramatis personae

I now must change
Those Notes to Tragic; foul distrust, and breach
Disloyal on the part of Man, revolt
And disobedience.

John Milton[1]

THE CAST

Bad John

When I was growing up in the Caribbean paradise of Barbados, there was always a specific character of special note in our society. We called him "Bad John." Bad Johns were fixtures not only in my native land but, if I can judge from the blues, calypso, mento, reggae, or soca songs that provided our daily carnival, were present in every Caribbean island, and apparently went by the same name everywhere, too. In Jamaica, they are also the Badman, Don, or Rude Boy to name a few of these apocryphal beings in what people generally call "badmanism." And the blues and jazz traditions of the US South suggest that these personalities were as much at home in the United States. They also answered to such American names as Bad-Bad LeRoy Brown, High John, Mack the Knife, and Stagger Lee.[2] They are central dramatis personae in the drama of life in many societies – a story about society's outcast – the delinquent, the deviant, the disruptive, the malcontent, the racialized, the untouchable, even the terrorist. The story of these characters is about whether or not they are able to find a way to become part of their society or social order, about how they can bring about meaningful social change only from within. Theirs is a classic tale about the folk.

Their story is about state formation and even reformation, about how individuals come together in a fraternity. In the end, for those of us in a social order we call "the West," this is a narrative about how a society can be democratic and inclusive. It is perhaps even more important that the story of how the society must change to fully incorporate even those citizens espousing the most radical change to existing social order, its beliefs, dreams, institutions, and traditions about social justice. There must be conversions, or metanoia, of those seeking to change society and, just as important, of society itself. For the individuals, theirs is also a different story within a wider, overarching narrative: about how, once in a society or fraternity, particular individuals can achieve all the possibilities and potentials that society offers – how they can be individual citizens, free to become whatever they hope or aspire to become. It is about how they can live a life that for them is a narrative idealistically ending with the words "they lived happily ever after."

This is a story of liberal citizenship. Linking together as individuals and a social order, these are the two narratives of liberal democracy in our time: the individual as a free moral agent imagined as a sovereign end unto himself or herself, and the society, both means to individual happiness and an end unto itself, as the sovereign determinant of what will be that happiness for its individual members. Can happiness arise out of these two conflicting views of sovereignty?

These prototypical characters, these Bad Johns, helped to populate the entire Americas, and everywhere they were always in conflict with the state. That this was so when I was growing up was yet another sign of how small and interrelated was *our* world in the Americas. It is also a measurement of how unnatural and tragic to the region are the imitation European societies that created nation-states for privileged ethnic groups and marginalized all other residents and citizens of different ethnicity and supposedly different race in these prototypical Eurocentric social orders called "Western states." The "vagabonds," as my grandmother called them, people for whom she felt there was no human satisfaction or love, were always a test of what we knew to be freedom or how we were to achieve the greatest desires of our hearts, how we could imagine ourselves living a story that ended with the moral affirmation "and we live happily ever after." The presence of these "criminals," as my grandmother would also call them, was as well a test of how reasonably we could engage with these malcontents and still remain, in our own eyes, free, and therefore in control of our happiness.

These Bad Johns were blessed with such natural attributes as above-average strength, abilities, and a perspective and sensitivity only they could have. These qualities gave them the ability to make everyone else singularly unhappy. In my memory, there is no equivalent female name, even if there might have been one or two women tyrants; they usually received generic labels such as "badwoman," "Jezebel," "loose woman," or "virago." These identities described behaviour that was perhaps more acceptable and partly embracable than that of the Bad John and spoke even to some degree of socialization. It was as if even the rudest woman was always already in society, already a social character. In a mythical sense, there seems to be no named female equivalent to the Bad John, to this perceived embodiment of pure negativity. Perhaps this is because, in this folktale that is an alternative to the traditional European model, the woman quintessentially represents creativity in its most positive forms.

But I want to suggest that naming Bad John categorizes a specific set of human virtues and natural attributes – the ability to harm society and to be unsocial – that is first a human characteristic. These societies traditionally associated these uncultured virtues with a specific group they gendered as male. Many modernist societies such as in North America or Europe have historically racialized such destructive virtues in a way that homogenizes traditional gendering into racialization that presumes the inferiority and superiority of certain members of the society. Sometimes they racialize and gender them, as in the case of black males.

Our desire in my formative society was to make these vagabonds fully human and worthy of our affection. We wished to instill in them whatever it took to make them more than the sum of their natural attributes, more than what was so *natural* to them. This was an exercise in *Bildung*; in a sense, they would be following their own unique path to a perfection that is meaningful only in a social setting. By seeking a collective happiness with others, they would move from a status of pure bestiality to becoming cultured and socialized. The process they would undergo would be as old as that Enlightenment philosophers and social scientists recommended – most notably, G.W.F. Hegel, Immanuel Kant, and all those social anthropologists contending with the morality behind turning individual people with very noticeable differences and diversity into a common social order with fraternity for everyone, equality of citizenship, and individual freedoms. Those thinkers hoped that people who are different and need accommodating within an existing order could do so without its placing rules or constraints on them. Their achievement must come from a pure heart, with no fear, malice, or feelings of loss and restraint. Society must accommodate them freely – fully and without reservation, as if they were always no different from anyone else, and they must be willing to accept freely the constraints of accommodation it demands and offers.

Bildung

Bildung starts with recognition of the natural forms of the individual and how to change those forms at the individual's behest to the benefit of "humanity," a term many people take to mean the majority, or those portions dominant enough to define what humanity is quintessentially. We usually understand "social perfectibility" to be the goodness of citizens – their willingness to sacrifice themselves for others. Society wanted to brainwash these Bad Johns into believing that the natural way is always bad, or that it was vastly inferior to what most people could make out of the raw resources that they inherited. *Natural* characteristics and values focused simply on survival and existence; humanity at its fullest was actually about the seriousness of living, about planning and achieving common goals, about having fun and bettering the existence in which people find ourselves. It was about passing time in a meaningful way.

A social order, then, as Kant bequeathed it to us as a viable prototype of fraternity, is when and where individuals would come together as separate, distinct, different, and diversified as their talents and qualities made them. In this setting, they would become the very best Nature intended for them while sharing and helping others to attain a lasting happiness – a perpetual peace, as Kant[3] calls it, and the peace that Hobbes describes in *Leviathan* as justice, as the primary reason for the creation of that *civitas* that is in design and practice a Christian commonwealth. John Locke claims peaceful coexistence is the only condition for which humans will give up the rights of living freely in a state of nature for social life. "The great end of men's entering into society, being the enjoyment of their properties in peace and safety, and the great instrument and means of that being the laws established in that society."[4] Ironically, what Nature intended for them would be the determination not of Nature itself but rather of the social desires and subsequent norms for collective happiness.

This was the Enlightenment spirit or attitude that society cultivated and that became our social ideal; it is the mark of our humanity as the highest refinement of our species. Such thinking occurs today in the socializing process – in what Hegel theorized as recognition of differences and diversities within a single unity.[5] This way of thinking still seeks to reconcile the many contradictions in society – a process that ideally is at the heart of what we call "multicultural citizenship" within a liberal democracy.

This attitude was clearest in the wish by individuals to be social rather than just *natural* and atomistic. The social was what people imagined and then proceeded to work on to make our living reality, as a work in progress, aim at leading us to a time when we would all have purity of heart vis-à-vis everyone else. The difference between what Nature gave us and the reality, or what *lived reality*, which we manufactured out of available resources, was the result of our work and effort. The social was not only what we constructed but how we worked together to transform ourselves and the landscape around us. These actions were at the heart of how we as social beings passed our time and marked a history that was uniquely ours. The spirit gave us motivation. This spirit was love and what in a multicultural setting we now call "recognition."

Prince Charming

In my mind decades later, I still carry the graphic image of a typical Bad John: not only of his physical attributes, but of his mental demeanour: angry, spirited, vexatious, troublesome, immensely strong, and a loner to the point of being anti-social. He was a force unto himself, a tyrant in any folklore. His morality – or lack of it – was always on display: in the gangling way he carried himself, in his stout, muscular build, squinty eyes, knitted forehead, bulky chest pushed out, and bulging biceps always at the ready. It was there in the manner in which he always demanded his own way and the many ways he mixed up right and wrong. Most of all, this was a man spoiling for a fight, with anyone, so impervious was he to reason.

In our minds, he was ignorant or simply *ig'grunt*, a term that didn't describe ignorance of formal schooling or illiteracy or innumeracy as much as it did lack of social skills and graces. As we said back then, this was "a man without knowing," or a man without a good conscience, a kind of brute beast existing at the animal level of mere survival. In our reality and by our thinking, this was the essence of someone who was lost and unsaved, a diabolical type of person who believed and acted as if only his world counted and everyone else was inferior and of little consequence. This was a charmless person, because such a person had no need for charm or cultural niceties.

It is not trite to say that the typical Bad John was no Prince Charming or Sweet Boy; he was no prototypical saviour coming out of history, out of the unknown, yet whom we might expect to be a saviour because we expected him to act out of purity of heart. Bad Johns and Prince Charmings: one the material, the other the dream; one steeped in fear, the other the source of hope; one an error Nature perpetrated on society, the other the truth or the embodiment of the existing ideal of what is good for society; one a rogue and a subversive, the other the embodiment of love and the divine law that is Polynices, loved by his sister in a tragedy such as *Antigone*; and both of them having a special place in the imaginations that our cultures instil in us.

They are opposites: one acting from malice and self-interest, the other from purity of heart – opposite ends of the same concept of fear and diremption and of love and unity, the act of cutting asunder and creating divisions where there would have been togetherness, a shared spirit as a unique self-consciousness or a united life. The two ends are like the opposite poles of an hourglass. One cuts and drive apart, creating disunity, a spirit of loss, and unhappiness. and the other heals and brings together in a fellowship of universal love. These collective memories start with all of those images of Bad Johns and Prince Charmings or Sweet Boys that populate fairy tales or children's bedtime stories all over the world.

MASKS

But we live in a world of irony, with no guarantees of morality, justice, and reason, which may at best arrive in unexpected and even contradictory ways. We do not have full knowledge, and often, when we do test what we think to be certain knowledge about ourselves and others, we come up empty or confirm the very opposite of what we think we really know. Indeed, it is no wonder that Greek theatre presented survival in a social order as wearing masks – that the same word represented mask and character – so that what we do determines who we are and who we are determines what we do, and some order or the other emerges out of all these seemingly uncoordinated and purposeless actions. Character and personality, the Bad John or Prince Charming, are not so much what we think we are but what others expect us to do or be, and this objectification at the same time determines what we are and what we do.

The mask we receive determines our character; our character determines the mask other people give to us, a kind of objectification that

Frantz Fanon captures so well in *Black Skin, White Masks*[6] – the quint-essential explanation of a tragedy, where race shapes the individual's experiences, who still hopes some day to exist in a comedy, acting and acted on as if race does not matter. One mask may hide who we really are; another might make us what we want to be. Tragedy speaks of how irrational we find the world and in return how existing social orders find any of us not yet fully integrated into it.

We live in an inverted world, compared to the one that we think we know. This realization can dawn on us when we face the brute facts of living. In this relation of lord and bondsman, we are sceptics. We really do not know. The stoicism in us often proves to be so content-less, so improvable, in what to our imagining is an unreal world. So in a world of prototypes of scepticism that we call "Bad Johns" and prototypes of stoicism that are Prince Charmings, we err on the side of uncertainty. We protest the existing social order and start by assuming sceptically that people we do not know are Bad Johns until *they* prove differently – until we can have that certain knowing that we associate with stoicism of an internally held truth that the wider world does not contest. This is the complete opposite of how we treat people whom we think we know as well as we know ourselves, those whom we presume always act out of goodwill and good faith– those whom we, stoically, assume to be inno-cent and as good as we until we find out different. Such is the story of the treatment of immigrants in most countries, especially in those this book considers.

Every new entrant in a society is a potential despoiler, some perceptually more so than others. Therefore, as ideal forms, most immigrants start out in Western consciousness as Bad Johns, and this includes women, whose gender this archetype of humanity subsumes in a patriarchal sense. They are the embodiments of society's history of error, and of those receiving them not knowing with certainty makes the new arrivals start out in their adopted country that way stereotypically – as potential purveyors of uncertainty. As strangers with strange ways, they need watching and monitoring. Some receive this image more firmly than others, particularly those whom society has already racialized as inferior and who can only with great difficulty shake the perception. Those whom society racializes as superior beings, as the Americas traditionally branded Europeans as racially white, might never have to really contend with that potential. Instead they would affirm their other potential iden-tity, that of a Prince Charming. More so, the dominant social perceptions of the prototype of the good – as the European male – make immigrants, now largely from non-Europe, the Others to the white Prince Charmings. Because they are Others who are objects of the imagination and perception of the dominant groups, society often places and positions these non-traditional citizens-in-the-making in inferiority. Therefore, when old-timers see immigrants through the lenses of European intentions in foreign lands as having the same initial desires as those who force their way initially on the peoples they found, they end up wearing the Machiavellian desires of colonialists, even though the immigrants may want nothing more than to integrate, to merge as seamlessly as possible. For as Will Kymlicka has shown, most immigrants to a country such as Canada come not to set up their own societal cultures, a kind of folkway, buttressing it with their own ethnic public institutions, but to become citizens and to take full membership in the existing liberal democracy.[7]

Historically and perceptually, North American and western European society constructs non-white immigrants as Bad Johns and positions them as such. As I have argued elsewhere, the newcomers arrive as representatives of the blackness of humanity before the norms and precepts of a specific society "civilize" them.[8] The big question for the protectors of society is whether they should allow the Bad Johns to have the same destiny as the Prince Charmings – proving their worth by becoming good citizens, that is, good workers, who, along with society, benefit as fully as society mandates for every citizen from what they produce. Do these newcomers face the same fates as the protectors and even owners of the social order want, the ideals they desired for the continuing happiness of the fraternity before the strangers entered the state to save the lifeless maiden under the glass?

The answers to these questions – and what determines our actions towards others – crystallize from our expectations of what contributed to a narrative or fairy tale that ends in happiness or perpetual peace. These are the stories that we receive with our mothers' milk, on our father's knees, and from our caregivers and other who socialize us. They are the discourses of our life and what help us to know what is really meaningful.

"At first glance," writes Alison Lurie, the Pulitzer Prize–winning novelist, literary critic, and essayist on children's stories,

most famous fairy tales seem so implausible and irrelevant to contemporary life that their survival is hard to understand. The story of 'Rapunzel' involves a heroine with hair at least twenty feet long, and

'Hansel and Gretel' asks us to believe that two children abandoned by their parents in the forest will find a house made of gingerbread. But these and other tales live on because they are dramatic meta-phors of real life. 'Hansel and Gretel,' for instance, represents the two greatest fears of children – that they will be abandoned and that they will be imprisoned. Many adults, if they think back, will remember one or both of these fears, though usually in a less extreme version. We occasionally felt neglected, disregarded, unsupported – unloved. Or we felt overprotected, overindulged, intruded upon – loved, but in a very possessive, almost scary way.[9]

This kind of fear we associate with Bad Johns, and the love of which Lurie speaks we link with the Sweet Boys or Prince Charmings. They are all necessary for *Bildung*, as they indicate the kind of self-examination and -education necessary for a project in self-construction – what we call "coming into consciousness" as a kind of maturity – that makes the individual aware of a distinctive past, the present, resulting circum-stances, and a future that reformulates past and present. This is an indi-vidual who is aware of time, of history, and of having a specific memory. Even adults find few characters as scary as Bad John, and in traditional folklore every young male hopes to become some young woman's Prince Charming.

Both the Bad John and the Prince Charming characters are representa-tives of time itself. They are the spirits of the era representative of change, which is time and history. Society spurns one and welcomes the other. It fears one and loves the other. Between them, they determine the essence of the nation-state and what, over time, it will become. In the language of street, they are both players, or as some would now say, "playerz": the Bad John the unscripted actor in his own drama, with others playing lesser role and seeking an outcome different from what he wants, and the Prince Charming playing in a game whose rules all participants approve.

In the end, society labels them "Bad John" or "Prince Charming" in the light of the *assumptions* it receives as perceptions of moral behaviour as fairy tales present it so as to encourage youngsters to imagine how they would react in socially appropriate ways under the most trying circumstances. In turn, these assumptions determine expectations that are projections of society on the individual or group; depending on these presumptions of hope or despair, society positions the newcomers.

So far nothing that the newcomer has done has determined his or her characterization. Indeed, these expectations and stereotypes suggest that a seeming Bad John might find that there is nothing he or she can do to change expectations, treatment, placement, and position in society. Yet Prince Charming types, wearing a halo of hope, might also find that there is also nothing they can do to make society in general think negatively about them. Social justice for the two characters has little to do with their actions and more to do with their apparent deservingness – whether society should treat them with the equality that it reserves for citizens as a primary assumption or whether it presumes them to be unequal and not belonging to the general citizenry, which it always ethically assumes to consist of good people. Their birth as social creatures has little to do with their natural abilities and lots to do with their social construction – with other people's assumptions about who they really are. With the dominant social narratives determining them socially, they receive the justice society deems them to deserve.

As symbols of love, Prince Charmings become representations of a nation's time and history by showing how it works out a specific lineage and fidelity in time and how this time becomes meaningful as the nation-state's history of moving towards its destiny or desired perfection. Time becomes meaningful when it becomes social. In this progress, citizens embody time individually, and the people do so collectively – concepts that speak to the sovereignty of the nation-state and its ability to determine what freedom is and how to achieve it.

Therefore, Prince Charming represents freedom and a special movement towards its achievement as the highest human desire – a trajectory and duration that make up the nation-state's history and its time, respectively. This is a freedom that gestures towards the future, to emphasize a better time ahead, which satisfies the desires of the heart; but it is also a form of existence that requires a constant negation of the past, except for those who falsely believe that there was a halcyon past, so that the present seems to be an attack on what the past has achieved, transforming the lived experience of the present into what people can only imagine – a reality that the past has not produced.

On the opposite side, as the symbolic opposite of love, the Bad John does not start out symbolizing the nation's idealistic future as a social entity. Rather, he represents the very opposite: a backwardness that wipes out the gains of collective living in peace and happiness in favour of a world of the injustice and vagaries of Nature itself. The Bad John does not represent the ideals and desires of the collective. He is not representative of the nation-state's time or an actor working out its history. He is the embodiment of fear itself, of finite limits of the universal that is the united life, a way of doing things in a historical society, a culture. The Bad John is the personality that challenges the past by trying to change what exists into an existence that might be utopian for him but that others might consider tyrannical. In this case, the optimism of life focuses on maintaining the past and seeing the future as a continuation of past and present, with no radical changes in way of life or the status quo.

The Bad John might very well be the fate against which society shapes destiny and desires, and, as with most things, a universal fate determines it. Society would have to overcome the Bad John and bring him into the nation-state's time and history. But, ironically, any particular Bad John is the newest and most privileged face of time, perhaps the embodiment of time itself and the face of the future, which by nature must signal an attack on the past and on historical identities in society's hope of producing a unitary future. For, using the current language of the street, the Bad John is he who keeps things real by challenging notions of what is authentic and essential. His ways and presence oppose the normal, the given, the accepted, and the ideal. For if the real is what conforms naturally to what we think and desire, how do we account for people such as Bad Johns and their actions? How do we account for the non-conformists in the world? And could there be freedom that is not non-conformity? Can there be freedom without slavery? The Bad John, unlike the Prince Charming who validates the ideal and even the false consciousness of living, is the individual who constantly reminds us that life is tragic and that the limit of living is death – a future that, ultimately, every individual or nation-state has in common.

Back in my formative years, such a person came right out of our mythology in Barbados: a veritable tyrant, self-made, a sovereign unto himself, disrespectful of any law but his own, and seeming not to have any care about either the past or the future. He was the epitome of raw, unbridled masculinity. His concern was merely to make the most of his daily activities, and this usually meant using other people physically and mentally to secure the most while living at his wit's ends. He could be arbitrary, with seemingly no reliable pattern to his thinking and actions; he was capricious, perhaps friendly in response to one gesture and another time snarling at the same gesture; and he was unpredictable. Overall, he was a destabilizing force, and whether he acted for good or evil, as the majority of us saw things, he usually decided his course on a whim. With each Bad John, society faces a question of sovereignty: who is the real sovereign – the state, which reserves to itself all powers of punishment and coercion, or individuals, who are laws unto themselves and retain the right to coerce others?

Such a man had the power figuratively to move mountains, either to create a path to a promised land or to put up insurmountable obstacles. Fools were we to cross his path, but blessed were we when he was on the same side as we – if residents of another village were to threaten one of us and a Bad John offered himself as a mediator or representative, he was the lamb-cum-lion. For him, life boiled down to a simple choice: to be loved or feared. The choice was that of becoming somewhat of a Prince in Western mythology or shape-shifting into a private citizen whom people love, not fear.

Often, this choice was not so easy after all, for to seek love would turn the Bad John into a mere object – just another working stiff working for a particular cause in society; evoking fear meant to remain a subject and a dictator of sort, the lord to whom nobody would give anything, and from whom nobody expected anything. The second option – fear – meant staying out of society or setting himself so far apart from everyone else that the result would be practically the same: one road led to acculturation and to becoming social; the other, to tyranny, fear by others, and lack of love. To choose fear would be Machiavellian in political thought; the route to love would be the choice that the Hebrew prophets and Greek philosophers suggested, which still inform our understanding of the route to justice and happiness.

As our history has taught us, any Machiavelli, especially the man himself, would reject the path of seeking love, on the grounds that the real world is one not of love and seeking it but of surviving by any means necessary – a characterization that marks life itself with never-ending, universal fear. This would be one of the most irrational expectations in a setting where we expect reason and rationality to reign and where everyone could confidently seek full humanity.

Perhaps it was for these reasons that I always associated Bad Johns with politics: they were the guys who in my youth became the "bodyguards" for politicians when there was a general election, every five years or so. They were the enforcers who would break our heads if we were not on the right side of an issue. Or they stopped other people from breaking our heads, again because we showed the right taste, opinions, and voting intentions. In the end, these actors were usually the deciders and enforcers of what was enlightening and of what good and evil could be, at least for us.

The question for the majority of the society was always how to control the raw power and energy in these characters, and in such a way that everyone would benefit. For these Bad Johns started out with advantages that most of us did not have: Nature had given them valuable endowments. Topping the list was their strength and other physical attributes. They had what the rest of us wanted and were unable to supply ourselves. In this regard, clearly, Nature had its favourites, people that it treated as if they were its natural offspring. Nature was unjust by human reasoning. Most of us she had simply adopted. Those of us so disadvantaged had huddled together to preserve what we called the society and thus protect ourselves. This involved our setting out reasonable rules about how we should live together, including even possible forbearance for those Bad Johns whom Nature seemingly would prefer to live on their own and whom it had prepared, by and large, for such an existence.

But, ironically, even a society of weaklings has a need for superhumans, just as long as it can control them and even convert them into heroes and protectors of the weak. Life seemed incomplete without their presence. When our society did not have them, we always seemed to long for what was missing. Such an acute feeling of loss could plunge everyone into a deep melancholia of constant grieving over an absence. This response was no different from the behaviour of the very religious among us – those who lived stoically in denial of worldly things while awaiting the Messiah who would repair loss and desire and restore the world to a condition where there was no absence, loss, and, therefore, no unreasonable melancholia.

To this end, life was a mixture of the material and what we knew to exist in the transcendent, in another world we usually associated with the spirit and future events and possibilities, particularly the dream of a seamless and indivisible unity. We expected the spiritual to constantly break into and influence our daily living, to bring us justice, and to make life meaningful in an otherwise dreary, arbitrary, and even unjust world. For this reason, we were undoubtedly rational idealists – for we believed justice followed cause-and-effect relationships and that history had taught us what was good and evil. Because we learned from history, we were moral and we were rational and conscious; we could project our wants and desires into the future and apply the lessons of history to attain them. Particularly, we believed that we could make our days better, perfect our lives, and create the state of affairs under which people of a later time would flourish in conditions more conducive to making happiness than any conditions we had yet encountered.

These were not just bread-and-butter issues involving survival from day to day; these issues implicated the ideal – they were about how we could create a better life and be happy. In this way, we had moved from living like animals who relied on beastly senses and inclinations to becoming human; we began to live rationally, desiring a higher and better standard of living than the existence common to all seemingly unthinking and non-planning animals. To this end, we looked forward to a time of justice, a time for the realization of our wildest dreams, when actions and thoughts produced the same results – the world that we rationally admired as the best imaginable, the world of absolute freedom, a world of full and flourishing humanness. This would be a world that the Spirit of the times would infuse, and those times would be notable for the freedom that makes them like no other in history – like nothing any Bad John could create on his own.

SPIRIT: THE MORTAL GOD

Before we go any further, let me explain the notion of the non-transcendental Spirit, as I use the term in this book; this is necessary because my discussion will be neo-Hegelian in that it departs from the common Hegelian assumption that the self is a dualism of separate spirit and matter, or mind and body, with the spirit or mind acting as the Lord over the matter and body. The spirit I am suggesting is in one sense like that of a *conscience,* a moral and ethical compass, as we use the word when we say that a person does or does not have a conscience or that someone is acting against his conscience or according to her conscience. This assumption flows from the recognition of a self-consciousness, whereby an individual or group also sees itself as having suffered diremption and sees that within it are diversity and difference. It is a subject fully knowing itself and knowing itself as an object – thereby able to know itself as if from a distance and free from personal desires that condition how the knower recognizes and accepts this object. "A self-consciousness," says Hegel, "in being an object, is as much 'I' as 'object' …

this absolute substance which is the unity of the different independent self-consciousnesses which, in their opposition, enjoy perfect freedom and independence: 'I' that is 'We' and 'We' that is 'I.'"[10]

This spirit is what results from a feeling of love, when two people come together and feel that they are one. Instead of feeling finite by dealing with another, we feel that we and the other have merged, so that all limits and boundaries that were markers of our individuality and self have combined into a oneness or unity. In a world that consists of the two lovers, there is now no individual boundary or limit: there is infinity within and universal, because what used to be personal limits now evaporate within the wider oneness or unity that now exhausts all personal potentials. The lovers have become absolute within themselves, just as a nation-state would seek to become self-sufficient by its own means, by meeting all its daily requirements for life, and ensure its propagation under its own rules and independence. Where this is true of two individuals, analogously the same applies to any number of human beings coming together to create the people, the nation, the state, or the country. The citizens must be in love with one another, and the nation-state is the child of the union – a child that right away will have one overriding concern: not how it should retain the past, but how it can reproduce itself as an absolute or a universal without limits across generations. Its highest task is to live as well as possible and to maintain life at all costs.

As Hegel suggests, "True union of love proper, exists only between living beings who are alike in power and thus in one another's eyes living beings from every point of view; in no respect is either dead for the other. This genuine love excludes all oppositions ... Love neither restricts nor is restricted; it is not finite at all. It is feeling, yet not a single feeling [among other single feelings]. A single feeling is only part and not the whole of life; the life present in a single feeling dissolves its barrier and drives on till it disperses itself in a manifold of feelings with a view to finding itself in the entity of this manifold."[11]

So society cannot accommodate love or this spirit that is a zest for life, and it does not accommodate any effort to enhance life. It occurs when a subject loses his or her self in another, thereby feeling not a loss of the self but a merging with the other and creating a newness, a new oneness, such that the finite boundaries of the individuals have now extended into an infinity of both. In this case, spirit or conscience is a morality that is also an ethical command or approach to life. A pure and free conscience in the Hegelian sense is one wherein the moral individual's thoughts are consistent with the ethical expectations of society. "The mortal element, the body, Hegel says, has lost the character of separability, and a living child, a seed of immortality, of the eternally self-developing and self-generating [race], has come into existence. What has been united [in the child] is not divided again; [in love and through love] God has acted and created."[12]

In this case, there would be reconciliation, harmony, freedom, and justice for the *self,* whether this self is the individual or a collective that is a community of society. This is a second sense in which I use the term *spirit*, somewhat similar to the usage by William James,[13] the American pragmatist, whose theory descends directly from Hegel's. James suggests that the self consists of three parts: the material, the social, and the spiritual. As German psychologist Urs Fuhrer suggests, the "social" for James refers to how other people regard and recognize an individual. The "material" describes tangible objects, people, or places that the self associates with itself. However, "the spiritual self is our inner self or our psychological self. It is comprised of everything we call *my* or *mine* that is not a tangible object, person, or place, or a social role. Our perceived abilities, attitudes, emotions, interests, motives, opinions and wishes are all part of the spiritual sense. In short, the spiritual self refers to our perceived inner psychological qualities."[14]

In this respect, I am groping for a meaning of "conscience" that reconciles, if I may say so, the classical Hegelian dualist position with its lordship-and-bondage relationship in the individual, imagining the self as a single entity that does not have separate warring parts. To this end, the relationship of lordship and bondage is an ethical one that then influences the morality of the individual citizen, who is fundamental to and not distinct from the society.

It is a relationship where an outward or social death akin to physical slavery occurs but without a metanoia experience; rather, it is the creation of the situation where the struggle is most intense within the individuals, even if outwardly or physically they appear to acquiesce and not to be struggling. But it is a relationship that derives from diremption or disunity – where at least two supposed sovereigns exist, one of which has to be destroyed in a tragic working out of an individual destiny against an overarching fate. Here I am incorporating Niebuhr's explanation that the human is a being with a conscience. This conscience is what makes human beings rational. Niebuhr explained that "the self is a creature which is in constant dialogue with itself, with its neighbors, and with God."[15] This self always finds itself always already in an enclosed system or ethical order – that is, a society, community, or country.

Neibuhr says that he bases this definition on the Bible, but I think it would be more useful for us if we were to replace – as I suggest below when we consider how to reconcile tragedy and comedy, irrationality and rationality, in Western tradition as a single system – the concept of God with that of an external sovereign: either the state or, from a wider perspective, an ethical order that we will call "the good." By invoking this notion of the good, I am borrowing from Charles Taylor, who argues in *Sources of the Self* that all human action takes place in relation to some good. As he says, understanding the modern identity "involves tracing various strands of our modern notion of what it is to be a human agent, a person, or a self ... Selfhood and the good, or in another way selfhood and morality, turn out to be inextricably intertwined themes."[16]

Both Niebuhr and Taylor appear to be thinking about the same thing when they use the poetic imagery of human beings in the likeness of God or, as we see below, the state. According to both of them, when we use that phrase, we should be talking about the effects of culture on individuals and on the nation-state – the source of culture itself.[17] With this in mind, we can understand why Hegel refers to the ideal unity or reconciled spirit as a Godhead. How do we create this unity and love for fellow citizens so that it appears as a natural and even moral development, as something that flows logically and freely out of our history and desires?

Social consensus deemed those Bad Johns incorrigible because it presumed them unwilling or unable to adjust to mainstream social standards; it simply left them to the mercy of time, the greatest of all levellers: time or life was the one thing that Nature had neglected to give a too-generous supply of to any human. Again, there appears to be a life lesson in this observation, another indication that life is a tragedy: the realization that, maddeningly in the end, Nature really has no favourite and is amoral, for it cannot classify actions as good or evil. It was always merely a matter of time before Nature devoured *all* its children. Both the weak and the strong alike were materials for Nature to use over time; and equally, both must change, and even end up as nought. Every day would weaken their physical strength and abilities and sap their power. But the message seemed most potent and sobering for the strong: on their own, the Bad Johns would come eventually to ruin – a fate that they shared with even the people whom a two-faced Nature neglected most in endowments. O, for a rational world as our dominant ideology and mythology promised us!

By the time the Bad Johns hit bottom they might have created havoc in society, but eventually they would be reduced to a mere shadow of themselves: they would continue to remain outside society as mere shells of their former selves. At the end, Nature in all its cunning may well seem to remove its protective hand from over them; their lifelong dependence on Nature and their wildness would teach them how to learn a valuable lesson: Nature might have favourites, but it has no heart and is unreliable. It is extremely arbitrary and capricious. Indeed, Nature is a mother that eats every last one of its children. Human society does not do that, if only because it appears to be of a higher order, deriving not from forms but from a never-ending and never-changing value of love. This is a relationship that is strongest among the children of Nature who have connection by blood, but just as strong in trusting relationships between people who seek to become fully human, such as in a marriage. And the Bad Johns usually found this out too late. Their choice really concerned how they would use up all their potential over their lifetime and what they would receive in return. Sticking with Nature would eventually lead to their achieving nothing socially – certainly not love. Switching to the social would give them a measure of justice – perhaps some welfare provision in ill health or old age, in those times when they were weakest, and, if they were truly good, a fond place in the people's memory and a sense of everlasting love.

With time, the Bad Johns became weaker than their societies and, ironically, late in their lives some even needed the protection of the state they had aggravated. In the end, not only would the Bad Johns in Nature have no social knowing, or what we commonly call a "conscience," but they would have no culture either: they would be incapable of appreciating anything, especially what humanity commonly accepted as good, and ultimately as human. They would not even be good human beings, so that they were likely to start life acting like animals and to die having made no noticeable improvement in themselves. And what a waste, where they started out more proud and powerful than their fellows of lesser talents or natural abilities but ended up worse. But, as often happens in the Americas, the Bad Johns and even the Sweet Boys might not be natives of the land of their residence or citizenship. They would be immigrants, and the adoptive society usually imposes its own measures of accommodation on them.

ACCOMMODATION

The measures that I just outlined above generally represent how the wider society would *accommodate* these bullies. Specifically in Canada, they would have to learn fear through a lordship-and-bondage type of relationship, in which Canadians of older lineage hoped to exploit a perceived flaw in the newcomers' supposed essence and nature. Thus emerged the belief that newcomers, despite their strange ways, are not fearless; that they are willing to risk their lives, but only up to a given point; and that, when a real challenge emerges, instead of "going for broke," they settle for a better life in Canada rather than returning to the state of nature whence they came.

Accommodation is action that first appears as a thought that the thinker may verbalize thus: "Why don't you go back to where you come from if you don't like it here and are not willing to accept your treatment and position?" Society's main intention is to instil fear in new arrivals who appear to be fearless, representing the very opposite of people wanting the accommodation in the first place, and to turn the newcomers into bondsmen in the service of a Lord whose business they must conduct for him. Accommodation in this case moderates between fear on the one hand and, on the other, a love that comes from a mere civic recognition of the individual's citizenship. If fear triumphs, marginalization and even ostracism may result. The civic citizenship would prove to be really meaningless, because the new relationship would be one not of equals but of true citizens who are the Lords and of mere immigrants who join the proletariat, living as if they are still outside Canada, enduring an existence inferior to their Lords', and never able to identify as full Canadians. Even though Canada has selected them painstakingly for suitability, once they arrive, it treats them as errors. It positions them in ways that suggest that they are not really up to scratch, that something about them is awry and un-Canadian, and that they are errors that will require correction and transformation to meet the perceived truth and dominant reality of who is actually and genuinely Canadian. Accommodation is the imposition of a citizenship lower than first class; it doesn't provide solutions for handling in a spirit of freedom the despair of perceived social disruption by *Others*, but rather shifts to another battlefield the real struggle between those acting out of fear and those performing acts of love. Accommodation is a veritable prison. Love transports the individual into a relation so thick that it is almost a blood connection – a lineage that is divine and primordial.

Occasionally, we have not had to wait long for a respite from our fears of social disruption. Time can move quickly: it can produce other Bad Johns who arrive later with their strengths and unique moralities, and it can quickly find places of accommodation for older miscreants. Such a newcomer imposes an order that the weakened Bad Johns have to accept, joining all others in society in awe of the new lord or temporal sovereign.

One development we might find somewhat hilarious is that of the deposed Bad John trying to pretend his rule has not ended. In this case, he might succumb to maudlin melancholia, the opposite of what we previously wanted when we kept lamenting the absence of a deliverer (see above on Messiah). Instead, this Bad John refused to accept his removal and replacement and kept on acting as if he had not fallen. In this way, he might be living in a fool's paradise, or simply refusing to internalize what had happened outwardly – that his previous self and his well-being have changed, and for good, as he will probably never experience a reversal of his fortune. Time has moved on; although he might yearn for a return to halcyon days, that won't happen. We will see his melancholia as unrealistic nostalgia, and it will encrust him in deep melancholia or depression. More than likely, he should simply deal with reality and "get a (new) life."

Alas, the replacement of a particular Bad John may simply have one tyrant give way to another – "swapped monkey for black dog," the Caribbean phrase – exchanging one embodiment of fear for another. Again, perfection would elude us. The good we imagine would still be beyond our reach. Tragically, as usual, achieving a life that was normal according to human capabilities still means settling for less than one desired. Ultimately, it means not only chaining the deviants that seem to be the cause of our troubles, but tempering our own wishes and desires, settling for less than a perfect life.

For this reason, one of the first things we learned in Barbados was not to think of ourselves as Bad Johns. Indeed, often when figures in authority were flogging us or a peer challenged us to a fight, the explanation society gave us was that we were being Bad Johns and somebody had to set us right; someone had to prevent us from becoming an irredeemable tyrant and show us that we were instead mere weaklings, that what we might try and even fail to do to other people time would definitely mete out to us in more than full measure.

TAMING BAD JOHNS

But our society had another, less violent way to incorporate these powerful forces. And this marks a distinction between the dominant Western norms of socialization in mainly Eurocentric societies and those of other societies. Usually, in the Caribbean, the woman in the Bad John's life took on this task: she would be the one constantly tempering him and keeping him satisfied. A force perhaps weaker than him physically but so much stronger mentally and psychically – the fully socialized woman

– would put him "under manner." Caribbean societies tend to be matri-focal and even matrilineal, although European-style law makes them formally patriarchal. Like a mediator who can operate at both the ani-mal and the human levels, she was the one to *teach* him culture and how to live reasonably. In a practical sense, she would not only offer him affection but "give him love" – that is, social respect. Just like the Biblical Eve, she would sacrifice her body and even her identity for necessity, for a dream that makes everyone so much more human. She was the one to give him knowing in the form of an acceptable conscience, that internal self-regulation that produces feelings of sympathy and concern for oth-ers. Giving him children – particularly some who would not have as many endowments from Nature as their father – was one way of encour-aging the tyrant to replace his selfish interest with the interest of others, so that he would always have to be weighing how his actions would affect the children and the way society treated them. "Under manner," and with an appropriate code of behaviour, he would be born again, resurrected psychically through metanoia.

Like a new mother, the woman would give him a new language – one of love and sociability; she would help him to learn how to communicate through symbols and institutions according to the method that we had all agreed to be appropriate for everyone who was human. In this way, she gave him a history or past in common with all the others, a present in which he became part of current human interactions and even follies and shared with the woman and the entire culture the hopes for infinity that is a collective presence in the future.

Literally and figuratively, she embedded him in society as a place of love. Indeed, he would take on a new language or way of thinking and imagining possibilities through which he would then judge what is good and evil – a social language that delimited what anyone may reasonably imagine and attempt. It was a way to prevent him from descending into melancholia and to replace his previous self and way of living. From this point on, his reliance on Nature would end, and in its place he and his fellow beings would construct a world according to commonly agreed ideals of a good life. Paradoxically, this happened even to the seemingly lowest among them, remoulding them all and positioning them to the same levels.

Often, these heroic women suffered physically for the rest of us. Often when the Bad John relapsed into his old ways, the women of the area commiserated, not about the backslider, but about the "poor soul" (the woman) who would have to start her efforts all over yet again. Our dominant Graeco-Christian mythology never cast Sisyphus as a woman, but then again *he* never had as tough a task. In this regard, socialization was not about forcing the weak members of society to conform – they would anyway, for that was why individuals entered into a society – but about weakening those that did not have a compelling reason to be weak. A tragedy from the perspective of the weak was when, seemingly against all senses of what is natural and good, the Bad John sacrificed the well-being of even those whom he had created, his children and family, by acting out of his selfish interests. Then he was truly incorrigible, beyond any perfecting as a human being.

But even here, again, the woman performs her role as the positive influence, by maintaining the family, often raising the children of the union and socializing them in the male's absence. The woman becomes appropriately "the mother who fathered" the nation. Caribbean social critic Rex Nettleford reflects on the region's crises since independence, usually when male politicians operate in a patriarchal framework in the public sphere. Noting that the era has seen the rise of "leaders" in both private and public spheres who propose new, foreign ideas of social and political management, Nettleford says wryly, "Many a Caribbean mother or grandmother has been just this kind of leader. Unfortunately she hardly gets a chance to preside over governments here ... Why, then, have not her sons, who dominate Cabinets and Boardrooms, turned out to be as good a[t] leading. I ask the Question of Caribbean women yet again: 'what has gone wrong with the socialisation process out of which have emerged such men?'"[18]

Without over-romanticizing, the result is that a socialization norm for the Caribbean is that of a woman who does not depend on the male for her fulfilment as much as the man needs her for socialization and the society needs the female for its continuity in all phases. Cultural critic Carolyn Cooper explains these roles, especially those in the region's modern-day dancehall culture, which presents the female as dancehall queen but still as mama. Most of all, she is strong and independent. Cooper recalls a blurb for a film on this cultural phenomenon that talked about "a modern-day Cinderella story, with no Prince Charming, but one very strong woman." And she comments, "The Caribbean stereotypes of the superhuman Black woman and the delinquent Black man meet the European fantasy of the nurturing Prince Charming; and part company."[19]

This approach to norm construction is not unique to the region. Madonna Kolbenschlag refers to such enduring practices in North

America: "Black women, and many first generation American women, have an inherited or conditioned sense of themselves as workers. In the case of the black woman, her role as a stabilizing force and provider in the black community for several generations [has] given her a strength and resourcefulness – a confidence and a sticking power, a success capability – that many middle-class white women lack."[20] She calls on white readers to break free of the restrictions of a society where they are part of dominant group: "The experience of black women presents a significant contrast to this picture. Research generally indicates that black women professionals exhibit more 'survival' capabilities than their counterparts in the white middle class. Assertiveness qualities are higher, initiative and momentum over the long haul are more consistent, dependency on mentors and husbands is lower, and in general self-sufficiency traits are much more developed. Studies indicate that women from white immigrant families are more likely to share these traits."[21]

Indeed, what we have been discussing is a form of folk socialization that springs seemingly organically from people whom modern Western society still sees hierarchically as very folk, who do not provide the ideals of *the people* in Westernized societies beyond those of western Europe. In reaching back for the aporia as we look for a new model that would create a truly just society, genuine multiculturalism demands that we consider these forms of socialization as candidates for adoption in a new ethical order.

Another way of controlling these Bad Johns was a collective one, through an appeal to a common morality. Backing up this appeal was force that derived not from the Bad John's notions of right and wrong but from the collective's. In this way, we hoped that the Bad John would find religion and change his outlook on life, becoming less selfish by joining a spiritual community subscribing to a universal morality. We hoped that this specimen of evil would find God, the same almighty sovereign that politicians in a democracy claim to be the voice of the people, whether it is to rebuke people into humility or to acclaim them with glory. In such cases, we hoped he found the Lord in a spiritual sense – the religion, coincidentally, of the very society he was shunning. We hoped he would undergo metanoia, a psychic death through conversion that would make him other to what he was previously. We prayed he would put himself under a covenant, where he would acknowledge his weakness and mortality, and as a result agree to accept a specific type of culture and to behave as it expected him to. By figuratively finding the Lord, then, he would, we anticipated, not only willingly place himself under manners but that he learns to behave, with acceptable actions for individuals in a society. He would come to believe on his own in a greater good and that there was a force beyond him capable of imposing its way on him at some crucial point. He would become a practitioner of society's ethics, often practising them unconsciously. His action would signal the death of the old spirit within and its replacement with a new spirit that is now the source of only good and socially acceptable deeds. This metanoia would complete his socialization, making him a cultured member of society who knew how to think and behave appropriately.

If all else failed, we hoped the police, acting with our authority, would intervene, in which case the strongest of the weaklings – the majority of society – would in effect combine their strength and subdue this individual, forcing the Bad John to accept a covenant of another sort, which made him part of the society while for all intents and purposes excluding him. This is the point at which fear triumphs over any desire to make the tyrant lovable. Then even further along we enable the enforcers of our laws and traditions to remove this deviant from society, mainly by imprisoning him until he becomes so weak he is no longer a physical threat after release. Again, time would be the great diminisher.

Failing this process, if the police were unable to subdue the righteous Bad John, we gave them the right to kill him – the ultimate in reasonable force – thereby ending his threat against us. Our final analysis acknowledges, then, that the sovereign is indeed the state ... until time – tyrant that it is – sends us another Bad John to teach us all over again

For such a person we would have no tears, whatever his ending. And we would be wise not to laugh, or not for too long or too openly. For even then our joy would not be complete, for we should know that, even within our human-made society, Nature is still an overwhelming force. Unfortunately for most of us, what time does to any specific Bad John it also does to all of us individually, for if it is so quick to humble its favourites, what might it do to those of us for whom it never had any time?

This is another important lesson for us: all of us are in common moving towards one thing – *death,* and the *dread* of death. We are all finite beings in a contest with an infinity of time, for a world without end is not of our experience and is something for which we can only dream and hope. Nature's favourites and the disadvantaged are both continuously degraded as we live. Indeed, this is what the equality of citizenship really means. As finite individuals, we will never arrive in a time of perfection, when all is just *good*, as good as we can imagine. In the end, our tragedy seems to parallel that of the Bad Johns, if only because we share the same time, the same cycles of life, and the same struggle to say to Nature that we should experience the good in the finite lives that we live rather than in the infinity of time that is Nature itself. The only consolation for us is to think beyond ourselves and attempt to bring more of what is beyond us – the infinity of time – into the good that is our finite existence, so that with each gain in longevity we lay claim to what used to be an evil and rename it a human good. The consolation is that as human beings we can dream of negating ourselves – or of reaching an evolutionary point in the future when the old self is still a part of us but overall we are new people no longer in thrall to the human condition that Nature creates. By negating our humanity, we would overcome all our natural flaws and emerge from the process a better species.

Or we might cast our eyes to the future, believing that at least people yet to come will be free of a specific tyrant and that their freedom will be the greater good, which might exclude us physically but to which we can contribute and help make happen. Similarly, we hope that others as weak as we are will share a special fraternity with us – that of knowing that the daily lot of people like us was and is not easy. Most of all, looking to the common ending we share, we might hope that we could persuade the Bad John who currently dominates us to turn away from his benefactor and cast in his lot with us, even if that means he must renounce the benefactor and some of his gifts. In effect, we have to convince the Bad John that, seemingly against all reason, in the long run it is better for him to live as a mere human being like the rest of us rather than as a distinctive and unequalled specimen of Nature.

One of the goals of socialization is to encourage the Bad John to realize that while he and society war with each other, they are really misguided proxies – the true fight is to blunt Nature by deciding which of the alternative ways of life is better than that with which Nature endowed them. Ironically, whether he knows it or not, in the eyes of Nature the Bad John is on the same level as everyone else in society. Both are trying to be human and free of the limitations Nature has imposed. The compromise is that we are creating a state of existence where, although we impose the existence of a state through our collective cooperation, Nature, with its endless time, still calls the shots. Our Lord, our state, must be benevolent: ever conscious of how easily Nature can destroy us all but also aware that the lord itself, even when appearing to protect us for our individual sakes, needs us for its own survival and for its very reason for existing.

Joining together, the Bad Johns and the rest of society can set aside their differences, accept their dread of their awareness of their pending deaths, and try to produce something organic and authentic to our environment and that outlasts our physical demise. Ultimately, that is what citizenship is: an organic relationship that extends across generations by living on after its most recent holders. It is a solidarity emerging from a common purpose that stretches across time. In this way, the state achieves its will to life, and the individuals, both those with a stated legacy and those without, can look to a common future as the best human species possible. However, this future by necessity must be different from what existed before. The question then becomes who has the chance to shape this future: the state, with its own fear of a collective death; the Bad John, with his own personal fear; or those weaklings in society, who as individuals fear a death that could very well come from the state, which always reserves the right to punish and even destroy deviants, as much as it can come from the Bad Johns entering the society or from Nature itself. Who calls the shots about the future becomes a question of sovereignty.

By the time this entire process is complete, we hope to transform our Bad John from one of Aristotle's "unfinished human specimen[s]" into one of us, a citizen of our state. This change would bring, we also hope, a new approach to life, making the Bad John into a Good John or a John the Good. The difference between the two conditions might not be obvious, but might reveal itself in actions. By then, giving up his absolute freedom would have forced the Bad John to become socially free. This is a freedom that is inert and develops in conjunction with other citizens. Living in a real world, rather than in the absolute freedom of thought, desire, will, and potential, is what constrains his freedom. Spiritual freedom, then, is the component that depends not on action but rather on a prevailing perception of good intentions.

Once the Bad John becomes socially free, from time to time he can escape into daydreaming of different times, and he might even long for that time when he was really free, as liberated as his thoughts and imagination. He might even on occasion join with other Bad Johns to reminisce privately and even act among them in narrow quarters as if they were absolutely free. But this would be mere comedy. The ex–Bad Johns, either as individuals or as a group of minorities, can live in this make-believe world just as long as they keep their thoughts and actions private. As soon as they have to deal with other people, when they have to enter the public sphere, they must put aside all notions of having absolute power, for in public they live as individuals and according to the rules of the inorganic and social freedom. They live by the ethics that bind everyone in a common citizenship. This is the tragedy of life at its most meaningless – of having to sacrifice the moral and the absolute for something inauthentic and even hypocritical, for a world of diversity, differences, pretend unity, and made-up values.

Comedy, then, is how we become a conscience, a site of tolerance, within a wider commune or society that is the source of tolerance. It is how we behave rationally in a world or social order that is not rational. This conscience is an individual that is self-legislating, seemingly authentic, and fully aware of itself, in full understanding of the human condition that afflicts human beings living in societies. It is in need of tolerance because of its strong views and perception of self and because of its superior and dominant relationship to the rest of the world – for in this sense this individual is like a god inhabiting a world of competing gods. These other gods are also as wise and knowledgeable as the individual god and have their own unique desires and dreams. They play out their desires and personalities within a system, which for the most part they all create as a separate and distinct entity, but which is indifferent to any particular action or god. For as an individual, this god's interest is only that it exists and preserves itself as the site for this interaction, even if at times it has to oppress any individual for this collective good. In the system, every individual tries to make what is an individual wish and desire universal – as that which the system should adopt, develop, and preserve as essential to its own existence.

Such understanding and comprehension speak to awareness that life is an existence within this wider consciousness that the conscience has come to recognize as a community or society that people have constructed through their actions across history, all of which amount to the morality that guides the members of a community and that normatively informs their behaviour. For this consciousness is not a natural thing – at least not as perceptually natural as the conscience. Unlike this tragic conscience, the wider consciousness as an entity of the world in which the conscience exists might not even be aware of the individual conscience and might have absolutely no desire to accommodate it. There is no symmetry of knowledge between the conscience and consciousness, for while the individual is aware of its own standing in the society, the consciousness might be totally oblivious of the individual as a separate and distinct being and worry even less about the individual's desires and dreams. So the self-consciousness often feels alienation, and, so as not to allow the mute and unknowing consciousness to wipe it out, must be the beneficiary of a kind of grace from the consciousness – a tolerance of its existence and a benign neglect that allow it to exist. While the consciousness runs under its own rules, laws, and traditions, the individual conscience can exist as if it is free from them for as long as the consciousness does not impose its ways on the recalcitrant individual and destroy the sources of negativity within the consciousness.

This is living in a world that actions in time and language determine. Actions are the intentions and the expression of the self as subject and tragic hero and, coincidentally, of actions of the community as history and centralized morals that are tragically against the hero. Language is the explanation to the community of the performance of this self as subject and hero and is the means by which the wider communes validate or tragically reject those individual actions as both separate intentions and expressions. But in a comedic setting, language is vital: it allows the individual to retain its *negativity*, and so it can allow the tragic hero to appear forever as free from the dictates of the wider society. Language became a means of defiance, of not giving in to what culture offers as given or to the positive freedom of having an identity that is separate and distinct from the commune. Thus, in this setting, an individual appears to be talking and acting in a play but also to be performing at least two primary but contradictory personalities: judge and criminal; lawgiver but also lawbreaker; the epitome of good and also the embodiment of absolute evil; owner of personal property and just a stakeholder in collective ownership; hoarding all this as his or hers under a personal notion of "this is mine" but also fighting to ensure the sufficiency of collective property for the undifferentiated; confessor to moral and ethical depravity and, absurdly, taker of the confession; the living trying to live in a community of the dead and dying.

In this way, the individual is, first, the tragic hero wearing its negative freedom and retaining the negativity to destroy any identity or culture the wider consciousness gives to it and to transform this situation; second, he or she is the individual who is simply an expression of the culture and way of life in the wider community and who willingly suppresses that way of life's negativity even to the point of self-alienation to fit snugly into the wider society and to heal any diremption of the unity of society into separate individuals and groups. The problem is that we are talking about a single individual, even if that individual shows split personalities. In all cases, the individual is never absolutely singular and self-owning nor totally an expression of a collective, not a mindless mouthpiece of its society, but the product equally of self and of society.

What I described above as comedic is what we generally now accept to be living in a society that is a seeming contradiction: it is liberal and democratic, and it is in further contradiction as a society consisting of individuals and groups that feel they are free in actions and thought to have their own gods, goods, values, behaviour, ethnicities, and cultures but that also in absolute knowledge recognize that for this living to be meaningful they need the validation of the wider society in which they live – they need to speak a language of tolerance that is authentic in the way they recognize the differences of others who in turn recognize the differences in them, and that in the end the *other*s and *them*s are the essence of the wider community.

They need to recognize that the community is ontologically multicultural and is multicultural through its actions too. And in speaking of thinking about themselves, to be authentic, radically democratic, and yet still liberal, they must be epistemologically multicultural as well. In this awareness, the epistemological would include the absolute knowledge of the contradiction: that within the society as inseparably both individuals and groups, life is tragic, all perception of the authentic self is forever being lynched on a tree, happiness is illusionary, but life is also comic, for we can believe that out of the lynching and heartbreak we obtain a better knowledge of who we are and, optimistically, can delude ourselves that we live in the best of all worlds and that what we have could always be so much worse.

Therefore, one of the first lessons that we have applied in our society, even if we counter-intuitively refuse to accept it, is the idea that good, or what could become the best, is often what used to be evil. Humans, then, construct good first in thought and then in action, through the negation of the natural, to make what was there at the beginning social and better. In this sense, if good is to grow and to prevent itself from becoming sterile and atrophying, it has to co-opt what society used to consider bad or evil, redeem it, and rename it as good. This, we learn below, was one of the few ways in which the forces of good could win the never-ending battle between good and evil: through a conversion or even rebirth from evil to good, resulting in a new good that now incorporates what was formerly evil. The evil that remains within what we generally consider the good and that shows up the divisions and lines of resistance is the tragic figure whose conversion is only partial but who exhibits or claims enough change for us to recognize him or her as none the less good. This is a good that is not organic. It is evolutionary, and the ultimate test for this good is usually what it produces or causes to happen in the very moment in which we invoke it.

With time, all that is evil may very well become good, even if all that is good was not always evil. Therefore, central to our understanding is something that lies deep in our unconsciousness, as deep as our religious claims as a Christian state, as part of what is we call "Western civilization" – and this is the often-hard-to-accept notion that it is usually those beings who think of themselves as good and as most deserving who have to change. Good must be changeable. The old-timers have to accommodate those newcomers whom they might view as being of lesser pedigree or even of an inferior race, those whom they might consider still "primitive" and culturally blind, and even those whom they might fear both physically – for Nature may have blessed such "Others" as its favourites and may rely less on the justice of the state – and culturally – for such Others may have different views of what to value and how to organize society. What good meant in the past, what it was intended to achieve, and who established it are never as important as what good means, produces, and aims to help, *now*. So "What good have you done for me lately?" is more than an aphorism: it is an ethical way of existing.

PART TWO
Practices against Social Diversity

3

A Hegelian – Christian Model

I heard old Queen Victoria say if we would all forsake
Our native land of slavery and come across the lake
That she was standing on the shore with arms extended wide
To give us all a peaceful home beyond the rolling tide.
Farewell, old master, this is enough for me.
I'm going straight to Canada, where coloured men are free.

Part I has offered a story of tragedy. In the case of Canada, it is about
how the social order, in whatever form it takes, never seems to make
sense for some liberal-democratic individuals. This is especially so for
those who do not share the dominant culture and find its mores and
norms immoral and meaningless. Similarly, citizens who swear by the
dominant ideals and ways of life find those of an opposite view equally
immoral and even ungrateful, especially if the latter are newcomers. But
what I reviewed in part I is also a tale of comedy, of how we can manage
to encourage the strong to act as if they are weak, and to comply willingly. It is how we try to make sense of seeming nonsense. Comedy is
also about how we, tragically, figure out not only other people but ourselves, and how we might come to terms with imperfections that make
us unlovable and bring less than absolute happiness into our own lives.
And by "unlovable," I mean lacking the kind of abstract liberal recognition that Charles Taylor says is the politics at the heart of multiculturalism.[1] This is an ideological or spiritual love that means total absorption
in a society. Mead and others call it "fraternity," a view that Taylor
appears to share in his decrying of this social insertion as one of the
major ills of the modern society.[2] In a nod to Hegel's earlier writings and
the way he treats this love as akin to religious experience, Mead says,
"[Fraternity] comes back to the attitude of neighborliness, the identification of ourselves with others, a common emotional interest in others.

This comes under the general term 'sympathy,'"[3] which in this book I call "the spirit of modernity." It is what the Marxists maintain is a false consciousness, and it is tantamount to what Niebuhr describes as the deception of being deceivers who still tell the truth, or the tellers of truth who must deceive to achieve their goal.[4] As the African-American theologian James Cone shows, differences in perspective and personal awareness determine not only comedy or tragedy but the reality that is life itself; "therefore when the master and slave spoke of God, they could not possibly be referring to the same reality."[5]

This would be mere comedy: to act on faith and belief in the face of even compelling and reasoned *evidence* to the contrary. It was ideological that long before anyone but a white male had served in office, many Americans could still believe that every child – regardless of race, ethnicity, gender, wealth – can grow up to become president. It is the same faith that allows us to witness a citizen's dastardly act and then presume him or her innocent. And it is the same kind of faith that is at work when we assert that Canada is officially multicultural, even though most evidence – in the form of decision-makers – continues to be mostly other than multicultural in spirit and other than ethnically and racially diverse.

Some observers may argue that the same differences arise when we talk about the state as a sovereign, and that the miracle and mystery of multiculturalism, as of any religion or faith, are how to encourage those lords and bondsmen or slaves – all embodiments of inauthenticity itself, for neither status is what those individuals really want – to live together in a society in which they all believe they are equal, even while they suspect or even believe otherwise. They act as if they are all, indeed, authentic and recognized as such. As Hegel argues, this is a super-sensible existence, one that turns upside-down everything that should otherwise appear *natural*. Life is an inversion, for what used to appear to natural instincts to be black is now white, sweet is sour, north is south. The loss of that once-certain way of knowing creates a gain: sociability or humanness, or, as the Hegelian scholar Howard Adelman states, human bondage. This comes from living in a society of laws and from enjoying life itself, a life that the sovereign, not the individual or specific group, determines and legislates. For comedy has to be the transcendence and even the inversion of our tragic experiences, and it is this act of overcoming that is empowering for those who not only believe in but try to live this faith. The release and freedom come in their action – by citizens remaining natural beings who do things but who are also social creatures who in effect do things in concert with others and according to a common plan. Thus the individuals or groups, in fulfilment of citizenship, remain the producers they naturally are – in these modern days, mere workers – but they coordinate their production and work and do it for a purpose: for the greater good of all, instead of only for individual gain. This is true even in the most liberal of societies; as Adam Smith argues, the invisible hand of the market, through the individual's action, is coordinating the common good.[6]

Hegel says as much in his discussion of the totality of life and of how individuals are merely components of this universal that is life itself – what they do for themselves they really do, often unawares, for humanity as the genus in general. "Life consists rather in being the self-developing whole that dissolves its development and in this movement simply preserves itself," he writes.[7] This is the tragic hero looking out for his own interest. It is also, as in the case of Canada, the hero in the thrall of the biological desires to preserve himself – desires that find expression sexually.

But the effects of acting out these personal desires do not end there, nor do they relate to the preservation of just the individual hero. A much wider tale is unfolding. "It is the simple genus which, in the movement of Life itself," Hegel explains, "does not *exist for itself qua* this *simple* determination; on the contrary, in this *result*, Life points to something other than itself, viz. to consciousness, for which Life exists as this unity, or as genus."[8] Consciousness comes to realize that it exists in an inverted world. Even what it thought to be actions for its best interest were in fact serving a higher calling. An informed consciousness can see itself as a comedian thinking it was performing the script of its own writing when all along it was merely following direction and acting within limits that came from above. Historically, then, if tragedy is the awareness of the practicality of actually living, comedy is about the imaginary and about when natural rules have lost the edge that would normally make living tragic, lonely, and often meaningless. Struggling to privilege either the personal good that is its primary interest or the greater good that is the unintended consequence and higher calling, the consciousness finds itself in a relationship of lordship and bondage. The genus or life itself is the lord, and the individual trying to assert its personal and private desires is in bondage to it. Life is more important than the individual person or group. And essential to life is *change*. Yet for many people, the very idea of existence is that of living in a changeless world, or one with the minimum of disruption – in effect, a tragedy wearing the mask of a comedy.

How we accept and incorporate change as natural to living is a main theme in our understanding of general multiculturalism as an ideal. It is why I take the starting position that life in general is a tragedy, for such is the human existence, and our understanding is that not all change is desirable. I also posit that we, as individuals and as societies, want to make ourselves, to become something that is of our own "image." This is our highest human desire. To achieve this ideal usually means undergoing change, and this is part of our concept of *Bildung,* an evolution that we hope our own wishes and actions govern. Such change would be akin to acting out a *destiny.* Changes that we do not desire, or anything that holds us in a grip from which we cannot escape, is *fate* – that over which we have no control and that places limits and boundaries on us. Fate is a plotline from elsewhere, so that, while under its sway, we perform only as if in a play that already has a script. There can be no improvisation. We are not free but are slaves to the script, directions, and props.

These concepts of tragedy and comedy are crucial to living in society, for, as social theorist Paul Meadows explains, they represent the many faces of and obstacles to change. According to him, observers of social change down through the ages often explained it as a social drama. The explanations usually come with "a plot-line, characters, dialogue, idea or theme, context of enactment, denouement."[9] These are all the elements of a modern drama, of which the primary form is tragedy:

> The form of change theory, reflecting the dominant cultural ontology or the theorist's own personal *Weltanschauung* (world view), parallels the historic framework of drama – tragedy, melodrama, comedy, farce, tragic-comedy. The scene has been a veritable kaleidoscope: the universe (as in cosmologies), history (as in philosophies of history), nature (as in process theory), the human psyche (as in varieties of humanism). The rational has been the play as portrayal of reality, and here there has been an impressive succession of scenarios: *Imitatio Dei, Imitatio Naturae, Imitatatio Historiae, Imitatio Vtae, Imitatio Personnae.* Sometimes the plot has been set forth in myth, sometimes in theology, sometimes in philosophy, sometimes in the arts, most recently in the monochrome methodology of the sciences.[10]

This evolution, as Meadows argues, has resulted in modern times in a specific explanation of social change: the suggestion that life is not an imitation of any kind or a mere mimicry of some higher being or force.

It is the real thing, and if there is a drama, it is between the self that exists and the self that it desires. We still speak of a method that uses drama to rationally explain society as desires and alienated lived experiences within a historical context. The individual as the central character in the play we call "modernity" was one of Hegel's main innovations. It is still an explanation that helps us to understand not only what we are still becoming but why we are unhappy at what we have achieved by our own efforts and free of any cosmological influences.

"In our own time," Meadows explains,

history becomes a drama of human beings as actors; there is a shift from external events; the accent is on character, not on plot, though sometimes (as in Freudianism) mythology provides a plot-line as suggestion of a developmental pattern of meanings. The plot is immanent, not transcendental; the dialogue is intensely personal, not cosmological and elevated; and the time span is individual, not cosmic or generational or epochal. This existential mood, re-enforced by a phenomenology which seeks to bring a subtle personal epistemology to the explanation of action in place of resonating externalism of earlier traditions, is the emerging dramatism (eschaton) of change theory today. In unison with the contemporary theme of freedom, this newest voice heralds an age which proclaims freedom *within history* just as earlier voices proclaimed freedom *from nature* or *from history*. The current mood of change theory is indeed biographical: the human being has become his own metaphor of reality.[11]

This freedom that our discussion asks us to consider as an option speaks to what I call "genuine multiculturalism," deriving from a radical democracy of individual equality. This way of knowing ourselves is necessary as we try to understand ourselves in this late moment of modernity. And because modernity itself is an attempt to know the self so that it can "to its own self be true" in actions and even thought, one of the ways it helps us explain what we have become and are still becoming is Hegel's phenomenology of knowing, specifically as he explains the movements of personal change in the tragedy of despair and disillusionment that he calls "phenomenology of spirit."

Indeed, what we are talking about is really telling stories about change and how identities emerge out of changing environment and times. As Hilde Lindemann Nelson suggests in *Damaged Identities, Narrative Repair,* our identities are imaginary, also emerging out of the dialectic of what we think of ourselves and what other people think of us. "Personal identities are narratively constructed" – as stories we tell about one another and how collectively we all fit into a pattern, system, state, or nation:

> Identities are constructed from the first-person perspective through the loosely connected stories we weave around the things about us that matter most to us: the acts, experiences, and characteristics we care most about, and the roles, relationships, and values to which we are most deeply committed. In the course of this narrative construction, we draw on stock plots and character types that we borrow from the familiar stories embodying our culture's socially shared understandings – the stories that ... [are] master narratives. Especially necessary to our identities is the narrative activity that takes place from the third-person perspective: other people weave the things about us that matter most to *them* into stories that also constitute our identities. Important too is our membership in various social groups, whose identities are themselves narratively constructed.[12]

Often, especially when we or observers construct us as a tragic hero, we have to repair those narratives about ourselves to affirm that we are comedic characters, lovable and wholesome. This way we escape historical oppression that starts with how others see us and how we not only internalize these projections but act them out, whether willingly or not. We seek to liberate ourselves, and to do this we have to both tell different and empowering stories about ourselves and convince the people important to us to not only accept those stories but share them as part as the real stories of their *own* lives and as part of the master narrative that is like train tracks leading them to some supposedly ideal time, some ultimate destination. Thus an identity emerges psychologically, in an internal dialogue between the self and its desires; and at the same time it surfaces socially, in dialogue between the self and others. Both the psychological and the social components are integral.

The story about multiculturalism shows us how to move from social tragedy to comedy. Multiculturalism is first and foremost an existence, a Hegelian force of life, before it becomes an explanation of living and then an ideal to achieve sometime, somewhere. Multiculturalism, therefore, is first a tragedy before it becomes idealism and comedy, the latter two nothing more than an inversion of the naturalism that makes life tragic. It is first ontology before it becomes an ethical relationship, this movement an attempt to create a unique way of becoming and acting human.

MULTICULTURALISM IN CANADA

I focus on the Canadian brand of multiculturalism because this model is the hallmark of this social construction, the world's first official multicultural state. I look at how, in a society, we can move from being feared to being loved. Here the emphasis is on the method – on the procedure and the way rather than on some goal or outcome. This is a story about a process that, I contend, critics usually malign for not bringing about what it did not even intend to produce: happiness for everyone. And it is for this reason that, looking around us at this time, we seem to feel and sense a deep melancholia; dominant groups in Canadian society may mourn what used to be and discuss how to accommodate those they perceive to be still not full members of their country, while many of the dominated mourn the loss or lack of opportunities, including the state's failure to make best use of them and the loss of the ideal of freedom that told them that in Canada they could be themselves, could be as authentic as they wished to be, without losing any sense of self. Therefore nobody seems to be happy.

As an organic being, as a state where historical claims and moralities face wide challenges, Canada then is an unhappy consciousness. It may feel despair, where some people see a one-sided expectation of happiness as abject failure rather than as an exercise in errantry, where we are simply following a path without a specific destination. One of the lessons available to us from this wandering is not failure per se but what there is to gain, the good that hides in evil or tragedy. This discovery of the unexpected adds to our storehouse of knowledge. And because we are supposedly moral and therefore learn from experience, knowledge influences the way we treat one another – if only by standing out as the lesson on what is *not* the way to good ethical relationships and citizenship.

Canada is a body in search of a proper way to keep its many parts from warring among themselves and even with Canada itself as the state. This is a struggle to determine sovereignty – particularly which entity should establish the conditions and ideals for an assault on the future, if Canadians still believe in a future together. As Pierre Trudeau, the idealist behind multicultural Canada, said, "if the citizens want to avoid being ordered about against their will, they must provide themselves with a protector in the form of a state strong enough to subordinate to the public good all the individuals and organisms that go to make up society."[13]

Such an entity would be, in the words of the English theorist Thomas Hobbes, nothing less than a "leviathan": in effect, a god that human beings create and establish as sovereign.[14] "This done, the Multitude so united in one Person, is called a COMMONWEALTH, in Latin CIVITAS. This is the Generation of that great LEVIATHAN, or rather (to speak more reverently) of that *Mortal God,* to which we owe under the *Immortal God,* our peace and defence."[15] As Hegel would say, this is a godhead – an act of living that produces the unity that occurs in loving and in fellowship, where a single act of "life is not different from life [itself], since life dwells in the single Godhead."[16] George Herbert Mead makes much of the search through history by humans for the god-like authority that is a sovereign, that as god brings rationality and order to an otherwise chaotic world. Noting that the ideal of a God with a perfect mind and all-knowing and all-powerful is a gift to modern times from Christianity, Mead states that this ideal of the god transferred to the state as the ultimate authority that is not arbitrary or irrational. Its antecedent was the power of the medieval church. "But the authority of the church came from an infinite deity, an infinite mind, whose knowledge you could not comprehend," Mead states. "You had to accept it simply because God spoke and gave his authority through the church. This authority got its expression not simply in the church but in the state. The sword was placed in the hands of the king by God himself. All institutions were conceived of as established by God."[17]

Ultimately, this god would become the state itself, a moral force that with time sees and knows everything perfectly even if it has to apologize for past mistakes that occurred in its name, as it seeks to bring about heaven on earth in the form of *natural* social justice. This is also the god-like being of which the sociologist Emile Durkheim spoke, the entity on earth that is a creature of time and space and that represents culture's belief in the goodness of life. "A religion is a unified system of beliefs and practices relative to sacred things, that is to say, things set apart and forbidden – beliefs and practices that unite into one single moral community called a Church, all those who adhere to them."[18] This unity produces what Durkheim calls "solidarity," and I, "fraternity." In its widest and most inclusive sense, the moral community is the nation-state as the embodiment of this spirit. This is a view that surfaces also in the work of such thinkers as Hegel, Marx, and Weber.

But at every point in the history of people's attempt to attain togetherness, it appears as if the country experiences only despair and failure. This is the only conclusion possible if we assume the correctness of a specific outcome that is the production of an ethnic country rather than seeing the methods that people tried as exercises in learning and in the fulness of living day by day, in what Hegelians would call achieving a "determinate nothingness." This is not the same as coming up empty at every turn or after experimenting with a specific approach. It is recognizing that even when we fail to attain a specific goal, we still achieve something, often the opposite of the goal itself. We gain knowledge; this new knowledge is now central to our greater appreciation of *all* facets of life – positives and negatives – so that we can know only retrospectively whether what we have attained is ethically good and a process that we want to keep. Concentrating on one side of this experience – *not* meeting a specific goal – sets us up for failure. Who can predict which path among the many available will lead us out of despair and into happiness?

Multiculturalism is about the path and what we can learn both positively and negatively along the way. As a path, it is a road of despair, a narrative in which the pages on happiness are blank. Multiculturalism will always be a failure as a specific goal if only because as a goal it would always presuppose a specific form of existence rather than a way of being. Someone will always see this way of living as the tragedy it is. Multiculturalism as a specific goal would be yet another moment of diremption, for it would seek stasis, an unchanging position that is contrary to life itself. Especially in a society that grounds itself in history, life is about trying things and finding out which of them work and, when one reaches a dead end, about what we can take away from the experience. It is recognizing that we are never really at home and that we are constantly in search of a better way to overcome the human condition. While we hope to end up in a specific state, such as a comedy, it is the process of becoming, of changing, that makes us more aware of ourselves and our possibilities and that is the real exercising of that hope. It is living.

What we see in the unfurling of *history* is the flourishing of "multiculturalism as tragedy," as Canadians come into consciousness as a multicultural society. This is analogous to the teenager who becomes aware of her selfhood and challenges the limits family and society impose on her. The teenager must find herself and figure out who she truly is, even if this means struggling with the old order of things and with herself psychologically and physically. The teenager has to come up against limits to really know her own personality and true character, to know all she can become and all she can achieve. Yet for this person, as for all others, her full personality and achievements become determinate only in death, the ultimate limit for all human beings. The teenager seeing herself as the centre of the world most likely looks like a comedy to the people around her.

Multicultural Canada is young. One of the main tasks it faces is determining what really *is* a multicultural Canadian and what is a multicultural culture. What is a multicultural culture good for, and what is it capable of achieving? Indeed, how should a truly multicultural being that is aware of itself as truly multicultural react? How does it live in this world with other states, some of which might not be *officially* multicultural? Searching for answers to these pressing questions can occur after this consciousness answers one main identity-related question: Does "being Canadian" constitute an evolution away from Canada's earlier identities and consciousnesses of being French, English, or any of the many different ethnic identities that have existed and continue to exist in a multicultural Canada? Are all of these different ethnicities and cultures merely parts of the Canadian body – an entity that by definition has to be bigger and more encompassing than any part or even all of them together? In this entity exist all the parts but also a spirit that is unique, which is a hybrid, capturing the identities and cultures of its many groups. This consciousness has to look at itself and, seeing itself with fresh eyes, decide if it is still "good" according to the contemporary standards and definitions of what is now *Canadian*.

This new awareness might be necessary even if only because to be the most current version of *Canadian* means incorporating many of the evils that, in a previous form, Canadianness shunned or even fought against. The consciousness that is multicultural Canada has to determine if the changes necessary for it to live as a new, multiethnic entity are good and desirable or whether it would be better to remain static as a consciousness that formed in a different time and that some people believe still optimal for today. But no sooner does the consciousness attempt to answer these questions than it faces a whole series of different questions, all resulting from incessant change, from life moving on and leaving a trail or history of more and still more questions but few answers, leaving in its wake no harmony, stability, or reconciliation among its disputing members. Indeed, in Canada today, there is no lasting harmony.

MULTICULTURALISM IN THE AMERICAS

Multiculturalism was never to be a cure for or way to eradicate the human condition of unhappiness. It never promised to produce truth, certainty, or clarity in human affairs. It never promised a perfect world in the immediate. Maybe such desirable goods are attainable some day, but not today, and such is the abject pragmatism that underlies the policies of multiculturalism. Multiculturalism never promised a unity that Canada – with its differences, its regionalisms, its divided and even antagonist jurisdictions of sovereignty and other forms of cultural and political diversity – has never had since Europeans first appeared on this continent. So, existentially, life in Canada is about dealing with tragedy.

Multiculturalism is about existing and not about the certainty that can come only with death, when the changes that produced unhappiness in life have fully run their course. Multiculturalism is about different beings finding themselves in the midst of living – *in medias res*, as the old saying goes – and simply having to make the most of the situation. All the while, these conscious objects know that even though they are capable of making the most "good," they are just as capable of making the most evil, by struggling for permanent dominance over each other. Indeed, the settlers' colonies that would later become the countries of the Americas emerged from the creation of fear among the original inhabitants, often in ways that we can trace directly back to Machiavelli's *The Prince*. Let us remember that specific monarchies colonized most of the Americas – Machiavelli would call them "principalities" – through acts of diremption. Instead of these tyrants physically setting up new principalities as a way of extending their reach and power, it was best and certainly cheaper for them to create colonies in far-off places. This is why I agree that multiculturalism in the Americas is an attempt to deal with a congenital flaw: that of states coming into being as settler communities, with tragic beginnings but somehow achieving comedic endings.

"The colonies will not cost much," Machiavelli states in *The Prince*, "so that with little or no expense on his part, the prince can send them out and maintain them, and he only injures those whose land and houses are taken to give to the new inhabitants, and they constitute but a small part of the state; and those who are injured, remaining poor and disunited, can never do him any harm, while all others, on the one hand, are uninjured and therefore should be easily pacified, and on the other, are fearful of doing wrong lest they should be treated like those who have been stripped of their property."[19] On one hand would be the demons of tragedy dispossessing those residents – the existing folk – who have; on the other hand would be the angels of comedy giving to those newcomers who are without but who are now in highly favour, those who would be the new folk, or the people. In Hobbesian language, this prince would be a leviathan, but, as we see below, he would be more akin to the tyrant of antiquity than to the ideal of a subject or citizen who finds love on earth.

The story of European colonization worldwide grows from this type of fear: courting those whom the marginalized love or who do not quite fit into the ruler's plans becomes a sign or an act of weakness; because of the diremption and severing of life and humanity into several individualistic parts, everyone wars against everyone else, instead of living harmoniously in love as a universal collective. For in this thought, as Machiavelli captured it, we have the making of a classic Hegelian unhappy consciousness: we are in a world of diremption, where each of the parts thinks that it is the essential and unchangeable and that all the others are inessential and changeable. Each part or group feels that it can attain a state of love within itself, but only by interacting intimately with itself and excluding all those with whom it might otherwise have meaningful intercourse. A happy self or consciousness is one that benefits not only from interacting with itself, but also from engaging satisfactorily with others.

This happy consciousness comes about in the form of the new state under construction in the Americas. In practice and thought, it is an unchangeable part of Europe: location aside, it has grown naturally out of European experience as a synthesis of the idea of European freedom and of how Europeans used their land and experience to bring about this liberty. In the classic case, it is the triumph of the idea of human freedom over the hostile environment of Europe – over Nature. It is akin to the consciousness's concern only with itself.

But in the Americas, this colonial society under white or European domination is a transplant and a stranger in lands already belonging to others. It is inorganic and is not a natural unity. Its dream is to some day, in the beyond, become natural to the Americas while retaining its European essence. This was how the European-engineered state would wish to become, naturally, a site of a new spirit of love for those people within its boundaries. Such is the higher unity of which Fanon writes, but the desires of all the members to feel a sense of inclusion oppose and seek different ends from those desiring fraternity with others. They are in different prison zones, according to Fanon and, as we saw above in the Introduction, to John Dollard, who documented the segregated life of southern US towns. I return to Dollard shortly. Throughout history, the dominated zones, existing in their inferiority, carried such names as Africtown, Africville, Brownstown, Brownsville, Haiti, Little Hayti, and reservations; today they are ethnic enclaves or ghettoes and government projects. In all cases, they live with poverty, lack of opportunities, and the other great social inequalities.

But there already existed a way of life that Others to the Europeans saw as unchangeable and as the essence of living in the Americas – a way of life that Europe would try to replace. This way of life is *natural* to the Americas, in that over generations it has become the synthesis of the dreams and experience of those native to land on which the new state was to arise. This way of life is the product of the relationship between the peoples of the Americas and the Nature in which they have always found themselves. Relationships of love already exist between the peoples of this land. The new state would, mythologically, be the Fall and an act of diremption that rends the love that exists.

Whether they like it or not, the Others and Europeans alike would have to live within the state, for it is still the site of Life itself. Those who do not see the Others as candidates for the intended state's love would none the less have to accept the presence of strangers within it and marginalize them or wipe out their presence through acts of physical genocide and/or cultural assimilation. The Others in turn must accept the European dominance and exclusivity as yet another version of hostile nature that they must overcome to someday create the ideal state.

Now, as a lived experience, as Life itself that is separate and distinct from thoughts and wishes, the Machiavellian-type state is on the scene. It is sovereign because of the dominance that Europeans imposed. But perceptually, it is at the same time the representation of the positive and the negative of existence – positive for Europeans and negative for all Others, including those who are left out and those such as the aboriginal peoples who would have no part in this imposition. And the state, as an entity created out of desires, is always aware of the internal conflicts, what I call a "congenital flaw," hampering its quest to become a unified state of love. It has to develop a spirit born in conflict, not wholesomeness, a conflict that leaves the state ultimately in a Hobbesian state of nature of all warring with all. There is no *natural* love either within its boundaries or without. It is a failed desire, not really different from Life as nature. Emerging from or a social construct of violence, these social arrangements can produce only further violence as an ongoing way of life or even culture.

Such are the lessons we should have learned from antiquity and that have been the gist of the ancient tragedies incorporating differences and diversity into a single whole; this is the story of why fear and hate result from such social construction and of why special acts of self-denial and self-abnegation and even self-sacrifice are necessary to create societies of love. We have plentiful evidence of this Hegelian-type lordship and bondage in the form of social extremes and inequalities. Theoretically, this is how the decolonization that Franz Fanon describes results in extremes:

> The zone where the native lives is not complementary to the zone inhabited by the settlers. The two zones are opposed, *but not in the service of a higher unity*. Obedient to the rules of pure Aristotelian logic, they both follow the principle of reciprocal exclusivity. No conciliation is possible, for of the two terms, one is superfluous. The settlers' town is a strongly built town, all made of stone and steel. It is a brightly lit town; the streets are covered with asphalt, and the garbage cans swallow all the leavings, unseen, unknown and hardly thought about. The settler's feet are never visible, except perhaps in the sea; but there you're never close enough to see them. The settler's town is a well-fed town, an easygoing town; its belly is always full of good things. The settler's town is a town of white people, of foreigners.[20]

An example of the social and empirical evidence that has for so long characterized the ethnic and racial relationships in this Machiavellian country, so apparent in the Americas for the purposes of our discussion, appeared in John Dollard's classic *Caste and Class in a Southern Town* (1937). In this text, the difference between caste and class is as obvious as recognizing which is the "right side of the track" for the railway of life: on one side is the black Southtown, and on the other is the white – the same existence, but manifestations of it as different and as stark as the extremes that Fanon describes for the marginalized and outcast and for the colonizers and entitled. "It is a small town," Dollard observes,

> just about large enough to qualify under the census as an urban area. It is flat as a tennis court but with a bit of a tilt, the white people living on the upper half. Should floods come, the Negro quarter would be first under water. Southerntown is bisected by a railroad, and its tracks divide people according to color, the white living on one side and the Negroes on the other ... On the white side of the town the houses are, in general, commodious, well painted, shrubbed, and neat. Fans buzz in them during the summer months. They are screened and as cool as they can be in this climate. There seem to be few houses of poorer grade on the white side, and one does not in fact see many unkempt white people in the town. The streets are paved in the white

area and telephone wires run through the trees. There is a cleared play-space for children around most of the house.[21]

The state as a social unity that should produce freedom, along with stability, fraternity. and even equality, is a tragedy, for the world by nature will not allow this desire to come fully into being. The state starts out in the Americas as a site for a tragic struggle over dominant ways to exist. It has discovered that even through diremption it cannot avoid Life as a universal and as a relentless master or lord that brings all its many parts into continuous intercourse so that Life itself can continue. The state as a particular is an unhappy consciousness, resulting from duplication within what is actually only a smaller universal in a wider array of particular desires that are themselves at odds with one another. As Hegel says, "Consequently, the duplication which formerly was divided between two individuals, the lord and the bondsman, is lodged in one. The duplication of self-consciousness within itself, which is essential in the Notion of Spirit, is thus here before us, but not yet in its unity: the *Unhappy Consciousness* is the consciousness of itself as a dual-natured, merely contradictory being."[22]

This contradiction widens because of the spirit or intentions of the state and because of the ethical order that this disunity produces: the state is for the protection and benefit equally of those who are deemed immigrant or alien to the Americas and of those who are not. Yet, Europeans intended it to be a new homeland solely for them, and hence off-limits for all other peoples not natural to the region, such as Africans, Asians, and Oceanics. Indeed, it was not even for all Europeans, but for those who were "essentially" Dutch, English, French, Spanish, and the like, which puts a finer point on the situation when particular identities prove to be universals themselves rather than essences. For in a Machiavellian world, there *is* no European essence. At the same time, from the other side, all those people whom the dominant Europeans – now with a racial definition, as white – intended to exclude saw the state as a site where they could actualize and maintain their ways of life as the unchangeable in human experience. Indeed, those others would have no essences other than the perceived essence that they are non-white, even though they might express endless numbers of particularities such as ethnicities and nationalities that they often present as estimations and representations of essence.

In general, even if some members within these groups might disagree, the groups wanted a state for many of the same reasons as Europeans

– as a place of love, justice, and happiness, and for human blossoming and flourishing – but wanted the state to take a form and structure more natural to *their* experiences and thoughts. This would mean transforming the state, as an expression of their desires, from a European instrument into something else. Yet the state would fulfil the roles humanity now almost universally associates with nation-statehood.

Therefore, every side saw *the state* as an ethical order flowing from justice as becoming in the beyond what they always knew to be the one unchangeable way of life. The intentions are all the same: to find justice. This ideal, however, they execute through different, particular forms. The state of unhappiness extends to all sides. As Hegel says, "The Unhappy Consciousness itself *is* the gazing of one self-consciousness into another, and itself *is* both, and the unity of both is also its essential nature. But it is not as yet explicitly aware that this is its essential being, or that it is the unity of both."[23]

Unhappy consciousness is, important, a state of being: such was always the state of the nation-state in the Americas, and this is why as a being the state in the Americas has always been multicultural. Unhappy consciousness is also a way of behaving, as when the state recognizes that it is officially multicultural and that to be ethical and just it should build relationships that recognize a multicultural state of being. The goal of unhappy consciousness has always been to bring about a unity of Spirit, where recognizing the being as the starting point and acting in good faith as a multicultural being are *natural*. The ethical order, in the forms of laws, must anticipate this future, where the state will treat all beings as citizens as if grace binds them together and their actions reflect an ethical order of natural unity and love. This spirit speaks to a unity of perception and actions as a form of devotion.

CANADIAN MULTICULTURALISM: CELEBRATING *DIFFERENCE*

Here is where rituals become the expression of this new ethical order, but, ironically, they can never be the full expression of the newness. These rituals are merely the enactment of ways of thinking, not the total expression of the new life. At the outset, this message did not permeate the practice of multiculturalism in Canada. Multiculturalism became almost exclusively the celebration of differences through various ethnic/cultural fairs – most of them mere exoticism. Each appeared as other and as inessential to the real/essential Canada, which the state still imagined as fundamentally a bicultural expression. To invoke an analogy that Hegel borrows from Christianity, such expressions of multicultural behaviour were "no more than the chaotic jingling of bells, or the mist of warm incense, a musical thinking that does not get as far as the Notion, which would be the sole, immanent objective mode of thought."[24] Empty, they lacked unity and love; they contained no spirit, not even that of the community they were supposedly reflecting. These rituals were only further representations of a divided consciousness, for such rituals seemed separate and distinct from actual life – from the quintessential Canadian day-to-day existence that is still *beyond* the rituals.

Genuine multiculturalism suggests that rituals must be at the same level as daily work and life. They should be expressive of the thanksgiving for the freedom the state provides. For while it recognizes that the state itself has a conflicted *essence* – in that the many individuals and groups within it claim their own existences and even separate essences – the components share a new history of their own making. That history is the story of the life experiences of the state itself. In a case where the state is the subject, these individuals and groups are mere implements and objects for a state that gives the beings their very essence. It is the state that gives them any meaningful life in the face of an ever-present threat of death to all forms of life, including that of the state. But for this life to persevere and even prosper, there must be one intention or common desire, something that must appear organic and natural to every individual and group. Indeed, one way of assuring death is for there to be no cooperation within the state and between the goals and desires of the state and of its members. This is the prototype of the state that is liberal in terms of pluralism and democratic as in ultimately multicultural in spirit and form.

For this newness and idealism of spirit to emerge, the seemingly unchangeable and essential – on reflection, mere properties in a multicultural universe – must, as in a Christian consciousness, die to achieve redemption. These particulars can then reappear in the state, each in a new guise – as an essential portion of the spirit of the times that sums up all the experiences of the Americas. And at the same time, ironically and even comically, they must appear as not essential at all to the Spirit. Instead, they start out in alienation vis-à-vis the Spirit and must now work towards becoming part Spirit. But even when they are in the Spirit, they would still be different and distinct because of their history. Their essence would be Spirit in a new world.

The prototype for this newness and for the living contradictions of knowing – of having an essence that is, paradoxically, also changeable – is basic to Christianity and its precepts of a universal church embracing radically different co-religionists. A good example of its application in the Americas has been the experiences of Africans during and since slavery, when they lived a "double consciousness" of being outsiders in a state not intended for them. As James Cone explains, this is the substance of their brand of Christianity, which allows them to exist as inessential Americans while knowing that some day they will overcome and gain recognition as the true Americans they always were. In this respect, the Africans and Blacks are different from people aboriginal to the Americas, who never developed the second consciousness of attempting to enter the Europeans' new state. As an act of consciousness, the native peoples recognize their own statuses as outsiders and apart in their own states and nations. Their relationship with the new state is strictly that of dealing with Death and Nature itself – as existing in a spiritless world where they cannot actualize their desires.

For those people of a different mind, the state as a site of human love became a Christian ideal. It is where death is not now physical but *metanoia*, the undergoing of a radical change internally or mentally, where the inner being or spirit dies because it has altered radically. Yet in practice, a Machiavellian way of life remains dominant in the region. Unhappiness is the social norm. Spirit and newness have to await a birth in a new day, when a spiritual death or *metanoia* has reduced all particulars to the ashes and dust out of which the newness will form. The Machiavellian way of thinking led us in the Americas to a loveless state.

MACHIAVELLI AND THE AMERICAS

Niccolò Machiavelli's life (1469–1527) coincided with the opening up of the New World to Europeans, particularly to those nation-states in western Europe fighting for dominance and for recognition of prototypical liberal and democratic citizenship within each country centuries later. His birth took place some twenty-five years before his fellow Italian Christoforo Colombo (Christopher Columbus) "discovered" the New World for the Spanish king and queen, Ferdinand and Isabella. Five years later the Venetian Zuan Chabotto (John Cabot) arrived on the coast of what is now Atlantic Canada and claimed the land for Henry VII of England. Two years after that the Italian Amerigo Vespucci led a mission that took him to South America; in 1507, geographers named the entire hemisphere the Americas after him. It was not until 1565 that the Spanish started a permanent European colony in the Americas, in Florida, which they called "St Augustine."

Machiavelli had made a name for himself as head of the Secondary Chancery in Florence, a job that allowed him to manage "the foreign affairs of the city and consequently thrust him squarely into the centre of Florentine politics."[25] This put him in the forefront of political discussion about the city republic's survival and about the possible formation of a strong, centralized, Italian federation free of French domination. In 1513, a version of his treatise *De Principatibus* (The Prince) began circulating; the first printed text appeared in 1532, five years after its author's death.

The publication occurred seven years before France started its first colony in the Americas on the Caribbean island of St Kitts, which the Spanish quickly wiped out. European settlement began in earnest when João Álvares Fagundes started a colony on Cape Breton Island, in what is now Canada, in 1521/22, although it soon failed. The European presence in the future United States started in 1607, when Britain's Virginia Trading Company settled at Jamestown, Virginia. Two years later, the company established a colony in Bermuda. Various trading posts or colonial outposts started soon after, including Manhattan, by the Dutch in 1624, and St Kitts and Barbados, by the British in 1623 and 1625, respectively.

Taking his idea of the efficacy of fear further, Machiavelli suggests in works following *The Prince* that the lessons of history worth retaining are those that chronicle what fear has achieved. In *The Discourses*, he notes that governments in civil societies tend to oscillate between tyranny and oligarchy when people forget their history – a history that should constantly fill them with fear. For example, he argues, the best forms of government are principalities or monarchies, aristocracies, and democracies; however, when people forget the conditions that caused them to set up one type, they end up with a corrupt form – principalities become tyrannies, aristocracies become oligarchies, and democracies become anarchies.

Coming out of a kind of state of Nature with no order to implement justice, people would, as acts of socialization and then stratification, give power to the most just person among them and make him a king. But since monarchy is hereditary, later kings might not be as just and might eventually become tyrants, ultimately leading the people to overthrow them. Fearing to repeat this experience, the people would then invest authority in the elites or that group of people who can best protect the people's desires. The government of the few becomes corrupt when a specific group within the elite obtains power and uses it to oppress the many. The many overthrow this rule and set up democracy. But that generation dies off, and ultimately the people forget the reasons for it – hence anarchy.

"The result was that with each person living as he pleased," Machiavelli says, "a thousand injuries were committed every day, so that, forced by necessity, or at the suggestion of some good man, or in order to escape all the licentiousness, they returned once again to princely rule; and from that they went back, step by step, towards anarchy, in the manner and for the reasons just given."[26] Indeed, life is a tragedy, and the resulting nation-state is weak, a likely prey to stronger neighbours that lack the good life citizens expect in a nation-state.

As a result, and with time, people devised a form of government that entails the best elements of monarchies, aristocracies, and democracies, so as to avoid the excesses of tyrannies, oligarchies, and anarchies and their attendant losses of freedom. That form is republican, where "each one of these [ideal forms] keeps watch over the other." This type, we can almost hear Machiavelli saying across time, has now matured into what we would call a "liberal democracy," which assumes that constitutional government is the best guarantor of freedom.

THE CANADIAN EXPERIENCE

As throughout the Americas, this point is central for understanding Canada: societies are artificial beings that must recruit individuals from elsewhere in order to construct a state and allow it to exist across time. In our mythologies, unlike those of countries elsewhere on the globe, Canadians and their American brothers and sisters were not divine creations in a land God gave to a special people. Canada and its siblings came about from a reverse ordering. First came the people who would claim the land; then they decided to create a country or countries there.

Now, did these people surrender all individual and national or group claims of sovereignty to a specific state? Did they willingly agree to share sovereignty, either with other peoples who might join them or with those they found already on the land? Even now, do they wish Canada to become a genuine organic nation, or do they expect to preserve historical claims and even extend them across time?

What commentators have often overlooked in the recent discussion of multiculturalism is the context in which Canada initially adopted the policy. When the new progenitors of Confederation decided to change the *essence*, or their imagination, of what was Canada, many citizens had considered the country ethnically white and culturally and historically European. Canada was to be a part of Europe in the Americas, a homeland for those Europeans seeking to continue their ways of life and to achieve their dreams in a new land. To make this happen, the outsiders, or European newcomers, gave themselves the right to take possession of all the lands they found, discovered, and desired. This was part of a Malthusian way of thinking, a belief that survival requires control and management of human and natural resources to cope with growing populations. This idea dovetailed with the social Darwinian argument that the managers of these resources should be the most culturally and biologically evolved beings – an idea that simply assumed that Europeans were superior and had a moral and paternal duty to help inferior beings.

According to Albert Sarraut (1872–1962), French minister for the colonies, colonial governor, and briefly prime minister twice in the 1930s, "Nature had distributed unequally across our planet a wealth and variety of raw materials; and while she has located in this continental extremity which is called Europe, the inventive genius of the white races and the technical expertise with which to exploit natural resources, she has concentrated the most abundant reserves of these materials in Africa, tropical Asia and equatorial Oceania, towards which the developed countries in their need to live and create, are directing their impetus and drive ... Must these immense expanses of land ... be allowed to lie fallow, abandoned to the thickets of indifference, ignorance and incompetence?"[27] Many in the British elites held similar views; not untypical, Lord Frederick Lugard, colonial administrator in Hong Kong, Nigeria, and Uganda, observed:

When Great Britain undertook the control of great regions in tropical Africa, she not only gave to her commercial rivals the same opportunities as were enjoyed by her own nationals ... She secured to their inhabitants an unrestricted market for their products ... She recognised that the custodians of the tropics are ... 'trustees of civilisation for the commerce of the world'; that their raw materials and foodstuffs – without which civilisation could not exist – must be developed alike in the interests of the natives and of the world at large..: The tropics are the heritage of mankind, and neither, on the one hand, has the suzerain Power a right to their exclusive exploitation, nor, on the other, have the races which inhibit them a right to deny their bounty to those who need them.[28]

In North America itself, we find the same type of thinking by Theodore Roosevelt (US president 1901–9) in his rationalization of American development. In *The Winning of the West* (four volumes, 1889–96), he said, "The settlers and pioneers had justice on their side; this great continent could not have been kept as nothing but a game preserve for squalid savages."[29] As a result of such attitudes, US Europeans waged relentless wars on Native Americans, dispossessed them of their land, and ultimately penned them in to what they called "Indian Territory." The same attitudes resulted in the US conflict with Mexico that led to the American absorption of part of that country. The land was for tilling, as Stephen Steinberg says in his book on construction of ethnicity,

> and as one politician expounded in 1859, 'no nation has the right to hold soil, virgin and rich, yet unproducing ...' On the eve of the Mexican–American War in 1848, Sam Houston [who supported creation of Texas out of Mexican territory and served as its president and later senator and governor] reasoned that since Americans had always cheated Indians, and since Mexicans were no better than Indians, 'I see no reason why we should not go on the same course now and take their land.' An editorial in the *New York Evening Post* also stressed the similarity between Indians and Mexicans: 'the Mexicans are Indians – Aboriginal Indians ... they do not possess the elements of an independent national existence. The Aborigines of this country have not attempted and cannot attempt to exist independently along side of us. Providence has so ordained it, and it is folly not to recognize the fact. The Mexicans are Aboriginal Indians, and they must share the destiny of their race.'[30]

Developments to the north were no different. As Canadian sociologists Vic Satzewich and Nikolaos Liodakis state in *'Race' and Ethnicity in Canada*, "The titles of the mid-nineteenth century pieces of legislation that were precursors to the 1876 Indian Act are telling indicators of the ways that those in power regarded Aboriginal peoples at the time. For instance, the 1857 Act for the Gradual Civilization of the Indian Tribes of Canada clearly suggested that Indian people were in need of careful guidance to transform them from their uncivilized state. In not very subtle terms, the legislation implied that there was something faulty about Aboriginal peoples and their churches but that these faults could be corrected through the mindful and benevolent actions of missionaries and the Canadian government."[31]

The aim was to take their land and natural resources and convert them into a piece of Europe. The newcomers were able to build new societies for their own exclusive use by mistreating or enslaving other peoples, making them do the building and hard labour, and keeping them outsiders by withholding full citizenship and its status and rights.

In this respect, the liberal nation-state, as dominant European thought fantasized it, had at its heart a practical contradiction: develop and manage the world's resources for the use of all humanity; however, the resulting societies would not be open to everyone, but rather belong to particular nation-states, which shut out all non-citizens, separating people from their resources. They could not go and live where their natural resources went, to the states that they developed.

But these liberal notions also have a philosophical contradiction at heart. On one hand, the nation-state should be a place of love through membership, where even the most tyrannical among the people could savour social love. On the other, society should be a place of fear – a site of clashes over ownership, especially over properties, of which the highest form is the individual. In the latter condition, only the strong can win, for this society is veritably still in a state of nature, or tragedy. Fear, therefore, drives every action and thought.

TWO MODELS

In this book, I argue that Machiavelli best captures such a consciousness of fear in his advice on state formation and governance. Proponents of the European model intended to fleece the rest of the world of its natural resources and to convey those to people natural to Europe who lacked such resources. In this model, Europeans as privileged people stay on the land and environment that had naturally produced them, retaining exclusive rights to the ownership of all natural and human resources. This way of forming a state was very different from what European colonies elsewhere would do. The model of the Americas is different: peoples from around the world, as Machiavelli suggests, move to the land where the desired natural resources are part of the landscape. In this setting, it is the natural resources that are natural to the environment and the people who are inauthentic, as they are outsiders, foreigners, and even interlopers. Worse, they are colonial, as Machiavelli discussed. Their approach is to clear the land of all that nature has given it, depleting natural resources and even in some cases causing the genocide and extinction of the land's human resources. This is necessary to build societies that they perceive as superior and more refined and to support ways of life that are European and perceptually unnatural to the area.

Once the Europeans have imposed and installed their order, the aim is to make it appear natural or organic to the state. This would be a place of love, the kind of place that young men and women sing of and die for – built in the image of the motherland and fatherland. Incestuous interbreeding would, they assumed, within a generation or two naturalize what was originally unnatural.[32] This comedic belief posited that a specific group of human beings could improve on what nature had provided, using the resources to make something new that Nature itself might not have thought of – but in their thinking, what they deemed to be new was the old European structure, a system that by then had become old even in Europe. The models in old Europe and in the Americas aimed to produce the same social outcomes.

By the 1960s, dreams of European colonialism and dominance were floundering as the two models – European and American – proved themselves socially bankrupt. At home and abroad, the world was changing, and many of the colonial dreams that Europeans had taken with them and imposed on the rest of the world now appeared immoral, unjust, and inhuman. The winds of change were blowing all over the world, bringing down colonial powers in Asia, Africa, and the Americas in their wakes.

Most of these winds seemed to blow out of the Americas, starting with the Haitian Revolution of 1805, becoming a whirlwind in the early 1860s with the US Civil War, which ended slavery, and eventually turning into a hurricane with the arrival of the US civil rights movement a century later. This last phenomenon changed the ideals that informed the practice of what is the modern state. This continuous movement for freedom spawned outbursts everywhere: in the Caribbean and Latin America, a desire for political independence and a socialist revolution granted power and influence to diverse groups; in Asia, independence movements freed the Indian subcontinent and led to Vietnam's liberation wars; in Africa, wars for independence waged in Algeria and elsewhere, and political independence emerged, starting with Ghana in 1956; and in Canada, struggles by various ethnic groups for cultural recognition challenged the practice of inequality. By then, the hierarchical British Empire, of which Canada was an independent and superior elder member, had given way to the club-like Commonwealth, with all member-states as equal partners.

This was also the time of the so-called colonialism in reverse, when peoples from the colonized lands began moving to Europe and to European outposts such as Canada and Australia. These new arrivals were following the natural resources from their native lands. They were seeking to enjoy benefits available in metropolitan centres that had prospered with the development and international husbandry of world resources. They had discovered that, under colonial management, most of the bounty of colonial powers' natural-resource harvests the world over had gone to the powers themselves.

With the arrival of the newcomers, the Europeans, who traditionally dispossessed other people, began to fear the same fate – losing their own homeland or place of love to foreigners and strangers from across the seas. Here was a side of the earlier contradiction that the colonial powers were not ready to handle: they needed the natural resources of the undeveloped parts of the word but not their plentiful human resources. When they accepted the human resources, they could not imagine these new people benefiting in the same way as they themselves. But the economies of the day demanded a mixing of peoples and resources.

How best, then, could a nation-state exist? Could it be possible to produce a single citizenship for all members of a society, or should some members have more privileges than others? Are all human resources equal in the state? The answer rested in solving the philosophical contradiction of the nation-state: Do all citizens equally deserve a sense of membership and belonging, of uncontested love? Are they willing to be loved, or should at least some of them evoke fear? Should society treat them as worthy of fear rather than of love?

These questions are still relevant today, for in a country such as Canada they go to the heart of the discussion on immigration. They speak to whether it might be possible to extract from immigrants the labour and other resources that the nation-state needs without giving them – as full human beings – all the same rights, privileges, responsibilities, and civic obligations as the earlier settlers? This is the sort of immigrant is Canada's equivalent of the Bad John or the tragic hero, the outsider who refuses full socialization and conformity to a specific culture. Such a character is the epitome of the fearsome, the opposite of perceptually the traditional and quintessential Canadian, who is naturally lovable, at least by other Canadians. It was as if Machiavelli's Prince was looking through the wrong socializing end of the telescope. And in terms of stratification, the feared was, ironically, the Other who had long been dispossessed, not the European as the colonial invader intent on civilizing nature and imposing a *natural* order.

CANADIANS AND NATURE

As Canadian cultural theorist Northrop Frye argued, central to the traditional social imagining of what is Canada and who is a Canadian is the *reality* of an outer and physical struggle against Nature. First, this is the struggle that people who are not ethnically natural to the land may wage. They may fight against the land and the surrounding vegetation to bring out of the primordial barbarism and primitiveness a "bush garden" fit for European living. They traditionally list among the barbarians all those peoples and cultures that are not European but whom they call "spooks" and "bogeymen" – the beasts who reside in the primitive and uncivilized forest and woods of our mythical imaginary.

Second, the social imagination necessary for love presumes conformity. All members of a society work together for a common good – overcoming the almost-overwhelming wiles of Nature. As Frye says, this is a struggle against a history of immediacy and not against the past and myth-making, where individuals struggle against ideals of accomplishment for its own sake that emerge from, in some sense, a timeless good. Under such conditions, two features stand out: these settlements – these bush gardens – take the form of a garrison; and they develop a garrison mentality, basing their culture on conformity and the rejection of individualism.

In such a setting, very unlike the social imagination that developed in the United States, the tragic hero in Canada becomes the individual alienated from the community who no longer benefits from communal living and love. Society fears this individual, who does not embody the image of love – the community. The society does not create tragic heroes who struggle against limits and boundaries in the society, such as when immigrants enter a society and refuse full socialization, unwilling to accept the society's images and intentions for them. In dominant Canadian thought, the tragic and even pathetic individual is the one resisting the state; in essence, the Canadian imagination sees such characters as actors in a comedy rather than in a tragedy and so not as part of their history.

As Frye states of Canada, "the conquest of nature has its own perils for the imagination, in a country where the winters are so cold and where conditions of life have so often been bleak and comfortless, where even the mosquitoes have been described as 'mementoes of the fall.' ... Small and isolated communities surrounded with a physical or psychological 'frontier,' separated from one another and from their American and British cultural sources: communities that provide all that their members have in the way of distinctively human values, and that are compelled to feel a great respect for the law and order that holds them together, yet confronted with a huge, unthinking, menacing, and formidable physical setting – such communities are bound to develop what we may provisionally call a garrison mentality."[33] It is a garrison just like Machiavelli described: a colonial outpost of soldiers in a foreign land.

Frye describes the historical or dominant social imagination of Canadians that sets up the rationale for the angst between old-timers and newcomers who remain outsiders and tragic heroes even when they become nominal citizens. "A garrison mentality," Frye states, "is a closely knit and beleaguered society, and its moral and social values are unquestionable. In a perilous enterprise one does not discuss causes or motives: one is either a fighter or a deserter ... The real terror comes when the individual feels himself becoming an individual, pulling away from the group, losing the sense of driving power that the group gives him, aware of a conflict within himself far subtler than the struggle of morality against evil. It is much easier to multiply garrisons, and when that happens, something anti-cultural comes into Canadian life, a dominant hard-mind in which nothing original can grow."[34] It is this type of thinking that today sees multiculturalism as a multiplicity of separate and distinct garrisons, each reporting to its own Prince back home, wherever that is, except that we now call these garrisons "ethnic ghettoes," as sites of abject alienation from that national spirit. The dominant fear is that these garrisons fracture the social love, generating a multiplicity of sites of fear masquerading as a united country.

To this end, Frye seems to be in agreement with the neo-conservative critic Leo Strauss, who states that modern society is a place where individuality is always under attack by the forces of conformity. A citizen has the choice either to share the group's "subjective certainty" and be just another friend and loved one sharing in common thinking and action or to continue to search for the self as an individual. In the latter, the individual searches for true knowledge that is wisdom, a quest that must place him or her at odds with the group. This searching makes the individual a true philosopher, a being independently searching for its own subjective certainty, truth, or morality. This quest begins in a state of nature among the fearsome and might best find fulfilment in a state of nature that privileges individuality; in effect, fear should always be present, even in the new state. "Friendship is bound to lead to or to consist in," Strauss explains, "the cultivation and perpetuation of common prejudices by a closely knit group of kindred spirits. It is therefore incompatible with the idea of philosophy. The philosopher must leave the closed and charmed circle of the 'initiated' if he intends to remain a philosopher. He must go out to the market place, the conflict with the political men cannot be avoided. And conflict by itself, to say nothing of its cause or its effect, is a political action."[35] Machiavelli could not have said it any better.

A Straussian philosopher, the prototype of the liberal individual, can be happy only outside of the society, resisting conformity and, in Canada's case, Frye's garrison mentality. Entering society, she or he becomes a mere tragic hero, struggling to maintain the quest for individual certainty but having to accept the common prejudices of kindred spirits. Comedically, this sharing of a common kindred spirit must now serve as a perfect substitute for the freedom and philosophic search of the state of Nature; morally, this has to be unacceptable to the true hero, whose concern is only with the love of the self.

Genuine multiculturalism would be an attack on a Straussian-Machiavellian mentality: ironically, the enemies of the defenders of the old state or bush gardens would coexist with the defenders themselves. More than that, the enemy would be *within* the individual defenders and would not appear to be outside or beyond them. Genuine multiculturalism therefore acknowledges the diversity of humanity, of all Canadians, and this diversity can produce the love that others fear. This is the way of living and understanding a civic identity, where, as Frye explains,

a sense of [national] unity is the opposite of a sense of uniformity. Uniformity, where everyone "belongs," uses the same clichés, thinks alike and behaves alike, produces a society which seems comfortable at first but is totally lacking in human dignity because there are no differences. Such are the horrors of living the life of the eternal same.

Real unity tolerates dissent and rejoices in variety of outlooks and traditions, recognizes that it is the human destiny to unite and not divide, and understands that creating proletariats and scapegoats and second-class citizens is a mean and contemptible activity, ironically, the opposite of the intended state of love. Unity, so understood, is the extra dimension that raises the sense of belonging into genuine human life. Nobody of intelligence has any business being loyal to an ideal of uniformity: what one owes one's loyalty to is an ideal of unity, and a distrust of such a loyalty is rooted in a distrust of life itself.[36]

This is an imagination that favours the tragic hero, where life for the most part is a tragedy. Recognizing this was to drag Canada into postmodern times, when, ironically, the lovable is diverse, fragmenting, and in conformity with the Hegelian type of unity, which recognizes the whole but also its many separate parts.

Multiculturalism as official policy was the de facto recognition of a seemingly primordial existence that produces diversity as the norm – as an already ideal state of being. This is what philosophical circles might call the "ontology," or physical formation of the world. It is the final recognition that the state is not a natural entity rising up like some mythological leviathan out of the land that is the fatherland or motherland, with a common mother tongue. This is an aberrant way of giving meaning to Nature, for it places in unchanging and, indeed, concrete terms the "us" and "them" of the world – those who are lovable and those whom we are to fear. Instead, the state is a social construction, which citizens touch and refine, just as people transport minerals away from their sources, where Nature had placed them, to add value. In a new land, people process them into something that is acceptable as socially new and "refined," just as diversity in Canada produces workers who shine with "true patriot love." The same would have to happen with people who do not appear "natural" to the Americas: they need social refinement or socialization according to the values of a specific culture. Therefore, the people of the American states, not being natural to the region, require social construction.

SOMETHING NEW

Multiculturalism in Canada is really an attempt to follow the process I described above by producing something that is genuinely new – something that is not Europe or any other part of the old history. What it produces has to be something that mixes natural and human resources freely, with no prior notions of social hierarchies or political dominance, so as to generate something "natural" to such an existence. Canada adopted official multiculturalism to solve a congenital flaw, an apparent birth defect that produced something unnatural. Nation-states in the Americas faced a discredited history of European colonialism and domination and the rational-idealist dream of a country where all members – no matter whence they hailed – could flourish equally and live happily together in a state of love without fear of violence.

The official policy was a search for a type of justice for a world that is basically multi-ethnic and racially diverse, justice for a people that come together not by nature but through migration. As a desire for justice, multiculturalism follows naturally from a pivotal point in the history of the Americas, the US Civil War, which wrote in blood the prototype for citizenship in a land of diverse peoples trying to making themselves into a nation within the moribund European model that sought a nation natural to the land. An alternative to such nation-state construction is to move away from basing patterns and practices on fear and thereby excluding other peoples, marginalizing difference, and rejecting diversity. So, then, the new justice since the Civil War rejects traditional models of nation-state formation, not diversity and difference.

Pierre Trudeau seemed mindful of these developments and of how they shaped the consciousness that is Canada. "Federalism is by its very essence a compromise and a pact. It is a compromise in the sense that when national consensus on *all* things is not desirable or cannot readily obtained, the area of consensus is reduced in order that consensus on *some* things be reached. It is a pact or quasi-treaty in the sense that the terms of that compromise cannot be changed unilaterally. That is not to say that the terms are fixed forever; but only that in changing them every effort must be made not to destroy the consensus on which the federated nation exists."[37]

To this end, in search for a malleable consensus, Trudeau seems particularly aware of the legacy of the American Civil War: "The advantages *to the minority group* of staying integrated in the whole must on balance be greater than the gain to be reaped from separating. This can easily be the case when there is no real alternative for the separatists, either because they have met with force (as in the case of the US Civil War) or because they are met with laughter (as in the case of the *Bretons bretonnants*). But when there is a real alternative, it is not so easy."[38] Not only does Trudeau see the centrality of the Civil War, but his example shows that he is aware that trying to satisfy human desires had caught him in either a tragedy of fear and violence or a comedy, with laughter at a futile battle against natural laws, including those that have sprung organically out of a particular way of life.

In the great big drama that is the shaping of the Canadian consciousness, Trudeau envisioned Quebec as analogous to the Confederate States
and the "rest of Canada" to the Union. In effect, Quebec had no choice
but to choose laughter over violence and crying, to become multicultural
so as to overcome the congenital flaw I have described for these nation-
states not founded for the people indigenous to the land. "We can safely
assume that the men who drew up the terms of the [Canadian] federal
compromise [in 1867] had heard something of the ideology of nationalism which had been spreading revolutions for seventy-five years. It is
likely too that they knew about the Civil War in the United States, the
rebellion of 1837–8 in Canada, the Annexation Manifesto [by Canadian
businessmen in 1849 advocating US annexation of Canada], and the
unsatisfactory results of double majorities [in the Province of Canada]."[39]

Too often commentators discuss multiculturalism outside of this
context. They often confuse cause and effect: they present multiculturalism as if the problems of diversity and of different ethnic groups'
living together result from multiculturalism. Frequently, they fight over
even the very idea of what Canada is and how it arrived at this particular juncture. This will be so unless they stop presenting or imagining
Canada solely as part of "the European civilization on which our nation
is grounded," as Canadian historian J.L. Granatstein claims, like many
who think this way.[40] In this light, Granatstein criticizes Canadians as
"lamentably ignorant of their past," for somehow believing, among
other things, "that the Civil War was a Canadian affair."[41] Indeed, it is
hard not to imagine the ideal person of whom he speaks to be ethnically European and racially white.[42] Imagining him or her this way pic-
tures Canada not as a consciousness that can hope for happiness only
by fully recognizing the conflicts within that makes any ideals of a
single essence farcical.

"History is important because it helps people know themselves,"
Granatstein says in *Who Killed Canadian History?* "It tells them who
they were and who they are; it is the collective memory of humanity
that situates them in their time and place; and it provides newcomers
with some understanding of the society in which they choose to live. Of
course, the collective memory undergoes constant revision, restructur-
ing, and rewriting, but whatever its form it reveals anew to each generation a common fund of knowledge, traditions, values, and ideas that
help to explain our existence and the mistakes and successes of the
past."[43] How true in a general way. In the specific, by his own reasoning,

perhaps today's generation should excavate through the overpowering European elements in this process to arrive at the core of modern Canada: the US Civil War and how even to this day it continues to change the entire Americas.

But every so often Canadians remind themselves that their history is not what Granatstein would have them presume. Take Tom Kent's version in the *Globe and Mail* on 25 April 2008. Kent immigrated to Canada in 1954 and served as principal assistant to Lester Pearson, prime minister 1963–8. In 1966, he was deputy minister of Citizenship and Immigration. Lamenting the diluting, as he saw it, of Canadian identity, he recalled that this was not the intention underlying the Canadian Citizenship Act of 1947 or the British North America Act in 1867.

"In the beginning," he wrote, "in the 1867 escape from colonies to nation, what it meant to be Canadian was plain. It was to be different from American. As the United States emerged from its bloody civil war, and found purpose in the manifest destiny of rolling west and potentially north, determination to have no part of it was equally strong in the British and the French." Canada was in effect an attempt to escape the shadow of the neighbours' civil war. "The BNA Act was soon supported by the National Policy of tariffs and the railroad. That was not enough, however, to build an economy from sea to sea. Farmers from a cold climate were needed to break the Prairie sod. It was immigration from central Europe that made it possible for Quebec and the old British colonies to grow into a nation state. We remained a dynamic economy. In the mid-twentieth century, particularly, remarkable and diversified growth called for many new workers. At first they came from Britain and Europe, but prosperity there soon diminished those sources. The temper of the 1960s in any case called for openness to all peoples, who have since come especially from south and east Asia."[44]

Unlike Granatstein and his ilk, Kent argues that the Civil War has had a lasting effect on Canada. Of course, he overlooks Canada's desire to be a white person's country, where a bright young man such as Kent could leave England and nine years later be special adviser to the prime minister. Later, he would co-chair a royal commission on newspaper ownership and concentration. There is no evidence to suggest such social mobility is still open to extremely well-qualified immigrants, which raises two questions: Is this so because, as Kent suggests, the country itself and the Canadian identity have changed? Or is it because the *sources* of immigrants and the diversity now present have changed the country's old character?

Multiculturalism, especially in Canada, was to solve a problem: how to convert a society that had different types of people into a single country, with all the people as citizens sharing a common solidarity and love for one another, seeking liberation and shared citizenship as equals?

Often observers present multiculturalism as having come into existence without a history or as if it was not part of an ongoing consciousness that hoped to realize full justice at some future time. We can deepen our understanding of it and its ideals if we place it in its socio-political context as an attempt to form a nation-state. In particular, I argue that we should read it as part of an unfurling of the quest for freedom in the Americas and as resulting from the struggle that shaped the hemisphere – the struggle over African slavery and the desires of black and African peoples for full inclusion in the modern nation-state. And thus we can gain much by reflecting on the common elements in the religious thinking and ideology of those dreamers who imagined Canada as a genuine multicultural state and of those blacks and African Americans who desired their full liberty and humanity – who wanted life itself. This is a point I develop more fully as we go along.

While we can read Canadian multiculturalism at the universal level as part of the modern quest for freedom, it is not purely a Canadian occurrence and does result in part from one gory and fearsome particular – the American Civil War. Pierre Trudeau alluded to this connection when he reflected on the social construction of the new Canada in the 1970s. He was struggling with provincial premiers over what should be the new Canada and where, ultimately, sovereignty should rest. He was a spirit of the times, an embodiment of the desires that sought actualization. In a Hegelian sense of recognizing what is the real battle instead of looking only at the combatants, he stated, "We were fighting the rebirth of the theory that Canada is the creation of the provinces rather than the creation of the sovereign Canadian people. The list of the powers the provinces wanted grew longer and longer, until I reached a point where I thought we had decentralized enough."[45]

If there is an innate flaw in the construction of Canada and other states in the Americas, it is that they started in the dominant ideology as settler communities, which dispossessed the indigenous peoples before the first waves of settlers claimed an unchallengeable and irrevocable ownership over their spoils. More than that, these settlements began at a time when many Europeans considered it normal and natural to enslave other beings whom they thought human but of lesser worth or spirit, to dispossess them of all that they owned, and to build settler communities by forcing their labour. This way they reduced the social inferiors, the non-settlers, the underprivileged, to the status almost of walking dead in the new societies and states they built. From then on, many settlers, most of whom were Europeans, sought to prevent their own dispossession, a Machiavellian fear that still resonates in some quarters of privilege.

This is an issue that, ironically, has come to be of little interest for the state that these acts of dispossession and repossession created. The state's primary concern is not to prove or preserve ownership by a specific group or people but to single-mindedly continue the state's existence across time. It should do so regardless of who might come to own or be owned by the state. Multiculturalism in Canada was an attempt to establish rules of behaviour to allow a national existence in the absence of or despite the impossibility of a final determination of possession and to enable a state to continue to exist in whatever form it had to. Here we may think of the wise words of the 2004 report by the Royal Commission on Aboriginal Peoples in Canada: "After some 500 years of a relationship that has swung from partnership to domination, from mutual respect and co-operation to paternalism and attempted assimilation, Canada must now work out fair and lasting terms of coexistence with Aboriginal people."[46] Indeed, with all its peoples.

As a collection of diverse peoples and individuals who sought out this particular land mass for a variety of reasons, Canadians must find a way to get along. They have to determine whether to build a society in which they fear one another, each other's differences and diversity, or to love one another by simply accepting all differences and diversity as natural – but not essential – to the creation of thick social relationships. "Getting along" means determining what elements to adopt from two seemingly opposite approaches: that of Machiavellian fear and that of the Hebrew prophetic and Greek philosophical traditions. And if these people are to be free, no one group or combination of groups can have dominance, except in a Lockean way, where such people consent freely to that condition. Consent, then, has to be an act of loving, the opposite of dominance and use of power with force. Multiculturalism is *essentially* about different peoples and individuals' getting along in a common cause. Again, as the royal commission acknowledged in 2004, "Canada is a test case for a grand notion – the notion that dissimilar peoples can share lands, resources, power and dreams while respecting and sustaining their differences. The story of Canada is the story of many such peoples, trying and failing and trying again, to live together in peace and harmony."[47]

Just as important, multiculturalism in Canada recognizes a particular history and truth: that because the country and its provinces started as settler communities, they could never evolve into supposedly natural state organisms like those in Europe, no matter how much the dominant European groups might desire them to. For as long as they could, Canadian elites held on to the notion that the country was a fragment of Europe in the Americas, that it was a part of European history and destined to become a European – read, white – country, like its prototypes in England and France.[48]

All the while, Canada itself was turning more and more to the wider world for its most valuable resources – people – so that the dominant dream and the living reality on the ground became binary opposites. With the arrival of diverse peoples from around the world, all of them looking to settle in Canada just as the Europeans did, the chances of Canada's evolving into a European nation-state or sovereign organism withered. And it is primarily because the Americas as nation-states are so different from Europe, Asia, and elsewhere, with their entrenched ethnic-nation groups, that multiculturalism is unique to the history of the Americas and to their internal power relations. The basis for this uniqueness is that the modern countries of the Americas were the creation *of* immigrants *for* migrants and refugees. What is more, many of the newcomers came and lived as chattel slaves, as property, not humans. Such were the *natural* resources for state formation.

"America is therefore the land of the future," Hegel said in a lecture series in the winter of 1830–31, "where, in the ages that lie before us, the burden of the World's History shall reveal itself – perhaps in a contest between North and South America. It is a land of desire for all those who are weary of the historical lumber-room of old Europe. Napoleon is reported to have said: '*cette vieille Europe m'ennuie*' [This old Europe bores me]. It is for America to abandon the ground on which hitherto the History of the World has developed itself. What has taken place in the New World up to the present time is only an echo of the Old World – the expression of a foreign Life."[49]

But if we judge by concerns today in the Americas over the scarcity of space and the integration of newcomers alongside those of old-timers, perhaps North America has become like the Europe of Napoleon's time. The old has also become decrepit in a new land, now growing dusty even in the eyes of the old-timers. And old spirits need revival, kisses from many Prince Charmings. As the American-born modernist poet T.S. Eliot says in *The Love Song of J. Alfred Prufrock*, "I grow old … I grow old .../I shall wear the bottoms of my trousers rolled."[50] To be old without dignity in a European-type society is indeed – as human beings as varying as Achilles, Odysseus, and even Machiavelli have taught through the ages – to be tragic.

4

Multiculturalism in the Americas

Hegel remarks somewhere that all great world-historic facts
and personages appear, so to speak, twice. He forgot to add
the first time as tragedy, the second time as farce.

Karl Marx[1]

Genuine multiculturalism, then, is more than mere formalism and its
seeming common-sense opposites, conformity and coercion – both sides
of which I am presenting as twins of the same dialectic, as faces of freedom and slavery. Both have the same beginning, and at times the same
genealogy of historical experiences. Their early separation into one or
the other occurs as acts of diremption, akin to a biblical fall or to a
tumble like a Humpty Dumpty – an apparent degeneration from freedom to slavery.

As the Latvian-American philosopher Judith Shklar describes it, this is
the splitting of an ego of sorts, or what we call a "consciousness," over
competing desires. The despair of slavery "begins when the ego recognizes itself as desire for both self-sufficiency and communion with others,
as it seeks knowledge. The ego can remain integrated even though it be
complex, but the possibility of a split between its two aims is always
there."[2] This is on one hand the desire to be a self-reliant individual and
on the other the competing desire for love. The initial tearing apart gives
way to a series of actions and thoughts about how to re-create this unity,
how to return to the idyllic and even naïve freedom. A new desire, this
time for what one has lost, emerges, and one must satisfy it, even as the
desires for separation maintain their hold. The desire to return results in
a journey of despair, fraught with failures. This journey of experiences is
akin to that of a tragic hero tearing away from what is known and familiar, the existing life, and setting off to make himself or herself in the
world – only in the heat of the journey does this traveller realize that the

success of a new freedom depends as much on himself or herself as on what the world offers.

In the world, the individual must also be part of a collective or society, in effect playing out the two desires that caused the diremption. Thus even in society, the initial split or rending remains, with knowledge from history telling the many travellers that converge together in any community that to achieve communion they must act as if the split no longer existed, as if individual self-sufficiency no longer mattered, even though the split is obvious to everyone. These travellers must live a comedy of their own making, where if they satisfy one natural desire they defer the other. The comedy is the redefinition of freedom in terms of a hierarchy of desires – where all desires cannot be equal, even if the society now constructs holders of the competing desires as free men and women or citizens.

Genuine multiculturalism is the opposite of diremption and disunity, for it is a spirit of oneness and unity in the plenitude of diversity and differences. It is all about finding love, unity, fraternity, and recognition in the crowd or the nation-state that is humanity itself, and it is about finding that self that is authentic and free, bereft of alienation and any other form of slavery. It is the practice of radical democracy, where the actions of the collective or state express and reconcile the desires of every individual. And genuine multiculturalism is about finding wholeness and wholesomeness in a state where the sovereign's power furthers the good of the state or collective, which means that the sovereign has no favourite children or citizens and uses and consumes all citizens equally.

This state is like the Christian consciousness, where even God must die every moment to resurrect in the next into love and new fellowship. The state is the prototype of this new spirit that is constantly undergoing death and rebirth, for the state is the love, fellowship, and values that are the synthesis of all that went before, what is happening now, and what will emerge in the future. It is the consciousness of time becoming immanent in the present and expressing itself in the individuals and groups that temporarily make up the state. But it is always more than what it seems: as time, it is dead and it is also yet to be born. In this sense, as Hegel and later Durkheim, Marx, and others would suggest, it is God.

Analogous, the sovereign is like the god that is always asking its human subjects or bondsmen to prove their worth to him. In our dominant mythology in the West, humans try to please their Lord by burning their bodies or the fruits of their bodies, reducing themselves to their essences

– dust and ash that the wind will so easily blow away. This is what they become as citizens: means of producing what the state needs. They are primarily producers of things and services. They are workers, all hoping to receive that social mobility that frees them eventually from the need to work and to please anyone. Yet despite their best effort at producing, some will come up short, including those who felt that they had a birthright or deserve one from the Lord. These tend to be those who felt that, culturally, they knew what the Lord wanted and that they had a privileged and historical relationship with the Lord. As the dominant mythology tell us, in somebody's eyes, the god that is the state will always make the wrong decision. But what is wrong for some is right for others.

In our day, its own necessity seems to oblige the state to favour workers who use their bodies to produce for the state and to meet its insatiable appetites for burnt offerings in the form of the children of the land. This is the state's raison d'être, as we see most vividly in the Greek tragedy *Antigone,* where the state as the universal political actor must repress private interests that are not in the state's wider interest. As Hegel suggests, this is the ethical order the state must promote, and in the case of Canada and immigrants, this is why the Antigones who support the existing order and resist change from the political have to die and lose their privileged positions in the ethical order. The state claims to love all members of the society equally and calls them "citizen." It gives them the same rights, standings, and privileges and might even enshrine this recognition in charters of fundamental freedoms and bills of rights. Even when there is much evidence to the contrary, all its members want to believe that the state loves them equally and might even favour them.

But this is a sceptical and even cynical world: the state truly loves only those who feed it and ensure its survival across generations. This is a god whose love is always open to purchase by transactions among bidders who never stop sacrificing in the hope of attaining a lasting affection. There is always the chance someone new might earn the name of "citizen" and for an extra price obtain privileged treatment. Such treatment may come from selling the soul to the Lord, in a Faustian way – promising to offer up the fruits of the body not only now but in the future. In today's world, the state must favour immigrants. They offer as burnt sacrifice not only their own bones, but of those of their children and their children's children. In a country such as Canada, there are more bodies coming from immigration for this Lord of the land, like the giant in the fairy tale "Jack and the Beanstalk," to imagine consuming. This Lord searches for the immigrant in this new land while singing, "Be he

'live, or be he dead, I'll grind his bones to make my bread." While fatten-
ing the interloper, the Lord will even call him "citizen."

Once the sovereign sets the conditions in this lordship-and-bondsman
relationship, individuals as personalities and groups – including the
newcomers – can compete among themselves. In looking to the future,
the state, as sovereign, becomes the god of the oppressed, the stranger,
the excluded, and the uncultured. It offers a new form of social justice
to the oppressed and excluded as enticement to make them good producers and citizens for its own sake. Therefore genuine multiculturalism is
about living a tragedy and also about hoping to overcome this fracturedness and deprivation of human desires by transcending the self and
the current state of existence. This is the hope of comedy. But this is a
transcendence that comes through a personal and then a collective conversion that result from learning and improving through life experiences
– by challenging existing beliefs and cultures and by knowing and
accepting the changes of life.

In Western countries such as Canada that claim to be multicultural, can
members of the dominant groups and ethnicities speak and fully understand the language of genuine multiculturalism? "Language" here means
how members of the society imagine themselves: the way they capture
what they are in words and actions.[3] This speaks to the memory of what
they were, who they are now, and what they hope to become. This language captures all facets of social life, including acceptable, ethical
behaviour. People who speak this tongue betray a particular common
sense, good judgment, good taste, and a tactfulness that is second nature
to their culture but that is indispensable to their sense of collective and
individual well-being.[4]

Powerful people and groups speak an abstract language of recognition
or fraternity that reduces life to concepts, thereby having a discourse,
essentially, about the past. They speak out of an easily assessable knowledge that derives from history, including what society has achieved so
far. Multiculturalism is the language that pushes concepts to be more
concrete, in order to be more inclusive and to capture the spirit of the
times and the dynamic actions that create a future that is often very different from the past. Therefore it pours new and different meanings into
old signifiers and even creates some new ones of its own. It gestures to
the future while negating the past, all with the aim of bringing reality in
line with ideals for the future. What happens, then, in a place such as

Canada, where the old-timers speak a historical language from the past, which describes as ethical the "accommodation" of some citizens?

To put it politely, there can be only misunderstanding when some members of society have moved on and might even be deliberately undermining history, the accepted, and the given. Their aim is the creation of a future that is ethically very different from both the past and from the struggle for dominance that is the present. Those lose coherence and full facility in the dominant language and its ability to capture fully the resulting imagination at its fullest. They do not share the society's myths or its dominant opinions and truths. Instead of seeing coherence in the system those assumptions produce, they see glaring and alarming contradictions. This way they challenge the prevailing wisdom of the years, in effect arguing that it is mere opinion and often causes egregious and harmful errors, especially in human relationships. Instead of freedom, they see slavery and conformity. They see the society as basically and chronically unethical and as hypocritical, even by its own mythological and religious standards. They look to transform current errors in human behaviour into the truth and reality of dreams and aspirations, into a future where a new myth can explain, fully and accurately, what reality actually is.

In the process, they aim to transform the notion of who is fully Canadian, incorporating in the concept all the country's diversity and difference into a single thought of what we imagine instinctively to be Canadian. They hope to overcome society's dominant historical perception of them as mere *errors*, as inauthentic and not genuine to the nation-state. And just as important, the influential newcomers differ enormously from the progenitors of the historical nation-state, whose successors now battle to preserve the language and culture of that founding era. Those heritors may have strong voices, but they are trying to communicate fully in a language that has now fractured and become obsolete, even foreign. The society, instead of being the unity that its history was to have produced, with its concrete language, finds itself at a new moment of creation. It is in a struggle over lordship and bondage that creates its own language and its own concepts to capture its new reality. The old has failed to translate the imaginary into the concrete through utterances. More than that, some of its competitors have come out of time or out of a supposed state of Nature that is beyond the civil society that they have now entered and are disrupting. In terms of the new language that the situation requires, they are now truly the barbarians.

The new fight is always different from any previous one, and any analogies to the past lose their usefulness and need refreshing and extending by new developments. The heat of the struggle updates the language. Can the entrenched and privileged members throw off the old morality of the culture that socialized them and that they defend? Can they adopt a new morality, adapt to an ethical code of genuine equality and democracy more in keeping with the times and the state's needs? Can they be happy fooling themselves that they can become content in unfamiliar circumstances? Can they exchange a tragic existence of constant struggle against limits and boundaries that others impose, so as to accept quietly the comedic reality of a new type of justice that improves on the old one, even if it is not as authentic or personally satisfying? Can individuals who believe in permanent social hierarchies become genuinely multicultural and love those whom they have feared historically?

The answers depend on the hold of rational idealism on all of us and on our belief in a good that emerges from our experiences, is available to the future, and is not immanent in our daily lives. As transcendentalists, we accept that the ideals and good of life are desirable but not readily achievable at this point. This can become our excuse for doing nothing. It can be the rationale for passivity, acceptance, and even apology for the status quo. Yes, we may argue, better will and must come, but not today, so why aggravate a bad situation through an exercise in immediate futility? Others might respond that what will be "good" in the future must be "good" now and that continuing acceptance of the opposite to this good is immoral, irrational, and unethical. Accepting the diversity and difference inherent in human relations and in social life is a prerequisite to enjoying, daily, what we know to be a better way of living.

In this day and age, very few among us do not believe that, ideally, the world would be better off without racism, ethnocentrism, and xenophobia. Most of us would admit to doing our bit to make sure this ideal becomes a living reality. Indeed, most of us can see the day coming – even if it is way out there in the distance – when society will reward only merit and when true citizenship will ground itself in equality. That will be a better time in which to live than today. We might argue even that such an era will perhaps come in our children's lifetimes, or those of our children's children, though not yet today. Rationally, we would also suggest that we should postpone such ideals, for there might be danger in moving too swiftly to attain them. In the meantime, we should make accommodations that will maintain the status quo and injustice, rather than reach for what we know lurks in the transcendent: the good that is somewhere in the future waiting for the right moment to break into history and daily living. The bondsmen and -women of society would continue working and making the culture that is our society, but they would never transcend themselves, to become like the current masters. The lords would simply remain the lords. Everything would freeze, even if such rigidity and lack of change are the very reality that we associate with death.

Obviously, these long-term rational transcendentalists seek justice not now, but in the indeterminate future. Therefore they do not share the impatience of people who want justice now. At this point, the language of rationalism breaks down. The lords and masters demanding justice that they deny others cannot grasp the language of those rationalist bondsmen and -women who want to realize their ideals now. Combining, the two groups speak the tongue not of fraternity and happiness but of a very unhappy consciousness. Life is tragic without the language that makes comedy possible.

For multiculturalism has always been a question of how the *Other* can find justice by overturning a society that offered justice for only a few. Multiculturalism's ideals of justice have always sought freedom in a land of slavery while totally aware that slavery per se is a fact of social life. Multiculturalism asks itself whether any specific form of slavery can be permanent and still just, or whether slavery is simply the act of using force and imposing conformity on another and is therefore unjust. In this case, what are slavery and justice? Rationally and ethically, can we, once we identify justice, ever defer it justly? The Stoics among us may claim that the deciding factors include compulsion and forbearance and that we should focus on who has the ultimate power to decide not only issues of physical movement but also those of political will. In contrast, the sceptics argue that life itself is slavery and that wanting or deciding to do something without being able to see it through is a meaningless exercise. Genuine multiculturalism listens to both sides and, in agreeing with both, also disagrees with them – the social language, it reasons, must encompass not only thoughts of justice but its immediate enactment. To be complete, it must be a working language in the truest sense, combining thought and its enactment as action.

Genuine multiculturalism is about speaking a new language of liberation, speaking from the position of the previously excluded, rejected, and non-preferred who now happen to find voice. Economics Nobel Prize winner F.A. Hayek was thinking along these lines concerning the effectiveness and ability of an *old* or existing language to express new ideals and concepts in changing times. "If old truths are to retain their hold on men's mind," he states in *The Constitution of Liberty*, "they must be restated in the language and concepts of successive generations. What at one time are the most effective expressions gradually become so worn with use that they cease to carry a definite meaning. The underlying ideas must be as valid as ever, but the words, even when they refer to problems that are still with us, no longer convey the same conviction; the argument do not move in a context familiar to us; and they rarely give us direct answers to the questions we are asking."[5]

Hayek wonders how much more, then, we would need a new language when the existing language's underlying ideas are not valid and revolutionary change is under way. How do we capture the new desires and hopes in appropriate terminology? We have no mechanism to express our thoughts – to give them life. Analogous, a universalizing god may have thoughts of perfection but prove incapable of implementing them – there is always a gap and level of intolerance between the master plan and what it produces in its image, between thought and action. As a social and political thought, multiculturalism has always been about using the dominant language of social justice to undermine the entrenchment and privileges of the dominant few who have anointed themselves as subjects at the expense of everyone else. In action, multiculturalism is about creating a new freedom out of the hopes and desires in the transcendence, as the thoughts and language of the enslaved materialize them, and about this idealistic and eternal freedom entering into human history as a daily occurrence. It ought to be the right language to describe and determine the present social order.

Ideologically, genuine multiculturalism is about the creation of a new kingdom on earth where everyone is free, where the scales of justices favour the oppressed, the excluded, the marginalized, and the stranger – where everyone is a minority. This is a freedom that the refugees in the garrison cannot imagine, enunciate, or shout from society's towers as they beat back the barbarians' army of change and the approaching new freedom; it is a language that enunciates a yearning for change. Some of those who count themselves as ethnically white and/or as either anglophone or francophone in Canada might not understand it, for their language describes the apparent Prince Charming as a Bad John. They see themselves as the *self* that is already sovereign and that has to protect its turf and interest. They know what is Canadian history and what is

Canadian time and which of the many diverse bodies in the world can make Canadian time and history. In actuality, Canadian time and history are the same thing – the working out of a desire for a future where a specific type of humanity they call "Canadian" can flourish and perfect itself. They can no longer understand the command of multiculturalism to radically other themselves and to see themselves and be treated as if they are "the stranger" or "the powerless."

Multiculturalism asks that the entrenched reach out in love and understanding to those who are not now like them and, in reaching out, not only to know the unfamiliar as well as they know themselves but also to learn a lot about themselves, some of which they might not even like. Many people enjoying privileges cannot readily imagine a social reality in which they are simply as free as any other citizen, as free as the many. They cannot find the words, incantations, or dances to halt the changes that advance the causes of those who speak the new language of nationhood, confederation, citizenship, and belonging in a liberal democracy. Canada is a country that is now beyond the imagination of those of ancient lineage; the next milestone on its route to freedom is up to newcomers. When the old-timers try to speak the language of multiculturalism, it sounds old, usually a fearful lamentation or a melancholic grieving for past times. Hegel diagnoses this malady as occurring when an individual can only appeal to a lord, living alien to its own desires, feeling contempt for its own condition: "The fate in which the man senses what he has lost creates a longing for the lost life ... And the man animated by this longing may be conscientious in the sense that, in the contradiction between the consciousness of his guilt and the renewed sensing of life, he may still hold himself back from returning to the latter; he may prolong his bad conscience and feeling of grief and stimulate it every moment; and thus he avoids being frivolous with life, because he postpones reunion with it, postpones greeting it as a friend again, until his longing for reunion springs from the deepest recesses of the soul."[6]

For, as Charles Taylor suggests, this is a feeling of loss, creating a perception of a decline in civilization and a malady in society.[7] The language rings hollow, emanating as it does from spaces of exclusivity and from the separation of its citizens into those with privilege and those without. For those seeking exclusive ownership and belonging, the language of multiculturalism always seems incomplete, fixed, rigid, and so unchangeable that it does not capture life itself. Worst for them though a bonus for the newcomers, its language is that of the state itself. Who, then, genuinely speaks for the state, and whose language does the state, acting in its own interest, use as it develops a voice that fully captures the dynamic of living?

It needs new vocabularies, harnessing concepts that exhaust the possibilities of multiculturalism, that transcend even the new, ultimate, and real worldview of today. It must go beyond the acceptable and expectable, beyond what seems real by today's standards and experiences, to reach the new thoughts of perfection and the absolute. This new language must imagine the impossible (for us) as natural and real; what we now consider unreal and even too abstract must find new meaning in what we find unreal and only thought.

Here then we must move beyond seeing and expressing the human existence in concepts. Current language can no longer contain the fullness of life. For no single worldview ever totally exhausts all of humanity – otherwise why would there be others? No particular ever exhausts the universal. In effect, humanity in totality consists of my worldview plus an x factor – x representing all the diversity of humanity, being bigger and more consequential than the worldview itself. This x amounts to an infinity, to all those potentials and opportunities that I do not now even think about. My worldview appears so tiny and self-centred, even preposterous, in comparison to x. The new language of multiculturalism must attempt, then, to capture in one worldview that x, so my new language can express all that is human. Looking back on my old worldview, I would notice how the old had been so old, limited, and even empty – rather than what some accommodationists and some ethnic egoists might have thought: that their language embodied not only the desires of humanity, but the very best of humanity.

Ultimately, freedom is a test of sovereignty, whether of an individual or of a group in society. Can there be an absolute sovereign in society? And if such existed, would it not also be an absolute tyrant? The choices that plural societies in the West face concern different levels of freedom, with their commensurate and countervailing regimes of conformity, violence, and tyranny and of experiencing love and fear. This is the tragedy of life, and it is representative of the tragic human condition that is at the heart of the mythologies and expectations about social life in the West.

Freedom and tyranny are not mutually exclusive; we cannot live totally free of tyranny, nor can we live, alternatively, in absolute bondage. As the Stoics have long taught us, people behind bars might believe they are free, as long as they can think whatever they wish. In this case, some of us would undoubtedly think such people are living in a fool's paradise, in a comedy or make-believe world. We might wonder about their sanity and question in what *reality* or world they actually live. Similarly, the person who moves around without hindrance and obstruction still might not *feel* free if unable to think freely. Such individuals would undoubtedly be tragic, feeling the pains and disappointments of having to strain against limits on their natural abilities. Yet we might also wonder about how they exist in a world that is practical, pragmatic, and reasonable, where reality is seldom as we imagine it ought to be.

In modern society, to our despair, we are neither fully free nor totally in bondage, and for this reason we are unhappy consciousnesses or malcontents. We are tragic figures or social persons. No state is totally benevolent, nor is it an absolute tyranny, for such a state of existence would be impractical and would be death itself and not life. The issue that plural societies face, especially settler communities, regards how much freedom and tyranny to design into them, as they are new, still under construction. Can freedom be the preserve of the few – those who would live on a higher plane of freedom, claiming lordship – with, below them, fellow citizens living in bondage?

Abraham Lincoln wondered whether a house could for long remain with some residents living free within it and others as slaves. The house was his analogy for the state, and it is still relevant for the United States and also for Canada. Either all the members of the house must be free or slaves, or pragmatic compromise must subject them all to the same combination of freedom and slavery.

As an act of their liberty, free members should get to choose the amount of slavery and tyranny they wish to have to endure. It is like giving everyone a say in determining what temperature to set the thermostat in the house, or how many windows to open. However, freedom can never be such that there are no limits and that individuals are not subject to some higher authority; life is about actually living and doing things and can never exist without action or change, where one person might prevent movement or a decision by withholding consent or even assent.

This is the legacy that is so relevant for those of us living in the Americas: we have a history of trying to develop societies with ideals of absolute freedom for a dominant group – liberal citizens; however, these citizens emerge at the expense of dominated groups, consisting of individuals on the margins or otherwise lacking the full benefits of citizenship. These societies as exclusive ethnic homelands have fortunately ended in failure, proving unpractical, unpragmatic, and ultimately not free, whether championing African slavery or white supremacy in a Jim Crow United States or the white man's country of Canada.

What I am describing is another reason genuine multiculturalism rejects the absolutes of both slavery and freedom, and why, as I argue elsewhere, multiculturalism is ultimately cultural and idealistic blackness.[8]

Multiculturalism in North America has been the response to despair, particularly in the mid-twentieth century, when it became very clear to Canada and many of its people that as citizens of a confederated state with consociational relationships they were unhappy and shared very little in common with one another. This was the despair that resulted from diremption – an idealistic and practical separation and severing of ties, emerging in practice in a separatist movement in Quebec that, in a quest for independence, sought to further break up Canada as it existed. The story of how Canada arrived at this position appeared in a multi-volume final report in 1969 by the Royal Commission on Bilingualism and Biculturalism (Laurendeau–Dunton Commission), whose mandate was to "inquire into and report upon the existing state of bilingualism and biculturalism in Canada and to recommend what steps should be taken to develop the Canadian Confederation on the basis of an equal partnership between the two founding races, taking into account the contribution made by the other ethnic groups to the cultural enrichment of Canada and the measures that should be taken to safeguard that contribution."

Further, this was the moment when it became clear in the national conversation that Canada could not function as a bicultural and bilingual country, as what many federal officials intended, but that there were people throughout the country who thought Canada *multicultural*.[9] This meant that the diremption was so bad that there was nothing whole except the collection of the many and diverse people in some loose and warring relationship. Canadians were living not in a state of love or recognition but in an atmosphere of hatred and fear. Every group and even region or province lived a finite experience, with few seeing themselves in the wider, horizon-less universal that is a confederation or union. This was truly a moment of despair. Facing this angst, the leaders of the day decided to change the gaze through which they were seeing Canada and to attempt to change the conversation – instead of seeing only the negative of a state that is multicultural, they tried to seize the positive, for there are both good and bad in any tragedy.

To this end, they started a new narrative and a new conversation that redefined justice and what is Canada. In this conversation, justice starts out by meaning that the country has to become the best that it is, which means the best *multicultural* entity it can be: Canada will define itself and seek recognition as it really is and intends to remain, officially a multicultural country that is a liberal democracy. Its purpose in life will be to become a "Just Society" (Trudeau's phrase) based on love and recognition of all citizens; its history would be a narrative of how past injustices were contingent moments on the way to Canada's becoming authentic and true to itself as a just society that is multi-ethnic. Staring from this tragic position, the new narrative has to be how a multicultural entity that is Canada overcomes its divisions and diremptions and, on the way to a happy ending and perfection, becomes the best it can be – a perfect multicultural country. For this is the new *Bildung*. In this piece, idealistically, every new arrival in the state, especially immigrants, would become a Prince Charming, a symbol of the love that is necessary for Canada to reach perfection.

This thinking may remind us of Hegel's suggestion that the attainment of recognition that goes with accepting unity in diversity does not amount to eternal happiness. Such unchanging bliss can occur only in the beyond or hereafter. Even when levels of knowledge are higher, life remains wretched. We find meaning in life in the things that we do as workers and citizens. Moreover, we rely on an external agent or mediator to tell us what is really reasonable.

Reason is comedy, making sense of the inverted world that is the very opposite of what we originally thought was the world. This mediator, now the state or a legislating sovereign, expresses for us, as Hegel explains, "a certainty which is itself still incomplete, that its misery is only *in principle* the reverse, i.e. that its actions brings it only *in principle* self-satisfaction or blessed enjoyment; that its pitiable action too is only *in principle* the reverse, viz. an absolute action; that in principle, action is only really action when it is the action of a particular individual."[10] Such an individual is what we call a "citizen," a full-fledged Canadian, who we all know exists as an individual but about whom we can prove this claim only in principle. Ironically and comedically, this particular individual is what we would once call a "universal." So all that remains to do is jettisoning all vestiges of the old self and its way of knowing in order to become reasonable or what we might even call "human" and "social." We become a citizen. The old dies. But even then we are not happy. To this end, unhappiness continues, or we mask it over, while the search for genuine individuality proceeds within a different framework – that of multicultural Canadian citizenship. "But *for itself*," Hegel continues, "action and its own actual doing remain pitiable, its enjoyment remains pain, and the overcoming of these in a positive sense remains *a beyond*."[11]

Multiculturalism's message is that we cannot afford to forget the story and lessons of transatlantic African slavery, the horrors of the Asian Kala Pani (travel over long, dark waters such as the Indian subcontinent to the New World), and the genocide of the aboriginal peoples throughout the Americas, particularly in Canada and the United States. Multicultural Canada took another step towards this decision not to forget – but also to dismantle the results of a past that it no longer can stomach – when in 2008 Prime Minister Stephen Harper stood in the House of Commons and apologized to First Nations peoples for Canada's imposing residential schools on them several generations earlier. Through his speech act, Canadian leaders made the past present, and it is only fitting as we relive these horrors in words that we seek absolution and reconciliation in love for them. Apologies for past wrongs can be morally beneficial and ethically responsible ways to start overcoming acts of diremption. "In the 1870s," the prime minister said, in the presence of a number of First Nations leaders, some in ceremonial dress,

the federal government, partly in order to meet its obligation to educate aboriginal children, began to play a role in the development and administration of these schools. Two primary objectives of the residential schools system were to remove and isolate children from the influence of their homes, families, traditions and cultures, and to assimilate them into the dominant culture. These objectives were based on the assumption aboriginal cultures and spiritual beliefs were inferior and unequal. Indeed, some sought, as it was infamously said, 'to kill the Indian in the child.' Today, we recognize that this policy of assimilation was wrong, has caused great harm, and has no place in our country. Most schools were operated as 'joint ventures' with Anglican, Catholic, Presbyterian or United churches. The government of Canada built an educational system in which very young children were often forcibly removed from their homes, often taken far from their communities. Many were inadequately fed, clothed and housed. All were deprived of the care and nurturing of their parents, grandparents and communities. First nations, Inuit and Métis languages and cultural practices were prohibited in these schools. Tragically, some of these children died while attending residential schools and others never returned home.[12]

And he continued: "We now recognize that, far too often, these institutions gave rise to abuse or neglect and were inadequately controlled, and we apologize for failing to protect you. Not only did you suffer these abuses as children, but as you became parents, you were powerless to protect your own children from suffering the same experience, and for this we are sorry. The burden of this experience has been on your shoulders for far too long. The burden is properly ours as a government, and as a country. There is no place in Canada for the attitudes that inspired the Indian residential schools system to ever again prevail."

This address followed earlier apologies to a number of ethnic groups, including the Chinese and Japanese Canadians, for wrongs the Canadian state did to them. This series of statements culminated in 2008 in a global apology to several ethnic communities that had suffered historically because of racist immigration policies and citizenship practices.[13]

Absolute freedom would be untenable for good social living. The main point here is not whether slavery and freedom can exist together but whether all members of the society would be subject to them in the same way, or if some would be freer than others or more enslaved than others. What is notable here is not the question of whether or not it is possible for people to exist together in different cultural states under different conditions of freedom and slavery, for this is possible. But they would exist as separate peoples and separate states. They would not be *a people* and *a state*. They would not be one people facing a common tyrant but several peoples facing several different tyrants, even if the tyranny emanated from the same source. For many people, that source has to be unitary and common to all, and this is why sovereignty ultimately resides in the state. Analogous, a single body cannot be absolutely sick and absolutely well at the same time, yet it can have a single existence wherein it enjoys a healthy disposition despite physical disease.

This question of different levels of freedom still hovers over American arguments over the incorporation of Mexican immigrants, the preservation or curtailing of civil liberties, and how far the state should go to limit those members whom, in the age of the so-called war on terrorism, the mainstream might consider threats to the state. In Canada, the same concern exists in terms of whether an entrenched mainstream – usually English and/or French, and Christian – should place accommodations on people whom it considers different and not of the same stock and intentions as itself. The problem becomes, eventually, one of determining the state's existence as the ultimate authority and its determination of reasonable limits on both freedom and tyranny. The concern is not whether the state would or must change towards one extreme or the other, for as long as there is life there are changes along the imaginary sliding scale of good and evil that places freedom and tyranny at opposite ends.

A crucial question of good ethical behaviour becomes how to manage these changes in such a way that will allow the state, as the final arbiter or sovereign, to still consider itself free; this is a freedom that, in the case of most states in the Americas, is now liberal democracy. Clearly, this is a definition of the state as the sovereign and not about an individual or a specific group. The state expresses its sovereignty through laws and orders. The Supreme Court of Canada has been at pains in speaking to this point:

> The consent of the governed is a value that is basic to our understanding of a free and democratic society [such as Canada]. Yet democracy in any real sense of the word cannot exist without the rule of law. It is the law that creates the framework within which the "sovereign will" is to be ascertained and implemented. To be accorded legitimacy, democratic institutions must rest, ultimately, on a legal foundation. That is, they must allow for the participation of, and accountability to, the people, through public institutions created under the Constitution. Equally, however, a system of government cannot survive through adherence to the law alone. A political system must also possess legitimacy, and in our political culture, that requires an interaction between the rule of law and the democratic principle. The system must be capable of reflecting the aspirations of the people. But there is more. Our law's claim to legitimacy also rests on an appeal to moral values, many of which are imbedded in our constitutional structure. It would be a grave mistake to equate legitimacy with the "sovereign will" or majority rule alone, to the exclusion of other constitutional values.[14]

In the final analysis, as appears in war – and in this time, particularly, of a war on terrorism – the general good of the majority must prevail. The liberal individual must seek its peculiar rights and freedoms within constraints and under even the benevolent tyranny – but tyranny none the less – of the utilitarianism of the common good. As the English scholar on jurisprudence John Austin has warned, "In the great majority of cases, the general happiness requires that *rules* shall be observed, and that *sentiments* associated with rules shall be promptly obeyed. If our conduct were truly adjusted to the principle of general utility, our conduct would seldom be determined by an immediate or direct resort to it."[15] And here is another place where we might argue with the liberal contract theories for presenting liberalism and contract theory as first principles. I am thinking of such statements as John Rawls's in his *Theory of Justice* – that society should never sacrifice the good of the individual for the utilitarian good of the state.

This would create a state with no real sovereign. Instead, we should think of the sovereign as the entity that brings the state into existence, which takes place through a struggle among those who thought they were essential to the state and who later found out that they were not; they will have had to agree to different arrangements to continue their existence. Once that initial act of state formation has taken place, a second decision must follow, about the quality and type of slave that the members of society would be; in effect, this decision concerns how much freedom social individuals should have. But, ultimately, when the state faces threats – from terrorists or people who might want to impose or entrench a specific way of life – it has to assert its sovereignty, and in the name of the common good. This is the only outcome for an order that rests on fear – that of the individual against the many.

In such a case, in the face of a utilitarian good, as Austin suggests, most liberal rights and much of the language of liberalism, as with any other ideology, become meaningless. If, he argues, instead of measuring the object of the greater question at hand "by the standard of utility, each party were led by the ears and appealed to meaningless phrases such as 'the rights of man,' 'the sacred rights of sovereigns,' 'an original contract or covenant,' or 'the principles of an unviable constitution,' neither could compare its object with the cost of a violent pursuit, nor would there be room for compromise. The phrases having no meaning, the objects represented by them are of course invaluable, and must be fought for 'to the bitter end' regardless of cost."[16]

Such is the lesson that the various states and individuals learned at the hands of Abraham Lincoln in the American Civil War: that, ultimately, the morality and ethics of a common good deriving from a wider love must dominate those of the state, individual, or group unless the preservation of those peculiarities is, indeed, the common good. And this is also the lesson that Canadians learned during the time of Pierre Trudeau when, instead of resorting to violence, they decided to create a new common good in the form of a new language of multiculturalism. In the process, they poured new meaning and significance into concepts that in the earlier struggle for ethnic dominance in Canada had become meaningless and loveless.

This prevailing and dominant definition of multiculturalism has built into it a specific trade-off between freedom and tyranny, with the exact positioning on the sliding scale flowing out of the history of the consciousness that is the state itself. Therefore the trade-off is traditional, cultural, and by necessity collective. The United States fought a brutal civil war in the 1860s and then, through the shakedown of the civil rights movement a century later, finally arrived at its compromise. Canada avoided a bloodletting in arriving at its compromise in the latter part of the last century. In this book, we recognize these compromises as "lordship and bondage relationships," speaking to the idea that the relationships are not natural but the product of force. This means that they are covenants rather than social contracts. They are mixtures of tragedy and comedy. In them, it is possible for some individuals and groups to feel they are absolutely free and loved and for others to feel absolutely enslaved and feared. Others would feel that they are neither fully free nor enslaved and that, all things considered, they are indeed free, as this is the best they can enjoy of all possible worlds.

Currently, the trade-off in Canada is such that individuals and groups may feel that they all share the same levels of freedom and that this freedom outweighs the amount of tyranny, conformity, and enslavement necessary for the existing state of life. The state is equally tyrannical or benevolent to all groups and cultures. This position is one of "official multiculturalism," meaning that that all cultures and their members share the same amount of freedom and tyranny. One way of looking at this regime is by recognizing that no single group is freer than any other, or that the state tyrannizes no single group more than any other. The state is an equal-opportunity friend or bigot. The question becomes how "individuals" fit in.

As officially multicultural, the house of which Lincoln spoke is one in which all groups and their members equally enjoy the same freedoms or have to fight the same impositions. And comedy looks at this relationship as the highest freedom, encompassing the least amount of tyranny possible, in the current situation. It is a comedy because members of this society deliberately fool themselves into believing that they are totally free, thereby ignoring the restraints on them. Some people go so far as to suggest that official multiculturalism is chaos – *absolute* freedom of sorts, as they feel that the state imposes almost no constraints, so that there are no unity and norms. There is no conformity.[17]

But the trade-off can change radically, to the point where Canada in a later moment might even countenance putting accommodations on specific residents and citizens such that the state creates a society of different citizenships, with power and privileges exclusive to a particular group. This is a pathway Canada has tread before, evident in its history of reservations, which imply the notion of exclusive and distinct homelands within the geopolitical territory, and of the expulsions thereto of peoples, whether ethnically they be First Nations, Acadians, or Blacks. This legacy created an image of a country that is not free and is not a liberal democracy.

A country such as this is colonial in the Machiavellian sense, where a specific minority group appears to be superior over all other groups. Canada is still trying to extricate itself from this sordid past, for when earlier residents set out to make the country a continuation of European, in particular English and French, history, they were also accepting the colonial legacies of, particularly, England and France. This legacy is obvious in the social stratification and racialization of peoples along the same lines as those of the erstwhile British and French empires. In rejecting the ideal of Canada as a white man's country, later Canadians were also turning away from colonial recommendations for their society. Particularly since the Second World War, the West has turned its back on the colonial type of nation-state that rests on the fear of Others and the love of only the self. A watchword in development currently is "self-determination" – "an inviolate right of a people to choose their levels of freedom and self-tyranny." During the second half of the last century, countries such as Canada and the United States roundly criticized those others such as the apartheid regime in South Africa and the communist Soviet Union for maintaining a colonial relationship among their own peoples that involved power and tyranny. Ultimately, the countries under criticism fell under the weight of their own systems and entered the fold of liberal democracies, to the point where some critics marked this realignment as the ending of the so-called struggle to shape the course of history in terms of how much tyranny and freedom are now essential for vibrant and free societies.[18] Official multiculturalism is the most recent expression of this self-determination as freedom.

Therefore, if Canada and the United States were to change to severely limit the freedoms of different ethnic and racialized groups, they would hardly be able to meet their own definition of freedom as a liberal democracy; they would appear to step back into an era of colonialism and its terrors. Some groups might welcome such a step, but others would consider it a return to slavery. The two countries would be rejecting, in return for retained privileges for a favoured group or two, what current standards and expectations generally accept as freedom and sovereignty. It would also be doubtful if these limits and accommodations could be possible in a truly capitalist country, one where the tragedy of the individual is always at stake but where the returns are that the individual always believes she or he has the right and opportunity – in effect, the full freedom – to transform the state to her or his advantage.

As John Austin suggests, a sovereign is pure subject; it answers to no one; it gives commands that others must follow. And as C.E. Merriam, Jr, says, from Austin's view a sovereign issues laws "as 'a command which obliges a person or persons and obliges generally to acts or forbearance of a class.' Law is essentially a command given by a superior to an inferior: God gives laws to man as his superior; men give laws to men as superiors, understanding here by the term superiority, 'might.' In any case the essence of the law is the command given from the superior to the inferior, and binding by reason of the sanction which the superior is able to attach to it. There are two great classes of law. The divine, set by God for men, and the human law."[19]

If there is a command giver, then there must be a non-sovereign who receives the law and habitually obeys. There must be someone or some group facing the option of conforming, which is a form of slavery, or of trying to assert its own rights to sovereignty by instead trying to become the command giver. To this end, difference results in a struggle for power and dominance, in being either slave or free. Genuine multiculturalism seeks to find a way where everybody can be sovereign, or rather, where nobody is equally a slave to the same things. A seemingly natural inclination to war gives way to supposedly equal instincts to want to live peacefully if the real alternative is enslavement.

With that in mind, this book is an attempt to show multiculturalism as diversity that ironically aims at producing social conformity even though nobody is going to be completely happy with the outcome. Unhappiness will accompany the act of having to conform in the first place or the amount of conformity that occurs, for any resistance in any form will produce only a conformity that will seem inauthentic to those who are absolute. To this end, tragedy permeates multiculturalism – but then it is no different from other ideologies that expect some members of society to surrender their ambitions for the greater good of the whole society.

Genuine multiculturalism suggests that this tragic experience will touch every citizen, not just some inferior individual or groups that would have to sacrifice for a common good that some elite individual or groups determine and maintain. The story of multiculturalism, as Pierre Trudeau explains it, is that everyone is a minority in the new society, with no individual or group permanently holding power and privileges over others. Sovereignty exists with the state, but its composition is always fluid, with different coalitions of individuals and groups holding the reins of power but for fleeting moments, so that the struggle of every minority individual and group becomes about how they can be part of the ruling coalition that will emerge in the *next* moment. It is a dynamic interchanging of people and power, and it takes place under the rubric of sovereignty. It is akin to the political haggling over the formation of the dominant mainstream that Canadian political scientist C.B. Macpherson describes as "possessive individualism" or, indeed, *minorityism*.[20]

This, then, is an argument for a critical or even radical democracy that I call "genuine multiculturalism."[21] It is the paradoxical notion that a single country or state can achieve speculative harmony as a common good when it practises a kind of conformity that recognizes that the state is most natural when it is most fragmentary and individualistic; a conformity that recognizes that the state is most human when those who believe that they possess a god-like right to its ownership and who dictate to newcomers what it is and should be realize that they must give up their ideals; a conformity that recognizes that the state is most human when the input of newcomers reformulates these ideals as they give up and sacrifice what is sacrosanct to them – their human bodies – in the hopes of achieving unity.

More than that, there is an onus on those who think they are the lords of the piece to give up what they have historically thought to be their leading role, and to give it up willingly rather that wallowing in melancholia or refusing to accept that they are losing or have lost prominence and power. As long as they live in melancholia – that longing for a previous time – instead of facing up to and accepting the new dynamics of the moment, those who have lost their privileges are unable to move on and wallow in the past. As a result, the society cannot move on but rather remains deeply divided regarding its ideals and principles, with one or more groups pining for the way things might have been in the past and others rejecting this past and longing for a future that is very different.

In the interim, both sides fail to become the new men and women of the moment, fail to become the vessels for the new times, and the common good tries to justify individual unhappiness.

In this discussion, contradictions abound, and in this sense alone the debate seeks to capture the spirit of Canada and multiculturalism – a living tragedy. Critical democracy and genuine multiculturalism come together in a social and philosophical order that comedically assumes for all citizens a common knowing, an agreed perception of what is *truly* Canada, especially and particularly on knowing the Canadian self in its perceived authenticity that tragically is inauthenticity to any one group. This might be the embodied self that is universally no more than a citizen or an individual claiming an identity flowing from a package of abstract rights and fundamental freedoms. In this case, the self creates authenticity and gives it to itself. It is also possible that the self may become the spirit: that it may become an analogy for the culture of a group of people sharing the same consciousness emerging from an identity it imposes on itself. In either case, it is not a primordial authenticity: it has no genesis in the creation of the state and citizenship. Democracy and multiculturalism in such a state would require the capturing of the majority will, but ideally a will that is a unity, an expression in which all groups have equality of opportunity and participation in their acquired or common authenticity.

This is an order that characteristically develops on the shifting sands of temporality, impermanence, and the uncertainty of human activities. It assumes the probability that life is safest for everyone when power spreads as widely as possible, thereby throwing the tyrant off-balance. This occurs when every individual and group has a say in the colonization of the future as an act of self-determination and in furtherance of this act of authentication. In the end, all actions wither or flourish because of the totalizing gaze of an absolute sovereign who is, in effect, a disguised tyrant. This is the totalizing morality that produces the ethical relations that rely on democracy for its expression. This is the unifying gaze that refers not to individual acts but to the commonality of the intentions behind them. That is what makes it democratic: the gaze is authenticity itself.

This arrangement also presumes the continuous cycle of destruction, transfiguration, and reformulation of any power alliance and coalition in human affairs. For the process to be democratic, there must be an understanding that a dialectical warring within the existing order of partners must happen. Here I am reaching for the radical definition of democracy as rule of *the people*, as some Greeks suggested originally, but I am also searching for an application that captures two strands in our conceptualization of this rule by the people. The first is Pericles' statement that democracy amounts to rule by the majority (of the people) and the second is Lincoln's assertion that the ideal form of democracy is "rule by the people, of the people, for the people." Indeed, this is where the modern struggle for sovereignty lies: in whether all of the many that constitute what we now call "the masses" should have power or any say in determining the future course for the nation-state. In other words, are all groups part of the people, or does *people* mean an elite group? Some quarters of the Canadian province of Quebec have suggested the latter. A number of francophones in Canada claim that their group should be able to place limits of accommodation on other groups – newcomers and immigrants – who are part of the people but whom they consider to be of an inferior pedigree and culture.

Countering this argument is the suggestion that there must be the realization by all residents that the members of the coalition can come together as one only in a speculative moment, but that in so doing they never give up their right to self-determination and freedom. Thereafter, they break apart for the good of the alliance itself and for that of the weaker individual member, for power should not rest permanently in the hands of any one individual or group or in a single, unchangeable arrangement. They form new alliances and power relations by trading off in a spirit of mutual love, not fear, one group or individual for another in a situation that, technically, excludes no group or person from the outset.

Idealistically, the aim is to preserve permanently this fluidity where, through goodwill and good intentions, power constantly diffuses and rests in all potential members. This is how I want to suggest that our concept of *the people* is constantly formulating, reformulating, and expressing itself. There is, to begin, the externality of the concept *the people* in a democracy. Just as important, it is within the dialectic of creation and death occurring through the constructing and shattering of unities moment to moment that democracy and *the people* perpetuate themselves. This they do by protecting themselves separately and collectively and by protecting their individual members, all of this happening dynamically in the whole that the concept of the people bounds.

But in the end – and this is the ethical and existentialist tragedy – in all probability, it is not possible to include every group or individual every time, even if that principle underlies the idealistic boast "we the people."

However, a severe problem arises if the coalition always leaves out *some* groups and *never* includes them, or if it must always include a particular group and can never leave it out, so that it becomes an essence of sort for the concept of *the people*.

In the latter case, we might think of a situation such as that in Canada where the anglophone or francophone groups must always be part of any moment's formation of the people. Is it now possible to have a Canadian expression that might temporarily exclude the English and / or French group? Similarly, can we envisage a day when a majority of US minorities might take a position contrary to that of the now-dominant whites, as happened in the 2012 presidential election? Genuine multiculturalism as radical democracy says yes, if that is what a majority agrees to and what is in the best interest of the sovereign or the state. In this case, is it possible for Canada to negate itself, taking marginal groups into the mainstream through an assimilation of power, thereby extending the identity and culture beyond even the definition of what dominant Canadians now hold for themselves? No identity can be fixed, and, as an act of freedom, dominant identities must change, for such is the story and mythology of the West – the idea that identities must be as universal as all the people claiming them.

In order to find a solution, we must leave one form of idealism for another, this latter being *majority rule,* which must by definition be a tragedy for some members of society and for society itself. As a free individual or group, everyone starts the moment indeterminate, without a prior right to hold on to power deriving from a previous arrangement, not even those of the former alliance and the former moment who might have paved the way for the arrival of this second moment. Rights emerge only socially.

Fully indeterminate, the power holders from the previous moment might freely choose not to include themselves in an arrangement where they feel that power is now too diffuse. In this case, they would be acting either like an Aristotelian-Hegelian god or like a barbarian, both of whom see themselves as outside of the pale of the new social order but who, for their own actualization, have to enter the social fold. For the end is but the moment when the alliance must crystallize, where people must make choices in terms of the circumstances of that moment. Ideally, the final composition will grow from a decision of inclusion that the self, not others, makes. This is how indeterminacy changes into determinacy, how a determined will is the rational, moral, and considered normal.

In this regard, critical democracy is the moral acting of a fully informed moral subject that is constantly finding itself at a new moment of creation. It is moving not only from indeterminacy to determinacy, but from a specific and *authentic* momentary determination into the indeterminacy of the next moment. New power relations grow out of the expiring ones. Thus, ironically and paradoxically, the self, in coming together as a unity, is also falling apart, fragmenting and fracturing into particulars; this is the moment when there are no prior claims, and while there might be "dead possibilities," as Sartre argues, the potential to create is limitless but also indeterminate. Once this group of subjects becomes determinate, it then attempts to transform the sovereign from a tyrant into an ally, making the state in its own image and giving the state the group's spirit and culture. Tragedy always colours the comedy of living, for a complete life has its moments of comedy and perhaps justice, if not happiness, in the tragedy of living.

Genuine multiculturalism is the ethical relationship that emanates from subjects acting critically as moral objects, each as an individual, with rational reflection determining the will. It is the crystallization of the faith and, more important, intention behind the act, of inclusiveness in the first movement of the dialectic that would also realize itself in the end that also severs this perceived unity. Acts have to find their ground ethically in love, the same way that we presume that all citizens act in good faith, not in the fear that causes us to repel those seeking inclusion in the social. This is the faith and idealism that a moment of reconciliation will include everyone and every group and that, if it excludes a group or person, it does so because of that group's or individual's choice, not because others objectively left out the group or person in the coalition; for this is an exercise in subjective determination and creation. To this end, critical democracy and genuine multiculturalism are fundamentally individualistic, intentional, and wilful, but, ironically, they gesture to an exercise in freedom achievable only within an embedded and wider relationship. This relationship crystallizes through a wider intention to be free within an alliance of power that can imprison through a demand for conformity.

My argument challenges the common-sense notions of society formation and preservation that are at the heart of much of the sociological and cultural discussion of Canadian multiculturalism. Chief among these is the contract theory that is so much a part of the leading conversations on multiculturalism and liberalism. Indeed, instead of searching for explanations of genuine multiculturalism through contract theory, I offer the position that it is best to analyse and understand multiculturalism as being a result of a society that begins with a covenant of sorts between groups of unequal power and proceeds to grow into a social organism that the dialectics of the struggle within the covenant shape. This way of thinking marries the thinking of Hegel and Austin to explain multiculturalism as a synthesis of sort between Hegel's German/Roman view of nation-state formation and the British system that was the model for the Machiavelli-like settler community that was to become Canada, which is closer to Austin's perspective.

With this in mind, I invite the questioning of some liberal tropes that many commentators consider fundamental to understanding a liberal democracy that is multicultural: that recognition must start from natural or constitutional rights that construct rational entities that are individuals or groups capable of respecting and being fair and just to one another. This is recognition of an otherness that is primordial and inauthentic to Canada. Such is the case when observers emphasize the hyphenated identity of Canadians to privilege some ethnic, racial, religious, or cultural signification. In my argument, multiculturalism is the privileging of the Canadian element and authenticity as the *necessary* element that makes everything else in such a hyphenated Canadian identity contingent and transitory.

Chief among these liberal tropes is the argument of recognition that Charles Taylor and many of his disciples present so ably – that multiculturalism is foundationally a struggle by one person or group of persons for recognition by another person or groups of people. This is an argument that Taylor clearly expresses in his seminal *Multiculturalism: Politics of Recognition*. This book was very timely in explaining multiculturalism in general and specifically the Canadian experience in time.

It relies heavily on a specific form of recognition: that of a subject, as Hegel puts it, coming into self-consciousness and realizing there are others in the world – a world that already exists. Similarly, as Heidegger says, this is the experience of *thrownness*, when the individual, realizing that it has fallen into a world that is already following a given order, has to adapt to this sense of alienation.[22] But individuals' real concerns are not with the world as they find it – that is merely sensual knowledge no different from that of other animals – but with transforming themselves by working (in Canada, for our discussion) to become the human beings of their dreams. This recognition flows from a clash of desires, which changes everything – the playing field and the two sets of actors. However, this common-sense notion that Taylor and others enunciates, has flaws, for it assumes that personality and human individuality antedate the state or the ethical relationship of so-called master and state. In this understanding, rights are prior claims and determine the individual or citizen. Rights, rather than relationships, ground recognition.

I argue that personality and privileged claims occur only within an existing ethical relationship and that a mark of this citizenship is the holding of rights. Therefore the main action occurs at the point of entry into the state, not so much with the struggle that follows this birth into citizenship. A good example of this is the experience and legacy of chattel slavery in the Americas, where slaves and their descendants held no rights in the nation-state. It was only when the descendants of slaves gained full recognition with human dignity by the states of the Americas that they acquired personalities, citizenships, and then rights.

Taylor's argument is that multicultural politics becomes a question of the Subject and the others struggling with one another for recognition as all subjects of one kind or the other. This is a fight for permanence and fixity, for changelessness, rather than for control of the changing or the mechanism that keeps the fluidity pure. This struggle for recognition seems to happen once, fixing the outcome in place. But human desires never remain constant for long, and every time they unfix, they engender yet another battle for recognition. These battles all fall within an envelope, and over time they appear as a never-ending struggle over ways of life and the belief that specific ways of life can produce happiness. All the parties remain forever in a struggle that resolves itself only when everyone recognizes everyone else as subjects. This is a recognition that never fully materializes, for this kind of recognition would always start at least a moment too late and then abort. The individuals have themselves changed, and what they recognize is at best an earlier shade of what has become a new being.

Here again, we can take the example of chattel slaves. Citizenship came too late for those who lived existentially and ethically as slaves and who fought against the institution. The sons and daughters of slaves are not the slaves themselves. Time has moved on. And so the politics of recognition stalls existentially as the politics of an unhappy consciousness – of a tragedy of ethical relations.

The participants are unable to progress to a site of freedom, where life is a comedy, as one would expect from the sons and daughters of slaves who are now citizens. This is so because those with status as citizens have agreed to the self-imposed limits of the collective. This form of recognition creates an insuperable chasm for individuals – they cannot enter the life of comedy and utopia that is in the transcendence, for that requires further change to their perception of themselves, which is not what they fought for. Even though they ground their existence on rational or transcendental idealism, they find themselves on the edge of human lived reality or experiences. Choice or other people acting with the best of intentions fix or overdetermine them. They cannot change, grow, and adapt. Across the chasm or gulf lie their dreams and hopes, what they hope to achieve. How can they cross this hollow expanse and not fall into the open grave, disappearing forever in an epistemological, onto-logical, and ethical black hole?

Here I want to take a different route from Taylor as I argue for what recognition is and what it is that multiculturalism recognizes. This book asks how we truly know what we are recognizing when we live in a world where identities are fluid and responsive to desires, and where fix-ing an object in a singular identity for any period may do it violence. Taylor's analysis seems unable to explain how a subject that is truly *itself* knows even itself from one moment to the next in a changing environ-ment. What happens when desires change, if to be human is the process of acting out desires? In other words, how does the individual or group know what it will become in the next moment, and how can it ever reach unchangeable recognition, consistent with its changing beings across time? Surely such a subject can know only what it used to be, not what it has changed into, for at any moment the individual is always in the midst of the changes. It can know only its historical desires.

Under Taylor's model, any recognition that the individual achieves or gives now may not be adequate or authentic enough in the next moment. Indeed, does the other's awarding this recognition – or the subject's doing so, for that matter – even know itself or its own desires from moment to moment? For if only the other knows itself – if the truth indeed lies outside of the subject – then this appears to be the opposite of what liberal multiculturalism now expects: that a subject conveys subjecthood onto others. Indeed, the relationship should be the other way around: multicultural subjectivity should arise only through the gaze of the other as it reduces the subject to passivity, making it less than an active moral agent whose essence and authenticity lie in what it does.

If this is the case, and I contend it is, it recasts the meaning of democ-racy in a genuinely multicultural state, for it would then be the *Others* or the unknown that determine the ethical relationship. Can the state then force immigrants, for example, to conform to the society, or should it grant them citizenship and a share of power with current citizens? First, anything to which it forces immigrants to conform, once it has formalized that, would always be a thing of the past. Life would have moved on, imprisoning the immigrants in the past. Under current practices, multiculturalism in Canada does not imply disempowering subjects and empowering Others. It is more likely to mean subjects' recognizing others as their equal – an act of tolerance where agency and determinacy rest totally with the subject. To this end, then, I argue, genuine multiculturalism cautions us to be willing to err – to act on faith that the new arrivals or immigrants are Prince Charmings. Only their actions – not fear or perception of them – would be the test of this faith. This is akin to the good faith that we automatically bestow on all citizens and that we withdraw only when they act in bad faith.

But how do we know who is the unchangeable subject? And, while we are at it, how can we know who or what is the unchangeable other? If we don't know, how can we achieve recognition? And how, collectively, do we know who *we* are, since we too are of fluid natures, characters, and identities? How do we know who is really the *who* we should recognize and who is really the *who* that is recognizing? The current politics of recognition leave us without answers, as it presents us with a struggle between entities whose essences are already knowable and on display, and it leave us in fear and without love; more than that, it gives us no way out of this vexing and, dare I say, tragic existence. The citizens might have dignity and nobility, but they would not be loved or loving.

This is not, apparently, my view alone about Taylor's approach, although I might be making the argument more forcibly. For example, some of his admirers acknowledge that his recognition struggle is between two entities who view themselves as already subjects of a specific hue and history who are seeking to become *the* subject. Therefore, missing from this analysis are those who are already Others or nonsubjects and who are now seeking recognition, arguing that they belong within the existing discourse of conversation on Canada. As such, Taylor's framework as it applies to Canada focuses on the struggle between groups he calls "French" or "Québécois" and another he calls "English," "Canadian," or even the "Rest of Canada." All other groups have lost their determinations, histories, and presences and have disappeared into one of the dominant groups – they are merely faceless and cultureless mercenaries, mere cannon fodder in this ongoing war. That is, until they appear to challenge the order that the French and the English have established among themselves – perhaps Muslim women wearing veils when they turn up to vote or black and darker-skinned people demanding social and political mobility at the seeming expense of the hegemons. Only then does the discussion shift to one of accommodation and, I argue, of who has not only rights but human dignity.

Guy Laforest's preface to his collection of Taylor's essays in *Reconciling the Solitudes* – only two solitudes! – captures this understanding of the turf, the war, and the actors:

> This book is aimed at several audiences. Citizens of Canada and of Quebec (those who believe themselves to be ordinary no less than those who think themselves as enlightened) will find here an original point of view on our interminable constitutional and political crisis. Charles Taylor captures all the essential *angst* experienced by those societies and people of North America who are eager for recognition and are worried about the dangers that threaten their identity and their sense of belonging. The intellectuals of Quebec and Canada will recognize here the voice of one whom they have regarded, for more than thirty years, as one of their most eminent colleagues. They will discover, sometimes to their surprise, what Taylor persists in wishing to say to those who occupy the other side of the Canadian duality. For although he always sees himself simultaneously as a Canadian and a Quebecker, he does not hesitate to calibrate his remarks in accordance with the roots of his intended audience.[23]

Well, what Laforest sees as Taylor's Canadian conversation appears now only as incessant and even incestuous whisperings between two groups, around such tropes as Quebec citizenship, Canadian duality, and roots. This debate may now seem parochial, even irrelevant. The others can eavesdrop – or ignore the conversation as none of their business. Canada as Taylor imagined, and even in its natural form, had long moved on from biculturalism and duality, so we must broaden the discussion to *recognize* this development. In the case of the state, what are we recognizing, and what is it – a tyrant or a benevolent and radical democrat – that recognizes us?

Contrary to Taylor and others, recognition must start with trying to know and fix the *who* that is to do the recognizing – the subject in the piece. We must figure out who we are before we can even think usefully about the rest of the world. Trying to achieve a true and genuine subject position – akin to Kant's moral imperative – is indeed a very difficult, slippery, and elusive thing. As free subjects, we must be slippery, elusive, and indeterminate – freedom demands no less. These characteristics are the very nature of freedom itself; to limit any of them is to make us less free, to make us into flat or stereotypical characters that are less than fully human. As ideally free subjects, we will still be imperfect, failing to reach the minimum levels of perfection necessary for active and effective citizenship; we would subsequently lose all the dignity that flows from the diversity and difference that Nature gave us and that we later brought into the society.

Taylor's politics of recognition for multiculturalism is at variance with Hegel's solution for moulding diversity and plurality into a harmonious state. As we saw above, Taylor's analysis of multiculturalism is more in keeping with the Fichtean-Kantian approach to identity, which, as Paul Franco suggests, assumes a subject needing another subject to grant it recognition – but, without actions, the subject cannot even know its authentic self. As Franco states, "In the human being, this opposition takes the form of the opposition between intelligence and natural drive, between reflection and impulse, or between reason and passion. And Fichte, no less than Kant, demands the subordination of the latter to the former, the subordination of the necessity of nature to the freedom of intelligence. The human being's final purpose, an infinite task never to be completely achieved, is [as Hegel says] 'absolute freedom, absolute independence from nature.'"[24]

However, as Hegel argues, this one-sided kind of freedom is not holistic – why do we have to see immigrants as either Bad Johns or Prince Charmings and not some combination of both? Rather, it emphasizes negative freedoms that lead primarily to an abstract liberal citizenship and, less so, to a more all-inclusive civic citizenship, which fully embeds the individual in the state and thereby renders him or her fully free, beyond merely exercising rights. As Franco suggests, in Hegel's eyes "such a notion of freedom leads to a community characterized throughout by the 'lordship of the intellectual' or 'concept' and the bondage of nature."[25] This is the very method of state formation, which produces what Hegel calls a "machine-state" with no soul, passion, or love for or between members. Missing are the dreams and the acting out of dreams that make animal-like beings human, that make individuals into persons and then the people. Hegel argued against this kind of state formation.[26] A Taylor-type solution of recognition flowing from the primacy of old-timers' groups, as sovereigns dealing with sovereigns in a confederacy, does not offer an exit out of the unhappy consciousness that is the tragic struggle of how individuals as fully liberal citizens fit into a society of equal members.

Another theorist on whom we shall be relying to help us fathom genuine multiculturalism as a tragedy looking for comedy is the Russian philosopher Nicolas Berdyaev, whom we met above. Berdyaev helps us grasp the moral compass that produced in multiculturalism an idealistic destiny. In many respects, he is an ideal companion for Hegel, for he resolves similarly profound issues of differences and diversity that usually result in such crises as intractable ethnic and racial disputes. Both Hegel and Berdyaev offer the same type of mythology that resolves the tragedy of the unhappy consciousness, which forces individuals to choose between competing notions of what is good and end up feeling unfulfilled, guilty, and inauthentic.

Just as important for us, both philosophers are Christian, and what they say will help us to understand the morality that underpins the search for justice and freedom in the West. They can illuminate the genesis of an ideology and the way of culture that is a tragedy. As William Faulkner stated, Christianity is the good that informs everything in the West. "No one is without Christianity, if we agree on what we mean by the word," he told the *Paris Review* in 1956. "It is every individual's individual code of behavior, by means of which he makes himself a better human being than his nature wants to be, if he followed his nature only. Whatever its symbol – cross or crescent or whatever – that symbol is man's reminder of his duty inside the human race."[27] The nation-state in its current form can still substitute for a collective Christian consciousness possessing absolute knowledge that its members lack, acting like a benevolent tyrant that is the expression of a general will or common good, having an individuality and personality of its own because it is immortal. Therefore, as in Christian thought, notions of death, resurrection, and rebirth – whether physical or in thought only – inform the ideals of social justice.

Another of the great tropes I engage is tolerance, which flows from a quest for recognition of rights. This is the liberal alchemy of critics such as Will Kymlicka and several generations of multicultural politicians, who advance it as the watchword for bringing about social justice and understanding in society. It is a possible answer to the problems endemic to the unhappy consciousness, especially when there are differences in power, prestige, status, and a sense of belonging. The granting and receiving of tolerance must by definition imply inequalities, a superior extending grace to an inferior. The invoking of tolerance as a social strategy or acceptable value, too, is more in keeping with the liberalism that postdated Fichte and Kant's model arising out of a master-and-slave struggle but that unintentionally led the actors into a struggle of lordship and bondage within themselves and then with each other.

In short, we ought to take an alternative look into how we form societies, how we socialized the *Other* that is in ourselves as well as those around us, and how we can produce states that, by encouraging us to conform, make us believe that we are free or that we will later achieve the liberty of our dreams. How can we have the socialization of sameness without the stratification of differences of power? Otherwise, how do we move from the tragedy of the unhappy consciousness to the comedy with the fairy-tale ending of living happily ever after if we are rejecting standard liberal norms of recognition based on historical and traditional cultural identities as well as rejecting tolerance as the way to accommodate differences and diversity? In this regard, this book recognizes that the raw material for ethical relations already exists or is already at hand, as Heidegger puts it. Therefore, identity cannot occur out of its context – the history of the world that began long before any individual's self-consciousness. What is already there: either the bonds of slavery or those of freedom, but bonds, harsh and difficult to break free from. In a practical sense, genuine multiculturalism points away from the old notion and rhetoric of recognition and tolerance.

To this end, Kymlicka is right in talking about the social mores that society has already negotiated and accepted. These arrangements have resulted in Canada in a way of life that defines the welfare state as a liberal institution with citizens who have equal rights to a standard of living that protects them by offering at least the minimum daily requirements to keep body and soul together. But this is a way of life that ensures the present generation's constant borrowing from the future: today's beneficiaries, especially those receiving pensions, are in debt to this generation's workers, investors, and immigrants; similarly, the welfare system also borrows from the future or from the deferred savings of the present generation.

For some time, the welfare state has been under assault physically and intellectually. The intellectual attack takes the form of the discussion of whether newcomers, even when they become citizens, should have all the entitlements of today's welfare spending. The alternative argument is that they should continue in their traditional role – deferral of immediate personal gain. In this way of thinking, Canada chooses them primarily for its own benefit and to help people who have claims on the state. This is how it recognizes them, at least epistemically. Therefore, objective expectations determine their socialization and stratification and result in an ethical kind of recognition that posits newcomers as somewhat inessential to the real Canada – a kind of *accommodation*, where they produce the labour, capital, and investment to maintain current living standards, subsidizing the old-timers, which pays their entry price. In return, the practical and concrete benefits would flow to their children and grandchildren (the "second-generation theory of immigration").

Times have changed, and there is conflict over the welfare state itself and who should benefit *now* – in the moment that genuine multicultural-ism stipulates is always the right time for social justice. Some old-timers demand their own welfare privileges and would keep immigrants and newcomers in an inferior position of gratitude; many highly educated and ambitious immigrants and newcomers want all the privileges and rights of citizenship in a welfare state and can move to other immigrant-hungry countries that offer better deals. The second group's argument becomes more lethal to the existing way of life when it demands not only full social citizenship but also complete recognition in the political and economic spheres.

For these immigrants are the essence of the self-made individual who rejects his or her mother and father (motherland and fatherland) to start anew and to achieve his or her desires. In Machiavelli's sense, they are the many Princes and Princesses who set out to launch their own colony in a new land, even knowing that they would start out a small minority. Yet they provoke fear, for they bring virtues and abilities to bear on their new society and would wipe out what is already there, just as the Prince's colonial army would under Machiavelli's advice. This is where the soci-ety has really to come to terms with its ideals of liberal citizenship – par-ticularly with whether citizenship should translate power into sovereignty and whether it is ethical to make some citizens appear to be free while society merely accommodates them or enslaves them.

Again, one of the major questions for a multicultural, liberal democ-racy is whether it can accept social inequalities of any kind. Particularly of interest: can the state itself tolerate, even create inequalities, especially those that the idea of citizenship should address? Instead of advocating a common welfare for all members, can it favour some and accommo-date others, and still truly be capitalist in the way it distributes justice, allows ownership of property, and protects the rights of individuals and minority groups? Here we may think of the British thinker T.H. Marshall, one of the first people to define equality of citizenship as the genuine mark of membership and belonging in modern societies. This perception is the basis for development of individuals' modern consciousnesses as political beings in a world of diversity. As political scientist Chris Armstrong reminds us,

> Marshall suggested a gradual historical trajectory along which citizenship rights have been progressively realized. These rights should be seen as threefold in nature: a full vision of citizenship requires, specifically, the satisfactory achievement of civil, political and social rights. Civil rights imply personal freedoms and equality before the law; political rights on the other hand principally involve the right to vote and hold public office. Such civil and political rights had been achieved in Britain during the seventeenth, and in the eighteenth/ nineteenth centuries respectively. The development of the third, "social" form of citizenship rights was a particularly twentieth-century phenomenon however, and can be associated with the great reforms of post-war Western liberal democracies ... Significantly the job of social citizenship was not to secure equality of condition, but to rein in otherwise productive inequalities sufficiently to protect the basic "equality of status" of citizens.[28]

This trajectory is equally applicable to Canada, as for this period when it struggled to be exclusively a white man's country, Canada was effectively a part of the British history and culture.

Now we must incorporate a fourth bundle of rights to allow individuals to assert their differences and human virtues within the state. Does this exhaust the ideals of a civic citizenship involving a commonality and sameness that multiculturalism suggests that we have? In the context, a true difference can be more important than civic sameness.

We cannot ignore prevailing ethical relations, and mere epistemic recognition of them, or allowance for difference and diversity within them, would not solve the intentions of the ethical relationship – happiness for everyone. Should Others coming into the society simply disrupt it? Should society treat them as unchangeable, with the Others – in this case, immigrants – having always to conform? If the Others must conform, then are they coming into a site of freedom? Do they enter with agency and subjectivity, or do they await determination in the eyes of Others to them, the existing Subjects? If this is the case, do they then have any self-determination, and if not, can they still be free? The result, I argue, is full recognition: both that which is epistemic and, in the same moment, that which is ethical. Combining, they offer the recognition that is fraternal love, a sense of belonging in the sameness of citizenship but also retaining the differences and diversity intrinsic to individualism. Everyone ends up speaking the right language for the moment, because the act of speaking, the language itself, and the moment of occurrence are all new.

Therefore I argue that there must be internal change so as to create a new and expanding fraternity. Change must occur within the existing state and within the immigrant – in the state, so as to allow all differences and diversity of membership; in the immigrant, who feels fully belonging to a new social entity and sharing the very essence of this group. Each and all would gain recognition, and by extension none would have to give or receive tolerance. All sides must be willing to negotiate constraints on their subjectivity, for no side can remain truly free at the expense of the other. Such would be an unhappy consciousness and, ethically, a tragedy for both. This would be the idyllic position that a moral agent would desire for itself. Therefore, once again we would be trying to avoid the rocks of the unchangeable that lies at the heart of Taylor's recognition, which is now the benevolence of tolerance in Kymlicka's argument for multiculturalism.

In this way, I answer the question Michael Ignatieff and others raise about the need for an ethical relationship based universally on love in society.[29] Can there be any solidarity in such a society? How can we not only love others but, just as important, have them love us, often when many of us are rubbing shoulders and elbows, pursuing different universals goals on the same stage? Many of us have no need to like some or any of us or have learned under different conditions to have no use or need for other people among us or to even hate them – we come from a position of fearing the *Other*.

As Jean-Jacques Rousseau suggests, citizens have to learn this love of or affinity for members of the same nation or state. This is the eternal story of the tragedy of human existence and how we live in a vale of tears while believing we are marching to a paradise, if in fact we are not already almost there. Tragedy and its companion, comedy, provide the quintessential narrative of how not only to achieve a multicultural, diverse, and plural order but to coercively maintain it as a singular functioning system that even polices itself by keeping the people authentic to their collective intentions.

Tragedy is the story of the internal struggle in each of us to be free while knowing that society demands that we willingly give up our freedom as a price for ensuring our freedoms. It is the story of how we must learn to love what we loathe, realizing that in our ethical relations the choice, if there is one, is often either to try to love freely or in a Machiavellian way to live in dread and despair as the unloved and the unloving. It is a play for which the stage, the props, and the actions all come together in a singular aesthetic work in process. Tragedy is the play about domesticating the powerful and teaching it how to love for the good of itself as part of a social order or consciousness in which there are many others besides the most powerful, all of whom must live together in the hope of prospering. They see themselves always as subjects that are rational moral agents and as objects only when it is strategic to position themselves as such – and never permanently. Identity and positioning are also in flux: one being is constantly giving way to another, of choice, and people and groups are always in a state of becoming. This, too, has to be the status of the sovereign, for the sovereign must be as perfectly as possible a reflection of the people and the people of the sovereign – there must be symmetry of reflection between the people in their coalitions and the sovereign.

Now that we have discussed the idealism of genuine multiculturalism, let us take a deeper look at tragedy and comedy themselves. For in examining these two forms of life, we can access the practicality of ever achieving the kind of recognition that is fraternal love or genuine multiculturalism.

5

Canada's Second Covenant:
The Charter of Rights

OTHELLO: Not I – I must be found:
My parts, my title and my perfect soul
Shall manifest me rightly. Is it they?
IAGO: By Janus, I think no.[1]
                    Shakespeare, *Othello*

Tragedies often confront us in our daily lives. This is a staple of the human experience or condition, and learning from them is what allows us to come up with theories and rules of life. Perhaps the most philosophical attitude we can take to these trials and tribulations appears in aphorisms such as "What doesn't kill me strengthens me" and "What evil there is must be for some greater good" – sayings that depict our resignation to the unchanging nature of some things in life and our need to somehow manage. And one social fact of life seems to be always with us: that as individuals, if we live alone or outside of a society, we cannot be indefinitely happy, we cannot be fully ourselves and reach our full potentials. We cannot be sovereign and live in society. We can know who we really are only by rubbing shoulders with others, by playing with them, and even by dreaming and working together – by in effect linking our bodies in an ecstatic embrace as if we were one. Although we may desire sovereignty at the individual level, we can achieve it only collectively, if ever. For this is the lesson at the heart of Western mythology: the story of a *soi-disant* sovereign Adam in a Garden of Eden awaiting a fall, so that he might eventually live forever through his descendants in societies. Adam, then, is the prototype of every Sweet Boy or Prince Charming and every Bad John. These figures are one and the same: *Bildung* characters acting out their own notions of evil and good to perfect themselves in life. Society evaluates the former type as good and the latter as evil, the former having the right values, common sense, good judgment, taste, and tact, and the latter, none of these traits. Other people confer the labels "goodness" and "evil" on them, even though their own actions may shape the evaluation.

Yet, living in a society, we must always be compromising, even becoming and acting hypocritical and inauthentic according to selfish standards, so that even in this social embrace we still cannot fulfil ourselves. We cannot reach our individual potential and truly make ourselves. We cannot reach the point where we can, on our own steam, realize all those dreams and aspirations swirling around in our heads, like the archetypal human being in Auguste Rodin's statue *The Thinker*. We may find the confines of dealing with others frustrating, cloistering, and even suffocating. Indeed, we still cannot be genuinely happy.

But then this is exactly what the prototypical Adam learned before he discovered fear and found that it heralded a certain type of wisdom. This is the fear that is the beginning of a lordship-and-bondage relationship. It is a fear that brings on trembling and awe, the possible loss of life and way of life, and the need to submit to a culture and way of life that is very different from the individual's ideal. This fear forced the prototypical human that is Adam to take the status of neither a full Sweet Boy nor a full Bad John pursuing a life of idleness and higher thoughts. Instead, as a bit of both, he and his female equivalent became simply workers in the service of a higher force or calling – a sovereign or a tyrant from which there seemed no escape. The worker's life is tragic, alienated, and unhappy. It features prohibitions and forbearances, rules that harness the individual's creativity, reducing life sometimes to drudgery.

We usually associate tragedy with fear or prohibitions that in their extreme are deadly but that generally are routine. As John Austin tells us, in our daily actions "we should not therefore ... be under the necessity of pausing and calculating upon each act or forbearance. To do so would be superfluous, inasmuch as the result of that process would be embodied in a known *rule*; and mischievous, inasmuch as the *true* result would be expressed by the rule, whilst the process would probably be faulty if it were done on the spur of the occasion. On the contrary, the inferences suggested to our minds by repeated experience and observation are drawn into *principles*, or compressed into *maxims*, and these we carry about us ready to use, and apply to individual cases promptly and without hesitation. This is the main, though not the only use of *theory*, which ignorant and weak people are in a habit of opposing to practice."[2]

Just prior to Austin, Hegel had suggested that, if society formalizes thought, desires, and intentions in laws, these enactments must be fully reasonable and harmonizing and must reconcile words and action, and society must live them as actualities. Otherwise, all that remains is the formalism of empty regulations with no reality in living expression and representing the seeming formlessness of life – where life appears to offer all the empirical evidence we may need but we have no way of making sense of these data.

Speaking of the formalism of laws and theories of ethical thought, Hegel states, "To say that they have no *reality*, means in general, nothing else than that they lack truth. They are indeed, not supposed to be the *entire* truth, but still *formal* truth. But what is purely formal without any reality is a mere figment of thought, or pure abstraction without that internal division which would be nothing else but the content. – On the other hand, however, since they are Laws of pure thought, and pure thought is intrinsically universal, and therefore a knowledge which immediately contains being, and therein all reality, these Laws are absolute Notions, and are inseparably the essential principles both of form and of things."[3] Such formalism is mere tragedy. Equally, this argument holds for superficial displays that do not go to and identify the heart of the matter – namely, comedy.

These principles and the instinctive way in which we apply our principles, thoughts, and ethical laws in practice make our ideology and our knowledge peculiar to our culture or living reality. Ultimately, this is how we formulate our morality and develop ethical practices for the specific, and even unique, way of life that is our culture.[4] "Speaking then generally," Austin tells us, "human conduct is inevitably guided by *rules*, in the form, for the most part, of general principles or *maxims*."[5] For it cannot be true as a rule that something can be true in theory and false in practice, for this would just be another way of saying that practice is misleading. In this respect, we may think of the remarks of Leo Strauss, who tended to privilege fear and distrust in human relations, decrying any "vulgar separation of theory from practice." As he explains, "there never was and there never will be reasonable security for sound practice except after theory has overcome the powerful obstacles to sound practice which originates in theoretical misconceptions of a certain kind."[6] In our way of thinking, then, theory is philosophical and is therefore "comedy," whereas practice is tragedy, because it is the truth of the living experience rather than the utopia of what could or even ought to be.

As Berdyaev reminds us, "The word 'happiness' is the emptiest and most meaningless of human words. There exists no criterion or measure of happiness, no comparison can be made between the happiness of one man and another."[7] Here he seems to be in good company across time with an array of scholars, such as Hegel and Kant, who still hold some sway today. Hegel, for example, argues in his *Philosophy of History* that what we call "history" is really a search over time by humans for happiness, for what to the explorer would be the magic elixir that turns tragedy into comedy. But alas, "The history of the world is not the theatre of happiness. Periods of happiness are blank pages in it."[8] Only a few pages earlier, we read: "History as the slaughter-board at which the happiness of peoples, the wisdom of States, and the virtue of individuals have been victimized."[9] Just think of all those Adams and even Prince Charmings who, over time, have amounted to nothing more than mere workers trying to please some ruler.

Equally as pessimistic, Kant muses that "the concept of happiness is such an indeterminate one that even though everyone wishes to attain happiness, yet he can never say definitely and consistently what it is that he really wishes and wills."[10] We see this relentless search for *happiness* as nothing more than comical, especially when we view the quest from the lofty position of rationality, history, and knowledge deriving from experience. If we do not have a gaze from such a lofty perch, akin to that of gods, or if we are blindly groping, then the process loses its comedic effect and becomes the very opposite. As the American social and political thinker Darren McMahon observes in *Happiness: A History*, we then have to learn the facts of life about the tragedy of happiness.[11] So we can never have long periods of happiness either as individuals or as a community. And thus it seems also that we can never be free.

In society, however, we can settle for something other than full happiness, for a partial bliss of sorts, so that we can determine in advance how tight an embrace we are entering, so that we can decide how long the partial bliss will last. Even if there are times when we can be free of such obligations, we can agree to limits and boundaries on both the upsides and downsides of our desires and wishes. What we might agree to is justice, but this is merely a compromise at best in terms of the absolute that is happiness, a situation where at times justice may not even be as *just* to us as we would naturally want it to be. And what we might agree to make just today we might not tomorrow, or we might have frowned on it in the past. The arbitrariness and capriciousness that we hoped to escape will still be with us, as will be the continuing uncertainty.

Justice appears in the guise of a chameleon, or even as the most abstract of paintings with its shifting meanings, understandings flowing from the shifts of time, of place, and of the individuals participating. Justice can be the working out of a tragedy if we believe that some form of happiness is still something attainable and that its achievement requires a continuous struggle against great obstacles. This is particularly the case for Canada, where, as a people, we supposedly still hold to the ideal of creating a homeland for all of us regardless of our birthplace and ethnicity – a home that offers everyone something we call "social justice," which we will all share equally. This ideal is the main social production of what we hope is a just society, an ideology that should contain all the maxims useful for Canadian life and a theory and practice that is still state policy. As Pierre Trudeau explained his vision for a multicultural Canada, "The aim of life in society is the greatest happiness of everyone, and this happiness is attained only by rendering justice to each person."[12]

Or life in society can be a comedy, if we start from the standard structural-functionalist position that the mechanisms for justice are already in place and all that we need to do is conform to them. If we do that, any additional struggle would be foolish. Instead of appearing to be an expression of a deep desire for freedom, it would represent nothing more than bad socialization. These disparate characteristics of social living that are possible as justice, then, can only be an arrangement. It is a process for limiting both happiness and unhappiness, but usually leaving us in neither state, at least not for long.

This changing arrangement – unlike happiness, which is ideally permanent – always needs defining and negotiating with other people. Its character is much unlike that of happiness, which, in its pure and seemingly authentic state, is usually another form of selfishness and is inflexible and uncompromising. To this end, if we cannot agree on the terms of natural justice, we can always fall back on law as the final arbiter of social living. US philosopher Karl N. Llewellyn argues that ultimate questions of morality and the common good may fall to the wayside in dispute settlement, so "let us acknowledge merely the obvious fact, in law, that law as is, is law. Justice may be an ideal; in actuality it is an accident."[13]

This is a truism that we may see around us daily in social matters such as divorce settlements, civil actions, or criminal matters, or when minority groups are collectively seeking social and individual recognition from society's dominant groups. In all cases, natural distributive justice seems to be missing, and only the law as is remains. Therefore justice as an intentional product of an ethical relationship must ignore everything that claims to be natural or to emanate from natural or universal law.

Justice is a social construction, even if its creation, ironically, aims to produce a new set of laws as genuine and good as if they were, indeed, natural. With time, socially constructed laws will come to seem natural, devoid of human imagining, and products of nature itself. Equally ironic is the growing presence of law courts in governing the social order,[14] suggesting that what started out as a moral order tends to downplay morality in favour of expediency and the functioning of the system, even if it works like a conveyor belt fomenting continuing injustice and general resignation to the comedy of this life.

But despite this caveat, an agreement to produce justice means surrendering sovereignty to someone stronger in return for ethical rules to settle, with finitude, disputes of sovereignty. In this case, the agreement is more a covenant between unequal parties than a social contract involving equals. As Jonathan Sacks argues in *Dignity of Difference*, "It is the conception of personal identity that lies behind the concept of covenant. Covenant is a bond, not of interest or advantage, but of belonging. Covenants are made when two or more people come together to create a 'We'. They differ from contracts in that they tend to be open-ended and enduring. They involve a commitment of the person to another, or to several others. They involve a substantive notion of loyalty – of staying together even in difficult times. They may call, at times, for self sacrifice. People bound by a covenant are obligated to respond to one another beyond the letter of the law rather than to limit their obligations to the narrowest contractual requirements."[15] Covenants imply the idea of a transcendental, all-embracing spirit.

It is this going beyond the letter of the law – this willingness to sacrifice the self for an/Other – that we call "love," and it is the very opposite of fear and selfishness. In our modern society, these ideals amount to what we call "citizenship," a covenant among members to form a specific group, share an identity, govern themselves as sovereign, protect one another, and share the good and bad times. This is citizenship as justice, freedom, and ultimately, we hope, happiness – all the handiwork of individuals working together in a specific society.

Explaining further, Sacks notes that the initial covenant sets the tone for everything that follows. Here he is thinking about the culture of citizenship through notions of identity and belonging and about the agreement on how individual members will relate to one another. The covenant creates the ground for social norms necessary for an ethical life – for the chance to create some semblance of happiness and to make it last as long as humanly possible. This is "where we develop the grammar and syntax of reciprocity, where we help others and they help us with calculations of relative advantage – and where trust is born, and without them [grammar and syntax] there would be no selves and no contracts. Contracts, social or economic, mediate relationships between strangers. But if we were always and only strangers to one another, we would have no reason to trust one another. The possibility would always exist, and always have to be taken into consideration, that the other will defect when it is his or her interest to do. A world systematically bereft of fidelity or loyalty would be one in which neither states nor markets would ever get under way."[16] In this sense, strangers are individuals or unknown sovereigns akin to the Aristotelian god or beast; when people know each other or share sovereignty and culture, they become persons, or citizens.

To this end, Sacks explains that the founding conditions help determine even the quality of justice itself, for evaluating the quality of the result: "Sociologists speak about trust, economists about social capital, sociobiologists about reciprocal altruism, political theorists about civil society. What these various terms signify is that social life cannot be reduced to a series of market exchanges. We need covenants as well as contracts; meaning as well as preferences; loyalties, not just temporary associations for mutual gain. These things go to the heart of who we are. They are the 'signals of transcendence' in the midst of a fast-paced world ... When contracts displace covenants and means replace ends, we are left with freedom without meaning, which is certainly more pleasant but not necessarily more fulfilling than meaning without freedom."[17] Socially, we love more than we fear. Ironically, we traditionally settle for a bit of both. For that is life – or so we offer as a maxim.

Thus the covenant is the initial act of creation that produces the inequity that is the basis for the notional social contract that develops equality. It is the basis of stratification that occurs within an existing state. Specifically, in the West, it is more akin to a second, secular, biblical-style covenant that offers to the Christian world an end to human tragedy and the beginning of a time of justice on earth. But before that contract comes into being, biblical life as presented is about the unequal struggle among members of the same group and between the group itself and other groups and about having to accept a series of covenants that never produced peace, far less happiness or even justice for everyone.

A SECOND COVENANT

But a second covenant of redemption presumes a first that was already a stratified world and therefore undesirable. In Christian mythology, the first was the lordship-and-bondage relationship in an earlier, fictive state of nature.[18] It took the form of natural law, where human beings found themselves in a tragic situation of natural inequality and of trying to assert themselves against a universal law that enslaved them. In this state, they reacted to base emotions and instincts that were the very stuff necessary for survival – for keeping body and soul together.

But the real struggle was over the "soul" and how to set it free from the base survival instincts. The struggle then was over the ideal and safe forms of living and how to make life meaningful, more than just basic and routine and focusing on staying alive – a state perhaps analogous to poverty today. This original state was a time of frustration, unhappiness, and injustice for humans, as they had to conform to a higher order that an Other that was a higher power imposed. If they resisted, they had to do so with cunning and stealth, for survival meant their accepting outward subordination to the racialized but powerful beings that were not human and therefore could not understand what it meant tragically to be human.

Their real struggle was for socialization and the creation of a fraternity to ensure freedom. Once they set up that framework, the question of stratification, or its appropriateness, becomes whether freedom should be absolute or fragmentary. Indeed, free persons in terms of a specific way of socializing might even covenant further to have less that absolute freedom but share the safety and other benefits of socialization.

History under this prototypical Christian covenant is the era and effort of slaves in bondage. It is the time they spent trying to assert their humanity. It ends when participants become free, when tragedy ends and comedy begins. This occurs when the individual believes that matters of the body are not really all that meaningful but rather that those of the soul are primary, though even the biggest fool knows that the two elements depend on each other for survival and that in some circumstances the body's desires must be paramount. In Western mythology, this history ends with a second covenant, which takes all that is old and reformulates it as new and even virginal. This is the kind of newness that I offered in the last chapter as the goal of multiculturalism in Canada, where the old materials that are the many peoples of the world would join with the resources of the land to create a new type of human – a Canadian whose essence, ironically, is multicultural or who, in contrast, has no essence at all. To pull this off would be as great a miracle as any in history, for it would refine materials that even the creating gods or Nature could improve no further – an entity to whom they could not give a new spirit or a soul free from the mundaneness of living. This would be the miracle of socialization whose product is the cultured being or citizen.

The second covenant repeals the old order of natural inequalities and the law that imposed it, forging naturally unequal beings into a unity flowing from the ideal of social equality. Its first task is to create the conditions for justice. Then its participants can agree on how to attain and mete out this justice – distributive justice. For Christians, this agreement is a function of their mediator, with the Universal agent helping human beings and their god to agree to a new covenant of love to replace the old one deriving solely from God's law.[19]

The new agreement provided redemption for slaves of the earlier law and promised life in a new state, more in keeping with a comedy than with a tragedy. This new covenant is a new *creation*, establishing new ideals of what is good and evil in the ensuing state. With notions in place of what is good, how then to distribute the good among the now-equal members? Whom to entitle in any later stratification? This becomes the issue of distributive justice, a kind of dividend for ownership of the means that produce the good that society now calls "social justice." This dividend is a measure of the freedom and welfare that exist in the new state. As such, the dividend can be most generous to individual members and stingy to the state, or vice versa, but this is a matter that is separate from the initial act of creation.

What we have just discussed is a crucial point of chronology that can illuminate multiculturalism. It is mainly an act of creation – the new covenant that determines what is the new good and evil – rather than essentially a method of distributing justice. Creation determines what the political and social organism will become, what forms it will take, and what it will be capable of doing. Multiculturalism in Canada is the attempt to end a state that is naturally a tragedy, a state that started with the creation of a settler community that racialized peoples, and to replace it with one that is a comedy, wherein its members believe that they are totally free of natural laws that placed limits on what Canada and Canadians could become.

For this reason, I disagree with theorists such as Michael Ignatieff who argue that multiculturalism is a social contract and culminates a revolution in liberal rights.[20] They have the order of creation backwards. They confuse the creator with the created and the desire for good and freedom with the manifestation of that desire. They conflate acts of socialization and stratification – or worse, they offer stratification as the primary motivator for state construction. This would be tantamount to assuming that the aim of creation of any state is an unhappy consciousness, with the attendant struggle for recognition, as the beginning of the state's history. In this case, there is no distinction between the creator and the created – as if a god is making an object of itself, this god that is made in its own image and by its own hands and thoughts.

A clear example of this was what happened in the first country to have a standard bill of rights. This was the United States, which effectively emerged through the Declaration of Independence and then the constitution. When the state had come into being, and only then, "the people" – which creature it had called into existence – enacted a number of amendments to the constitution. "The people" did so in an effort to define their new nation's character and to determine how it would mete out justice and how citizens would experience their new republic. This all took place because independence had produced not happiness but an unhappy consciousness.

These amendments became the US Bill of Rights, which limits the sovereign's powers and promises inviolable guarantees, or *rights*, to all citizens. In effect, the document limits any additional changes that the creator can impose on itself. It is only in the second stage in this evolution of the people as a constituted entity, when they recognize rights, that the liberal individual whom the first stage created could decide that there would be no additional changes to definitions of its Self. But this stratification of humanity into who do and do not have rights and power followed socialization, the calling into being of Americans as a fully constituted self that created itself with its own identity and unique reasons for existence.

Those who look to mythology or spiritual life for proof of precedence would note that God issued the Ten Commandments to the Chosen People only after they had constituted themselves as a people and entered into a covenant. These commandments not only dealt with issues of behaviour and forbearance to produce a culture or way of life for the weaker members – the people – but also limited the behaviour of the omnipotent creator. Like a two-edged sword, the document enjoined the people to obey the lawgiver, who had to enter into its culture and respond to what it did and did not do. Ironically, the covenant's constraining the omnipotent in effect negates any omnipotence. Once the people of Israel lived as he commanded, then the god of the covenant had to keep his word.

With God's abiding by the ideals – the spirit – and letter of this agreement, the covenant allowed both human beings and God to achieve what they had bargained for – justice. In this regard, the covenant was at the same time a tragedy and a comedy for both sides, and neither scored a clear triumph. The rights of the minorities – the weaker parties‧ – allowed individuals to retain those features of their individuality not subject to socialization and cultural eradication. The Bad John still had the right to assert his individual interest over that of the common good and to do so in a comedic way, by convincing everyone to agree that, paradoxically, this very act of asserting the individual good was de facto the same as the common good. This is the argument for minorities in liberal democracies: ultimately every individual is a minority because everyone else can gang up on that individual and enslave her or him. What keeps the majority from acting tyrannically is not just the law of the land, but the spirit of the covenant – the pre-covenant ideals, the love that antedated creation of the state and must have existed in the state of nature as an everlasting virtue.

As the British-based political scientist Jennifer Jackson Preece explains in *Minority Rights*, "'Minorities' are political outsiders who challenge the prevailing principles of legitimacy. This explains why the identity of those persons who constitute a 'minority' changes from one political and historical context to another. And it immediately discloses how minority questions enter into both domestic and international politics – for what defines legitimacy within a community also has a fundamental effect on relations between communities." Even if we agree that every individual has what we might call "human" or "universal" rights, these can guarantee justice only within a state. They become limits on the state or any other potential tyrant within that community of individuals or states that would make any member less than human. Again, as Preece states, "For at its core, the 'problem of minorities' is what Isaiah Berlin has termed a 'collision of values' between diversity and community to which there can be no permanent resolution."[21] Without resolution, the only reasonable approach might be to rely on trust, faith, and hope – virtues that existed before the state and that ground the optimism that led to its development. At their most basic and foundational, these are issues primarily of socialization.

Once a country decides to be multicultural, members of this new covenant can make a second decision, about what form the country should take and how to divide up power. For example, if Quebec, as historically some people in the province including the government from time to time aspire, were to decide to separate from Canada, it would immediately start out as demographically multicultural as it had been before its status changed. In current practice, it would express its yearning for independence through a referendum, which would merely articulate its desire for freedom and a different form of justice. The new country would start out multicultural in nature, whether it was officially so or not.[22]

A major question of justice would be to decide after independence whether to establish this new country in an act of stratification for the good and benefit of only the *French*, however it might define them, or if there should be any stratification. That it would be primarily French would be a question of distributive justice, not a covenant of creation – unless, in the most unlikely of cases, its pre-independence population would purge itself, most likely through assimilation, of all non-French elements. Even now, the current question of how to accommodate some Quebec residents in an obvious regime of structural inequalities is one of social justice and citizenship. Once a covenant has formalized that desire for creation and attendant socialization of all members in a common identity, it then becomes a question of what form the expression should take.

The new country can decide to be a democracy or a tyranny. And even if it chooses democracy, it can take on any of the variant political forms that exist or that it could imagine, from liberal democracy through social democracy to communism or any other variant of the members' choosing. The same would be the case for places such as the Basque country, Chechnya, Kurdistan, Puerto Rico, Scotland, Tamil Eelam, Tasmania, or Wales, places where there are nascent desires to form separate and independent countries distinct from the encapsulating polity.

This, too, was the story behind the impasse that led to the American Civil War: the Northern states wanted a place of freedom for all humanity, and the Southern states fought for the right to live in an organism that ensured freedom for an elite group, including the freedom to own other human beings as chattel. That initial desire to call a nation of specified humans into being would need first formalization in a covenant and then a social agreement over what would make the fraternity happy. This is where what is a mere idea first becomes concrete: it is that magic moment of creation. Indeed, here we might want to reflect on the creation of what Will Kymlicka calls "societal culture," which we can pair with the explanation above by Sacks.

"By a societal culture," Kymlicka writes, "I mean a territorially concentrated culture, centred on a shared language, which is used in a wide range of societal institutions, in both public and private life (schools, media, law, economy, government, etc.). I call it a societal culture to emphasize that it involves a common language and social institutions, rather than common religious beliefs, family customs or personal life-styles."[23] Here Kymlicka stresses the social, whereby the culture comes about *after* human reflection and the building blocks are the human and physical resources available to the covenanters to produce a specific way of life. More than is usual with a specific identity, this societal culture typically emerges from common values or folkways, and in current Western liberal democratic thought the essential value is respect for law as the foundation for the given order or society.

Undoubtedly, we must see this thing we call "the social" as a living organism, as Thomas Hobbes says – a kind of mortal god that eventually has more power than its very creators.[24] And in doing this, we might want to consider Hegel's idea of spirit as the will of a god-like creature or sovereign to ultimately find happiness. This spirit, if it is the will of the modern state as Krabbe described it above, has the same goal for all its citizens: to provide them with happiness and justice in a land of freedom. The societal culture – as an expression of the sovereignty that the cove-nant expresses – is what gives the law and enforces it. Sovereignty is the culture that binds in lordship and bondage the rule givers, as Austin sug-gests, and the people who must obey.

American philosopher George H. Sabine and political scientist Walter J. Shepard seem to extend Austin's thought: "The fundamental concept of the theory of the modern state is law."[25] It privileges the lawgiver as the sovereign or the lord of the drama that is either a tragedy or comedy, depending on the observer's gaze: from above, it exists as a comedy for the lawgiver; from below, a tragedy for those social unequals who must obey. As these two scholars wrote,

> It is obvious that law is one expression among others of what is called generally the civilization or the culture of a community and that the development and effective working of any such system of common evaluation is not independent of other factors of culture. It depends, for example, upon the free interchange of ideas which is certainly rendered easier, if not made possible, by a common lan-guage. It may be aided by a common religion; it is certainly weak-ened by a wide divergence of religious ideas, especially if these ideas find expression in antagonistic religious institutions. A common law is evidently very closely related to that intangible complex of ideals which we call nationality, for the latter is very largely though not ex-clusively just the ideal of a common law and of a common political institution to express such a law. A common law cannot flourish

except where there exists a common mentality in which it can thrive, and it may be laid down as a general proposition that the thinner and weaker this common mentality is in a community, the narrower the range of interests that can reach an accepted valuation in that law. When the basis of common agreement is slight, the law must be more general; more must be left to local groups where a better basis exists.[26]

These reasons, including belief in law's primacy, render Canada a multicultural liberal democracy. Multiculturalism expresses the good it has created and is still engendering. Liberal democracy is the form that that intentional good will take and the framework that will facilitate its genesis. This ethical formulation, which a second determination of the methods for achieving the goals for which the nation-state is created forms, establishes the norms for existence. The desire that such norms could become universal means that the creators intend this new state to be a comedy. The faulty reasoning that presents multiculturalism as a culmination of a rights revolution or of a desire for liberal democracy can emerge only within a debate that sees Canada as an old country merely changing the makeup on its face so as to absorb diversity from elsewhere. It cannot assume that at the moment of its creation Canada was diverse and that such diversity remains present at every subsequent re-creation.

That current debate of a fully developed Canada merely adjusting to change also founders over whether multiculturalism is a creative act or merely a method for distributing power and justice. Seeing it as a method produces sociological and political angst over the equitable distribution of its dividends. This is akin to the argument that a capitalist system should more equitably distribute its dividends, which is a separate issue from determining if a capitalist system is desirable in the first place. It is for these reasons that I offer genuine multiculturalism as a non-stratifying form of socialization – an imagined place and time where, hierarchically, race does not matter. Combining it with radical democracy might lead to a socialization of absolute equals, with no reason or desire for stratification.

In Canada's case, most policies, laws, and regulations imply or state that government enacts them for a multicultural country. It is because of this confusion over the distribution of social justice to individual citizens that much of the debate about multiculturalism concerns whether its primary purpose is to protect minority rights.[27] This protection may be one of its functions, but its main goal is to preserve a state where diverse groups of peoples, ethnicities, cultures, and perceived sovereignties and moralities can live under one absolute sovereignty and where, according to the rules of the sovereign and the comedic spirit of believing, they are all actually sovereign and equal.

The confusion implies a single, historical act of creation for Canada that brought it out of the tragic state of nature. As we see below, this reasoning overlooks developments from the mid- and late 1940s and primarily from the 1960s, when a second-type covenant developed. A new Canada emerged, rejecting first an earlier unitary monoculture and then pluralist biculturalism. This sea change set the stage for a new comedy to play under the banner of multiculturalism. And Canada repatriated its constitution and entrenched therein a Charter of Rights and Freedoms after it had become officially multicultural. Repatriation and entrenchment did not create a new country so much as formalizing its shape and personality.

In this light, we are discussing only the formal or institutional creators of Canada – i.e., the need for a second covenant to determine new forms of existence. When we talk about individuals' acts of creation, which individuals produce one by one, we see another form of socialization. And this creation begins anew with the arrival of every immigrant. Genuine multiculturalism suggests that the *spirit* or life force of creation must see the institutional and individual creational processes as a single act for the benefit of all. Indeed, we should perhaps see these individual acts as having primacy over acts of stratification, of secondarily determining what positions and statuses individuals should hold in the new ethical realm resulting from this reformulation. By giving primacy to socialization, we accept that individuals created the institutions of the state for the common benefit of all individuals, and not exclusively for any specific group, no matter how socially constituted. The resulting stratification is another function of socialization, which has made Canada a liberal democracy that in terms of sovereignty privileges ranks individuals ahead of institutions, with the state holding this common sovereignty of all the people.

This process is important, for it allows us to grasp cause and effect in current Canadian society. In particular, it helps to shed light on the discussion of authenticity and on the issue of tolerance, which is so much part of the debate on multiculturalism. First, it illuminates the position and placement of so-called visible minorities and non-white immigrants in Canada. If multiculturalism speaks of the creation process, then these groups are as much the creators of Canada as any other. This is why, I would argue, formally there can be no meaningful difference between those citizens who are born in Canada and those who come from elsewhere. They are all equally creators of Canada.

In this way of thinking, Canada is an act of creation in process. Its socialization remains incomplete. Canada is still at the point of what the American critic and philosopher Richard Rorty's "being described as if for the first time" – in the process of developing its own stories about itself. In this way, it is determining how, in the social-scientific and philosophical language of today, it wants other people and nations to recognize it. The process of description involves creating a specific language or vernacular that contains all the past histories, achievements, and aspirations of Canadians. This new tongue provides a new way of looking at the past and of explaining what is happening in the present and what we can hope for in the future. It explains the dominant morality and ethical relations, an arrangement and description of a specific reality that is still emerging in Canada. This new mode of communication is still in flux and can manifest itself in French, English, or any other language, but none of these alone would convey the meaning, thoughts, and imagination of this new "spirit," for it is the tongue of the gods creating Canada in all its diversity and in a way that the old speakers of the old language simply cannot. It is the language of the Canadian god looking into the void and speaking the words to give form to its creations: "In the beginning was the Word, and the Word was with God, and the Word was God." But, as Statistics Canada shows, such thoughts and intentions now express themselves more and more in an ever-changing, multicultural tongue, a *patois* consisting of the more than 200 languages in use in Canadian homes, and less and less in the official languages of English and French.[28] With this language in place, the sovereign can later review what it created and how it has stratified and assess how good the creation is.

But because it has not yet fixed its own description, Canada differs from other actually, if not officially multicultural countries, such as the United States and some in Europe, the Pacific, and Africa, where the master narrative does not incorporate the "foreigner" or "outsider," nor is it developing a new, more comprehensive form of expression of the full complement of what could constitute the national self. In these countries, there is already a dominant descriptor, such as the notion that Britain is a British country, the United States is an English-speaking country, or, at the heart of Australian culture and nationalism, something already exists that is essentially Australian, with its own form and content, and to which all newcomers must conform in order to become Australian. This process, contrary to what is happening in Canada, is what Rorty would call a "re-description," where the old mythology, fantasies, or established realities are facing challenge and reconsideration. But instead of these old realities receiving a new description, we end up with the old describing the new and making it fit into the old reality.

In the process, two things occur. First, the old ends up, in effect, rewriting the old narrative all over, but in so doing it unintentionally achieves a second thing: it describes the new as now having an experience and a relation to the old, something that previously did not exist in the consciousness. This is akin to what Rorty says happened to Marcel Proust in writing *Remembrance of Things Past*: "At the end of his life and his novel, by showing that time had done to these other people, Proust showed what he had done with the time he had. He had written a book, and thus created a self – the author of that book – which these people could not have predicted or even envisaged."[29] This was because Proust was a self at the beginning of the process.

This is not the case for Canada, for it has not yet come fully into consciousness as a self; instead of having a single author – a specific person, tribe, ethnicity, or founding people – the author describing and bringing Canada into being is indeed a collection of "these people" who are all part of the juggling to hear and to describe. At best, Canada is still a consciousness trying to discover its true self, including what forms it can take. It is a book that is still being written – and so far all the pages on happiness, as Hegel would intimate, are blank. But the pages about the future are also blank. Such a reality – if the book is technically already "written" and all that needs to happen is for it to unfold more blank pages about the achievements of happiness – does not bode well for the future and for hopes for happiness. Therefore, the search must be to find those Canadian Prousts who can write a fitting story about Canada and in the process soil the pristine whiteness of the pages about future developments and successes. Because it is an unhappy consciousness, and thereby a tragedy, the creation is not yet complete of Canada as ultimately a comedy where "they live happily ever after" is the norm.

This means that the form that Canada will take as a result of this expression of freedom is not final or clear. This form – and the corollary of how to distribute the good – are still up for grabs. An open process leading to negotiations, or a tyrant's impositions, could institute and formalize them. Democratic negotiations might take the form that political philosophers suggest is natural to a social contract where individual members bargain away freedoms in return for common assurances for a peaceful existence or, less formally, in the daily, informal referenda of people living together. Or some tyrant might become the final arbiter of the good and the decider for everyone else and impose a form. The form that helps the creators to achieve common desires for the state would be good, and the form leading them off course would be evil. These are the two positions – democracy and tyranny, respectively – that, from its inception, multicultural Canada has determined which form is good and which is evil and if it should adopt either for itself. In between these two polar positions lie an infinite number of combinations of the two. Most important to the adoption of the appropriate model is the guiding principle that Canada sees itself as a liberal democracy. The final determination of what is good would depend on which method helps Canadians to achieve and maintain an ethical order consistent with what modernity defines as a liberal democracy.

My argument is for a radical, egalitarian democracy, close to the end point for maximum democracy. It would allow room enough for every Prince Charming, Bad John, or Sweet Boy and for every Sleeping Beauty, Snow White, Cinderella, and Rapunzel to create a new life in a fairy-tale-like drama. This is a matter of socialization, and it answers the question of what form the ethical order should take.

The second question is that of tolerance, for most observers assume that Canada is a tolerant society, because its entrenched citizens of mainly European descent are accepting of members of other groups. In this society, there are subjects and objects among Canadians – actors in their own drama and players in others' dramas, respectively. The latter group consists mainly of comic characters who delude themselves that they are subjects and tragic heroes. Tolerance, then, is something that an enlightened subject extends to an object, to a being of lower ranking. Since tolerance surfaces after initial creation of the state, it is purely part of the good and is something of concern only as a form of distributive justice and an issue of democracy. It is not, then, a part of the universal desire for freedom that is prior to the state.

As a result, *tolerance* often seems a coded term for the ingratitude of the visible minorities who receive a gift from the old-timers. Instead of accepting it willingly and humbly, the suggestion goes, these ingrates simply abuse this kind-heartedness by making greater demands for respect and recognition. Such is the tenor of much of the discussion in the public media on the quality of tolerance and the expected rewards for such generosity. As part of a discourse on ethics, tolerance is presented as a gift for the old-timers to offer or withdraw without a loss of freedom to anyone. In this way, it is simply a norm of good behaviour while formalizing structural social inequalities.

I propose an alternative stance: this type of tolerance is not consistent with multiculturalism's being part of the magical spark of creation. If all groups and members are equally subjects and of the same social standing, then no one can expect this form of tolerance. Subjects do not give one another tolerance voluntarily and discretionarily, as a benefit from one to the other, thereby inadvertently giving multiculturalism its character and personality; instead, tolerance is an inherent part of the personality of the created. It is as much an expression of freedom in Canada as multiculturalism itself. Here we can reflect on Berdyaev's observations: "The paradox of good and evil – the fundamental paradox of ethics – is that good presupposes the existence of evil and requires that it should be tolerated. This is what the Creator does in allowing the existence of evil. Hence absolute perfection, absolute order and rationality may prove to be an evil, a greater evil than the imperfect, unorganized, irrational life which admits of a certain freedom of evil. The absolute good incompatible with the existence of evil is possible only in the Kingdom of God, when there will be a new heaven and a new earth, and God will be all in all. But outside the Divine kingdom of grace, freedom and love, absolute good which does not allow the existence of evil is always a tyranny, the kingdom of the Grand Inquisitor and the antichrist."[30]

An intolerant Canada would be an irrationalism or even an absurdity in this way of thinking. Tolerance would be part of the tragic charter of Canada and by definition would be a strength that would become the kind of weakness that produces horrors for the country and its citizens. Tolerance would be a value deriving from freedom itself, rather than something that Canadians in their freedom can decide, as a matter of choice, whether or not to exercise. Mainstream Canada expects more recent citizens and immigrants to be equally tolerant of one another and of Canadians native to the land or claiming an ancient lineage. The network of tolerance should be like a web connecting all groups and people without placing any of them in a hierarchy. A value of tolerance would be part of the founding good that determines what Canada itself is. It would not be a unidirectional benefit or gift from the superior and entrenched to those of a lesser claim and privilege.

Tolerance would be part of the natural process of determining social justice, so that there would be no question of gratitude or supplication. It cannot be contingent. If it is a gift, it must be one from primordial freedom to all the various expressions and determinations of this freedom, for it must be a necessity of identity itself. To be otherwise would be unacceptable: the American anti-slavery advocate Martin Delany sneered in a letter to the white abolitionist William Lloyd Garrison that a one-sided approach that leaves some groups subservient to others is untenable. What is now on offer as tolerance in much of the discussion about accommodations of differences and diversity in a Canada that is constitutively and demographically multicultural, even if not all quarters officially recognize it as such, would be another version of what Martin Delany called the "mere *sufferance*," which was an extension of slavery, not liberty.[31] Delany was commenting on such inequality in 1853, when much of the discussion was about the new American society that would emerge out of the death of African chattel slavery: "I am not in favour of caste, nor separation of the brotherhood of mankind, and would as willingly live among white men as black, if I had an *equal possession and enjoyment* of privileges."[32]

In keeping with Delany's view, multicultural groups would not only be the beneficiaries of the gifts of tolerance but would themselves be the benefactors and givers, for otherwise they would not be genuinely Canadian. To paraphrase American pragmatist Sidney Hooks, this kind of tolerance was an attempt to acknowledge and come to terms with understanding that, in North America, religious and other forms of tolerance flowed not from conviction or principles "but from the plurality of religious sects (and ethnic groups), no one of which was strong enough to crush the other."[33] Tolerance emerges at the same time as the tragedy that is the human condition, and, just like the human condition, it is never partial to one side or the other. Like the two-edged sword, it can cut on both the downswing and the upswing. The difference this time is that the cuts derive from love, not fear.

I am here trying to isolate in theory and practice the fundamental difference between multiculturalism as an actual state of existence and what we might call "multiculturalization" as mere policy reflecting an essential group of citizens' extension of tolerance to others, primarily to immigrants whom they construct as ethnically and racially different. Multiculturalization can be no more than the acceptance of Othering and another expression for accommodation.

Worse, as seems to be the practice currently in Europe, it can be a political fad; in some European countries there is much political discourse about multiculturalism, in the sense of acceptance of difference and marginalization within a wider culture. Take the case of the incorporation of Eritrean immigrants in Greece. The government claims its policies are multicultural because they extend greater humanity to non-Greeks; but it also states that Greece is essentially a Greek state and that Greek history and traditions make Greeks superior in the state. This might be *multiculturalization* in action, the difference as distinct as that between claiming to cook a curry and using "curry" as a mere spice in some other dish.

Multiculturalism would mean that Eritreans would be no less superior than the Greeks; that they would exist and be so embedded in the society that there would be no conception of Greece as a state without instinctive acceptance of an Eritrean presence. Genuine multiculturalism hollows out the perceived essential centre of the modernist state and refills it with a social construct of humanism, an ethical code of behaviour, and a multicultural identity. A country's humane incorporation of immigrants can be the essence of multiculturalism. In my contention, genuine multiculturalism is about *citizenship*, not about immigrants. Immigration simply becomes a tool within a multicultural state for securing future citizens, and the concept applies to those it recruits not so much in their immigrant phases but in terms of what limits and boundaries a liberal society can place on them as full citizens.

Therefore, multiculturalism is a form of pluralism. Pluralism is an expression of a specific culture or way of existing, but it is not necessarily genuine multiculturalism. A multicultural state can be also illiberal – and we need only reflect on colonial societies of European-style states with aboriginal peoples – but such a state would not be just; all citizens would not share the same justice or partake of it equally. Therefore, if a state is essentially Greek, French, or Scandinavian, then it cannot be multicultural in spirit, no matter its demographic makeup. It might be plural and even practise a form of liberal democracy; however, if a state of Greek or French and Scandinavian + other cultures + other cultures + to the nth degree has no essence, then it is multicultural, a specific form of pluralism. This would be the case where the universal that is the state, the union, the confederation, is culturally black and indeterminate in general, with pockets of cultural whiteness and purity within its wider scheme. Many sites of supposed ethnic and cultural purity might add up to a pure site of existence such as a state or country, but never can they become a site of cultural or ethnic purity unless a political setting so constructs them.

Genuine multiculturalism does not come about because of a constitution; rather, the constitution has a specific flavour – some say "odour" – because multiculturalism produces the constitution as an act of seeking justice for an a priori universal state. The document becomes the socializing act to create a civil state by members of a society that in a prior state of nature were already multicultural. It seeks to codify the attitude and approach – the Spirit – basic to radical democracy and genuine multiculturalism. This is a perceived state of human existence in any part of the world where actions and intentions are in harmony and where there is this inauthentic and social construct of authenticity. Increasing immigration or expanding the diversity of its sources does not change the multicultural nature of Canada or any other country. This would be like assuming that an already pregnant body can become more pregnant. Pregnancy exists: the stages may change, but it is a state of being, and so is multiculturalism. Genuine multiculturalism occurs when the traditions and laws of daily behaviour make multiculturalism second nature in thought.

6

When Tragedy Becomes Comedy

What is looked upon as an American dream for white people
has long been an American nightmare for black people.[1]

Malcolm X

In a common-sense way, the maxims at the start of the previous chapter
capture a contradiction immanent to life. Their irony gives them a generalized truth that is not always the case, while they remind us that we
always face the certainty of despair and hope – often from the same
source. Despair and hope are dialectical, for they can be opposing, and
at times even complementary, parts of the same whole. The sayings also
speak to the possibility of change for the better or the worse and to how
every thought and act appear pregnant with the possibility of producing
either a tragedy or a comedy. For tragedy, as some say, is when something bad happens to you, while comedy is when it occurs to another;
both effect a change in status. In other words, comedy and tragedy flow
from the same *actions* and which occurs depends on whether the object
of the action is sovereign or subject: tragedy happens to lords, comedy
to bondsmen. The two come together to determine life or fate.

As Geoffrey Brereton argues, "A 'tragedy' in ordinary usage always
implies disaster, usually resulting in death. When death occurs in the
natural course of things and cannot fairly be called disastrous it is hardly
a 'tragedy.' To qualify as one it must take place in unexpected and strik-
ing circumstances. It must, at least, be in some way remarkable."[2] It
must result from a person or group's choosing a specific destiny or life
course that runs counter to fate itself, generating tragedy when the naturally weaker party, with stronger head and will, runs up against an
uncompromising opponent that appears to be fate itself.

The American social and political thinker Darrin McMahon goes further, defining tragedy as one of the outcomes in the never-ending human

search for happiness. As the ancient Greek historian Herodotus shows, nobody can escape the fate that the gods have decreed for her or him, and drawing from history McMahon writes, "No one who lives is happy. Where human agency is frustrated, human choice contradictory, and human suffering inevitable, happiness, if it comes at all, is largely what befalls us. That is the tragic predicament."[3] Happiness as a chance occurrence, and therefore unplanned, is quite a remarkable thing for those of us who believe that human effort, whether political leadership, increased knowledge, or painstaking planning, could lead us to such an end.

As McMahon notes, ancient Greeks came up with the term "tragedy" (*tragoida*) as roughly what we call a "play" at the springtime festival to the god Dionysus.

> [As] any reader of the great playwrights of the period – Aeschylus, Sophocles, and Euripides – will know, fifth century BCE Athenian 'tragedies' seldom have happy endings. On the contrary, they return again and again to situations in which seemingly innocent figures are overwhelmed by circumstances they cannot control. Forced to make impossible choices between the irreconcilable alternatives, the likes of Agamemnon and Antigone, Orestes and Oedipus, Electra and Medea are hunted down by gods and pursued by familial curses, overwhelmed by fate and defeated by the very nature of things. And although those figures inevitably contribute to their own undoing through hubris and folly, the crux of the tragic dilemma is that there can be no easy resolution of conflict, no decision without grave costs, no simple, happy ending.[4]

Thus tragedy is about unhappiness and about the loss of the wholesomeness of a *Self* living authentically and free, according to its own rules, which fulfil the desires that would make this self happy. It is what we hope will happen to the Bad John and what will, if there is a sense of justice, never happen to a Prince Charming or Sweet Boy. Tragedy is the death that stems from the realization that the individual will not find lasting happiness either outside or inside an embrace, that there is no authenticity and happiness either alone or in relationships with others. It is the realization that what previously seemed to be the norm and universal is general and abstract.

The exception to this banality of living only to die ultimately is a death that is truly exceptional – one that is chosen as an act of living. Death's universal attributes, which make humanity quake with fear – its unity and legendary abilities to homogenize all outcomes and dominate all humanity by reducing all individuals physically to nothing – cannot survive an encounter with diversity and difference that is a departure from the usual scripted ending, with a death that the person seeks or that makes him or her stand out as an exceptional human being in the way he or she courted death. This is a morality tale about the puncture of ideals as site of purity and conformity and of the recognition of the histories of living instead of the dominance of a particular history masquerading as a universal. The exception does not survive either as the nonconformist in the state or as the exceptional state that is itself nonconformist and impervious to change. This death is similar to Thomas McCarthy's reminder: "As we know from the history of social and political thought, significant shifts in thinking often come about as a result of challenges precisely to what have previously been taken for granted as natural, unalterable facts of social life – class-structured distributions of the social product, gendered divisions of labor, race-based hierarchies of social privilege, ethnocultural definitions of citizenship, and the like."[5] Change is tragic, for whether people desire it or not, it speaks to finite limits: its embodiment is the tragic figure that society must contain; its stage, the society that must transform itself the moment the change agent materializes and kills the old while itself dying as a pure ideal. In the instant of change, we have the tragedy of death and the emergence of hope in a brand-new beginning – both at one and the same time.

Tragedy is having to deal with the death of the desire to produce a world that is most perfect in our imagination and is pessimistically recognizing that, as finite beings, we never have enough time to produce perfection. It is also coming to terms with awareness that our notions of perfection are always suspect, even if our intentions appear good,[6] for we never possess absolute knowledge, not even that infallible knowledge about our own selves. Change is a reminder of human imperfections.

Tragedy extends a personal loss to other people, who make it personal and share the unhappiness. When we look at it this way, we may understand why the idea of *sharing* – empathizing but also claiming and taking possession – is central to any radical-democratic notion of a genuine multiculturalism. "A country, after all," as Pierre Trudeau once stated, "is not something you build as the pharaohs built the pyramids, and then leave them standing there to defy eternity. A country is something that is built every day out of certain basic *shared* values. And it is in the hands of every Canadian to determine how well and wisely we shall build the country of the future."[7] Another time he stated, "The answer is

NO to those who advocate separation rather than sharing, to those who advocate isolation rather than fellowship, to those who – basically – advocate pride rather than love, because love involves coming together and meeting others halfway, and working with them to build a better world."[8]

This is what pragmatists such as the American John Dewey refer to as "transmission."[9] Transmission is the renewal of the self either individually over a single lifetime or in a community; it is a sharing of experience and attendant knowledge across cultures and across generations – analogous to the ongoing education that teaches the young members of a community about the community's past, its present, and the possibility of its future.

This sharing would be the antidote to the fear that a society favouring anything other than assimilation and compulsory hegemony would lead to a kind of pluralism, with independent and seemingly sovereign cultures living in an array of ghettoes or ethnic enclaves. There would be no communication between them, as has often happened mythically in the Americas because of the garrison mentality and the Machiavellian colonies that are European outposts in a strange land. Such is the kind of thinking that to this day is expressive of concerns over European-style multiculturalism, a pluralism that starts in every nation-state with a national ethnic core at the centre of inferior and lesser communities. Each community is struggling to work itself up the hierarchy of belonging, perhaps eventually disposing the "authentic" old-timers.

Here I am thinking of French sociologist Alain Touraine's pluralism, where "the dark side of this multi-culturalism is the danger that every culture will be trapped into one particular experience that cannot be communicated. Such cultural fragmentation would lead to a world of sects and a rejection of all social norms ... where it is dangerous to situate or judge individuals purely on the basis of their membership of their community. That would result in the triumph of a generalized racism."[10] Sharing, especially as second nature, removes these concerns. It is an act of loving, of transcendence of self and others. Sharing as love helps undermine the reason, which Touraine implies, that the nation-state was better off in some halcyon time when it was a unity, a time before it fragmented. Instead, the need for sharing would imply that fragmentation is the original and "natural" order and the goal is to bring a unity as a social reality out of such diversity and difference. Sharing, then, is the recognition of the interdependence among individuals and groups and of how, in the Hegelian lordship-bondage relationship, individual members and groups can hope to enjoy the fulness of life itself, of all that is humanity, only by freely taking from others and giving back to them – learning through sharing what, in the case of Canada, it means to be fully human and yet fully Canadian.

This is the kind of analysis that students of symbolic interaction think explain how we become human. As the theorist Robert Prus suggests, this pragmatic process of knowing and action as human allows us to share "the viewpoint that people act toward things in deliberative, purposive manners and in terms of the meaning they have for those things."[11] This humanity emerges collectively as members of the community interact through social institutions. It also crystallizes as we creatively devise roles for ourselves in a society whose institutions and agencies represent the skeleton, its human relations the flesh that clothes them. For individuals, it is how we discover ourselves intimately by finding out how we behave in given situations and contexts – how either we flourish and grow fat because of specific experiences or die from them. How, as the modern rap artist 50 Cent exclaims, in a creed from the streets, we "get rich or die trying." Genuine multiculturalism is quintessentially pragmatism – it is about processes and techniques and about the way we interact, share, socially.

And while multiculturalism, like happiness, is the state that we as individuals hope to enter (or maintain, if we think we have already found it), it never develops fully as form and spirit working together. For instead of a lasting happiness, it can generate only time-sensitive justice. Because it comes from human relations, it will remain the seemingly authentic self's search for happiness and will, tragically, find only human justice at best. Even more tragic, without good intentions it might not find justice at all. It becomes a comedy when that self realizes that it can be neither authentic nor happy, far less both, but that, like a fool in paradise, it can pretend to be a little bit of both – enjoying the embrace and its accoutrements without dwelling on how much of its own self it is giving up.

Tragedy encompasses at least three dimensions: that of the hero or presumed individual sovereign; that of the audience, which interprets and evaluates actions in terms of a cultural code of good behaviour and which, as George Herbert Mead reminds us, is always a significant other; and that of the relationship of the hero interacting with that of the audience as major components of the performance itself. So that while we might describe Canada as multicultural in form – a diversity of people, languages, customs, traditions, and rituals – it might still not be multicultural in spirit: all the institutions and agencies governing social relations that, as in a play, may be mere props whose use and positioning provide meaning to onlookers and to actors themselves. In response, the actors position themselves onstage in relation to the props that are so structurally and systemically important to the play and to what the audience understands. These props can convey only a specific and scripted meaning, so that even if the play boasts of celebrating the many colours of Jacob's coat, the overall result might still not paint a pretty picture. There might still be no organic fusing of props, actors, audience, and play to produce the experiences for everyone that reconcile coat, wearer, and observers because it satisfies the desires of all elements in the play. This would be the case if the elements were not committed to the same overarching narrative but were each acting according to separate perceptions of what the play and audience are about. Together, these elements certainly might not produce happiness, for that failure in human experiences is now a given, just as they might fail to produce even genuine testimony to the ideals and, if the play is living reality, to the achievement of justice.

In tragedy, the loss is that of the tragic hero. On the stage, movie theatre, or home entertainment system, tragedy ends usually in death and comedy in marriage. In all cases, it is the audience that is the last to leave the burial or pyre or feast. By then the presumed sovereigns – the actors – have gone on to mourn the trials and defeats of life or to celebrate the triumphs of continuing living.

And in talking about tragedy as what happens to an individual, as rational idealists we can apply insights from Hegel's discussion of history and the human quest for happiness to a nation-state or a specific group of people. "To *explain* History," he argues, "is to depict the passions of mankind, the genius, the active powers, that play their part on the great stage; and the providentially determined process which these exhibits, constitutes what is generally called the 'plan' of Providence ... But in the history of the World, the *Individuals* we have to do with are *Peoples*; Totalities that are States."[12] This way we can analyse the collective actions as if they emanated from the same spirit or consciousness.

As the American theatre critic Walter Kerr warns us, true comedy is not *funny*. More than that, comedy is always contrived. It seems to be unnatural and forced, and only an interruption in the interminable tragedy that is life itself. And here is a major irony: "Comedy," Kerr states, "at it most penetrating derives from what we normally regard as tragic."[13] Comedy appears through a back door we call "tragedy": "The more I attended to comedy the more I found it contradicting itself: what is funny had better not be laughed at, laughter is an inadequate response to what is truly funny ... *Something* inside comedy is not funny. The form refuses to define itself on its own terms, defies explanation as an independent, self-contained eruption of high spirits, simply will not be claimed as an uncomplicated good companion. It does more than acknowledge an ache: it wishes to insist bluntly, even callously, on its often overlooked secret nature."[14] Indeed, he argues, life is *first* tragedy. At creation, life is tragic. For this reason, tragedy usually surfaces prior to comedy. Humans, not the gods of creation, create comedy. Therefore, in a multicultural sense, those acting out new forms of creation are merely comedic – if, that is, we assume that the creation process is already complete.

This view of the privileging and even superiority of tragedy to comedy is not widespread. Critic Julian Gough lamented such a privileging of tragedy, particularly currently in the West. About the modern realistic novel, he states,

> Two and a half thousand years ago, at the time of Aristophanes, the Greeks believed that comedy was superior to tragedy: tragedy was the merely human view of life (we sicken, we die). But comedy was the gods' view, from on high: our endless and repetitive cycle of suffering, our horror of it, our inability to escape it. The big, drunk, flawed, horny Greek gods watched us for entertainment, like a dirty, funny, violent, repetitive cartoon. And the best of the old Greek comedy tried to give us that relaxed, amused perspective on our flawed selves. We became as gods, laughing at our own follies ... Yet western culture since the middle ages has overvalued the tragic and undervalued the comic. We think of tragedy as major, and comedy as minor. Brilliant comedies never win the best film Oscar. The Booker prize [for fiction] leans toward the tragic ... The fault is in the culture. But it is also internalised in the writers, who self-limit and self-censor. If the subject is big, difficult and serious, the writer tends to believe the treatment must be in the tragic mode.[15]

But few of us in our daily lives are gods or absolute sovereigns of our domain, and some of us are merely the fools. We often find ourselves struggling against limits of all sorts, including our own desires and the demands of other people. Most of us are still trying to achieve our "human" potential in this life. These limits do not appear to enhance what we consider to be naturally good and desirable for ourselves. For life to be a comedy would be for us to laugh in the face of reality and our own desires, which may serve more as a copout than as a mechanism for dealing with the dying trials of living. As Kerr notes, "Compromise, resignation, doubt, frank disbelief on all sides, the denial of dignity, the reminder that victory changes nothing and that the bumbler will go on bumbling – these are the indispensable ingredients of a comic 'happy' ending. Without at least one of them, the ending must forcefully call into question the issues of 'happiness' and 'forever after.' Comedy is not lyric, not rhapsodic, not reassuring; putting its last and best foot forward, it puts it squarely down in dung."[16]

Maxims of the types we examined above usually gesture to the unpredictability of human affairs: that good may come out of evil just as easily as vice versa. In other words, justice is arbitrary and beyond our control. It can smile or frown on us, and often the choice between them has nothing to do with what we want or deserve, nor with our actions. There is no guaranteed cause and effect in human relations: life works itself out usually very different from what we planned or intended; retribution is usually heavier, less forgiving, and more unmerited than we expected, while others may feel that the justice we receive is not nearly heavy enough. In such circumstances, all we can do is to accept our lot and seek to triumph over fate by trying to remain human. Or we can rebel and become even more tragic.

Smiling and sometime singing the blues in the face of such capriciousness and powerlessness place the seal on our "natural" humanity. It might not be happiness, but it might be justice. Life might be tragedy and it might be comedy, still, we are never free, never happy, unless we, in a genuine act of pragmatism, define our happiness and freedom to fit into what is happening around us. According to Kerr, "Comedy, it seems, is never the gaiety of things; it is the groan made gay. Laughter is not man's first impulse; he cries first. Comedy always comes second, late, after the fact and in spite of it or because of it. Comedy is really the underside of things, after the rock of our hearts has been lifted, with effort and only temporarily. It appears in the absence of something and as the absence of something. Man's primary concern is with the rock, with his heart, with tragedy; that is where his hopes lies, strange though the taste of hope may be."[17] Indeed, his use of the word "gay" may offer a suggestive double-entendre for today's readers: while Kerr may have intended simply "happy," the current meaning "homosexual" is quite appropriate to the language of multiculturalism. This is to speak of the person living in full social freedom, especially free from the conformity and sexual slavery of living in a strictly heterosexually normal society. And it also speaks of how the use and acceptance of traditional symbols can change – where new content and meaning pour into an old symbol and form, such as the signifier "gay," and how its old meaning can die and re-emerge as something else, in keeping with a new spirit and different intentions.

I use the dialectic of tragedy and comedy to explain genuine multiculturalism in this way: tragedy is the quest for freedom; tragedy is the recognition that humans have limits, some of a nature that seems to conspire to prevent what human beings imagine as freedom. These processes of *thinking* of freedoms and *acting* within limits are the dialects of multiculturalism, the yin and yang of tragedy and comedy. I am not even talking about multiculturalism today in Canada, which I see as not radically democratic enough, still too intent on forcing spontaneous freedom into a liberal community.

I am writing about a transcendent multiculturalism: a practice that is an ideal that now appears beyond our grasp. It is like the notion of going beyond the practicality of life to aim for the spiritual or even divine – a way of capturing the fulness of humanity, but in a way that produces justice if not happiness. I argue effectively two things. First, multiculturalism recognizes that our daily lives are tragic when we are on our own, and that other people may make our lives less tragic or even a comedy. Genuine multiculturalism is quintessentially pragmatism – the perfect philosophy and culture for the Americas, which have had to develop a new way of life by compromising between the absolutism and theologies of the old world and the practicality of having to create new societies where, technically and idealistically, freedom reigns, in that every individual or group has the right to and expectation that it will challenge the dogma, beliefs, and doctrines of those old countries.

Second, multiculturalism promises us a hope for happiness – not a guarantee, mind you – when we are embracing one another, perhaps not even monogamously but polygamously. For indeed, in this postmodern world of genuine multiculturalism, we may aim for fidelity and the belief that there is only one god, but we can be authentic, certain, and dogmatic only about our own. Once we enter into wider social relationships, once we have left the private world of authenticity, we have stepped into the polygamous bedroom of the state, the social, and the political, where not only is there more than one god, but there are also many lovers and sexualities, each hawking its own path to happiness.

This is the rock of genuine multiculturalism, and it is forever resting on our hearts. Each day we roll it up the hill, only to wake up the next morning to see it is still resting on our heart yet again, at the bottom of the hill.

Mythologically, we are entering our father's house with many rooms, but where even the builder is searching for freedom. This is a liberty that can come about with the help only of an Other, or what the builder considers its absolute opposite. Therefore, the creator of the house is neither authentic nor free, either before or after it constructs the building. However, in place of complete freedom and even happiness, the individual produces something and in the process feels momentary satisfaction, which appeases its desire temporarily.

This is where I employ the notion of the *embrace*, extending Howard Adelman's reading of Hegel on how the archetypical Adam and Eve, representing the first human beings, came into full knowledge and consciousness by coupling with each other as a positive step towards escaping from Eden to form a society of their own making. Until then, Adam believed that he was the only authentic being, that he was pure thought and therefore superior to all other material beings. He believed that this woman, Eve, was merely a projection of him. Indeed, in his naïveté, he thought the soft, sweet voice of reason he heard as he went about his business was God – or what some would interpret as conscience – not realizing who was truly God and divine in such a relationship and from where the socializing conscience comes. That was until Eve, the supposed quintessential Other, or the material body in this drama, took matters into her own hands by engaging in an embrace that gave Adam a new knowledge of and understanding of life.

The prototypical Bad John entered society: the potential Prince Charming did not know his true and "authentic" role in the piece, and someone had to fool him into acting that part. Thinking he was all mind and no body, Adam was, like a Prince Charming, afraid to catch girl cooties or worse – mononucleosis. He ended up with a special knowing: that his life was moving towards its own limit of death and that he needed Eve to produce the life that would keep his genes, and possibly thoughts, alive in a future that would survive him. This is the opposite of the Sleeping Beauty or Snow White story, for, as if in a comedy, the woman should become the tool of patriarchy. Eve was not only a temptress but equally the socializer. She was all woman, and in some ways Adam's superior.

All that the supposedly sovereign Adam turned out to have was a desire to keep living, but he alone had no method to achieve his ambition. Adam at this stage of consciousness was the male equivalent of the Greek Kore, who to grow and make a society has to be enter in a relationship with an other. Kore would become a Persephone, as part of an ongoing series of biological and social changes throughout her life. But in many respects, men tend not to change to the same extent.[18] Adam wanted to become a god, an Aristotelian being that would not die. He wanted to see all human struggling as comedy that did not befit him. Adam was incapable of recognizing that, tragically, he and the species he thought he embodied would fail at some level crucial to life itself. However, comedically, he had to learn that even if he failed physically, he might succeed at another level, by pretending that the fruits of his loins could indeed enable him to live forever.

This embrace shatters the natural reality while creating a make-believe world out of the shards. The result is a reality that is a social construction, very unlike the previous state of nature that, he thought, had all freedom and no limits. It is an escape into what Adelman calls "human bondage" – to be human and social but still not free. It is an unhappy consciousness. At one level, this might appear quite funny, but at another, more rational level it might just be pathetic, an exercise in self-delusion by the original Adam. Eve had to show Adam, the first Bad John, what he required to become a real Sweet Boy of the action – how to be a real Prince Charming. This Eve was the one giving the kiss of life to a socially dead male for the greater good.

In creating a new organism, Adam and Eve transferred all that they were – including their desires to live and to maintain life – to their offspring and to society in general. But they also transferred to their offspring Adam's idealism and desire to transcend the mundane of merely corporal living, for in a short time they were dead, but life still had to continue, as the heroes of this piece lived forever after, making eternal the story's dénouement. The wider society's main task becomes an obligation to preserve, at all costs, life as a desire, even if, ironically, it has to accept the death of its physical founders, Adam and Eve, in order to do so.

As a seeming absurdity, the creation had become more important than the creators. But if the process of creation has not ended, these new creatures would become the next generation of creators, and so the cycle continues infinitely. The love of the creators that would produce new creatures, and even the love between creatures themselves for their own regeneration, must include the kind of active love-making of which Adelman is talking. Adelman's point is similar to the suggestion by Christian theologian and philosopher Paul Tillich that love – no matter how we define it – "is united with sexual attraction or fulfilment ... It is always true."[19] For as Tillich further explains, "There is an element of libido even in the most spiritualized friendship and in the most ascetic mysticism. A saint without libido would cease to be a creature. But there is no such saint."[20] For, after all, this is the love that is not only the desire for but the fulfilment of the need to overcome separation and divisions for a unity.

Adelman explains, "Adam and Eve ate of the Tree of Knowledge of Good and Evil and Adam knew Eve and Eve knew Adam. And self consciousness is thus only assured of itself through sublimating this other, which is presented to self-consciousness as an independent life; Self-consciousness is Desire. Convinced of the nothingness of this other, it definitely affirms this nothingness to be for itself the truth of this other, negates the independent object, and thereby acquires the certainty of its own self, as true certainty, a certainty which it has become aware of in object form."[21]

Now certain of their authenticity through their usage of each other, as Adelman explains, these two beings "become conscious of their mortality, consciousness, which saw the world out there as objectification of self, now must take account of the self as an actor. Man has set out on the path of history; thought operates through that which is acted out by passion. Emotions and thoughts are sundered so that feeling ignores thought and thought distorts feeling."[22] Thought produced tragedy, feelings produced comedy, and together they make up human history.

Yet in our dominant mythology, which stretches back to the ancient Greeks, out of the hug and embrace comes, as Plato suggests, humans' opportunity to create beauty. And for Plato, beauty is a value higher than good: it is love itself. Beauty is nothing to fear, as would be the case with the sublime. This creativeness is for him the essence of love, resulting from an embrace of thought and emotion as one, for it transcends and antedates all other urges and desires. It is the chance for humans, in a sense, to trick themselves, by doing one thing and producing something else – by acting at the level of mere human facing their own mortality and hoping to produce something different and everlasting, something for them that is eternal and divine.

Through the gaze of an all-knowing entity as unifying thought and emotion, such endeavours are the ultimate in the contradictions of comedy. But who among us is ever this unified? And, indeed, has it not been long a tenet of Western thought that to become the philosopher king of pure thought is the height of self–affirmation? Such attainment would require a diremption of thought and passions. Indeed, has not one of the biggest claims of Western thought been the privileging of men as rational and superior beings of thought and of women as inferior beings whose essence is the passions?

Here in this description is an attempt by humans to create something new and at the same time permanent while knowing the seeming impossibility of producing anything out of nothing. But here, as prototypical social beings, they dig into their subconscious looking for the germ that they can make into a new creature, maybe even producing the next mythological God-man that can reconcile all contradictions in human life. More than likely, if history is any predictor, they end up producing only what they can create in their own image – they reproduce mortals like themselves, through procreation. Because, physically, their kin are different from them, they fool themselves into thinking that what they have produced is the very opposite or other than what it is: immortality; for they want to believe they have escaped the limits and boundaries of their own Nature. But this can be only a fantasy. The comedy of believing the child is the next Messiah or God-man lasts only so long before the parents' eyes open to the realization that they simply reproduced their own image. More than that, through socialization they now have to breathe the spirit or desire for life into this individual, make this being a person, while the state makes it a citizen. This is so because the laws of Nature bind them: humans can beget only humans; they cannot really create nothing new but rather can only redistribute what already exists.

Yet human beings know in themselves that they have created something new, for every human being is special, unique, and good – at least, until another set of laws takes over: those of the society, where each person can continue a tragic existence of struggle against the laws or accept that she or he is just human, no different from all others before, and must abide by the laws of society and give up most of individual freedom and creativity. Just as with the progenitors, they push the primordial desire for freedom and creativity back into the subconscious, where it waits until another hug or embrace liberates it in the hope of creating a life that is truly free and authentic. When the truth hits home, in time, the individuals realize that reality has tragically dashed their dreams. What they have produced in the eyes of the immortal is a comedy.

Plato's discourse *Symposium* captures this sense of comedy through a conversation that is a series of eulogies to the god Love. But the words appear, comically, to be doing the very opposite of all that Plato claims, with Socrates in the end turning a light-hearted discussion on Love into a serious search for the truth about human beings as part thought and part passions. And comically, even while the participants at the beginning claim, as pure thought, that they will be drinking wine only for a special occasion and will not become drunk as usual, by the end of the night wine overcomes them all. It is bacchanalian revelry, where everyone is drunk and experiences tragedy passionately as comedy: emotions rule thought.

But before the intoxicant fully takes hold and mental perceptions change, Socrates, in a rather bothersome way, convinces his dinner companions to agree that, ultimately, love is about life and that it cannot continue without the magical moment of creativity. Generally love, while an act of beauty and a good thing, is a longing not for the beautiful per se "but for the conception and generation that the beautiful effects."[23] "And why all this longing for propagation?" Socrates asks, before answering himself: "Because this is the one deathless and eternal element in our mortality. And since we have agreed that the lover longs for the good to be his own forever, it follows that we are bound to long for immortality as well as for the good – which is to say that Love is the longing for immortality." Fear is the opposite, the recognition of our mortality. In Socrates' mind, it is what causes true lovers, as men loving men, to undergo diremption and momentarily engage in heterosexual sex – that is, for procreation and to fulfil social responsibilities, just like paying taxes – and the comedy of ensuring eternal life.

To this end, Socrates, in the moments before his death – a suicide to fulfil his social responsibility – as he prepared himself for the final pleasures of life and for the comedy of an afterlife, he chose to be alone with his true loves: the men. Socrates asked that his wife and children – his social obligations – go away before his final escape into physical death. Similarly, at the end of their lives women in ancient Greek mythology reverted to a kind of Kore state, where, as Hecates, they spend their last days with other females and giving advice to young women on how to navigate the pending changes of life.[24]

And as Socrates, the main character in the *Symposium*, explains,

For here, too, the principle holds good that the mortal does all it can
to put on immortality. And how can it do that except by breeding,
and thus ensuring that there will always be a younger generation to
take the place of the old?

Now, although, we speak of an individual as the being the same so
long as he continues to exist in the same form, and therefore assume
that a man is the same person in his dotage as in his infancy, yet, for
all we call him the same, every bit of him is different, and every day
he is becoming a new man, while the old man is ceasing to exist, as
you can see from his hair, his flesh, his bones, his blood. And all the
rest of his body. And not only his body, for the same thing happens
in his soul. And neither his manners, nor his pleasures, nor his suffer-
ings, nor his fears are the same throughout his life, for some of them
grow, while others disappear.

And the application of this principle to human knowledge is even
more remarkable, for not only do some of the things we know increase, while some of them are lost, so that even in our knowledge
we are not always the same, but the principle applies as well to every
single branch of knowledge. When we say we are studying, we really
mean that our knowledge is ebbing away. We forget, because our
knowledge disappears, and we have to study so as to replace what
we are losing, so that the state of our knowledge may seem, at any
rate, to be the same as it was before.

This is how every mortal creature perpetuates itself. It cannot,
like the divine, be still the same throughout eternity, it can only
leave behind new life to fill the vacancy that is left in its species
by obsolescence.

This is not the disposition of a biblical Adam, nor even of Narcissus.
And this is why every tyrant whose main tool is fear still desires the
people to love him – to shift from mortal to immortal, at least in memory
– and why this story of an everlasting search for a fraternal embrace is
as old as the stories of the Greek tragedians.

But that moment of peace, of recognition of the self in the world, a self
of several parts in a world of infinite parts, is magical.[25] It is the genesis
of both the ambitions and the Prometheus-like quest for freedom from

all human bondage and also of the realization that even freedom itself is bondage, that in the end everything that is human must by nature be finite and passing. As Cedric H. Whitman states, this moment of embracing also is partly comedic, because of its subversive elements in the way the actors – at the mercy of human desires – fly in the face of natural laws. It is a moment of *poneria,* the term from which later emerged "pornography," for images of illicit sex or sexual pleasure, especially outside wedlock or good taste. The Christian religion usually understands *poneria* as the wickedness of using other people for personal gain.[26] But many of us still enjoy the spirit of *poneria* in Milton's *Paradise Lost,* which stars the Devil as much as the prototypical Man, Adam, even if both represent the Other to God.

In this spirit, the final two chapters below offer *poneria,* as play, as the key reconciliation, leading us all, as players in a game whose winners and losers we do not know and whose only rules are what matter in the exercise. "Play clearly represents an order in which the to-and-fro motion of play follows itself," says German philosopher Hans-Georg Gadamer. "It is part of play that the movement is not only without goal or purpose but also without effort. It happens, as it were, by itself. The ease of play – which naturally does not mean that there is any real absence of effort, but refers phenomenologically only to the absence of strain – is experienced subjectively as relaxation. The structure of play absorbs the player into itself, and thus frees him from the burden of taking the initiative, which constitutes the actual strain of existence. This is also seen in the spontaneous tendency to repetition that emerges in the player and in the constant self-renewal of play, which affects the form (e.g., the refrain)."[27] Play is most beautiful and most socially satisfying when there is no individual intentionality – when a specific outcome is desire for the benefit of one over another and the ensuing activity becomes merely a game where only one side can win.

Play is the ideal situation; as observers often comment, we could all become most human or social and yet most natural and individualistic when we are at play, releasing our creativity, improvising with and riffing off one another, learning and advancing together, without trying to dominate one another. Play is where we can have other than lordship-and-bondage relationships, such as when under multiculturalism we aim for a setting where all the participants are lords or all are bondspeople, where all are subjects or all just ordinary Others and even objects of a state. This is where, as Pierre Trudeau envisioned, everyone is a minority, or where everyone is an equal citizen possessing the same fundamental rights and obligations to themselves and the state. There is no need for intentionality to maintain a specific – historical, even – form of social stratification.

American classics scholar Cedric Whitman notes that "*poneria* in modern Greek indicates not wickedness, but the ability to get the advantage of somebody or some situation by virtue of an unscrupulous, but thoroughly enjoyable exercise of craft. Its aim is simple – to come out on top; its methods are devious, and the more intricate, the more delightful ... *Poneria* is wonderfully useful in politics, business, love-making, and family fights. Far from concealing its triumphs, one boasts of them; for though the word may be translated simply 'cleverness,' it also connotes high skill in handling these challenging aspects of life in which the agonistic tendencies of Greek psychology find a field of enterprise."[28]

By incorporating the notion of *poneria* in our analysis, we can imagine a world purely of human desires without boundaries, and utterly free, such as might have been the case when natural law ruled everything, even the creators of the current world. This is, in the biblical story, when the world was void and without form, before the magic words came, "Let there be light." Suppose that the only law that existed then was something that we now call "freedom" and that this freedom had no form; just like the mythological Adam, it was merely desires, and as such was sheer indeterminacy, what I have described elsewhere as ultimate blackness.

This form had no morality, for it never had to choose, never had to decide on what to award hierarchically the label of "good" and what the label of "evil" and then to fill choices in between on a sliding scale. And like Adam and Eve, this freedom needed to express itself through creation, so it created the first workers, and they, also feeling the urge in themselves to create, produced the current world. To the second god or gods fell the tasks of determinacy and making choices between good and evil, between seeing things as white and seeing them as black.

What, then, happened to this natural urge for freedom that was there in the beginning? Did it simply disappear, or did it conform to the new moral code that the secondary act of freedom called into being? And suppose that this original being or nothingness did not agree with what the sons and daughters of the gods have created and labelled good and evil; suppose that it felt inauthentic and alienated in the emergent society; and suppose that this is how people still feel the original desire today. Does it conform, or does it then continue the act of creation by imbuing today's sons and daughters, the progeny of the original sons and daughters, with its pure and unadulterated desires for freedom? Will it deem it necessary to drive them on, tragically, to transcend the boundaries and limits of their society? Does it end up existing in relations of lordship and bondage, still looking to the day when it can truly be free, when it can *become* free and achieve recognition as what it knows itself to be: pure freedom?

In pushing the newer creatures to greater heights and extremes, would this force not be encouraging *poneria* and blasphemy and what today we may call "sedition" and "subversion"? Here we may think of the Greek myth of Prometheus, in which the hero's stealing of fire against the gods' will set humanity on a path of improvement, flourishing in societies of their own making. Similarly, disobedience also plays a role in the Garden of Eden. The common thread suggests that humanity, to develop fully, had to challenge God's order in order, like the divine, to "know good and evil" – not merely the image in the mirror but, à la Frankenstein, the maker of the image as well.

And just as important, what kind of consciousness can this urge for freedom create if those desires, which antedate creation, must now go underground? This is what happens when the freedom does not feel that the creation fufils its pre-construction desires and intentions. In this case, to be authentic and genuine it cannot remain on the surface of creation but must hide, waiting for a moment when, in another act of disobedience or social subversion, it can break loose and re-create creation, this time perfecting social conditions to accord with the original blueprints. If the new construction meets the ideal, then instead of becoming a consciousness with freedoms to fear, it would become one that would love and fully accommodate the desires for freedom. This freedom, as a human expression, creates its own moments of *poneria*.

Let us now assume that every new immigrant arrives out of the original nature of freedom. How can she or he not be a practitioner of *poneria* in the receiving state?

What we are looking at here in *poneria* is a psychological urge that appears to be pathological in any consciousness, producing alienation, fragmentation, and even a death wish. We must challenge life by pushing it to the limit, for it is only risking death, looking into the abyss of non-being and nothing on the other side, that substantiates life. There is a lingering sense of immaturity, as desire cries out in the darkness, reminding us of its presence and of its need to be at the centre of all activities. We end up with a sick consciousness, and this bad health can intensify as life further frustrates and contains the desire, so that, in the darkness of non-fulfilment, it cries out tragically. In this way, its tragedy is like that of the being that realizes it has a seemingly incurable disease but that it must fight to defeat the malignancy. Comedy is more akin to that person recognizing that death most likely will come from the disease but, in an attempt to delay the inevitable and to preserve life, uses medicines to control the continuing deterioration. Tragedy always assumes that better will always come, just as soon as it breaks out from any obstacles in its tracks. Except that when better comes, ironically, the initial condition turns from tragedy into comedy and then back to tragedy.

The issues that I raised above should trouble us throughout our discussion as we look at the tragic experiences of those Canadians who have come to this country because of desires that we may consider primordial. Immigrants personify these desires – they are modern-day Bad Johns when we fear them and Prince Charmings when they seem potential saviours. These desires certainly antedate their arrival and citizenship, perhaps even the creation of their native countries. Suppose immigrants are in the thrall of an ancient and natural desire for freedom that did not find authenticity, happiness, and recognition in the native country, and this dissatisfaction propelled them to look for someplace more authentic. For otherwise, why would rationally free people leave their homelands, where they are among people like themselves and in a culture whose freedoms and values they cherish?

What happens when the new country turns out not to be authentic either, to be nothing more than a site of slavery and compulsory conformity – a site just like the one Eve found herself and Adam living in and that they had to flee in the hopes of becoming fully human and free? What happens to that original desire for freedom? By *nature* can it avoid tragic consequences? Or does it just roll over and pretend it is in a land and time of comedy?

But so far we have looked only at this natural, pre-creation freedom from one side. Suppose we were to try to understand the desire as it may work itself out in the attitudes of old-timers who see themselves as being formed at the only creation that matters to those of primarily naturalized Canadians? These old-timers are Canadians who claim an unbroken lineage back to the time when desire for freedom caused their ancestors to create a site of freedom they called "Canada" out of primordial and aboriginal land. This new land established a new moral code to regulate all creatures or citizens of this country. For example, they all have to accept unquestioningly that all citizens are equal. But suppose that some of them do not agree and as a result still find the new space inauthentic and alienating to the primordial spirit of freedom as they understand it? Particularly, what if they believe that there should be a qualitative difference within the body politic, especially between those with a higher and superior claim and those without, even if the state no longer recognizes such historical claims – namely, members of ancient lineage versus (bad) johnnies-come-lately?

And, in addition, there are those who are aboriginal to the land and who never created Canada or considered themselves its creatures. Yet they must reside near those Others and even come up with an acceptable ethical code to govern their own behaviour. What happens to their initial, primordial desire for freedom, which had expressed itself in them in their aboriginal way? Does it seek to dominate all others? Does it become subservient and colonized? Or does it try to create a new spirit of equality? In this narrative, at what point do aboriginal people become creators in the Canadian sense?

How Canada rationalizes and reconciles these dilemmas is important and helps to tell the story of multiculturalism and the socialization of Bad Johns. For here we have several forms of determination, each with its own notions of what is good and what is freedom, but with no certain sense of a common good and of common or fundamental freedoms. Ultimately, this becomes an issue of how we reconcile natural law, or what remains of it, with the law that society has constructed so as to eliminate inauthenticity and alienation and forge a single notion of the common good and fundamental freedoms. Thus, paradoxically, the society to end tragedy is in itself a site of tragedy.

Universal freedom starts out as conflicted and seems certain to remain so until it can find its authentic form – when it resolves its internal contradictions. To this end, it uses the state, as the embodiment of the desire for life, to find the latest authentic form of itself, of freedom. As we recall, Hegel saw the state as the embodiment of happiness, so that if the state is happy, so are its citizens and residents; if it is unhappy, so are they. We may recall the statement by some wise men that a happy wife means a happy life, a clear recognition of the divine source of happiness and love in a heterosexual marriage.

Therefore, while the embrace allows the self to know the self, it also launches a struggle for mastery, as radical feminists and other theorists of political identity keep telling us. This is a moment not only of a new creation, but of creating something that is an expression more of free will than of mere necessity, as a leaf floats in a stream. It is going back to that moment when there is neither good nor evil, just a creative act that hopes and intends to produce good, happiness, justice, or some other indeterminacy in the momentary joy or bliss.

At the same time, it is a moment of infinity, for it is both the ending of one reality and the beginning of another; and, absurdly, it is neither, but just a continuation of all that has gone before, pointing to all that is to come. Genuine multiculturalism, then, is that positivistic and even utopian belief that the state can manage the sickness in the body politic effectively and that not only will it postpone death indefinitely, but in the interim humans will find a cure to all that ails, frightens, and sickens them. Genuine multiculturalism is a tragic attempt to capture the body and spirit of life and the living and to reconcile them in a form of good, and even healthy, living that can exist only as a comedy. It is a search for a different body as an expression of life and immortality – in effect rejecting what is the old and known for the new that is also unknown and untried.

In multicultural Canada, this approach suggests that history rests with the new and not with those citizens of ancient lineage, who have already proven to the desires in the form of the state that they are not immortal. There is nothing *new* about these old forms. The immigrants have yet to prove themselves. They start off with the promise of being new. The state must accept them as good and wholesome, and as preferable to the old and known. This is until, just as Adam and Eve realized when they reproduced mere copies of themselves, the immigrants themselves lose their status and prove that they are mortal too.

But current immigration theory argues that this newness does not wear off until at least the third generation, when many descendants consider themselves unhyphenated Canadians – now natural to the lands. They become equal to the old-timers, joining them as they prove inadequate to the state for its primary purposes. Then they are old – no longer new. Genuine multiculturalism continually makes the old and ancient new or knocks the shine off the new instantly, making it of the same vintage as the old.

Just as important, the pragmatism of multiculturalism in Canada leaves us hoping for an ideal one state or one world for social inhabitation – where we do not have to inauthentically separate our private and public lives and where we can be fully human at all times. This way we would not have to deal with the split, alienated beings that we are in modern society. In the desired one world, we are at times mere liberal abstractions, particularly when invoking our minority rights and freedoms. This is also the case when we display more of our humanity, of the culture that makes us feel complete when we are at home, in our churches, mosques, or synagogues, when our bodies are merely one of many in a culture.

Instead, we often discover ourselves in two rival states: one that is secret and fully tragic and authentic – comedic for show and pretending to collective ethical precepts – and another, secret one in which the battles for recognition, authenticity, and indeed individual happiness still rage. The latter is where the true tragedy and comedy link dialectically, where a struggle for lordship and bondage is under way every day. This is where the "authentic" individuals believe they can extend the authenticity of the private sphere into the public and where, tragically, they face challenges at every turn, where their authenticity and happiness are constantly under attack. Meanwhile, in the more "public" world, inauthenticity and unhappiness already reign, and people undertake any embrace to satisfy the carnal more than to demonstrate the authenticity and happiness that accompany an enduring state of love.

Finally, in its practical, pragmatic, and *realpolitik* sense, multiculturalism is a covenant of lordship and bondage: the struggle to see life as either tragedy or comedy and also to see if there can be any genuine justice in a society. This is an important point. Another of the frustrations of multiculturalism in current practice is that people often see it as a social contract – one that makes everybody a subject and does everything possible to protect and preserve their subjectivity.

As John Rawls writes in *A Theory of Justice* and even according to Pierre Trudeau, the social contract tries to retain the subjectivity of reason and rationality that emanated from the European Enlightenment as the dominant view in modernity.[29] Multiculturalism seeks to diffuse that subjectivity into socialization, love of fellow humans, and faith that even in weakened and most human conditions, others would love the individual.[30] Seeing multiculturalism as strictly a social contract – particularly trying to turn its actors into abstract liberal props – undermines most of the dynamics that are still prevalent in a world where actors struggle to make their private world dominant in the public and where they have not yet given up the fight for authenticity. Canadian multiculturalism is the covenant story of life, a tragedy that becomes a comedy through faith in justice – justice that may at times be asleep, may not be colour blind, and is always in the transcendent.

If we see multiculturalism as a social contract, do we look at it as a master–slave *dialectic* or as a *relationship* of lord and bondsman / woman? I use the terms deliberately, even though both connections are relationships and dialectical. However, "dialectic" suggests very obvious tensions and negations, and even impermanence. It suits perfectly a story of actors choosing and wanting to improvise, even with a script, and perhaps amending the script and outshining nominal stars. The improvisation that is life itself comes out of the subconscious, which yearns for freedom and sustains the conflict between conscious and subconscious that creates the creativity of the imagination trying to produce a new reality. This script, then, results from the ill health and pathologies of the nation-state as much as it aspires to engender a wholesome and healthy unity that captures all the various elements of life.

As for "relationship," I am clutching at the notion of an inherent misrecognition or false consciousness at play between two or more parties, none of whom knows enough to recognize the *authenticity* of the others and earn their recognition. The term focuses on the dialectic's speculative moment of temporary peace and seeming harmony, when a subject meets its match and realizes its finite limits. In a fraternal embrace, at least for the time being, the subject decides that life is a comedy, so that it can still hope for some justice in the relationship and decides that it is not a tragedy, where the evils of existence are nature's guarantees of injustice and death. Indeed, we spend our daily lives performing the dialectic of freedom, an infinity that can produce the despondency and despair of tragedy or the faith and hope that is comedy.

Every new moment holds tragic and comedic possibilities: which ones we see, recognize, or choose depends on whether we have faith or not, or on how pessimistic and despondent we are. Individuals have the power and freedom of transformation: of making the next moment tragic or comedic. For if we do not have faith, all moments are, indeed, completely tragic. Any such faith must come from within us, planted by society sometime in our history and expressing itself in our hope that our compatriots will react to love, protect, and preserve us as we innately believe they are capable of doing and willing to do.

In a real sense, we have here two fundamentally different *attitudes* to socialization and society formation: on one side, a tragic, Hobbesian vision, a perennial state of nature that we can see today in the rampant capitalist ethic of competing rational egos and unfettered individualism, and on the other, a kinder, gentler form of socialization presuming a need for shared risk, a desire that emanates from and recognizes the inherent weakness, fallibility, and finitude of humanity and individuals' need to control their egos and even submit them to the majority's wishes and well-being.

My two examples appear in the choices and ways of life that are Canada and the United States. I see a Canada that, in its humility and its acquiescing way, strives to offer, but cannot guarantee, justice to all its citizens and to the world. This is a Canada that embodies what I call the hope and promise of life that is genuine multiculturalism. The opposite, American case currently offers a tragic figure that in its own righteousness and absolute truth and knowledge seems willing to impose its subjective view on many other people, whether they be fellow citizens or the rest of the world, or is willing to die in an attempt to make the world conform. Both countries are tragedies, even from their own selfish perspectives. Both are also comedies if we shift the emphasis.

In our Western civilization, we have learned to live with tragedies big and small in the hope of making some progress towards a better life and world. We hope we have learned from them by adding to our storehouses of knowledge of what is good and what is evil. Generally, we hope that both tragedy and comedy teach us about living – our lives and those that we share with other people in a world where we struggle to recognize and know the distinction between tragedy and comedy, between the personal and the collective, between what makes us cry and what makes us laugh until we cry, and how we can have choice and control over the forces for good and evil within our lives.

Two lessons on tragedy stand out: first, it helps us to understand why there is so much unhappiness in our lives and that, ironically, the trouble is often of our making; second, that it might appear trivial yet ultimately be more significant in a greater scheme of things. Indeed, there is a greater good. Most things in life connect to other things. And tragedy teaches us that any meaningful change must happen not in the Other, but in *us*. We have to become new, as if we are starting out all over, without a history and without the state knowing what we can achieve and what our limits are. Such a change from what has become *us* over the years, and from what we are comfortable with and feel safe about, can be a real tragedy, especially if we believe we are already perfect and if our material conditions fool us into believing we have escaped the conditions and concerns of most other human beings. It is just as Socrates explained in the section I quoted above: realizing that the old men or women we have become have gone through many changes, each in its own moment producing something new and different, but all of them later becoming old

– and even recognizing them as unchangeable. But even the elderly undergo change – none greater than physical death and the disappearance of the body itself.

Each change is a reach for comedy that degenerates back into tragedy, the same type of tragedy that is always lurking and appears never to have changed during the process. For the comedy of happiness is usually unintentional and fleeting. We may hope that this would not happen to us, for, at least in Canada, official multiculturalism has also told us that we are perfectly imperfect, and such wisdom can be a promise to a fool or an indictment of our personal failures. Let us now look at when the past haunts the present; when shades of the old overpower the new; when fear dominates in the present and gestures to the future; when those individuals who emerge in one generation become true creators or even veritable Prince Charmings.

7

The Legacy of the US Civil War

Then in violent, frustration, he cries out to God or just no one
Is there a point to this madness and all that he was ...
Is just a tragedy.[1]

The Used

A spectre, a pending destiny, or even fate haunts Canada, and it is all so American: the spectre of the US Civil War, which settled by force issues of sovereignty at the state and individual levels seemingly once and for all. If sovereignty rested effectively in the state, then it was at the universal or federal level as a special type of organism that is almost uniquely that of the Americas; and if this sovereignty belonged to the people, then the very concept of "the people" had changed radically in the Americas – from meaning "European and white" to including all other groups, including Africans and other dispossessed, the truly "wretched of the earth," whom many settlers and citizens did not even consider fully human.

The US Civil War proved irrevocably that no state organism in the Americas could ever be *European* and *white*. It took Canada until the second half of the twentieth century to come fully to terms with these lessons. When it did, Canada came into full consciousness with the proverbial musket pointing at its head, when the country faced a struggle over state or provincial and federal rights and ultimately a realization that all brands of humanity, and definitely not Europeans only, were *the people* and sovereign in Canada, with the crown as their ultimate representation. However, the people did not all have equal privileges: the Europeans and assimilated English or French were the lords of this piece. The bondsmen had non-assimilable ethnic and cultural identities.

Canada's decision to become officially multicultural occurred during cataclysmic times for it and its southern neighbour. Both countries were overhauling the structures they had developed since colonization and particularly since the American War of Independence, which began in 1776. The old systems intended both nation-states to be countries for white men, modeled just as Machiavelli had recommended. But the 1960s were pivotal. The civil rights movement threw into doubt all those plans. This was when American blacks – called "negroes" if only because they had no real citizenship of any specific country but rather were identified purely by a racio-ethnicity – demanded full membership in the nation-state and recognition as African Americans. The result once again tested the state's sovereignty, and, just short of another physical civil war, the US experience showed that sovereignty had to abide at the universal or national level, at that highest social or human level. To arrive at this point, while the entire world looked on again, US citizens endured the wrestling for power between the Union and the states, with the military sometimes staring down in the form of various national guards over universal civil rights. More and more, state rights had to give way to universal civil rights over such issues as educational desegregation, voting rights, and the integration of all groups into American institutions. These demands found expression on both sides of the US–Canadian border.

Often the US government reserved the right to step in and even override state jurisdiction in cases where it felt that the state was not protecting individual human rights. The national authority was redefining who is an American and what the ethical relations governing all citizens should be. In so doing, it was redefining the limits of state powers and sovereignty.

At the same time, in Canada, the nation-state was in doubt as Anglo-Canada and Franco-Canada stared each other down, bringing into doubt whether the entity we call "Canada" had a future. Many observers saw a real possibility that Canada might fracture into two nation-states, one English and the other French, perhaps both with very weak national authorities. The first fracturing might lead to future diminution, with the English-speaking part eventually becoming part of a wider United States, as we can see in the advocacy of various pro-American lobby groups on either side of border. For this to happen would be the realization of some Canadians' fear of their neighbours who believed in a manifest destiny: at the most sanguine, American politician James G. Blaine (1830–1893), briefly secretary of state in 1881, saw Canada as like a ripe apple ready to fall into the embrace of the United States, which did not even have to shake the tree or even climb it – truly a comedy for the Americans, but equally a tragedy for Canadians.

Such Canadian fears – particularly that the Union armies victorious in the Civil War would simply keep marching northward – helped inspire Confederation in 1867. The anxiety resulted perhaps in part from the open support that some Canadians had given to the Southern cause during the Civil War, even to the point where the Confederacy had considered Montreal as a possible site of government, at times on a par with Richmond, Virginia.[2] The fear acted itself out through a classical lordship-and-bondsman relationship, where the way of life – not the basic animal desires for an individual life but the desires for a specific quality of life that "the people" held – would be at stake.

In the aftermath of the American conflict, Canadians did what was necessary in their scheme of things to maintain a way of life that was as similar as possible to what existed for them. Ironically, this meant their rejecting the past in terms of what they conceived of as the ultimate in human desires and dreams and clinging instead to a new human desire, which animalistic survival techniques kept in check. This is the pragmatism that is multiculturalism as Canada officially designated it in the 1970s, where ideals of justice and freedom exist but reconcile the soul and spirit of the people with the demographic reality of the diversity that is actually the Canadian people. This was the only way Canadians could imagine themselves continuing as a liberal democracy.

Another meaningful development in both countries during the civil rights movement was a sea change in immigration policies – a reimagining of who would become citizens. The US Congress passed a new Immigration and Nationality Act in 1965 to end a very restrictive policy. The racist Immigration Act of 1924 had effectively limited immigration to countries with sizeable US expatriate communities according to the 1890 census – namely, European. The act explicitly excluded Asians. The openly racist eugenicist Madison Grant had argued in a popular book, *The Passing of a Great Race* (1916), that open immigration was destroying his country or, rather, the dream of and desire for a perfect America. Grant and other people claimed that northern Europeans, or Nordic people, were the superior peoples of the world. Canada in 1919 had already prohibited the immigration of members of "any nationality or race deemed unsuitable" to the ideal racial and ethnic composition of the country.

The 1965 US immigration law sought to balance the annual intake of immigrants from the Eastern and Western hemispheres. Two years later, Canada stopped limiting immigration to mainly Europeans or those of European descent living in the Americas. It introduced a universal points system that evaluated each applicant, thereby attempting to remove the biases towards the states that it had favoured.

These developments happened partly in response to the new spirit abroad throughout the Americas that inspired the civil rights movement. But as good as it was at creating new conditions and creatures, the movement was only the child of the earlier US Civil War and before that of the Haitian Revolution.

The legacy of the great American struggle is real in Canada. It speaks to the question of whether there can be two sovereigns in one state. Either the sovereignty of the federal and highest socially constructed state will be the victor, as with the North's victory over the South or, alternatively, state sovereignty will come out on top, as would have been the case had the South won. This was the dilemma in which the United States found itself with the Dred Scott legal decision of 1857, a ruling for states' rights that would eventually succumb to the Civil War and the thirteenth amendment to the constitution. Scott was a slave who went to court to contest the legality of his position as a slave in Missouri and the United States. The federal government, in 1820, had accepted the Missouri Compromise, which prohibited slavery above the parallel 36°30' north. The US Supreme Court upheld state sovereignty over that of the wider federation. First, it ruled that blacks were not citizens, whether they were free or slaves. Second, it decided that Scott was not a citizen of Missouri and, in a move that tied citizenship to the state rather than to the nation, that a single state could not make a black "a citizen of the United States, and inure him with the full rights of citizenship in every other State without their consent." Third, it ruled that citizens had constitutional property rights and that, as a slave, Scott was property; the right of ownership stemmed from state authority. Therefore, Scott had no case: only citizens, and not property, could come before the courts.

So far to date, we have seen the ebb and flow in Quebec of one sovereign (Ottawa) struggling with another (Quebec City), with no clear resolution. One of them may well have to die for there to be the emergence of a true, singular conscience. The US North was able to use an issue of civil and human rights to impose its sovereignty throughout the states in the unity. The human rights issue in this case was slavery – in modern language, it concerned the accommodation of Africans in a new country. By seeking to hold some Canadian citizens and Quebec residents in "accommodation," Quebec is living out the fantasy of some of the Confederate South, living a kind of counterfactual American history where the bad guys of state sovereignty and rights would have triumphed over the good guys of federal sovereignty and nationalism.

The struggle over sovereignty between Quebec and Canada is a continuation of the lord and bondspeople's struggle for recognition that the US Civil War and civil rights movement seemed to have finally settled. Quebec is not willing to accept the same fate as the American states. Creatively, Canada and Quebec have been finding ways, in the spirit of pluralism, not to settle the issue of sovereignty according to the script developed for the Americas. Both sides are still searching for something that is genuinely new and that would allow all parties to live happily ever after. That they have not yet found such an ending means that they remain unhappy consciousnesses living recognizably tragic lives. They still await the certain death that their belief promises will allow them, like a Sleeping Beauty, after receiving the kiss to rise up pure and desirable into a life of endless comedy.

What remains questionable for Canadians is whether human rights will also be the issue for the next major development in the struggle between the federal and provincial sovereigns in Canada. If so, the flashpoint might be the civil rights of how to accommodate the supposed Others in society, whether they should have full liberal-democratic freedoms throughout Canada or whether, as was the argument in the American South, rights were and are fully for special privileged groups and merely accommodate others – indeed, objectify them – almost as if they are property to position and place at the pleasure of higher subjects. This argument, that civil or human rights could become the spark of life, might not be far-fetched; indeed, it might express that irony in human actions that is at the heart of tragedy.

Yet it is hard for Canadians to ignore the reality that produced their southern neighbour and the implications that such a history have for them. When the fires of Quebec separation seemed to be raging at their hottest in 1998, the Supreme Court of Canada, as the final institutional arbiter of self-determination, asked two eminent lawyers for their opinions as to whether the province had a unilateral right of secession. Their responses were that "there may be developments in the principle of self-determination according to which not only colonialism but flagrant violations of human rights or undemocratic regimes could lead to a right of unilateral secession."[3]

The lawyers and the court agreed that these conditions did not exist in Quebec. Suppose accommodations in Quebec made the province undemocratic, amounted to flagrant abuse of human rights, or made some citizens feel they were in colonial bondage. Would the rest of Canada, and the world in general, have a right to intervene unilaterally? The Supreme Court seemed to be anticipating such a development: "Since Confederation, the people of the provinces and territories have created close ties of interdependence (economic, social, political and cultural) based on shared values that include federalism, democracy, constitutionalism and the rule of law, and respect for minorities. A democratic decision of Quebecers in favour of secession would put those relationships at risk. The Constitution vouchsafes order and stability, and, accordingly, secession of a province 'under the Constitution' could not be achieved unilaterally, that is, without principled negotiation with other participants in Confederation within the existing constitutional framework."[4]

In this ruling, the court invoked an earlier decision that allowed the federal government and the rest of Canada to impose their way on Quebec vis-à-vis patriation of the constitution in 1982: "It did, however, have the important effect that, despite the refusal of the government of Quebec to join in its adoption, Quebec has become bound to the terms of a Constitution that is different from that which prevailed previously, particularly as regards provisions governing its amendment, and the *Canadian Charter of Rights and Freedoms*." While the court was arguing for negotiation of differences in Canada, what should happen if negotiations fail on "Canada's commitment to the protection of its minority, aboriginal, equality, legal and language rights, and fundamental freedoms as set out in the *Canadian Charter of Rights and Freedoms*"?[5]

Something else in the court's thinking is reminiscent of the US precedent. It restates its claim that federalism is "the dominant principle of Canadian constitutional law."[6] With the enactment of the Charter, that proposition may have less force than it once did, but there can be little doubt that the principle of federalism remains a central organizational theme of the constitution. Less obvious, perhaps, but certainly of equal importance, federalism is a political and legal response to underlying social and political realities. "The principle of federalism recognizes the diversity of the component parts of Confederation, and the autonomy of provincial governments to develop their societies within their respective spheres of jurisdiction. The federal structure of our country also facilitates democratic participation by distributing power to the government thought to be most suited to achieving the particular societal objective having regard to this diversity."[7]

Once again, the precedent might be the American Civil War. If the Canadian civil war is not physical, it certainly is spiritual and intellectual, first over what people should imagine as Canada and then over how to render that imagination real or actual. Again, the US federal government did not always have to use force against the states to get its way. Often, the mere threat of the federal authority did the trick – that and an appeal to people's moral goodness.

It is possible to make a reasonable argument that much of Quebec's angst over the accommodation of certain non-French groups is a reminder of what might have transpired in the United States if the South had won its war of secession. It might also tell us what might have occurred had distinct black states emerged in the South, as some black nationalists advocated. Like Quebec, the South or a separate black homeland might have sought to maintain and preserve a specific society for the exclusive benefit of a specific ethnic group. That group would have had a superior claim, and all other groups would have had to adjust their expectations and freedoms accordingly. But, undoubtedly, the Southern society or the black homeland would have faced pressure as it interacted with other societies, both in the form of trade and in the presence of non-citizens as residents. What if non-citizens had pushed for full freedoms and for full recognition as citizens? Undoubtedly the state would have denied their claims or forced them to curb their ambitions and to accept accommodations – otherwise the very reason for Southern independence or for establishing a state only for blacks might have seemed meaningless. The quest for freedom would constantly attack the structure of the state, forcing it to give in to the forces of liberty for greater and greater groups, or reducing it to a police state and a tyranny even for those it aimed to privilege. Indeed, recent history tells us that this would be true, for it is the story of what happened in South Africa under apartheid.

In Quebec, those people pushing for accommodations of Others might very well find themselves like actors unsure whether they are Bad Johns or Prince Charmings. They might look back to the thinking of similar characters in Margaret Mitchell's epic, Pulitzer Prize–winning novel *Gone with the Wind* (1936), her sarcastic paean to Southern US life and the great loss that was the Civil War. Ashley Wilkes appeared to be a Prince Charming, loved by the Southern belles, going to war for the great Cause of "King Cotton, Slavery and States' Rights." Ironically, on the battlefield he finds himself thinking traitorous thoughts. "These summer nights I lie awake, long after the camp is asleep," he confesses in a letter to his wife, Melanie, "and I look up at the stars and, over and over, I wonder, 'Why are you here, Ashley Wilkes? What are you fighting for?"[8] And answering these questions, he transforms into a Bad John: he realizes that there was no real good reason to fight this war and that in the final analysis he was fighting for specific patriotic or nationalist symbols. The real enemy was not the Yankee soldiers, but time and change. "Perhaps that is what is called patriotism, love of home and country. But, Melanie, it goes deeper than that ... These things ... are but the symbols of the thing for which I risk life, symbols of the kind of life I love. For I am fighting for the old days, the old ways I love so much but which, I fear, are now gone forever, no matter how the die may fall. For, win or lose, we lose just the same. If we win this war and have the Cotton Kingdom of our dreams, we still have lost, for we will become a different people and the old quiet ways will go ... I lie and look at the boys sleeping near me and I wonder ... if they know they are fighting for a Cause that was lost the minute the first shot was fired, for our Cause is really our own way of life and that is already gone."[9]

Life is change, and killing off one aspect of change or the harbingers of change does not stop universal change or life itself. This is because the killer is as much a part of life as the victim, and removing or annihilating the other simply affects life in its entirety or universal, dirempting the killer and cutting him off from life itself. This leads to feelings of internal reproof, of shame and guilt, all part of what is an unhappy consciousness that divides not from others but within itself. These are the roots of lamentation. The individual is suffering a loss in the form of a spiritual fall – a fall from the ideal of having a pure heart, from sharing fully and completely the spirit of the time, from living in a world of solidarity and recognition that we call "love" to individuality, fears, and feeling out of keeping with the general mood of the times.

For in acting against change, the individual is acting against life itself – the part acting against the whole – and for this reason cuts itself off from the whole, or what we call the "Godhead" – the state or the spirit of the times. The individual has created an enemy for itself within the universal of life, an Other to itself within the overall framework of a proposed united life. This is so because, as Hegel attests, life itself is "immortal, and, if slain, it appears as its terrifying ghost which vindicates every branch of life and let loose its Eumenides [fates]. The illusion of trespass, its belief that it destroys the other's life and thinks itself enlarged thereby, is dissipated by the fact that the disembodied spirit of the injured life comes on the scene against the trespass, just as Banquo who came as a friend to Macbeth was not blotted out when he was murdered but immediately thereafter took his seat, not as a guest at the feast, but as an evil spirit."[10] Change is not stoppable; it simply returns in a different form – in this case, as something alien and opposing the unchanging.

This is tragedy, as Hegel suggests. The accommodationists would face the same challenge if they attained their cotton kingdom of a French-only Quebec. Likewise, they would change from Prince Charmings to Bad Johns, at least in the eyes of the international community and according to their own consciences.

It is for these reasons that the current debate in Canada is about the integration into the nation-state of visible minorities, usually with a somatic base in skin colour and cultural standard of non-European perspectives. Canada has successfully integrated all the Europeans into an assimilated whiteness and privileges them as lords of the land. Still there is always the spectre of the US Civil War, and later the civil rights struggles of the 1960s, as the only mechanism – as the prototype of the Americas – to fully decide sovereignty in what started as a settler society. These models produce an organism that is American in the widest sense, deciding sovereignty and *the people* in favour of the universal in terms of both state powers and the composition of the people that exercise this sovereignty. Ottawa's imposition of the War Measures Act in 1970 in Quebec for an insurrection, whether it perceived one or merely imagined it, sending federal troops into the streets and allowing the federal government to rule by decree, reminds me of the American struggles between the states and the Union almost a century earlier. Indeed, Abraham Lincoln effectively launched the civil war by similarly claiming an insurrection at work. In his Proclamation Suspending the Writ of Habeas Corpus of 1862 in response to the start of the Civil War, he wrote, "it has become necessary to call into service not only volunteers but also portions of the militia of the States by draft in order to suppress the insurrection existing in the United States, and disloyal persons are not adequately restrained by the ordinary processes of law from hindering this measure and from giving aid and comfort in various ways to the insurrection."[11]

Furthermore, even the discussion on accommodation within multiculturalism is an eerie reminder of the post–Civil War debate in the South. The Canadian debate, which began most prominently in Quebec but resonates in the rest of Canada, even uses the same term: "accommodation." This term reminds me of the accommodationist "Atlanta Compromise" of the black activist Booker T. Washington on how to begin integrating former slaves into the American mainstream. In 1895 he told a predominantly white audience at the Cotton States and International Exposition in Atlanta:

> Cast it down in agriculture, mechanics, in commerce, in domestic service, and in the professions. And in this connection it is well to bear in mind that whatever other sins the South may be called to bear, when it comes to business, pure and simple, it is in the South that the Negro is given a man's chance in the commercial world, and in nothing is this Exposition more eloquent than in emphasizing this chance. Our greatest danger is that in the great leap from slavery to freedom we may overlook the fact that the masses of us are to live by the productions of our hands, and fail to keep in mind that we shall prosper in proportion as we learn to dignify and glorify common labour, and put brains and skill into the common occupations of life; shall prosper in proportion as we learn to draw the line between the superficial and the substantial, the ornamental gewgaws of life and the useful. No race can prosper till it learns that there is as much dignity in tilling a field as in writing a poem. It is at the bottom of life we must begin, and not at the top. Nor should we permit our grievances to overshadow our opportunities.
>
> To those of the white race who look to the incoming of those of foreign birth and strange tongue and habits for the prosperity of the South, were I permitted I would repeat what I say to my own race, "Cast down your bucket where you are." Cast it down among the eight millions of Negroes whose habits you know, whose fidelity and love you have tested in days when to have proved treacherous meant the ruin of your firesides. Cast down your bucket among these people who have, without strikes and labour wars, tilled your fields, cleared your forests, built your railroads and cities, and brought forth treasures from the bowels of the earth, and helped make possible this magnificent representation of the progress of the South. Casting down your bucket among my people, helping and encouraging them as you are doing on these grounds, and to education of head, hand, and heart, you will find that they will buy your surplus land, make blossom the waste places in your fields, and run your factories. While doing this, you can be sure in the future, as in the past, that you and your families will be surrounded by the most patient, faithful, law-abiding, and unresentful people that the world has seen. As we have proved our loyalty to you in the past, in nursing your children, watching by the sick-bed of your mothers and fathers, and

often following them with tear-dimmed eyes to their graves, so in the future, in our humble way, we shall stand by you with a devotion that no foreigner can approach, ready to lay down our lives, if need be, in defense of yours, interlacing our industrial, commercial, civil, and religious life with yours in a way that shall make the interests of both races one. In all things that are purely social we can be as separate as the fingers, yet one as the hand in all things essential to mutual progress.

Washington preferred marginal economic progress through self-sufficiency for blacks rather than full citizenship rights, such as equality. Accommodation offers no advance in the pursuit of human desires for those in bondage but rather ensures enslavement at the basic level of survival and menial production for the benefit of others. Washington had some African-American supporters and was very popular among whites, who saw him as placing a damper on the aspirations of the ex-slaves and helping to prevent any meaningful threat to the status quo.

W.E.B. Du Bois emerged after Washington's death as the period's most effective African-American leader. In his seminal work *The Souls of Black Folk*, he totally rejects such a stance: "So far as Mr. Washington apologizes for injustice, North or South, does not rightly value the privilege and duty of voting, belittles the emasculating effects of caste distinctions, and opposes the higher training and ambition of our brighter minds – so far as he, the South, or the Nation, does this – we must unceasingly and firmly oppose them. By every civilized and peaceful method we must strive for the right which the world accords to men, clinging unwaveringly to those great words which the sons of the Fathers would fain forget: 'We hold these truths to be self-evident: That all men are created equal; that they are endowed by their Creator with certain unalienable rights; that among these are life, liberty, and the pursuit of happiness.'"

Still, the legacy of the American Civil War continues to influence both the US and Canadian federations with the ideology of racialization, of determining which groups and immigrants are white and which are black. As American sociologists Michael Omi and Howard Winant note in *Racial Formation in the United States*, the difference between who could become white and who remained black solidified following the Civil War. The racial category of "black" had evolved with the strengthening of slavery's hold on American society. It would help explain the "melting pot" theory, which saw immigrants of many ethnic groups becoming a common American: "By the end of the seventeenth century, Africans whose specific identity were Ibo, Yoruba, Fulani, etc., were rendered 'black' by an ideology of exploitation based on racial logic – the establishment and maintenance of a 'color line.'"[12] Initially, *white* meant "Christian," then "English" and "free." During the nineteenth century, the meaning continued to change to categorize other non–Anglo-Saxon groups and immigrants who, while free in a land of slavery, might not be Christian or English. "In the nineteenth century," the authors state, "political and ideological struggles emerged over the classification of Southern Europeans, the Irish and Jews, among other 'non-white' categories."[13] This resulted in classification of all Europeans as "white" – "authentically" American.

According to Omi and Winant, "By stopping short of racializing immigrants from Europe after the Civil War, and by subsequently allowing their assimilation, the American racial order was reconsolidated in the wake of the tremendous challenge placed before it by the abolition of racial slavery. With the end of Reconstruction in 1877, an effective program for limiting the emergent class struggles of the late nineteenth century was forged: the definition of the working class in racial terms – as 'white.' This was not accomplished by any legislative decree or capitalist maneuvering to divide the working class, but rather by the white workers themselves. Many of them were recent immigrants, who organized on racial lines as much as on traditionally defined class lines."[14] This kind of social construction became the norm in North America and, as I have argued elsewhere, helps explain official multiculturalism in Canada.[15]

We can see the acceptance of this approach to nation building and social integration in various studies that show Canada as a vertical mosaic, with its hierarchy of whites and whiteness at the top and black and blackness at the bottom.[16] And until official multiculturalism became a national policy, the ideals and norms of Anglo-conformity and Franco-conformity shaped nation building. In effect, they were twin components of the same ideals of whiteness – *biculturalism* – that were, according to Omi and Winant, a legacy of the US Civil War. Some Canadian intellectuals appear ready to accept that the approaches of the two countries were similar. "Perhaps immigrant groups did not 'melt' as much in Canada as in the United States," says Canadian historian Howard Palmer, "but this is not because Anglo-Canadians were more anxious to encourage the cultural survival of ethnic minorities. There has been a long history of racism and discrimination against ethnic minorities in English-speaking Canada, along with strong pressures for conformity to 'WASP' ways ... Anglo-Canadians have been no worse, and perhaps slightly better in their treatment of immigrant minorities than other major immigrant receiving countries such as the United States or Australia."[17]

The policy of multiculturalism of 1971 never offered to reduce doubt about the fragility of the Canadian state or to impose any other dogma than multiculturalism itself as an ideology or theodicy. In its pragmatism of trying to save the nation-state's at any cost, it does not offer absolute answers. It depends on a healthy scepticism that reminds us that all of us, since we are human, are creatures of a history that has culminated in a consciousness relevant only to today, only to this particular moment. To this end, the policy reminds us that history has taught us that many of the things we now call "good" were previously "bad" or "evil." Canada did not prefer many of today's citizens, when they were immigrants.

The society misrecognized many Sweet Boys as Bad Johns and positioned them as objects of fear, so what we call "evil" today might not be "good" tomorrow or the day after, when we have further evolved. In the larger scheme of things, only the state will know with time what is truly good and evil, which citizens are the true Prince Charmings and which the Bad Johns. Individuals will not be around long enough to really *know* much that time in its infinity will eventually reveal.

Therefore, it is healthy to be sceptical. For the people whom society is accommodating today might be the ones doing the accommodating tomorrow, just as some of the groups now clamouring to accommodate others were themselves on the receiving end a generation or two earlier. Indeed, life seems always to follow some rule of divine irony, so that it might not be wise to wish for others what you would not wish for yourself. To this end, in the hopes that we will influence the development of the universal consciousness and our individual selves within it, multiculturalism expects us not to abandon the banner of Enlightenment to be independent and autonomous and to knowingly run the risk of becoming a tragic hero.

Rather, multiculturalism acknowledges some very firm and serious brute facts of life: that there is always fragmentation and disunity and even a tendency in Canada to produce disunity. Northrop Frye equated this longing with a death wish or with living in the shadow of death.[18] Indeed, multiculturalism argues that this tragic vein is a holdover from the Enlightenment period and is a consequence of how we have tried over the ages to construct societies according to the contradictory ideals earlier of Enlightenment and now of modernity.

In this respect, then, multiculturalism is about sovereignty, especially in a society where many individuals and/or groups claim to be sovereign. It is about coexisting and trying to get along, especially in a situation where every person or group thinks itself as privileged, superior, and having exalted claims to ownership of the place and its culture. Multiculturalism says that if everyone cannot be a sovereign at the same time, at least they can all be subjects, without losing face or feeling inferior. In an act of *poneria*, we can all build a golden calf of our own to replace what we all may consider to be our true and authentic sovereign.

Since this idol is not *real* and does not have a specific form, colour, religion, or any other mark of difference, it can be something that every individual and group can find acceptable and non-threatening. It is rational. This is the sovereignty of law. For we want to be free and secure at the same time, and tragedy, as Bernard Williams tells us, builds on changes and contradictions, particularly when the pillars of our society and social order come under attack, especially by outsiders.[19] In such a case, how can we have freedom that is not slavery for others, and how can we have security without demanding and enforcing social conformity, which is, in enlightenment terms, the anathema of freedom? And so the circle that is Western civilization or society continues, tragically, unbroken. Multiculturalism is only the most recent tragic face of Western civilization, the latest in a trunk full of masks that represent every form of official plurality and diversity in the history of the West. And that, in itself, is very ironic.

COMEDY: THE BEGINNING OF A NEW HISTORY
OF THE LOVED

The Canadian state intended official multiculturalism simply to make the country more human, to begin to reduce any people's sense that they are yet absolute, super, or even godly, and in the process to offer a way of attempting to perfect themselves. This, it hoped, was achievable, as it argued that, as a society, it is better that everyone tries to get along together rather than endlessly crack one another's heads. But even when Canadians were not beating each other over the head (i.e., most of the time), not imposing their ways and moralities on one another, not frog marching others into conformity, accommodation, and assimilation, or cultural genocide – even then, multiculturalism did not promise happiness or freedom from tensions, anger, and disappointments.

Multiculturalism is, indeed, about humility and even humiliation and self-abnegation – not the kind of thing we associate with superheroes or people any divine power choosing to fulfil some destiny. Rather, it places us all as the children of fate, of contingencies that make us the way we are but that, through some stroke of luck, magic, or bad fortune, could have made us better or even worse. It is the recognition of the sigh of resignation that, indeed, it could have been worse. However, at the same time it embodies the hope that, since there never was any real plan, life could have been, and still can be, better for us as human beings. Without any guarantees, let us manipulate the fates as much as we can to make life better; let us still hope for a society where everyone can flourish.

As children of the Enlightenment, multicultural citizens should accept that their citizenship is a compromise between the good and evil of our existences and try, piece by piece, to convert more of the evil in society into good. It is about what the French philosopher Michel Foucault called the "politics of power," where we accept that the very things that, in one context, can provide our freedom might in a different one enslave us.[20] For while anthropologically and philosophically as human beings we want to be totally free, living only according to our own understandings of freedom, at the same time, as human beings, we also have to live in societies and we can become fully human only by placing ourselves under the rules and laws – the guidance – of a society that tends to be paternalistic. The human condition, then, is a tragedy. Multiculturalism is about enduring the tragedy.

To this end, as a practice in pragmatism, multiculturalism is an exercise that aims at producing practical, reasonable citizens. As the eminent British legal scholar John Finnis explains, practitioners of this type of social ordering, especially in the legal sphere, are "practically reasonable, that is to say: consistent; attentive to all aspects of human opportunity and flourishing, and aware of their limited commensurability; concerned to remedy deficiencies and breakdowns, and aware of their roots in the various aspects of human personality and in the economic and other material conditions of socials interaction."[21]

Again, we see that tragedy, at least in the Aristotelian sense, deals with the fate of the noble. Here I am thinking of all those peoples from around the world that have at different times been colonial subjects, who as truly tragic heroes found themselves fighting against enslavement by outsiders who considered themselves god-like in their superiority over their would-be slaves – the people they perceived as lesser beings. Canadian society has always expected these newcomers to conform to the directions it gives them, so historically expecting them to accept with as little struggle as possible their positions in society. They have always been the ones receiving accommodation, just as, in their native land, they were the ones undergoing colonization and enslavement for the good of those who saw themselves as more powerful and important. Yet today we hear the dominant groups protesting that today they are more enlightened and more humanitarian than their predecessors, that they would never have hated, colonized, enslaved, or practised genocide against anyone, and that they simply wish to have a good life without stopping others from doing the same or from sharing in the good life the dominant groups already know to be good. What could be so bad about wanting this arrangement, and even mourning and remonstrating over the lack of such a universal goodness? This debate itself is one of the beauties of multiculturalism, which sought to extend *nobility* in the form of equality to all those people whom a Eurocentric world has not thought notable enough to be truly free.

Rather than offering us a script in which good always triumphs over evil, multiculturalism seems to leave us on our own to improvise, for it itself does not seem to know the outcome: these struggles for dominance are not between evil and good but rather between various goods. And what a tragedy it is when different versions of the good collide. As Berdyaev suggests, "Tragedy means a conflict between polarities, but it need not necessarily be a conflict between good and evil, the divine and the diabolical. True depths of tragedy become apparent when two equally divine principles come into conflict … The greatest tragedy is suffering caused by the good and not by evil, and consists in our being unable to justify life in terms of the distinction between good and evil. Tragedy existed before the distinction was made and will go on existing after the distinction has been transcended. The most tragic situations in life are conflicts between values which are equally noble and lofty. And this implies that tragedy exists within the Divine life itself. The appearance of evil and of the diabolical is something secondary."[22]

And, definitely, despite much discussion and expectations to the contrary, the government did not intend multiculturalism principally to create quintessential liberal citizens, although, with the country's success in just having groups live together non-violently, liberal citizenship became more than just a hope, even if not yet a full reality for everyone. Liberal-democratic citizenship is ultimately just a specific expression of the most recent covenant that produced the Canadian state. Within this form of existence, while some individuals and groups may value liberal intentions highly, at times the state's main concern must be utilitarian.

Second to the state's own preservation must be its equally utilitarian desire to produce the greatest common good, an ideal that must be universal in scope and that often brings itself into conflict with individuals and groups worrying only about narrower liberal rights. An example is the untenable position in which Quebec finds itself when privileged groups demand accommodation for other, non-privileged members.

And her again we may think of Finnis's argument for the practical, reasonable citizen. This approach to citizenry is an attempt to convince people whom we think have no genuine reason or reasonableness in their actions to agree to a specific legal or social order. We would want them to at least feel a "moral disinterestedness" towards others in the society. And adopting this attitude would be to follow a common good. For this way of living would be a practical way of feeling they can still achieve justice in society without bothering about what others are doing. We would strive for an accommodation that, in practice, accommodates everyone as an object in society, while at the same time everyone feels that, theoretically, she or he is the subject doing the accommodating.

And here Finnis reminds us that Aristotle and before him Plato had long argued for the "cardinal principle of method in the study of human affairs – viz that concepts are to be selected and employed substantially as they are used in practice by the *spoudaios* (the mature man of practical reasonableness)." Further, he reminds us that in the *Republic* Plato argues "that the lover of wisdom can understand the concept of men of other characters, while the converse does not hold; in other words, the concerns and understanding of the mature and reasonable man provide a better *empirical* basis for the reflective account of human affairs."[23]

Such an assessment is still true today, for in our society nobility is the norm, not the exception, as in pre-modern times. Enlightenment and modernity teach us that every citizen of a Western country has social nobility, which we now call "human dignity," for citizenship presumes and produces equality. This equality, as a measurement of the common good, might bring us all down to the lowest level – a level for non-citizens – but that exists to raise every last one of us up to the highest level, so that, as the US army promises, we can all become what we want to be. The Enlightenment promise that is the beginning of tragedy supposes that each and every one of us can be as great as our dreams.

Somehow, the liberal individual has to find a way of expressing itself and still be authentic to the state and to itself.

More than that, multiculturalism seldom receives praise for its achievements: for keeping at bay the tyrant – so often today, forcing accommodation on others – that lurks in all of us and for peacefully ensuring the survival of a diverse group of people, whom history and common sense tell us a state should never intentionally bring together in an experiment in nation building.

Mainstream media in Canada recently presented a series of articles more critical of multiculturalism's success than the "ethnic press."[24] Most of the discussion offers an accommodationist approach to integration or the search for unity: immigrants and members of "visible minorities" need to adapt and to adjust their expectations, desires, and even dreams to fit into the existing Canada. It tends to reduce these groups to the stereotypical role of the Bad John, rarely associating them with the Sweet Boy.

The idea of the receiving society's adjusting over time is a non-starter and even far-fetched. Lynda Hurst writes, "The post-war immigrants originally addressed by the policy (mainly European, nominally Christian) have been replaced by a wide range of culturally and religiously diverse groups. The old assumption that integration – a sense of belonging to Canada – almost always occurs by the second generation no longer holds up. Breaking the silence that usually surrounds the subject, some analysts are asking whether it's time to rethink the policy, revamp it to reflect the new, 21st-century 'mosaic.' In no way at present, they say, does it encourage newcomers to move from immigrant 'them' to citizen 'us.' Nor does it stress that Canada holds certain non-negotiable values – the rule of law, sexual equality, freedom of expression and tolerance. If nothing else, they argue, *that* must be made explicit."[25] These critics point more to the work still to do to produce a deep form of multiculturalism and to the major obstacles. As multiculturalism entrenches itself, it has finally become a policy that deals with power and who should own it in Canada.

Often in current speculation, it appears as if rationalism has disappeared and everything has turned upside-down. The focus seems to be on how Canada can remain a culture of freedom. In such a setting, conformity and even the privileging of the common good over that of the individual may appear to be evils. But "evil" appears to become "good" when the race and ethnicity of Canadians change. In debates on the placement of visible minorities – primarily immigrants from outside European – the mainstream argument switches to privileging conformity and the enforcement of norms and expectations. The actors in this piece are not all equally noble, as some people perceive them as lesser beings than old-timers. Somehow the slavery, conformity, and accommodation that are anathema (at least for themselves) to the privileged groups, especially those of ancient lineage, become acceptable for people who are less than authentically Canadian. And the egalitarianism of multiculturalism genuinely challenges this stance by deeming everybody noble.

In this way, the discussion seems to be about two different realities within the same reality – for some citizens, liberal-democratic norms and rights, and for everyone else, conformity and even slavery to a higher common good, acceptance of a higher social order, and then and only then liberal-democratic norms and rights. In effect, what is good and what is evil in the first order switch around in the second. Members of the second order fight tragically, from their perspective – or comically, from the firsts' perspective – to merge the two orders into a single reality. Multiculturalism holds on to the ideal of what this merging could bring: if society considered all citizens equals and evaluated them by the same standards of good and evil, this transcendent morality would become the new day-to-day ethical order. Until this utopia arrives, members of the two orders subsist in a tragedy like Antigone's, having to choose between two competing notions of good and make one of them evil. No matter which one they choose, they are likely to violate that defining standard of the other order.

Another argument concerned the kind of society that we should become; the first recognized that we are and *always have been* multicultural, just that our compatriots spent most of our history denying this reality, looking to produce a metaphysical and transcendent country that at most is monocultural or bicultural, but eventually acknowledging the tragedy of trying to make a silk purse out of a sow's ear. Multiculturalism, then, is about how we as a collective of diverse and different groups and individuals can exist together and be our *natural* selves, about how we can all pretend, just so that we can all get along together, that we are *authentic*, even when we are not so in any way that genuinely matters, except in our pretence and in mimicry of what we take to be authentic.

In this regard, Canada is not yet a fully developed consciousness, for it is still a work in progress, and this is the greatest problem that confronts our nation-state: Many entrenched and elite group members talk and act as if Canada has reached that stage or behave as if it had done so in the past but had since degraded.

Instead, Canadians are still in the process of creating *reality*, even if it be deliberately to delude themselves into the appropriateness of a false consciousness because the real thing is too frightening or unfathomable in all its diversity and depth. Especially from the 1960s on, the new Canada emerged with the notion of *second chances*, which now animates justice in multicultural Canada: an old and dominant Christian notion of justice has undergone a sea change since Canadians recognized that their state has always been imperfect. "Nevertheless," Mary Stewart Van Leeuwen writes, "substantial healing is possible. Created in God's image and thus possessing agency and self-consciousness, human beings can reinterpret the past and re-envision the future, even given the very real constraints that biology and history place upon us."[26] In this sense, and hinting at its American parallels, pragmatically, multiculturalism is as much about faith as it is about actions and dealing with human relations through institutions and traditions that reflect people's yearning for the day when they can live like the god of their imagination, who not only created them but whom they also create.

This makes the reality in which they live a human construction out of a state of nature, governing itself by rules, norms, and expectations of behaviour that citizens have agreed on as appropriate house rules. And by definition, this makes the new reality a tragedy acting as if it is a comedy, for the human imagination is never at rest. It is always looking to create new possibilities and, indeed, realities. So that when it constructs itself in one way, as an act of free will and creativeness, there will be human beings who can think of innumerable ways to improve the new creation and make it more *real* – more human. To limit their ability to produce any of these possibilities would be to make these thinkers into tragic heroes or to reduce them to comic figures, in effect revealing them as slaves who believe that they are still free. For at the heart of the living experiences in the Americas, of which the Canadian experience is a prime example, lies the need to come to terms somehow with a very tragic flaw – a flaw that is congenital and requires treatment as a sickness or disability that, comedically, should not unduly affect the social organism's ability to live.

8

Canada: Forging a Single Consciousness

They wield their votes at the U.N. not as legitimate representatives
of their own fellow citizens, but as two-faced members of the global
club of tyrants, who hold sway through force and fear.[1]
> Claudia Rosett, "A Tyrants Club,"
> *Wall Street Journal*

Historically, official multiculturalism in Canada emerged in the early
1970s out of the frustration of various groups trying to determine
whether they should all exist according to Anglo conformity, Franco conformity, or no conformity at all.[2] In the end, they chose none at all – or
so we hear, for there are many people who still argue that life in multicultural Canada is an exercise in conformity to the ideals of either a Franco
or an Anglo mainstream, or to a hybridized Anglo-French culture.

As I see it, what happened back then is instructive: Canadians chose
multiculturalism as their identity and as a formal ideology, a move in
keeping with my argument that peoples and societies tend to see themselves in the image of their newest members, as part of the evolution of
a more universal identity. Many Canadians began to downplay somewhat their old English and French identities and instead allowed newcomers, some of whom refused assimilation, to help shape a new identity.
Some of the new arrivals had argued that their presence showed that
Canada was multicultural rather than bicultural. This stance set the conditions for starting to fold the old French and English identities into a
wider, newer identity – that of multiculturalism. In the end, the new
became more representative of life in the state, and the state – while
claiming in effect that all citizens reflect its image – finds the newer members playing a role in revising its own image.

Because there is no cultural or official conformity in the Canadian
imagination, Canadians seem to be working towards an idealistic

conformity to abstract ideals and identities – *multiculturalism*. Multiculturalism does not take a specific form but exhibits values, such as tolerance, pluralism, love, sharing, concern about the future over the past, and even political correctness in its vulgar forms. This might be the height of contradiction: on the one hand, choosing to exist as a single nation-state, but, on the other hand, having an existence that is completely novel.

With multiculturalism, Canada was symbolically going back to the beginning of its social time, to before it in effect decided to reject or downgrade other peoples and become a white man's nation. Now it was suggesting that it could be the world; that the image of its people is the demographic likeness of humanity itself. Symbolically, while crafting a nation-state out of humanity, Canada was not really seeking to leave humanity behind. Rather, it was ready to argue that all humanity was capable of becoming Canadian, again rejecting the previous approach that Canadian identity meant adopting an exclusive and fixed personality separate and distinct from the rest of the world.

This new choice depends for success on reliance on faith and good intentions, making it an exercise in rational idealism, falling just short in the quest for a utopia. And therefore, because Canadians seem consciously not to be searching for a utopia in the common usage, they have settled for a state of existence that is at best a comedy and at worst an ongoing tragedy. How, then, should we grasp this seemingly irreconcilable contradiction: as a conforming multiculturalism or as a unity that displays diversity and differences? Multiculturalism in Canada is a tragedy, and Canada itself is a Hegelian unhappy consciousness, aiming to produce good works and perfect outcomes. For reasons not of its own making, Canada lives the tragedy of finding itself falling short of its goals and often feeling miserable with itself for failing to achieve ideal outcomes. As an unhappy consciousness, it and its citizens must live in a world in which they are always falling short of perfection, and this is what unsettles them. In an untenable position, the outcomes are never as good as people imagine: happiness from what they have achieved, for in terms of material goods the country continues to flourish, economically and in international repute as a developed country that is a liberal democracy; unhappiness over the difference between the actual product and what people had imagined and over the realization that no group or individual can always have its way on matters of importance.

Contradictions, by their nature, show the limits and boundaries of an ideology. As French philosopher Paul Ricœur argues in *Lectures on*

Ideology and Utopia, a successful ideology solves its internal contradictions, or at least appears to do so, if only to safeguard the ideology itself.[3] As with most contradictions, meaning is equivocal in this exercise, where what people imagine does not always match what they live. Meaning is not as clear as philosophers, sociologists, politicians, social scientists, and media commentators would like. For in their minds, diversity and plurality, the hallmarks of multiculturalism, are anathema to conformity, with its expectations of rigidity, assimilation, homogeneity, and hegemony, with its intentions for a unity of power and lack of subjectivity and agency for others. Multiculturalism, in this case, is the epitome of fragmentation and disruption, of diffusing power, warring factions, and lack of clear identity. That is not the multiculturalism we are discussing here.

Rather, we are talking of multiculturalism that, ironically, ends in a unity. Conversely, it is a conforming statism that ends in a multiculturalism that is fragmentary but not a fracturing unity. It is a common good that is always refashioning itself but never breaks into pieces, if only because humanity itself is impossible to attain through distinct and discrete groups. It is the identities that people project on these groups that might change, because of changes in categorizing and social construction.

But in the end, humanity will still be more than the sum of its many groups, categories, and identities. The fluidity of humanity and what it does, the forms it chooses, will remain. There will be an underlying unity, a oneness of the universal human experience. The brand of multiculturalism that Canada proposes – but has not attained – and which I term "genuine multiculturalism," tries to capture this oneness within the Canadian geographical borders. Such a way of living tries to create this unity where the accord matters most, in the imagination or in what this book presents as part of the transcendent. In this special place, multiculturalism resides with ideals as pure as eternal justice, happiness, and freedom. The question for Canadians is how to bring the transcendent into daily life: how to attain that freedom that they know is possible in their thoughts and dreams and integrate it into their living reality.

Key to this multiculturalism is how Canada socializes diverse and different peoples from around the world as Canadians. At its most idealistic, socialization is an attempt to keep moving citizens closer to the ideal, to making the country and citizens as perfect, just, and free as possible. This means, as British social philosopher T.H. Green suggests, that they should imbibe a common morality so that their ethical relations flow from internal dispositions rather than through the force of law.[4] There would be no compulsion or forced conformity. In other words, how is it possible to inculcate in people with many differences in race, culture, ethnicity, religion, languages, and moralities a love for their new country and their fellow citizens? This is the kind of love that grounds patriotism and even jingoism; where an individual would willingly sacrifice himself or herself for others who are practically strangers; where he or she would, as a tragic hero, give up personal gains and good for what is morally and ethically a higher and universal common good.

This is an exercise dependent on each individual's recognizing that he or she is inferior to the common good or that individuals can obtain genuine and worthwhile recognition only out of a universally accepted common good or order. Theirs is the morality that fires the imagination, as Benedict Anderson shows, that ideologically produces *our* country, state, and nation in an unbroken symbiosis of authenticity.[5] For while the faces of this specific multicultural country might be the same as the rest of the world, within the country itself there would not be the problems and differences of the world.

The difference here is that all members of this country would have drowned their many differences in a new hybridized culture and way of life. They would have created something new out of the old ways, so that the old lives and differences that went with them would matter no more. What would bind these peoples in a unity would be their new faith and ideology, flowing from the values that are now common to all members and that have become the skeleton of their very being. Faith and hope suggest that it is possible to achieve these goals, to make life a comedy; something else, including the stories of history, tells us that this might just be a pipe dream, that we have trapped ourselves in a tragedy of existence with no seemingly good way out of it.

We are talking about changes that must occur to a state that is a constantly evolving ethical consciousness: What must the state do through its institutions and agencies to reciprocate the love that it expects of these citizens? And how can it act like a parent, loving its citizens even before they love the state and one another? This is a state whose task is always to capture, in any given moment, what is the universal and higher common good that standardizes the dreams and aspirations of *all* members. As Green suggests, the state's purpose as an ethical consciousness is to create the conditions through a covenant that allows all its citizens to try to achieve the goals that they establish in common.

The argument for a comedy is in understanding the contradictions of this ideology. For genuine multiculturalism, this is a moment when not the few but the many hold power and in a system that seeks to forge out of the many a singular spirit or consciousness. This is what the German philosopher Martin Heidegger describes as a "theyness," what Hegel calls a "consciousness," and what, ironically, Charles Taylor says is essential for the construction of the modern individual and personality.[6] However, what I am talking about is a socializing act – where the individual disappears in the collective. This is what happens when, as Aristotle says, a god or a barbarian enters society, where individual appetites and behaviour begin to conform to a common good. This is how the tyrant or dictator finds genuine love among the people.

But this is a society that is always in flux and in which change is imminent. This is so much so that because of the dynamics of history, the state never knows in any era what its true nature is, if indeed it has one. The state is always groping to know in what form it will attain permanent happiness, where citizens will be happy, and where everyone will prosper. But those conditions never occur, for history is a narrative of disappointments and of the state's groping in the dark to know its optimum form and the likeness of its optimal citizens. All the state knows with some certainty is that what it was in the past and is even now does not provide the ideal of happiness, and that to reach the ideal, it must change.

The problem is that the state would like to have a teleological path to this happiness, but this is vain thinking because nobody knows what exactly this happiness is. In the end, the state has to select one of a series of options or paths to the utopia, which means that its freedom consists in having to choose from the infinite paths to this happiness without knowing what the happiness is, without knowing when it has attained its ideal form. To this end, it seems speculatively prone to unhappiness, quarrelling over different paths, and racking up a history of changes that move it nowhere near the ideal of happiness. This is its tragic history.

Alternatively, it can choose a specific path, declare this the sole path to happiness, and reject all others. But this would be to extinguish freedom as choice, and, as the communist revolutions of the last century and the various religious and secular homelands over time have proved, this one path does not produce the intended result. More than that, the process – or lack of process – is likely to increase unhappiness and frustration.

Therefore, at no time is the state authentic in terms of its goals. Much negative comment on Hegel's method claims that it aims for a particular totalizing ending. Typical is American Christian theologian Sheila Greeve Davaney's suggestion in *Historicism* that "in the Hegelian vision each moment is an element in the upward, if indirect, movement of reason. Furthermore, history unfolds in a necessary manner; its stages are inevitable and predetermined by the *teleological* pull by spirit."[7] This thinking is part of the notion that Hegel's master system assumes, according to Austro-British philosopher Karl Popper, a tripartite process of thesis-antithesis-synthesis, where the system becomes a particular, teleological outcome – the end of history.

This position seems at odds with another statement by Davaney on Hegel's dialectical process and its likely outcomes. "The dialectical process," she says, "is one in which each claim is incomplete and contains contradictions and tensions. Such internal contradiction gives rise to contrary assertions that also are incomplete and internally conflicted. These in turn give rise to new ideas that contain the possibility of reconciling these differences, not by denying them or choosing one over the other, but by taking up the oppositional truths and preserving them together. In this interpretation of knowing, truth results from a process of development in which truth is emergent, not given; it is to be made, not simply discovered."[8]

But what is also true is that this truth is neither final nor homogeneous: it is rife with particulars and differences and, as Davaney claims, is just the most recent truth claim that "is incomplete and internally conflicted." Only as a comedy would the truth claim be final. Otherwise, if it is a tragedy, the fraction and attempt at healing lead only to many more fractions. Hegel has indicated that there is no such tripartite system and that his analysis ends not in a particular but in a new universal that generalizes all the immanent particulars. In this case, there is no specific or particular form of happiness. So instead of the hope's streamlining and focusing itself, it fractures and defuses and calls into view more of the options in the infinity of paths and interpretations of happiness.

If there is telos, it is one not of unity but, ironically, of greater diversity. We should bear this alternative reading in mind in also determining what individuals or particulars the state has to homogenize through recognition. For, just like the state, the individual is searching for happiness but also failed and is changing as its concepts of freedom and the road to a particular ending evolve. Thus to recognize epistemically the individual at any time is to recognize flux and an unhappy consciousness – for at that moment of recognition the individual would be in the process of rejecting what it has become and then looking for a new change that would move it towards its ideal.

In this respect, the state and the individual citizen mirror each other, as universal and particular. Neither is happy unless it pretends. For even when appearing to be happy, *human* nature causes individuals or society to dream up more and different desires to make them even more perfect and in the interim recognize that they are not indeed perfect, and this knowledge makes them unhappy. This starts the recognition struggle all over again, until it ends in another version of the lord-and-bondsman relationship.

Only by coming into civil society do individuals in this sense become *human* or *cultural* beings, personalities that attain rights and the chance to perfect themselves into an image of their own making. They become sociable by entering the social. The trick here is to make the image of their own making the same as that the state desires, so that the perfected individual becomes a human who embodies the abstract citizen of the state. In this sense, the individual is just another member of the society, having no meaning and being outside of what the state offers to every other member. This perfecting art that fully humanizes the individual is the living out of the terms and dispositions of citizenship in the state. Essentially, it is the product of ethical relations that govern how people get along together.

There is collective significance in vesting power in a general will or new spirit, one in which the individuals are in harmony and unite in purpose, so that what the state does in the name of the collective is no different from what the individual or group does. The individual or group's morality merges perfectly with that of the wider collective to which it belongs and with which it is in total symbiosis of purpose. The ethical relation that the state founds and produces is the same as that motivating individuals and groups.

This relationship importantly reflects self-recognition, providing what philosopher Jacques Maritain calls a societal "concrete behaviour, [a ...] *concept* of itself" that is essential for the achievement of freedom in a civil society or the social.[9] The recognition of freedom flows from the *concept* of what and who the society and its members are. All of these notions of the self rely on a freedom that the society maintains and preserves as a common good and in which citizens see genuine reflections of themselves. It is a society in which they feel acceptance and have the right to determine the prevailing social norms and mores. Therefore, full citizenship for everyone is a testament to the freedom of all persons. This is the equality that is at the heart of radical democracy, with all its egalitarian possibilities for citizenship and actual power. As Maritain says, "A genuine democracy implies a fundamental agreement between minds and wills on the basis of life in common; it is aware of itself and of its principles, and it must be capable of defending and promoting its own conception of social and political; it must bear within itself a common human creed, the creed of freedom."[10]

For instance, we may think of Maritain's criticisms of the "bourgeois" democracy that caters to the atomist individual who effectively remains outside society or enters its "neutral boxing ring," which subjects all ideas, thoughts, and principles to Hobbesian-type battles for dominance. This metaphor offers no concept of a collective self. There is no social. Here society is mainly one individual against another, where the outcome can be only the good of one and the vanquishing of the other in a master – slave relationship. "Just as it had no real *common good*," Maritain says of such a society, "it had no real *common thought* – no brain of its own, but a neutral, empty skull clad with mirrors: … it had become a society without any idea of itself and without faith in itself, without any *common faith* which could enable it to resist disfiguration."[11]

The main difference of persons having many things in common is that the actions unfold in a culture or consciousness that takes a higher social significance than the drama unfolding among individuals, for this culture is ultimately the true site and stage of freedom. The individuals or separate atomic groups become the actors on this stage. This is so even if they, ironically, in their full freedom, have the right to change the course at any moment. In this way, democracy allows individuals to retain their identities and personal goods but also encourages them to seek a just outcome to any of their struggles.

Radical democracy bridges these gaps and helps to reconcile the contradictions. The American philosopher Rex Martin considers "what particular institutional process[es], if any, are apt in the formulation, maintenance, and harmonization of civil rights" in society. The theorist T.H. Green, Martin notes, had ignored this question in his analysis of social rights and obligations as part of the universal common good. In Martin's words, "Active civil rights require an agency to formulate, maintain, and harmonize them. They require an agency to identify and establish ways of acting or being treated that we can reasonably suppose to be in everyone's interest. Democratic institutions – universal franchises, contested voting, and majority rule – can effectively perform this job and provide the setting required by civil rights. Democratic procedures are a stable and relatively reliable way of identifying, and then implementing, laws and policies that serve interests common to the voters, or at least to a majority of them."[12]

The primary determinant of a collective identity and culture therefore is not who or which ethnic group(s) hold or retain power, but for what good they use the power. Power is the output, the theatrical play that is the stage, the performers, and all the creativity and improvisation that generate a successful show. This is the good that occurs when all components work together towards a single end. The common good has to motivate the use of power, and that universalism into which individuals disappear should be an act of achieving a morality. What then is the intention of the acts of power? In the power-play drama that is multiculturalism, attention focuses not only on the actors in their many different and exotic costumes and masks, but also equally on the stage where they perform and on the relationships between the actors, their props, and the stage itself.

The entire play is more than the people mouthing the words or performing the script, it is more than the script itself, more than the scenery, and more than the setting that concretizes the play – as a whole, the play is more than these three relationships. It is a common good that emerges from a specific cultural perspective. As the French philosopher, dramatist, and critic Jean-Paul Sartre and others state, this is the authoritative gaze that demands conformity and consistency. It is the gaze that Sartre's fellow French philosopher Emmanuel Levinas states leads to the question, "Where is your brother?" We cannot merely answer with another question such as "Am I my brother's keeper?" It is a gaze and a command to be responsible, to look deep within the self and to speak truthfully not only about the other, but about oneself and one's relation to the others – both those outside and, particularly, those inside one as a subject. It is a command to perform according to a specific cultural authority.

Knowledge and understanding must on one hand ideally focus on what this consciousness now a-building is learning and communicating. But on the other hand, since the materials enter the Canadian consciousness from elsewhere, and since even the youngest child, we assume, starts life with received knowledge and morals, how to exclude all these experiences and this knowledge from these social relationships? This reality is real only in thought, as a linguistic expression, so that the actual experiences might be unreal and fanciful – like living in a dream or in a prison where the inmates are in charge, which would be pure comedy or worse, farce. This reality can have a transferable or common meaning only as a language, expressing a shared viewpoint of what we think we know of the world we inhabit, which, to make sense to us, cannot be "natural" or beyond human contamination.

The new reality becomes then a mixture of these several worlds, with their own styles of life and crazy or authentic meanings. But we hope that the mixture can produce only a hybridized, inauthentic, and make-believe world according to extant rules, just as when we measure for a recipe in a cookbook, which crystallizes other cooks' experiences, which we must apply faithfully while adjusting things to suit our tastes and the available materials. The resulting new world is like a product made from recycled or slightly processed materials, perhaps with flaws or even so beautiful and perfect as to be unusable.

In this world, what happens when words such as "accommodation," "citizenship," "equality," "freedom," and "justice" acquire different meanings, or none at all? What happens when institutions that we think undergird reality cannot communicate with one another or with people who rely on them to create meaning in their lives? What kind of reality would it be for those whom this social construction leaves behind? Here we might think especially of individuals still searching for their own reality, even though newcomers act as if they have already found or created perfection. In Canada's history, there was never an idyllic past, but rather recent acceptance that the creation of this country, along with its southern neighbour, disrupted an idyllic period in North America. And this longing for an idyllic past still informs the melancholia haunting Canadian multiculturalism.

By the time the two countries entered the dominant European and Christian mythology, they were already helping to replace the proverbial Eden. They also reflected the idea that men and women had been created or born free but everywhere were in chains. The founders intended Canada and the United States to be part of a solution to human agony and to the tyranny that humans make. As people such as the English social philosopher John Locke argued, all the world was America,[13] and, as Hegel noted, a hybridized and creolized American hemisphere was the future of the world,[14] which would leave behind the rest of the world's ailments and pains for a better time. But as we saw above, this was an America with natural resources, and Europeans and others had to leave home to exploit them. Therefore, the Americas in this mythology probably represent Adam and Eve's new home after their expulsion from Eden. For the Americas were not natural to the settlers, they were not idyllic, like their native lands, and they lacked a distinctive ethnicity and culture.

Therefore, if they were going to create gardens of Eden, social construction would be necessary, through human thoughts and efforts, in another quest to naturalize the unnatural. Men and women would construct them as places that produced a Christian justice. And we today are still striving to reach the point where, as a collective, we can look back on what our society has brought out of the void of history and the shapelessness before human intervention and pronounce it good. Multiculturalism makes us both creator and created, much as the child is indeed parent to the adult – John Finnis's "practical reasonableness."

One of the contradictions of official multicultural Canada is that its policies or ethical behaviour should transcend any particular religious faith. There is no official religion of the public sphere, or rather all and any religion is official. Yet Canada aims to produce a specific form of justice on a day-to-day basis, and even into the future. Judaeo-Christian precepts underlie it, which adds to the contradiction: how can a state that still has special statuses for Christmas, Easter, and their notions of rewards for people who have "been good or bad" and of members having second chances make room for citizens with different ideals of justice and social renewal?[15] The challenge for multiculturalism, then, is how to take the religions of the world – particularly the fundamentalist segments of Christianity, Islam, or Judaism, with their own notions of *the* good and *the* evil – and convert them not into a single religion or theology, but into a theodicy or ideology that always questions these very ideas – all with the hope of letting us live peaceably together?

The culture that has produced the archetypes for Canadian justice can serve as a lesson on how to move human existence from a tragedy to a comedy. Here, I am thinking of the hybridization of Western civilization, with its dominant Greek and Christian pillars, each with its own notions of tragedy and comedy and of how to reconcile or resolve them. For our study, we must agree that both the Greek and the Christian archetypes locate the resolution in the individual self – in people who feel they are the most authentic and have full knowledge about perfection and absolute happiness.

From the Greek, there is no clearer archetype than Oedipus, whose search for perfection and happiness ultimately made him the cause of all imperfection and unhappiness. More than that, he showed that the individual can destroy the common good. Christianity presents the image of a saviour hanging naked from a tree, wrestling with whether he himself was truly a god or human and settling for less than perfection, which is death of the self, to rise again so as to reconcile this issue. This tragic and necessary death of the unchangeable to achieve later reconciliation is the foundation of the Christian consciousness, a spirit that Western states embody, even if they do not say so. In the daily living out of the spirit in the state, the gods of the piece must face the despair of knowing that

God is dead but that God has also risen and will achieve full reconciliation of life and death in another world. For happiness to occur, it can
come only in time and under different assumptions; as for spirit, this
world cannot be its home, even if it has to dwell here. Still, the message
is clear: tragically, we have imperfection and tyranny in us, and meaningful change must come from within and not from external compulsion.

Canada is just like the child taking its first tentative steps, having to
determine what to accept from the received knowledge that comes out
of its past and what it should try to find out on its own. This is an emerging consciousness that must rely on errantry: it must remain sceptical,
even about what it thinks it knows about itself, and it must remind itself
that it is fallible – as a young child, it has made some bad decisions,
which beset it with guilt, agony, and the fear that even when it intended
good it could produce evil; that while it tries to ensure its own longevity
it might be creating the conditions for its own demise. History has taught
us that what Canada thought was the truth and the most ethical turned
out to be neither. Canada must always temper the optimism of hope with
the pessimism of the current situation and the past: with the reality that
humans can hurt and tyrannize each other – and that even in Canada
enslavement and forced conformity have terrorized specific types of people over the generations. Therefore it must always question the wisdom
of trying to build a future on this kind of a past.

    Until it has emerged fully as a consciousness, Canada is always just
beginning its correct and corrected history, beginning the narrative of
how its citizens, as a special but constantly changing people, really
learned how to get along together and stopped tyrannizing one another,
intentionally or otherwise. Therefore we cannot say that it has not yet
written this history. No country has achieved such glory, if only because
the people have never been recognized as fully constituted. That is why
Canada's new journey along the path of multiculturalism is so full of
hope and expectation, for failures have not yet tarnished it, as the human
condition assures us they will.

    In the first place, the story is about how, as a single consciousness or
community, we control the strong members by forcing them to surrender
to our wishes. Here we are talking about social justice and social inequalities and how to rectify them intentionally and meaningfully. A different
perspective shows a story about how, conniving, we can force the strong
to surrender, but willingly, without their becoming anti-social. This is a
postmodern narrative, with many diverse and varying actors following
different scripts or paths to what each thinks is freedom.

Often there appears to be no script of all, a kind of "malaise of modernity," as Charles Taylor calls it, or a situation in which the actors find themselves, as Hegel argues, in drunken, bacchanalian dance – and each imbibing from her or his own bottle, too. Not only are we having fun drinking our poison of choice, but we also bring the concoction or witch's brew to the frenzy. It is how we can convince the Bad Johns to believe that they are so much part of our society that whatever we want they want and that whatever they fight for is also for us. In this respect, we need to reassure them that there is no difference between them and the society, even if they continue to see a fundamental one between us and them as individuals and as a group – whether in another political party, village, area, island, nation, or state.

In this way, notions of state formation and retention play out first as tragedy – how do we socialize the Bad Johns? – and then as a comedy, when we fool them into believing that they have no interest separate and apart from us. And there is the additional comedy when the spotlight falls on us and the folly of our belief that we really know and understand what is happening and that we – not the Bad Johns – are in control. Therefore this is a story about controlling tyrants, or about producing real democracy, where individuals have the freedom that results when their country can see, hear, and recognize them and embeds them in its culture. This is the story of wanting freedom that is not slavery or of desiring a slavery that is still freedom.

As I have said elsewhere, it is a case of having your cake and eating it, too[16] – of determining that if there must be a society and if there must be tyrants and Bad Johns, then it would be best, first, if *you* were the tyrant or Bad John and, second, if you were in control of the tyranny and the Bad John. Some people would call this a weird form of pragmatism. Others would call it licensed freedom. In most cases, it is what we usually call "democracy": putting yourself under the tyrant of your own making. And ultimately the questioning of all structures and forms could imprison even a tyrant; therefore this too is a story of how we can have structures without resorting to mere formalism and formulas, where a structure or a way of achieving a common end simply morphs out of the given context, what some would call the "historical material-ism" or what I call "material dialectics."

As I write this book, issues of tragedy and comedy are playing themselves out around the world. My vantage point has shifted. I no longer reside in Barbados or occupy the identity solely of a Caribbean. The Caribbean is one of those places that, depending on your perspective, is either an ideal state of nature or a civil society, but it has never strayed from its multicultural roots. The world tends to see the region either as a tragedy – a state of nature still trying to make order out of the disorderly – or as a comedy – a bumbling civil society, where people add to their own misery simply because they do not know better. Such was the view of the Nobel laureate V.S. Naipaul, who sees the comedic nature of Caribbean tragedy in the fact that its people have not yet acquired the knack for living in a society of rational laws.

My new vantage point is Canada, a place that seldom seems a state of nature, but one that needs constant reminding that within its hearts nature lurks – there is always wildness, a non-conformity, a multicultural habit that needs guiding and shaping if there is to be any structure at all. Rather, Canada presents itself as, in theory, a model of a civil society for the world to copy. Yet some observers differ, seeing Bad Johns in different disguises on the streets, in its politics, and in culture, and a plethora of Sweet Boys and Prince Charmings – all those immigrants who want to help it to a new life.

Unlike the Caribbean, Canada might be multicultural in form but not quite yet in spirit. Multiculturalism in Canada demonstrates what becomes of the long struggle over ways of life when a society diffuses power among people who were powerless in colonial times. In a colonial era, "the people" generally means "the masses," or those whom the colonizers keep in bondage. Multiculturalism hints at the sea change when these masses take over and diffuse power: they may still see themselves as the masses, even though they have all become lords, doing away with the traditional masses. Genuine multiculturalism transforms concepts such as lord, bondsman, bondswoman, and the masses through a radical democracy that gives power to the masses – now all the people, with their social inequalities and natural diversities. The masses – no longer historically *vulgar masses* – now include the sovereign and are the sovereign in terms of their human desires. The masses are now noble.

When Canada reaches that stage, it could stop reminding itself that it is a multicultural state and that it should interpret all its laws accordingly.[17] A truly multicultural Canada would know that it had left the realm of tragedy for comedy and that its social institutions and agencies give the same treatment to all citizens, who genuinely believe that they are all equal, even if they are only fooling themselves.

This vantage point reveals to me two crises of socialization, with Bad Johns aplenty. One is the consciousness that is Canada itself, as it struggles to incorporate some very strong people – immigrants: the mythological gods for good or evil who roam in states of nature. Like most receiving countries in the West, such as the United States, Australia, and the members of the European Union, Canada finds itself seemingly in terror of the assumed wreckage that immigrants can unleash on its society. Some citizens see immigrants as strangers, ugly geniuses, and cultural barbarians who can overwhelm and even destroy what is good about the existing society. More than that, the newcomers may take away something from a special group: the absolute right to a country, its resources, its culture, and its future – its very freedom and sovereignty. This despite these nations' claim that immigrants are building them. These immigrants are also people whom Canada calls the brightest and best – people who may have no need for Canada but whom Canada needs for its continuing existence. As Statistics Canada has been saying with increasing rapidity and even alarm, these immigrants are Canada's future.

Some mainstream Canadians see the immigrants differently, however: they are outsiders and perhaps terrorists, people with different and alien cultures whom Canada must tell not to stone their women and not to cover up their faces on the streets. Rather, they should just act like everyone else. A few columnists in national newspapers may seem to suggest that certain immigrant women trade in those dark, heavy burkas for the skimpiest of bikinis, just to show that they value living in a free, liberal society. They present these immigrants as the barbarians, and Canada as a fully formed state with a salient culture beyond the gate.

This type of exaggeration has inspired a few critics to blame immigrants for most of Canada's problems – its having "no real culture" anymore, its identity problem, its having no real values, too many people now holding dual citizenships, and those Bad Johns abusing tolerance. This tempest in a teapot points to the question "Does a *real* Canada exist?" This query arises because some old-timers may see immigrants not as human beings equal in life desires and aspirations to citizens but, in Hegel's sense, as mere *things* to use and even discard. They shear them of most of life itself, particularly of the good attributes of humanity. In this projection, some immigrants become types and abstractions, such as purely workers, criminals, terrorists, and cultural defilers.

The state may give points to applicants for immigration depending on specific qualities so it can mechanically select the "brightest and the best." Officials may assume that specific characteristics predict human behaviour, paying little heed to history itself, which has shown humans to be largely unpredictable. However, the questionable certainty of such predictability arises when we view immigrants not as fully human but as mere *things* or abstractions.

As immigrants settle – some perhaps initially near family, friends, and co-nationals – these perceived Bad Johns supposedly banish Christmas trees from public places; alienate some mainstream Canadians who do not see themselves in the faces of the newcomers; cannot read street signs, markings, or graffiti; rename urban centres with monikers such as "Bramptonadesh" or "Bramptonistan"; and even help inflict on Canada one minority federal government after another.[18]

In all of this, the hecklers seem to have been missed the irony: that Canada has for generations been a community of communities, with immigrant groups living in their own neighbourhoods. Historically, almost every major Canadian city has had its own Little China, Little India, Little Portugal, Little Greece, and so on. Most of these areas produce multicultural flair and internal national dynamics during such times as the World Cup of soccer or the Olympics. Some communities in regions of Canada have sported their national identities, including the Ukrainian flavour of the west, the Scottish in Ontario, and the Gaelic in Nova Scotia's Cape Breton.

Now, and without leaving these communities, many of these occupants are ethnically white and may think of themselves as "good" Canadian citizens, assimilated into the Anglo or Franco mainstreams. They and others no longer see their communities as enclaves or ghettoes – places where "immigrants" live – even though that dominant mythology suggests that their inhabitants should have long ago become natural to the land.

So, despite its creation of reserves and homelands for its aboriginal peoples, Canada had its genesis in a practice of socially constructing communities within communities. The current angst by old-timers surrounding nation building in receiving countries such as Canada seems to relate primarily to the compatibility of those whom it traditionally did not prefer as immigrants or ultimately as future citizens.

The first irony seems to be that there is seldom talk of a Little England or Little France in Canada, partly because of the expectations that, even though officially multicultural, Canada is English and/or French. This appears most noticeably in Quebec, which claims to be officially francophone. The second bit of irony is that these communities within the larger Canadian community worry over what they call "ethnic ghettoes" of so-called visible minorities. What makes them ghettoes is that they are enclaves with residents who are *ethnics* – not "authentic" Canadians.

However, most recent discussions seem to centre on the Islamic presence in Canada, especially during the international war on terrorism that has made authorities in immigrant-receiving countries anxious about domestic fanaticism or terrorism. Canadian governments have symbolically associated perceived threats with things Islamic and with the fear of a so-called "clash of civilizations" between Muslims and Christians in a plural society. As history shows, old and even discredited ideals do not just die: they go underground until they can emerge in different guises and await reconciliation in new national narratives. Some mainstream Canadians may think that this country is, or aspires to become, a *European* country. This ideal remains even two generations after adoption of official multiculturalism – the ultimate in new world pragmatism and hybridity.[19]

In the eyes of the state, the identity and sovereignty of Canada are no longer united and whole but severely fractured almost to the point of misrecognition. Nothing about Canada, the country where multiculturalism has been an exercise in recognition, is recognizable anymore. This is definitely not what a modern state should have to endure. And what is generally true for Canada is also true for the West: that place that has long socialized mythological Bad Johns out of existence, where Prince Charmings have become the ultimate in the practicality of citizenship – dedicated workers with a middle-class existence of licensed or permitted freedoms that leave them still feeling that they are absolutely free. Overall, we may indeed wonder about what has become of modernity as the basis for the West and for the escape from tyranny and fear.

From the mainstream perspective, the tragedy in this crisis is how to make these immigrants as weak as other Canadians, how to make them feel – or fool them into believing – that they need Canada more than any other place in the world. In this respect, the struggle in Canada is tragic, for it is about social inequalities and hierarchies that test the notion of who and what groups should have power, privileges, and entitlements in society. This is a story in which citizens concentrate on the inequalities and social alienation that is the tragedy of living, rather than on the imaginary social oneness that everybody has a hand in creating. It is a reality that comes from concentrating on what *is* rather than on looking ahead and imagining what might be, and from acting somewhat foolishly, as if that world-to-be had already become a reality. In the current debate, the Bad Johns of the world, including those who think they own Canada, have not yet lost themselves. So, too, for the Sweet Boys. All must become good, loyal, and patriotic citizens who produce for the state – both the material products that improve the quality of life and the future generations that will sustain the state across time.

Theirs is a struggle that resembles the struggles of social classes that societies have constructed according to gender, sex, race, ethnicity, or any other form of identity to disempower these people. Such labelling is a tragedy because its aim is to control the very strong, those who are capable of disrupting and even destroying the current status quo and its norms, socialization, and social stratification. It reveals a struggle between radically different moralities and notions of how to understand daily existence. One social order sees the other as seeking to overthrow and supplant current ways, which it fervently dislikes. Canada is still a narrative of people who refuse to believe, who won't allow themselves to slip into the imaginary, who know that they are still not free and are unable and unwilling to fool themselves otherwise.

And it is a tragedy of a special kind: trying to live in two separate worlds at the same time, a tragedy that Hegel sees as occurring when discrimination exists between citizens of the same state or social order. Canadian sociologist David McGregor describes a negotiation between an unreal secret or external world and the socially construction that is the real world we all inhabit, with people ultimately feeling strangers in both.

This is the tragedy of living in a multicultural liberal democracy, of negotiating the contradictions of liberalism, with its individualism, and democracy, with its collective notions of majorities, common good, the sacrifice of individual selves, and the primacy of "we the people" in everything. This tragedy stems from a conflict over the appropriate stratification of society – a structural and/or functional argument for different classes of citizenship. The conflict arises when some people find that they do not enjoy the same rights as members of elite or special groups. This even though the society espouses ideal, some would say "comedy," that all citizens possess the same rights and privileges.

Yet stratification gives some members elite positions because of historical claims or traditional class structures. As Hegel says, "Those who are in authority are very likely to execute such rights as legalized rights on account of the interest they may have in preserving them. But in a case of this kind their right will be merely the unrighteous right of the barbarian, and they must themselves appear to us in the category of barbarians, at least, who resolved to carry out and perfect what is essentially injustice."[20] And as Hegel adds, "To this type [of conflict and tragedy] belongs the legalized lordship exercised over slaves or serfs, the right to rob a foreigner of his liberty, or to sacrifice the same to the gods."[21] Canada today!

There is an echo here of Aristotle and his notion in the *Politics* that only gods and barbarians do not need to live in societies and therefore are beyond the need for socialization.[22] Foreigners should have full citizenship, he insists, on the same level as native-born individuals, when they hold office in the state. I keep saying in this book that, following on Aristotle and Hegel, politics and social positioning in society are the material of tragedy in the way they marry citizenship and political rights.

Hegel mentions the "rule of Aristotle" – that tragedy engenders fear and compassion. "Strictly speaking," Hegel adds, "we experience neither fear nor reverence when confronted with rights which only exist among barbarians and are the misfortune of uncivilized times."[23] Canada's positioning of immigrants vis-à-vis citizens provides an interesting reading of the conflict in a multicultural society, which, Hegel suggests, casts the entrenched groups as barbarians. *Quel* irony: perhaps we have misrecognized the causes of the crisis? Maybe the real Bad Johns are the old-timers – the folks with power and clout, with their privileges and status, with their permanent dominance of John Porter's vertical mosaic – who need multicultural socialization? Do those who believe and act as if they *own* the state now need to adapt to the new reality – to a genuinely multicultural state? With their putative ownership, they are hamstringing even what a Prince Charming can hope to do and achieve.

Well, as we saw above, any good tragedy relies on irony – and one of this book's biggest ironies is Canada's finding itself in a Greek tragedy we call "An Unhappy Consciousness." Some of the biggest tyrants in our Canadian drama are those characters who believe that they are the true Canadians and that everyone else should be secondary to them.

Yet the situation would become a comedy if Canada could get everyone to accept her or his status and inequality – if it could convince these immigrants that they can have no meaningful existence outside of the Canadian state and that their well-being is the same as Canada's. It is to their advantage to be weak – it guarantees them a better life, in order and stability and in the probability of a better future for them. They would be acting according to deterministic laws that ensure their freedom and survival, and their job would be simply to accept their placements within the system that is the manifestation of these laws.

It would be a comedy when the greater good that law guarantees – perhaps in a social contract, but most likely in a covenant, which captures the natural laws of the universe – and which provides the certainty that individuals cannot do on their own. Only within the collective can these citizens aspire to have the absolute knowledge on which to base their absolute certainty, preservation, and perfection. Social inequalities would be likely, to allow the system or collective to function as efficiently as possible. That is why a heated debate continues over the positioning of immigrants and whether they should have full power or some lesser position.

Were any of this narrative to be true, for us to be in the midst of comedy we would have to believe that most of the immigrants coming to Canada, all those we cherry-pick from around the world as the brightest and best, all those coming from the elites of their home societies, would have to be in a false consciousness. They would have to believe that they are ideal for promoting the greater good of a society that does not recognize them as intrinsic to its community. They would have to be willing to voluntarily sacrifice themselves and their dreams – a fate they were unwilling to accept back home, where they enjoyed a "natural" sense of belonging and had their friends and family around them – so that they could simply exist here. They would have to be unwise to believe that this would be justice. And if there is no hope of justice, then there is no comedy but simply tragedy. Without justice, there is ultimately only an appeal to cold, hard, and inflexible laws, which becomes a tragedy for people to whom the laws may appear unnatural, irrational, and unjust.

In this battle of wills, then, the tragedy can be for only one of the two sides, as our common sense tells us that these views of society and of who should belong cannot coexist forever. Canada is not about different societies, even though it is multicultural. It is still an exercise in producing a unity, a single self-consciousness, and so it will have to be a tragedy either for the immigrant or for the old-timer, as these two positions are incompatible.

But instead, life might just be unfurling according to its own divine irony. It might be the initial story of two suitors beating themselves to death in a struggle to win the affection of or even dominance over their beloved. But when they catch the drift of what happened while they were so busy fighting each other, they realize that the beloved has made off with the butler or some lesser social underling whom they invited into their house to take care of it while they fought each other. Not only that, but the beloved and the new favourite are off making a future together, and neither of the original suitors is likely to have dominance over what the new couple is planning. Indeed, it now appears that the focus of the story has shifted to the immigrants (the new favourites) and the beloved.

The original suitors now feel so marginal that they beg the beloved to turn back the clock to allow them to correct their mistakes, to allow them to keep a more watchful eye on the social underlings to prevent them from becoming their superiors. It becomes a story just like the current one about Canada and all those visible-minority immigrants and how to accommodate everybody one way or the other.

For the French and English in Canada, the reality of this story is a tragedy. Somehow they have lost control over the script. All they can demand is that the beloved move forcefully to domesticate the Bad John that snuck up on them. They can hope to merely accommodate the Sweet Boy and Sleeping Beauty or Snow White too, rather than giving them the traditional gifts of freedom in the form of the key to the city and allowing them to ride off on the horse to live happily ever after.

For the immigrants, what is unravelling in time might be a comedy until the beloved also discovers their faults and possibly jilts them for some unproven stranger, for some other Bad John or, preferably, some Sweet Boy. Then they would be performing a tragedy.

And for the beloved that is the country Canada, all this struggling, all these disappointments, and all these elations are just … well … life, with no malice intended nor offered. These ups and downs can happen to anybody, for such is life itself. It is existence at the animal levels of survival and amorality. More than that, the beloved does not and cannot have time or sympathy for anyone no longer among her favourites. For that, too, is life – the beloved's life. And as long as the beloved has life, well, life is, indeed, a comedy – even if it seems otherwise for everyone else.

With this anecdote – or warning – in mind, let us now take a closer look at what constitutes tragedy and comedy in our daily existence as a multicultural Canada.

9

Citizenship with Difference:
The CBC and I

In like manner, the beginner who has learned a new language always
translates it back into his mother tongue, but he assimilates the spirit
of the new language and expresses himself freely in it only when he moves
in it without recalling the old and when he forgets his native tongue.[1]
                                                                    – Karl Marx

In the summer of 2001, I took part in a most frustrating exercise. The
participants may have viewed it as a tragedy; observers who knew more,
it might have seen a comedy. CBC Radio, the radio arm of the Canadian
Broadcasting Corporation, had commissioned me for what both it and I
thought was a relatively easy project. The aim was to identify differences
within multicultural Canada and to isolate power conflicts between
groups – or at least that was what I thought.

We were "working out the politics of recognition" vis-à-vis immigrants
in Canada. I wanted to reveal the difficulties some immigrants encounter
as they move towards citizenship, focusing not only on the civic components – a passport and voting – but also on how the mainstream imagines the immigrants. Were foreigners achieving their goal of becoming
what we might call "fully human" by gaining citizenship? In order to
determine this, we had to view the new citizens as having all the rights
and capabilities to effect democratic change: civic rights, the ability to
participate in politics, including running for and winning high office, and
a share in the country's prosperity (criticism was growing in some quarters that poverty was becoming more of a concern for immigrants).

I wanted then for the program to assess whether or not newcomers
could claim Canada as theirs as much as old-timers. I hoped to examine
how much the wider society feared or loved the recent arrivals and how
much this attitude made their lives in Canada comedies or tragedies.

The exercise was a small forerunner of the wider debate that was to sweep Canada in 2007 over "accommodation" of immigrants and of difference in a multicultural society. In our CBC project, a leading institution was exploring the meaning of accommodation vis-à-vis Canadian citizenship. I was looking at how we socially imagine newcomers; for me, this issue goes to the heart of Canada's commitment to genuine, egalitarian multiculturalism and to citizenship as a true marker of equality and social justice.

I was thinking primarily of the practical tests to the limits of section 6 of the Canadian Citizenship Act of 1946 as amended on rights and responsibilities: "A citizen, whether or not born in Canada, is entitled to all rights, powers and privileges and is subject to all obligations, duties and liabilities to which a person who is a citizen ... is entitled or subject and has a like status to that of such person."[2] A host of legislative and official policies reinforce this provision, including the constitution, which states that Canada is officially multicultural and that governments should see and administer it as such. What in this context does "multicultural" mean? And isn't citizenship, as philosophers and social scientists long told us, a recognition of love akin to membership in an extended family,[3] where only belonging – not individual performance – matters and is the qualification for love? If this is so, then it is an unusual family that fears rather than loves many of its members.

The Multiculturalism Act of 1985 defines its subject, building on social legislation to make the country egalitarian in theory and to allow all members full liberal citizenship. In its preamble, it states: "The Government of Canada recognizes the diversity of Canadians as regards race, national or ethnic origin, colour and religion as a fundamental characteristic of Canadian society and is committed to a policy of multiculturalism designed to preserve and enhance the multicultural heritage of Canadians while working to achieve the equality of all Canadians in the economic, social, cultural and political life of Canada." The act stipulates that the government intends to "(f) ... encourage and assist the social, cultural, economic and political institutions of Canada to be both respectful and inclusive of Canada's multicultural character; (g) promote the understanding and creativity that arise from the interaction between individuals and communities of different origins; (h) foster the recognition and appreciation of the diverse cultures of Canadian society and promote the reflection and the evolving expressions of those cultures."

The Multiculturalism Act creates mandates for the government and even indicates how it should administer and monitor the policy. In a Hegelian sense, institutions such as the CBC embody the Canadian spirit

– in terms of historical development, but also as a means of achieving national desires in the future. They speak the Canadian socializing language, and so if Canada is building a just society that is a multicultural liberal democracy, then it must reach those goals and intentions through its institutions. Specifically, the act mandated the minister of multiculturalism to "(*a*) ... encourage and assist individuals, organizations and institutions to project the multicultural reality of Canada in their activities in Canada and abroad; (*b*) undertake and assist research relating to Canadian multiculturalism and foster scholarship in the field; (*c*) encourage and promote exchanges and cooperation among the diverse communities of Canada; (*d*) encourage and assist the business community, labour organizations, voluntary and other private organizations, as well as public institutions, in ensuring full participation in Canadian society, including the social and economic aspects, of individuals of all origins and their communities, and in promoting respect and appreciation for the multicultural reality of Canada." One might well assume that crown corporations such as the CBC would be aware of the intentions and political will of Canadians as reflected in the legislation and would also be leading the charge on this policy.

At this time, two social issues have come up for discussion: accommodation of certain members of minority groups and accommodation of outsiders, even native-born Canadians. It is within this context that the incident below becomes relevant. The other side of accommodation is what we can learn from the role models of happy assimilation. I am asking, in the manner of Austin and Hegel, whether Canada practises what it preaches about multiculturalism. For me, the ideal test should be its treatment of newcomers, particularly immigrants, and whether they receive social justice. To avoid both mere formalism and a focus on appearances, we have to place the test in ethical relations – in deeds, the acts of actual living.

On reflection, it seemed clear to me that the parties in this narrative about me and the CBC were bumbling along on a question of sovereignty, attempting to determine who can tell Canada's story and whether all Canadians, particularly those from abroad and not Christian, were in fact equally Canadian, equally part of "the people." A wider question for me: when visible-minority immigrants became citizens, could they immediately benefit from the Canadian welfare state and experience real political and economic advancement? This question is equally relevant today. In effect, could – and can – these immigrants overcome the stereotypes that defined them as Bad Johns?

This difference in perceptions of citizenship that both the CBC and I detected was harming many immigrants, through lower earnings and through "dumbing down" and de-skilling, especially because of non-recognition of foreign credentials. In our mythological language, these immigrants were Bad Johns, who had to undergo mental pain and social diminution to socialize into the new society. Governments' actions and policies were frustrating and alienating them, turning them into unhappy consciousnesses.

State employment has always been a primary form of accommodation. This type of story about citizenship and its limits dates back to Aristotle. Idealistically, the CBC and I hoped to identify these conflicts from *real* life and package them into a radio program of six reports for a general audience. We imagined that we could help Canadians to understand their differences and become more tolerant and accepting of others, and generally make Canada a more enlightened and rational country.

The exercise ended in failure. Despite the best of intentions on all sides, we would find ourselves in an intolerable situation, which appeared to offer no good escape. Tragically, this left us with only options that appeared equally bad for both sides, further distancing us from our initial intentions. We could not reach our goal while remaining true to what we believed right and moral. Our good intentions floundered because their underlying assumptions proved unchangeable. We could not develop a fraternal legal spirit, for we were not speaking the same socializing language with the same ideals of social stratification. The content of the proposed programs was diremptive, even if we had agreed on form and whose the voice should be. We simply did not have the same perspective on life.

I wanted to feature only immigrants, meaning for me Canadians who had started life outside the country, while the CBC understood "immigrant" as meaning anyone who was not white. The broadcaster approached second- and third-generation Canadians of visible minorities for interviews. I wanted success stories, such as former BC premier Ujjal Dosanjh and Justice Selwyn Romilly of the BC Supreme Court. Despite some opposition from the network, we did interview both of them.

Instead, CBC wanted to focus on immigrants who had lined up outside Canadian high commissions, consulates in India, and embassies elsewhere to apply for a landed immigrant's visa. Its producers wanted to look at how these immigrants failed to integrate in Canada because they had poor language skills or because no one would accept their credentials or their work experience.

I was keen to show how some of the brightest and best people from around the world were willing to leave home in search of success in Canada. My point was to highlight how many of them actualized their dreams and to ask them how they communicated their experiences back *home*.

The log-jam seemed ubiquitous. While the CBC wanted to show that jobs and economic concerns should be the main criteria for selecting immigrants, I wanted to argue – as the Immigration Act suggested – that immigration was about choosing new citizens who would eventually hold various functions, with society hoping to ensure its future by reproducing new citizens. I envisioned the six episodes dealing with Canadians living in Canada as members of a Canadian fraternity, with the only difference that some were born here and others elsewhere; the CBC wanted the bulk of the programming to be about foreigners seeking to join the Canadian fraternity. I wanted to tell stories about possible Prince Charmings living a tragedy, to see how they encounter and if possible overcome the fates that prevent them from actualizing their dreams as full Canadians. The CBC, seemingly, wanted stories about Bad Johns, all those characters whom lack of socialization prevented from becoming Canadian as of yet, operating behind masks of differences and diversity in what I might call a "comedy," which real Canadians could easily see.

Finally, I wanted to be the storyteller – to indicate the storyline and explain the story and its actors. The contract specified that I would offer my perspective and the voice of an immigrant who became a citizen and had the experiences to relate to others who have gone through similar changes. Instead, the CBC wanted me to act like a traditional Canadian. I was not willing to simply mouth somebody else's script – not if the CBC would present it as my perspective.

In the end, the only reasonable course was the death of the project and all its good intentions and idealism. But by then, two other metaphorical deaths had occurred. In my eyes, I had witnessed the death of the CBC as a medium that was able to deal with complicated issue of culture without imposing a dominant viewpoint and while upholding the broadcast act's ideal that its programming reflect all regions and people of multicultural Canada to Canadians.[4]

In the CBC's judgment, it had witnessed the metaphorical death of me as someone who could be flexible and accommodating and could become a team player by sacrificing his particular ideals for what it deemed a universal good. The producers, even if they offered accommodation for differences and diversity, as the embodiment of the social traits of the outsider on the inside, saw me as not being accommodating.

In the end, neither CBC Radio nor I could transcend our selves, and I felt as if I was experiencing my social death.

Perhaps not surprising, I can see elements of comedy and tragedy in this sad story. I thought I was creating a story of tragedy: of how the dreams and ambitions of well-educated, heroic figures evaporated in the Canadian reality. On reflection, I now think that the CBC producers thought that we were making a comedy: a story chronicling in all seriousness how so many fools unfamiliar with the Canadian notion of justice continued to run afoul of the expectations of multicultural Canada. If there was a comedic element, they must have thought it was those not-yet-fully-Canadian species from foreign lands and cultures who believed that they could get off the boat one day and take on the mantle of tragic hero the next, looking to cut themselves loose from all the limits and boundaries that framed Canadian society as the good. Again they had no intention to make such living funny or comical – merely an indication of what happens socially to people not fully socialized when they run up against entrenched societal norms and values.

In effect, the CBC was going to present these fools for heroes as the elements that disrupted and even threatened the good life, instead of joining and preserving life in keeping with their own natural instincts. Rather than following the examples of role models– outsiders who had become insiders – the fools were seeking to make their ways in the world, each following his or her own way, looking to work out a separate individuality, acting the script of a tragedy, and refusing to follow the comedic approaches of their role models. And I, as the chief fool who grasped the pain of the death of these tragic figures, and having come to recognize the folly of "kicking against the pricks," was for the CBC perhaps an excellent leading man for its comedy of redemption. For me, this was a story about some Bad Johns and some Prince Charmings; for the CBC, apparently, it was all about socializing Bad Johns. The problem for both of us involved recognizing and accommodating change.

Parliament mandates the CBC to reflect a Canada that is a status quo. This is a Canada that already exists, that has regions with their own cultures, and where specific groups already dominate. Parliament's requirement assumes cultural norms integral to Canada's cultural and social life. What I wanted the CBC to reflect was the challenges facing those norms and their possible replacement. I was curious about the status quo not as a lasting ideal but as Canadians might transform it. I assumed that the real Canada does not yet exist, that foliage developing over time has hidden it, and that we needed to clear away much of the Canadian bush to see the tangled garden underneath. Thus, for me, Canada was a work in progress: we should deconstruct its norms rather than support and preserve them. How could the CBC handle such change, when that was not its role? We quickly arrived at a dead end; we had driven into an alley of unhappiness.

What happened with the CBC and me is no different from what is happening in most institutions and agencies across Canada. Both of us started out thinking that we had a common agreement on what we thought constituted Canada, its ideals, and the true meaning of Canadian citizenship. Borrowing from the definition of a *societal culture* that I offered above, we began with an ideal very similar to what Kymlicka says is vital for the construction of a liberal democracy, and especially one, I would add, that is officially multicultural. For, as Kymlicka states, "Societal cultures with a modern liberal democracy are invariably pluralistic, containing Christian as well as Muslim, Jews, members of just about any the other religion in this multi-faith world, and atheists; heterosexuals as well as gays; urban professionals as well as rural farmers; conservatives as well as socialists. Such diversity is the inevitable result of the rights and freedoms guaranteed to liberal citizens, particularly when combined with an ethnically diverse population. This diversity, however, is balanced and constrained by linguistic and institutional cohesion; cohesion that has not emerged on its own, but rather is the result of deliberate state policies."[5]

Therefore I refer to this understanding to help frame a discussion of the role and behaviour of social institutions and agencies in a multicultural liberal democracy. How do these institutions, as the real agents of sovereignty in the land, incorporate and account for change, dynamism, and creativity, especially when the transformation comes in the forms and ideas of outsiders?

Particularly, these changes come in the guise of the immigrant whom the recipient country considers first a foreigner and then, ultimately, a full citizen. How should society incorporate the changes and the actors, and at what levels? What freedoms should they enjoy, and should there be limits on their ability to work for serious change in society? Or rather, how should the actors, as fully independent and democratic citizens, exercise their rights in society and participate in all aspects of decision-making?

And mind you, this is a society whose members, as free moral people, should be able to help transform it to suit their genuine liking.

Whenever we discuss these issues, lurking in the back of my mind is Prime Minister William Lyon Mackenzie King's statement in the House of Commons on immigration policy in 1947. His words reflect what we have been calling a "garrison mentality," with Canada as in effect an elitist state for one superior group, particularly white and/or European. As if reflecting Machiavelli's admonition to be fearful, King said, "There will, I am sure, be general agreement with the view that the people of Canada do not wish, as a result of mass immigration, to make a fundamental alteration in the character of our population. Large-scale immigration from the orient would change the fundamental composition of the Canadian population. Any considerable oriental immigration would, moreover, be certain to give rise to social and economic problems of a character that might lead to serious difficulties in the field of international relations. The government, therefore, has no thought of making any change in immigration regulations which would have consequences of the kind."[6] The term "Orient" refers to places that Europeans deem exotic and has changed over time, often, as Edward Said shows, meaning the Muslim world. King would have applied the term to source countries for many of today's immigrants. This was not a statement rife with love for foreigners, whom the prime minister perhaps saw as living an existence closer to the "natural" than he might have seen as appropriate – he was talking about Bad Johns, not Sweet Boys.

In 1971, Pierre Trudeau informed the House about his government's new policy of multiculturalism. "There cannot be one cultural policy for Canadians of British and French origin, another for the original peoples and yet a third for all others. For although there are two official languages, there is no official culture, nor does any ethnic group take precedence over any other. No citizen or group of citizens is other than Canadian, and all should be treated fairly." He added, "A policy of multiculturalism within a bilingual framework commends itself to the government as the most suitable means of assuring the cultural freedom of Canadians. Such a policy should help to break down discriminatory attitudes and cultural jealousies. National unity, if it is to mean anything in the deeply personal sense, must be founded on confidence in one's own individual identity; out of this can grow respect for that of others and a willingness to share ideas, attitudes and assumptions. A vigorous policy of multiculturalism will help create this initial confidence. It can form the base of a society which is based on fair play for all."

Leader of the Opposition Robert Stanfield – whom many people have called "the best prime minister Canada never had" – responded: "I wish to state immediately, Mr. Speaker, that the emphasis we have given to multiculturalism in no way constitutes an attack on the basic duality of our country. What we want is justice for all Canadians, and recognition of the cultural diversity of this country." He saw duality as *maximizing* diversity.

This perspective still informs some circles that believe that diversity in Canada means exclusively its French–English differences. All other differences must fit within English or French modules and disappear from consciousness. This is the opposite of Trudeau's multiculturalism policy, which stressed the willingness to share.

Trudeau explained "the view of the government that a policy of multiculturalism within a bilingual framework is basically the conscious support of individual freedom of choice. We are free to be ourselves. But this cannot be left to chance. It must be fostered and pursued actively. If freedom of choice is in danger for some ethnic groups, it is in danger for all. It is the policy of this government to eliminate any such danger and to 'safeguard' this freedom."

Later Trudeau would attempt to lead the country into official multiculturalism by showing how the Canada of modern times is new and different from the Canada of old. Ideologically, it subscribed to the ideal of social justice for all citizens that he had outlined in his writings about a just society; it made its laws fairer in terms of who could become immigrants and then citizens, and it and the provinces repatriated a constitution, adding a Charter of Rights and Freedoms that put flesh on the skeleton of a liberal citizenship. Creating Canada as a just society also meant trying to institute a thick solidarity among all Canadians on the political and economic front. This would require a strengthening of federal sovereignty, and Ottawa invaded provincial jurisdiction to standardize social and economic life for Canadians in all regions. Full citizenship meant that every citizen should enjoy civic, political, economic, and social welfare and recognition of identity claims; all citizens are equal, whether native born or immigrant.

Of course, as with any construction of consciousness, not everyone shared these ideals. It was clear from the political rhetoric and even from the presentation by the media that some powerful voices always remained in opposition. Should power relationships change, those in opposition would institute a new order and impose new meanings for justice and freedom.

Apart from the laws that determine the responsibilities and obligations of multicultural citizenship, a more recent authoritative position on Canada and minorities has emerged, and it may be at odds with King's statement. The Supreme Court of Canada has stated that

the concern of our courts and governments to protect minorities has been prominent in recent years, particularly following the enactment of the *Charter*. Undoubtedly, one of the key considerations motivating the enactment of the *Charter*, and the process of constitutional judicial review that it entails, is the protection of minorities. However, it should not be forgotten that the protection of minority rights had a long history before the enactment of the *Charter*. Indeed, the protection of minority rights was clearly an essential consideration in the design of our constitutional structure even at the time of Confederation ... Although Canada's record of upholding the rights of minorities is not a spotless one, that goal is one towards which Canadians have been striving since Confederation, and the process has not been without successes. The principle of protecting minority rights continues to exercise influence in the operation and interpretation of our Constitution.

If the courts are of the same mind as Trudeau, then they acknowledge the legacy of the US Civil War on Canada and the historic positioning of ethnic and racial minorities in the country.

A major issue concerns how Canada is to produce a healthy society through immigration: can it do so simply by relegating immigrants to the status of the subconscious, where there will always be a tragic fight for recognition and for a hearing and respect? Which of the two approaches, as we see with King on one hand and the Supreme Court of Canada on the other, captures Canada as a liberal democracy that is officially multicultural and where all citizens are equal in the share of welfare? And as a corollary, if the immigrants are part of the Canadian subconscious, what type of creativity and resourcefulness are they producing and offering to Canadian culture as they struggle to overthrow their lordship-and-bondage relationship with a more dominant culture? Bearing all of these things in mind, how is it possible to transform the tragedy of Canadian living into a comedy?

This dilemma of living in social ill health and even pathology while desiring a healthy and happy consciousness is a major one in immigrant-receiving countries. Plural societies such as the United States,

Britain, and even Australia, even though the latter two claim to be multicultural, handle the change through a Hegel-type relationship of lordship and bondage. The newcomers are simply slaves or bondsmen and must agree to accept a secondary role in society. Those of ancient lineage and dominant pedigree tolerate them and position them on the basis of their own desires. They call the newcomers "citizens" and give them the outward trappings – a passport, the right to vote – but do not allow them full equality.

Of course, sometimes the opposite happens, as has been the case in Canada, where some immigrants, as the archetypal Prince Charmings, have become citizens ahead of those with a longer, but inferior, lineage in the country. An example is the speed of naturalization for western European immigrants, ahead of visible-minority citizens whose families have been in Canada for generations. As American ethnographer Stephen Steinberg states in *The Ethnic Myth*, the settler societies in the Americas traditionally differentiate true citizenship along the lines of race.[7] One resulting myth, as he suggests, is to ignore the "essentially negative basis on which (ethnic) pluralism developed [in the New World]."[8]

This kind of pluralism has its origins, Steinberg says, in conquest, slavery, and exploitation of foreign labour. Many Europeans, even if they had belonged to ethnic minorities and were despised back home, considered themselves superior to such groups as Native peoples, Africans, and other peoples of colour. Here we see preference for Prince Charmings and Sweet Boys over Bad Johns. And because the Europeans knew how to live and behave in European cultures, they could easily adapt to the new societies.

Within this Steinberg-type framework, attitudes such as racism, ethnocentrism, and xenophobia still arise today, holdovers from a hypothetical natural law that needs refining and changing to produce the equality and egalitarianism of citizenship and still essential in European-style societies. These attitudes preserve a fundamental belief that antedates modern citizenship. To proclaim a new multicultural Canadian citizenship is one thing, but justice will not be multicultural if the society remains officially and practically Eurocentric and merely accommodates other groups in a way that minimizes their full citizenship.

When racism, ethnocentrism, and xenophobia appear, we see conflict between an old good flowing from natural law and the dominant current good, which positions and recognizes all people as equal, raceless, and at home. To this end, those who suffer such stings and limits are players in a tragedy, fighting against "natural" limits that may still appear. They require hubris and a strong will to struggle against these limits, to seek freedom to try to discover and actualize themselves. They consider themselves moral: fighting for a specific notion of the good, especially when they see a just society that is a multicultural liberal democracy.

To this way of thinking, racists, ethnocentrists, and xenophobes are fools and comedians, unwilling to accept a new order not based on natural law. These practitioners appear unethical and unjust. Unhappiness arises in society because neither side likes this arrangement. People with these old ideas feel guilty because they have sacrificed their true and authentic desires yet still do not meet the terms of the compromise. Therefore they still search for freedom. The desire for freedom acts like a repressed malady in the body politic and constantly requires stronger and stronger drugs to produce the mask of healthy living. Living becomes socially unhealthy.

What I have just described is pluralism at work: it assumes a competition between morals and ethics, and it provides for the recognition of pockets of natural law within the social ethical framework. There are real battles going on between good and evil, and apparently either can win this struggle for lordship and bondage. It is part of the making of an unhappy consciousness, where neither party feels fully free and genuine. It is a struggle of tragedy, even though those who are in superior positions might desire it to be a comedy.

The other desire is that for a genuine multicultural state that aims to move beyond mere pluralism and ensure that every individual is genuinely equal to the others and should have all the rights and freedom of citizenship. This multiculturalism seeks sameness among citizens and legitimacy for each vote, desire, or intention. This social construction is purely ethical, working for social justice in a just society. If it does not totally repeal a natural law such as recognition of ethnicity, for example, it at least deems that principle to be foreign and lacking universal appeal. In addition, this natural law and its sense of freedom, which antedate the just society, is not enforceable. It is purely voluntary: an act or result of freedom itself, rather than its determinant. It is objective rather than subjective and available only for particular and specific usage.

Ultimately, what matters in this framework is the laws and ethical expectations of the social construction that has banished the hold of natural law on citizens – people who are ethical subjects at home in what they are creating. Such individuals will have ceased to be tragic and will be all of the same comedic consciousness, believing in this false consciousness that they have returned to the erstwhile Garden of Eden, away from a place of good and evil, back to a place of limitless freedom. Under this scenario, differences of any form would not count – every Canadian would be, first and foremost, abstractly the same. Only when they put on the garments of full citizenship should they be able to decide how they want to differ from one another, acknowledging that that difference should never wipe out the sameness that is the beginning of their social relationship and their Canadian reality.

Such a dream aims for a life that has moved beyond the unhappiness of tragedy into the merriment and celebration of comedy, into the full embrace of individuals as genuine selves celebrating their perceived authenticity and then moving on together to construct a new reality. Each individual would have an equal and democratic say in the continuing construction, and they would enjoy full recognition and equal responsibility and privileges in the constructed reality. To pull this off, Canadians and individuals as a unity would genuinely leave the world of tragedy behind.

However, this new reality would be a social construction and contrivance, and so many people might just wake up to the reality that it is not an ideal reality for them. It would be just like the morning after the wedding celebration, after all the embracing and toasting, when the main actors awake and ask themselves what the heck has just happened. And instantly, they are into a different reality, one that is authentic and tragic. Once they have broken the embrace that produced the unity, the participants instantly find themselves in a world of confrontation primarily because of their differences and in a reality that maximizes and makes these differences real.

What I have just outlined is an issue of the reality of incorporation that I have encountered in many fields, as a journalist, an author, and later an academic. In all cases, people must make choices. One of them is engagement with an institution that already has a culture, which no longer seems to the new arrival to be ideal or representative of wider society. In other words, the institution's official ideology is neither really democratic nor multicultural.

This is especially the case in Canada for such institutions as the media and academe, which embodied a now discarded good – making a white man's country. They now seem predominantly white institutions, even when operating in a multicultural environment, for power and prestige still rest with whites, who remain dominant. How can these institutions change yet still keep to their original mandate? Indeed, how much new wine can society pour into old skins before it destroys them? In such a case, we can only pour purer and more enlightened *intentions* into them.

By undertaking the project with CBC Radio, I was really attempting to test something that even the staunchest of traditionalists have long acknowledged. This is the idea that what drives these institutions and agencies is a psychology, and that their behaviour usually flows from their perceptions of the social importance of their interlocutors. As the conservative Friedrich Hayek, who might disapprove of the social engineering in multicultural policy, warned, this kind of psychological change alters people's character. "This is necessarily a slow affair," he said, "a process which extends not over a few years but perhaps over one or two generations. The important point is that the political ideals of a people and its attitude toward authority (as what it postulates as the common good) are as much the effect as the cause of the political institutions under which it lives. This means, among other things, that even a stronger tradition of political liberty is no safeguard if the danger is precisely [that] new institutions and policies will gradually undermine and destroy that sprit."[9]

We hear similar sentiments from liberal theorist John Rawls, who argues for equality of citizenship as the benchmark for social justice in a liberal democracy. He proposes seeing any citizen as possessing two types of goods, one bundle that he calls "primary," and the other "secondary." Possession of the bundles makes the individual a citizen. In the first bundle, "each person has an equal claim to a fully adequate scheme of equal basic rights and liberties, which scheme is compatible with the same scheme for all; and in this scheme the equal political liberties, and only those liberties, are to be guaranteed their fair value."[10] In the second, "social and economic inequalities are to satisfy two conditions: first, they are to be attached to positions and offices open to all under conditions of fair equality of opportunity; second, they are to be the greatest benefit of the least advantaged members of society."[11]

So were mainstream Canadians surrendering to a new form of tyranny? Or was directing institutions to recognize and reflect non-dominant groups altering mainstream perceptions of who is truly Canadian?

The second main participant in this drama is newcomers. They could accept current ways, cultures, and social realities but would thereby cease to be genuine and would not be helping the institutions to broaden their scopes and activities. Apart from a few new and diverse faces, nothing would have really changed. Alternatively, they could try to remain authentic and to do only what their conscience says is right, even if they have to go against the institution's tradition and history. In this case, they could either be Prince Charming or a Sweet Girl or be a Bad John or his female counterpart. Then they might bring new ideas and approaches to the discussion, but perhaps alienate the older hands and experience alienation themselves. The point here is that the state decides who is Sweet Boy or Bad John. As sovereign, it creates the conditions and environment – the stage of this drama.

Neither of the Canadian choices brings happiness, either to the existing institutions or to the newcomers, who stand a good chance of appearing intruders, interlopers, or even barbarians. Colleagues could ostracize them, cut them off from fraternal love, even accuse them of not being team players, an act of diremption that ironically the team itself perpetrates.

They would simply be the existing culture's latest manifestation of a Bad John much in need of socialization. But since the culture, at the beginning of this piece, is suspect and even undesirable in so many ways, to what should a Bad John socialize? Herein lies the comedy within a tragedy, or the tragedy that refuses to move on to be a comedy, even if only to give momentary respite. In the end, it is the state that makes us a Prince Charming or a Bad John. Let us now look at how my dealings with the CBC positioned me as a Bad John.

MEDIA, IMMIGRATION, AND CITIZENS

The contract that brought the CBC and me together in 2001 was, as we saw above, for me to create six one-hour shows on immigration an issue that was of growing concern to Canadians and to the national broadcaster, whose mandate is to reflect Canadian culture to Canadians.

This debate has spawned political rhetoric, newspaper headlines, and columns and a growing number of publications by the popular press, academic presses, and think tanks. In the late 1960s, Prime Minister Pierre Trudeau began implementing his vision of a just society, and in 1971 Canada became the world's first officially multicultural country.[12]

Charles Taylor's *Multiculturalism and the Politics of Recognition* (1994) outlined the congenital battle between English and French ethnicities.[13] In the author's eyes, this struggle was taking place within a wider and almost civilizing framework, in keeping with developments in modernity. He argues that the modern nation-state subscribes to a notion of dignity that prescribes equality for all members regardless of "natural" differences such as race, ethnicity, gender, sexuality, place of birth, or language. "As against [the traditional] notion of honor," Taylor says, "we have the modern notion of dignity, now used in a universalist and egalitarian sense, where we talk of the inherent 'dignity of human beings,' or of citizen dignity. The underlying premise here is that everyone shares in it. It is obvious that this concept of dignity is the only one compatible with a democratic society, and that it was inevitable that the old concept of honor was superseded."[14] The ideal of dignity resonates most strongly among personalists and people who argue that the basic difference between one-dimensional individuals and well-rounded personalities is dignity. This is what makes every human special, what makes him or her god-like and yet sociable. "Finally," says the personalist Jacques Maritain, "we turn to religious thought for the last word and find the deepest layer of the human person's dignity consist in its property of resembling God – not in a general way after the manner of all creatures, but in a *proper* way. It is the *image of God*."[15] It is dignity that takes individuals beyond abstract liberal beings to socially embedding in the community, which they can transcend. For this reason, the influence of personalism as an ideology on Trudeau and other people of like mind can help us appreciate the radicalism behind official multiculturalism in Canada. This dignity is the difference between remaining a sentient individual focusing on immediate matters – survival, awareness of surroundings – and becoming a fully sensitive, self-conscious human. Canada's introduction of official multiculturalism – a symbolically US Civil War–type fight, I suggest – momentarily diffused much of the tension between the two "founding peoples" by advancing the claim that while Canada was officially bilingual, it was multicultural and recognized all individuals, ethnicities, groups, and cultures.[16] In a multicultural Canada, and emerging from the ashes of their bloodless war, the two founding nations became, collectively, the mainstream, presenting a seemingly unified position on Canada and its future. However, since the ideal of human dignity that comes with a peculiar Canadian flavour and intention is what attracts new citizens the world over to the country, we must ask ourselves whether the newer citizens are in a struggle against the recovenanting bilingual mainstream or whether the mainstream widened itself enough to automatically include *all* diversity.

This type of liberalism in a plural society can be deadly for everyone, particularly when it is no more than what Hegel would call "bleeding heart liberalism," which is likely to deepen the tragedy of an unhappy consciousness. More than that: this outcome is what I argue we can expect from "a politics of recognition" – effectively, recognition of the presence of difference in the body politic that associates no real needs or desires, no extra power, with those whom it marks as "different." Such multiculturalism sees difference as purely a marker of being non-Canadian; it extends recognition for purposes not of inclusion but of continuing social exclusion.

The failure of my radio project was to bring home to me the dangers and limits of seeing a politics of recognition as the key to living happily in a multicultural society: that is, the recognition of one person for another. This kind of recognition is central to all those worshipping at the "liberal temple of tolerance for others" of modern Canada. It is also a warning to people trying to change the world for good solely through the exercise of good works for the Other and through others. Here, the emphasis is on bringing change to the other, perhaps in a beneficial way that uplifts the other to a point of subjectively recognized equality with a benefactor. Such an approach can also be generous recognition that places the subject in position of superiority and dominance, from which it has the time, luxury, and good intentions or desires to confer a status of equality on an inferior suffering the evils of inequality.

Such is the recognition of amelioration, which flows from good intentions and tolerance and has become the hallmark since the 1990s for popular analysis of multiculturalism and citizenship in a liberal democracy. It is a recognition in which the subject, as the powerful partner in an ethical relationship, sees the evil in the world as outside of and foreign to its own body and, from a detached position, believes that it can enter the world and effect positive change without undergoing any meaningful transformation itself.

But I propose that this is a form of recognition that can illuminate power relations within a genuinely multicultural country. This is the recognition not of another, who is an object that is equally and unchangeably another subject whom we momentarily misrecognize as a lesser thing, nor of another subject that ought to sport all the clothing and equality of a liberal moral agent. Rather, it is the recognition of a subject whom we perceive differently and whom we trap in an unchanging identity or stereotype that we impose.

This recognition occurs not through a change of gaze or subjectivity, when we attempt to see the world from the perspective of an I by seeing evil as nesting de facto in an intersubjective miscommunication and misunderstanding. Rather, it occurs *within* a subject over its dealing with the world and allows the subject to realize, often to its horror, that, as an individual, it is responsible for much of the evil within its own world. For example, it might have treated Prince Charming as if he were a Bad John, and vice versa. This is the recognition of the self's fatal misperception of the self. And, traditionally, this is the kind of recognition that is central to good tragedy.

This recognition is internal to the body and is also projected onto the individual's body as a primarily moral consideration that only later becomes an ethical one by informing the treatment of others. Tragic recognition is subjective before it can become intersubjective. It calls for drastic action, not vis-à-vis the world but by and to the individual by itself – corrective action often so radical that it destroys the subject – or at least its tyranny – to save it from further harm partly of its own making. What it might have to destroy is the method and mechanism of determination – the process that decides who is the Bad John and who is the Prince Charming.

External recognition can lead to indifference, to a kind of stoicism whereby the individual feels that he or she has nothing to do with the evil or unhappiness and no power to effect change. Or it may lead to a type of scepticism that is the uncontested acceptance of the world as it is, with its attendant evil – a world in which there can, perceptually, be no justice and which it is even foolish to try to change. Once again, there is no onus for a moral agent to become active or for the agent to even be moral.

Internal recognition is different and, ironically, more disastrous for the subject. For it grasps what lies at the heart of tragedy – the evil already in the subject before it encounters another and that reconciling tragic relations in an ethical state requires reversal of what seems good. It also indicates what to eradicate and what to venerate (usually the former) to make tragedy into comedy, despair into hope, and the feared into the beloved. This recognition derives from an absolute knowledge of the self as if it were an object, and it suggests that the solution to tragedy is death. A personal death is what makes life tragic and not comedic.

Such recognition goes beyond opening up oneself passively to the possibility of harm by an Other, or of simply turning the other cheek – acts once again of generosity by one subject to an Other, or by a superior and enlightened being to an inferior and unsophisticated being, even if in response to a moral command. The tolerance and open-mindedness that emanate from the recognition of an external evil lead to a dead end of inactivity or conformity by a more duplicitous route. In the end, the subject does not change; it continues, like the misguided fool in a comedy, to wreak havoc from its good intentions. It has no way to end this tragic and unhappy experience where nothing turns out the way it planned, where its actions for the good merely extenuate an already bad situation. The subject's initial good, which is the cause of the evil, remains inviolate.

The recognition that I am proposing, because it occurs within the individual, is enough to propel the individual to do something to heal itself from division and conflict. But it is not enough in itself: it commands the individual not just to treat the symptoms but to look for the root cause of the unhappiness. In this search, the separate acts of recognizing and reconciling conflate into one continuous act that is a dialectical relation within a whole system, the same way as night follows day to complete a twenty-four-hour period.

My undertaking to produce for the CBC a series on immigration enmeshed the institution, the state, and me in a debate as old as Canada and as current as the social imagination of what is and could become Canada and Canadian. The discussion was – and still is – about what Canada should look like in the future. It is about the reality that should and could be Canada: either a reality reflecting old ideals or a reality that accepts fundamental change. Depending on the perspective, this is the scripting of a tragedy or of a comedy.

One of the strongest voices in this discussion on forming the Canadian nation-state comes from the status quo – a group with a distinct profile and psychology. Some of its members may see themselves as the historical mainstream and possess strong views of what is Canada and who are Canadians. These views retain vestiges of the old order, when some people imagined a European country in the Americas, whose citizens were somatically white, European in culture, and aristocratic in way of life.[17] The arguments from this group indicate that, psychologically, some members have not fully come to terms with who or what modern immigrants are or with their proper roles and functions. We can see this uncertainty in the debate over whether immigrants are aliens or strangers who should be happy to be incorporated peripherally or whether society should see and treat them as already future citizens, part of the unchangeable that is Canada, with the same rights and entitlements as any other Canadian.[18] Perceptually, this argument constructs immigrants as willingly accepting limits on standard liberal rights and conditions as members of society. Some old-timers may think these limits acceptable because they imagine immigrants improvising circumstances, incapable of or unfree for full self-determination.

10

Crisis 2001: Not Enough People!

Nobody seemed to know where John called home
He just drifted into town and stayed all alone.[1]
Jimmy Dean, "Big John Bean"

Immigration, including the role of immigrants in Canadian culture, became a national issue by the summer of 2001, when Statistics Canada reported an ethnic and demographic makeover under way. The impact was analogous to the point in Hegelian analysis when Eve had to teach the facts of life to a rationalist and self-centred Adam, an archetypal Bad John. Just like the exemplary Adam, Canada was coming to know itself as a tragic hero: it was ageing and dying but wanted to live forever. As a self-consciousness, it had to realize that it was ultimately a *desire*, which has led it into a relation of lord and bondsperson in which it faces its ultimate master – death. This pending death is the cause of the fear wracking Canadian social life. Change is the death of the old and of the status quo. Here we see change that is a death even before its arrival in a new setting or context to start all over again. It is death that drives the immigrant to leave a homeland and to seek life in this new land.

Having killed its old self, the new entity, wearing its burial clothes and the ghost of a previous life, haunts the receiving society by portending the social order's demise as a perfect social construct. It is a death in the hope of a Christ-like resurrection into a new world – into a beyond that is the other of the previous lived experience. However, this death and resurrection must occur in the now, when the here and the beyond collapse into a single moment and time. As Hegel explains from a distance, "For this consciousness has been fearful, not of this or that particular thing or just at odd moments, but its whole being has been seized by dread. In that experience it has been quite unmanned, has trembles in every fibre of its being, and everything solid and stable has been shaken to its foundation."[2]

Comedically, Canada had no means of translating that desire to avoid the spirit's material death and leave its old self the same and as authentic as it imagined itself.[3] Comically, the slave that is Canada today, thinking it is still its own master, has to attempt to turn what is otherwise Nature as an overlord and potential killer into a social experience – to overcome the natural limit or finitude that is death through its susceptibility to unwilling change. It attempts to do this by accepting others or immigrants who are "naturally" different and by working on them to make them socially Canadians.

Thinking they are working for themselves, Canadians are – tragically or comically, depending on perspective – mere slaves working for a master that nature imposes. "Through his service he rids himself of his attachment to natural existence in every single detail; and gets rid of it by working on it," as Hegel wrote.[4] Canadians of ancient lineage find that they are not masters naturally, or even socially, for in turn they see the immigrants as a different form of death – a death of their own dominance in Canada. The realization that they must accept immigrants, and then their acceptance of the newcomers, constitute a death: the old has passed away, along with its ways of doing things. The equation of life has lost its balance, because change has thrown off its proportions and alignment. Immigrants should have been the bodies doing the bidding of old-timers in their attempt to cheat the ultimate master, death. Now, the oldsters find them merely another form of death, threatening their old image of Canadians, and that they themselves are in bondage. They can remain alienated in this changing world, even as an unintentional consequence of their action or because of an action whose intentions they knew but they were not free not to make, or they can accept this spiritual death or metanoia as the realigning of *life itself* and accept that they are simply one element in this life and must always be seeking harmony with the times and with life itself.

In all cases, this would be an end-of-life confession that Canadians of ancient lineage are not the masters of their own faith. The gods they thought they were must die, even in the act of trying to avoid that death. For merely by thinking about their possible death, they have started to conceptualize themselves as mortal. With the first thought of their own death, then with the second thought of the need for immigrants, and, third, in actually allowing immigrants among them, they have died symbolically several times. Their world and their inviolable position in it have crashed in despair, reducing them to a mere nothingness – the dust with which they and the immigrants will have to restart building a new world.

Should the immigrants automatically take a bondsman's position in the new world or expect and even fight for equality if not superiority. If they go for superiority, both sides will be starting out to rebuild what time has discredited, meaning they are logically most likely to end up retracing the old journey to a new moment of despair. Times might have changed, but not the outcome. By choosing equality, they would be trying something, and, since this is terra incognita, who knows what it would bring? In this newness, they would be venturing forth on a journey that they could reasonably expect to end in hope. But for the journey of hope to start, all the voyagers must come to an absolute knowledge – that they are all mortal and as such equally dependent on one another for survival and for preservation of the state.

Ironically, Canada could *not* decide how to greet the newcomers. Should it welcome with open arms its potential saviours, who turn up perceptually as representatives of Nature, and submerge them fully into a citizenship of acceptance and love? Or should it fear them – for representing subversive elements unhappy with current levels of freedom and perhaps keen to destroy the social entity Canada? Sporting unsatisfied desires, the newcomers could be looking to decide how to do things in society, which should therefore fear and even control them to limit the potential for damage and obstruction.

Still, there is another irony at work: the Canada that Canadians are working on in opposition to the master that is death is the external representation of what they desire: survival or life. This is their authenticity. The slave is making the world and acting out history through its actions. It is producing its own social world, absent of nature.

In Canada, this social world turns out to be multicultural – seemingly the very opposite of what the old-timers wanted originally, but, comically, all they can produce outside of nature. And the same thing is happening to the immigrant, who, in opposition to its dual master – that is, nature and old Canadians – ends up producing its own Canada as a social entity, also multicultural. The aims and form may differ from the old-timer's multicultural Canada, but the joint effort expresses itself as multiculturalism as an intention and as a universal with different particular shapes. The key difference will most likely be over stratification, or distributive justice.

The result is a comedy of errors of misrepresentation by Canadians of ancient lineage, who do not recognize that they share dependence for life with the slave. Instead, they act as if they are not even slaves to death but are masters of the immigrants. In a Hegelian sense, they believe they are free and independent and that the immigrants need them, but not vice versa. The immigrants are living a tragedy: they recognize that death is a natural enemy, and they know that, at least temporarily, Canadians are the master – they impose limits and boundaries on the newcomer. The immigrants must accept this way of life until they can do better. So they work to make the world better and freer for themselves. The Canadians see themselves as stoics, whereby the thought of freedom is crucial to their being; the immigrants see themselves as sceptics, struggling physically against limits and boundaries and recognizing that Canadian justice is merely a thought for them – something in the transcendent or, as Hegel would say, "in the beyond."

In this drama of intra-dependence, neither the stoics nor the sceptics are happy, because neither gets recognition as the heroes they think they are. They are unhappy consciousnesses, and they produce multiculturalism with prototypes: stoics that are Prince Charmings and Sweet Boys, Bad Johns who are sceptics or perceived as pure negativity or social blackness.

LIVING DESIRES – SHIFTING TRAGIC EXPERIENCES

At least two factors accounted for this realization that it is the desires that drive this performance, even if Canadians started out by misrecognizing themselves and even the type of drama in which they found themselves. Statistics Canada had been reporting for some time an impending population crisis. First, Canada was not producing enough people to naturally sustain levels of population development and social growth. In effect, it was the hero looking up at the sky and howling against Providence – against a necessity that seemed to be organizing the cosmos in a way that would frustrate the country in its quest for freedom and everlasting happiness. In a world where the natural good is the continuation of a nation-state called Canada from one generation to the next, this meant that the country had come to rely heavily on foreign-born migrants for growth if it hoped – and hopes – to achieve this perceived good. Canada might lose full and exclusive power over an issue it perceived as central to its control over its fate and destiny. *Life itself*, or the ultimate Canadian desire, could not be found even within its own body.

Second, the demographic changes were forcing change in socialization and in national identity and culture.

While the Hegelian and biblical Adam would have to settle for becoming a father, the Canadian consciousness ran the risk of having to settle for step-fatherhood – a clear break in its natural or ancient lineage – from the social construction of a relationship that starts out unnatural. Instead of producing future citizens by direct bloodline, or *jus sanguinis*, Canada increasingly has to domesticate foreigners.

Mythologically, Canadians must take creatures not of their body and blood and try to make them into their image. Many immigrants become citizens – new Canadians – through *jus soli*. As a code, "new Canadian" extends even to infant offspring of landed immigrants or naturalized Canadians.[5]

In a 2010 report, Statistics Canada rationalized the need for Canada to track population changes: "Owing to persistent low fertility and strong immigration, Canada has seen its population rapidly change in recent decades. Thus, from one census to the next, there has been an increase in the proportion of persons born abroad, persons whose mother tongue is neither English nor French, and persons belonging to visible minority groups."[6] In a seemingly comedic diagnosis, Statistics Canada was in effect intimating that the apparent threat to the country's existence came from within: Canada was not producing enough babies. In any fairy tale, Canada is the Sleeping Beauty under the glass case, her life juices seemingly draining out, waiting for her Prince Charming – the revitalizing touches and kisses of immigrants. For only then can Sleeping Beauty (or Snow White) spring to life and do what she has to to live happily ever after.

But discussions about Canada's physical survival may sometimes mask a more meaningful debate about the country's purpose and which ways of life should dominate. What are the human desires for the country? This is where the decision focuses on choosing between human values. This moral discussion is what gives Canada the peculiar form of dignity that is the main battleground, more than the desire to make sure that Canada always has people. If Canada is to be a means to an end, the end has to be a specific quality of life that we can call "freedom" in a Canadian sense. This quality of life represents Canadians' desires as we generally understand them. The means to get there are simply the resources available, including human, able to remake Canada in keeping with those dominant desires but to become fully human themselves. Immigration has always been about the same thing: which values should dominate in a lordship-and-bondage relation. Human desires have not really changed over time, even if animal methods and expressions for achieving goals have evolved, particularly through physical and symbolic fights by animal combatants.

Therefore the ongoing discussion on immigration and on the diversifying population is at heart the same as that popular up to the 1960s. That was when many people assumed that the dominant Canadian values should be British and perhaps French and that, as a human expression, Canada was to be a country for Europeans. Since the 1960s, the ideal of what makes Canada human has changed from requiring a demographically white natural base to having no preference. However, the dominant human desire is to have immigrants with values that allow them to fit neatly into the existing covenant, and for both immigrants and old-time Canadians to agree on this. As it turns out, this is an order that racializes humanity, making some ethnic groups superior to others. Most modern immigrants fit into the groups at the inferior end of the hierarchy.

While this arrangement might be acceptable to people who like the system, why would highly skilled and ambitious immigrants – Machiavelli's self-made individuals and potential princes – settle for an inferior positioning? While Canada might easily meet immigrants' animal desires for the materials for daily minimum requirements, as human beings the newcomers would be hollow. They would be unable to achieve ambitions and dreams to make themselves fully human, superior to the images that Canadians have of them. Unless they can feel a chance to exhaust their natural abilities and penchants and thereby construct the greatest human being they are capable of becoming, they are likely to view Canada as tragedy instead of comedy.

Already, visible-minority immigrants have transformed the country's demographics, thereby leading to a debate over the good and evils of immigration. Should immigration maintain Canada as unchangeable in all respects, primarily demographically and culturally, or simply ensure its survival as a concept or form, regardless of its people and cultures? Is the ultimate good the survival of a nation-state we call "Canada," a civil site for the perfecting of humanity, which is most meaningful at a universal level, or is it maintenance and preservation of a particular and historical identity?

If the latter is the case, the particular and different identities and cultures within Canada will be the changeable matters that, from time to time, submerge their particularities into a higher universal Canadian identity and culture. To this end, Canada will always emerge as a good that continues everlastingly as a concept, regardless of its inhabitants. The good that was Canada has been changing, primarily since the overhaul of immigration in the 1960s.

Over this time, life in Canada's major cities evolved from a seeming monoculture or English and French biculturalism to a polyglot of languages, cultures, and religions, full of youthful exuberance and cosmopolitanism, brimming with symbols of cultural life. In contrast, the rural areas tended to remain staid, provincial, and virtually monochromatic culturally and ethnically. These developments over a forty-year span coalesced to make immigration a hot issue at the turn of a new century, as Canadians discussed the number of foreigners to take in each year, how to select them, and how to incorporate them into society.

While a country such as Canada is undergoing dramatic change, partially because of globalization, its makeup has shifted. Demographically, it is becoming a genuinely multicultural state, mostly because of changes in immigration patterns and increasing reliance on immigrants for population growth. Canada is, ironically, suffering the pangs of freedom that have hit most liberal democracies. The problem is a declining birth rate accompanying an ageing population.

Statistics Canada reported that Canada's birth rate, which had been declining, hit an all-time low in the 1990s and 2000s. It issued its brief findings in April 2002:

> Canada's crude birth rate (the number of live births for every 1,000 people in the population) fell to its all-time low in 2002 in the wake of another decline in the number of live births. The crude birth rate dropped to 10.5 live births for every 1,000 population, the lowest since vital statistics began to be produced nationally in 1921. The rate has dropped 25.4% in the last 10 years alone. In total, 328,802 babies were born in 2002, down 1.5% from the previous year. It was the 11th decline in the past 12 years. The fertility rate, an entirely different measure, estimates the average number of children women aged 15 to 49 will have in their lifetime. It fell slightly from 1.51 per woman in 2001 to 1.50 per woman in 2002, which was only marginally above the record low of 1.49 set in 2000.[7]

For Canadians of ancient lineage, this was startling news. It is against this background that I had agreed to supply the programming for CBC Radio as we saw in the last chapter. Indeed, in a subsequent report, Statistics Canada indicated that the ageing of the population is accelerating, so that by 2036 "the number of people aged 65 years or over would surpass the number of children aged less than 14 years or under. This shift, a first in the history of the Canadian population, would occur between 2015 and 2021." The country's working-age population was to decline to 60 per cent from 69 per cent by 2009.[8]

To compensate and to keep the population growing, in line with the national dream or idealized good, Statistics Canada has called repeatedly for more immigrants for at least the next twenty years. In *Projections of Diversity of Canadian Population* (2008), it speculated on what Canada would look like by 2031. "The results show," it reported, "that regardless of the scenario of future change considered, the ethnocultural diversity of the population will continue to increase significantly over the next two decades, especially within certain census metropolitan areas [CMAs]. Three Canadians in ten could be a member of a visible minority group in 2031, and the corresponding proportion in the Toronto and Vancouver CMAs could be two times greater."[9]

Reinforcing this dynamic of change, Statistics Canada attempts to quantify "the ethnocultural diversity of the Canadian population." It makes projections for visible minorities, religions, and mother tongues in 2031:

- Approximately three Canadians in ten (between 29 per cent and 32 per cent) could be a member of a visible minority group in 2031, regardless of the projection scenario. Canada would then have between 11.4 million and 14.4 million persons from visible minorities.
- Visible minorities would be over-represented in the younger ages, with 36 per cent of the population under 15 in 2031, in contrast to 18 per cent 65 or over.
- The most numerous groups in 2031 still should be South Asians, at 3.2 million–4.1 million, up from 1.3 million in 2006, and Chinese, at 2.4 million–3.0 million, up from 1.3 million in 2006.
- The fastest-growing groups should be Arabs, increasing by between 806,000 and 1.1 million by 2031 (from 276,000 in 2006), and West Asians, rising by between 457,000 and 592,000 (from 164,000 in 2006).
- The number of non-Christians would more than double by 2031 to 5.3 million–6.8 million, or 14 per cent of the population, up from 2.5 million in 2006, or 8 per cent. Among the non-Christians, about one in two would be Muslim in 2031, rising from about 35 per cent in 2006.
- Christians would represent fewer than two Canadians in three in 2031, down from three in four (75 per cent) in 2006 and 90 per cent in 1981.

- People with a mother tongue other than English or French
  should make up from 29 per cent to 32 per cent of the whole in
  2031, up from 20 per cent in 2006 and less than 10 per cent
  in 1981.[10]

Current trends show that most of the immigrants will come out of
states of nature from countries that, as recently as a generation ago, were
not on Canada's preference list. "If immigration were to continue to
come mostly from non-European countries," Statistics Canada states,
"the population of foreign born persons residing in Canada would continue to change over the next 25 years. In 2031, the percentage of visible
minorities who were foreign-born would reach 71%, the percentage of
allophones more than 77% while the percentage of persons having a
non-Christian religion would be approximately 32%. The corresponding proportions were respectively 54%, 70% and 24% in 2006."[11]

Foreign-born Canadians would rise from 20 per cent of the population in 2006 to between 25 per cent and 28 per cent in 2031 – the highest level since Confederation. Indeed, by 2031, 46 per cent of people
aged 15 years would be foreign born and have at least one foreign-born
parent, up from 39 per cent in 2006.

But even so, a lot changed in just the generation prior to these studies. The difference is already apparent in the major cities, with their
many different colours of skins, religions, languages, and other cultural
markings, each city containing a mix of these cultures and cultural
institutions. The living experience of mainly French and English cultures – the "two solitudes" (the title, from Rilke, of Hugh MacLennan's
iconic, Governor General's Award–winning novel of 1945) "warring
within the bosom of a single state" (Durham Report, 1839) and with
an aboriginal Other – has blossomed into a vivid, living experience of
organic multiculturalism.

The particular strain that we want to isolate in the Canadian dialectic
is one that we see on the streets and the playgrounds; it is more universalizing and inclusive than even "official" multiculturalism, which still
carries much of the baggage of the mythological two solitudes.

As part of its attempt at reconciliation, Canada rejected an immigration policy that seemed previously to try to create a whiteman's country through subjective selection principally of Europeans[12] from states
that Ottawa felt had in effect grown out of states of nature. Instead,
Canada moved to an objective points system to ground a universal
immigration policy. It idealistically treats all applicants as equal,

regardless of their histories and cultures, seems to assume that all the world is the same type of a state of nature, and selects migrants with high levels of social and economic capital able to fit easily into Canadian society. Many of the people urging such an approach were from neither "solitude."[13]

This policy has transformed the demographics of Canada, primarily in the large urban centres such as Toronto, Montreal, and Vancouver – the primary destinations for about 70 per cent of immigrants. Visible minorities, as a group, are fast becoming the majority there, dethroning the English and French. More of the values from their "states of nature" are now integral parts of Canadian culture.

This mixing has also brought Canada international acclaim for its multicultural policies, and a growing body of academic literature suggests that Canada is now an example of ethnic and racial peace for other multi-ethnic and plural countries.[14] Canada's values are those of the world – of the original state of nature from which all human desires congenitally spring.

Alongside the changes to immigration since the 1960s came a major overhaul of the Canadian Citizenship Act, which now implements the principle of *jus soli,* under which a Canadian citizen is anyone who has lived in the land for a requisite period and who agrees to live by its norms and precepts.[15] Newcomers who arrive as landed immigrants can become citizens after three years of continuous residence, as long as they have not become a financial charge on society or committed a serious crime.

One other plank in creating a just society was patriation of the British North America Act, as the Canadian constitution, from Westminster and entrenchment therein of a Charter of Rights and Freedoms. Both actions aimed at making Canada fully a liberal democracy.

The Charter reinforced in the social consciousness the specific foundational rights (due process, democratic, economic, mobility, and so on) not only of citizens, but also of landed immigrants and visitors. These rights determine relations between citizens, immigrants, and residents in what is in effect a Canadian social contract.[16] Among these are presumably the rights to participate in the construction of Canada, to change its philosophical and sociological conceptions of Canada and Canadians, and even to make a clean break with the Canada of the pre–Just Society era. To complete the circle, the Charter stipulates that the courts must interpret the constitution as if Canada were already a de facto multicultural country.

But the existing debate often omits a third important angle: the view of immigrants in a Canadian space, and their goals and dreams. Many observers seem to assume that the two older groups have assimilated these people and passed on their notions of what and who is unchangeably Canada and Canadian. There is still a tendency in mainstream Canada of unconscious and implied "conformity" that long typified Canadian society and that multiculturalism rejects.

My CBC radio show was to suggest that, while Canada had become a self-consciousness desiring life, it now had to confront one more struggle, over lordship and bondage, between life and death – a testing of desires from a state of nature – in the form of a struggle between the Canadian of ancient lineage and the minoritized immigrant. Which would dictate the terms of the new life? Who would decide the appropriate socialization of Canadians? Which side of any debates between old and new Canadians over socialization and then stratification should the state, as sovereign, support?

If it were to turn out to be the immigrants, then Canada would be in a tragedy, where the new heroes would ultimately have to come to terms with a new reality that might frustrate all their ambitions. This is where more of the desires from the nation-state overwhelm those of the civil society. In this case, Canadians of ancient lineage, as bondsmen, might seek to undermine the new reality in the hope of achieving something new, different, and more authentic. But the dominant immigrants would view their activities as merely comedic, a quixotic struggle against all the logic of the new reality and its expectations for justice.

However, if the old-time Canadians were to remain dominant, they would see the entire episode as a comedy, for they would have created a reality that produces justice for their favourites. Civil human desires would overwhelm the natural ones. These older Canadians would also see this reality as a comedy by newcomers crazy enough to believe that they are as equal as the older Canadians or that they can change the laws that underpin existing reality and give it its everlasting spirit.

In the 1960s, the latter scenario – the old order thinking that it must suppress the life force of the new – was developing. As a result, Canada was becoming an unhappy consciousness: two sets of actors were fighting for the true good, which they defined from their perspectives. How was Canada, as the state, to determine which human desires are good – the ones in the existing civil society, or those from a state of nature still crying out for inclusion, recognition, and membership? As a self-consciousness, Canada desired life but could not produce life, and it would not give way to its potential saviours. The mechanism for deciding what was good indicated that those immigrants could *not* be good; they could be only Bad Johns. Therefore the old Canadians were unhappy: they worried about maintaining their authentic Canada and about preserving their way of life.

Similarly, the immigrants were and continue to be unhappy. Seeing themselves as Sweet Boys, they come to Canada for "new life" – both for themselves and for the country. But while the new society expects them to provide for its greater good – to give the seeds of their body, like Adam, for a new life – instead, like Eve, they find that this new life is the same as the old one: it still excludes them and even writes them out of the national narrative. It considers them inauthentically Canadian. The old ways of thinking, the misrecognized ideas of life, still dominate, so ·that the immigrants find there is no new life for them and that, tragically, they must fight for the freedom they imagined. The state must be the mediator between the opposing sides. But the state is an untrustworthy mediator, for it has an interest that transcends those of both types of citizens and is likely to side with the combatant it finds most useful: the side that promises – if not guarantees – the state's future. In this regard, the current immigration debate reflects in its one-sidedness elitist Canadian perceptions about immigrants. It sees immigrants as exclusively *Others* or not fully Canadians, who yet want all the rights available in a liberal democracy. This discussion therefore lacks the enlightened knowledge that would result from incorporating their viewpoints, as possibly nonconforming subjects as well as Others, in a conversation about life in its many aspects.

IMMIGRATION: SURVIVAL THROUGH GROWTH?

What then was the climate in which my CBC Radio programs were to take shape? It is worthwhile lingering in that moment. Canadians arguing for a hefty increase in immigration as a route to national survival appear to have seen their case strengthen in recent years. Consistently, succeeding censuses have shown two serious problems – a declne in birth rates and funding for the social safety net.

First, Canada has a steadily declining birth rate; if the trend continues, within a decade it will not be reproducing itself naturally.[17] Census figures of 2002 showed a birth rate lower than that of 1946, when the population was much smaller. The *Globe and Mail* offered the stark headline, "Births Decline Again." "Canada's fertility rate tumbled to a record low in 2000, and fewer babies were born than in any year since 1946. The data released Thursday by Statistics Canada reflect a world-wide trend that is pushing the median age in developed countries beyond 40, reinforcing government assertions that increased immigration is necessary to maintain a viable work force."[18]

The country's rates of fertility – the average number of children for women between 15 and 49 years of age – dropped to 14.9 per thousand women, down 2.8 per cent from the previous year. This was the lowest level in 56 years and the tenth consecutive year of decline. In 2000, for example, Canada had 327,882 babies from 30.8 million people. This compared with 343,540 births in 1946, when the population was 12.3 million, and a peak of 465,000 in one year at the height of the baby boom of the 1950s. The last time the birth rate reached 2 per cent or greater was in 1972.

The statistics present other worrisome demographics. Older women are having more babies than younger females, but smaller families – reflecting a general trend in liberal societies. Indeed, only the group 40–44 saw an increase, up to 5.9 per thousand women from 5.5 in 1999. The tendency to have no children or have children later is most apparent among women 35 or younger, a period of higher fertility.

Statistics Canada says these findings follow Canadian women's tendency to start families later than women in, for example, the United States, "where access to medical services can be more expensive than under Canada's universal health-care system." For example, the birth rate for Canadian females 15–19 continued to decline, down to 17.3 per thousand in 2010 from 18.9 in 1999. As a result of such trends, Canada's population grew by only 4 per cent between 1996 and 2001, its lowest five-year growth rate ever, and as high as it was only because of immigration. According to the *Globe and Mail*, Patricia Tully, a senior analyst with Statistics Canada's health division, opined that Canada's options are quite clear and grave: "If a population can't replace itself through what we call natural increases – which is fertility rates being higher than mortality rates – then the population will decline, unless there's immigration."[19]

Second, national survival may be in jeopardy because of problems with funding universal health care – a seeming hallmark of the country and of its values and citizenship – because of an ageing population.

Canadians have been reflecting on the report of a federal commission in 2002 under Roy Romanow, former premier of Saskatchewan, into the future of health care, a system whereby the federal government pays for minimum levels of health care for all citizens and landed immigrants. The document urged Ottawa to spend billions of dollars more annually to prevent the health system from becoming more like the US approach.[20] In Canada, individuals do not pay directly for health care and hospitalization; political debaters often cite health care as an example of Canada as a more caring and more community-spirited nation than the United States, which has seemed in constant turmoil over the subject. Medicare and other forms of government assistance, including mandatory employment insurance and a government pension for older people, are prominent features of the Canadian social safety net, and many politicians and commentators use them to justify higher levels of personal taxation than Americans experience.

But the funding of the social safety net in Canada appears to be in crisis, once again because of demographics. The 1996 census and several updates by Statistics Canada show an ageing population; over the next 20 years the number of people 60 or over will increase from 4.2 million to 8.6 million. This growth may well increase costs for medical care and pensions, which recipients will expect and will have been paying for through taxes and insurance premiums. A proportionately smaller group of younger people, themselves paying insurance premiums, would need to make up any slack. Therefore the state needs more people of working age and hence hundreds of thousands of immigrants, perhaps even more than current numbers.

Current statistics indicate that, all things remaining the same, only about 7.8 million native-born Canadians will enter the country's workforce in the next two decades, leaving a shortfall of 800,000 vis-à-vis those who will be retiring. Three solutions suggest themselves: raising retirement age from 65 years, reducing benefits, and increasing immigration. The first two options would undermine the government's commitment to the elderly and tarnish Canada's image as a humanitarian space with effective and generous cradle-to-grave social assistance. David Baxter, executive director of Vancouver's Urban Future Institutes, observes: "The picture, if we don't do anything, is quite distressing ... We're living with the consequences of the children we didn't have. So let's quit debating about whether there's going to be a labour shortage or whether there's going to be a health-care crisis or if there's going to be a pension problem."[21]

The federal government's solution certainly involves immigration. Prime Minister Jean Chrétien rejected fiscal incentives to new mothers or for bigger families. First, Canadian women, he noted, have consistently demonstrated that they are not in favour of having big families or of having children early. Financial incentives won't change attitudes that value personal liberal freedoms and the self-actualization for women that translate into (or come with) small families. Second, Canada needs more people soon; an incentives program would take decades to have any effect.

According to the *Toronto Star*, Chrétien's solution was immigration. His "government will not adopt any policy changes to encourage Canadians to have more children but it would try to increase the number of immigrants in a bid to meet the demands of a rapidly aging population."[22] "We see that the population is not growing as fast as it should," Chrétien acknowledged in response to census reports that so many baby boomers are heading for retirement. Canada, he reported, was working on reforming a "very open immigration policy" to simplify procedures and admit people to the country more quickly.[23]

The federal government and sympathetic demographers argue that Canada needs levels of immigration equal to or greater than those record peaks of the 1900s and 1910s, when over 3¼ million people arrived, at, in some years, four times current rates proportional to existing population. The figure for 1913 – just over 400,000 – is the highest ever. These boom years followed a massive exodus to the United States and coincided with the rapid settlement of the Canadian west. Ottawa has been proposing to increase the annual intake indefinitely to about 1 per cent of the population, or about 300,000, up from an average of 237,000 in the last decade – a figure that already some quarters consider excessive. However, even target levels may not be enough. Indeed, the Organisation for Economic Development and Co-operation (OECD) has suggested that Canada may need as many as half a million people annually for 20 years to maintain sustainable levels of growths and the existing safety net.

According to then Minister of Citizenship and Immigration Elinor Caplan "If the projections are correct, and if immigration is the only policy lever pulled, maintaining a constant ratio of retired to working people would require annual immigration levels of at least 430,000 (over the next 20 years). I say 'at least' because this figure is all of these arrivals to be of working age, which of course, is extremely unlikely owing to family sponsorships and so forth. I can't help noticing that this figure of 430,000 exceeds the Government's long run target of annual levels of 1 per cent of the population. Indeed, it is nearly two and a half times the number of immigrants Canada accepted last year."[24]

Therefore Canada seems in dire need of many more immigrants very soon. Despite its promise in consecutive general elections to increase immigration to 1 per cent of the population, the federal Liberal Party (in power 1993–2006) failed to act, not even meeting its much-lower annual targets. It was not until 2010 that the Conservative government allowed numbers to rise.

Part of the reason for Canada's unhappy consciousness – arguing vigorously for more immigration but failing to meet modest targets – is the dialectical forces that have coalesced against the government on Canada's immigration needs. They argue that Canada should in fact cut the current level back drastically. Proponents of immigration argue for selection criteria that attract more suitable candidates who are more likely to fit in.

The contradictions and unhappiness arise through misrecognition of desires. The need for additional bodies responds to a basic problem, almost that of animal survival. But what do Canadians really desire for their country as a human expression? Do they want citizenship to mean real equality? Do they want to limit some citizens to life at a natural level? Or do they want everyone to try to share and achieve the same desires for recognition of their full humanity?

These arguments take Canada almost back to the immigration debates of the 1960s, when the policy debate took place within the wider discussion of who is Canadian, what is Canada, and what kinds of ethical relations are appropriate. In the 2000s, immigration was central to the national debate about the country's present and future. It was therefore understandable that the CBC, the national broadcaster, would want to deal with this issue seriously. I wanted to include some people whom the debate, I felt, too easily excluded.

IMMIGRATION: MAINTAINING THE OLD WAY

Coinciding with Statistics Canada's publication in 2001 of the latest updates on population trends, three groups of reports attacked the very notion that Canada needs large numbers of immigrants. One group argues that Canada does not need more immigrants at all. Another maintains that if it does, it should choose the right types and classes and dictate to them their conditions of entry. This second group clearly sees immigrants as Bad Johns. Hailing from the state of nature – instead of European civil societies – they could never be Prince Charmings who could take the maiden's hand and disappear into society. And, because they're Bad Johns, even naturalization would never bring them unconditional love – full citizenship. They can only be feared. A third group of critics argues that immigration weakens society and offers no net economic benefits; society should lay out specific conditions, such as how to police the newcomers and integrate them.

One thing that the three groups appear to agree on is the suggestion that the push for more immigration was a plot to keep the Liberal government (1993–2006) in power and to weaken Canadians' hold on their destinies. They also believe that the government has consistently pandered to immigrants for their votes at the expense of "Canadians" and the "national interest."

In *Immigration: The Economic Case*, public intellectual Diane Francis pooh-poohs Statistics Canada's findings and the common implications that readers have drawn from its reports. "Hand-wringers turned out in droves and repeated the same old myths: Bring in even more immigrants because it's important that Canada be bigger than it already is; it a big empty country; and more immigrants will reduce the problem of an aging population."[25] She continues, "This revealed a complete misunderstanding of 21st-century economics. The we-have-lots-of room school was rooted in the early 20th-century 'last Best West' drive to give away empty farmland to skilled and unskilled people in order to populate the frigid Prairies and create freight for the railway. Canada is no longer a gigantic horizontal band of farmland along the U.S. border that requires millions more labourers to till its soil as a means of lifting us into the economic big leagues. And Canadians do not need to foster a bigger internal market in order to grow world-class industries and become exporters and world-beaters."[26]

Francis writes that "size does not matter any more" for Canada. Not only does it not need more people, but econometric studies show that "doubling or tripling" annual immigrant intake would have little effect on the ratio between workers and retirees. Arguments for more people are relics of a different time and different circumstances, primarily when Canada was developing and could rely mainly on its domestic market for economic growth. But since then, such arguments have succumbed to "two revolutions and a major policy initiative: the industrial revolution, the technological revolution and free trade. Since 1989, and the launch of the free trade agreement with the United States and Mexico, Canadian business had had access to the largest, most prosperous marketplace in the world. Since then, exports have tripled."[27]

Moreover, Francis maintains that immigration policy over the fifteen years previous "has been a dud," leaving immigrant families poorer off. Canadians should learn from another model: "Sweden has dealt success-fully with the issue of [economic growth] without immigration. It has done this by maximizing the potential of its existing work force: through education, by passing laws to encourage part-time work for parents, by ensuring daycare spaces and by providing incentives for people to post-pone retirement or work part-time. Most important, its industries have expanded aggressively into export markets and invested heavily in auto-mation and technological advances, greatly enhancing the productivity of the work force. Studies show how such productivity gains can offset any harmful effect on an ageing population that is growing faster than the work force that supports it."[28]

Francis further contends, "Canada has enough people to maintain its lifestyle and create wealth in order to look after an ageing population. The brain drain to the United States is a problem, but strategic (or more selective) immigration can replace those who leave." Canadian immigra-tion policy is "wrong-headed" because it lets in too many unqualified and elderly immigrants.[29]

Of similar mind is Martin Collacott, the author of *Canada's Immigra-tion Policy: The Need for Major Reform*. Collacott worked for 30 years with the Department of Foreign Affairs (and International Trade), including stints in China, as high commissioner to Sri Lanka and Maldives, and as ambassador to Syria, Lebanon, and Cambodia.[30] An accompanying press release from the sponsoring Fraser Institute com-ments, "Canada's current immigration levels undermine tolerance and acceptance."

According to Collacott, there is no justification for higher immigra-tion.[31]

The federal government justifies large-scale immigration on the basis that it is essential to economic growth as well as to offset the aging population and the increasing proportion of retired persons to work-ers. These rationales, however, are not based on facts. The govern-ment's own research indicates that immigration and population increases play a minor role at best in economic growth. It is equally clear that only overwhelming levels of immigration would have any

significant effect on reducing the aging of the population and avoiding higher dependency ratios and that there are much more practical
ways of dealing with these issues than through immigration.
Similarly, the government's claims that we require immigration in order to cope with an anticipated shortage of skilled workers is of
questionable validity.[32]

Collacott suggests that immigration is a burden to taxpayers and often
results in the ghettoization of immigrants. Modern technology might
slow the integration of immigrants, primarily those of the family class,
and "more attention needs to be given to issues concerning crime in
immigration communities. The relationship between immigration and
crime, as one recent study indicates, remains largely unexplored."
Another area in need of additional study, especially since the terrorist
attacks in the United States on 11 September 2001, "is the degree to
which foreign-based terrorist groups have been able to function with
relative ease in the midst of some immigrant communities."[33]
Collacott maintains that the current approach to immigration will
transform Canada: "Immigration is having and will have a major impact
on what sort of country we are to be in the future. It is too important an
area of public policy to be left to special interest groups and efforts by
political parties to increase their political support against the interest of
the country. Immigration policy must be based on careful consideration
of what is best for Canada as well as the well-being of those allowed to
come here as immigrants."[34]
Similarly, Daniel Stoffman, a consistent critic, takes issue with the
current approach and its results in *Who Gets In: What's Wrong with
Canada's Immigration Program – and How to Fix It*.[35] Its publicity
states that the author "points out that our immigration policy is based
on two false premises: that immigration provides substantial economic
benefits, and that we need a huge influx of younger people to offset the
aging of our population. Both assumptions he persuasively refutes. Add
political correctness, diversity masquerading as multiculturalism, and a
voting public that has not yet made immigration an election issue, and
presto: you have the most generous, insecure, and muddled immigration
system in the world."
Like most Canadians, Stoffman heartily supports responsible immigration and a compassionate refugee program. But we have neither, he argues,
and it's time for Canadians to rescue the system from politicians and return
it to its original foundations of national interest and humanitarianism.[36]

Something else is noticeable about these various critiques: in a debate on immigration in a multicultural country where many citizens are newcomers, these were all that appeared when the debate seemed liveliest. Indeed, the debate was one-sided and anti-immigrant, perhaps reflecting a very narrow group of elite citizens who ran the national debate.

A variant on their view is the stance that the poor quality of immigrants and their inability to fit in are endangering what is intrinsically Canada and Canadian. This angle emphasizes the growing number of immigrants from visible minorities who have claimed racial and other forms of discrimination. Martin Loney calls his book *The Pursuit of Division: Race, Gender and Preferential Hiring in Canada*, parodying the myth of a pursuit of unity and equality under the rubric of order and good governance.[37]

Loney challenges a growing body of work that criticizes Canada's integration of immigrants, claiming that systemic barriers, such as racial, class, and ethnic discrimination prevent newcomers from full self-actualization as moral liberal agents.[38] Such systemic biases include hiring preferences for people with Canadian schooling; the failure of professions such as medicine, engineering, and accounting to accept or even evaluate foreign qualifications or work experience; and the large numbers of highly qualified immigrants in major cities unable to get suitable work, many of whom end up, as sociologist Jeffrey Reitz claims, subsidizing the Canadian economy through low-paying jobs.[39]

Loney argues that this "politics of grievance" results in reverse discrimination against "long-term Canadians." Here, he points to federal employment retraining for immigrants and to the selection of immigrants unsuitable for the job market who "could also seek to benefit from preferential hiring policies." "Such policies often give new immigrants opportunities to access employment vacancies not open to long-term Canadian residents. Large numbers of Canadians with teaching qualifications have been unable to obtain work in their professions, but in Ontario some recent immigrants with teaching qualifications gained overseas have been able to gain more favourable access to opportunities by enrolling in a York University program, partly funded by the Ontario Ministry of Education."[40]

Loney does not see discrimination against certain immigrants in the labour market and argues that if newcomers do not find the professional jobs that they expect, it is because they are ill equipped. He says that this situation simply reflects a "politics of grievance" by feminists and visible minorities seeking preferential treatment, thereby subverting that national good of equality and universality of treatment for everyone.

> Immigrants taking advantage of Canada's generous admission policies may hold unrealistic expectations about their economic prospects. The expanding economy, relatively low unemployment levels, and the absence of massive public sector debt afforded earlier generations of immigrants opportunities that are not open to many contemporary arrivals ... In Canada the dominant attribute of failure to discriminate rather than the weak labour market and low skill levels of many immigrants may have explosive social consequences. The claim that the labour market is profoundly discriminatory is endorsed by a range of government and government-funded organizations. It would be surprising if many of those who had entered Canada with high hopes of social and economic mobility, only to find few well paying jobs and limited prospects, did not conclude that their failure was due to skin colour.[41]

Certainly many members of visible minorities in Canada are immigrants, a result of demographic changes flowing from more open changes in immigration policies since the 1960s. Critics of hiring practices and failure to absorb many immigrants into appropriate positions have pointed out that many females who are disadvantaged are also immigrants. As Loney contends, "the same transformation is evident in the rapidly spreading diversity training cult. Where once liberal values gave support to the idea of treating people equally and recognizing that ethnicity, skin colour, sexual preference, and gender were not defining characteristics, now we must learn that such characteristics are indeed defining and that people must be treated differently, depending on which they exhibit. Sensitivity is to be encouraged through official endorsement. The only group not entitled to such protection are heterosexual white males, whose caricatured world views and ostensible privileges provide much of the diversity training script."[42]

With Canada in the throes of nation-building, there seems to be no middle ground in the debate on immigration. However, this was not the first time that the country has been in such a position. Every time the two sides have clashed so openly and fiercely, opponents believed that the nation's future was at stake and that Canada and Canadians, by putting limits on immigrants and their ability to function, were being benevolent and liberal.

This then was the climate in which I was to produce the CBC Radio series on immigration. How then could we determine what justice and freedom are, and tragedy and comedy? How could we understand the Canadian consciousness and what official multiculturalism means in a liberal democracy where citizenship is de facto social equality and official justice? How could we ensure that any portion of this series was not one-sided, but attempted to convey the views of Other Canadians – especially as some observers saw them as helping to undermine things that some elite members consider *authentically* Canadian?

11

Massey and Culture: From Bi to Multi

When I was just a little girl
  My momma used to tuck me into bed and she read me a story
It always was about a Princess in distress
  And how a guy would save her and end up with the glory
  I'd lie in bed and think about the person that I wanted to be
Then one day I realized the fairy tale life wasn't for me.[1]

Tata Young, "Cinderella"

There is then perceptually a problem with Canada as a practical and pragmatic entity, and there are problems in the way that we as citizens and critics imagined multiculturalism and its achievements. A being or consciousness is – in Hegel's sense – in need of a tragic ending that offers an escape. The classical strain of thought in Western philosophy privileges acts and forbearances that are moral and ethical, qualities that we associate with the supersensible and with God, the absolute, the unchangeable, reason, and rationalism in a world that we thus treat as if it is the product of dual systems of knowing. In this approach, the rational is what motivates us. Logic legitimates our desires, as well as our ideals and our dreams, but it is usually at odds with our common sense, which relies on experiences and situations in a "practical" real world.[2]

But we always believe that we can behave as moral agents, as subjects who are free. We are unhappy unless we see ourselves as sovereigns. We gain this freedom, this *notion* of freedom, from the identity that we want for ourselves in an absolute sense. But this is an infinity, as Hegel says, that flows from reason, which comes to us out of our traditions. It is received knowledge. It is culture.

Therefore our cultural ways of knowing, their preconditions, and their attendant and necessary perceptions are what ultimately determine how we act and behave. They are the "real" bases for our ethical order, and this is why such issues as racism and other forms of hurting and excluding people because of ethical differences still persist in a multicultural Canada, despite the Charter of Rights and Freedoms, provincial bills of rights, and our commitment to international human rights agreements. We may still on occasion act as if these "knowings" are mere political correctness, not what we genuinely feel and know – what our culture really wants and what history shows us as the most practical, pragmatic, and even efficient method for social stratification.

Perhaps a "real" Canada is hiding behind the living experience of Canada as a multicultural setting. There is a conflict regarding who is the actual rule giver in a house divided. The jurist Austin reminds us that what is correct in theory and what occurs in practice must be the same: "They who talk of a thing being true in *theory* but not true in *practice*, mean (if they have a meaning) that the theory in question is false: that the particular truths which it concerns are treated imperfectly or incorrectly; and that, if applied in practice, it might mislead."[3]

Such actions or practices, as we saw above in part I, would follow maxims and rules of their own and would therefore be in conflict with the sovereign. In our society, there can only be one sovereign. If it supports multiculturalism, then subjects who practise something different would be acting unethically and challenging the sovereign.

Because of its history, institutions, and idealism, Canada is still very much a Christian state trying to convert its practices and institutions to reflect its ideal of multiculturalism. This even though most Canadians would claim that their country has no official religion and that nothing about multiculturalism is official – except multiculturalism itself – and that all religions and other forms of cultural identity are equal.

But is this true? Do Jews, Muslims, Confucians, Hindus, Buddhists, and even atheists have equal standing in Canada? I argue that they do not. Even as a professed multicultural state, in its ideals and even its practices, Canada is still very much a Christian state, one where Christianity is the "folk" religion in the same way that Canada is still officially a bicultural country.

Examples of this theodicy abound in every season; as faithfully as spring gives way to summer, it to autumn, and that to winter, so too are the seasons and festivals of Easter an unofficial start of spring, and later comes Christmas, the moment of justice "when every child shall get his share" and when the dispenser of justice, who has been "checking his lists" on who has been good or bad, determines just rewards. As Elvis Presley often intones on the radio around that time, "He doesn't care if you're a rich or poor boy. He loves you just the same. Santa knows that we're God's children." Later in the same song, "Here Comes Santa Claus," Presley tells us that "peace on earth will come to all if we just follow the light. Let's give thanks to the Lord above, 'cause Santa Claus comes tonight [and] that makes everything right."

In this moment of carnival, there will indeed be justice, if only for a moment, but it sports a specific hue. It is a Christian justice – a situation that would become eternal if we were to reach the day when "they all live happily ever after." Supposedly, every day in this mythology would be Christmas – with its declaration of peace on earth and goodwill to all men (and women) – perhaps one of the most ontological multicultural endings to the universal tragedy of life.

We see these expectations in the dominant culture: in the way the public media privileges Christian festivals and holidays, assuming that they are the norm, while largely ignoring those of other religions, those of the seeming "outsiders." Indeed, in practice – where it is the celebration of an official holiday from work that may encompass gift giving, making merry as a public activity, and showing exceeding tolerance to others, even those we do not like throughout the year – does there not lie the assumption that every genuine and good Canadian is Christian at heart, if not in outer manifestation? And do many people not take it for granted that every Canadian, especially those who receive many and continuous appeals to give to the poor and needy, is a potential vessel for the Christian spirit of goodwill?

At times, it appears that Canada is a country of many sovereigns, each with its own theory and practice of what is real and what is the good life. At times, people in powerful positions seem oblivious to the intentions of the supposed sole sovereign, who has decreed official multiculturalism and that, in good Christian justice, Canadian agencies and institutions should treat all citizens as equal.

Even though many commentators see Canada as the first postmodern state, it is still at heart striving to be a modernist state in the European style. This is in effect a Christian state, where reason – the height of ultimate attainment in the state – seems to take a Christian form. The ideals of the state are Christian. The notions of the citizen and of belonging build on the notion of a Christian world family. Canadian rules, laws, regulations, and traditions flow from a morality that emerges from of a Christian knowing. Our heroes and villains wear Christian clothes, and many people assume that the Christian norms of moral and ethical behaviour and what is deviant from them are universal. Canadian concepts and ideals of justice are still very Christian. This is the Christianity that underlies the seemingly dominant and conforming culture in Canada. Indeed, as I argued above, if the state is the modern god, Canada's is Christian.

This has even become a *secular* religion: it emphasizes a unity of everyone through ceremonies and rituals of a Christian origin, and that faith's sense of community in the notion of the congregation now applies to the understanding of the national polity. A thin veneer of secularism attempts to present public policy as being free of religious taint and to free the state sovereign of the mysticism that once hallowed any absolute power that claimed direct links to God. It is this culture that shapes every immigrant and to which every naturalized or native boy and girl, regardless of his or her religion and earlier culture formation, must conform if that child is to have a feeling of belonging. And most important, if this creed is true, every boy and girl must be eligible for a share – fair or otherwise.

If these individuals do not conform in practice to the dominant culture, they will merely be members of a cult within Canada – a cultural group that the dominant group's loathing, fear, exclusion, and sense of difference separates from the main culture. It is not part of the mainstream – the general body. Neither does it possess the goodwill that forms the spirit in this body. Its members do not profess the subjective religion or spirit of freedom, but that of the alter, one where they become passive entities in the state and where they would not have the freedom that gives them an identity at one with the state or its agencies.

In this sense, they have no moral fortitude, and they should expect an ethical relationship that positions them as not fully belonging among the genuine members of the state or citizenship and of not having full entitlement. The practitioners of other cults would not, therefore, count as fully human – an identity exclusively for those whose *actions,* subconscious or otherwise, are consistent with the prevailing ideology. The underlying assumption is that only the values that our society inherited from the folk religion of Christianity make us fully human as Canadian citizens.

Canada has changed radically over the last half-century – but which Canada? The outer Canada that is the nation's demographic makeup? The peoples contingent to the real Canada? Or the genuine and real Canada that lives in morality and ethics and is the product of a reason that can only be Christian in orientation? I believe that a truthful answer would show that an officially multicultural Canada is a Hegelian and Christian unhappy consciousness. Canada is therefore a tragic figure even in the eyes of its own reason. Tragic figures are like the dead that cannot die. They need to die socially and spiritually, to retransform, and to rise again in a new culture – not as the walking dead, but as new entities at the beginning of a new history and time, with their own reason and ways of knowing, free from the reason and ways of knowing that previously dominated. For not only would they renew themselves through this type of death, but so too would be their culture and the society itself. A new dynamics of dominance would be at play.

The old self must arise again out of a world in which there seemingly can be no justice, for there is no reconciliation between the apparent dualism of a world of make believe and a real world of genuine feelings, knowing, and reason. It would resurface into a new spirit with expectations of hope, a connection, through ideals of equality with other social beings, that I call "genuine multiculturalism."

In this analysis of Canada, one other thing is important about tragedies: their endings are often ironic. This too I think would be the case for genuine multiculturalism in Canada: in seeking to undermine the hold that Christianity has on our senses of what is good, moral, and ethical, we would in fact be practising one of the most Christian of acts – a belief in real justice that can come to us only after death that is the acceptance of change, a belief in a new world and a resurrection and rebirth that would make us all whole again and bind our fracturedness, fragmentation, and alienation. This would be a belief in an idealistic rationalism that has been the synthesis of Western thinking and that is at the heart of a Christian sensibility that explains to us how we can make sense in our separate lives, how we can live ethically as communities and states, and why in the face of all our existential angst and unhappiness we should strive to be happy, moral, and ethical. Ironically, it would be a religion that, if we can judge by the death of the tragic figures, would boast vitality, dynamism, and that bacchanalian revelry that is life itself; its aim would be the celebration of full freedom following on the full recognition of identity in a specific culture at a specific moment.

This is a death, as Hegel says, that allows a human being to die in his or her own individuality and particularism and to subsume himself or herself fully in the universal, which for us is the state – demographically plural and socially and ethically multicultural. The norm gives way and returns as a new norm of what used to be abnormal. "Death loses this natural meaning in spiritual self-consciousness, i.e., it comes to be its just stated Notion," Hegel explains; "death becomes transfigured from its immediate being, viz. the non-being of this *particular* individual, into the *universality* of Spirit who dwells in His community, dies in it every day, and is daily resurrected."[4]

Tragically, the individual might fear this death more than a physical demise, for it seeks to overturn the very idea of who the being thought itself to be and to wipe out as meaningless everything it holds dear as achievement and history. This is a death after which there would not even be a monument to the individual, which, to participate in the future, would have to come in the guise of a new creature. This is a fate traditionally for only evildoers such as murderers and practitioners of genocide and of other acts of inhumanity when in our judgment as a social consciousness we rule that it would have been better that they had never lived. If there is any consolation in this moment of despair, it is that this erasure and death are happening to all individuals, all the time – and they are necessary to put them all on a new path to a place of greater enlightenment and real freedom.

Ironically, in asserting it has no official religion, Canada cannot help but to be Christian in ideals. Otherwise, there would be no historical meaning to the idea of Canada itself, to the tradition of Canada as a place of social justice.

THE THEORETICAL BACKGROUND
FOR A CANADIAN TRAGEDY

Since the 1960s, recognition has been central to the drama that is Canada as a multicultural liberal democracy. Recognition helps position Canada as a civil society, where life is rational and reflective and values specific ethical norms. Canada is therefore a site of freedom that expresses itself through fairness and justice as ethical ideals. Canadians are rational moral agents who possess fundamental rights according to their own Charter of Rights and Freedoms.

Every day we see issues of recognition on display, particularly in education, politics, language, and culture, areas of life often tragic if they operate with lack of recognition. Recognition transforms them into comedies or, less desirable, farces and absurdities. Recognition indicates that the foundation of the civil society is fully in place and that individuals, whether citizens or visitors, should perform according to a script that grows from an innate faith that every action contributes to a greater good or that the good will arrive through the solving of contradictions and conflicts inherent in the script.

These conflicts serve a common good: even if they must inevitably abide by the rational laws that govern the culture, they provide a way to overcome the society's limits in a dialectical manner. The good they serve is that of Canada as a demographically plural society that offers equality of opportunity and recognition for everyone before the law and the state. This is a good that positions Canadians, in their rainbow of colours and Babel of languages, as living peacefully in an officially bilingual and multicultural liberal democracy. Let us look at how this became practical through the working out of the tragedy that is history.

Canadians and Recognition: The Practice

Giving recognition a pivotal role is part of wider academic attempts to illuminate the discussion of who is a Canadian and the meaning of life in Canada. Indeed, even the notion that Canada should have a national culture and literature assumes a need for others to recognize Canada as already a civil society and, perhaps even more important, for Canadians to see themselves and their civil ethical relations as distinct. Canadians must be able to recognize themselves in their literature, music, films, broadcasting, sports – indeed, in every facet of their national life. And where there is not already a national image, there should be a concerted effort to create one.

Such was the recommendation in the 1951 report of the Royal Commission on National Developments in Arts, Letters and Science (1949–51) – the Massey-Lévesque Commission – which profoundly shaped the Canadian national image. It contributed to federal and provincial efforts to create a national identity and culture that is recognizable both at home and abroad as distinctly Canadian. Its main aim was to discover if there was anything "national" about Canadian life and, if there was not, to suggest how to construct a nation out of diverse peoples and cultures. Its terms of reference stated "that it is desirable that the Canadian people should know as much as possible about their country, its history and traditions; and about their national life and common achievements; that it is in the national interest to give encouragement to institutions which express national feeling, promote common understanding and add to the variety and richness of Canadian life, rural as well as urban."

This commission was to determine what was uniquely Canada and whether, as a unity, Canada was achieving the common good and, if not, how it might do so. Indeed, while it was at work, the government explained what it desired: recognition of Canada by the rest of the world and Canadians' awareness of who they were, what they had accomplished, and how to preserve and build on that success. Prime Minister Louis St Laurent had instructed the commissioners when he appointed them in 1949, "Because of the many contacts which you and your colleagues on the Commission have had with the public throughout Canada, it occurs to me that you might be prepared to advise the Government on two other matters which are not specifically included within your terms of reference. The questions I have in mind are the following: (a) Methods for the purpose of making available to the people of foreign countries adequate information concerning Canada. (b) Measures for the preservation of historical monuments."[5]

Through its recommendations, the commission provided the basis for Canadians to see and then treat themselves as a distinct people with a peculiar view of the world and for them to demand such recognition from others. This epistemic recognition is an acknowledgment that Canadians have a specific living experience that might very well lead them to see the world as real in a way that is different from other points of view. The prime minister, as the executive expression of sovereignty, was asking for a narrative that forced these two aspects of recognition together into a story of Canada as a self-consciousness with a certain past, present, and future. The commissioners were like the servants of the prince in the Cinderella story: carrying only a fragile glass slipper, they had to scour the land for the right-fitting foot – for what would fit snugly into the ideal of a bilingual and bicultural Canada.

The Massey Commission noted the existence of tradition that constituted a history of Canada. However, this was a narrative or tradition of deep and abiding conflicts and appeared to be running out of steam, for it was uncertain whether or not Canada could meet the future as a united modern state.

The commissioners highlighted an irony in Canadian life – a tradition that can continue and maintain itself only through *change* and by doing things differently in the future: "But tradition is always in the making and from this fact we draw a second assumption: the innumerable institutions, movements and individuals interested in the arts, letters and sciences throughout our country are now forming the national tradition of the future. Through all the complexities and diversities of race, religion, language and geography, the forces which have made Canada a nation and which alone can keep her one are being shaped. These are not to be found in the material sphere alone. Physical links are essential to the unifying process but true unity belongs to the realm of ideas. It is a matter for men's minds and hearts. Canadians realize this and are conscious of the importance of national tradition in the making."

This would be only one of the ironies that have shaped Canadian life as Canadians come to an awareness of who and what they really are culturally and in terms of their identity. Ironically, the future that Canadians had hoped would be a continuation of the past, the very order of life for which they had fought and many of them died, needed amending so that they could continue to live in a country they called "Canada" and even to strengthen its warring factions into a single nation. Indeed, the future would not be the past, for at least they would no longer be "warring in the bosom of a single state."

There would be one spirit and possibly one essence and one people. This would be the start and paradoxically the continuation of the tradition that Canadians would preserve and carry into the future. Canadians were upholding a common good, but one rife with ironies. From one viewpoint, it was a continuation of the old regime with a few changes to ensure its health. From another, it was the end of one era and the beginning of another, with a distinct break between the periods. This good that was conceptually Canada contained two dialectical forces warring for dominance and to decide who and what Canada consisted of. The commissioners' task was to bring a united Canada out of such a tragic existence and free it from its existence as a Hegelian unhappy consciousness, an existence so common in tragedies.

The desire for objective and subjective recognition is partly the reason that, traditionally, all levels of government in Canada pour huge sums of money annually into the arts, to subsidize and award prizes to literary and other artistic works, to fund publishing, and to help underwrite the costs of movie and television documentary production in Canada. The aim is to bolster Canada as a fully formed civil society. Yet, in providing funding and other support, the government is acknowledging an irony: that the Canadian identity is also a work in progress, that it is still as fragile as a fledgling and in need of what is akin to parental support until it can be weaned.

Active support for the arts has its genesis in the assumption that it is good to create a Canadian spirit and culture, a view that resulted from the royal commission. This sentiment suggests that it is a civic evil for a country not to have a national literature, one that sets it apart from the rest of the world but also that, as I argue below, captures the difference and diversity in the Canadian nation-state, ultimately producing an authentic expression of the national spirit.

The evil that the commission identified, or tried to eradicate with its recommendations, was that Canada was a fractured and decentralized country. It had too many particular identities competing for recognition with the universal Canadian characteristics. As a result, commissioners also identified another civic evil: the strong perception that some identities had more privileges than others. This perception flowed from the recognition and veneration of specific cultural and linguistic characteristics. To this extent, for example, the commission thought English, as a language expressing Anglo culture, more important and "Canadian" than French and Franco culture. Other languages and cultures did not even enter into consideration.

The injustice that the commission identified stemmed perceptually from forcing non-anglophones to conform to a particular, fittingly Canadian way of life. This made many francophones see their present ways as inferior and not genuinely Canadian. Recognition for them would come through comparison to an ideal that was beyond their reach and that many of them did not share. However, people assuming that Canadian society was a fact had implemented the ideal strictly as an intersubjective act.

In this way, the original intention of a society of recognition as an act internal to the appearance and orientation of society itself as a single unit, not simply as the struggle between parts that must ultimately conform, changed. The assumption that the country was still a-building requires an assumption: that it is possible to reconcile the goals of the old construction and the new. This would be a Canada in which Canadians would see themselves as they are now, as they were in the past, and as they will be in the future. Ironically, the Canadian that now exists would be the same as the ideal Canadian of the past, except that it would have become a new ideal for the present and future. But this ideal would also capture the ideal of the past. It was this existential and ethical struggle that made Canada an unhappy consciousness and a living tragedy.

Accepting the intersubjective form of recognition meant that the search for happiness started with recognizing a priori notions of good in order to make each notion a subject rather than an object. The next step was intersubjective equality between these new and fully recognized subjects and the Others in society – including a way of treating both non-conformists those superiors who embodied the ideal. At the time of the Massey Commission, this was primarily the relationship between, on the one hand, the French and English, whom it recognized as equally, fully Canadian subjects, and, on the other hand, those of lesser cultures and languages who were not fully Canadian.

The Massey Commission was an exercise in creating Canadian recognition, both domestic and foreign, and related to knowing who and what is truly Canadian, in the same way that a jeweller might wish to know the separate and indispensable parts of a fine watch. But it was also the kind of recognition that would allow the jeweller to lay out watches side by side, each with its own price, so that no one could misrecognize their respective quality of one for that of the other. These two forms of distinctions might occur within the jeweller's assumptions, which purchasers might share: that it is good and worthwhile to have a watch. This is separate from recognizing that a watch, as an object, produces something good and valuable.

Different watches, because of their internal components, might produce different goods, but these are outcomes or products that either party can rank for the purpose of making choices. Disagreements may arise, however, when a purchaser does not share the jeweller's opinion of a watch's value and meaningfulness. They might differ over the value of parts or the number of diamonds – not necessarily over what the watch is good for. But then again, while one person might see the watch as primarily a timepiece, so that how many diamonds it has does not necessarily matter, but too much stainless steel might cause it to tarnish. Here, the difference might be that of a supposed *essence*, of what the object really is in its primary and unchangeable form: watch or adornment. The parties may dispute the watch's external value and the internal components as well.

We are discussing, at a minimum, a three-way recognition: the watch as a distinctive object; the value and importance of its components and their differences, which collectively make the watch worthwhile; and the value of what the watch produces. Most of the discussion on multicultural Canada has been about the first form of recognition.

This commission was one of several major examinations that were to set the stage for policies to create a national character that subsumed various particular identities in a fraternity that is Canada. These studies and the debates they generated resulted in the recognition of Canada as a multicultural society that recognized a host of ethnic groups within the whole. They would also point the way to Canadians seeking a solution to what I see as the tragedy and despair over the future of their country in what Pierre Trudeau would eventually call a "Just Society." In the process, Canadians were perhaps unwittingly acknowledging that they were actors in a tragedy, a drama that, according to the rules from antiquity that govern this genre, always seek solutions through justice.

Assessing Canada's progress towards this goal of justice and an authentic cultural identity relates to the interminable discussions over whether a given book or author is Canadian enough to claim any major awards. Usually, this argument takes the form of external recognition. For example, does an artistic work have to gesture to Canadian geography or history to be Canadian? Is it enough to claim Canadian identity for the art to appeal to values central to the debate internal to Canada, or does the work belong elsewhere as part of an overall worldview? In the latter case, is it enough that the work may appeal to Canadian ideals that are universals while clothing them in particulars from elsewhere?

The Massey Commission acknowledged these concerns: "Moreover, students of Canadian literature still find themselves faced with the question of the form that this Canadian national literature will take. Shall we have some day a national literature 'which includes without distinction the English and French parts of our literature?' This seems to be impossible, states the author of our special study on letters in French Canada, 'since the very structure of present-day Canada, which is based upon the loyalty of the French and the English-speaking groups alike to their origins and to their different language traditions makes impossible in Canada the existence of one homogeneous literature that would not be clearly differentiated.'"[6]

This was a literature still searching for "its centre of gravity" because of vigorous influences from Britain, France, and, to a growing degree, the United States. Not only did the good of Canada derive from British and French characteristics, but it also seemed to be in a dialectical relationship with Britain, France, and the United States as its sources of inspiration. For this commission, the model of what was Canadian had already become clear, even if it was the grafting of a Canadian sentiment onto consciousnesses and models that were already present in the mainstream depiction of Canadian society. But as the final report stated, there was a second issue of recognition: "If we have properly understood what we have been told, the Canadian writer suffers from the fact that he is not sufficiently recognized in our national life, that his work is not considered necessary to the life of his country; and it is this isolation which prevents his making his full contribution. It seems therefore to be necessary to find some way of helping our Canadian writers to become an integral part of their environment and, at the same time, to give them a sense of their importance in this environment."[7]

Usually, this means some critics' conferring of recognition on a work of art or on an artist who might not have been born in Canada or who located a particular work within a physical geography or space that is Canada in a practical sense. Often absent from the debate is the idealistic notion of Canada as a spirit that resists the limits of physical geography or confinement to a too-rigid and particularist narrative. In this case – when the debate focuses on a dynamic internal to the artists or works, to a self-recognition invariably at odds with an external recognition, often gratuitous – it becomes meaningless. This dialectical struggle generates another contradiction or irony when, as Canada has recognized as a good since the Massey Commission, foreign groups recognize particular works as Canadian or as superb examples of the Canadian spirit, while domestic critics consider these works to be less than fully Canadian.

BI AND BI

The Massey Commission led Canadians to begin constructing a real "nation," aiming much of their effort at encouraging their compatriots to recognize themselves as epistemically Canadians. This meant their privileging a national identity over a regional or provincial one, and then ultimately seeing themselves first as Canadians and only secondarily of different ethnic backgrounds. This self-recognition as beings that are Canadians, even though they might differ in how they celebrate their Canadianness, crystallized following another royal commission: perhaps an even more important study of what Canada is and whether it had a future as a bilingual and bicultural country. In effect, Canada as a social consciousness or fraternity was assessing itself in terms of its own ideals. The commissioners would be examining every major action that Canadians had taken to bring them to this point, of manifest evil, where they did not think they could go on any further without creating greater evil.

In a sociological sense, these arbiters were determining Canada's success as a confederation in which provincial powers dominate. When Canadians had set up their confederation in the mid-1860s, they had, according to one historian,[8] looked at all the powers of sovereignty that mattered and assigned the crucial ones to the provinces and the rest to the federal government. This was an original sin, for what emerged was not expressive of the intention, unless it was avoiding a Frankenstein's monster of a strong federal state. The US Civil War had driven British North America's elites into as weak a confederation as possible so that they could protect provincial rights and powers while providing for collective security against a victorious US North. Now, in the 1960s, Canada seemed a house divided, and it wanted to avoid civil conflict. The thought of Canada as existing in practice, as the fathers of Confederation had intended, had died. The concept of Canada would re-emerge but different.

In an ironic twist, the Royal Commission on Bilingualism and Biculturalism (Laurendeau–Dunton, 1963–9) went beyond the Massey Commission and found that while Canada was officially substantially bilingual French and English, its peoples were multicultural. It therefore suggested that Canadians had been, in effect, misrecognizing themselves epistemically and ethically as culturally French and English. Instead, they were actually of many more cultures.

This was a pivotal moment in Canada's recognition of itself. And it was tragic, for the old, bicultural perception had to die socially to ensure the survival of the true and genuine Canada, which was multicultural to the core.

Shortly after receiving this report, the government in 1971 completed the tragic rituals: it killed the old ideal of Canada as bicultural and installed the ideal of multiculturalism, as the natural order of the country and its citizens. The evil that nestled within the Canadian bosom – seeking recognition for Canada as bicultural – had to disappear so that the real, multicultural Canada could receive full recognition as the genuine national good.

Laurendeau–Dunton would lead to recognition of Canada as multicultural, unlike Massey, which found the country bilingual but did not contest the bicultural assumptions. Both royal commissions had recommended policies to capture the Canadian spirit that they discerned and realize it in national institutions and agencies. Dialectically, the two commissions found two different Canadas and proposed different ways to achieve an agreed-upon good to ensure preservation of a united Canada as a civil society. Canada recognized that the evil in its ethical relations was not that it was forcing other groups to conform to an imposed national identity that was British and Anglophone, but that it was trying to make *countless* cultures conform to a previous dominant ideal.

Canada's success and happiness as a place for "recognition" has earned such universal approbation that many people promote it as a shining example of multiculturalism for the rest of the world.[9] Most observers are talking about objective and intersubjective recognitions, rarely about the essence of reconciliation in a tragedy: personal, internal recognition that produces a radical conversion. Tragic recognition comes with the realization that there is a difference *within* what previously seemed homogeneous and unitary, that the conflicts and contradictions are not the result of differences resulting from socialization. Rather, it is the acknowledgment that the differences stem from conflicting natures within the body and that the stage on which they are acting themselves out is not really a civil state but still a state of nature without a single covenant to govern ethical life.

Liberal tolerance would suggest that people who already recognized themselves as the ideal should generously extend the hand of friendship, tolerance, and love to those of a lower status and standing. In a just world, the latter would recognize themselves as lower and inferior and realize the generosity of those trying to help them and see that they might even be offering them more than their due. Ethical relations would aim to maintain the idealistic norms of good and evil, of superiority and inferiority, and assess individuals and groups' conformity to these a priori expectations.

According to social theorist David Goldberg, tolerance, the central plank in a politics of recognition in a late-modern liberal democracy such as Canada, creates perhaps more problems than it solves: "Liberals may admit the other's difference, may be moved to *tolerate* it. Yet tolerance ... presupposes that its object is morally repugnant, that it really needs to be reformed, that is, altered. Thus, liberals are moved to overcome the racial differences they tolerate and have been so instrumental in fabricating by diluting them, by bleaching them out through assimilation or integration. The liberal would assume away the difference in otherness, maintaining thereby the dominance of a presumed sameness, the universally imposed similarity in identity. The paradox is perpetuated: The commitment to tolerance turns only on modernity's 'natural inclination' to *in*tolerance; acceptance of otherness presupposes as it at once necessitates 'delegitimation of the other.'"[10]

Yet it is only when both parties recognize who the individuals and groups really are that they can deal effectively with issues of power as a determinant of justice. This means not simply shifting the gaze from individual to individual but focusing and even restricting the gaze, so as to examine the very legitimacy of that which was given – starting the process by questioning the justice that the parties assume to be inherent in a specific good or standard of conformity. This involves probing what they seek to uphold – that which they posit as the good – to see if there is any evil within it.

As well, the subject must probe itself as the ultimate determination of morality: how should a responsible moral agent act, when to not act is effectively neither a moral choice nor good? This moral agent expresses its freedoms in actions that are not arbitrary or contingent, whimsical, or in keeping with the times. Instead, it grounds its actions in reason that is purposely dispassionate and free of the effects of human nature, of its appetites, and of emotions that emerge by chance. This is a freedom, as Hegel says, that requires "being at home with oneself in one's other," a freedom that one makes free of caprice by recognizing the otherness that both is within the self and is equally the self.[11]

Such is not a dialogic discourse hoping to produce recognition of equality among already fully determinate and independent wholes. It is an intra-dialogic discussion between parts of the same whole, and it is a recognition that the apparent unity has flaws and needs corrective action from within – that the flaws within are causing the unit to produce other than what it intended as good. Its greater self-awareness allows it to grasp that it can produce only what its parts are capable of producing and that, according to more enlightened standards, the best this system can produce is not good. Canada found at a pivotal point in its historical development in the 1960s that it needed this kind of introspection. This soul-searching would cause it, as a whole, to recognize the *multi*cultural character of the unity it thought it embodied.

The other two forms of recognition analogously go to an issue of deeper or genuine multiculturalism – the authenticity of the country's component parts and validation or rejection of what the country intends to produce. The traditional dialogic intersubjective discourse on recognition in Canada usually overlooks these forms of recognition because of two underlying assumptions: that there is already an ideal ethical order and power structure for recognizing the ethnic groups and visible minorities within the Canadian unity and that Canada's type of multiculturalism is flawless, even worthy of export to lesser countries. But this is not the full story of how Canada became officially multicultural, even if the outcome reflects the a priori understanding of what Canada's good is.

POLITICS OF RECOGNITION: PRAGMATISM OF CANADA

Charles Taylor's *Politics of Recognition* has become the standard for discussions on Canadian multicultural identity. In it, Taylor depicts the development of Canada as a nation-state as a drama that we can explain in the classical terms of a tragic tale. In so doing, Taylor applies notions of speculative philosophy to modern issues of politics and political philosophy, presenting the drama of a people's working out a peculiar consciousness as part of a universal that is Western civilization.[12] This consciousness is a specific way of life, the product of competing dialectical forces on a stage that is northern North America.

Taylor adapted his explanation and method of analysis from Hegel, who applied the analogy of tragedy and comedy to explain the triumphs and defeats of human life in history in his seminal *Phenomenology of Spirit* and *Philosophy of History* – a tragedy of the human spirit that reconciles itself in a comedy of idealized living. This is the story of the Divine, as an act of trying to know and recognize itself as an essence, enduring the tragedy of the human condition as it seeks to know the limits of its powers by recognizing in a real sense who it is and what it can do and become.

Hegel was also a dramatist, presenting the development of Western civilization and its Christian ideology as a tragedy in search of a comedy. As he suggests, the reconciliation of tragedy occurs "as a point of transition to the otherwise to be contrasted province of comedy."[13] He adds, "Comedy possesses, therefore, for its basis and point of departure that which it is possible for tragedy to terminate, that is, a soul to the fullest extent and eventually reconciled, a joyous state, which, however much it is instrumental in the marring of its volitional power, and, indeed, in itself comes to grief, by reason of its asserting voluntarily what is in conflict with its aim, does not therefore lose its general equanimity."[14]

Similarly, Hegel places recognition as central to tragedies and comedies, along with irony. For as he says in his *Philosophy of History*, if the history of Western civilization is a book, then its pages on happiness are empty. This is the case even for the great men and women – the tragic heroes of history – who embodied the spirit of their times, took a commanding position on the local or world stage, and helped to shape a consciousness that might have been local, regional, national, or even global. At the heart of the dialectics of this drama is a relation of lordship and bondage, a fight between the spirits of freedom and of tyranny that shaped the consciousness. The result is a culture of freedom in which its members recognize a consciousness as free humans producing a way of life to maintain, preserve, and ultimately extend their freedom. This freedom derives from recognition, the kind that Hegel acknowledges lies at the heart of a good drama, primarily a tragedy. Before him, Aristotle, in one of the first treatises on tragedy, had identified recognition as an essential element.

Taylor equated Hegel's lordship-and-bondage analysis to a master-and-slave struggle or dialectic that explains the formation of civil societies in Western thought and history. I show below that Taylor eventually found both in Hegel and in world history a struggle of master and slave rather than of lordship and bondage and warned of its severe implications for our present understanding of multiculturalism. This difference between a master–slave and a lordship–bondage relationship is important enough to leave unexplained a kind of relation that Hegel identifies as one in which society is caught on the horns of a dilemma because it is neither fully a civil society nor a state of nature, where factions appear as lords and lawmakers unto themselves. This was what Hegel identified as a situation in history marked by satyr in ancient tragedy and by an unhappy consciousness in modern times.

Taylor's analysis sees little or no irony in the outcome of the politics of recognition whereby he explains multiculturalism. He perceives the struggle as a master–slave one and perhaps did not want to follow a Hegelian analysis through to its idealistic ending. Indeed, Hegel has faced criticisms for his idealism, and Jean-Paul Sartre too did not follow his own analysis to the idealistic ending of the phenomenology of Being.[15]

Taking a similar route that eschews the idealism – which quality, I argue, permeates multiculturalism – Taylor finds no exit from the unhappy consciousness that is multiculturalism. Without idealism, multiculturalism offers no hope, no expectation that at some point – perhaps one that we may never reach – all the demographic particulars in Canada will fuse into a common entity. This would be the good of a Canada that is an infinity of people, possibilities, opportunities, and cultures and at one and the same time a single unity.

This ideal that I have introduced as genuine multiculturalism occurs when Canada is no longer an unhappy consciousness. That we can have genuine multiculturalism with power that is diffuse and dependent on participatory politics is another plank in this idealism. In taking this tack, I am pressing Taylor to what I believe is a natural ending to the tragedy he described, a tragedy that I would argue he tacitly acknowledged derived from idealism, if only because his is a Hegelian analysis. This is the tragedy typical of two brothers warring over one prize, a theme common to Greek and Christian tragedy. In Canada's case and in Taylor's analysis, the two brothers are like the archetypes Cain and Abel, who fought over the norms of civil societies, presented here as European – two nations that are French and English.

By pushing Taylor's analysis, I am looking within the dialectic of history that he describes and claiming that seeing multiculturalism as a struggle of recognition between anglophone and francophone cultures misrecognizes the Canadian being or body. More than that, I am privileging the traditional norm in tragedy that would have the real recognition of multiculturalism as a tragedy occurring within the subject as a rational moral agent.

In this respect, we need to push Taylor's politics of recognition into a truly multicultural world by highlighting three things that he overlooked. They are personal recognition as the first step to understanding the unhappiness in society, the need to reverse the knowledge of the main characters in the drama, and recognition of the ironic outcome in terms of a new intersubjective relationship that has different notions of good and evil. Taylor insists that recognition of these principles is essential for a Hegelian analysis to explain Canada and its designation as a multicultural liberal democracy.

Therefore my aim is to dig deeper into Taylor's Hegel-style analysis, not to prove or contest Hegel's analysis of tragedy and speculative Western history per se, but to apply Hegel's method. I want to offer a second view on Taylor's project, in which, using Hegel's model, he started to explore the Canadian body but discovered only what his time could use. Perhaps Taylor was being very Hegelian, for, as Hegel suggests, no person can jump over her or his shadow, so that any observations we make and any knowledge we acquire reflect our times and their issues.

Taylor locates his analysis within the master and slave's struggle for political dominance in Canada that was indeed a physical fight for objective recognition. This was primarily a struggle between English and French Canadians for dominance, which started at the beginning of Canada and that has shaped the contours of the country. At various times, it has forced the country to confront its mortality, when it faced the possible break-up of the federation, most notably in efforts since the 1960s by some people in Quebec to secede from Canada.

It has involved such issues as which language or languages should have dominance and which culture should have privileges. It played itself out in the drawing up of the constitution and in its implementation, particularly provisions recognizing the French factor in a country that English and anglophones previously dominated. Two forces in a prison or exitless stage work out how to share the space and which should be dominant, if either. For Taylor, resolution began in the 1970s with official recognition that Canada was a multicultural state. Everything since then has maintained this ethical order as good for Canada and for all its constituent ethnic groups.

Taylor's work was speculative philosophy on the formation of a particular type of civil society. However, while it claimed to focus on multiculturalism, it really dealt with how Canada came to be bilingual rather than bicultural, as the Massey Commission intended. Taylor saw the struggle as primarily between two combatants, which produced two official languages, English and French.

Language, however, is not the only component of culture. According to Pierre Trudeau, "Anybody who really wants to learn a language can do so. But you can't learn an entire culture."[16] In this respect, a language is useful for communication – its practical use and function – but less so for preservation of a culture.[17]

However, Canada is not a bicultural country; rather, it is multicultural, which implies recognition of more than two combatants. Canada became such through an introspection that produced personal recognition, whereby Canada as an actor discovered itself as a Hegelian body that was a universal and a community of communities, because of the various constituent groups. This process involved three types of recognition: of universality, of object and subject, and of the moral equivalence of the other in an ethical relationship that recognizes and positions all members socially as subjects.

While Taylor accepts the commonly held myth that Canada was founded by two European nations, he ignores the constant presence of Others within the Canadian body. First, the First Nations and Inuit peoples are aboriginal to Canada and still maintain their own civil societies. Second, there always existed foreign elements that were not French or English. Canada has always been a site for immigration, even if it did not always incorporate them and considered specific groups undesirable and unnecessary.

These groups still maintain a presence even if they did not early on receive official recognition as Canadian. The prevailing myth did not include them as part of the Canadian good, even though that good always contained elements that were struggling for inclusion or even domination. Ultimately, these groups acquired enough mass and a presence to overthrow the prevailing norm of a bicultural country. They helped to install the new official norm of a multicultural country.

As we saw above, Canada recognized itself as multicultural following Laurendeau-Dunton's exploration of its bilingual and bicultural nature.[18] In the midst of the commission's deliberations, Canada came to a new realization: that it consisted of a multitude of cultures and languages, each wanting recognition as having pride of place in Canada, which this discourse presents as offering the immigrant perspective on multiculturalism. The recognition that made Canada officially multicultural differed from the politics of recognition that Taylor has presented as necessary for such a pronouncement.

Taylor's recognition is external, one subject acknowledging another. Canada's was internal, much like in tragedy, where the protagonist grasps that the evil lies within. The Canadian government realized the presence of differences other than English and French and decided to act. This accounts for Canada's ethical position as multicultural because of its multiple ethnicities, even if it was bilingual.

Another indication that this recognition was personal and internal came from divisions between Ottawa and Quebec City, which never officially recognized Canada's multicultural character. For the government of French-speaking Quebec, multiculturalism was an attempt to undermine the importance of the French difference in Canada. It saw multiculturalism as an issue not of political or cultural recognition, but rather of what this recognition means within the Canadian body. Partly in response, Parti Québécois governments mounted two attempts at Quebec sovereignty via provincial referendums in 1980 and 1995. It presented these as, in effect, a struggle for objective recognition that would result in the physical death of the Canadian state as it was then and its rebirth in a reversal that was a separate Quebec nation-state and a Canadian federation without Quebec.

However, the results of the second referendum showed that the debate in Quebec and other provinces was more multicultural than many people had at first expected. A growing group of people who identified themselves as neither French nor English played a decisive role in the very narrow outcome. By voting solidly against secession, they helped to defeat the bid for separation. The leader of the secessionist forces, Jacques Parizeau, shot back, "It's true we have been defeated, but basically by what? By money and the ethnic vote." He had identified what he thought was the evil within Quebec society, which was what many of his opponents saw as the good within the universal Canadian society.

A few weeks later, Parizeau told students at the University of Alberta, "The Jewish Congress of Canada, the Greek Congress of Canada and the Italian Congress make a very good fight against sovereignty." Still later, he explained that while he knew of Haitians who supported Quebec sovereignty, he was yet to meet a Jamaican who did. All these comments amounted to the laments of a tragic hero recognizing that power had slipped, or was slipping, beyond the recovery of a single ethnic group, no matter its historical roots in the province. Ironically, Parizeau had to look within the body politic and, to his disappointment, grasp that the *pure laine,* or pure wool, Québécois, descendants of the original French settlers, were becoming just another minority. They had lost the effective power of the majority in a liberal democracy – to shape the destiny of a country where the majority, as it coalesces around any issue, decides what matters. Even in Quebec, what was previously evil was becoming the universal good.

And this realization has caused the secessionist forces to rethink a possible path to independence. They know that their numbers cannot support a majority. In addition, a third-space group outside the two "charter" groups of Quebec and Canadian society as a whole could now decide the outcome by siding with either side. Effective power has changed, even if there is no official reversal to recognize the heads on which power rests. Indeed, much power rests in the hands of immigrants, those who do not fit neatly into the traditional myths of Canada as a country of one or more homelands to be determined and brought into existence as the resolution of conflicting anglo and franco nationalisms. With significant numbers in the body politic, the group that is seen as "immigrant" because neither English nor French is not merely to be integrated or accommodated into some pre-existing myth about Canada. As citizens of Canada and residents of Quebec, they have a strong hand determining the future, and one of the choices open to them is to reject equally both anglo and franco nationalisms in a Canada that is genuinely multicultural and a liberal democracy.

The tragedy continued, as a democracy moves the wheel of power not by justice but by majority vote, so that a mainstream that is a coalition of groups of interests effectively rules. Power in Quebec is still largely in francophone hands, even if they must rely on other groups. In a Hegelian way, this mainstream has internal conflicts, with different and at times irreconcilable notions of the good. There is still a false consciousness of power, primarily because Quebec has not gone through the pain and tragedy of an internal search for recognition.

For this reason, the Parti Québécois government had to admit to a paralysis while in power: while it still wanted independence, it recognized that Quebec was a multicultural state where French historical claims may be unravelling with passing time and shifting demographics. To this end, the party vowed that it would call another referendum only when the odds of winning were high – highly unlikely. We can speculate that the unhappiness continues, primarily because the actors have not recognized the good and evil that rest within them. There has been no appreciation of the ironic outcome that would require the recognition of a new good – that power should not be the preserve of the English, French, or some combination thereof – and a new evil, the idea of reserving power for an English–French reconciliation within Canadian and Quebec society. These new goods and evils centre on the multicultural nature of both the universal and the particulars of Canada.

As a result, this drama that started as a search to discover whether Canada was essentially English, French, or both played out to an ironic ending: the country realized that it was in fact more fractured and more *multi* than it had expected. It had progressed much further towards multiculturalism than it had originally thought. First came the discussion of whether Canada was uniformly English with a French Other or consisted of two Others that were French and English, neither of which was dominant. Instead, the dialectical process showed that it was a country consisting of many more Others.

Epistemologically and phenomenologically, this like a person's maturing by realizing how his or her body really works and recognizing that it has many more parts and organs – some of them not visible or recognizable – than it thought. In this way, the body that is Canada continues dialectically to give up more knowledge of itself, leading to an ironic outcome, such as a reversal of what it previously posited as its full complement of knowledge about its body. Such awareness emerges not from its intersubjective dealings with other bodies or from knowing that it exists as a body, but primarily because new information about the body's components negated its previous understanding. This is an internal, personal recognition.

In the early 1990s, when Taylor was writing, many Canadians were following the battle between the English and the French – the largest groups. But times have changed, and open immigration since the 1960s – ironically, an attempt to preserve the country – changed the dynamics. Quebec never accepted multiculturalism partly because it understood that it would transform the society and its dynamics of power. Quebec nationalists have always maintained, as Premier René Lévesque, who led their first separatist government, suggested, that multiculturalism was an Anglo ploy to swamp the French.[19]

Quebec fought for and received some control over the selection of immigrants to the province. It wanted newcomers who supported the French identity within Canada. However, it failed to attract enough francophones and had to accept immigrants whose first language was not French; proved unable to retain all its immigrants; and could not convince the majority of even the francophones who had immigrated first and foremost to Canada to develop allegiance to Quebec. It invoked the notwithstanding clause in the constitution, which allows provinces to override liberal rights in the Charter of Rights. Such action implicitly recognizes a good that is different from what the polity posits as the universal good. Quebec's invocation maintained an old good – conformity to French ideals and mores – at a time when multicultural Canada claimed that such conformity was an evil.

These struggles in Quebec and Canada over the treatment of difference and diversity in the national body masked deep changes in Canadian society. Canada is much more multicultural and multilingual today that even at the time of Taylor's writing, and even more so than in the period on which Taylor was commenting.

The conflict within Canada is not so much between what John Porter calls the "charter groups," the French and English,[20] but between a mainstream that is historically English or French and the many ethnic and immigrant groups trying to gain admission, and even dominance. Reconciliation, as Hegel would suggest, would involve looking at the dynamic forces in the mainstream and recognizing them as dramatis personae within the unfolding drama. In another sense, this is an analysis of tragedy, which is, as Hegel argues, the struggle of individuals colliding with the wider culture. That culture is all-encompassing, like the Canadian mainstream, and allows recalcitrants no escape into a private world of self-virtue and -actualization without their harming the culture that gives their lives meaning.

Here is where seeing Canada as a tragedy hoping to become a comedy can help explain it as a multicultural country – the Canadian universal with many disparate parts (Hegel-style particulars). Taylor's politics of recognition extends only to a bicultural Canada. There are several reasons for this limitation, the main one of which I explore in this book.

First, Taylor's notion of recognition is too narrow – two combatants struggling over how to treat and recognize the other. This is an external recognition. Yet Canada's recognition that it was multicultural, not bicultural, was *internal*: it happened within Canada itself. This is a key point. The recognition that great tragedians looked for was internal and not external: the tragic hero realized that she or he was culpable – that hubris which is pride, ambition, or a desire for a specific goal had corrupted her or him. Good and evil are inside the soul, not external to it.

Taylor's recognition contributes, à la Aristotle, to a simple tragedy, with fewer lessons and less drama. Indeed, American philosopher Mark William Roche argues that sometimes the genre does not involve even subjective recognition. "Complex self-sacrificing tragedy" usually does not invoke public recognition; rather, "it belongs to the idea of the great hero that she acts even without being recognized; indeed, the greatest hero avoids recognition."[21] For the hero, it is enough to have acted morally – a recognition that is internal.

Second, most of the great tragedians have looked for an ironic ending. This ending relates to internal recognition and ends usually in the death of the hero in order to achieve a greater good. The hero's death is ironic: the figure had been all along at the mercy of desires aiming at achieving a *life* of what he or she perceived to be the good; now the hero realizes that the only route there is through death. Ironically, death will bring the *everlasting* life that is good, a Christian concept that Hegel presents as essential for understanding Western civilization. Thus tragedy demands an ironic outcome. Taylor does not flesh out the irony in the Canadian multicultural play.

Third, great tragedians looked for reversal as a way to end the day – shifting the play from tragedy to comedy – like the point in any fairy tale that ends with "and they all lived happily ever after." This can be a comedy deriving only from hope, as common sense tells us nobody had ever been happy indefinitely – Hegel claims that the pages on happiness are blank in the book of history, and so far nobody has ever lived forever. Such are the tragedies of life, that everything human must die and decay, for humans contain the seeds of evil and corruption that cry out for recognition. But within them too are the good and the everlasting, primarily hope of some-day transcending the limits that are the evil within the body and the world in general. It is this hope that also speaks to the good of humans.

Good tragedians know that the good at the play's end must reverse the doom and gloom of pending death at the beginning of tragedy. This is the hope that all human tragedy will someday play out as comedy, with a happy ending, when everyone realizes that the hero is not evil but sim-ply misguided and that only the presence of evil permits exorcism of an evil genius within to save the world. Rather, the fool simply sees the light, learns from her or his mistakes, and ultimately marries – the mythic, mystical new birth that promises everlasting life as an initiation of the process leading to a stream of subsequent births. Therefore rever-sal is key to the working out of tragedy.

Taylor does not account for a reversal in Canada's speculative philoso-phy, which oversight limits its application to genuine multiculturalism. This is true Hegelian multiculturalism, which considers all the body's parts, good or evil, equally important to its functioning. If one part of the body is evil, it all is, and if one is good, then goodness is everywhere. If there are both good and evil parts, an internal struggle ensues. The inher-ent division makes it conflicted, sick, or an unhappy consciousness.

On the question of power in Canada, genuine multiculturalism would suggest that the mainstream of Canadian life would be a site for the struggle between the many parts of the nation-state. It is there that the struggle for dominance will take place, there that ultimately acts of death and rebirth will happen, acts of tragic despair and comedic hope, and there that the old good will constantly be in a state of reversal. At any given point, any particular tragedy with its unity of time and place within this universal narrative must end with a reversal – with a death that gives way to hope. This too is lacking from Taylor's analysis.

This new analysis could inform Canada's debate in political philoso-phy, primarily those liberal analyses that restrict themselves, like Taylor's, to the politics of recognition. One result of Taylor's analysis is that Canada's recognition of equalities renders it an unhappy consciousness, with the body's parts in civil war, and nobody, even good people, seems happy. Therefore, as we can see in the discussion on racism and anti-racism, some members of the same group that should be the likely win-ner will usually condemn as merely liberal pabulum any measures to improve the lot of some groups. It is enough at this moment to recognize that Taylor's groundwork presents multiculturalism as a struggle for recognition. In chapter 12, we examine Taylor's analysis more fully; then I draw a sharper distinction with him over recognition and a lasting solution in tragedy. Hegel clearly articulated this solution, and Taylor was applying his methods in equating multiculturalism to a political struggle for recognition. In addition, we focus there on nobility, which critics from Aristotle on have identified as necessary for good tragedy. Unfortunately, Taylor did not follow through on his Hegelian analysis, or perhaps a misreading of Hegel left his analysis seeming like a tragedy without a speculative moment of reconciliation.

I now turn to why I think the principles of tragedy can illuminate the social and cultural issues that are emerging in Canada as a work still in progress – as not yet a comedy for all its citizens.

PART THREE
Accepting Diversity, Promoting Social Equality

12

Tyranny v. Freedom: Strauss v. Kojève

I let you down
Let me pick you up
I let you down
Let me climb up you to the top
So I can see the view
from up there
Tangled in your hair.[1]

Dave Matthews Band, "Rapunzel"

Men in great place are thrice servants: servants of the sovereign or state;
servants of fame; and servants of business. So as they have no freedom;
neither in their persons, nor in their actions, nor in their times.
It is a strange desire, to seek power and to lose liberty: or to seek
power over others, and to lose power over a man's self.[2]

Francis Bacon

In a famous exchange about the time Canadians were examining the idea of official multiculturalism, two leading theorists – conservative US philosopher Leo Strauss and left-leaning French philosopher Alexandre Kojève – debated about what it took to produce wise and good government in a modern state. Strauss wrestled with the question of the sovereign individual and whether one can remain authentic while living in a society – can he or she live happily ever after? Strauss starts always with the desires of the individual in discussing freedom and tyranny. He sees a "crisis in modernity" because neither the individual nor the state knows what they really want. Slavery ensues, for the strong, especially when they make a collective as a state, usually become tyrants.

Kojève speaks out of a tradition that would contain particular differences and hence individualities and recognize them in a social union. Freedom can be relevant only to a specific place and time. The folk determines freedom, living by a narrative of how social justice would emerge or what would bring it about. The way out of tragedy is to live – as I would say, comedically – in a universal and homogeneous state. The individual must merge with the people and the culture. As Aakash Singh says, such a state is "a global society consisting of all nations, all of which are free and equal, populated by men and women who are all free and equal, all enjoying affluence, all enjoying justice." Such a nation–state would be a homeland that is effectively a diaspora for the world: every nation on earth would recognize that where they live is not ideal-istically back home but is the best that they have. Pragmatically, this exile would have to be home or be made into one.

I contend that the widespread thinking about modernity, tyranny, and freedom that this debate crystallized heavily influenced the multicultur-alism that emerged in Canada in 1971. The creators of this new vision hoped for a Kojève-type homogeneous state that would universalize all peoples from around the world as Canadians. At the same time, the indi-vidual was to be sacrosanct – this being the epitome of freedom. Canada is to be a multicultural liberal democracy – a seeming contradiction that pits the individualism in modernity, whom we can trace back to Plato, and Hegel-style collectivism. I also contend that the Strauss–Kojève debate explains multiculturalism as a tragedy hoping to become a com-edy, for its contradictions remain irreconcilable in terms of Plato–Strauss and/or Hegel–Kojève.

Strauss and Kojève were debating what reality is and how any group of people, or even a single individual, if she or he wishes, can create a truly authentic and real existence. How can they be at home and attempt to "live happily ever after"? How to move from tyranny and slavery into never-ending happiness? Nicolas Berdyaev may help us again, par-ticularly with his notion that our values and desires for freedom are not only primordial and seemingly unchanging, but antedated our exis-tence. For mythology still helps us assess whether we are living comedy or tragedy.

Strauss and Kojève were debating the life of the tyrant in the light of Xenophon's tragic dialogue *Hiero or Tyrannicus*. The tyrant Hiero visits the poet-philosopher Simonides. His host asks him about the difference in "pain and pleasure" between his earlier private life and his years in power. Hiero confesses that he can no longer remember the pleasures of a common life, but he remarks wistfully that he knows now that that was better, because people cannot love a tyrant, and everything he does makes them despise him more.

As they together enumerate the staples of private life – the pleasure they derive from the sights, sounds, and smells around them, from food and drink and sex, from knowing good things and bad things, and from a good sleep – all that we might call "folkways" – the tyrant pleads concerning each that he is worse off than the common person. The private individual takes more pleasure from what is around: can enjoy each special food and drink as something new and fresh, as a treat. For the tyrant, sex is usually loveless, because the partner is seldom in love but responds to some other motive, such as fear. Sleep never comes easily, for betrayal lurks constantly. Most of all, the tyrant lives in constant fear and cannot trust anyone. All this is completely foreign to the common citizen. "I guard against drunkenness and sleep," Hiero explains, "as if I were in an ambush. To fear the crowd, yet to fear solitude; to fear being without a guard, and to fear the very men who are guarding; ... to trust strangers more than citizens ... to desire to keep the free slaves. And be compelled to make the slaves free – do not all these things seem to you signs of a soul distracted by fears?"[3] It is not unusual, Hiero explains, for a tyrant to consider suicide.

When the poet finally offers his advice, his reasoning is blunt and seemingly contradictory: the tyrant must improve the common good if he wants society to love him. The stoic that is the tyrant must seek meaning in a world of scepticism. Ironically, the tyrant's private good and the people's common good must merge – probably only through the ruler's cunning or deceit or through his figurative death and subsequent rebirth as a lovable tyrant. At the same time the tyrant must still believe that he is most important, even if his valuation must come from the beyond – the wider society. He needs the folk not in order to rule over them but for them to love him fraternally.

In no other way could he reconcile the desire to be loved and to be a real-world tyrant, so life would be tragic and unhappy unless he changed one or both of these desires. "But enrich your friends with confidence, Hiero," the poet concludes; "for you will enrich yourself. Augment the city, for you will attach power to yourself. Acquire allies for it. Consider the fatherland to be your estate, the citizens your comrades, friends your own children, your sons the same as your life, and try to win victory by benefiting all these. For if you master your friends in beneficence, your enemies will be unable to resist you. And if you do all of these things know well, of all things among human beings you will acquire the noblest and most blessed possession; for being happy, you will not be envied."[4]

As Aakash Singh notes, later scholars have focused on the way the dialogue ends, with the poet having the last word and painting a utopia. Hiero says nothing more, perhaps realizing the philosopher's cunning in telling him of a utopia without giving him a roadmap, thereby shutting him up and in effect paralysing him. Indeed, this ending may parallel God's command to Adam and Eve to go forth and multiply and take dominion over the earth but eschew sex and eating of the tree of life. It echoes the wise advice of the Oracle of Delphi on how to find happiness. As we saw above, Machiavelli rejected this approach out of hand because its very assumptions are baseless: a tyrant has to be practical, and so he should inspire fear from other people, especially potential enemies. Machiavelli's advice has resonated ever since, although many followers have remained like Hiero, struggling to reconcile fear and love and to make even people who fear them just as happy. And perhaps the answer is truly ironic and the stuff of tragedy, for Hiero suggests, somewhat innocently, that suicide might be a real option. In the next chapter, I propose that a social death might suffice – metanoia suggests resurrection into something better.

The debate between Strauss and Kojève can help us understand at least two of the daily contradictions in an officially multicultural Canada. First, what do we mean by "justice"? Is it "just us" that has to sacrifice itself for a greater good – perhaps, paradoxically, preserving an un-equable, non-egalitarian social order? The American philosopher Richard Bell observed, à propos of South Africa's Truth and Reconciliation Commission, that for too long much of "justice" has involved the few and strong oppressing the many and weak by administering justice from the top down, for retribution, and keeps the strong strong while doing nothing to empower the weak. "The very idea of justice should be testament to our humanity. Rather, the idea of justice seems to follow political, ideological, or religious dogma throughout the world. Instead of promoting or restoring a sense of human well-being and peace, community reconciliation, and an individual sense of virtuous living, justice has come to reflect a more retributive spirit and too often reflects an abuse of power."[5] As the American theologian Walter Brueggemann says, "The case is clear. Justice must be rethought from the bottom of violated bodies up to more compassionate policy formation."[6]

Second, even officially multicultural Canada does not offer a de facto escape from tyranny. We human beings are always fleeing, even though we rarely know where we are heading, and one person's Garden of Eden

can be hell for others, who find themselves mere humans in such a setting. Often, even those who would create justice for us cannot see why
we turn away, spurning their efforts *for us*. Even to the most benevolent
tyrant, we are all ungrateful brutes, especially when we, through self-will
and determination, reject what the master knows with certainty to be a
superior level of justice.[7]

Doesn't such a tyrant deserve pity? This question has even wider
implications if we remember that there is a tyrant in all of us. Can a
tyrant ever be *happy* and *authentic*? And if the tyrant cannot, can a non-
tyrant? Any of us could become either a despot/bully or the beloved
democratic hero whom people would approve of and think great – or so
we think. Alas, the human condition does not seen to demonstrate this
kind of cause and effect. Paradoxically, there seems to be no real justice,
whether we are authentic or not.

Coming to terms with these two contradictions is important, for the
belief that justice is a *social construction* has long held, making it col-
laborative or dialogical – it has to involve more than one person, hence
its need for a social setting. And here we may recall Strauss's opening
position: we are more authentic as atomic individuals – in other words,
as potential tragic heroes – than when we dare to give up our freedoms
and become mere slaves or subjects in society. He warns us that we
should hand over our personal sovereignty to the state only very carefully, if ever. So if we cannot have justice in society, where even comedy
is not justice, can we obtain justice by remaining non-social or even anti-
social? Is citizenship really worth anything?

This debate is broadly about multiculturalism as it exists in the "reality" that at heart Canada is still Christian in its actions. Justice is the
purview of people living an essentially, if unofficially, Christian life. In a
Hegelian sense, Christianity's redemption is that it allows believers to
live as unhappy consciousnesses, with a seeming split personality, where
the individual is the central entity in the secular, "public sphere" and
absolutely inessential in the divine or spiritual. This is a world that is
tragic: the stoic must become the sceptic, on the road to the eventual triumph of stoicism. So the individual lives sceptically – keeping stoicism in
check – in a world of comedy, where boundaries and limits exist but do
not now appear as such. In addition, some non-Christian values might be
now acceptable in the public sphere or marketplace that is Canada.

Non-Christian values may very well have become dominant – in effect,
making Canada ontologically a site of comedy as the expression of specific human desires. But from a hegemonic perspective, even if acts of

fidelity in Canada do not require swearing solemnly on a Bible, Christian norms still dominate. Public life still tends to relegate non-Christian values to the state of nature within all of us – the cultural and private sphere, which contains the bulk of humanity and that which is not Canadian. As Leo Strauss argues, "Modern philosophy, which is the secularized form of Christianity, created the idea of the universal and homogeneous state"[8] that now seems the general ideal for the Western nation-state. He claims that it created the folk.

But in a conflicted world, this is still a state of lordship and bondage, where no one can readily prove what is real or lift it up as authentic. It is a world where reality and authenticity always need context, where what might seem real and authentic in one case might not in another. This is the comedic world, multicultural by definition, where private and public, secular and spiritual/divine, and whiteness and blackness exist not as moments of diremption that are specific or segregated spheres but as integral elements of the same whole. The only reasonable approach to life there is pragmatism – mediating the differences between spheres within the whole. For the whole is love itself, whether as solidarity or as recognition.

Canada's dominant notions of justice privilege people of a specific faith, and this too is at the heart of Quebec's painful discussion on the reasonable accommodation of Others – Canadians who can be inauthentic and happy but ideologically must conform to secular, mainly Christian practices.

To appreciate this, we can examine the genesis and history of the dominant reality. The debate between Strauss and Kojève can frame our understanding. We might also call again on Charles Taylor – this time, on the development of social imaginaries in the West[9] in the evolving consciousness that is a specific state, province, city, or community. It evolves, we assume, in response to some idealistic notion of the good for which its founders intended it – its *spirit*. Taylor, along with Strauss and Kojève, shows us how the Christian notion of justice undergirds the spirit of a modern society such as Canada.

This debate of the early 1970s began with Strauss's monograph on Xenophon's *Hiero or Tyrannicus*.[10] He posits that the liberal individual can become wise enough to become a benevolent leader and citizen of sorts – a kind of philosopher-king. Such an individual can seek to be happy in the prototypical state where rulers, as both tyrants and individuals, must respect the very laws they produce. The glue for all this would be knowledge, most important, of the self. Central to this discussion are traditional assumptions about sovereignty and tyranny that we saw above, particularly that the sovereign's mood determines the sovereign and subjects' happiness and well-being. A benevolent tyrant, if unhappy, would make *the people* unhappy. Thus the temperament of the sovereign tyrant creates the reality of the people. In a rational idealistic world, law – acts of pragmatism – would underpin social reality. Where there is no law, there can be no lasting reality and certainly no justice. The universe – a natural reality – provides the materials for this reality. But the first natural reality is uncompromising and individualistic. It is diverse and plural, with diversity also equating to difference and an innate struggle for dominance. Civil society's role is to perfect this way of living. Under the secondary regime, citizenship would emerge from a Kant-like cosmopolitanism privileging all individuals as unique with their own morality.

All the differences that we now observe in humanity are accidental and not essential to the citizenship, just as in the natural world apples might be so diverse that we might see them as distinctly Golden Delicious, McIntosh, and so on; however, if we are making a homogeneous thing we call "apple juice," we would have to use apples – Golden Delicious, McIntosh, both, or neither – not pears or oranges. They are all Bad Johns existing by their own unchangeable codes of behaviour. This is true whether we speak of apples for juicing or humanity for nation-state construction.

Most of the first-order diversity and pluralism would be available for social construction, for, if you take materials out of nature and build with them, you must acknowledge that all objects have a constitution that makes each unique. Otherwise, it would be like expecting a fairyland where bears can talk and death merely suspends sleep in the wait for a kiss. And because they are Bad Johns entering societies not totally of their making and must water down their Kantian imperatives, they are tragic characters.

After deciding to live with others, these atomists actualize themselves within the state, with little room to act out desires as inviolable individuals who can shape and hold fast to a prior image in this tyrannical state. In this respect, the individual enters the negotiations as an unchangeable being. The state becomes a reflection of her or him, imposing one person's perspective first on that person and then on her or his environment. This relation implies that "it's my way or the highway." Such is the existence of a loner, who creates it by choice.

This Strauss-type thinking permeates Pierre Trudeau's argument for multiculturalism, through his elevation of the liberal individual over the state as the starting point, not the end. For Trudeau, individualism always comes prior to the civil state: it crystallizes in the state of nature and develops this humanity and individualism in the civil state. To this end, the builders may make the state disappear or will it out of existence, but not the concept of individuals, the original builders. If, however, the individual disappears, then there are no more builders and there is nothing more to build. For Trudeau, multiculturalism assumes that individuals and groups come into the nation-state sporting their full humanity – the values they will have in the state of nature. Civil society is where citizens agree on which of humanity's values will form their new ethical order.

A multicultural Canada would therefore reject many values from the state of nature and also any model of them that its members keep. Multiculturalism becomes dynamic as new members keep moving out of the state of nature into the civil society. Every newcomer adds more of its humanity and its values to the Canadian pool. Each newcomer by definition causes unhappiness and even headaches for those who feel reconciled and want to believe they are living comedically. In return, all the newcomers enhance the possibility of freedom and of social justice's moving closer to its image in a state of nature, which would recognize and reconcile all of humanity and make it happy.

In opposition to Strauss, Kojève argued that good government in a modern state accepts changes in time and being. Even then, he was a leading voice on Hegel and his speculative thought on modern state formation as recognizing differences in unity.[11] This was how modern citizens actualized themselves – negotiating recognition, even with the self, from moment to moment. Self-actualization is never-ending, a work in process and progress, and an education about the genuine self in any individual or group. Often the individual may not recognize itself, far less know with certainty the others that inhabit the same world. Everything is unreal until the people in that world determine what is real by naming themselves and then explaining how each named object will behave under conditions that create the new reality that they desire.

Individuals recognize and actualize themselves by acquiring language, specifically the definitions of and rationale for rules and the means for communicating with and between the social institutions on which this reality rests. This acquisition transfigures all the differences, diversity, and pluralism of its materials and resources, like going through the refiner's fire or entering the social melting pot. All the resources would emerge with equal importance and status, even though they would not have changed physically. They would have traded in multiple values and "authentic" uses for new ones, which accord with the new reality that is the state where all diverse groups and individuals are, as in a fairy tale, equal and can now live happily after, at least in their imaginations. Anyone believing this ending is undoubtedly a joker – a mere comedian.

As Kojève tells it, recognition comes through personal endeavours that convey love and honour by others for the modern individual. All this takes place within a specific consciousness that is the state as part of a quest for freedom that idealistically reached an end of history, where the individual's actions correspond and externally reflect personal wishes and appear consistent in this way and harmonize these distinctive desires consistently. This consciousness is evolutionary.

Kojève sees a new type of *modern cosmopolitanism* at the heart of this debate on social integration. It assumed the withering away of the state and the elevation of the individual, not as a liberal democrat, whom Strauss read out of the pre-modern Xenophon and later history, but as a person seeking self-actualization in a state he or she wished, which might not come to be in his or her lifetime. And in this progression, the individual moves from tragic hero to at least tragic comedian, but overall to joining the comedians in a play consisting of modern society. Therefore the end of history is always at hand yet never comes to pass. The fairy-tale ending is always at least one further refinement of the social construction away. The reality of living in this state is that reality is unreal; reality still has to be established.

In a battle for recognition at the state or individual level, the original state must perish, to give way to an ideal – a universalistic state. The new state must cater to the generalities of existence and focus on attaining the common good. The individual's desires must become secondary to a wider ideal, a form of the common good, which replaces his or her previous dreams. This is the tragedy facing all liberal individuals as a particular modern state socializes them, but equally the state becomes tragic as its individuals shape it democratically as they determine and work for the common good. Instead of remaining seeming tyrants as Strauss suggested, citizens must become slaves to a higher tyrant. Worse, they must give in to a tyrant that is not natural or authentic. How can any self-respecting tyrant be happy, be satisfied, with this upside-down world?

We can see the influence of this idea in Trudeau's positions on the state's fragility and on how it must constantly change. And this is what happens when minorities as individuals or groups enter the civil state and challenge its social order. While Strauss accounts graphically for humanity's changes as it moves towards a civil society, Hegel and Kojève show us how to look at the issue from the other side: what happens to the emergent state and how it can handle the demands for change and retain any happiness or justice. This is usually the situation when immigrants, as we saw above, call for renegotiation of existing ways of life and positions of dominance. When they become citizens, they expect to bring to the never-ending negotiating table more of the values that society had rejected earlier. They and other challengers are always asking for inclusion and recognition of many previously discarded values as official and as Canadian. There is constant demand for reconsideration, which old-timers may consider an endless appeal to fairness on old and discredited grounds, but which newcomers would view as a new argument that deserves free and full examination.

Such is the dynamism of multiculturalism. And so, I argue, substantive change occurs to the state: in the end, the individuals coming out of the state of nature are eternal in a Straussian sense, but the state that they are helping to build is not. For the civil state to exist, it must change more and more to accept and accommodate the wishes and ideals of those representing the state of nature at its purest. In a pluralistic world, multiculturalism, demographically and culturally, would be the purest form of humanity and justice. For citizenship to be meaningful in terms of equality and ownership, democracy would have to take into account the multiplicity of interests and values that multiculturalism represents. Following Kojève's explanation, for citizenship to equal true equality, democracy would have to be radically egalitarian, again shifting the balance to the margins, which represent qualities, values, and intentions that seem to suit the state of nature, not the civil society. This thus explains much of the contradiction in Trudeau's official multiculturalism, how Straussian individuals end up as Hegel-type folk as persons or citizens living organically in a culture and even homeland of their own making.

At its most utopian, a Strauss–Kojève reconciliation would be a civil state that has a citizenship cosmopolitan to the world of individuals who undergo an ontological sea change to citizenship within the particular state. In this effect, the state would be the *world* to all intents and purposes, even if, legislatively and in terms of sovereignty, it acted in and possessed a form as if it were separate from the rest of humanity. This would be paradoxical for the state, accepting diversity without seeing it as difference, without an inherent or built-in hierarchy of rights, privileges, and belonging that effectively nullifies citizenship. It would also be ironical: while the state seeks to present itself as a unique particular, in practice it would be acting universal, the world within its bosom, without recognizing that it cannot be both at the same time. Indeed, what would tragedy be without irony?

Taylor suggests that citizenship is about sharing dignity and humanity, implying, as the English theorist Derek Heater suggests, two contradictory ideals – cosmopolitan citizenship and state citizenship. First, the cosmopolitan form assimilates diverse members and groups under a single civic identity. It goes hand in hand with a Stoic philosophy that argues for a universal oneness through all humanity. The laws of nature that produce this oneness are superior to the laws of any group as an intention to limit its membership and to treat members and non-members differently. Heater asserts, "Stoicism asserted that man and God (or the gods) are rational beings and that because all men are the sons of God and because of this common attribute of reason all men, of whatever race or social status, slave or free, are equal ... Moreover ... all men the world over and without distinction are capable of attaining this status by developing their rational facilities. Thus is the concept of citizenship opened up to universal application. However, a good citizen must obey the law. That indeed is tautologous; but what law is a citizen of the world to obey? The stoic answer was 'the law of nature,' a code consisting of fundamental principles of justice emanating from divine reason and discernible by man through the exercise of that same facility."[12]

Second, in state citizenship, only individuals and groups native to a specific polity can have membership. The state is exclusive and prevents the naturalization of those who might qualify under a cosmopolitan membership. Over the years, through its various attempts at assimilation, Canada tried and failed to perfect a model of civic citizenship for specific groups and individuals, with continuing membership for only a specific group.

Beginning in the 1960s on, it changed to a cosmopolitan model. Immigrants did not have to give up their natural culture and distinctiveness; the new approach enhanced rather than diminished their authenticity by joining them to a wider group whose membership is open and whose ideals they can shape; and preserving their naturalness required the state to protect the things that make them distinct and diverse. The last idea led to human rights codes that permitted all citizens to remain distinctive. Therefore a Stoic-type multicultural citizenship makes citizens as equal as they choose and as different as they want to be, while it protects, maintains, and even enhances these individual differences.

But there are other ways that human citizenship can let individuals achieve this dignity of humanity. Traditional citizenship theory suggests that, apart from conferring rights and responsibilities, citizenship includes two other bundles of components – *political* and *economic* or *welfare*. The British theorist T.H. Marshall theorized citizenship this way, and his views became prominent just as Canada was developing its Citizenship Act of 1947. The political bundle of rights guarantees the right to be part of the sovereignty that the US Declaration of Independence captures in the phrase "we the people" – namely, to help in the continuing creation of their nation-state. They can stand for political office, vote, and hold their political representatives accountable. In addition, these rights may place limits on what representatives can do, how long they can hold office, and how often there should be elections. We consider below these rights' role in multicultural citizenship, especially in light of the entrenchment of the Charter of Rights and Freedoms, which guarantees "democratic rights."

Reconciling Strauss and Hegel–Kojève in thought is easier than doing so in our living experience. Such is the challenge of official multiculturalism as policy and practice. The state and its form of cosmopolitanism would be highly imaginary – its appearance offering one picture while a utopian bent idealizes another. It would be part of Kant's imaginary "schemata of understanding" (*Critique of Pure Reason*), which hints at a compromised third space between the living reality and the utopia.[13] This would be the making of the most ironic of beings in modernity: an unhappy consciousness in Hegel's sense, which I contend is Canadian multiculturalism as an exercise in humanism and cosmopolitanism. It is a story with a long back story in the discourse on modern Western states such as Canada.

Let us now look at this state of unhappiness before we examine the prevailing method for reconciling of such unhappiness: how we can think of and even accept an intentional tragedy as a comedy – living with two faces.

TWO MODELS OF UNIVERSAL REALITY:
ALEXANDER AND THE CHURCH

For Kojève, the new political cosmopolitanism flowed from two models: the world empire of Alexander the Great and the Christian church.

Alexander the Great's Stoic-like idea of binding all the world's peoples into a single state created the blueprint, he argues, for the dominant form of cosmopolitanism that informs the ideal of state formation. This became the bedrock of the social imaginary of equality and constructed sameness. The model recognizes difference and diversity, but also wipes out, even reverses, any inequality flowing from citizens' differences and diversity. Difference, diversity, and plurality do not have to bring inequality. Instead – and rather counter-distinctively – individuals should see all the diversity, difference, and plurality only as equality, reducing everything to an agreed-upon abstraction that determines social usefulness.

According to Kojève, "What characterizes the political action of Alexander, distinguishing it from that of all his Greek predecessors and contemporaries, is the fact that it was directed by the idea of *empire*, that is, a *universal* state, in the sense at least that this state would have no limits (geography, ethnic, or otherwise), *given a priori*, nor any *pre-established* 'capital,' that is, a geographically and ethnically *fixed* nucleus destined to dominate politically its periphery ... Moreover, by obliging the (enemies) Macedonians and Greeks to enter into mixed marriages with the 'barbarians,' he certainly had in mind the creation of a new ruling class which would be independent of all rigid and *given* ethnic support."[14]

According to Kojève, "Instead of establishing the domination of his *race* and letting his *Fatherland* reign over the rest of the world, [Alexander] chose to dissolve the race and do away with the *Fatherland* itself"[15] – an early prototype of the multicultural state. Alexander's approach suggested the possibility of citizenship that does not tie individuals to the land but rather allows for a seemingly unnatural relation based on ideas. A good example, as we saw above, is what happened in the Americas: settler colonies founded nation-states to makes citizens of people ethnically *unnatural* to the land. There was not a specific race of people that both sprang naturally from the earth and lived harmoniously in a state that was a development of the land.

Canadians claiming ancient lineage might not find much succour in Kojève in their zeal for privileges, or sympathy for their expectations that newcomers should have no say in important matters, that they must accept what is already extant, and that they must shut up and conform. Ironically, Kojève seems to suggest the complete opposite – a position comedic only for old-timers.

A multicultural state would be able to use this approach to base citizenship not on an exclusive relationship with a territory. People in all their diversity could go to that land and there subscribe to a common citizenship – to behave in a way so as to achieve some common goal.

The other prototype for the modern state, and for multiculturalism, is the Christian church, which Kojève acknowledges is very different from the idea of a state. However, he finds in it "the *philosophical* idea going back to Socrates which, when all is said and done, acts *politically* on earth and which continues today to determine the political acts and entities aiming at the actualization of the *universal* state or empire."[16] The Christian model provided two ideas: intention as an analogy for desires and the transcendence of a universality and homogeneity of people that fully actualized in the beyond of either heaven or hell.

For Kojève, the new political cosmopolitanism resulting from these two models assumes Hegel's lordship-and-bondage reading of history,[17] or what Kojève calls a "master–slave narrative." "For St. Paul there is no 'essential' (irreducible) difference between the Greek and the Jew because they can BECOME Christians, and this not by mixing their Greek and Jewish 'qualities' but by *negating* them both and by 'synthesizing' them in and by this very negating them both and synthesizing them in and by this very negation into a homogeneous unity not innate or given, but (freely) *created* by 'conversion.' Because of the *negating* character of the Christian 'synthesis,' there are no longer any incompatible 'qualities' or 'contradictory' (=mutually exclusive) 'qualities.' For Alexander, a Greek philosopher, there was no possible 'mixture' of Masters and Slaves, for they were 'opposites.'"[18]

Again, this reasoning offers little support for old privileges: as soon as once diverse and different people enter the state, they *become* the state: there can be no further mixing of ancient lineage and more recent pedigree. They are now equal, interchangeable, and the same. To be different would be for the emerging reality to be akin to Strauss's, where individuals are all tyrants and nobody yields to another – a state of nature or a time and place that are not social. Some people might like this, but it will not construct an authentic reality involving not happiness forever but justice.

The adaptations that Kojève describes would construct a reality with expectations for a specific, Christian type and quality of justice, even though we Canadians, like Americans, might talk about the separation of state and religion. As well, people of other faiths must be "tolerant" enough to accept their position.

The further result is, as even some Christians recognize, the unreal reality that "salvation history only begins with the good acts of God's creation. Human beings, in their desire to 'be like God knowing good and evil' (Gen. 3:5) have inherited very ambiguous tendencies. Both individually and institutionally, we are capable of great sinfulness toward God and our neighbours. We do not live *in* but *after* Eden. The result is that we approach life not just as if we were looking 'in a mirror dimly' (1 Cor. 13:12) but also as if we were looking 'in a mirror, distortedly.' People's ambivalent attractions to a distorting mirror comes from the realization that what they see reflected therein both is and isn't themselves. There is enough of our original image and mannerisms reflected to make us recognize ourselves, but the accompanying distortion can be truly disturbing."[19]

What then is *reality*, if it is always distorted? And do its appearance and realness change when the God of this founding mythology is no longer some supernatural being in the transcendent but the state or nation? In the state, we have created this god, and we both define the standards that this being should judge us by and determine how they constitute justice, so that our daily lives refashion us, shape us, and give us second chances and makeovers to create all of us anew, so that the state will now find favour in us. Does this reality change when, in the end, our sense of justice is always like Christmas, when tragedy ends and comedy begins but, more important, when justice comes from a being who "knows" everything, has all powers, and can justly reward us with that which we desire most or with merely a lump of coal? Seemingly in a farce, the self-consciousness that is official multiculturalism answers "Yes" to all these questions, wondering only later what the answer really means in such an unreal world.

MODERNITY'S COMPLETING THE BEDROCK

So what is this *reality* into which we try to incorporate the proverbial Bad John, whether immigrant or the next baby born in the country? Canadian theorist Northrop Frye describes this reality as a culture, a way of life that a special group of people living in a closed society produce. This closure, Benedict Anderson argues, may involve a common stoical belief that all members are alike and follow the same patterns and that, teleologically, they had the same beginning as a nation-state and may share the same ending.[20] The sense of oneness translates into *sovereignty*, whereby the group considers itself as a unity and power unto itself, free to determine its reality and the form of justice and to work towards these goals.

This unity then presumes the freedom to operate without restriction or molestation – or eventually freely – in a specific geographical area that Frye calls "a world of domesticated animals' model in the West, based on both classical Christian metaphors such as the sheep, itself a metaphor for citizen." "The human form of the mineral world, the form into which human work transforms stone, is the city. The city, the garden, and the sheepfold are organizing metaphors of the Bible and of most Christian symbolism, and they are brought into complete metaphor identification in the book explicitly called the Apocalypse or Revelation, which has been carefully designed to form an undisplaced mythical conclusion for the Bible as a whole. From our point of view this means that the Biblical Apocalypse is our grammar of apocalyptic imagery."[21]

Canadians founded their society on Christian principles and ideals. They planned their institutions to produce a distinctly Canadian justice, which grew from a Christian reading of life and its fulfilment. Multiculturalism as a policy may have changed the ideals of Canadian identity and the components of its culture, but not the bedrock justice, which still expects all residents, of whatever religion, if any, to conform to Christian practices. Some public holidays, though growing more secular, still mark special moments in the annual Christian cycle. Which of its conflicting stoic and sceptical founding principles should it elevate and privilege? Does it stoically believe that there are no differences in the Canadian body, for the individual expression of difference and diversity is inessential, or does it tilt to extreme scepticism? Does it argue that the true Canadian will emerge in the beyond and that what is now on display is a mélange of groups, one of which is essentially and authentically Canadian while all others are not? Or does it settle for a simple form of scepticism by saying that the world is unreal and real at the same time and all we can do is be pragmatic, for we are not living in the past, when people really knew what is true, nor have we yet attained that point when, after all human bodies have become dust we will know again what is true.

In a moment of pragmatism, we can assume that all bodies have become dust, but instead of finding the essence we now have new materials to construct beings that would contain equal parts of essence and of what is inessential. In this moment, we also remember history's lesson about when we imagined an essential Canadian consisting of specific properties – usually geographical and ethnic. We discovered that each seeming property turned out to be universal, so that the property had some unknown or hidden essence. We learned that essence was not a property but a value. These new beings are copies of themselves – a comedy of achieving in the here and now what once seemed possible only after a real death.

The multicultural Canadians we make from dust would have the forms of all humanity, of every region and ethnicity. Culturalization would instil in them Canadian values, so their Canadian personalities would express their citizenship. It would socialize them as *Canadian*, educating them in social norms, mores, and ways of living according to Canadian ethics. This social construction reformulates what nature provided. Stoically, multicultural Canadians would be equal in all areas of citizenship, even if sceptically they would not appear equal or copies of each other but would act and behave as they wish, with one exception.

In the public sphere, they would put themselves totally under the society's prevailing ethics, even if they do not fully agree with the rules. Then, in this sceptical moment of individual inauthenticity, of internal unhappiness, they work to remake the rules and ethics towards what they would be if life were as real to them as they would want it, if there were no diremption and happiness was natural.

Frye's explanation of culture resonates with the work of cultural theorist Terry Eagleton, who writes:

> Culture is said to be one of the two or three most complex words in the English language, and the term which is sometimes considered to be its opposite – nature – is commonly awarded the accolade of being the most complex of all. Yet though it is fashionable these days to see nature as a derivative of culture, culture, etymologically speaking, is a concept derived from nature. One of its original meanings is 'husbandry', or the tending of natural growth. The same is true of our words for law and justice, as well as of terms like capital, 'stock', 'pecuniary' and 'sterling'. The word 'coulter', which is a cognate of 'culture', means the blade of a ploughshare. We derive our word for the finest of human activities from labour and agriculture, crops and cultivation ... Perhaps behind the pleasure we are supposed to take in 'cultivated' people lurks a race-memory of drought and famine. But the semantic shift is also paradoxical: it is the urban dwellers who are 'cultivated', and those who actually live by tilling the soil who are not. Those who cultivate the land are less able to cultivate themselves. Agriculture leaves no leisure for culture.[22]

Picking up on reality as a social construction, or as an exercise in planning, Frederick Hayek reminds us that there can be too much social engineering. "'Planning,'" he tells us, "owes its popularity largely to the fact that everybody desires, of course, that we should handle our common problems as rationally as possible and that, in so doing, we should use as much foresight as we can command. In this sense every-body who is not a complete fatalist is a planner, every political act is (ought to be) an act of planning, and there can be differences only between good and bad, between wise and foresighted and foolish and shortsighted."[23] Yet too much planning, he worries, robs individuals of their creativity and amounts to slavery or totalitarianism.

But his real concern is more with the *outcome* of planning. Planning reflects the creationist need to transform and streamline, what Berdyaev calls the magic of imagination, imagination being the source of all human creativity: "There is such a thing as the magic of imagination. Imagination magically creates realities. Without it there can be no works of art, no scientific or technical discoveries, no plans for ordering the economic or the political life of nations. Imagination springs from the depths of the unconscious, from fathomless freedom."[24] The problem for Hayek is what happens when morality enters the picture and imposes values of good and evil on the creation. This magic and spark of the imagination characterize tragedy, which becomes a comedy only after the magic of creation has passed.

In explaining social imaginaries and proposing how this "magic" translates into living experience, Charles Taylor postulates that citizens gain civility from constructing the reality of social consciousness. Some critics may consider this behaviour social or political correctness, but effectively it prescribes how a "civilized" and "cultured" person with *knowing* should behave. And ultimately, it is a construction of power – a hierocracy between people who must always act civilly and the more powerful, who alone may take moral holidays of bad and nonconform-ist behaviour. It is a special claim to ownership of the goods, services, and welfare of this social imaginary; a possessiveness for individuals who own the history of all that this setting has thought and produced.

This civility comes, Taylor says, from members sharing the same back-ground and from understanding and performing specific rituals: "The background understanding that makes [a ritualized act] for us is com-plex, but part of what makes sense of it is some picture of ourselves as speaking to others we are related to in a certain way – say, compatriots, or the human race."[25] Taylor is doing more here than just grasping norms that underpin social practices: "There also must be a sense ... of what makes these norms realizable" – confidence in the reality.[26]

Shaping this common background is the courtesies that are norms of the society – for Taylor, such characteristics as mutual respect, especially since the fifteenth century in European societies of quasi-equality. People understand government's role because a code of law forces rulers and magistrates to exercise their functions properly, and they grasp the individual's place in a still-hierarchical society. Taylor writes, "I mean by this term [recognition] not an absence of hierarchy, because court society was full of this, but rather a context in which hierarchy has to be partly bracketed because of the complexity, ambiguity, and indeterminacy noted above. One learns to talk to people at a great range of levels within certain common constraints of politeness, because this is what being pleasing and persuasive requires. You can't get anywhere either if you're pulling rank or ignoring those beneath you or so tongue-tied you can't talk to those above."[27] Civility teaches social graces, which include the norms of hypocrisy and duplicity. It shows how to lead life as a comedy – but not as a full-length farce – and that the lone tragic hero is redundant.

In taking culture as the way of life within the city-state, we assume that those people do not share this social construction of reality stay behind in states of nature. They remain barbarians, primitives, foreigners, immigrants, and any other concept that indicates a different reality from us, less free and good than ours. "Because of the projection on them of the image of 'natural man,'" Taylor explains, "savages were held to lack these things [of orderly government]. But what they really lack in most cases were the makings of what we think of as a modern state, a continuing instrument of government in whose hands was concentrated a great deal of power over the society, so that it was capable of remolding this society in important ways. As this state developed, so it came to be seen as a defining feature of an état policé."[28]

We can almost hear Leo Strauss and his allies lamenting the state's tyranny and the quashing of all that is natural in the individual – of what would truly be for them a comedy.[29] But we can guess at Taylor's conclusion from Kojève's earlier analysis, especially his growing expectation of social conformity and equality, even within a spirit of egalitarianism or democracy. "The mode of government required by civility also assured," Taylor explains, "some degree of domestic peace. It didn't consort with rowdiness, random and unauthorized violence, or public brawls either in young aristocratic bloods or among the people."[30] This requirement might also generate expectations of tutelage for uncivil people until they have so matured. Canada still insists that landed immigrants wait at least three years for citizenship – showing, by not running afoul of the law, that they are civilizing themselves. Babies do not have to wait.

This civic construction leads ultimately to a sense of ownership. The individuals own the state, and the state in effect owns them. Individuals in theory have rights to the benefits and privileges of the social well-being their state produces, just as shareholders do vis-à-vis the benefits and dividends of the companies they collectively own. But, according to people who see only the comedy in this type of justice, the state, like a company, has first claim on the benefits and dividends, whereas those who emphasize individuals' ownership would see a tragedy, with the collective entity having the final say. But the core issue concerns ownership – individuals having a claim on the state, or vice versa.

The answer decides the social justice – the tragedy and comedy – of the social reality that is theoretically for the benefit of the individuals. The owner is indeed personal, so the new reality subsumes the individuals and makes them inseparable from it. The authenticities of the state and the individual merge or mesh together. But in return, the individuals lose something: they move from being concrete individuals to being abstract and general; from true subjects to objects of the society; from individuals whose knowledge of truth in the world matters most to *thing*s and beings whom others know. They lose their spirituality and become less philosophical and anthropological in the traditional sense, as they become objects of sociology, psychology, politics, and the law. Instead of being the centre of the world, they become merely new members of the group. Personal characteristics give way to group traits; an individual moral code to an ethical code that transcends it; tragic heroes to comedians, while the collective consciousness looks down on them and smiles as they seek to assert who is more important: the state or the individual.

This way of thinking usually considers the justice of the moral social order to be superior to any other. This then gives us the makings of patriotism and the willingness to die, even physically, for our country. It also explains the construction, when we mix diverse groups of people, of racism, xenophobia, and ethnocentrism. What remains common among diverse people living in a reality consisting of several realities or of one dominant reality and others that it thinks inferior? Do the inhabitants of the shared space exist in a single reality, a hybrid of the several realities, or in a setting of one or two major realities contesting inferior ones? This then explains multiculturalism and why it seems to define existences that include entities such as communities of communities, ethnic ghettoes, and mainstream and ethnic others.

MULTICULTURALISM, DISTORTIONS, AND JUSTICE

The debate between Strauss and Kojève, particularly the latter's position, frames this discussion on Canadian multiculturalism as a Hegelian unhappy consciousness, where seemingly inexplicable contradictions challenge its best intentions. The two main concepts of pluralism – official federal multiculturalism and Quebec's interculturalism – dialectically oppose each other. Quebec's policy recognizes cultural differences, discourages "ethnic enclaves," and requires linguistic assimilation. It is within this provincial debate that some voices are pushing for accommodations on some immigrants and minority groups.

Warring within the bosom of an officially multicultural Canada are two clear models. Unlike those of Alexander and the Christian church, each has a priori conditions, and neither seeks to compromise with the other. Instead, they squabble in a relation of lordship and bondage, where each symbolizes a specific culture or way of life and is unwilling to countenance or give way to the other. Each sees itself as the nucleus and the other as the periphery, yet they have to coexist as one single and homogeneous culture, with happiness for everyone and nobody fearing tyranny.

These models are in conflict and undermine the notorious contradictions of multiculturalism. The models offer a Kant-type cosmopolitanism of freedom for society to work out pragmatically, because absolutism in either leads to death. Multiculturalism grounds itself in the individual, reducing a fully formed individual to an abstraction – a citizen in terms of the Charter of Rights and Freedoms. In this egalitarian approach, the individual antedates the state and enters it only for its benefit. Quebec's interculturalism, in contrast, presents an inviolable state as its essential nature. A strong, centrist Canada would build a unity out of five distinct regions,[31] a unity to care for and protect the individual, who can attain his or her full potential and humanity only within a singular state.

The literature focuses on the second model: Taylor sees multiculturalism as a politics of recognition – in effect, a by-product of the struggle within a European group, among English and French ethnicities.[32]

This model does not speak to the egalitarianism that attracts the modern immigrant to Canada in search of social mobility regardless of race or ethnicity. It does not gesture to a rapidly changing Canada that incorporates minority groups. Also, it does not have a dominant status for First Nations peoples, unless they too seek assimilationist recognition as either English or French.

Either model leads unintentionally to an analytical or common-sense understanding rife with contradictions. Their only reasonable reconciliation appears to lie in Kant's imaginary third space, which has a role for a mediator and negates any essence for a free "conversion" to a new creation.

How can this reconciliation come about, and how would it affect politics? This is where the communitarian form of liberal democracy – the strong and inviolable individual and state, as Kymlicka and others argue, for example – can do little to make Canada less unhappy. Ditto for Joseph Carens's calls to limit newcomers' rights and privilege the existing state, as in Quebec.[33] The Kant-type solution – acceptable to such modern liberal thinkers as Carens, Kymlicka, and Rawls – paralyses cosmopolitan multiculturalism in interminable conflicts over privileges, recognized histories, and states of being Canadian.

These approaches do not explain dialectically the new cosmopolitanism at the heart of multiculturalism as a concept. They offer no syncretic understanding of what Kymlicka and others call "multicultural citizenship" and "notions of belonging." Indeed, this failure accounts for continuing discrimination, racism, and the argument of Bengali-Canadian sociologist Himani Bannerji and others that multiculturalism is a fraud on Canada's visible minorities. Critics always present genuine multiculturalism as requiring too high a price for dominant groups, which do not really want to start over again socially each day à la Hegel's schema. Their old perception of themselves as Canada's essence must give way to awareness that they are just another minority. Instead, they want to cling to past privileges and conquests, even though they now hear that these symbols of social status are evil. They cannot see the way forward as beginning with concrete action *today*.

Social resurrection and forgiveness are not, however, automatic for them and come only through grace and recognition that embodied they are the expression of social love. Forgiveness requires confession of past evils, whether intentional or not; even the elites must be willing to accept punishment by all members of society for their sins. But this judge is now simply a collection of other mortal evildoers, who will forgive their equals, just as they constantly do themselves. They would be sinners and judges, elites and subjects, dead and living. Their actions would represent a future different from the past, which they also now represent in the old, discredited selves from before their social death. They would all be evil and good – quintessentially human, not gods – even if they do hope to someday eschew the evil in themselves and be all good, like the gods in their thoughts.

Until that day, they would walk together according to a new morality so as to avoid all those mistakes that, if they take place again, would be unforgivable evils. To avoid unintended consequences, they follow an ethical code that changes with every death and resurrection. Every individual would contribute to the society's ethical code and could propose values that he or she brought into the state. Each would represent those particular interests, which would fit into a common good that, as a universal, recognizes all particulars. Negotiations for the code would be ongoing, constantly making room for new offspring and (adopted) immigrants. A common perspective would emerge, exalting love and recognizing the equal value of each member. It would close the door on a history of hurts and open a new one on hope. This new time and place would have no original sin and would abolish, even transcend the congenital racism of the Americas in the here and now.

What I offer is a cosmopolitan that James Clifford talks about when he outlines the postmodern state, where "people and things are increasing[ly] out of place,"[34] where there is no authenticity, and where many of the things that should work together for the common good are seemingly in oppositional relationships. Without any semblance of order or a strong centre, this situation hints at what Jacques Derrida called "the madness" of striving for a certainty that can only be illusionary (delusional?) as we seek a priori and universal conditions along with full freedom. Equally, this is Derrida's "madness" that allows subject and sovereign to constantly forgive the unforgivable in order to accommodate reconciliation.[35] I described this kind of multiculturalism in *Where Race Does Not Matter: A New Spirit of Modernity,* where we cut through the Gordian knots that we inherited from Alexander the Great and Christianity.[36]

Neither model of Canadian multiculturalism can attain current conceptions of justice. They offer good intentions, or what Kant's *Critique of Practical Reason* considers purity of heart,[37] which still sees one way of life dominate over the other as superior and worthy of ascendancy. Even such profound liberal essays as John Rawls's *A Theory of Justice*[38] and Trudeau's writings about a just society and the positions of Kymlicka and Carens do not plumb the depths of the new cosmopolitan spirit in Canadian multiculturalism.

First, in the resulting social order there was not the "the purity of heart, [where the desire,] if one can attain it, would be to see clearly and to act with grace and self-command from this point of view" – that of a higher and universal reason.[39] This purity is a willingness to allow a legislating good that is universal and rational to overrule private inter-ests. Rawls offers these words in anticipation of objections to his theory from Kant's *Critique of Practical Reason*: "Thus morality must have more power over the human heart the more purely it is presented. From this it follows that, if the law of morals and the image of holiness and virtue are to exert any influence at all on our minds, they can do so only in so as they are laid to heart in their purity as incentives unmixed with any view to welfare, because it is in suffering that they most notably show themselves."[40] The morality of the universal or a priori position of the Canadian negotiations did not appear pure to everyone. Their failure had more to do with political expediency – some would call it "pru-dence" – than with the process's reasonableness or moral "purity." Second, entrenched interests were unwilling to figuratively set aside their individual privileges – Rawls's veil of ignorance – crucial for (re)negotia-tion of the social contract. Rawls also emphasizes justice as fairness, a concept that Pierre Trudeau worked for in federal–provincial intergov-ernmental conferences, which usually ended in failure.

When they negotiated, many of the representatives of the English and French communities could not set aside their historical rights and claims, ignoring Trudeau's new spirit of egalitarian cosmopolitanism. They could not see themselves as equals with groups that they considered newcomers, who became ethnic-cultural groups only on arrival in Canada or whom the mainstream traditionally excluded. As power elites, they could not put on Rawls's veil of ignorance to help reconsti-tute Canada. They continued to act out a Hegel-style lordship-and-bondage relationship, elevating existing group rights and moral maxims. They acted with certain knowledge of themselves and their partners and out of a history of conflict that they envisaged continuing. In Canada, we see this conflict playing itself out in Kymlicka's assertions of the primacy of "societal cultures" in multiculturalism and liberalism and in Carens's objection to such a position.[41]

When Canada fails to reconcile the idealism and the practice of social contract theory, politicians, citizens, and immigrants must constantly compromise their ideals of universal laws of behaviour. Trudeau had a similar view: "Justice to me is a warm spirit, born of tolerance and wis-dom, present everywhere, ready to serve the highest purpose of rational man. To seek to create the just society must be amongst the highest of those human purposes. Because we are mortal and imperfect, it is a task we will never finish; no government or society ever will. But from our honest and ceaseless effort, we will draw strength and inspiration, we will discover new and better values, we will achieve an unprecedented level of human consciousness. On the never-ending road to perfect justice we will, in other words, succeed in creating the most human and compassionate society possible."[42]

In championing multiculturalism, Trudeau adopted Kant's solution to Canada's problems. Quebec desired recognition as a distinct entity, while Canada wanted to build a liberal heaven with free identities, no discrimination perpetuating historical wrongs or tyrannies concerning race, ethnicity, religion, language, disability, or any other categorization. Similarly, the state would not become arbitrary in its dealings with individuals and regions. But the state would be tyrannical protecting the common good. Trudeau, during the October crisis of 1970, went even to the extreme of imposing martial law against those Canadians (Québécois) who, he thought, endangered the survival of the state.

Trudeau himself was enigmatic: he wanted a Just Society that would recognize groups under the law for their cultural essence, but also to select immigrants to form these groups and to realize full freedom of identity and actualization by allowing them the citizenship and social mobility that would complete them as fully human beings – but only as individuals. Being Canadian would be just another cosmopolitan experience, with Canada and Canadians' representing all the world's peoples and ethnic groups, yet bearing their particular enculturation, which would privilege them as social liberal democrats.

Trudeau relied on Kant's view of imagination for his schema of multiculturalism, much in the mould of Benedict Anderson's "imagined community" as a utopian place of self-actualization and state formation.[43] The heart of this understanding consists of both the country and its individuals as citizens, which may not always share the same interest or common good. This is what people must imagine for the "empty" concepts of Canadian citizenship to make sense.

However, Trudeau's universalist cosmopolitanism, as Kojève shows, presented a contradiction. The imagined unity lies not with the state but in each citizen's universal humanity and the possibility of each group as a cultural entity with a Canadian universe. In Trudeau's view, a Canadian is a person of good intentions towards everyone, especially fellow Canadians, but equally vis-à-vis potential immigrants. He or she acts in good faith towards other Canadians, and even towards those who are not; he or she does not discriminate negatively against anyone. Canadians are tolerant and love humanity. They recognize themselves as free, even to the point of being diverse in their equality.

This recognition of freedom sits at the heart of the imagined schema of multiculturalism. It is the basis for Canada as a liberal democracy; this is what Kymlicka and others imagine when they present a Kantian argument of liberalism. The problem for Trudeau, and for Kymlicka and Carens alike, is the inherent contradictions, especially over what can and cannot change in the empty Canadian national time. Is it the state or the individual who can or cannot change? Which of them is the genuine liberal entity?

My argument is that Kymlicka and Trudeau cannot get out of the Kant-style analytical contradiction of understanding without "killing" the tyrant or "unchangeable" that is the concept of either the state or the liberal individual as sacrosanct. And since multiculturalism emphasizes the liberal individual, we are in a bind, for is that not what repatriation of the constitution and entrenchment of the Charter of Rights were all about? Or is it, as Carens suggests, the exalting of the liberal state that is the changeable? This is the argument against Quebec's secession and for a strong Ottawa, for official bilingualism throughout the country, for transfer grants from rich to poor provinces, and for federal intervention to ensure uniform standards in such provincial areas as education and health. This stance sacrifices the individual, as when Carens argues for limits on immigrants to Quebec in, for example, Bill 101, which forces them to send their children to French-language schools. The benevolent tyrant is a strong state, even if its actions defy the laws of the land – the tyrant's imposing's laws on minorities – and reasonable expectations and agreed honour and virtues.

An examination of the dialectics of Canadian multiculturalism raises the possibility that, as Trudeau hoped, time will undo this failure. Even then, the result might not be what he wanted. I return below to vulgarity in multiculturalism despite the concept's purity, as Kantians such as Carens, Kymlicka, Rawls, and Trudeau saw it. But let us first look at the circumstances, arguments, and compromises of Canadian multiculturalism so far.

ROOTS OF UNHAPPINESS: TRAGEDY OR COMEDY

My main explanation for the failure of Trudeau's approach to Canadian multiculturalism as a form of social justice unfolds on two fronts. First, some commentators suggest that Canada has not yet settled on a single model of multiculturalism as a cosmopolitan ideal and practice and is still experimenting. The body politic contains varying conceptions of multiculturalism, so that it is often unclear which dominates. In this respect, there is still no definitive spirit of multiculturalism in Canada. Modernity still seems to be a long way from its purported end of history.

Trudeau had two models: hub-and-spoke, centring on a form of biculturalism, and hubless, with open multiculturalism and a liberal and majoritarian form of state. The latter reflects Trudeau's egalitarian ideal of citizens being first and foremost liberal individuals who may then decide to take on an ethnic or racialized identity. It argues that diversity does not necessarily translate into inequality or into different levels of freedom because of recognized differences within the diverse body politic. And it places Canada firmly on the road to Clifford's socio-anthropological ideals and to the philosophical and political ethics of Derrida's notion of madness and forgiveness. In seeming opposition, the first model privileges ethnic or group cultures and places them in a racialized hierarchy. It argues for difference as the essence of Canadian multiculturalism and for a country that has grown from historical norms of good and evil and that recognizes the main characters in this tragedy.

At the centre of Canada in the first, hub-and-spoke, model would be a hardcore somatic and cultural whiteness consisting of Canadians of ancient lineage and the largest ethnic populations: the (mostly Anglo) Caucasians. Surrounding this hub, like spokes, would be a polyglot of somatic and cultural Others from various ethnic groups. It is hard to see how this method would produce Trudeau's Just Society. How would individuals, simply as citizens, and not reflecting any contingencies of birth, enjoy unhindered opportunities? This is the complete opposite of Kojève's presentation of Alexander's model.

Trudeau felt that peripheral groups should have the opportunity to join the Canadian mainstream. In effect, the mainstream and power elites would be a fluid mixture, changing over time and in keeping with the numbers. The main determinant for dominance would not be like Plato's esteem for history or ancestry, or what Leo Strauss calls the "indigenousness of citizenship";[44] rather, the individuals of groups would constantly renegotiate, reformulate, and re-create their relative strength along the lines of Kojève and Derrida's cosmopolitanism.

Trudeau argued, from a utilitarian position of the common good, for majoritarian rule, which logically requires egalitarian multiculturalism: "Democracy genuinely demonstrates its faith in people by letting itself be guided by the rule of 51 per cent. For if all men and women are equal, each one the possessor of a special dignity, it follows inevitably that the happiness of fifty-one people is more important than that of forty-nine."[45] Yet, as Trudeau insisted, one person might be right and ninety-nine wrong, so that the "one person must always have the right to proclaim his or her truth in the hope of persuading the ninety-nine to change their point of view."[46] The egalitarian-majoritarian model is the more Rawls-like of Trudeau's models and the one that he favoured, but that he did not get from the social construction of the state and citizens.

This model limits what could be the true spirit of this new cosmopolitanism, something that might reshape Canada, tipping it into seeming madness but generating creativity, renewal, rebirth, forgiveness, and the eternal present of the never-ending process of becoming. Perhaps Trudeau later saw this possibility and settled for the safety of the known and acceptable, thereby compromising and settling for the second model.

13

Rawls and Trudeau's Just Society

All power tends to corrupt and absolute power corrupts absolutely.
Great men are almost always bad men.

Lord Acton[1]

Beginning in the 1970s, the government of Canada became officially
multicultural, constructing a modern, pluralist nation-state. Canadians
renewed their social contract to make it more inclusive and less a fragment of Europe.[2] Pierre Trudeau's leadership (prime minister 1968–80,
1981–4) featured repatriation of the constitution with, at last, an amending formula, and entrenchment of the Charter of Rights and Freedoms.
Trudeau spoke of a new beginning for Canada, with negotiations among
individuals, not groups: "The liberal philosophy sets the highest value
on the freedom of the individual, by which we mean the total individual,
the individual as a member of a society to which he is inextricably bound
by his way of life, and by community of interest and culture. For a liberal, the individual represents an absolute personal value; the human
person has a transcending social significance."[3]

Trudeau said that it was during this renegotiation that Canadians
decided to protect their liberties and fundamental freedoms: "The
Canadian Charter ... sought to strengthen the country's unity by basing
sovereignty of the Canadian people on a set of values common to all,
and in particular on the notion of equality among all Canadians."[4]
Efforts were also under way to ease tensions between French and English
and to ameliorate the conditions of the First Nations people.[5] According
to Trudeau, "The very adoption of a constitutional charter is in keeping
with the purest liberalism, according to which all members of a civil
society enjoy certain fundamental, inalienable rights and cannot be
deprived of them by any collectivity (state or government) or on behalf
of any collectivity (nation, ethnic group, or other ...). They are 'human

personalities,' they are beings of a moral order – that is, free and equal among themselves, each having an absolute dignity and infinite value. As such, they transcend the accidents of place and time, and partake in the essence of universal Humanity. They are therefore not coercible by any ancestral tradition, being vassals neither to their race, nor to their religion, nor to their condition of birth, nor to their collective history."[6]

The reconstitution of Canada also had a demographic component. Until the 1960s, its immigration policy aimed substantially at sustaining a white man's country – reflecting Northrop Frye's "garrison mentality" and emphasizing Anglo- or Franco-conformity and preferential admission of European immigrants[7] from western Europe and from the British Empire, the Commonwealth, and the United States. The government actively discouraged peoples such as blacks, Chinese, eastern Europeans, Jews, and Southeast Asians.[8]

Canada has since moved to a points system, which aims to give all immigrants, as liberal individuals, an equal chance of acceptance. Universalized criteria test for individual excellence, not for group norms or characteristics. As Kojève suggests, anyone can theoretically *become* a Canadian by meeting a specified yet universal standard. The theory is that immigration helps maintain and preserve multiculturalism and liberalism. As I suggested above, multiculturalism places Canada always at a moment of new beginning, and every immigrant can help renegotiate the social contract.

Also in the period, Quebec held referenda on sovereignty association, first in 1980 and then in 1995. Western Canada's alienation arose, still fuels much national debate, and at election time can somewhat polarize easterners and westerners. Attempts to draw up a new constitution at Meech Lake (1987) and Charlottetown (1990) seemed to fracture the country even more, when ratification failed. Minority groups that are neither English nor French and immigrants of colour continue to agitate for greater inclusion in the state and more access to its power and perks.

Rawls's theory of justice, on which theorists such as Carens and Kymlicka rely, calls for parties to "make explicit the conception of social cooperation from which it [justice] derives," while not losing sight of "the special role of the principles of justice or the primary subject to which they apply."[9] Pierre Trudeau often faced less than full and open cooperation and, especially from groups in Quebec and western Canada, outright hostility to federalist positions. For repatriation of the constitution, the Supreme Court of Canada pushed the entrenched groups towards a grudging compromise. When they were entrenched interests, they often did not seem to overlap in any way but were presented as binaries.

As a result of failure to establish a regime morally acceptable to everyone, Canada found itself in a Hegelian type of unhappy consciousness,[10] with growing dissatisfaction on all sides with the prevailing ethical relations that constitute multiculturalism. People who had had to make compromises still await a moment of triumph – below the surface, the competition does not dissipate completely. Symptoms of frustration and alienation arise despite the best intentions of all parties.[11]

Trudeau had in the early 1980s reluctantly settled for the hub-and-spoke model of multiculturalism. Clearest evidence of this compromise was his hesitation about a "notwithstanding" clause in the constitution as a route to political peace. This clause allows provinces to override individual rights – such as the right to an education in the language of the individual's choice – that Trudeau wanted to make sacrosanct by entrenchment. He was always calling on Canadians to press their politicians to get rid of this clause. Idealism had in effect met *realpolitik:* no matter how much he had wanted a new Canada that recognized individuals and their right to shape their own destiny and their country's, some representatives of group interests and even of regions would not allow it. They were unable to forgive the unforgivable, in Derrida's sense. They were, at the socio-anthropological level, unwilling to uncouple difference and inequalities, even if they recognized that the country was indeed diverse.

Instead of dealing with individuals meeting to decide their social conditions and to establish the pillars of social justice, Trudeau contended with the kind of multiculturalism that Charles Taylor sees as a struggle for recognition among groups.[12] Primarily, many French Canadians demanding recognition and some English Canadians refusing that squeezed Trudeau. This was a struggle for control of the hub. This tug of war marginalized recent immigrants who had neither English nor French as mother tongues as separate and discrete ethnic groups. If they wanted to move to the centre, they had to align with one of the main groups.

Many immigrant groups refused assimilation and asked for recognition, thereby leading to the policy of multiculturalism. Taylor's model of multiculturalism as the politics of recognition seemed not inclusive enough. It left out First Nations peoples, immigrants, and so-called visible minorities, primarily because they refused to enter the debate as allies of the dominant groups, the "given."[13] Trudeau wanted to recognize the new arrivals as liberal individuals. He did not want them to be faced with an original position that had already decided all the "givens," which were unchangeable. Instead, they needed the freedom to decide if they wanted group recognition, "where numbers warranted."

As we saw above, Taylor's model describes a master–slave struggle between two primary groups, whereas Trudeau wanted more of a Hegelian lordship-and-bondage covenant first between individuals and then between several groups of different social strengths and levels of power. These groups would enter into an existing state that individuals had constructed and to which they would swear commitment and loyalty. However, the groups are always "cheating" by attempting to shift the advantage in their favour. This covenant acknowledges reason as an impure legislator, a product of a specific time and history – a time and history that might be tenuous and that some groups might consider immoral and wish to change.

Another line of argument assumes the notions of necessity and expediency that have always lain at the heart of the debate on multiculturalism in Canada – the *realpolitik* that forced Trudeau's hand. This time around, we see the driving force as Canada's increasing demand for immigrants to compensate for an ageing population and continuing decline in its fertility rate. A stream of reports from Statistics Canada has pointed to a population crisis starting as early as the 2010s.[14] That is when Canada's population will probably start to decline unless annual numbers of immigrants (now about 260,000) rise significantly. Some research indicates that Canada may need to double its annual intake for at least ten years to maintain economic growth and to have the population base to maintain current expectations for social welfare.[15]

But immigration is still not an easy issue for Canada, and the sources of current immigrants seem to make it even trickier. These are Third World countries, whose immigrants Canada would normally racialize as black, Chinese, and Southeast Asian – not groups that it traditionally sought out and which it would not position at the hub of multiculturalism.[16] Undoubtedly, more immigrants thence should not matter for a multicultural host country with Kojève's "purity of heart," where all individuals and ethnic groups are equal.

But political expediency shapes decisions. Below the surface and for powerful interest groups, Canada is still not as multicultural as it may appear.[17] The heart of multiculturalism is still impure, for Canada places immigrants and other individuals within groups in a hierarchy of power and equality.

Whether good intentions (prudence) of a pure heart or bad faith (political expediency) shape decisions on immigration to maintain the evil of group advantages, the result is still the same: a Hegel-type unhappy consciousness, where none of the parties are happy or feel keen to accept the state's reasons for conforming to its ideals. Again, that the reality is not the same as it appears indicates some of the problems with an abstract, Rawlsian approach to a social contract and with allowing people to locate themselves as liberal individuals within a society that they have found *in media res*.

TRUDEAU, RAWLS, AND A JUST SOCIETY

Several Canadian intellectuals have argued that Rawls's theory of justice underlies Trudeau's work.[18] An exemplar is Yvon Pichette of the Canadian Armed Forces, who looked at how Rawls's thoughts influence Canadian liberalism, even in the military: "Rawls says to us that to assure the stability of a society, it is absolutely necessary that there be a consensus between citizens of goodwill to have justice. This must be the case even though the citizens may otherwise be divided and far apart in their original beliefs. To achieve justice, they must be reasonable. The Canadian Charter of Rights and Freedoms is an example of the type of consensus and of the attitude that is needed to assure stability through the consent of reasonable citizens so that there might be consent and stability in the state" (my translation from French).

Several of Trudeau's statements in speeches read like paraphrases of *A Theory of Justice*. Trudeau was a law professor at McGill University in Montreal, and in his first cabinet post, as federal minister of Justice (1965–8), he reformed the Criminal Code and famously said, à propos of homosexuality, "The state has no business in the bedrooms of the nation." His ideals for a Just Society sound very much like Rawls's vision, where fairness and justice prevail:[19]

> The Just Society will be one in which all of our people will have the means and the motivation to participate. The Just Society will be one in which personal and political freedom will be more securely ensured than it has ever been in the past. The Just Society will be one in which the rights of minorities will be safe from the whims of intolerant majorities. The Just Society will be one in which those regions and groups which have not fully shared in the country's affluence will be given a better opportunity. The Just Society will be one where such urban problems as housing and pollution will be attacked through the application of new knowledge and new techniques. The Just Society will be one in which our Indian and Inuit population will be encouraged to assume the full rights of citizenship through

policies which will give them both greater responsibility for their own future and more meaningful equality of opportunity. The Just Society will be a united Canada, united because all of its citizens will be actively involved in the development of a country where equality of opportunity is ensured and individuals are permitted to fulfill themselves in the fashion they judge best.[20]

But Trudeau was a student of Lord Acton and valued Acton's aversion to nationalism that also recognized individual groups as almost semi-autonomous. His position on a state that by necessity recognized the diversity not of individuals but of groups came directly from Acton. As Trudeau states, "The co-existence of several nations under the same state is a test, as well as the best security of freedom. It is also one of the chief instruments of civilization ... The combination of different nations into one state is as necessary a condition of civilized life as the combination of men in society ... A state which is incompetent to satisfy different races condemns itself."[21] Canadian was not a nationalism.

In one of his earliest essays, arguing for a strong central state that was a confederation of provinces, Trudeau quoted Acton's *Essays on Freedom and Power*: "All power tends to corrupt and absolute power corrupts absolutely. Great men are almost always bad men." It is from this source that we can trace Trudeau's ideas on diversity, some of which appear illiberal. Trudeau often appeared as a contradiction: on one hand he supported individualism against a concentration of power in the Canadian state, but at the same time he wanted a strong state to balance the creeping powers of the provinces. Similarly, he advocated fundamental rights for the individual yet introduced policies that forced the state to recognize its obligations to groups. Trudeau argued for majority rule emerging from consensus among individuals but also wanted a kind of liberal democracy that recognized minority groups. As Acton would suggest, he struggled to recognize group cultures and to even give a nod to group language rights for the French while he fought against "ethnic nationalism, where one or two groups are dominant."[22]

These two sides of Trudeau were often in conflict in public life, resulting in the two models of multiculturalism in his proposal for a Just Society.

TRUDEAU'S MULTICULTURALISM AND A JUST SOCIETY

Canada's unhappiness over its governance is always present in the debate on multiculturalism. This argument stipulates that, in a liberal democracy, numbers are crucial – to borrow a phrase that seems to be disappearing: "where numbers warrant." For central to the image of a bilingual, multicultural Canada is the ideal that numbers matter: the majority that votes for a specific way of life should be able to impose it on the rest of society. So that this tyranny of the majority does not take over the liberal democracy, Canada has tried to protect sizeable minorities by recognizing them within the state and giving them special powers "where numbers warrant."

Trudeau even appeared to have left the door open for Canada, if numbers warrant, to become officially multilingual, or to remain bilingual, but not necessarily in English and French. He said that if there were as many Ukrainians as French, they would have as much right to official recognition and power as the French. This thinking was the basis for his proposal to share power proportionately or on the basis of numbers. As he explained, if enough citizens so wished, Canada could change its official languages. "Historical origins are less important than people generally think, the proof being that neither Inuit nor Indian dialects have any kind of privileged position. On the other hand, if there were six million people in Canada whose mother tongue was Ukrainian, it is likely that this language would establish itself as forcefully as French. In terms of *realpolitik*, French and English are equally Canada because each of these linguistic groups has the power to break the country."[23] Trudeau thus gestures towards an egalitarian model of multiculturalism with strict equality of citizenship, making decisions only as part of the general will that is the democratic expression of a numerical majority of citizens.

The questions he was addressing were how much of a state was unchangeable and whether it must always protect the power or rights of groups with long-term historical claims. In terms of Alexander the Great, he was foreseeing the death of the fatherland through radical, undesirable change. In arguing for the cultural rights of the living over the dead and for the power in the numbers of the living, Trudeau asked, "Can Haitian Quebeckers, for instance, protect certain aspects of their own culture by claiming protection as part of the French-speaking collectivity? ... Can neo-Canadian Quebeckers of whatever origins choose to renounce their heritage and origins so as to share with 'old stock' Quebeckers the protection sought by the French-speaking collectivity? Or are we dealing with a frankly racist notion that makes second-and third-class citizens of everyone but 'old stock' Quebeckers?"[24] Needless to say, Trudeau presented the Haitians as ethnically black in a province that is predominantly French and white – his very point.

In explaining multiculturalism idealistically, Trudeau sometimes seemed confused. He gave at least two answers – spoke-and-hub and all hub – each with implications for sharing power. He saw as Canada's highest internal aim reconciling all its many ethnicities and groups, harmonizing the wishes of individuals and the state and governing them with immutable rules of abstract reason that transcend group characteristics as determinants of power. This world might well have no stable norms, always open to negotiating what is good and what is different, including the state itself. It would not be a nationalism.

Trudeau wrote, "The die is cast in Canada: there are two main ethnic and linguistic groups; each is too strong and too deeply rooted in the past, too firmly bound by a mother-culture, to be able to engulf the other. But if the two will collaborate at the hub of a truly pluralistic state, Canada could become the envied seat of a form of federation that belongs to tomorrow's world. Better than the American melting-pot, Canada could offer an example to all those new Asian and African states who must discover how to govern their polyethnic populations with proper regard for justice and liberty. What better reason for cold-shouldering the lure of annexation to the United States? Canadian federalism is an experiment of major proportions; it could become a brilliant prototype for the moulding of tomorrow's civilization."[25]

So which model did he want? I think it is the diffuse power of the all-hub model, for even in talking about the other, he was still saying "where numbers warranted." Once the English and French ethnicities lost their entrenchment – effectively, the numbers that let them impose or prevent things – they would become like any other ethnic group. That fatherland would vanish, and their status would resemble that of Ukrainians and Haitians, for they too would exist outside their fatherland.

SOCIAL CONTRACT AND THE SEED OF DISUNITY

The praise for Canada at home and abroad hides some deep contradictions, for multiculturalism and the Charter of Rights still have strong foes. Critics and some leading federal politicians continue to argue that multiculturalism brings no real or lasting national cohesion, panders to groups with grudges, or that it is an attempt to buy the votes of minority groups by appeasing them at the expense of sound policy-making and governance.[26]

Some people still feel that Canada should be at most an officially bicultural country. Some extremists want it uniculturally English, or

French, as with the separatists in Quebec, who want independence or a loose association.

In each case, a fatherland or a homeland has privileges. Trudeau stead-fastly defended a strong, centralized Canada as a state for homeless lib-eral individuals who may then choose to adopt a specific culture as a new homeland. This would be a land they – not their parents – gave to themselves. This would be a land and culture of their own creation in the present. However, Trudeau appeared to stop short of advocating group rights, although he encouraged groups to preserve and maintain their cultures and ethnic identities: "The variety of cultures in Canada undoubtedly contributes to the country's richness and prosperity."[27]

Similarly, opponents, especially some Conservatives, also rail against the powers of courts and judges over Parliament. Canadian courts have become more interventionist and have struck down or significantly amended laws that Parliament passed; they have, for example, disal-lowed laws preventing same-sex marriages and restricting racial profil-ing by police, especially against blacks and other minorities.

Criticisms come too from the margins of society that multiculturalism is no more than an attempt by the English and French to keep power, influence, and privilege. According to Himani Bannerji, "In the multicul-tural paradigm, where difference is admitted, structural and ideological reasons for differences give place to talk of immutable differences of ethnic cultures. In both paradigms as the focus shifts from processes of exclusion and marginalization to ethnic identities and their lack of adap-tiveness, it is forgotten that these official multicultural ethnicities, so embraced or rejected, are themselves the construct of colonial – oriental-ist and racist – discourses. It is not surprising that many Western coun-tries, including Australia and its infamous *terra nullius* clause regarding its aboriginal people, looked to Canadian official multiculturalism for ways to manage a colonial history, an imperialist past, and convoluted liberal democracy."[28] Official multiculturalism "represents its polity in cultural terms, setting apart the so-called immigrant of colour from the francophones and the aboriginal peoples." This relationship pits "Canadian" culture against "multicultures" and makes whiteness the core value and dominant culture.[29] Here is an immediate contradiction in the policy aims of a multicultural liberal democracy.

The result of these policies, however, is clear in a very practical way: the Canadian polity is diverse, but, as Bannerji argues, an old-guard mainstream continues to wield the real and effective power. By this accounting, multiculturalism is trickery and deception in practice for non-white Canadians. Canada appears as an unhappy consciousnessin a battle between the changeable and unchangeable parts of its own nature and ideals. Universally, it needs abstract immigrants who are the best and brightest, but it cannot decide where they should come from, where they should settle, and what they should become in Canada.

A JUST SOCIETY AND NEGOTIATED COSMOPOLITANISM

Trudeau found it difficult to get the mainstream to show the generosity of spirit necessary to negotiate a new social contract. Rawls indicates that meeting this condition is vital procedurally for the attainment of justice as fairness; as well, the negotiators must be capable of cultural amnesia vis-à-vis earlier privileges. They must return mythologically to a time before humans ate from the tree of knowledge of good and evil. "Among the essential features of this situation is that no one knows his place in society, his class position or social status, nor does anyone know his fortune in the distribution of natural assets and abilities, his intelligence, strength, and the like. I shall assume that the parties do not know their conceptions of the good or their psychological propensities. The principles of justice are chosen behind a veil of ignorance. This ensures that no one is advantaged or disadvantaged in the choice of principles by the outcome of natural chance or the contingency of social circumstances."[30]

Trudeau had no weapons other than an appeal to what he deemed to be reason. When his reasoning and even cajoling did not produce the result he intended, he had to compromise and to rely instead on time to enlighten Canadians about their traditional positions. He found himself in the absurd position, of which Kant disapproved, of trying to impose a maxim – the elevation of common good – as a universal law of behaviour, especially a law that, by its nature, seeks to achieve greater levels of heteronomy in the nation-state.

Why should anyone, as a moral subject, give up a privilege, particularly if doing so might result in a losing position? Perhaps Rawls would answer that it was for such a question that he developed the idea of a fictitious original position of ignorance.

But this reasoning becomes circular, which might explain why Rawls and other Kantians appealed to the goodness of the human heart. As he states, "We may remind ourselves that the hypothetical nature of the original position invites the question: why should we take any interest in it, moral or otherwise. Recall the answer: the conditions embodied in the description of this situation are ones that we do in fact accept. Or if we do not, then we can be persuaded to do so by philosophical considerations of the sort occasionally introduced."[31]

Rawls says that where there are still doubts about assuming ignorance, the solution, in a nod to diversity, lies in different arguments that eventually conflate all arguments into one. From this position, the doubter can look at the social world and, relying on reason, aim for the particular conclusions. "Without conflating all persons into one," Rawls states, "but recognizing them as distinct and separate, it enables us to be impartial, even between persons who are not contemporaries but who belong to many generations. Thus to see our place in society from the perspective of this position is to see it *sub specie aeternitatis*; it is to regard the human situation not only from all social but also from all temporal points of view."[32]

But if diversity equals difference, which equals inequality and which the unhappy consciousness? Rawls is beginning to sound a lot like Hegel at the end of the *Phenomenology of Spirit*, looking for an ethical relationship neither of intentions nor of the goodwill or good faith of the parties. Hegel seeks a position of absolute spirit with absolute knowledge that is not blind and that accumulates within time and history, often through painstaking trial, error, and compromise. Rawls seems to aim for the same absolute position, but *without* knowledge, so that individuals can ultimately still descend behind the veil of ignorance.

In a Hegelian sense, Rawls looks for an Absolute of naïveté and innocence. "The perspective of eternity is not a perspective from a certain place beyond the world, nor the point of view of a transcendent being; rather it is a certain form of thought and feeling that rational persons can adopt within the world. And having done so, they can, whatever their generation, bring together into one scheme all individual perspectives and arrive together at regulative principles that can be affirmed by everyone as he lives by them, each from his own standpoint."[33]

This answer sounds too Kantian: reasonable people self-legislate the unchanging moral imperatives by which they would live. Kant states, "Thus practical laws refer only to the will, irrespective of what is attained by its causality, and one can disregard this causality (as belonging to the sensuous world) in order to have the laws in their purity."[34]

This reasoning forgets that reason can be deceptive and that these moral agents, as self-determining wills, live with other people in a world of heteronymous and competing desires and must be pragmatic – even hard of heart – about desires. They do not live in isolation and are not immune to others' words or actions or feelings. Kant reminds us that in a practical world, "no man asks, when he is concerned only with the agreeableness of life, whether the ideas are from the sense or the understanding (purity of heart or reason); he asks only how much and how great is the pleasure which they will afford him over the longest time."[35]

Relying totally on reason as both end and means to focus this purity of heart also still does not explain why a moral agent should even open up to reason, even from a more enlightened source. In effect, what remains is Hegel's bleeding hearts, who can only hope that their personal wishes will somehow materialize. This puts a heavy load on reason and on the expectation that humans will not act unreasonably or in politically expedient ways, something that no one with a Straussian sense of history would willingly concede.[36]

But then Rawls argues that the common good is not a sufficient reason to override the individual's best interest. He seems to leave idealists such as Trudeau with no way out of their moral dead end. Barring the use of force, such an idealist cannot impose reason on the reluctant, even if they are ill informed, misguided, and unreasonable. This is a point that thinkers such as Jeremy Waldron consistently score against liberals such as Kymlicka, asking how they achieve a *final solution* in such circumstances.[37] Force is the extreme opposite of tolerance – that moral virtue on which Rawls and others erect liberalism. The result for the idealists and those with whom they have an ethical relationship is to become unhappy consciousnesses, as Hegel explains in *Phenomenology of Spirit*. Even the best intentions and dreams come to naught or produce unhappiness instead of gratitude. Idealists end up in a form of semblance and duplicity as an alienated spirit instead of in wholesomeness and authenticity.

There are reasons for this, and Hegel explained them when he took on Kant and his moral imperatives. For Hegel, the culture determines notions of what is good, evil, reasonable, and even tolerant, and this is why the absolute position ends up as a kind of end-of-history narrative: it is the point at which the spirit has learned all there is to know about life as culture. It is also a position where norms and differences are at their clearest, or where they reconcile. This position is the complete opposite of that of Rawls's ignorant negotiator at the beginning of history. The best negotiator for Hegel is the person who knows it all. This is a person who has a grounding in history and who, if she or he is not at the end of history, runs the risk of refutation by others who possess greater knowledge and who arrive on the scene later.

What is more, cultures are what make some individuals, even though occasionally great men and women will arise, people who change the culture. Culture is what gives the moral individual a conscience like Kant's or Rawls's purity of heart. Yet when the individual genuinely disagrees with an intended a priori position, he or she must, in Rawls's sense, agree to an opposite imperative that also emerges in the name of culture. Which imperative in good conscience to follow? Kant suggests that the end result is remorse at best and moral paralysis at worst – and therefore no freedom.

The ideal final position, Hegel argues, would incorporate the known wishes and desires of all members of societies, which can happen only through privileging a greater good over individual goods, so that the state justifiably legislates the resisting individual, or, as Rousseau states, forces him or her to be free.[38] If we accept this thinking, it will probably, in the materialist world, be extremely difficult to create Rawls's conditions for justice.

Rawls knows how the positions we inherit can inhibit creation of the sense or condition of fairness that underlies his theory of justice and which is necessary for negotiation in ignorance. Yet even he will not insist on a retreat from these privileges – a volunteerism that undermine his moral imperatives. "No society can, of course, be a scheme of cooperation which men enter voluntarily in a literal sense; each person finds himself placed at birth in some particular position in some particular society, and the nature of this position materially affects his life prospects. Yet a society satisfying the principles of justice as fairness comes as close as a society can to being a voluntary scheme, for it meets the principles which are fair. In this sense its members are autonomous and the obligations they recognize self-imposed."[39]

Yet Rawls is here assuming a closed society or "a closed system isolated from other societies."[40] Pierre Trudeau was not so fortunate. A confederation, by its very nature, cannot be a closed society or system. There are at any time dialectics and dynamics at work within each unit. between units. and between the system and any number of units. This was certainly the case for Canada, as a federation, in its relations with Quebec and the other provinces and for Quebec in its relations with the other provinces.

In all cases, these units sought to "cheat" on the existing contract in a bid to further their gain or sought release from their original "birth" position. Quebec, for example, is forever seeking to withdraw from and re-enter, on its own terms, the confederation or some version of it. Even in dealing with Canadians as individuals, Pierre Trudeau was not operating in a closed system. Migrations within the confederation were problematic, as in Quebec and Ontario's dispute over construction workers or various provinces' honouring or not of welfare claims by migrants from other regions. This was one reason why Trudeau fought to entrench mobility in the Charter of Rights, allowing for more voluntarism and for individuals to "cheat" on their life chances by moving from an area of poor prospects to another that offers better chances. There were also questions of international migration and of Canada's continuing need for new citizens. All these factors create a fluidity, openness, and instability that are the very opposite of Rawls's conditions.

Trudeau found this to be the case, and he eventually settled for hub-and-spoke multiculturalism. This model had greater cultural legitimacy, for even though it may be racist and impede self-actualization for immigrants and recognition for minorities, it was the product of a specific history. Multiculturalism had to take into account the dominant sensibilities and cultures. Trudeau tried to change these, but he could only go so far.

Ultimately, as Rawls suggests, Trudeau had to appeal to Canadians' "purity of heart." He called to them ultimately to do away with the "notwithstanding" clause and to have a Charter of Rights without letting group concerns impede individual social justice.

However, although he could not realize the ideals of a Rawls-type theory of justice that he espoused in his writings about the just society, Trudeau did not abandon the theory. Rather, he held fast to its ideals and abstractions to the very end, and he even encouraged Canadians to do the same. Such a theory, he said, allowed us to keep searching for a rational and universal notion of justice and to keep working for a just society, and it gave us benchmarks to judge our success. Trudeau's ideals tell us to try continually for a schema where race does not matter and where diversity does not necessarily mean difference and inequality.

PRACTICE AND REALITY: LIVING THE UNREAL

In practice, Canada holds out egalitarianism (all hub) in its recruitment of immigrants, while a bicultural mainstream with less influential ethnic groups surrounding it (hub and spokes) is the reality that newcomers encounter. A contradiction in Canadian immigration causes unhappiness: Canada selects newcomers, as quintessential liberal individuals, for their personality and individuality but uses stereotypical ethnic and racial characteristics to place them. Personal aspirations that it seeks abroad collapse in the face of ethnic or racialized group aspirations – ethnic nationalism – in Canada.

Immigration is the wild card in the deck for Canadian multicultural-ism. Dominant groups will have to decide whether to incorporate new immigrants as ethnic groups or as individuals. Current practices would suggest ethnic groups, which creates a real possibility that the French and English will eventually have to give way to bigger and more success-ful groups and lose control of the agenda. In the 2004 federal election, for example, newcomers contested several constituencies in immigrant-rich Ontario and British Columbia; in several ridings, all the candidates came from the same *ethnic* group. This trend is also noticeable in provin-cial and municipal politics.

If dominant groups allow society to incorporate immigrants as indi-viduals, they will more probably retain control by offering social mobil-ity via a meritocracy rather than social advancement via a group. This approach might be more successful if, as the advertisement I quoted sug-gests, Canada continues to favour high-skilled and rich immigrants, many of whom might prefer personal social mobility to group advance-ment. Effective co-opting would place the individual over the group and might resuscitate a more liberal notion of social justice, even if the hypo-critical world of *realpolitik* makes it a vulgar form of Rawlsian justice.

This is the type of justice that Rawls frowns on: "If one supposes that the concept of justice applies whenever there is an allotment of some-thing rationally regarded as advantageous or disadvantageous, then we are interested in only one instance of its (justice) application."[41] Indeed, this vulgar parody of Rawls would amount to Hegel's duplicity and deception – ultimately causing an ethical relationship that is an unhappy consciousness, the very thing we sought to escape. The result will be a cycle of levels of an increasingly unhappy consciousness, with no obvious way to break the cycle from within. In the end, this might be a story not so much about "purity of heart" as about the cunningness of reason.

When it comes to power, in a practical and material sense in Canada, individuals are not abstract at all; instead they arrive as social constructs with the innermost layer of their clothing that of a presumed group or ethnic affiliation. This is not what Trudeau wanted for Canada. However, this was what he got, and the unhappiness prevalent today stems in part from the realization that the politics of the day did not allow Trudeau to go as far as he wanted – to become a Rawlsian in practice. This accounts for much of the continuing unhappiness in the cosmopolitan world abroad, which imagines a liberal democracy that is officially multicultural, which does not square with the living reality of those newcomers who see a work in progress where they can fulfil their individual and personal dreams. Canada then is still an unreal world, not yet metaphysically comedy.

To make the best of this untenable situation, Canadians dwell publicly in two worlds: in one, they secretly yearn for authenticity and for a Straussian tyranny; in the other, they subscribe to the dominant ethos, but because it makes them feel so inauthentic they see every day as an opportunity for a moral holiday of sorts. Nods and winks suffice, and even special handshakes if they're in the inner sanctums of real power, while publicly they smile and speak the orthodox language of the dominant social reality. We look next at this public doubleness.

14

Rethinking the CBC and Me:
From Tragedy to Comedy

It is in dying to self that we are born to eternal life
Prayer of St Francis of Assisi

In the story I told above in chapters 9 and 10 about my experiences with CBC Radio, I started with the narrative assumption that both the broadcaster and I were free to make our choices and to come up with our own ways of producing a series on immigration. I also supposed that both of us were operating in an environment that desired, welcomed, and accepted change and where one could challenge, even reformulate, the existing order. My assumption, equally, was that both CBC and I felt we were trying to help Canada, its citizens, and immigrants to achieve collectively a higher good that transcended and improved on the country's accomplishments. We felt a desire within the country to strive for this higher good, particularly one that would bring people from many countries, cultures, and ethnic backgrounds into Canada and help them become active and participating citizens. In this light, there was no good in maintaining barriers between naturalized Canadians and newcomers or even just-about-to-be citizens.

Undoubtedly official multiculturalism has failed to facilitate full transcendence for all groups of Canadians – especially those it racializes as whites and positions as privileged old selves and those it racializes negatively as non-whites as socially inferior. Fluidity of social mobility is still beyond reach when some people have positions as too good to fall socially and others are not good enough to rise.

Justice therefore would come through change, not through retention of the current order. It would not happen if society assigns newcomers to a specific place, where they should be happy and grateful. Justice would come from Canadians' recognizing that they were generally unjust and acting to right this wrong. They would help shape a social acceptance of immigrants that would allow newcomers to feel full participants in an ethical relationship emerging from attempts to meet equally the concerns of both the "old" and the "new" Canadians. Justice therefore would still lie in the transcendent, something to aspire to rather than already in our grasp and needing nurture and protection before something snatches it away.

The assumption then was that Canadians would want to share in symmetrical relations by living in the collective that is the state. The ethical relationship between old and new Canadians would not distinguish between subject and object, thus fulfilling the goal of the Citizenship Act, "A citizen, whether or not born in Canada, is entitled to all rights, powers and privileges and is subject to all obligations, duties and liabilities to which a person who is a citizen … is entitled or subject and has a like status to that of such person." No individual would have advantages in dealing with the state. Further, the relationship between new and old Canadians would look the same to both groups. The Canadian ideal of multiculturalism for us was justice to receive, attain, and even shape.

Suppose, however, that all our assumptions were wrong. That turns out to decide whether my relationship with CBC Radio was tragedy or comedy. If I was wrong, I was participating in an exercise in which I was unaware of, or unwilling to accept, limits that people or a force that knew better than I had put in place. This force might very well be a national consciousness that developed in Canada through centuries of experimentation, dialectical change, compromise, and reconciliation. I would be running up against the wisdom of history. Likewise, the CBC would have been participating in a comedy. It too might have been misguided and have lost sight of the real Canada by seeking to pander to those who do not represent its historical reality. In another sense, equally comedic, the CBC would have been helping me to challenge the good in society only to realize that society is already sound and healthy and that any change would be only to a lesser good. Politically, that would be an evil rather than a good, and so not justice.

Perhaps neither the CBC nor I was willing to accept rational rules that almost guarantee the continuing success not of individuals or groups but of society. This too would have made the situation a comedy. These would be rules based on knowing what is good and suitable for individuals and groups within society, so that in the end society would benefit and these individuals and groups would be better off. There is nothing good to gain from disrupting a system of rational laws, for they generate a common idea of what is just and normal. In yet another way, the CBC and I were perhaps in a comedy about our abilities, wherein neither of us had the mental or physical wherewithal to pull off what we intended, simply because it was untenable – like a well-meaning drunk trying to reason with the proverbial pink elephant.

In virtually every aspect of our relationship, the CBC and I might have been acting out a comedy – I especially, for telling it that I knew things about society that it did not know. In this case, I would have no notion of justice; I would not have the skills of a seasoned documentary maker, like the help the CBC provided; and I would not have had the understanding and social graces to act in a way consistent with the historical relationship between the CBC and its traditional listenership.

For the CBC, the comedy would emanate from its thinking that it could get an outsider-cum-immigrant, a Canadian who by nature is unchangeably an outsider/immigrant, to grasp its task and what it means to be truly Canadian. No matter how hard it spun, it could not turn straw into gold: I would never be able to fully understand its mandate – the demographic, historical, and cultural constraints under which it must prepare uniquely Canadian programming – simply because I was not part of this elite culture. In this respect, the CBC would have lost sight of the bigger and truer picture and misrecognized minor actors fundamentally unable to become noble and estimable heroes. Going into the contract, I did not believe the CBC was acting comedically – why would it court my perspective unless it believed that it could objectively give me a new one as I collaborated with its producers?

As Hegel explains, "The comic comes, therefore, rather into play among classes of a lower social order in actual conditions of life, among men who remain much as they are, and neither are able or desire to be anything else; who, while incapable of any genuine pathos, have no doubt whatever as to what they are and do."[1]

If we were acting out a comedy, both of us would be no different from a fool with a new script, bumbling over lines and fumbling over props, until someone or something mercifully saves him or her from mislaid claims to grandeur – subjective blindness. Again, as Hegel says, that hallmark of comedy "is the imperturbable self-assurance of such characters one and all, which becomes all the more emphatic in proportion as they prove themselves incapable of carrying into effect that which they project."[2] They hold on to this attitude "no matter what comes next or where it carries them."[3]

Enlightenment might not require our physical deaths, as with tragedy, but rather one or both of us seeing the errors of our ways and stopping the madness of fighting an unbeatable foe. In most cases, the foe is the self, trying to impose its wills and desires on other people and to make universals. Death would be an act of forgiveness – something spontaneous and illogical, not following naturally from any deserving or any actions by others. It is a death that is akin to what Natan Sharansky explains as escaping from a totalitarian regime into full freedom, where "appeals to the state, to nationalism, to religion, indeed to any ideology, seem empty ... It is no surprise that having experience this liberating feeling, you find yourself a born-again Democrat."[4]

Death would help us to overcome the pain and the lamentations of history and the despair we have suffered individually. Death would quench the desire for revenge and the desire to make things right so that the present and the future simply replay history, but with no major difference – we would always get our way. This would be a history in which we may see ourselves as Hegel calls us, "beautiful souls" – the kinds of being that the Hiero tyrant wanted to be – but because we would always be existing in an actual world that is unsympathetic to us, we would be no more than madmen and madwomen. But death changes all that and opens the world to a new beginning – one that comes from forgiveness. This death is metanoia, a personal change that is death of perspective and perception. It is death that comes with a renewal, a transfiguration, and even a transcendence of the old, into a new being mentally and a new situation fraternally.

This is a starting over again in which we are in control, for we are forgiving ourselves and others, and in which we are remaking the world – even reaching back in history to cleanse it not of the taint of others but of our stubbornness. We give ourselves the possibility of a new beginning, for the world is perceptually still our projection, but one in which we recognize the necessity of loving and caring for others like us – similar self-consciences and tragic heroes on whom we rely for everything, including for our very being and sense of who we are. This is the rebirth that Hannah Arendt describes as the forgiveness that produces natality and the spontaneity, unpredictability, randomness, and even liveliness of a life without diremption.

Arendt tells us that "the new beginning inherent in birth can make itself felt in the world only because the newcomer possesses the capacity of beginning something anew, that is, of acting."[5] This natality – and by extension, in our case, rebirth – she sees as actualizing freedom and its newness, including the possibility of all things, even the surprising and unexpected. "It is in the nature of beginning that something new is started which cannot be expected from whatever may have happened before. This character of startling unexpectedness is inherent in all beginnings ... The fact that man is capable of action means that the unexpected can be expected from him, that he is able to perform what is infinitely improbable. And this again is possible only because each man is unique, so that with each birth something uniquely new comes into the world."[6] Metanoia gives another chance to start over again – with all the potentials and possibilities present in moments of creation or birth. Each rebirth would offer a chance for (re)making in the image of the god of the piece, resulting in an escape into comedy. This rebirth or resurrection would be social construction of new identities and new relationships, now within an inclusive master narrative that omits no one and recognizes everyone in the thick fraternity of love.

We would simply conform and find our place within the existing order. We would bring our expectations and our intentions in line with the prevailing mood. Yet someone or something might intervene in a way we cannot expect – a *deus ex machina* – and save us from prolonging our own agony, which possessed socially redeeming values. Perhaps this is what happened when terrorists struck in the United States on 11 September 2001 and the ensuing discussion about the existing social order temporarily transformed issues of immigration, citizenship, and security. Were such a change a pure tragedy, it would have resulted from our recognition of the sheer power within us to do evil and of how, because of our firm convictions, we were willing to destroy in order to achieve what we knew was within our grasp. Tragedy would have left us facing the dread of knowing that unless we stopped ourselves, no one would intervene to protect others from the harm we could inflict on them. Once we recognized this, we would have the knowledge that there is no high moral agent that can contain and restrain us, for ours is an unjust world without proportionality, moderation, or compromise. We would be unjust even to ourselves if we lived according to our moral code and to what we perceive as our standing in or relationship with the world. One key to whether we are tragic or comedic rests therefore within our assumptions, while another is our intentions and whether we could recognize justice even if we fell over it. Yet another key is the method we use, or that which society mercifully offers us, to end the comedic experience. My issue with the CBC remained a tragedy. Even if I had experienced a moment of metanoia, into whose likeness would I change? The goal of this piece was the state and its image as official multiculturalism. I would still be out of step with an institution, the

CBC, which is really, I see on reflection, in a struggle with the state – not with me, for the state and I are seeming allies on diversity and differences in multicultural Canada. Maybe the CBC would need remaking in the state's image and have to learn its official language of socialization.

In this chapter, I am discussing the philosophical and ethical differences between tragedy and comedy to show multiculturalism in Canada as phenomenologically a tragedy that results existentially in Hegel's unhappy consciousness. This is a necessary step if I am to demonstrate that multiculturalism is more than a politics of epistemic recognition, for anything that is human and recognizable as such in one moment changes in the next. Such is the tragedy of the human condition, of living itself, where freedom, justice, and happiness are usually only temporary at best. The comedy where "they live happily ever after" exists only in the transcendent, along with freedom, justice, and happiness as natural forms. Societies have traditionally presented themselves as sites of freedom, where individuals can receive justice according to how they view and understand themselves and their world. Justice occurs ontologically when the individual's internal perspective matches that of the external, when his or her idea of what is good is identical to the good that society produces. Justice occurs when society fulfils agreed-to intentions with fidelity, when there is no alienation because of either surplus or deficit between the contents of the subject and object of a mental act.

It is only when justice is possible that individuals can move from a tragic existence to a comedic one, where they live by authentic rules that represent the moral and ethical relations on which they agree. Tragedy occurs when citizens disagree over how to achieve justice or even over what it is.

This is a struggle over the freedom to reject a specific moral and ethical approach to life that seems at odds with the surroundings. The bridge between tragedy and comedy is socialization, which prepares an individual for a comic existence, needing not a search for justice but rather a distribution of justice; an individual who remains at heart a god or a beast lives a tragic existence, still searching for justice while everyone else is in agreement. The tragic individual might be lagging behind the collective and need "advancement," or perfecting, as Aristotle would say, to a higher good that society has already achieved. Or she or he may be ahead of society and trying to drag the others up to a higher level of social good. In either case, tragedy is fluid and dynamic, unlike comedy, with its determinate ethical order, where the dialectics of history are already at rest and the search for justice and freedom is complete.

I show here that societies have historically presented socialization as tragic, primarily for people so strong that it has to sacrifice them for the collective good. Philosophers and social scientists have long grappled with how to make the sacrifice a willing act – always tragedy's intention in its mimicking of life, with individuals dreading something for some internal reason they themselves cannot fathom. To lay out this case, I give examples of tragic and comedic "heroes" in Canadian history since the country adopted official multiculturalism in 1971. Finally, I show how immigration and the changes in Canadian demography present Canada as a tragedy. This chapter ends with a discussion of whether Canadian literature as a narrative intending to show multiculturalism as a site for justice is by nature tragic or comedic and why some types of writing seem emblematic of Canada and others exemplify something different.

MULTICULTURALISM: POLITICS OF TRAGIC RECOGNITION

As Canada's prime minister from 1968 to 1984 except for nine months in 1979–80, Pierre Trudeau oversaw its transformation from an essentially Anglo country with a bilingual province into a bilingual country and then a multicultural nation-state. He saw multiculturalism as the culmination of the search for a Just Society. Canada would have a strong, centralized identity that the world community would recognize intersubjectively as such. But it would also self-reflexively recognize that its own universal body contained difference and diversity, a point many theorists have overlooked. Multiculturalism would provide a justice that would end conflict between the universal identity and the identities of the different and diverse particulars. Individuals would receive their just deserts whether asserting universal or particular characteristics, as long as fellow citizens recognized them as Canadians.

In his attempts to reformulate Canadian society, Trudeau must have been thinking of literary critic A.C. Bradley's definition of tragedy and of a particular type of tragedy that Hegel describes.[7] Bradley was commenting on Hegel's use of tragedy to reveal universal human aspirations for a free and just society, whose way of life is a culture of freedom. Bradley cites Hegel to the effect that tragedy examines the waste of human potential. As literary critic Geoffrey Brereton argues, "The notion of waste is frequent in the tragedies of 'life.' ... Waste is a failure to make a proper use of something."[8] It results from humans' inability to realize all the good potentially within them and arises because of an internal flaw or because of some external obstacle to full self-actualization. This is a misuse of what Aristotle calls the "soul's faculties" and occurs usually in a state of nature.

Trudeau appears to have been thinking along these lines when he said, "I used to think of all the wasted potential in the organization of societies that don't give equal opportunities to all."[9] As he further explained, "The aim of life in society is the greatest happiness of everyone, and this happiness is attained only by rendering justice to each person ... For where is the justice in a country in which an individual has the freedom to be totally fulfilled, but where inequality denies him the means? And how can we call a society just unless it is organized in such a way as to give each his due, regardless of his state or birth, his means, or his health?"[10] By the time he left office in 1984, Trudeau had overseen entrenchment in the constitution of the Charter of Rights to ensure freedom for individuals despite state of birth, individual means, and health, but also trumping their religions, sexualities, races, ethnicities, and more. However, he was arguing that this individual was a citizen in what was on its way to becoming a centralized federal state, meeting his two main requirements for full recognition.

In Trudeau's mind, justice was not only happiness, it was freedom, which he identified as the highest value in society. Freedom is individuals' ability to determine for themselves what is good for them and to believe that they can fairly achieve such ends. It is what turned individuals into subjects and fully determined subjects into citizens. This is the reason for individuals to live in the state: the promise of justice. "If men and women could not direct their collective effort to that end," Trudeau writes, "they might as well go off and live all alone in the woods and on the hills,"[11] as Aristotelian beings, I guess. Without freedom, humans cannot hope for true fulfilment and citizens will cannot realize their full potential. Individuals, either separately or as a group, will not be able to achieve the highest order of freedom, which is determining and pursuing their own destiny. According to Trudeau, "In my thinking, the value with the highest priority in the pursuit of a Just Society had become equality. Not the procrustean kind of equality where everyone is raised or lowered to a kind of middle ground. I mean equality of opportunity."[12] This is socialization into a fraternity without automatic or ascribed stratification.

This equality of opportunity starts with prior recognition of the individual as a self-determining subject or agent. For Trudeau, multiculturalism was the best expression of this freedom and equality, because it allowed members of different ethnic groups to be Canadian without having to conform exclusively to a singular ideal of what a Canadian is. Individuals could realize their full potential as Canadians through as many means as they can imagine. However, all Canadians start from the same base position – an equality emanating from socialization in Canada. How they express this equality is another matter. They do not have to conform to a specific method, for the essence of freedom in Canada does not come from a formula or a specific model to which everyone must conform. In this way, Canadians are intentionally in a symmetrical relationship. Multicultural citizenship is not recognition of a Canadian physically, but rather of the individual's heart and mind, where the real "Canadianness" lies – a universal essence based on equality. Citizenship changes – an internal exercise that appears in an assortment of forms. As Trudeau explains, "There is no such thing as a model or ideal Canadian. What could be more absurd than the concept of an 'all-Canadian' boy or girl? A Society which emphasizes uniformity is one which creates intolerance and hate. A Society which eulogizes the average citizen is one which breeds mediocrity. What the world should be seeking, and what we in Canada must continue to cherish, are not concepts of uniformity but human values: compassions, love and understanding."[13]

However, in its implementation, Trudeau's multicultural Just Society would involve primarily objective and intersubjective recognition, which grows from the recognition of cultures. The tension between internal and intersubjective recognition would remain uppermost in the Canadian consciousness, tragically establishing limits and boundaries on citizenship. Trudeau himself, for example, defended a symmetrical relationship in arguing for a form of idealism that appeared to consist of internal recognition as the basis for an ethical relationship: "National unity, if it is to mean anything in the deeply personal sense, must be founded on confidence in one's individual identity; out of this can grow respect for that of others and a willingness to share ideas, attitudes, and assumptions. A vigorous policy of multiculturalism will help create this initial confidence. It can form the basis of a society which is founded on fair play for all."[14]

In pursuit of these ideals, Trudeau often started with a search for intersubjective recognition to fathom the internal. Perhaps he did so because internal recognition is metaphysical and is visible in action. The external becomes a stand-in or analogy for what has happened within, out of view. This may help explain why multiculturalism has traditionally worked in terms of subjective or mainly epistemic recognition – recognition of how a rational subject displays inner good intentions through good works. These actions could of course be ambiguous, complicating interpretation, so that what some well-meaning individuals consider acts of charity, love, and goodness may seem evil to other observers. People on the receiving end may perhaps remember the seeming benefactor's past wrongs and evils. A gesture that appears kind may turn out to be evil, which may have been the doer's intention.

In the end and in general, Canadians found out that the action might be in keeping with an ethical order that still denied them their full subjectivity and flowed not from an inner conversion but from an evil that remained undetectable. What they mistook for civil society was still a state of nature. They were still very much in a tragedy, even if the perpetrators thought it a comedy. The difference became one of really knowing when the perpetrator is fully a subject and hence equally an object in an ethical relationship and that the two positions are identical. In effect, the unhappiness would stem from one primary cause. Ironically, this duality was the source of what Trudeau intended as the path to happiness. The cause would be a reliance on reason.

Trudeau wanted to build a Canadian nation-state that was rational and just. The system would work mechanically, turning out justice and dispensing an agreed-upon fairness to all. Once individuals had witnessed benefits of such a system, it would win them over. They would abide by its rules and adjust their behaviour in line with a superior and more "real" way of life. Unfortunately for Trudeau, humans are not that rational. Indeed, history has taught us that to be human is to be irrational – to have an imperfection that prevents us from becoming mechanical and robotic, on the one hand, or like gods on the other. The gremlins in human systems make things human; they embody our irrationality, that element that pushes us towards achieving our full potentials and faculties.

This push included achieving both possibilities for good and evil, or, as Hegel would say, the infinite that is always already in the finite, the rational, and its Other, the irrational. These opposites are indispensable parts of the same system. A politics of recognition must rely on a rational world for success. This too is part of the lesson of Charles Taylor's analysis. However, when the world is not rational, recognition leads to a dead end that, as Hegel says, is an unhappiness, where the tragedy has not fully ended but continues to play out in different guises. Reconciliation that ends tragedy requires more than epistemic recognition as a subject or citizen. It requires feeling in the thrall of the consciousness, which is the product of socialization. For full recognitions to happen requires a catharsis or purging of the inclinations to act differently from the prevailing social mores. This can happen only when, after recognition, the further step of reversal takes place.

Trudeau would introduce far-reaching policy changes into the Canadian body politic with a view to ending the Canadian tragedy by offering a way to find justice in society. In so doing, he would give a nod to the intersubjective recognition that is the basis of analytical and common-sense approaches to politics and philosophy. As he explained, this was a justice "born of tolerance and wisdom, present everywhere, ready to serve the highest purpose of rational man."[15] To this end, he led repatriation of the constitution and entrenchment of the Charter of Rights. His government changed the Immigration Act, made it easier for immigrants to become citizens, and intensified assistance for artists to produce works that reflect the true spirit of the country and its people.

He did all this to recognize the sovereignty of individual Canadians and of Canada. In addition, he based this justice on reason, in the belief that people would put aside emotionalism in discerning what is right and then act in a reasonable way. And significant, he sited the struggle for justice in the mainstream, which works out differences over particulars and universal characteristics: "In politics, particularly in a federation, problems are not settled once and for all; negotiations never stop."[16] Thus one tragedy reconciles itself only briefly – the arrival of comedy – before it gives way again to the reality of injustice in an irrational world and the tragic nature of life.

By his admission, Trudeau's policies did not lead practically to justice in society. He left office, he admitted, with Canada perhaps weaker. He argued that one tragedy of Canada was that it was always living in the shadow of its own demise – the ultimate step in an attempt for reconciliation in a complex tragedy in which the bid for a just compromise defies the actors' best efforts. Trudeau seemed unsure whether this ambiguity is good or bad for Canada. For one thing, "no nation is eternal. The glue that holds it together, the thing that makes nationhood, is the free will of a sovereign people to live together ... Every citizen, every family, every group, every region must feel that the chances to fulfil themselves to the utmost are greater within a united Canada."[17]

If Trudeau did not get the outcome he wanted, perhaps this was because his political philosophy could deal only with intersubjective recognition. His policies perhaps had less impact than he desired primarily because they would change the outer image before the inner feeling. His approach flowed less from an internal conversion than from the need to project the image of unity. He left us with his ideal of a place that would offer all groups and individuals, particularly those historically outside the mainstream, the chance to live freely within Canada as Canadians. The state should recognize them fully as Canadians. Trudeau argued, "Canadians continue to cherish the value system which has made them among the most fortunate of all the world's people. A system which embraces human relationships – tolerance, friendship, love, laughter, privacy; a system which pays heed to the beauty of our country and seeks to preserve the balance of nature; a system which accepts the inevitability of change but which at least consciously encourages only those changes that respect, rather than exploit, the human spirit; a system, in short, which regards individuals as ultimately beneficiaries."[18] But, ironically, as citizens they would be liberal individuals under the umbrella of a Charter of Rights and still awaiting full escape into a comedy of equal persons in form and spirit.

Trudeau decried the idea of achieving justice only via the physical death of the nation, of Hobbes's moral god: "This country and this constitution have allowed men to live in a state of freedom and prosperity which, though imperfect, has nevertheless rarely been matched in the world."[19] To his chagrin, Trudeau would admit that Canada had not arrived at a moment of justice or happiness for everyone, and neither had the state ended the original warring from within. There was not a singular commitment to an ideal of which things Canadian would be a mere representation. On the contrary, there was much unhappiness over what it has produced: perceptually, it is still a land of tragedy. There is still no genuine spirit of fraternal love.

As he implied, the chorus that is ideally public opinion was quite loud in the Canadian tragedy. It protested the unhappiness in the land. Trudeau said, "Talk to the people. Read the media. Listen to the grumblings. Canadians aren't happy with their fate. And this, in spite of the success of our country."[20] People were acting out their scripts not from conviction or conversion but out of a feeling of coercion; moral command and obligation were missing even if the political power existed to make individuals conform. As an array of recent publications indicates, many Canadians believe multiculturalism unjust, rife with preference or reverse discrimination.[21] Many more feel that it is not living up to its higher ideals of freedom.[22] It is not as clear a representation of the real world as Trudeau and others intended it to be, for too many Canadians think that they are acting out a script that leaves them feeling inauthentic and shackled to a false good. This form of multiculturalism is not genuine, for there is no unrequited fraternal love.

At one level, this unhappiness shows up in interethnic rivalries, in differences between regions, and in Canada's struggle to maintain an identity that is separate from the more powerful United States. And the lack of justice would show up as well in Quebec's efforts to reject most of the components of Trudeau's Just Society by refusing to sign the constitution and then using its "notwithstanding" clause to go against the spirit of equality and liberal egalitarianism that is at the heart of a Just Society. This unhappiness stemmed in part from ambivalence in Trudeau's own thoughts, such as his building of a multicultural society to replace an ethic of biculturalism.

"Bilingualism unites people," Trudeau stated, while "dualism [biculturalism] divides them. Bilingualism means you can speak to the other; dualism means you can live in one language and the rest of Canada will live in another."[23] As he further explained, his fight was always for multi- rather than biculturalism, as "there are a lot more than two cultures in the country." As well, "Bilingualism is a tool that doesn't necessarily imply you're of French or Anglo-Saxon culture. It implies that you see it as a necessary and useful step to recognize the languages of the Europeans who first settled what became Canada. Anybody who really wants to learn a language can do so. But you can't learn an entire culture. Besides, I have always believed in the superiority of the multinational society. The variety of cultures in Canada undoubtedly contributes to the country's richness and prosperity."[24]

With the country's becoming officially multicultural, the unhappiness that remains part of the Canadian condition stemmed from the very nature of this recognition. As Trudeau suggests, it was the classical liberalism of "Rousseau, Hobbes, and Locke" on how individuals can retain their freedoms within a wider society. This is partly an objective recognition, the same kind he had to grapple with over recognition of the French culture and language as integral to Canada. Trudeau also sought objective and intersubjective recognition for minority groups within Canada. All of these goals were to help make a place that is less tragic for the dreams of individuals and groups.

However, while he hinted at the need for personal recognition – the type that makes Canada and Canadians look within themselves for their true nature – he put less emphasis on this form of self-knowledge. He himself started with firm notions of what is good and evil in Canadian society, even if at times he too found them inherently contradictory but part of a dialectical process that would produce a singular good – a strong and united multicultural nation-state that allowed for recognition of differences. After he left power, he would rejoin the political fray over manifestations of these dialectical forces and the possibility that they might destroy the seemingly united, but unhappy, country, that was still working to build a Just Society.

This unhappiness is on display not only in politics, but in the arts as well. One can see it in the reception of specific works of art, primarily literature, that seem out of keeping with the spirit of Canada. Powerful forces in the mainstream continue to try to speak for Canada and impose a particular view. Trudeau had always argued that all Canadians can speak for the country and have a say in its destiny.

Much of this discussion on recognition in Canada revolved around who is a Canadian and whose experiences are relevant in depicting those of Canadians. This is an issue of nobility, of who has the requisite pedigree to be Canadian, who has the right to speak with authority on what constitutes Canadian identity, and who has the power to confer such recognition. The result is not "tolerance, friendship, love, laughter, privacy; a system which pays heed to the beauty of our country and seeks to preserve the balance of nature,"[25] as Trudeau hoped, but unhappiness. The recognition that Trudeau fell back on to explain Canada's multicultural character did not offer a full solution to the tragedy of an unhappy consciousness: while he understood Canada's tragic character, his analysis, like Taylor's, did not focus on personal recognition.

As a result, there was no reconciliation in the tragedy that Trudeau and Taylor diagnosed as Canada. Instead, Trudeau's multiculturalism appeared to suffer the type of fate that Hegel had predicted for a state that constructed citizens according to natural rights. The unhappiness that Trudeau lamented was for a type of state that Hegel characterized as a struggle for lordship and bondage because it miscast civic life as a fictitious master–slave fight between atomic individuals who were rational constructs, sporting their liberal attributes but appearing hollow and empty from having no civic duties, concerns, or responsibilities. Hegel states, "That state as conceived by the intellect is not an organization at all, but a machine; and the people is not the organic body of a communal and rich life, but an atomistic, life-improvised multitude. The elements of this multitude are absolutely opposed substances. The unity of these elements is a concept; what binds them together is an endless domination. This absolutely substantiality of points makes the basis for an atomistic system of practical philosophy in which, as in the atomistic system of nature, an intellect alien to the atom becomes law in the practical sphere under the name of *Right*."[26]

This is a discussion about whether Canada as a universal state has left behind its tragic existence. Much of the literature and art that critics treat as not Canadian, or even as un-Canadian, stems from its depiction of a land that, though officially multicultural, lacks justice. This work challenges the notion that Canada's ethnic groups have attained justice along with all other groups, have full representation in the mainstream, and have an equal say in determining the country's future and its artistic expressions and culture. It questions the myth that Canada is a site of justice, with tolerance, compassion, and love of others. It asks whether merely recognizing differences and diversity in the form of others allows the subject to generously confer equality, forbearance, and open-mindedness on those otherwise inferior and unworthy to share in the Canadian good life. This work looks at whether change in Canada is intersubjective rather than internal to the subjects.

Justice will occur when different groups see a full reflection of themselves in the universal that is Canadian culture or a societal culture, and also feel an indispensable part of the Canadian whole. It will be present when no individual has to fear dying without fulfilling her or his potential for good, primarily because of external constraints. There will be justice when individuals and groups feel that they can capture the quintessence of Canadian culture in their own ways – by fully using the individuality of their intellect, potential, and creativity, without having to conform to a dominant group's model. Justice remains a question of whether some groups are more worthy than others of setting the stage for conflict or for its resolution.

Much of the discussion in Canadian culture still revolves around conformity, even if it makes allowances for differences. It masks the efforts of an elite group, the heir to a particular legacy, to determine by right what is indeed universally Canadian but from a particular perspective or gaze. Its members have a different view of justice and of what is good for Canada than do outsiders. The body is revolting against itself. This is the story of a societal culture in conflict – or a universe of warring societal cultures unable to imagine themselves as a unity. In this respect, justice is the antithesis of hegemony, of the ability of a specific group to impose its good on everyone else. When this dominance happens, the body as a universal becomes sick, conflicted, and unjust, as it cannot represent the disparate ideas of good to which all members aspire.

These battles over justice and good play themselves out in the Canadian mainstream, either as part of the social consciousness à la Taylor and Hegel or as the societal culture that Kymlicka portrays. The result is not an era of justice, as Trudeau hoped, but rather a long period of angst, division, and difference and of everyone's feeling that the world is not rational, fair, or just. Therefore Canada, even as a site for multiculturalism and as an agent for building a Just Society, is still typical of the universal human condition: it is a tragedy in search of a solution to end a deep unhappiness.

Isomorphism and analogy – life as tragedy or comedy – this is the continuing story of Canada, even as a multicultural liberal democracy. Society results from intentionality, the nexus of justice that everyone expects, and meaningful sacrifices by individuals for a higher and common good. We now turn to why this is so and examine the principles of tragedy and how we can apply them analytically to multicultural Canada.

ENDING TRAGEDY FOR COMEDY AND JUSTICE

Howard Adelman is a member of the Toronto Hegelian school, which interprets Hegel differently from the European master–slave analysis. For Adelman, there is never a time when there is not a sovereign or when the sovereign is totally in control. People and culture do not just appear on the scene. As Heidegger suggests, people, when they become conscious of themselves, always find that they have been *thrown* into the midst of something. They are *in medias res*: life had started before them and will most likely continue when they have gone. Some have a difficult time fully accepting the latter. As objects that find themselves in the midst of things, they explore societies that are consciousnesses – ethical relations – that have evolved with time. Earlier struggles, compromises, disputes, and harmonies emerging through the dialectics of history and time have put their stamp on these consciousnesses, and the same process will continue. Nothing is every fully formed, stable, or everlasting.

These consciousnesses have evolved into a specific way of life that is a culture for a specific group of people – or, on a greater scale, a *civilization* – under the guidance, enlightened or otherwise, of a sovereign in some form. No matter when history began, that point was already *in medias res*. The beginning arose out of a previous consciousness: it was thrown into the midst of other happenings. As part of surviving the jolt, individuals need socialization into momentary consciousness. This process is the stuff of tragedies, comedies, and utopias – depending on the writer's perspective.

We enter a society that has its history and culture and that really cares very little about us, except for our usefulness. We often see the sovereign as unwise and likely to make mistakes. We find ourselves either lords or bondspeople. There are no negotiations. If we are born into the society or consciousness, it shapes and moulds us. We have no choice. Indeed, it expects us to comply and not be anti-social by resisting too much. Success takes the form of citizenship, which it confers on us as a right of belonging and that indicates our willingness to abide by its expectations. We must allow this process to make us, as much as the quality of the material allows, into an ideal citizen.

This then is a lordship-and-bondage relationship. As an individual, the citizen has no chance to appear at the beginning of the consciousness or to negotiate the founding ethical relationship, or social contract. Social contracts rarely happen; citizens are born into a covenant, or they place themselves under a covenant with a higher authority in return for its protection and privileges, while it retains power of life and death. Covenants work best when individuals are mere abstractions, identical, without any peculiar or specific needs and desires that need entertaining. It is for this reason that a Charter of Rights would be the linchpin of the covenant between citizens and their government, the state.

T.H. Green sees covenants not as proceeding from a hypothetical state of nature. "Such a theory [of a state of nature]," Green states, "can only be stated by an application to an imaginary state of things, prior to the formation of societies as regulated by customs or law, of terms that have no meaning except in relation to such societies. 'Natural right,' as right in a state of nature which is not a state of society, is a contradiction. Without this there might be certain powers on the part of individuals, but no recognition of these powers by others as powers of which they allow the exercise, nor any claim to such recognition, and without this recognition or claim to recognition there can be no right."[27]

Immigrants, by definition, are entering into a lordship-and-bondage relation when they go to a new country. There is no likelihood of their sitting behind a veil as abstract individuals to negotiate the conditions of their entry and the rules for their participation in society. They have no say in the formulation of any social contract. Indeed, newcomers exist in a state of nature and want to enter a civil society to become fully human. This is as true for babies born in the society as it is for new immigrants – both need socializing to meet the prevailing ideology's standards of human perfection.

Immigrants, particularly refugees, face a stark choice: "Take it or leave it." If they grumble at conditions, the society may tell them to return whence they came. They might receive tolerance, but this is more of a privilege than a right. They have to conform to and fit in with existing mores and civil values. For them, socialization is a tragedy, for it sacrifices them to a higher good. For society, socialization is merely a comedy, preparing the outsider to recognize that it has already worked out its social relationships; it knows the rules and norms necessary for the common good, and the outsider simply has to conform, willingly or by force.

This comedy would be one of society's having to make the exercise a significant tragedy for the individual. Whether we are native born or immigrants, our task is to convince the sovereign or master to see things our way, which at the beginning it seems incapable of doing. Therefore we must encourage the sovereign to change. The sovereign's task is to get us to abide by the mores and virtues of the day and not to be disruptive – to socialize us according to prevailing morals and ethics.

But we do not always see the sovereign's determining us, so we resist. However, the sovereign apparently does not need any of us as individuals. Therefore there is not much for the lord in this relationship to gain from recognizing liberal rights or the possessions of individuals. But the sovereign does need us as a collective, otherwise there would be no society. So individually, we put ourselves in a covenant with a sovereign, which becomes our lord and we agree to be in its bondage, but only as long as it keeps its promises to us – promises that we prescribe by constructing appropriate forms of behaviour in bills of rights. And it promises to recognize our wishes and desires – in effect, agreeing to be always in conflict with us, because our wishes and desires are infinite and always changing.

The result is that society is always tragic, in the form of an unhappy consciousness. Instead of just living, we play with ourselves and one another; we are always acting according to some desire or ulterior motive. We want to win and not to lose. As individuals and groups, we are never happy with our lots or positioning or sovereign, and the preferred groups – such as the day's majority – are unhappy because they feel incapable of meeting our demands. They see us as ungrateful and our desires as insatiable. Life is a tragedy for those of us in bondage and a comedy for those who have played by the rules and feel they are receiving justice; for in this case the resulting relation is one where even the sovereign cannot produce a common good that is happiness for everyone.

In the disagreement between Taylor's and Adelman's approaches, I side with the latter. Indeed, much of the discussion in this book owes a great deal to Adelman and his analysis of Hegel's lordship and bondage as the foundation for ethical relations in a diverse and plural modern democracy.

Adelman's analysis provides a way to introduce immigrants as a class with cultures, histories, hopes, and even physical appearances all seemingly distinct from those that observers historically associate with Canada. However, rather than seeking to dominate other peoples, they are simply trying to produce a better life – not only for themselves but for everyone with whom they come in contact. They are not the Machiavellian-type invaders or Princes looking to colonize. Life is most meaningful when they can satisfy or even satiate their desires, usually through meaningful work – when their jobs are as challenging as they reasonably expected and when they feel, that they have the same chances at the life they want as anyone else. Therefore reconciliation for them comes from recognizing that they are entering a game that is already in process but whose participants are constantly changing and whose aim is not so much to enrich the lives of some participants but to make the play and challenge as meaningful as possible to everyone. Again we may think of Hans-George Gadamer's emphasis on free-styling and unscripted play. "The player himself knows that play is only play and that it exists in a world determined by the seriousness of purposes. But he does not know this in such a way that, as a citizen, he actually intends this relation to seriousness of creating a common good of a better life. Play fulfils its purpose only if the player loses himself in play. Seriousness is not merely something that calls us away from play; rather, seriousness in playing is necessary to make the play wholly play. Someone who doesn't take the game seriously is a spoilsport. The mode of being of play does not allow the player to behave toward play as if toward an object ... The players are not the subjects of play; instead play merely reaches presentation ... through the player."[28]

This is not the game that immigrants usually encounter. The game they enter on arrival often has a motive and a determinate outcome. They enter a Canada that has its own history, has produced a sovereign, and has established its powers and boundaries through a historical struggle for domestic recognition. The players have, by and large, arrived at a consensus about their play, their roles, and the outcome. They have already divvied up power. They have an order, and they know that the sovereign has agreed to the rules they have negotiated. They have already agreed to a common good and to individual positions in the struggle for its attainment.

Now along comes a new group of people who in a bid to gain entry must profess willingness to abide by the prevailing virtues and mores. They enter a game that starts out fixed, with an outcome that does not depend on the players' individual ability or on how well they work together. Sensing the loading of the rules against them, immigrants say they agree to buy into the play as it is and to take the parts others hand to them. However, this is merely, as Hegel suggests, dissemblance or duplicity – hypocrisy and subterfuge. The newcomers have not yet gone through the crucible that would imprint the prevailing morality. They are still in conflict: the actions old-timers expect are not natural for them. Theirs are unhappy consciousnesses in the thrall of different rules and expectations.

Along the way, the newcomers change their mind or show their true colours; in effect, they show that they had never genuinely bought into this ideal. As pure exteriority, they simply said what was necessary to gain admission. Now that they are in, they want to change the play, recast roles, bring in a more impartial sovereign, and overhaul all ethical relations. Tolerance has earned their seeming ingratitude. Both sides find themselves in positions of inauthenticity, which makes them unhappy. Or, as the immigrants may argue, the paternalism and insincerity that they had to accept as the price of entry have given way to subjectivity and a true will to power. One person's liberation is another's enslavement.

How can they move out of this unhappy consciousness towards the ideal of reconciliation? How in the existing ethical relationship does a society move beyond a tragedy to a comedy and ultimately to a utopia? Here I build on the work of Adelman and John Burbidge, especially the latter's understanding of reconciliation in Hegel's ontology and epistemology. This is where the idealism that is the hope of multiculturalism and a Hegelian approach to epistemology and ethical relations shine through in the Canadian analysis and experience. And this is where the idea of a common faith and morality as a component of the prevailing ideology and as part of the socialization process is crucial. Faith is necessary for an understanding of some of the leaps necessary for reconciliation of some of the prevailing ideology's existing contradictions. This is the comedy that results from positive freedoms. It is the ideal *Bildung* experience – the perfecting of the individual or community according to its own desires and work. It is the acting out of this faith, a game whose outcome everyone assumes to be good for everyone but in which the authenticity of the play depends on everyone's upholding the rules and just playing. In this case, Canadians of ancient lineage must be willing to become mere players and even to put their country's future in play, all the while having faith that newcomers will play the same game as they – one with no end and no real winners and losers.

Otherwise, there seems no possible way out of the unhappy consciousness that produces a liberal democracy that is a tragedy for individuals and groups that find themselves in a lordship-and-bondage relationship. The prospects of release are even slimmer if we start from a master-and-slave social contract. I am grateful to Burbidge for informing me about Jonathan Robinson's depiction of Canada as a Hegelian ethical relationship from inception, which, I would argue, is one of lordship and bondage.[29]

Adelman and Burbidge provide a line to Canadian political theorist C.B. Macpherson[30] and his Hobbesian approach which illuminates Taylor and in so doing moves his analysis beyond a struggle for bilingualism and biculturalism to genuine multiculturalism. Taylor relies heavily on the French–English struggle for dominance in Canada, which, I would add, largely co-opted or omitted other groups and cultures.

For while Adelman and Burbidge argue that reconciliation must happen in the subject and through the unchangeable's changing, there must be an outward reflection of this inner change. This occurs through new ethical relations and recognition by others, which Taylor analyses in a wider spectrum. Internal change becomes exterior – making itself knowable and discernible – only through actions. The living experience or the ethical relations of day-to-day living lie at the heart of the ideal of genuine multiculturalism and radical democracy as an exercise in power and belonging. This is a case that must go beyond reliance on the externality of the Charter of Rights.

However, I argue, *pace* Taylor, that reconciliation must begin *within* the perceived subject and then extend outwards. Such is the order of meaningful change: where the subject as an act of freedom has to look within itself and discover the good or evil within. This is the historical recognition essential for the poetics and aesthetics of tragedy and, to a lesser extent, comedy. It leads not to recognition of others as subjects or to tolerance towards them by making them subjects, but to a reversal within the subject as an active moral agent and major adjustments to save itself and to provide reconciliation. The onus is on the subject to compromise, within. The subject, as the lead actor, must see itself as the evil and perhaps even anti-social character in this play. This is where the norms of behaviour are the same for lord and for bondsman, for tyrant and individual, for minority and majority. It is where the individual internalizes the ethical norms of society as moral imperatives, including Macpherson's liberal rights of possessive ownership and acknowledgment that they spring from a social consciousness that limits while liberating.

Similarly, the society or sovereign must recognize that this is the same society that is a collective of individuals that gives it freedom to act with individuals' consent but keeps it accountable to their desires and need for a greater good. The sovereign, as protector of of individuals' rights, must change and adapt as the individuals change and adapt, for the freedom of both parties is always relative. The sovereign must reach a place where it sees the externalities; what were once internal desires now express themselves as subjects to the sovereign.

What is tragic here is that the individual might find that it is itself the hindrance to reconciliation, and that if it were to disappear – that is, to die – others might enjoy peace and happiness. For this reason, tragedy has to have *recognition*, *reversal*, and an *ironic outcome*: knowing that they all relate to the subject, seeing and recognizing the subject as good or evil according to the subject's own morals and standards, make reconciliation possible. This is the basis for the hope that a tragedy can become a comedy and finally a utopia. This approach is contingent on my argument that free people often do not know who they are until they know they are not free. Often they do not know what they will become or how they will get out of the tragedy or comedy into utopia. They frequently have to give up old notions, especially if utopia calls for reconciling living, sensual experiences and the reality that is hoped for and conjured up as an ideal of the mind. Often individuals have to recognize that, like gods, they can be both good and evil.

This book is substantially about what we might called "the Canadian spirit" and how it appears as a multiculturally diverse body. For example, I might not go as far as Kymlicka appears to by suggesting that the Canadian model of multiculturalism is exportable. We are still defining it, contextualizing and tweaking it to suit the needs of a specific time, place, and people – ours. This is what makes it unique and unlikely to work as it is for all seasons and places as a Hegelian analysis should perhaps do.

How does multiculturalism in Canada handle differences and the simultaneous desire for sameness? Here is where we find Kymlicka useful, especially his notion of societal cultures with organic forms of social capital and currency of authenticity. But these forms of social capital embody specific virtues and mores, especially those of liberalism. Can these mores and virtues ever change and Canada remain the same? If so, what about Canadian culture as the history or a special consciousness: do we want to uphold it, retain it, and set it on the shelf for future Canadians?

If it is not changeable, what about Pierre Trudeau and the supporters of multiculturalism that Canada had rejected a history, past, and culture of exclusion, racism, ethnography and ethnocentrism, and preferential treatment? How would we ever move into a land of genuine multiculturalism as a site of natural authenticity? Can we ever have a state in which people feel sovereign, especially if their composition and demographics differ from what they were and will be? In effect, Kymlicka's position proposes that immigrants, especially those who do not share the prevailing virtues or mores or who change their minds and desires here, can feel able to help build a multicultural liberal democracy. Can they retain, even enhance their possessive individualism and attain recognition and thereby feel that the prevailing consciousness fully accepts and protects them?

Kymlicka, even if he does not name it as such, gestures to a Canadian spirit of compromise and reconciliation, perhaps as the basis for any attempt to formulate a workable multicultural society. In this I agree with him. It is this spirit of compromise, which may lead to a series of reconciliations as part of the dynamics of living, that could emerge if we adapt Macpherson's possessive individualism within an elastic ethical relationship of lord and bondsperson. This reconciliation will require recognition, reversal, and irony. This is why multiculturalism in a liberal democracy is a tragedy, even if its actors hope for eventual recognition as players in a comedy or finally a utopia.

I believe that genuine multiculturalism is possible in practice as a form of radical democracy and quite feasible with possessive individualism in a Macpherson-type market where everything is changeable – particularly the sovereign. Such change is the only way out of an unhappy consciousness, which tends to be a tragedy for everyone, into a comedy, with at least some hope of happiness and justice for some citizens, and ultimately into a utopia, where everyone lives happily ever after. What these Canadian theorists and thinkers have done is to take up a challenge that is at least as old as Plato, that we hear in music on the radio, in the streets and clubs, in political rhetoric and in folksongs, and in the ideals that we share for the future, so deep is it in our culture. For it is there in Polonius's admonition in Shakespeare's tragedy *Hamlet*: "To thy own self be true."

But this search goes back even further, at least to the ending of Plato's *Republic*. The ideal life and world are ultimately contingent on individual choice: the choice of each individual looking within itself and being true to the real person, a truth and a choice that will determine the individual's future life and happiness. This is an act of recognition, looking within the self and spotting what is real, whether it is for good or for evil. If it is good, then the individual may live and probably move on to a life of comedy or utopia – if that is possible in a collective setting.

Indeed, utopias are never attainable, because they cannot grow from an individual's idealistic wishes; by definition, a utopia has to be a collective experience, and to impose one person's desires and wishes on the group would invert the expectations of possessive individualism and liberal rights and would lead to life under the tyranny of an individual. Utopian hopes are tyrannical, like the static utopia in the biblical myth of the Garden of Eden. As Plato has Socrates say to his interlocutor in *Republic* in their discussion of the utopian civil state, "And there, dear Glaucon, it appears, is the supreme hazard for a man. And this is the chief reason why it should be our main concern that each of us, neglecting all other studies, should seek after and study the thing – if in any way he may be able to learn of and discover the man who will give him the ability and the knowledge to distinguish the life that is good from that which is bad."[31]

Such a being, or "the thing," as Socrates calls it, exists only within each of us individually. Indeed, this is the tragedy of life: that before we can move on to a comedy or utopia, we must individually be true to ourselves. But how do we know what is true and genuine when every individual is continually in a state of change? How do we know what is true and unchangeable, especially when we live a society that is a covenant between a lord and bondsmen? How do we achieve the kind of recognition that is the same externally as it is internally for a rationally moral agent? Can we be part of the majority but still hold on to our minority and individual statuses while knowing which is the true entity?

Genuine multiculturalism, as a liberal democracy, is ultimately a speculative attempt to deal with an issue that comedically seems so simple but is always so elusive – to thy own self be true. It is a search that holds the possibility of sinking into the deepest despondency and soul-destroying despair that routinely make life a tragedy but also offers the potential of the ultimate happiness knowable and livable only in a utopia. Indeed, these are the things that Canadians have grappled with for a long time. For they have lived it all in both the theory and the practice of a society that aims to be a Just Society. This is the idealism of a genuine multicultural state that practises radical democracy. That Canadians have not yet arrived in such a land and time is, indeed, the story of why multiculturalism is by nature a tragedy.

15

Tragedy: The Comedic Folk Saviour

Languages diverse, horrible dialects,
Accents of anger, words of agony,
And voices high and hoarse, with sound of hands,

Made up a tumult that goes whirling on
For ever in that air for ever black,
Even as the sand doth, when thewhirlwind breathes...

These have no longer any hope of death;
And this blind life of theirs is so debased,
They envious are of every other fate.[1]

Dante, *The Divine Comedy*

What is usually describe as the politics of recognition is then nothing more than grasping for a form of sense-certainty in the mistaken belief that it is the most sensuous form of knowing. We think we know who we are as Canadians through our determination or social imagining of what a Canadian is. And whether or not we derive this through such laws as the Canadian Citizenship Act (1947) or the Immigration and Refugee Protection Act (2001), we do not end up with a concrete definition that seems to fulfil our requirement. For example, the Citizenship Act can go only so far in telling us what types of persons Canadians are and how they should treat one another:[2] "A citizen, whether or not born in Canada, is entitled to all rights, powers and privileges and is subject to all obligations, duties and liabilities to which a person who is a citizen ... is entitled or subject and has a like status to that of such person."[3] The rest of the act enunciates the procedure for such people to gain citizenship. A citizen is more a type than a specific thing. In the Immigration and Refugee Protection Act, we learn the basic difference between Canadians as a group and the rest of humanity, or in this context non-Canadians: "Every Canadian citizen within the meaning of the *Citizenship Act*," it states, "and every person registered as an Indian under the *Indian Act* has the right to enter and remain in Canada in accordance with this Act, and an officer shall allow the person to enter Canada if satisfied following an examination on their entry that the person is a citizen or registered Indian."[4]

Instead of understanding fully what Canada and Canadians are, we end up aware of what they are not. We deal in universals of life and treat them ethnically and racially as particulars of citizenship. This creates a stream of errors, of misidentification and misrepresentation. The world is not as it appears. It is an inversion that is itself undergoing inversions. In these movements, certainty disappears and there is no fixity. The concepts of Canada and Canadians are always changing. We want to say one thing about what they are and end up saying something else, what these concepts are not. This world of inversion is a comedy, where we are not sure against whom or what we are fighting, if we should fight at all, if we should love and/or hate – we know none of the things that we once knew with certainty. Our demands for certainty are by nature tragic.

It is as if we have all become criminals and deviants and as if this change is the only way we can enjoy justice, for the law of the land needs law breakers just to prove its worth. Justice is meaningful only when it visits us as individuals. To make the individual whole, he or she must first be broken and destroyed. There must be metanoia – an inner death of spirit, even if the physical body remains the same. The physical body is now in thrall to a new sovereign, by a socializing spirit that causes it to produce ethically acceptable behaviour. Jesus' "Do unto others as you would have them do unto you" becomes the law of good behaviour under this sovereign, especially a sovereign that answers to a Christian sense of justice. But acquiescing to this law does not quite satisfy natural desires and inclinations for a justice of revenge. If an individual takes revenge against another, he or she would be accepting a social order in which what the other did to him or her he or she can also do to the other. It is not what we would expect of a socialized person, a citizen.

So something as naturally desirable as punishment for and revenge of a wrong against the tragic hero transfers to the state, while the foes love one another, leaving to the state the nasty job. For this is now the real law that replaces all other mere appearances of law giving, including those in nature. And as Hegel explains, this old law, "which bids me confront him as himself a person who does not treat me as such, and in fact bids me destroy him as an individuality – this law is *turned around* by the principle of the other world into its opposite: the reinstatement of myself as a person through the destruction of the alien individuality is turned into self-destruction."[5]

The tragic hero in this way loses him or herself but in return becomes a citizen with new responsibilities to the state and receives the equivalent of IOUs for redemption against the sovereign. Civil society becomes dominant, and civil rights replace universal rights. Hegel explains further, "If, now, this inversion, which finds expression in punishment of crime, is made into a *law*, it, too, again is only the law of one world which is confronted by an *inverted* supersensible world where what is despised in the former is honoured, and what in the former is honoured, meets with contempt."[6] The new spirit emerging through metanoia clashes with the old way, which refuses or cannot accept the new ethical order. Such is a tragic world of irony. This is more of a revelation for insiders who have to adjust to the additional inversions society requires. It is less so for immigrants who leave home for a land of inversion, where their culture will not have the same currency. Often they have to act as if their first responsibility in Canada is to undergo punishment, even a metanoia-like death – public rejection as cultural beings through their oath of allegiance or naturalization. This is truly a punishment and death, for individuals have meaning only in their culture. The culture that they know and that produced them deeply affects their personality and character. To renounce this culture is simply to *other* themselves radically – an act of diremption that discounts the love they had always known.

But the oath taking is also redemptive, and a restoration within a new family, as a new object of love. It is a folk initiation. According to Hegel, "The punishment which the law of the first world disgraces and destroys a man, is transformed in its inverted world into the pardon which preserves his essential being and brings him honour."[7] Actions of giving and receiving love celebrate the new citizenship and renew it daily. "Finally," says Hegel, "the *actual* punishment has its *inverted* actuality present in it in such a way that the punishment is an actualization of the law, whereby the activity exercised by the law as punishment *suspends* itself, and, from being active, the law becomes again quiescent and is vindicated, and the conflict of individuality with it, and of it with individuality, is extinguished."[8] So in the end, it is all appearance and show: appearance that *is* the reality. On one level, there is no real and actual punishment, just the symbolic mouthing of words that makes a Bad John into a Prince Charming so that theoretically everyone can live happily ever after. All this is the working out of a comedy, where instead of death at the end, there is life and love, history and recognition. There is a change from the old, not to nothing but to something that may well be better.

In addition, on our path to genuine knowledge of ourselves, we end up struggling with our experiences and discoveries. Instead of finding the world as reason tells us it ought to exist, experience makes us run up against harsh, brute facts that refuse to conform to our knowledge. The world is full of limits against which we are always struggling. We live in an alienated world, and we are perpetually unhappy because we feel we are in a lordship–bondage relationship. Either we agree that the world is not real because it is not what reason tells us it should be, or we reject the way the world appears to us.

In the first case, we are in servitude to our desires, for what we think is essentially the ultimate in human existence, even if we have to live in a world that is impervious to our humanity. In the second, we acknowledge that what we encounter is the real and authentic. In this case, the relationship is one where we privilege the living experience, as we encounter it, over what we really believe ought to be – and so we cannot become fully human and trap ourselves in our original nature.

In either case, we are unhappy and our lives are full of tension. There is no justice, no law that reconciles the form and content of life. Living is full of emptiness and is, by nature or appearance, tragic. Life has no meaning. We cannot find ourselves in the world, for it has no certainty or fixity, not even in ourselves. This is so because as we grow from our experience, we find that we, like the world, are also changing, so that often in all our possibilities and potentials we do not even know who we are from one moment to the next.

The struggle between internalities and externalities that is the politics of recognition has led us not into certainty but into a history of emptiness, of having no real and unchanging content, and of discovering that we are sojourning in a world that is meaningless to us. This is akin to what Canadians faced in the mid-1960s when Laurendeau and Dunton's famous Bi andBi commission set out in the early 1960s to prove Canada's self-certainty that it and its people were bilingual and bicultural. This was an exercise in experiencing a loss, of that which it thought with such certainty to be but that proved untenable. Instead, the commissioners reported that Canada and Canadians were *not* bicultural, but rather something they called "multicultural."

It was at this point of deepest loss, when Hobbes's mortal god appeared most human and mortal and when much of a seeming organic fraternity or recognition turned out not to be, that Canadians recognized the emptiness in themselves, as they defined themselves as an experience – a way of existing that they called "multicultural." They had apparently left the world of tragedy and the perdition of sense-certainty for the contrived world of perception, that of multiculturalism, which renders the appearance and reality of things the same.

This was also what had happened at mid-century when the Massey Commission had set out to prove that a Canadian culture existed, if only because such was Canadians' self-certainty. That exploration too discovered no such certainty, but rather that a culture that is essentially bringing together and collecting up universals into a particular is itself always shifting and changing – always in the process of becoming – and that this seemingly natural changefulness was effectively the essential element of this seeming culture.

This was true again when Canada announced that the country and its people were officially multicultural. This was an effort in self-certainty, leading again to the discovery that the assertion had no real content. Worse, within the seemingly multicultural Canada, the powers that be continued to search for proof of two founding cultures and ways of life, of specific unchanging liberal values, and for an ethnic hierarchy – accommodating and enslaving new people, while allowing old-timers to do the accommodating and determine levels of tolerance. Genuine multiculturalism, however, moves towards full knowledge, or truth. It recognizes too that all the shades we have gone through – all the many metanoia deaths – have led to self-certainty, which turned out to be its very other, the farthest from the truth, from knowledge of the real and authentic.

We keep looking for a particularity we call "the Canadian" as a single indivisible folk and end up finding merely universals, all the many things, elements, and beings of life. Here is how Hegel would explain this history. This thing,

> which can be called simply 'thinghood' or 'pure essence', is nothing else than what Here and Now have proved themselves to be, viz. a *simple togetherness* of a plurality; but the many are, *in their determinateness*, simple universals themselves. This salt is a simple Here, and at the same time manifold; it is white and *also* tart, *also* cubical in shape, of a specific gravity, etc. All these many properties are in a single simple 'Here', in which, therefore, they interpenetrate; none has a different Here from the others, but each is everywhere, in the same

Here in which the others are. And, at the same time, without being separated by different Heres, they do not affect each other in this interpenetration. The whiteness does not affect the cubical shape, and neither affects the tart taste, etc.; on the contrary, since each is itself a simple relating of self to self it leaves the others alone, and is connected with them only by the indifferent Also. This Also is thus the pure universal itself, or the medium, the 'thinghood', which holds them together in this way.[9]

Intuitively, Hegel's choice of "salt" and "whiteness" seems quite appropriate in our Canadian context. As we saw above, and as I have explained elsewhere, there is a specific historical definition of whiteness[10] but one that we have proven to change from moment to moment and that can serve as racial and ethnic short hand for determining who should have pride of position in Canada. Whiteness can be an assimilationist construct, with no essence of being. This is because we think we know with certainty what is white or, as in the accommodationist or separatist argument in Quebec and elsewhere, who is the salt of the land. This is the claiming of the essence of the here and now that is our community or country. Instead, we end up finding that salt and whiteness are universals consisting of other universals. Internal to them is a logical complexity. Individually, they are collections of universals and have no essential or necessary elements – they are merely what they appear to us to be at this moment in history.

So at this point in our journey along the road of despair, we end up with perception as a way of knowing, one in which objects and things contain properties, not an essence. Genuine multiculturalism in a specific country is the *thing* that collects up the many, the particular that consists of the many universals, the nation of many ethnicities and cultures of the world, of humanity, and of life. It is the spirit common to all the parts that makes its difference. In place of the universal – Hegel's property itself – in genuine multiculturalism, we see the universal of sharing, that act of clutching to parts or fragments of wholes. At any time, as a member of the folk, I can be a Canadian as a particular, and, without conflict, I can also embody some signifier in an adjective with hyphenation, as in French-Canadian, black-Canadian, Muslim-Canadian. More than that, in multicultural Canada I can also choose to share my particularity with those of other universals, so that in the current example I can be a Canadian who is also French and also black and also Muslim, until I run out of universals to share. The immigrant can be Prince Charming, Sweet

Boy, Bad John, or any other deviant at various different moments – or all of them at the same time. Such a person can simply be a social being – a citizen – full of potentials and possibilities both of the good and of the other. In the same moment of birth and death and even rebirth, the person embodies all the potential for good, as in any moment of creation or rebirth; but in the instant of death, the same person is all that its history has shown it to be as a tragic mortal. How then does the individual share what are now not just separate identities but properties of him or her?

How does this sharing – in effect, a deliberate and conscious attempt to create a mechanistic fraternity in the absence of one that is organic and permanent – work in an ethical setting that is a liberal democracy that is now officially and constitutively genuinely democratic? Again we can borrow from Hegel: we should share our bodies rather than consume them in a kind of self-masturbation, no matter how pleasurable we might consider self-pleasuring to be – no desegregation, just an indiscriminate mixing of bodies. This is the solution to mistaken efforts to exclude some groups from the sensuous pleasure of nation-building. But this exclusion is in fact impossible, because those who would exclude do not have the powers to alone carry on life and limit the universal properties in the nation. Indeed, those who would exclude immigrants are dependent on them and on those of once non-preferred pedigrees if the universal that is their nation-state Canada, or an independent province that is Quebec, is to exist and have life. The one is inseparable from its many parts.

Hegel provides us with two distinct analogies – infinity and truth – for good behaviour. Infinity allows us to submerge ourselves blindly in history and just follow where it leads us, all the while adding to our storehouses of knowledge. We relish the dynamics of living and the encounters of life, none of which we can really plan or fully anticipate. Here we are looking at the explanations of history, the kind of values that we can associate with living. These values would become the basis for our laws, the ethics that codify how we ought to behave and cooperate as a society. The law would socially eradicate all differences, making us all equal in the eyes of the sovereign. Making laws is merely a by-product or secondary characteristic of living – it does not explain life itself. This is a bothersome acknowledgment for liberal thinkers who suggest that defining citizenship by law and charters of rights completely protects citizens; their exclusive reliance on the law simply reduces individuals to explanations or abstractions. This can just be another attempt at diremption. Law can *legislate* a code of behaviour, but not a spirit This is not the fulness of life.

Hegel's other model invokes truth – a consciousness acting as if it has the *truth* and not a mere explanation of life's developments. This consciousness is not aware that that there is diversity and difference in each movement from one way of knowing to another. It does not acknowledge that "on the contrary, in this movement the Understanding has as objects positive and negative electricity, distance, force of attraction, and a thousand other things which constitute the content of the moments of movement."[11] In other words, diversity and continuing indeterminacy remain beyond the explanation and the laws of the period – and such are the facts of life.

We cannot reduce life to a mere explanation or to an abstract law. Like animals that simply eat grass and twigs and thereby put them to good use instead of reflecting too long on them to make sense of them, the sensuous animal should *engage* this diversity. It should act on the diversity and differences that are life and must also, to remain a part of life, let the diversity and difference act on *it*. There must be mixing and commingling, as none of the properties or universals in this piece is independent of the others and self-sufficient. There must be *sharing*, especially of bodies, to make a community. There must be not only the thought of love but lovemaking, too. Otherwise, how would we know what would emerge in the next moment out of this diversity and difference? Who would produce the next generation as part of the continuing search across time for the authentic self?

Hegel asserts tellingly, "The reason why 'explaining' affords so much self-satisfaction is just because in it consciousness is, so to speak, communing directly with itself, enjoying only itself; although it seems to be busy with something else, it is in fact occupied only with itself."[12] The true spirit of love involves communing between self and others and in a juxtaposing of bodies where positions of lordship and bondage are constant slipping away with the past and re-emerging in new contortions in anticipation of the approaching future – of the new being emerging out of this diversity. Instead of engagement with the self, there should be engagement with the infinity or diversity. The transcending of the body that law constitutes leads to a fuller life, with meaning and understanding in communal activity.

As Adelman argues, it is only in the sexual act that beings that are human find their humanity. As Hegel suggests, "Consciousness is aware itself *as this actual individual* in animal functions"[13] while seeking to defeat the ultimate enemy – death – which is always renewing itself and against which the state arises as a thought as means of overcoming. Sex is one of the most animal functions in our society, which often treats it at such in a negative sense. As a method for self-renewal, it is still the only weapon we have against the enemy in any guise, the ultimate expression of *poneria* – the fundamental idea of human creation of and by humanity itself for human benefits – and of the hope of overcoming the human tragedy when people take on limits and boundaries in a vain attempt to avoid the enemy. Hegel states that these animal functions "are no longer performed naturally and without embarrassment, as matters trifling in themselves which cannot possess any importance or essential significance for Spirit; instead, since it is in them that the enemy reveals himself in his characteristic shape, they are rather the object of serious endeavour, and become precisely matters of utmost importance."[14]

Judith Shklar argues that sex, significantly expressing the desire for self-preservation, produces what is ultimately a Hegelian erotic ego. This ego is also creative, with the need to reproduce and to make the world anew. Thus it not only extends itself in time, it is also remaking the world – so much like the tragic hero who leaves home to make himself a person but struggles to choose between self-sufficiency and communion or social love. "This erotic ego desires to project itself," Shklar states, "to externalize itself, to reproduce itself and so to escape from the confines of the given. It is not content merely to consume, it desires to recreate itself. It seeks an-other self-consciousness, in order to become 'we,' even as both remain egos. The erotic ego enters into communication and interaction with a projection of its own self, with another self-conscious being."[15] This may explain the violence of patriarchy, wherein the erotic ego must, in a Machiavellian kind of colonizing, preserve an other's otherness so as to have the space and difference for egotistical self-fulfilment through inequality and separateness. What happens to it when it does not view sex as primarily procreative and starts out the encounter with another as a fraternal relationship in which sameness is the norm. Does that ego still have the need for diremption as a way of finding its true self, just as Socrates and his colleagues discussed in Plato's *Symposium*?

In loving an Other, it loves itself. In this act of loving, of actually creating deeds and actions, it takes part in a discourse that we might call a "language of loving" and re-creates the very idea of who or what the ego is and what its uses to itself and to society are. A new language is under construction, which will express the desires and needs of the new creatures participating in this loving and emerging from these acts of love.

Sex is the classical metaphor for the work and production of things by beings who are simultaneously object and subject, giver and receiver of pleasure, but who share, both selfishly and unselfishly, the ultimate value in a liberal society: their bodies. Out of these seemingly meaningless actions that happen in the guise of personal gratification come a common good and, at the personal level, something that is both of our essence, whatever that is, and also separate and distinct from us, as if nature or the state itself made it. Ultimately, sex is the celebration of the body as the authentic temple of authenticity in a world of dependence that finds its apex in the family and its creation. This is the real world, not that which is beyond in transcendence, but, according to James Cone, the African-American and black liberation theorist, a world where transcendence occurs daily and where the God of the universe stoops to walk with and comfort the downtrodden. Perhaps it is for no other reason than just this that we generally accept the Universal Declaration of Human Rights (1948), which begins "Recognition of the inherent dignity and of the equal and inalienable rights of all members of the human family is the foundation of freedom, justice and peace in the world."[16] These words identify the elements common to the reasoning of social thinkers throughout the modern era who have wrestled with the nation-state as an inherent contradiction – as a site of a particular way of life for a unity and also as a place that contains all the diversity and differences of the human species – and as a historical construction or social consciousness.

This reasoning reflects my thinking about how to incorporate differences and diversity as independent elements in the universal and for the particular that, as a specific property and not an essence, is a particular society we call "Canada" – where the enemy arrives in the guise of acute need for children or for immigrants and hence dependence on the rest of the world. Sex speaks to interdependence in the unhappy consciousness – which exists among all Canadians and negatively between their nation-state and the rest of the world. And the universal and oneness that is Canada or Canadian can express itself only through a diversity of things and ways, of universals and particulars; and this is its force of life.

Appearances so diverse and different are those of a non-sensual and real way of existing. This expression is sometimes the *I* or single subject in a body or community and at other times an objective *you* in our way of *othering*. Idealism brings appearances and seeming reality and authenticity to one single expression. In Hegel's philosophy, this is to reconcile the *I* that is also a *we*, moving to end diremption and end up in love by engaging the diversity, not by limiting forms of explanation or even by well-meaning laws.

In Canadian multiculturalism, the fruit of a specific history in Western thought and action, this quest for recognition is a movement to discover how people who represent the rest of the world are in fact authentic and real Canadians – the true children of this mortal god. For life itself is a contradiction, as full of irony as the idea of a god that is mortal, as contradictory as the idea of Canadians who are from a state of nature that is the rest of the world. We can rationalize the answer only in and through perception, so that while we see the world as constitutive of tragic experience, we can perceive it and even delude ourselves into thinking of it as a comedy. Perception is what emerges when sense-certainty implodes: when we remain explaining the paradox of a life that we live as one and experience in many different and diverse forms. Perception rationalizes unity in diversity and equality in a world of differences.

This thinking is what explains genuine multiculturalism as a living experience. It is idealistically radical democracy, where all those universals that are properties in the particular social construction that is the commune or country have voice and agency. They can speak fully for themselves and are not voiceless subalterns. They can do things that express their thoughts of love, thereby expressing the authenticity that is the ultimate in their freedom. And by doing and acting out their desires, they can be moral – they can demonstrate that they have learned the lessons of their own loss and emptiness from a history of errantry. For such learning is also an exercise in knowing the self and becoming fully free and human. If individuals cannot be happy, they can at least have justice by first determining what it is and how to achieve it. They can negotiate what they recognize as justice, rather than waiting for some transcendental being to bestow such knowledge and awareness on them. As tragic characters, they can set their own limits and determine natural boundaries, rather than letting others do so. They can be not only thinkers but actors too, not only lovers but loved.

As citizens, they are in the world of smoke and mirrors, but they know that they have built it. This is the environment in which they hope to become perfect and in which they all hope to flourish. And they will do this with their own hands or from their own bodies. In this way, they create a new spirit of the age in which individuals are infinite because they are universal, constantly changing, so that when they come together as one in love, solidarity, or recognition, there is no real end or limit to what they can share with one another and in their embodiment as a group. There is nothing beyond the world as it appears. As Hegel claims, "Appearance is the arising and passing away that does not itself arise and pass away, but is 'in itself', and constitutes the actuality and the movement of the life of Truth. The true is thus the Bacchanalian revel in which no member is not drunk; yet because each member collapses as soon as he drops out, the revel is just as much transparent and simple repose."[17] This is just like the Platonic comedy where everyone drinks too much before they can figure out what love is, for they always fail to move beyond the appearance of the thing without realizing that the appearance is also a manifestation of the real but just *a* manifestation and not *the* definitive one. As the host of TV's *Flip Wilson Show* used to say – at about the time when Canada was introducing official multiculturalism – "What you see is what you get." Canada and Canadian exist merely as Canadian *thought* attempting to become *real*. Yet the Canada that Canadians (whoever they are) now see in all its diversity and difference is the real thing, which this moment in history delivered.

SEEKING RECONCILIATION

So what is the relevance of our discussion? If we were to ask Leo Strauss, he would tell us that tragedy is about the diremption and even destruction of humanity. At the least, it is the paring away of all that makes us truly human and unique in our own way so that we can become a common citizen. So much so that we resemble domestic animals in zoos or homes that no longer have even the instincts of their species – they cannot survive in nature or, ironically, in civil society without becoming totally dependent. They cannot even think for themselves and simply become followers.

Such thinking abounds in the differences Strauss sees between how we look at tyranny in the classical setting and what it has become today: "Present-day tyranny, in contradistinction to classical tyranny, is based on the unlimited progress in the 'conquest of nature' which is made possible by modern science, as well as on the popularization or diffusion of philosophic or scientific knowledge. Both possibilities – the possibility of a science that issues in the conquest of nature and the possibility of the popularization of philosophy or science – were known to the classics ... But the classics rejected them as 'unnatural,' i.e., as destructive of humanity. They did not dream of present-day tyranny because they regarded its basic presuppositions as so preposterous that they turned their imagination in entirely different directions."[18] Therefore, to Strauss, anyone trying to hold on to the entirety of humanity in our current society is, effectively, a tragic hero.

But if there is really a universal law for humanity, it seems to be that the goal of our living is to make life a comedy. This means that tragedy must end, and its traditional dénouement is death. After death comes *Other* than the current life, other than the tragic beings we are, the opposite of what we were alive. This is a view as old as the ancient Greeks – we find it when Socrates in *Republic* notes: "A man who has lived in his former life in a well-ordered regime, participating in virtue by habit and without philosophy, will choose for his next life 'the greatest tyranny,' for 'mostly people make their choices according to the habits of their former life.'"[19] When we transcend this life, we choose its very opposite.

This is a significant point in our discussion. It speaks to the current debate over Canada's immigration policy and how it is trying to choose immigrants who already share our values. Socratic thinking would suggest that we do the opposite. Counter-intuitively, we should select people with *opposite* values and transform them through a social death, so that they will desire to become the opposite of what they were. We will complete the process by teaching them our philosophy or ideology. Prophets and philosophers have long argued that civil society should perfect humanity – helping people to realize all the abilities, potentials, and virtues that nature has bestowed on them, but for society's own good.

Even Machiavelli, an arch-foe for us in this discussion, eventually concedes later in life that tragedy is not the ideal form. It attracts only people who value themselves as self-made individuals and who desire to become Princes, lording over others and making the world absolutely in their own images. Such figures having no sense of commitment or belonging might be willing to deny and negate their own parents and lineage so as to make a unique mark on the world. The drawback of this is that there is no solidarity, no liberty, no equality, only misery for everyone. Theirs are lives of fear and suspicion, and they might even deny their parents and destroy their children for personal gain. They show little respect for history and no concern for the future: the present consumes them. They represent the epitome of selfishness, for they base their actions and concerns solely on their desire for survival in the moment, rather that the higher and more rational human desire of creating a better world. They are definitely not humanists or of the folk or the unselfish and defanged subjects of current post-humanist times. They embody the archetype that in the Sleeping Beauty fairy tale asserts patriarchy, gesturing to a society that is one-sided and bereft of diversity and difference. For comedy to occur, they must change before we can conclude, "they live happily after."

According to Machiavelli, a life of misery is not ideal. In *Discorsi* (The Discourses), he seems to reject most of the advice he had offered in *The Prince*. He praises the common good and lauds republican government as the ideal for good living. The greater good trumps the individual good, and planning for a better future is more humane than having absolute power and independence within a lifetime. "Therefore," he says, "the salvation of a republic or a kingdom does not lie in having a prince who governs prudently during his life, but one who organizes the state in such a way that even after he dies, it will survive on its own."[20] States that rely on one man tend not to last too long. The same is not true of those founded on ideologies or religions. Machiavelli himself underwent metanoia, for he changed intellectually.

The best thing that secular and spiritual princes can do, according to *The Discourses*, is ensure that the people have a spirit that works towards achieving the common good. This gives them unity of purpose or joins them in seeking to find a path that can turn their tragic lives into comedies. This spirit becomes the state's religion or ideology. More important, once the state commits itself to new spiritual ideals, the leaders must give them their full support. If this observation is correct, it further bolsters the claim that justice in Canada would have to favour the poor, immigrants, and those whom multiculturalism is socializing into full citizens. "Therefore, the rulers of a republic or a kingdom should preserve the foundations of the religion that they profess, and once they have done this, it will be easy to keep their state religious and, in consequence, good and united. And they must support and augment everything that favours their religion, even if they think it is false, and they will do this more, as they are more prudent and more knowledgeable about natural phenomena."[21] Machiavelli says that when people follow this path, regardless of the truth or falsity of the religion, it becomes easier for the people to believe in miracles, so that the prudent sovereign "makes everyone believe in them."[22]

With this ideology in place, the sovereign's next step is to trust the people's wisdom because they tend to act instinctively out of the common good. To this end, the Machiavelli of *The Discourses* tilts towards the democratic republic, which elevates the interests of the people, all of whom have committed themselves to a singular common good. The main regulator would be the law, because the people are more likely to react to reason, to the words of a good man, than to a tyrant who speaks only of power and force: "When a people is truly unrestrained, one need not fear its foolish actions; one does not have to be afraid of present evils, but of that which could arise, since a tyrant might appear in the midst of so much confusion. But the contrary is the case with wicked princes: one fears present evils while feeling hope for the future, since men persuade themselves that the ruler's wicked life may lead to a resurgence of freedom. Thus you see the difference between the two, which is between the things that are and those that are to come."[23]

Machiavelli presents democracy as a comedy that could only by accident revert to a tragedy; tyranny is tragedy, where the hope and prayer are always to end this condition, to enter a comedy. And in so wishing, Machiavelli seems to imply that Socrates is right: that people always want to come back as the opposite of what they were, or if such a status means happiness, they would remain what they are.

Therefore we seem to have found agreement that the ideal is to overcome the tragic human condition by creating conditions of happiness for a comedy that will allow people to live happily ever after. How to do this? Here is where we turn again to Hegel.

UNHAPPY CONSCIOUSNESS: MODERNITY'S LEGACY

In *Phenomenology of Spirit,* Hegel says that the "*unhappy consciousness* is the consciousness of self as a dual-natured, merely contradictory being."[24] This discontent occurs when the individual realizes that, even with the best of efforts and intentions, his or her thoughts and actions are irretrievably in conflict and there seems no way to reconcile them. For Hegel, there are three metaphors – unchangeable, changeable, and mediator – at work in an unhappy consciousness, and they must participate in the solution. This is an analysis about perception and about who has the power to maintain others in stereotypical perception a dominant group or person has the others.

The first metaphor is what we will call the "unchangeable." This is the condition in which a dominant view exists and members believe that a specific ideology, approach, or way of existing is the ultimate good. Any change would make matter worse. For example, people might assume that a specific way of life is the *only* possibility and that any other would need accommodation, for what exists ought to continue immutable.

The second metaphor is that of the "changeable," that which is subject to death. Alternatives are available to what exists, making what the seemingly permanent changeable, malleable, and transformable. For example, immigrants arrive, challenge the existing order and values, and demand change; they become the agents of change from their state of nature.

The third metaphor is the "mediator," who tries to bridge the gulf between the seemingly unchangeable and people seeking change. In our discussion, government agencies and institutions play this role. In sum, the unchangeable represents people who think they live in a comedy and who look down on those tragic carriers who are the changeable, and the mediator encourages each side to consider the other's perspective.

This progression from tragedy to comedy requires metanoia-like death and resurrection. The seeming unchangeable dies, as does the mediator, transcending the limits that are producing the tensions and contradictions inherent to an unhappy consciousness. Through death, they become the same as the epitome of the changeable all along. Having switched perspectives, they must join the changeable in the hope of an afterlife that is the inverse of what they took as normal life, which proved to be tragic. This death is the negation of natural abilities and virtues. Resurrection, in Western mythology, brings transcendence across limits. A willing death brings freedom in reconciliation, which derives from hope and the faith that comes in a *new* mediator that is love. This is the love that accepts humanity in the many forms that nature produces. It takes this diversity and makes it into a civil society by hybridizing all the differences into a new type of humanity – equal citizens. The forms might change, but the values or the spirit of the individuals find renewal, and in such a way that all forms will be able to see their old selves and forms but also see a new and different present and future self. This is the ideal of Christian justice – again, a building block of multiculturalism.

Hegel's phenomenology portrays the development of human existence as a search for freedom. It outlines a Christian or catholic world and developments or movements over time in the creation of specific cultures within a civilization that is idealistically a comedy. Modernity is its most current moment, and modernist states are the most recent determinations of its ideal. For Hegel, the ideological explanation of this civilization is the search for reconciliation in freedom of the conflicting parts of human duality of body and mind – of tragedy and comedy. As he says in *Philosophy of History*, "The State is the Divine Idea as it exists on Earth. We have in it, therefore, the object of History in a more definite shape than before; that in which Freedom obtains objectivity, and lives in the enjoyment of this objectivity."[25] He is referring here to a state that comes out of the morality of a revealed religion that values beliefs, faith, and perception, such as Christianity, and that is an idealized unity.

Alternatively, it could come out of an ideology, as such theorists as Durkheim, Weber, and Marx suggest, with similar foundations.

With particular relevance for this chapter, this dualism in humanity occurs through individuality and collectivity in two specific ways: first, as individual humans who are body and spirit, or mind and substance, and, second, as humans who form societies but who tend to be individualistic and to seek happiness through self-actualization, including social mobility, yet are gregarious and need societies to share collective risks and to achieve self-sufficiency. In all cases, humans aim to exist in an idealized place of safety, stability, and predictability, where they are free to exercise self-determinacy, to imagine what they want to become, and to transform into the image in their imagination. They want the luxury of a place that is changeless and fixed by nature, not by inclination, but that by nature allows them to change as they choose or incline.

Reconciliation of these dualisms has religious and ideological overtones, for Hegel is ultimately a Christian philosopher. He sees History as an attempt common to all religions, all histories, and the consciousness of humanity to bring forth a unity out of dualities. At the same time, it is an effort to recognize, preserve, and carry forward, intact within epistemology, the distinctiveness of the parts of the duality. In this way, as I indicated in the previous chapter, the rationalist transcendentalist ideology that underpins societies in the Americas derives from norms and concepts that Christianity culled from Hebrew, Greek, and African mythologies and philosophies.

Recognition of differences within society and their ultimate reconciliation fit easily into a Christian framework, with the spirit of the nation-state standing in for the universal God, who reveals himself in most recent manifestations as Christian. As Peter C. Hodgson says in *G.W.F. Hegel: Theologian of the Spirit,* this explanation is tantamount to providing ontological proof of God's existence and the manifestation of God's will and intentions.[26] We can fathom these intentions by analogy from examining the various ways God expresses itself in Nature and through human actions, thereby discovering God's putative energy. This approach is in opposition to the cosmological argument that starts with God's existing prior to the creation of the world and hence changelessness. The preferred method is to prove, not assume, that an essence exists. By using Hegel's analysis, we can discern speculatively the existence of the essence of the *Canadian* spirit, whether cosmology or ontology decides, and we can inquire who or what an immutable Canadian essentially is. As Hodgson comments on Hegel's method, "The task of speculative philosophy is to demonstrate the unity while also explaining difference. It does this by showing that the concept or logical idea simply *is* movement by which it determines it to *be*; that is, it is the dialectical movement of the self-determination of being. This is the result of the science of logic, and Hegel believes that it supplies the demonstrative force lacking in the original form of the ontological proof."[27]

Hegel presents this logic or system as a dialectic between what others perceive as the unchangeable and fixed concept – the essence of being – and the difference that occurs within the seemingly changeless body that causes constant change. How reconcile this unity and fixity with that which, on closer examination, is constantly changeable? This is as much a question for the individual with a separate mind and body, whereby one has to react to a change in the other, as for a society acting as a collection of separate and disparate peoples with different and varying wants, desires, and intentions.

In the Hegelian dialectic, tragedians are those who practise Stoicism; scepticism is for those believing that they are already players in a comedy. The two approaches reconcile in a death that occurs when the Stoic and the sceptic realize that both must give up their independence and join a wider, unified being or community. It is this body that destroys them and then reassembles them as individuals and as citizens with no conflict between the new identities for the community or for the individuals as part of a wider whole. But in so doing, the community also destroys its old self, and in incorporating the transformed materials it reassembles itself as part of a new entity that is the wider and all-encompassing whole.

John Burbidge writes in *Hegel on Logic and Religion: The Reasonableness of Christianity* that reconciliation occurs in the unhappy consciousness when individuals, seeking a truth that they perceive as unchangeable, can transcend the contradictions of change that occur within them as a result of the search.[28] This change must therefore come from beyond the individual, in the form of a force that can reconcile the changeable and the unchangeable while negating them. Similarly, reconciliation would come only when the unchangeable moves, finding relief in a force beyond itself.

This development towards reconciliation is a three-step move. First, the individual as self-consciousness recognizes that there is an unchangeable and accepts this as part of the dualism; this is a surrender to the immediacy of intellectual feeling or intuition. Second, the individual "turns not outward towards an objective embodiment of the unchangeable, but inward into its own awareness of itself. Its own desire and labour are to be the means of reconciliation."[29]

Tragedy and comedy are thus two expressions of the same individual way of life or culture. Even then, there is alienation in the form of labour and desire. For what the individual produces, the very best of its efforts acting on its desires, it still does not consider a reflection of its essence or its true self. This is still unsatisfactory, because the individual members are still short of what they initially wanted or desired. They have freedom to, and can, create, but the result does not contain the crafter's soul or true spirit.

This is the point in Hegel's analysis – the third step – when the body and mind have recognized their connection: one must take instructions from the other in the hope of placing a soul in its creation, and the other needs a body for its soul; but neither has a mechanism to make this happen. They need a conduit that is external to both of them.

They search for the missing mechanism in an outsider, a mediator who represents both the changeable and the unchangeable. But they thereby acknowledge that they are not free to achieve their desires on their own. Both need each other and the mediator for maximum motility and affectivity as individuals and as a whole. They have placed themselves in bondage to a lord that is partly of their own making but that also contains the spirit or body that was always beyond them. The mediator is a joint creation of body and mind, and they, in fashioning it, are free to create but are also both in bondage through a need for each other and for the mediator, who takes over and becomes their vehicle for actualization. As Burbidge explains, "They receive from the mediator directions concerning what they are to do. In total obedience, the individuals surrender the positive value of self-determination. Even their own satisfaction in achievement must be sacrificed. They are told to use meaningless formulae, to confiscate products of their own labour, to abstain from eating, and to mutilate their bodies."[30]

Death occurs in three steps. The first is the death of the body or changeable, and the second is metanoia – the death of the mind or unchangeable. A third step follows, when the form of the mediator itself dies. The three steps occur simultaneously in the death of the mediator. This three-fold death is necessary for the three components to resurrect in a new reconciliation. In this case, the new mediator is not an embodied spirit but a spirit that contains traces of the previously unreconciled body and mind in the incarnate mediator of the previous moment.[31]

In the Hegelian analysis, as in Christianity, this point is the death of Jesus on the cross so that there can be a resurrection and the start of the Christian era in Western civilization. As Hegel says, "*Christ has appeared, – a Man who is God, – God who is Man; and thereby peace and reconciliation have accrued to the World.*"[32] Hodgson explains, "[Hegel] is describing here a process by which the divine being's individual self-consciousness (as Christ) becomes universal, becomes the religious community. Death is transfigured from the nonbeing of the historical individual Jesus into the universality of spirit, which lives, dies, and rises daily in the community. Particularity dies away in universality, representation in concept. What dies in the death of the mediator is not only 'the already dead husk stripped of its essential being,' but also the abstraction of the divine being. The abstract supreme being must die, along with the historical mediator, in order for the concrete universal, world-encompassing spirit, to be born."[33]

Spiritual or intellectual death is necessary to enable transformations to the unchangeable as concept or being, to the changeable as being and concept, and to the process that is the mediator that links the unchangeable and changeable in an ethical relation. As Harris explains, "In the world of our lives, God is dead. He has left us only a grave, an empty tomb to fight about. That battle itself is hopeless; only after defeat is accepted can the quest for salvation in actual thinking properly begin."[34] Therefore transformation is all-encompassing, as in this dialectic nothing stays the same – neither the actors nor the process that is their ethical relation. Burbidge argues that death, as awareness of finitude and the radical limit for individuals, plays a crucial role in Hegelian analysis: "The central significance of Christianity for Hegel lies in the fact that ... its dogma reported that God himself had in fact become a finite man and had died. In other words, the radical negativity of self-chosen death is also affirmed to be a central constituent of the divine life."[35] Hegel states that the fear of death is the beginning of wisdom; at other times, he says this of the fear of God.[36] This seems to suggest that God and death are the same in his analysis, a crucial point that I develop below for understanding how the reconciliation of an unhappy consciousness can occur.

But what is this phenomenon that is death? According to Burbidge, Hegel presents it as something that happens through a threat from another self-consciousness. But death could occur also at the individual's choosing, cancelling the possibilities that are beyond the limits of a finite person. In some Western mythologies, choosing one's death is always preferable to dying at another's hand. As Droge and Tabor say in *A Noble Death: Suicide and Martyrdom among Christians and Jews in Antiquity,* this choice is the difference between the good of becoming a martyr and the evil of committing suicide – both destroying the self at one's own choosing.[37] Why would the changeable and the unchangeable accept death? And how, out of this choice, is a self-imposed death good? Hegel suggests that the motivation has to come from the hollowness that is each entity's hopelessness and despair for a solution that only come from outside both of them. The solution comes in the form of Love, and it occurs ethically through Love and the act of loving. Love comes only through grace and not by entitlement or right. It expresses itself as hope and faith, it is the act of having those goods, and it is acting on them confidently. Here again, in our analysis, love is fraternity that results in complete recognition of the personal as society entrenches it.

These mythologies accept such a death for a greater good and not for narrow individual gain.[38] Each expression of Love embodies hope and faith. In love lies hope for reconciliation and for resurrection as a new but different being that contains both the changeable and the unchangeable; faith is the belief that the hope will materialize – that there must be a resurrection – and love is the expression of the combined whole. The acceptance of death is the limit of epistemology, is the finite. Faith and hope are the transcending of these limits and finitudes into the realm of the infinite that is also the unchangeable. Love is the new mediator, it reconciles everything. In this approach, Hegel draws heavily on Western mythologies.

Burbidge shows us something more from Hegel's analysis: the epistemological question of what in a Christian mythology is evil and when, ontologically, evil arrived in the world. Hegel suggests that if God projects something (and this is questionable), it is goodness. Noting that Hegel says that humans' fear of death is the beginning of wisdom and knowledge, Burbidge adds that in Hegel's analysis death helps shape the individual's development towards absolute knowing and ultimate freedom. Death dissolves points of finitude as they occur – a negating role – often cancelling or removing obstacles in the dialectic to absolute knowledge.

Burbidge traces three consecutive processes of death as part of Hegel's system. Citing attempts at reconciliation in the unhappy consciousness, he notes, "While there is here no physical death, he self-consciously attempts to exterminate its individuality. In this process the first negation is the finitude of change and decay which is not consciously produced but consciously acknowledged. The second negation is the process of self-mortification, but the third negation is the awareness that the mediated process of self-mortification is the concrete dynamic of unchangeable reality itself."[39]

Ultimately, humans know they are free when they have the choice of their own death without the attendant fear and terror. This comes with the acceptance of dying, for an individual, in a bacchanalian way symbolically accepting death as a mechanism for overcoming the fear of death and its limits, "becomes aware of the positive fact [that] he is free to create *ex nihilo*, and the prospect of genuinely moral action opens up" and that death itself is a creative act.[40] This is the death that, as we saw above in this chapter, creates a greater good in much the same way that it turns a Bad John from an antisocial character into a cultured being. Therefore it is not an absolute finite point, even if it is a specific and physical one for the individual. To this end, the individual becomes a martyr for a greater cause, and the self-induced death is not suicide.[41] Burbidge's analysis of evil in Hegel's philosophy throws new light on the role of death in his logic. Burbidge notes that Hegel's three-step notion of death, as a series of negations and rebirths to a higher consciousness of knowing, explains the arrival of evil.

In this analysis, God created the world out of nothing and, within the world, humans in his own image. This means that the Christian God is infinite and without limits. Humans, as created beings, are not; they are finite and incomplete. Through them, particularly when they thought that they could become gods and demanded recognition as equals and then acted on this thought, evil entered the world. According to Hegel:

> Man, created in the image of God, lost, it is said, his state of absolute contentment, by eating of the Tree of the Knowledge of Good and Evil. Sin consists here only in Knowledge: this is the sinful element. And by it man is stated to have trifled away his Natural happiness. This is a deep truth, that evil lies in consciousness: for the brutes are neither evil nor good; the merely Natural Man quite as little. Consciousness occasions the separation of the Ego, in its boundless freedom as arbitrary choice, from the pure essence of the Will – i.e., from the Good. Knowledge, as the disannulling of the unity of mere Nature, is the "Fall", which is no casual conception, but the eternal history of Spirit. For the state of innocence, the paradisiacal condition, is that of the brute. Paradise is a park, where only brutes, not men, can remain. For the brute is one with God only implicitly [not

consciously]. Only Man's Spirit (that is) has a self-cognizant existence. This existence for self, this consciousness, is at the same time
separation from the Universal and Divine Spirit. If I hold to my abstract freedom, in contraposition to the Good, I adopt the standpoint of Evil... Persistence in this end-point is, however, Evil, and the
feeling of pain at such a condition, and of a longing to transcend it.[42]

Burbidge comments, "When finite men and women seek to become
self-contained and independent as he [God] is thought to be, they break
apart the homogeneous fabric of the universe and introduce the difference between good and evil. *For evil is the self-contained refusal to allow
oneself to be incorporated into the larger totality.*"[43] Indeed, we are back
to the Aristotelian being that is either a god or a brute and needs socialization to become human – a citizen. Selfishness in the form of not
changing and undergoing this process is, mythologically, the beginning
of evil.

According to this line of thought, evil arrived when humans, in their
tragic condition, first decided that they wanted to become as culturally
comedic as gods, thereby disrupting the natural order of the cosmos.
They decided to transform themselves out of their primordial and natural state of existence, with only the desire for survival, into an idealistic
human way of life: a comedy that foresaw an end to the tragic human
condition. They believed that there could be a successful separation in
the condition of humanity, a break with history to create a new history.
The result of these efforts, in Christian mythology, is that humans discovered, to their chagrin, the utter alienation of knowing not only that
are they the exact opposite of gods and by nature must have a tragic
existence, but that they are the creators of evil and must live in agony
and despair. Their despondency symbolizes the limits of what they know
they are capable of achieving, even if their desires run ahead of their
capabilities. The ethical relationship they must endure is that of a tragedy and the negativity of failing to achieve human ideals; it produces a
second-class status that sees humans and God as separate and distinct
opposites instead of complements in a whole. This is an ethical world
that valorizes comedy, goodness, and the everlasting as seemingly the
natural state of gods, with tragedy as bad or evil because it appears
humans' natural state.

This is an exercise in inversion and irony. It is a diremption that is
necessary to heal the original diremption – the loss of the personal to
heal the loss in the collective that is all humanity. Death for the collective

or for the common good is the only meaningful death, for to die for oneself has no meaning or real purpose – it is self-defeating as thought and act. It is even evil. Meaningful death must be at least for an Other. This too appears in the metaphor of the open grave – of the unknown that faith explains as an escape into freedom by an earlier human and as a hope that later individuals in their collective Otherings will achieve the same. Death is the first negation of individuals' physical finitude: it is the transformation into non-beings of an infinity knowable only instinctually and by faith, as Plato and later Machiavelli seem to suggest.

But there is a second stage, when the divine or the unchangeable become human and die to remove evil, allowing for human reconciliation with God. This death "cancels particularity and finitude so that the incarnate one continues to live universally. Not limited by space and time, he dies and is raised again daily in the worship and devotion of the Christian community."[44] This second death therefore negates the historical selfish attempt at comedy by producing a reconciliation that comes through the efforts and Love of God, not through human initiative. Thus it restores the previous order, where humanity starts out in its tragic condition but attains a form of comedy. But this comic condition can occur only in the transcendent and in the afterlife, in the mediator, Love, which ironically represents human tragedy. Life on earth and in the here and now remains tragic for humans, even when there is love. This reconciliation comes through faith, belief, and perceptions.

The third stage, Burbidge says, is when God leaves the transcendent that is above human existence, becomes human, and then dies. But this too leads to despair when humans realize that God has died and that there is no escape from the evil that is the separation of the empty grave of Christianity. Without hope and faith, the believer faces the apparent emptiness of a religion. A religion like Christianity offers hope and faith in the justice and righteousness of a state. With no hope, there would be only nihilism and despondency. The faith and hope within Love negate this despair. As Burbidge argues, "The painful awareness of the death of God allows the spiritual integration of human with the divine not only in dogmatic theory but in actual fact. In other words, in the revealed religion of Christianity God is negatively defined as dying, not only in the objective content, but in the subjective, existential consciousness of the believer. And when this takes place death does not just define the limits of finitude, nor cancel the mediator's particularity, but it reveals the fundamental identity of the human and the divine. Both become actual by negatively dissolving the negative through their negatively determined isolation (whether abstract beyond or self-contained evil) is cancelled."[45] For this realization to occur, an Other has passed through that door to freedom, and this tells the subject that it can too, but by also becoming an Other.

The phrase "open grave" holds both the notions of despondency and hope. There is despondency, for the individual knows that she or he will be the substance that fills the open grave and causes it to be open no more. Simultaneously, there is hope: the belief that some earlier evil-doer, by sacrificing himself in the hope of transcending limits for the *Other,* had gone into the grave and escaped it. That the grave is open is a symbol of escape and freedom. It is the equivalent of a door through which a slave has escaped, rather than the portal through which a free person will lose her or his liberty and enter bondage when the cell door locks from the outside. As Harris says, "We must live in the hope of joining him [who previously escaped] when we pass through the portals of death."[46]

Christian mythology holds some clear implications for comedy and tragedy. Reconciliation occurs when the unchangeable becomes changeable, when God becomes human, when comedy becomes tragedy – as the mediator hanging on a cross symbolizes. There is a change as well for humans when, in the Christian faith, they aspire ethically to become comedic in an existence as, idealistically, God, while still remaining human in their daily life. They remain tragic, but within a comedic existence of faith, belief, and perception that is new – that death has tested. Death is not an absolute ending but a metaphor of transformation and hope, and this, as Burbidge says, is "why death plays such an important role in" the development of Hegel's *Phenomenology* and in his method of knowing the truth and the epistemology of good and evil.

A Hegelian analysis seems to suggest that, according to Christian mythology, there is still another stage of negation that is necessary for reconciliation – one that negates comedy and transforms it back into tragedy of different hues and colours. Love, without the taint of human evil, must come from beyond time, entering into History – not created inside history or at the start of history, where it would be subject to human morality. Indeed, as James Cone argues, this explanation is at the heart of understanding the experience of blacks and blackness in modern society as not only a way of surviving the tragedy of living but a means of having hope for better life.[47] This thinking calls for a reversal of what history has constructed as good by a return to the moment of creation for a symbolic rebirth, where the decisions of a future society occur on the basis not of what is good exclusively for a specific group of people but of what is good for all humanity and equally good for the specific group of people that they will most affect.

For it was in that first moment after creation, in time, that humans became moral agents and created evil. Their first act towards the creation of wisdom and knowledge was to create a seeming comedic existence that was the thought of a physical separation out of the human condition. Their second act was the performance of a comedy, acting as if they had already escaped the tragic condition of other human beings. Reconciliation calls for the reversal of these two acts as counter-moves. This requires returning, through a three-step movement in death in Hegel's explanation of the Christian rational transcendentalist ideology, into tragedy, but now with a hope – for it is the hope that is new and makes the existence new – of escaping into comedy. Really, we are back where we started, but this time we have love, understanding, and solidarity among all individuals and groups, trying as a common good to escape the tragic human condition by finding a new measure of justice.

There is one other implication of our discussion so far that we may consider: can humanity produce idealized societies? Can it aspire to comedy out of tragedy without eventually ending up as an unhappy consciousness? The answer seems to be "No," for humanity is by nature always tragic. This then is why multiculturalism calls for death of both the changeable and unchangeable – both the Canadians of ancient lineage, who in a Hobbesian sense see themselves as epitomizing the mortal god that is the sovereign state, and the newcomers – and for the death of the stage whose image reflects all Canadians. And at the same time this is why multiculturalism remains a tragedy for some Canadians and a hope of comedy for others. For those Canadians of ancient lineage, it is a comedy, the realization of all they have desired. They cannot see any further changes. They have maximized their desires. For the newcomers, it is a tragedy, for the order limits their natural abilities and virtues. Using their natural abilities and virtues, they cannot achieve their potential to become as human as they imagined. The state, which is the spiritual and temporal embodiment of the desire of both the old-timers and the newcomers, finds itself as an unhappy consciousness, still experiencing a tragic existence.

Western mythology suggests that death or metanoia is the path to social reconciliation. Canada – that is, the state, those of ancient lineage, and the newcomers as well – must die, negating natural desires and in a new life moving on to the quest for new human desires: those that people negotiate in the grave that is Canada, from which they expect the impossible – the miracle of resurrection. And not only must the three metaphoric representatives of Canada die now, they must be ready to die frequently – as often as a new tragic figure enters the piece and demands changes to allow their full humanity that is civically Canadian. In this process, as the mythology suggests, Canadians of all sorts can hope only for an idealized freedom while living in mental slavery. The result is that old and new Canadians recognize that they are in false consciousness if they believe that the solution to their struggle is a new relation of lordship and bondage where one group has dominance over the other and determines who and what a new Canadian is. Instead, they find that each is in a new such relationship – but this time with the state as lord and themselves as slaves. More so, each group has entered into this relationship unintentionally but also willingly. This is so because groups can find a solution to the impasse between them only by going beyond their individualities and virtues and accepting a new order that they now view as better than slavery and as freedom. As a living reality, it is not freedom but bondage, except that it is different from all previous bondages, for it contains aspirations for full freedom and no fear of a new lord. The lord tells both sides who and what a Canadian is, and since this definition does not fully capture what they want for themselves, the two sides continue to struggle for change. It is, however, the state as sovereign or lord against whom they must struggle, for the state's definition of the culture of a multicultural Canada would always be a culture and history of slavery for all members of the society.

Kojève has a good explanation of this process, which, as we saw above, he describes as master and slave relationship instead of lord and bondsperson. I prefer the latter metaphor: with multiculturalism and immigration, newer Canadians do not have any choice in the type of Canada they enter. To have a life that befits their ideal of the best for themselves, they have to accept the lordship that already exists in Canada, even though it is a covenant they never stop duplicitously fighting to achieve their natural desires. In the end, the tragedy of the situation is that the newcomers act as if they are in a struggle with old-timers only to find out that the lord is different and non-human – a being that is a human and yet not human, a being in which they can see themselves and in which they are still foreign. "And if the Slave accepts this new divine Master," Kojève explains, "he does it for the same reason that he accepted the human Master: through fear of death. He accepted – or produced – his first Slavery because it was the price of biological *life*. He accepts – or produces – the second, because it is the price of his *eternal life*."[48]

In this sense, the citizens of whatever vintage live seemingly in two worlds at the same time: one that remains a tragedy, for it is slavery and a lower form of humanity with social constraints on natural virtues and abilities, the other a mental world of comedy that is transhistorical and already exists because of faith and instinct and is located where the citizens are already what they dream of becoming. So they live, contradictorily, as both slave and free – as tragedy and comedy at the same time. This means that they continue the struggle for freedom that is natural to a tragic existence while refusing to work and construct the Canada that they think already exists; if only in transcendence, they delude themselves into believing that this is their real and authentic reality.

RECONCILING LOVE AND FEAR: TRAGEDY AND COMEDY IN OUR TIME

Change in the hope of transcendence is necessary on all sides. However, old-timers pay perhaps the biggest price for change – they felt all along that they were the ultimate in Canada and Canadian. Now they have to recognize that what they thought unchangeable is not so and reconciliation requires something radical and drastic in their own thinking – something akin to the Western myth of God dying to engender an equitable relationship with its own creations and inferior beings. Once this new idea becomes a definition of humanity or Canadian, how to identify the actions necessary to achieve the new ideal? Now of a single mind and spirit, fearing no longer themselves but the state, citizens can work together towards freedom – anything other than their current slavery and, à la Plato and Machiavelli, the other world for which they hope in the future.

Within such a setting, it is natural to be happy and pessimistic at the same time. The citizens can believe that justice already exists or is still beyond their grasp, in which case they need to do more work. However, ironically, even genuine multiculturalism would not be freedom for citizens. Full freedom would require each side to overcome the slavery that is multiculturalism, to have arrived in a time when they are no longer slaves in any form, when they are as free as they could imagine. But, contradictorily, multiculturalism is all the freedom they have, and they have to use the tools that they have to create a path to what might be the ultimate utopia, overcoming the ethnic and racial restrictions of the current condition and eventually ending up in a genuine, egalitarian, multicultural, radical democracy, which refashions even the state in the image that everyone desires.

The former ethical order abolishes all social differences; the latter privileges differences and recognizes them as freedom through self-determination and individuality. It is a bourgeois type of living that recognizes not the fulness of humanity but the abstraction of rights, such as owning property, including – highest form of all – the particular self. This is a kind of democracy where rights holders are lords who hold no one in bondage and slaves vis-à-vis the state. This way there are only thick relationships – between fellow citizens or fellow lords and also between the state as the powerful sovereign and individuals, who are equally powerful in their own rights.

The egalitarian world would be the triumph of the social and living in a society that improves ultimately on what Nature started with; the other world is living in a state where there are no limits on the virtues, values, and abilities with which Nature endows every individual. Life would no longer be an absolute tragedy, but neither would it be an absolute comedy – it would be both and also neither, depending on the individual perspective. This is why it would be so important for all Canadians to share the same perspective, to have a common spirit.

Multiculturalism suggests that these new and enlightened Canadians would try to limit their pessimism, to preserve all the happiness they have achieved and simply find a way to get along in a culture of bondage until they are fully free. In the meantime, they go about their work of constructing Canada with joy in their hearts, looking for vindication in a future that they already know to exist in thought only as a Just Society but of whose form they are unsure. So they try all forms, including some that they have never before seen or known, in the hope of arriving most quickly at one that produces genuine freedom.

Here I return to embrace as a means of coming into consciousness, extending Adelman's idea of finding love through mutual negation of one another – through playing with one another.[49] In this way, they expand the horizons of each lover with the addition of the other, so that in culmination, instead of playing individually on a small stage, they act out their lives on a bigger platform, with no externality as far as the senses can tell, for the other that was signified the external is now within their universe. This embrace should lack ulterior motives if individuals are to be acting out a modern tragedy that lacks a plot, without the confining hands of the fates. The only intentions would be those of good faith flowing from recognition that everyone is simply enjoying the performance, for that is all there really is to life: enjoying the "hour upon the stage" (*Macbeth*) or, in these more frentic times, the fifteen minutes of fame that American artist Andy Warhol said the world gives everyone.

This is the way to break the tensions between animal and human desires, for in this embrace there would be no higher desire than love and being loved. There would be no desire to transcend the identity anyone has on encountering the other – no need to see the encounter as a means of ultimately determining winners and losers, belongers and not, citizens and foreigners. Indeed, the embrace should be indiscriminate and indeterminate – a random act expressing fraternal love and recognition, an instantaneous satisfaction of the desire for unity, with the morality to be determined later, maybe in the morning after the bacchanalian revelry. What makes it justice is that the actions are acts of love, where the give and take allows the exchange and keeping of power. And justice would be more grace-like in nature than if it emerged from a cause-and-effect, proportional measurement of deserved and disseverment.

In any case, the desire of fear and to be feared would evaporate, as the participant would be operating ideally in a moment of love, in much the same way that societies assume that all members are operating out of a common good. Intentions would lessen if not disappear, and the embracers would be conscious of who they are but also conscious of only the moment. In this embrace, no distinction would exist between the Bad John, the Prince Charming, and the Sweet Boy, as it would throw a veritable blanket over them all, hiding their historical identities. Everyone would be just a player, savouring in the licentiousness of *poneria*, of living in a world where there are no lords and bondspeople – just players who are lovers. Everyone would retain his or her authenticity even while creating a group existence that incorporates all the different authenticities. This wider existence would be just life itself: happening and not responding to any intentions: life as a bacchanalian revelry – the only way, tragically, to enjoy it. This would be the reconciliation and renewing urge for life and the frivolity of living that must spring from the deep recess of the soul to overcome lamentation for things past. Such would be the frivolity of life and of loving – the elements necessary for a new spirit that has reconciled itself to change as an indispensable part of a historical society that is alive and adaptable. This would be genuine fraternity and recognition.

For in this setting, Canadians would be real and living beings produced in time. They would not be some abstract concept: while the idea of the Canadian might exist in thought, no single individual to represent the thought exists. Rather, Canadians would be more than the concept, which means that in their actions they would be negating the historical notions of who they are and should be. They would be overcoming the fixed identities of themselves and their actions, particularly the ethical relations of how they get along with one another; they would be creating a future that calls for the destruction of what was venerated, hollow, and even taboo in the past.

The future would be other than what they experience, and the experience would be enjoyable to people who are at the same time other than they but also by the lovers or the seeds from their bodies that live on beyond them. For in this struggle of intertwining, new life would be under creation – a new spirit breathing into the bodies of clay, a new spirit or consciousness now common among all the lovers and what they have created. When they rise up, figuratively leaving their lovers' beds, it would be as if they were escaping an empty grave – a chasm that shows they are leaving as a new type of human being that has within itself an experience and even a fear of existing on the other side; a grave that awaits the next time they have to return to this place of rest and struggle, when their human desires once again face challenges, as inevitably they will and must for them to remain human, by some animal motive. Sleeping Beauty and Prince Charming would have become new in the experience of the kiss. This would be the comedy that recognizes the human desires of multiculturalism: living bodies that were once dead but are now enjoying a new and different life. Collectively, this would be the social death or acceptance of change our mythology and the comedy that arises from the death imagined – just like when the newcomer to the kingdom, Prince Charming, kisses the socially dead, stirring both animal and human desires, and Snow White or Sleeping Beauty, she of ancient lineage, arises as if a new person, the old and the new now linking together to live happily ever after. None of this would happen if the kiss were between Sleeping Beauty and a Bad John, or in a state that was not willing, as a leap of faith, to change its belief that Prince Charming will always be a foreigner and stranger or that Sleeping Beauty can come to full life and bloom without him.

GENUINE MULTICULTURALISM AND RADICAL DEMOCRACY

Now I want to link the act of embracing to the notions of sharing and of death and resurrection that are at the heart of genuine multiculturalism.

Sharing in the conscious and mechanical sense is a special type of embrace, one in which the individual comes to know itself through actions, and where, at least momentarily, all existing morality disappears and gives way to something new. Here even the symbolism is important, for it would capture competing desires: the need to be loved and the desire for safety that results in fearing the object that should be loved. In this universal love-making, all bodies would be mere objects, things to use, as if they had undergone a death that has left them without a spirit. There is thus a ghoulishness in this love-making, a macabre dance resulting from the intertwining of bodies, but a dance that liberates people from human desires by reducing everything to the most basic, primitive, and primordial.

In effect, this is a return to the pre-social within a social embrace – a contradiction and irony in itself – whereas philosophers such as Kant can argue that each individual is truly an end and not a means to achieving some ulterior motive or desire. The struggle of minds that transcends the intertwining bodies would determine whose human dreams for a specific way and life, whose values, are so important that they are worthy of risking the dreamer's life. With human and animal desires clinching, there would be a symbolic return to the moment before the act of creation, or, better, to the biblical struggle between the brothers Cain and Abel for the affection and approval of their God. They would be letting their God, which ultimately is fate, determine the outcome: which way of life is worthy of validation and of preservation into the future.

This time we have learned from history and mythology that the winner must not kill the loser, for even the God of the piece can, and will, make a wrong decision, if only because there is a choice to make and the loser will disagree with it. We would have to accept that what would be born out of this embrace is a new spirit, wherein the divine has locked itself into a prison of sorts by now having to support and validate its choice as the basis for a new covenant with both those figures it favours and the rest. Spiritually, we would have a new definition of love that is most likely to be morally significant in terms of its relation between the divine and the losers; but it would also be a morality that shapes the relationship between the state and the winner and that shapes the shadow fighting between the winner and loser within the limits of the new covenant.

This embrace would also be carnal and at the animal level. As an act of *poneria*, in defiance of the gods and even of logic, this embrace is at times whorish and lascivious, and it produces what can at best be only miscegenation as a kind of hybridization. This is equally the idea of social construction, the rebellious notion of human beings as acts of their humanity seeking to make more perfect what nature or some god has made certain according to non-human ideals of perfection. The blue blood that would be at stake for those Canadians of ancient lineage would have gone. And there would be unhappiness, from brooding over what had disappeared and from the negation of the once-unchangeable Canada. Instead, there would remain only the larceny of just living, of having dirty hands and thoughts, and of pressing new boundaries – all that resting in the symbol of those immigrants seeking to become Canadians as part of their human desire for freedom.

Reconciliation into a new spirit that is Canada and an identity that is Canadian would be the act of playing, of passing between at least two different worlds that have to collapse into one – of recognizing that in this embrace of life, the same actor is subject and object, user and used, tragic and potentially comedic actor. But, then, that's life. This embrace is likely to produce not only a new spirit, but a new animal as well: Canadians who, in animal form, spring from the bodies of many different cultures but who as human spirits imagine themselves fully in the image of the state that made them, even if, ironically, in the physical sense they are actually making a new state.

I am arguing here what we have long known to be a living truth: that life itself ultimately must be the murderer of any concept, for a concept by definition is always too limiting and abstract to capture life. Life is the synthesis of time in any moment. It is the real and the authentic, and as the real it is always in a struggle with thought and the historical baggage of the concept. This is a primary lordship-and-bondage relationship. If Canadians are indeed the agents of time, if time is their essence, then for them to be free they must dominate and even kill the old concepts of who they are. But at the same time, they can never be so history-less as not to have a point of reference – which is equally the future that is the new desires and the past that effectively represents the errors of their ways. By their ethical actions, as life itself and as time, Canadians must kill the old and historical concepts of who they are. Canadians who see themselves as representing an entrenched order must willingly suffer metanoia for the greater good.

But they also have to take from the present the identity that their ethical relationships give them – an identity that usually those agents of time help shape. The Bad Johns and the tragic heroes of Canadian identity would strongly influence the new image – the same folks who would now be free to become the main actors in a genuinely multicultural Canada that is as radically democratic as the times demand. For, in this drama, they are the *real* Canadians, the embodiments of time and the agents for change: as Kojève says, "The Real resists Action and not Thought. Consequently, there is true philosophical 'Realism' [as opposed to idealism] only where philosophy takes account and gives an account of Action – that is, of History – that is, of Time."[50] And what is true for philosophy is also true for the humanities and the social sciences – for human life itself.

The moral of the tragedy seems to be that for as long as Canada needs immigrants, the old Canada as presumptive god will have to die in acts of metanoia, not only for its own survival but for it to remain, at least in thought, stoically free. What would be most distinguishing about this sovereign Canada is not its presumed godliness, but tragically its mortality, that it is merely human. For such is what it means to be a mortal god. That is the tragedy of genuine multiculturalism, one in which the abyss of life is always awaiting and in which only faith can decide if Canada is an empty grave of hope, as the Christian story of Easter suggests, or simply a hole, as in the view of the sceptics, awaiting its next victim with no hope of a tomorrow. Freedom is a different desire from the animal wish for survival. But the arrival of new immigrants also points to the resurrection or re-creation of a Canada that is more representative of humanity and hence, in human thought, free, even though it must always be mindful of its animal instincts for survival. With the arrival of every new immigrant, seemingly a barbarian out of a state of nature, comes a challenge to all those who believe that they have worked out a comfortable arrangement with fate and that they are the rightful masters of their universe.

The immigrant will demand changes, thereby throwing both the immigrants and the representatives of ancient Canada back into a tragedy to determine whose way of life to approve; otherwise, if the ancient Canadians were so entrenched and privileged that no one could touch them, they would see the new fiasco as a comedy of the newcomers' struggling against impervious limits. Rarely would immigrants, especially those of different religions and other social values, feel they were entering into a comedy. They must always come ready for a fight – to better themselves and to make the new country in their image, a situation wherein they would be very fortunate to begin anew with any love. It would then be up to the state and the Canadians of ancient lineage to transform these expectations into a comedy by loving rather than fearing the newcomers. This is where the biggest test of human values will take place. Will Canadians of today love the immigrants of tomorrow as much as they love themselves, or will they place the new Canadians in prisons of accommodation?

The message on the bodies of the new immigrants is clear to old-timers. It states starkly that they must change or die, for the times are indeed a-changing, and the times are making new women and men who in turn are making themselves into new Canadians. For the old will have to become new, as new as the newcomers who represent the change. For those seeking to preserve the past, this is a message that they must reject. In this case, Machiavellian fear would prolong the sense of tragedy and the unhappy consciousness that is bereft of love. Those who are open to the times and worry more about the future will see the arrivals of these strangers and their prophetic message as signalling the end of tragedy and proclaiming a new gospel about entering into a new land and time, into the times of a comedy with the expectations that we will all *live happily ever after*.

These immigrants would either be all Bad Johns or all Sweet Boys and Prince Charmings – in which case Canada would be unreconcilable as totally tragedy in the first case or absolute comedy in the second. Neither extreme would be the Canada we know as a living experience. In their humanity, native-born Canadians themselves are not of one extreme. We do not want to accept that Canada is still a hostile state of nature, as tragedy, nor do we want to totally fool ourselves that Canada is already a just state. It is a construction in process; we are making time by rearranging what makes life a tragedy, by trying to produce in the future a true comedy.

In this case, we must assume that all those people making the new Canada, whether immigrant or native to the new land, intend to be good – to eventually enter a land we call "Canada" that is good and just. Because good is changeable, we must presume that all those developing Canada as collectively part of their own *Bildung* are intentionally good and are good and worthwhile Canadians – all potentially Sweet Boys and Prince Charmings. We should treat them as Bad Johns only when their contraventions of the ethical order have proven themselves to be those of Bad Johns. Like any criminal or deviant in our society, they should always have the presumption of innocence and good faith until such presumption and faith are not reasonably supportable.

This is the equality of citizenship that flows out of this reconciliation, where, at the outset, difference and diversity simply mean difference and diversity and not, automatically, inequality. This equality would have its basis in faith and at times would even appear contrary to our common-sense understanding of what is natural and why some of us are seem-ingly more deserving than others of advantage and privilege. For practical purposes, there would be no need for accommodations on any groups just because of their "natural" differences and diversity. Accommodations that limit the aspirations of individuals or groups would simply be unethical and would not be of the common good. Individuals would believe that they can achieve their own *Bildung*, a self-construction that perfects and causes to flourish their best attributes and virtues.

They would be *free,* expressing their positive freedom by becoming what they imagine to be the ideal and best for themselves. What they become as self-made individuals would be the effect of what they initi-ated with what they can become in the future in mind. The final product that they become would be the result of their own efforts to transform themselves in a way that realizes the highest desires of their individual hearts. Through their own efforts, they would have realized the poten-tials that they have recognized in themselves and that they chose of their own free will to make real.

These individuals would be exercising their negative freedoms as well. There would be no limits on them, at least not without their consent. In particular, there would be no external limits that force them to conform to ideas of some tyrant of what is best in life for them. In this regard, what work they did would have the highest meaning for them, for it would be how they consume time remaking the world in their own image. They would be creating their own history, rather than working to achieve the ideals of some higher and superior lord whose interest differs radically from theirs. They would be making, therefore, a *meaningful* contribution to the *Bildung* of Canada, rather than spending time and their best efforts and attributes creating a way of life that during the process leaves them feeling alienated and unfulfilled.

Overall, these characters would be living both tragedy and comedy at the same time. But because they will probably feel that they are achiev-ing the justice they want for themselves, they would have every right to believe in a fairy-tale ending to the *Bildung* story of their lives. From their perspective, their living would be more a comedy than a tragedy. Life would be doubly reconcilable: as individuals who are happy with how they have perfected themselves and as members of a society where all citizens are helping to create a country that all individuals agree to be just for everyone and where possibly, eventually, they will all encounter true happiness. In this case, all citizens would be genuinely free, equal, sharing a form of solidarity that makes them think and act to the best of their intentions and in good faith, as if they were a single unit.

This, then, is the promise, and indeed the comedy, of genuine multiculturalism: that, with the materials to hand, we can create the folks who enjoy the highest quality of justice. Together, the different scenarios represent an irony and contradiction that is the fulness of life. But in a world that still appears either black or white, with marks of cutting and healing, diremption and reconciliation, tragedy and comedy, multiculturalism has ultimately and unintentionally developed two faces. For, contradictorily, multiculturalism sees itself as neither comedy nor tragedy if only because – like life itself – it is neither and yet it is both. Only fraternal love or its lack can really determine what to make of this drama that as a tragedy tells us there is no social justice but that as a comedy tells us that as long as we are alive, we can hope for a new life after death. For without the comedic hope that we shall all live happily ever after, our societies as they have emerged through time will have to let go of the belief that we live in liberal democracies where all citizens simply by virtue of being citizens are equal. No longer could we believe in fairy-tale endings – or in multiculturalism.

Notes

PREFACE

1 Peter Li, *Destination Canada: Immigration Debates and Issues* (Don Mills, ON: Oxford University Press, 2003).

2 Statistics Canada. *Census Snapshot – Immigration in Canada: A Portrait of the Foreign-born Population, 2006 Census.* www.statcan.gc.ca/pub/11-008-x/ 2008001/article/10556-eng.htm <5 April 2013>.

3 Typically, this is how the myth of these nationalisms is presented historically: "Francophones have long seen themselves not only as a distinct collectivity but, for over two centuries, as a collectivity rooted in Quebec. Inevitably, that has meant seeing (Canadian) Confederation on a dualist basis, as the creation of two founding peoples, with Quebec as the centre of the francophone people. Historically, English Canadians saw Confederation very differently, starting from the premise that they were part of a British nationality that transcended Canada. At the same time, English-Canadian leaders came to see Canada itself as a 'compact' among the colonies that formed it. To that extent, there was the basis of a common framework through which English Canadians and French Canadians could understand Canada. They might disagree over precisely who the parties to the compact were – whether colonies and provinces, or nations and 'races' – but at least Confederation itself was a compact among collectivities, however defined." Kenneth McRoberts. *Misconceiving Canada: The Struggle for National Unity* (Toronto: Oxford University Press, 1997), xiii–xiv.

A problem with this old school of thinking is, first, that it is hard to think of a time when the French and English Canadians as separate nationalisms had a lasting understanding about what is Canada. Second, and most important, this discussion of what constituted Canada too often limited itself to institutions, systems, and frameworks – colonies, provinces, nations, or races. Seldom did it focus on people – those individuals who actually live with and run those institutions and systems for supposedly the good of all the people, rather than for the good of nationalism. But perhaps just as egregious, this founding myth assumes a Canada that has already been fully *founded* and perfected. To a consociational compact, there can be no meaningful contribution by those not founding it: the aboriginal/ indigenous people who were never part of the initial compact (although recent reformulations by the federal government incorporated aboriginals as founding peoples) and individuals Canada has chosen as future citizens according to an individualistic points system that sees the newcomers as liberal individuals and not first and foremost as representative of any country, tribe, province, nation, race, or other collectivity.

4 Cecil Foster, *Blackness and Modernity: The Colour of Humanity and the Quest for Freedom* (Montreal/Kingston: McGill-Queen's University Press, 2007).

INTRODUCTION

1 Aristotle, *Politics*, trans. C.D.C. Reeve (Indianapolis: Hackett Publishing Company, 1998), 1253a–28–9.

2 Ian Burkitt, *Social Selves: Theories of Self and Society*, 2nd ed. (London: Sage Publications, 2008), 1–27.

3 This disbelief might be strongest among those people who see a discussion on multiculturalism in Canada as primarily among members of a dominant settler colony determining how to integrate in the body politic two other groups: the indigenous people, who have been dispossessed, and Canadians who are stigmatized as "immigrants" by those, even as later arrivals, sharing the ethnicity of the dominant groups when the settler colony was established and entrenched. See Will Kymlicka, *Multicultural Citizenship: Liberal Theory of Minority Rights* (Oxford: Clarendon Press, 1995) and *Finding Our Way: Rethinking Ethnocultural Relations in Canada* (Toronto: Oxford University Press, 1998.) The immediate problem with this approach is that until issues of possession and belonging – yes, legitimacy and jurisdiction – are settled by the aboriginal/indigenous peoples, all discussions on the fairness of multiculturalism remain hollow and, indeed, *unjust*. In the case of those called "immigrant Canadians," who have entered the settled colonies no matter how long ago but are not among the dominant group because of ethno-racial differences, isn't it true that their presence continuously unsettles what the dominant groups have produced and

expect? To this end, much of what I offer as genuine multiculturalism will be from the perspective of the *unsettlers* in such a discussion.

4 Isaiah Berlin, *Four Essays on Liberty* (London: Oxford University Press, 1969), 158.

5 In *Where Race Does Not Matter: The New Spirit of Modernity* (Toronto: Penguin, 2005), I argue that ideal multiculturalism aims to remove secondary and seemingly extrinsic social categories and identities that prevent all citizens from enjoying social equality. I contend this is the case where social hierarchies discriminate on the basis of race and racialization. I looked at how Western states' using notions of natural superiority and inferiority to determine who belongs intrinsically had led a country such as Canada into a social and political dead end. Canada adopted official multiculturalism to escape this historical impasse, to subsume all the differences and particularities in a common and inclusive universality of citizenship, One can make similar arguments for the types or hierarchies of social discrimination that cite such social categories as gender, ethnicity, sexuality, language, religion, place of birth, physical ability, which presume natural traits and can lead to social inequality. Most Western bills of rights do not outlaw social discrimination because of class, for neither nature nor intrinsicality is its sole determinant. Any of us might hit the jackpot in a lottery and thereby change our class, even if our nature never appears to alter.

6 Joseph Campbell, "Folkloristic Commentary," in *The Complete Grimm's Fairy Tales* (New York: Pantheon, 1944), 841.

7 Ibid., 864.

8 Anthony D. Smith, *Nations and Their Past: Opening Statement, The Warwick Debates*, www.lse.ac.uk/collections/gellner/Warwick.html <8 March 2011>. This reminds me of the suggestion by American political scientist Walter Lippmann that societies in the America(s) are the very opposite of those that value ethno-symbolism: "We are all of us immigrants in the industrial world, and we have no authority to lean upon. We are an uprooted people, newly arrived, and *nouveau riche*. As a nation we have all the vulgarity that goes with that, all the scattering of soul. The modern man is not yet settled in this world. It is big. The evidence is everywhere: the amusements of the city; the jokes that pass for jokes; the blare that stands for beauty, the folklore of Broadway, the feeble and apologetic pulpits, the cruel standards of success, raucous purity. We make love to ragtime and we die to it. We are blown hither and thither like litter before the wind. Our days are lumps of experience"; *Drift and Mastery: An Attempt to Diagnose the Current Unrest* (Madison: University of Wisconsin Press, 1985), 112. In this, he seems to echo the towering figures – Alexander

Hamilton, John Jay, and James Madison, who wrote articles in 1777 and 1778 that editors published as *The Federalist* in 1788 – who helped define the new republic: "I have as often taken notice, that Providence has been pleased to give this one connected country, to one united people: a people descended from the same ancestors, speaking the same language, professing the same religion, attached to the same principles of government, very similar in their manners and customs, and who, by their joint counsels, arms and efforts, fighting side by side throughout a long and bloody war, have nobly established their general liberty and independence"; Alexander Hamilton, James Madison, and John Jay, *The Federalist: With an Introduction and Notes by Robert A. Ferguson* (New York: Barnes and Nobles Classics, 2006), 14.

9 Alana Lentin and Gavan Titley explore recent attempts by some western European countries to introduce multicultural policies without changing underlying structures of the state. This result was merely the old racism appearing in a new guise, placing much of the blame for any seeming crisis of identity and belonging on outsiders, whom, even after becoming epistemic citizens, they still do not consider fully socialized. See Alana Lentin and Gavan Titley, *The Crises of Multiculturalism: Racism in a Neoliberal Age* (London: Zed Books), 2011.

10 Ironically, the incorporation of aboriginal peoples as an act of their freedom presents a mighty challenge to multiculturalism. And again this challenge speaks to how much multiculturalism is a child of the experiences of nation-state formation in the Americas. The problem is that even genuine multiculturalism assumes the conversation starts with a plurality of peoples from different geographical and cultural origins assembling in a land that the people collectively want to make a homeland. But in the Americas aboriginal peoples already possessed the land these peoples from elsewhere want. As liberal individuals, and as their name suggests, aboriginals have refused to give consent to membership of the new state other groups are developing. They steadfastly remain outside those states, often refusing to recognize them or to seek their recognition. How can these fundamental differences be reconciled? A solution to this challenge is beyond the scope of this book, except to claim that whatever is the solution, in a practical sense, the society that emerges would still be multicultural by nature. It would be at this point that the main arguments for a genuine multicultural state as an ethical or social order would have some currency. And it is also for this reason that genuine multiculturalism as a discourse begins as a discussion about liberal individuals achieving fully recognition and freedom – something that can occur only when individuals choose membership in a

society, even if it means making secondary or even rejecting any earlier affiliation or membership in in any natural groups or nations. Indeed, ironically, genuine multiculturalism argues that in places such as Europe indigenous people who claim that they are intrinsic to states carrying their name and supposed cultural memory would have to die and give way to a state in which immigrants and other non-indigenous people are recognized as fully members of the folk.

11 Orlando Patterson, *Slavery and Social Death: A Comparative Study* (Cambridge, MA: Harvard University Press, 1982). Delegates to the first women's rights convention in Seneca Falls, New York, in 1848 seem to have had a notion similar to social death in mind when they list among typical grievances against their enslavement by men: "He has made her, if married, in the eye of the law, civilly dead"; Declaration of Sentiments and Resolutions, Seneca Falls Convention, 1848, in *Race, Class and Gender in the United States*, 8th ed., ed. Paula S. Rothenberg (New York: Worth, 2010), 512.

12 Cecil Foster, *Blackness and Modernity: The Colour of Humanity and the Quest for Freedom* (Montreal/Kingston: McGill-Queen's University Press, 2007).

13 Pierre Elliott Trudeau, *The Essential Trudeau*, ed. Ron Graham (Toronto: McClelland & Stewart Inc., 1998), x–xi. Also see Michel Vastel, *The Outsider: The Life of Pierre Elliott Trudeau* (Toronto: Macmillan of Canada, 1990); Christina McCall and Stephen Clarkson, *Trudeau and Our Times: Volume 2 The Heroic Delusion* (Toronto: McClelland & Stewart, 1994); Ramsay Cook, *The Teeth of Time: Remembering Pierre Elliott Trudeau* (Montreal: McGill-Queen's University Press, 2006); John English, *Citizen of the World: The Life of Pierre Elliott Trudeau Volune One: 1919–1968* (Toronto: Alfred A Knopf Canada, 2006); John English, *Just Watch Me: The Life of Pierre Elliott Trudeau 1968–2000* (Toronto: Alfred A Knopf Canada, 2009).

14 Guy Laforest, *Trudeau and the End of a Canadian Dream* (Montreal: McGill-Queeen's University Press, 1995).

15 Richard M. Zaner, *The Way of Phenomenology: Criticism as a Philosophical Discipline* (New York: Pegasus, 1970), 78.

16 Cecil Foster, *Where Race Does Not Matter: The New Spirit of Modernity* (Toronto: Penguin, 2005).

17 John F. Walsh. *After Multiculturalism: The Politics of Race and the Dialectics of Liberty* (Lanham, MD: Lexington Books, 2008), 16.

18 Kat Glass, "U.S. Census: Everyone Will Be a Minority by 2042," *Miami Herald*, 14 Aug., 2008, www.miamiherald.com/news/5min/story/641325. html <21 July 2009>.

19 Sam Roberts, "New Demographic Racial Gap Emerges," *New York Times*, 17 May 2007, www.nytimes.com/2007/05/17/us/17census.html <17 May 2007>.

20 Yoav Orgad. "Before the Majority Becomes a Minority,"*Haaretz,* 21 July 21 2008 www.haaretz.com/hasen/spages/1003772.html <21 July 2008>.

21 Nikolai Berdyaev, *The Destiny of Man*, trans. Natalie Duddington (Westport, CT: Hyperion, 1979). 84.

22 John Locke, *Two Treatises of Government*, ed. Peter Laslett (Cambridge: Cambridge University Press, 1998).

23 In this book, I stay away from the debate on whether Hegel was racist in the way he depicted Africa as a place where the universalizing spirit of life/modernity was dead or nonexistent; G.W.F. Hegel, *Lectures on the Philosophy of History*, trans. J. Sibree (London: George Bell and Sons, 1878). Elsewhere in his work, Hegel appears more ambiguous, and as I argued in chapter 12 of *Blackness and Modernity*, he seems, in *Phenomenology of Spirit*, to view blackness as the creative force in the universe. Judith Butler, Jacques Derrida, and other scholars have argued that much of today's social and political thought owes a debt to Hegel. See Stuart Barnett, *Hegel after Derrida* (London: Routledge, 1998), and Judith Butler, *Undoing Gender* (New York: Routledge, 2004). Certainly, Caribbean thinker C.L.R. James agreed: *Notes on Dialectics: Hegel, Marx, Lenin* (London: Allison and Busby, 1980), as did the communitarians, pragmatists, and personalists who shape any discussion on multiculturalism. I aim to take what is good out of Hegel and ignore any racism, as do Butler, Derrida, and such black/African-American intellectuals as W.E.B. Du Bois, *The Souls of Black Folk* (New York: Modern Library Edition, 1996), Frantz Fanon, *Black Skin, White Masks* (New York: Grove Press, Inc., 1967), and Martin Luther King, Jr (see Rufus Burrow, Jr, *God and Human Dignity: The Personalism, Theology and Ethics of Martin Luther King, Jr.* (Notre Dame, IN: University of Notre Dame Press, 2006).

CHAPTER ONE

1 John Milton, "Paradise Lost," in *Paradise Lost and Paradise Regained* (New York: Penguin, 2010), Book X, ll. 1099–1104.

2 Frantz Fanon, *The Wretched of the Earth*, trans. Constance Farrington (New York: Grove, 1963), 41.

3 Cecil Foster. *Blackness and Modernity: The Colour of Humanity and the Quest for Freedom* (Montreal/Kingston: McGill-Queen's University Press, 2007).

4 Charles Fourier, "The Right to Work Denied," in *The Utopian Vision of Charles Fourier: Selected Texts on Work, Love, and Passionate Attraction*, ed. and trans. Jonathan Beecher and Richard Bienvenu (Boston: Beacon, 1971), 137.

5 Reinhold Niebuhr, *The Self and the Dramas of History* (New York: Scribner, 1955).

6 Northrop Frye, *The Bush Garden: Essays on the Canadian Imagination* (Toronto: House of Anansi, 1971), ix.

7 James H. Cone, *God of the Oppressed* (New York, Seabury, 1975).

8 Hannah Arendt, *On Revolution*, rev. ed. (New York: Viking, 1965), 107.

9 Samuel Moyn, *The Last Utopia: Human Rights in History* (Cambridge, MA: Harvard University Press, 2010).

10 John Rawls, *A Theory of Justice* (Cambridge, MA: Harvard University Press, 1971).

11 Trudeau, *The Essential Trudeau*, 17–18.

12 Thomas Axworthy and Pierre Elliott Trudeau, eds., *Towards a Just Society: The Trudeau Years*, trans. Patricia Claxton (Toronto: Viking, 1990); Trudeau, *The Essential Trudeau*.

13 I am borrowing "ancient lineage" from Toronto author Morley Callaghan, particularly the way he used it in the eponymous short story. Callaghan implies that an ancient lineage that hides from change and outside interaction atrophies and dies. In Canada, any historical claim to an ancient lineage must be fake; it is a history that fooled itself into believing what it had made up. See Morley Callaghan, "Ancient Lineage," in *Canadian Short Fiction*, ed. W.H. New (Toronto: Prentice Hall, 1986).

14 Isaiah Berlin, *Four Essays on Liberty* (London: Oxford University Press, 1969), 134.

15 George H. Mead, *Movements of Thought in the Nineteenth Century*, ed. Merritt H. Moore (Chicago: University of Chicago Press, 1936).

16 Hans-Georg Gadamer, *Truth and Method*, 2nd ed., trans. rev. Joel Weinsheimer and Donald G. Marshall (London: Continuum, 2004), 15.

17 Thus, as I argue in *Blackness and Modernity*, the living female in the dominant mythology is black until she enters service for the greater good – as a producer and guarantee of a future for a patriarchal state. For her to be mythologically white, she must be in the service of the nation-state.

18 Jane Billinghurst, *Temptress: From the Original Bad Girls to Women on Top* (Vancouver: Greystone, 2003), 10.

19 Ibid., 10.

20 Ibid., 4.

21 John Dollard, *Caste and Class in a Southern Town*, 2nd ed. (New York: Doubleday, 1949), 59–60.

22 Ibid., 57.

23 H. (Hugo) Krabbe, *The Modern Idea of the State*, trans. George H. Sabine and Walter J. Shepard (New York: Appleton, 1922), 9. This reminds me of Aristotle's observation in *Politics* that tyrants aim for their own pleasure while a king, akin to Krabbe's "rulership," seek the common good of the people.

24 Charles Taylor, "The Politics of Recognition," in *Multiculturalism: Examining the Politics of Recognition*, ed. Amy Gutmann (Princeton, NJ: Princeton University Press, 1994), 28.

CHAPTER TWO

1 Milton, "Paradise Lost," Book IX, ll. 5–7.

2 Lawrence W. Levine, *Black Culture and Black Consciousness: Afro-American Folk Thought from Slavery to Freedom* (Oxford: Oxford University Press, 1977).

3 Immanuel Kant, "Ideas for a Universal History with a Cosmopolitan Purposes" [1784: AA VIII, 15–31], trans. H.B. Nisbet, in *Kant: Political Writings,* ed. H. Reiss (Cambridge: Camridge University Press, 1991); Immanuel Kant, "Perpetual Peace" [1795: AA VIII, 341–386], trans. H.B. Nisbet, in *Kant: Political Writings.*

4 John Locke, *Two Treatises of Government*, ed. Peter Laslett (Cambridge: Cambridge University Press, 1998). sec. 134.

5 G.W.F. Hegel, *Phenomenology of Spirit*, trans. A.V. Miller (Oxford: Clarendon Press, 1977).

6 Frantz Fanon, *Black Skin, White Masks,* trans. Charles Lam Markmann (1967; reprint London: Pluto, 1986).

7 Will Kymlicka, *Finding Our Way: Rethinking Ethnocultural Relations in Canada* (Toronto: Oxford University Press, 1998).

8 Foster, *Blackness and Modernity*.

9 Alison Laurie, "The Girl in the Tower," *New York Review of Books* (1 May 2008), www.nybooks.com/articles/21318 <29 April 2008>.

10 Hegel, *Phenomenology*, 110.

11 George Wilhelm Friedrich Hegel, *Early Theological Writings*, trans. T.M. Knox with Richard Kroner (Chicago: University of Chicago Press, 1948), 304–5.

12 Ibid., 307.

13 William James, *The Principles of Psychology*, vol. 1 (Cambridge, MA: Harvard University Press, 1981/1950).

14 Urs Fuhrer, *Cultivating Minds: Identity as Meaning-Making Practice* (London: Routledge, 2004), 13–14.

15 Niebuhr, *The Self and the Dramas of History*.

16 Charles Taylor, *Sources of the Self: The Making of the Modern Identity* (Cambridge, MA: Harvard University Press, 1989), 3.

17 For example, Taylor says. "But like so much else in human life, this 'instinct' receives a variable shape in culture ... And this shape is inseparable from an account of what it is that commands our respect. That account seems to articulate the intuition. It tells us, for instance, that human beings are creatures of God and made in his image" (ibid., 5). Similarly, Niebuhr states, "In the western tradition, composed of Hebraic and Hellenic components, Hebraism supplied the poetic metaphor to designate human uniqueness. In the Bible it is affirmed that God made man 'after his image and in his likeness.'... It was left to the Greek philosophers to define the uniquely human more precisely. They did so by equating the divine element in man with his 'reason.' ... Obviously the rational faculty is a very significant part of the unique capacity which is indicated by the metaphor 'image of God'" (ibid., 3).

18 Rex Nettleford, *Inward Stretch, Outward Reach: A Voice from the Caribbean* (London: Macmillan Caribbean, 1993), 22.

19 Carolyn Cooper, *Sound Clash: Jamaican Dancehall Culture at Large* (New York: Palgrave Macmillan, 2004), 127.

20 Madonna Kolbenschlag, *Kiss Sleeping Beauty Good-bye: Breaking the Spell of Feminine Myths and Models* (1979; reprint San Francisco: Harper & Row, 1988), 103.

21 Ibid., 102.

CHAPTER THREE

1 Taylor, "The Politics of Recognition."

2 Charles Taylor, *The Malaise of Modernity* (Toronto: House of Anansi, 1991).

3 George H. Mead, *Movements of Thought in the Nineteenth Century*, ed. Merritt H. Moore (Chicago: University of Chicago Press, 1933), 23. As Mead explains, fraternity is the glue in a seemingly rational state: "In so far as a member of the community both enacts and obeys the laws of the community, a rational state is possible. If laws express the will of the whole community, the individual is able both to enact them and to obey them as a member of the whole community. And such laws could express the will of the whole community in so far as they expressed the rights of the members of that community, for rights exist only in so far as they are acknowledged, and only to the extent that those who claim them acknowledge them in the

person of others. That is, no man can claim a right which he does not recognize for others. No man can claim a right who does not at the same time
affirm his own obligation to respect that right in all others ... If men are
capable of recognizing rights as well as of claiming them, then they are capable of forming a community, of establishing institutions whose authority
will lie within the community itself" (13). Thus citizens of the state are
both master and slave unto themselves in the particular and master and
slave unto the state in general.

4 Reinhold Niebuhr, *Beyond Tragedy: Essays on the Christian Interpretation of History* (New York: Scribner's, 1937), 3–24.

5 Cone, *God of the Oppressed*, 11.

6 Adam Smith, *Adam Smith Today: An Inquiry into the Nature and Causes of the Wealth of Nations*, simplified, shortened, and modernized by Arthur Hugh Jenkins (1948; reprint Port Washington, NY: Kennikat Press, 1969).

7 Hegel, *Phenomenology of Spirit*, 109.

8 Ibid., 108–9.

9 Paul Meadows. *The Many Faces of Change: Explorations in the Theory of Social Change* (Cambridge, MA: Schenkman, 1971), 1.

10 Ibid.

11 Ibid., 3.

12 Hilde Lindermann Nelson, *Damaged Identities: Narrative Repair* (Ithaca, NY: Cornell University Press, 2001), 71.

13 Trudeau, *The Essential Trudeau*, 51.

14 Thomas Hobbes, *Leviathan*, ed. J.C.A. Gaskin (Oxford: Oxford University Press, 1996).

15 Ibid., 114.

16 Hegel, *Early Theological Writings*, 229.

17 Mead, *Movements of Thought*, 11.

18 Émile Durkheim, *The Elementary Forms of Religious Life*, trans. Karen E. Fields (New York: Free Press, 1995), 44.

19 Niccolo Machiavelli, *The Prince and Other Writings*, trans. Wayne A. Rebhorn (New York: Barnes & Noble Classics, 2003), 12.

20 Fanon, *The Wretched of the Earth*, 38–9 (my emphasis).

21 Dollard, *Caste and Class*, 3. Dollard also shows how quality of life differs vastly depending on the side of the tracks. It tends towards inferiority in "nigger town," as the book describes, and superiority in the white side. For a full description, see 1–15.

22 Hegel, *Phenomenology*, 126.

23 Ibid.

24 Ibid., 131.

25 Machiavelli, *The Prince*, xv.

26 Ibid., 162.

27 Terence Ball and Richard Bellamy, eds., *The Cambridge History of Twentieth-Century Political Thought* (Cambridge: Cambridge University Press, 2003), 112–13.

28 Ibid.

29 Stephen Steinberg, *The Ethnic Myth: Race, Ethnicity and Class in America* (New York: Atheneum, 1981), 16.

30 Ibid., 22.

31 Vic Satzewich and Nikolaos Liodakis, *"Race" and Ethnicity in Canada: A Critical Introduction* (Toronto: Oxford University Press, 2007), 40.

32 Robertson Davies, *The Merry Heart: Selections 1980–1995* (Toronto: Penguin Books, 1996).

33 Frye, *The Bush Garden*, 225.

34 Ibid., 226.

35 Leo Strauss, *On Tyranny*, rev. ed., ed. Allan Bloom (Ithaca, NY: Cornell University Press, 1975), 208.

36 Frye, *The Bush Garden*, vi.

37 Trudeau, *The Essential Trudeau*, 118.

38 Ibid., 119–20.

39 Ibid., 128.

40 J.L. Granatstein, *Who Killed Canadian History?* (Toronto: HarperCollins, 1998), xiv.

41 Ibid., xvii.

42 Unlike Granatstein, others are not always as clear about the history that explains the present Canadian living experience. For example, Canadian-born George Elliott Clarke often asks why Canada has to construe everything black in terms of the American experience. "Given the gravitational attractiveness of Black America and the repellent force of a frequently racist, Anglo-Canadian (and Québécois *de souche*) nationalism, African-Canadian writers feel themselves caught between the Scylla of an essentially US-tinted cultural nationalism and the Charybdis of their marginalization within Canadian cultural discourses that perceive them as 'alien.' Hence, African-Canadian writers are forced to question the extent and relevance of their Canadianness (that notoriously inexpressible quality)." Clarke singles me out for "insist[ing] that 'the reality for many blacks in Canada may be closer to what they see in the streets of New York or Los Angeles than what many people assume as being their reality'"; George Elliott Clarke, "Must All Blackness Be American? Locating Canada in Borden's 'Tightrope Time,' or Nationalizing Gilroy's *The Black Atlantic*,"

Centre for Language and Literature, Athabasca University, www.athabas-cau.ca/writers/geclarke_essay.html). However, in an introduction to his anthology of African-Canadian writings, Clarke writes, "As a child, I became African American. My soul instinct. At four, lodged near Halifax with my parents and two brothers, I lived heart-pure. One April day, three young white boys, passing our home, pitched rocks and yelled 'niggers' at my brothers and I. Unstung by the word, I hurled it back – with choice stones – at their surprised eyes. Alerted by the commotion, my father shooed the white children away, ushered us sons indoors. Before a stunned mirror he sat us, uncupboared two bowls of sugar – one white, the other brown – and preached, gently, that 'some white-sugar folks don't like brown-sugar folks.' ... From that moment, I was, irredeemably, African American ... I felt only semi-Canadian. I was not alone" (xi).

43 Ibid., 5.
44 Tom Kent, "Canada Is Much More Than a Hotel," *Globe and Mail* (25 April 2008). www.theglobeandmail.com/news/opinions/article680876. ece <28 April 2008>.
45 Trudeau, *The Essential Trudeau*, 172,
46 Royal Commission on Aboriginal Peoples, *Looking Forward, Looking Back* (Ottawa: Indian and Northern Affairs Canada, xxx), www.ainc-inac. gc.ca/ch/rcap/rpt/lk_e.html <5 Feb. 2008>.
47 Ibid.
48 Foster, *Where Race Does Not Matter*.
49 G.W.F. Hegel, *The Philosophy of History*, trans. J. Sibree (1956; reprint New York: Dover, 2004), 867.
50 T.S. Eliot, *The Waste Land and Other Poems* (London: Faber and Faber, 1940).

CHAPTER FOUR

1 Robert C. Tucker, ed., *The Marx–Engels Reader*, 2nd ed. (New York: Norton, 1978).
2 Judith N. Shklar, *Freedom and Independence: A Study of the Political Ideas of Hegel's Phenomenology of Mind* (Cambridge: Cambridge University Press, 1976), 11.
3 As Charles Taylor observes, "We become full human agents, capable of understanding ourselves, and hence of defining an identity, through our acquisition of rich human languages of expression ... I want to take 'language' in a broad sense, covering not only the words we speak but also other

modes of expression whereby we define ourselves, including the 'languages' of art, of gesture, of love and the like"; Taylor, *Malaise of Modernity*. 33.

4 Alexis De Tocqueville observed about the changes in language that followed the French Revolution of 1789: "The revolution followed its own course. No sooner did the head of this monster make its appearance, than its peculiar and terrifying character emerged. It first destroyed the political and then the civil institutions; it changed the laws and then the customs, procedures and even the language"; *The Ancient Regime and the Revolution*, trans. and ed. Gerald Bevan (1856; London: Penguin Books, 2008).

5 F.A. Hayek, *The Constitution of Liberty* (1960; reprint London: Routledge & Kegan Paul, 1976), 1.

6 Hegel, *Early Theological Writings*, 233.

7 Taylor, *Malaise of Modernity*, 1.

8 Foster, *Blackness and Modernity*.

9 Hugh R. Innis, *Bilingualism and Biculturalism: An Abridged Version of the Royal Commission Report* (Toronto: McClelland and Stewart in co-operation with the Secretary of State Department and Information Canada, 1973).

10 Hegel, *Phenomenology of Spirit*, 138.

11 Ibid.

12 "'We're Sorry,' Harper Says: Text of Address in House of Commons," *Toronto Star* (11 June 2008), www.thestar.com/News/Canada/article/441556 <20 March 2013>.

13 Prime Minister Harper issued this apology and also announced creation of a Community Recognition Program worth $25 million over four years as part of an effort at social retribution. The program aimed "to commemorate and educate Canadians about incidents which, while legal at the time, are no longer consistent with Canadian values" – specifically, internment of "enemy aliens" during the first and second world wars under the War Measures Act; the Head Tax and other immigration restrictions against Chinese Canadians; the *Komagata Maru* incident of 1914, which affected Indo-Canadians through restrictions under the Immigration Act's Continuous Journey clause of 1908; and the *St. Louis* incident of 1939, which affected Jewish Canadians in the context of the era's restrictive immigration policies. www.cic.gc.ca/english/multiculturalism/programs/community.asp, <8 July 2011>.

14 Judgements of the Supreme Court of Canada, Reference re Secession of Quebec, [1998] 2 SCR 217, s. 67.

15 John Austin, *Lectures on Jurisprudence: Or, the Philosophy of Positive Law*, abr. Robert Campbell (London: John Murray, 1913), 32.

16 Ibid., 30

17 Keith Banting and Will Kymlicka, "Do Multiculturalism Policies Erode the Welfare State?" e-mail exchange, 19 Sept. 2004; David Bennett, ed., *Multicultural States: Rethinking Difference and Identity* (London: Routledge, 1998); Neil Bissoondath, *Selling Illusion: The Cult of Multiculturalism in Canada* (Toronto: Penguin, 1994).

18 Francis Fukuyama, *The End of History and the Last Man* (1992; New York: Avon, 1998).

19 C.E. Merriam, Jr, *History of the Theory of Sovereignty since Rousseau* (New York: AMS Press, 1968), 136.

20 C.B. Macpherson, *The Political Theory of Possessive Individualism: Hobbes to Locke* (Oxford: Oxford University Press, 2011).

21 "Genuine multiculturalism" is loaded with idealism. While it may be normative, it resides in the future and emerges from everyday concerns for justice and even happiness. It is a natural outgrowth of a Christian ethic and thus shares some things with the religion itself: neither has ever gone fully into practice, and both rely on symbols rather than on practice. As Nicolas Berdyaev states, any social order that comes with its own hierarchies and social inequalities is not consistent with the earliest, revolutionary Christianity. Such an order saps the ideology of its creativeness or of the fiery spirit at inception. The resulting formalism is a result of expressing the spirit of the ideology in laws, which depersonalizes the process and robs it of its creativity. The same is true of the idealization and practices of multiculturalism. Thus multiculturalism too is tragic from inception, for it has conflicting goals for what should happen in practice and in theory. There is then a difference between idealized genuine multiculturalism and its daily practices. I argue that idealized multiculturalism ought to be the norm of daily practice – perhaps signalling even more the greater tragedy at stake by privileging one good over another.

22 Martin Heidegger, *Being and Time*, trans. John Macquarrie and Edward Robinson (Oxford: Blackwell, 2000).

23 Charles Taylor, *Reconciling the Solitudes: Essays on Canadian Federalism and Nationalism*, ed. Guy Laforest (Montreal/Kingston: McGill-Queen's University Press, 2007), ix.

24 Paul Franco, *Hegel's Philosophy of Freedom* (New Haven, CT: Yale University Press, 1999), 55.

25 Ibid., 55.

26 Hegel says the following, as Franco quotes him: "[Fichtean] natural rights offer us a picture of the complete lordship of the intellect and the complete bondage of the living being. It is an edifice in which reason has no part and which it therefore repudiates. For reason is bound to find itself most explicitly in itself self-shaping as a people (Volk), which is the most perfect organization that it can give itself. But that state as conceived by the intellect is not an organization at all, but a machine; and the people is not the organic body of a communal and rich life, but an atomistic, life-improvised multitude. The elements of this multitude are absolutely opposed substances. The unity of these elements is a concept; what binds them together is an endless domination. This absolute substantiality of points makes the basis for an atomistic system of practical philosophy in which, as in the atomistic system of nature, an intellect alien to the atom becomes law in the practical sphere under the name of *Right* ... *Fiat justitia, pereat mundus* is the law, and not even in the sense Kant gave it: 'Let right be done though all scoundrels in the world perish.' But rather in this sense: right must be done, even though for its sake, all trust, all joy and love, all the potencies of a genuinely ethical (*stlichen*) identity must be eradicated root and branch." *The Difference between Fichte's and Schelling's System of Philosophy*, trans. H.S. Harris and W. Cerf (Albany: SUNY Press, 1977), 148–9, in Franco, *Hegel's Philosophy of Freedom*, 55–6.

27 William Faulkner, "The Art of Fiction No. 12," interview by Jean Stein, *Paris Review* (spring 1956), www.theparisreview.org/interviews/4954/the-art-of-fiction-no-12-william-faulkner <20 March, 2013>.

28 Chris Armstrong, *Rethinking Equality: The Challenge of Equal Citizenship* (Manchester: Manchester University Press, 2006), 24–5.

29 Michael Ignatieff, *The Needs of Strangers* (London: Chatto & Windus, 1984); Beverley McLachlin, "The Civilization of Difference," Fourth Annual LaFontaine–Baldwin Lecture, Halifax, NS, *Globe and Mail*, 7 March 2003.

CHAPTER FIVE

1 William Shakespeare, *The Tragedy of Othello, the Moor of Venice*, ed. Michael Neill (Oxford: Oxford University Press, 2006), I.II.30.

2 Austin, *Lectures on Jurisprudence*, 27. Austin adds, "'Tis true in *theory*; but, then 'tis true in *practice*, says Noodle, with a look of most ludicrous profundity. But, with deference to this worshipful and weighty personage, that which is true in *theory* is also true in *practice*" (28).

3 Hegel, *Phenomenology of Spirit*, 180.

4 Explaining how this thinking becomes second nature to us, Austin says, "If I believe (no matter why) that acts of a class or descriptions are enjoined or forbidden by the Deity, a sentiment of approbation or disapprobation is inseparably connected in my mind with the thought or conception of such acts. And by this I am urged to do, or restrained from doing such acts, although I advert not to the reason in which my belief originated, nor recal [*sic*] the Divine rule which I have inferred from that reason" (*Lectures on Jurisprudence*, 28).

5 Ibid., 28.

6 Ibid., 199.

7 Nicolas Berdyaev, *The Destiny of Man* (London: Geoffrey Bles, 1937), 74.

8 Hegel, *Philosophy of History*, 26.

9 Ibid., 21.

10 Immanuel Kant, *Groundings for the Metaphysics of Morals*, trans. James W. Ellington (Indianapolis, IN: Hackett, 1981), 27.

11 Darrin M. McMahon, *Happiness: A History* (New York: Atlantic Monthly Press, 2006); Mark Kingwell, *Better Living: In Pursuit of Happiness from Plato to Prozac* (Toronto: Penguin, 1998).

12 Trudeau, *The Essential Trudeau*, 16.

13 Karl N. Llewellyn, "On Philosophy in American Law," *University of Pennsylvania Law Review* 82 (1934), as quoted in Peter J. Stanlis, *The Relevance of Edmund Burke* (New York: P.J. Kennedy, 1964).

14 This presence has resulted in heated debate over the role of the courts in a liberal democracy such as Canada, especially in the light of their constitutional role to interpret the law of the land, particularly, in Canada, the Constitution and the Charter of Rights and Freedoms. This issue arises at such moments as when the courts extends civil rights to minorities, such as gays and lesbians, women (in power and influence, if not numbers), and aboriginal and other ethnic groups, at the expense of what some critics may consider the common good of the state or the majority. Should there be any limits on democracy as the will of the majority or even of the dominant group(s) and over limits on the ability of unelected courts and judges to 'make' laws and even nullify laws that they rule abrogate or intrude on personal and minorities' rights in favour of a wider common good.

15 Jonathan Sacks, *The Dignity of Difference: How to Avoid the Clash of Civilizations*, rev. ed. (London: Continuum, 2003), 151.

16 Ibid., 151.

17 Ibid., 157.

18 The Bible formalizes this first covenant: "And he [Moses] took the book of the covenant, and read in the audience of the people: and they said, all that the Lord hath said will we do, and be obedient. And Moses took the blood and sprinkled *it* on the people and said, Behold the blood of the covenant, which the Lord hath made with you concerning all these words" (Exodus 24: 7–8, King James Version).

19 A propos of this second covenant, Jesus states at the Last Supper: "A new commandment I give unto you, That ye love one another; as I have loved you, that ye also love one another. By this shall all men know that ye are my disciples, if ye have love one to another" (John 13:34–5).

20 Michael Ignatieff, *The Rights Revolution* (Toronto: House of Anansi, 2000).

21 Jennifer Jackson Preece, *Minority Rights: Between Diversity and Community* (Cambridge: Polity, 2005).

22 Quebec Premier Jean Charest wrote a letter that appeared in major news-papers, admonishing those who criticize the province for being intolerant and anti-immigrant. He did so in the midst of a heated debate on whether Quebec should place accommodations on some residents – mainly non-white and non-Christian. Charest wrote, "People in the rest of Canada, in the United States and in France are wondering what's going on in Quebec, where we've earned a reputation for openness and tolerance. People are wondering what's happening here at a time when we need to open our doors to others because we're short of workers, because some of our regions are in a demographic decline, and because we're having fewer children. In Quebec, our tradition has always been one of protecting mi-norities and of openness to others. We are ourselves a minority in North America … Would René Lévesque, a great democrat, have accepted a bill creating two classes of citizens, a proposal that renounces the basic demo-cratic principle that we all have the right to vote, the right to participate in how our society is governed? This draft legislation by the PQ goes against the values of Quebec" (Jean Charest, "Quebecers Must Remain Open," *Montreal Gazette*, 30 Oct. 2007), www.canada.com/montrealgazette/story. html?id=oebbbae9-e293-4888-98ab-0908d8abface&p=2). The "social con-tract," if there is one, must occur after society has created the organism, and the act of creation is always one of covenant between the creators and the created.

23 Anthony Simon Laden and David Owen, eds., *Multiculturalism and Political Theory* (Cambridge: Cambridge University Press, 2007), 34.

24 Thomas Hobbes, *Leviathan*, ed. J.C.A. Gaskin (Oxford: Oxford University Press, 1996).

25 George H. Sabine and Walter J. Shepard, *Introduction*, in H. (Hugo) Krabbe, *The Modern Idea of the State* (New York: D. Appleton and Company, 1922), lxxiv.

26 Ibid., lxxv.

27 For the centrality of rights in the discussion, see Will Kymlicka, *Politics in the Vernacular: Nationalism, Multiculturalism, and Citizenship* (Oxford: Oxford University Press, 2000); Anthony Laden and David Owen, *Multiculturalism and Political Theory* (Cambridge: Cambridge University Press, 2007); Susan Moller Okin, "Is Multiculturalism Bad for Women?" in Joshua Cohen, Matthew Howard, and Martha C. Nussbaum, eds., *Is Multiculturalism Bad for Women?* (Princeton, NJ: Princeton University Press, 1999), 7–26; Alvin J. Schmidt, *The Menace of Multiculturalism: Trojan Horse of America* (Westport, CT: Praeger, 1997); Charles Taylor, "The Politics of Recognition"; Ignatieff, *The Rights Revolution*; and Lesley A. Jacobs, *Rights and Deprivation* (Oxford: Clarendon, 1993).

28 Statistics Canada, 2011 Census of Canada: Topic-based Tabulations: Detailed Mother Tongue (192), Single and Multiple Language Responses (3), Age Groups (7) and Sex (3) for the Population Excluding Institutional Residents of Canada, Provinces, Territories, Census Divisions and Census Subdivisions, 2011 Census. www12.statcan.gc.ca/census-recensement/2011/ <17 March 2013>.

29 Richard Rorty, *Contingency, Irony, and Solidarity* (Cambridge: Cambridge University Press, 1989), 102.

30 Nicolai Berdyaev, *The Destiny of Man* (London: Geoffrey Bless, 1937), 148.

31 As quoted by Carter G. Woodson, ed., *The Mind of the Negro as Reflected in Letters Written during the Crisis, 1800–1860* (1926; reprint New York: Russell & Russell, 1969), 293.

32 Ibid.

33 Thomas Paine, *The Essential Thomas Paine*, intro. Sidney Hook (New York: New American Library, 1969), xi.

CHAPTER SIX

1 Malcolm X, New York City, 1 May 1962, as quoted in James H. Cone, *Martin and Malcolm and America: A Dream or a Nightmare* (Maryknoll, NY: Orbis, 1991), 89.

2 Geoffrey Brereton, *Principles of Tragedy: A Rational Examination of the Tragic Concept in Life and Literature* (Coral Gables, FL: University of Miami Press, 1968), 2. As I show below, this is a very narrow, and often

misleading, definition both of tragedy, as it does not imply the character's wilful courting of this "disaster," or choosing to become tragic, and of the character's nobility in facing up to and accepting the consequences of his or her actions and choices, knowing well in advance that they may even be fatal.

3 Darrin M. McMahon, *Happiness: A History* (New York: Atlantic Monthly Press), 9.

4 Ibid., 8.

5 Thomas McCarthy, *Race, Empire, and the Idea of Human Development* (Cambridge: Cambridge University Press, 2009), 40.

6 Joshua Foa Dienstag, *Pessimism: Philosophy, Ethic, Spirit* (Princeton, NJ: Princeton University Press, 2006).

7 Trudeau, *The Essential Trudeau*, 182 (my emphasis).

8 Ibid., 180–1.

9 John Dewey, *Democracy and Education* (New York: Macmillan, 1916).

10 Alain Touraine, *Can We Live Together? Equality and Difference*, trans. David Macey (Stanford, CA: Stanford University Press, 2000), 30.

11 Robert Prus, "Symbolic Interaction and Classical Greek Scholarship: Conceptual Foundations, Historical Continuities, and Transcontextual Relevancies," *American Sociologist* 35 (spring 2004): 5–33.

12 Hegel, *Philosophy of History*, 13–14.

13 William Kerr, *Tragedy and Comedy* (New York: Simon and Schuster, 1967), 16.

14 Ibid., 15–16.

15 Julian Gough, "Divine Comedy," *Prospect* (26 May 2007), www.prospectmagazine.co.uk/2007/05/greek-comedy-modern-literary-novel/.

16 Kerr, *Tragedy and Comedy*, 78–9.

17 Ibid., 19.

18 Sharon Morgan Beckford, *Naturally Woman: The Search for Self in Black Canadian Women's Literature* (Toronto: Inanna, 2011).

19 Paul Tillich, *Love, Power and Justice* (New York: Oxford University Press, 1954), 32.

20 Ibid, 33.

21 Howard Adelman, "Of Human Bondage: Labor and Freedom in the *Phenomenology*," in John O'Neill, ed., *Hegel's Dialectic of Desire and Recognition: Text and Commentary* (Albany: State University of New York Press, 1996), 176–7.

22 Ibid., 178.

23 For this and the following references, see Plato, "Symposium," in *The Collected Dialogues of Plato including the Letters*, ed. Edith Hamilton and

Huntington Cairns, trans. Michael Joyce, Boillingen Series 71 (1963; Princeton, NJ: Princeton University Press, 1999), 207d–208b.

24 Ibid.

25 According to Berdyaev: "The faculty of imagination is the source of all creativeness. God created the world through imagination. In him imagination is an absolute ontological power. Imagination plays an enormous part in the moral and spiritual life of man. There is such a thing as the magic of imagination." Berdyaev, *Destiny of Man*, 75.

26 *Poneria*: iniquity, wickedness; evil plots with regard to another person or other people, hateful prejudice (Matt. 22:18; Acts 3:26).

27 Gadamer, *Truth and Method*, 105.

28 Cedric H. Whitman, *Aristophanes and the Comic Hero* (Cambridge, MA: Harvard University Press, 1964), 219.

29 Rawls, *A Theory of Justice*; Axworthy and Trudeau, *Towards a Just Society*; Charles Taylor, "Modernity and Difference," in Paul Gilroy, Lawrence Grossberg, and Angela McRobbie, eds., *Without Guarantees: In Honour of Stuart Hall*(London: Verso, 2000); Emmanuel Chukwudi Eze, *Achieving Our Humanity: The Idea of the Postracial Future* (New York: Routledge, 2001); Stephen Toulmin, *Cosmopolis: The Hidden Agenda of Modernity* (Chicago: University of Chicago Press, 1992).

30 John W. Burbidge, *Hegel on Logic and Religion: The Reasonableness of Christianity* (Albany: State University of New York Press, 1992); John Burbidge, *Being and Will: An Essay in Philosophical Theology* (New York: Paulist Press, 1977); Adelman, "Of Human Bondage"; Axworthy and Trudeau, *Towards a Just Society*; Trudeau, *The Essential Trudeau*.

CHAPTER SEVEN

1 The Used, "Poetic Tragedy," lyrics by Robert Edward "Bert" McCracken, Branden Steineckert, and Jeph Howard. *The Used* (EMI Blackwood Music Inc. © The Used Movement Music, 2002).

2 See Clair Hoy, *Canadians in the Civil War* (Toronto: Mcarthur & Company, 2004); Adam Mayers. *Dixie and the Dominion: Canada, the Confederacy and the War of the Union* (Toronto: Dundurn Press, 2003); Robin Winks. *Canada and the United States: The Civil War Years* (Montreal: McGill-Queen's University Press, 1998).

3 As quoted in Terence Ball and Richard Bellamy, *Cambridge History of Twentieth-Century Political Thought* (Cambridge: Cambridge University Press, 20??), 122.

4 Judgments of the Supreme Court of Canada. *Reference: re Secession of Quebec [1998]* 2 SCR 217, scc.lexum.umontreal.ca/en/1998/1998rcs2-217/1998rcs2-217.html <18 Dec.e 2007>.

5 Ibid.

6 Ibid.

7 Ibid.

8 Margaret Mitchell, *Gone with the Wind* (1937; New York: Pocket Books, 2008), 292.

9 Ibid, 293–4.

10 Hegel, *Early Theological Writings*, 229.

11 Abraham Lincoln. *Proclamation Suspending the Writ of Habeas Corpus* (Washington, DC: 24 Sept. 1862) teachingamericanhistory.org/library/index.asp?document=425 <20 Nov. 2007>. While Trudeau did not use the word "insurrection" in his speech to the nation announcing the implementation of the War Measures Act, such action can occur only during a war. Section 2 states, "The issue of a proclamation by His Majesty, or under the authority of the Governor in Council shall be conclusive evidence that war, invasion, or insurrection, real or apprehended, exists and has existed for any period of time therein stated, and of its continuance, until by the issue of a further proclamation it is declared that the war, invasion or insurrection no longer exists."

12 Michael Omi and Howard Winant, *Racial Formation in the United States: From the 1960s to the 1980s* (1986; New York: Routledge, 1989), 64–5.

13 Ibid.

14 Ibid.

15 See Foster, *Blackness and Modernity.*

16 John Porter, *The Vertical Mosaic: An Analysis of Social Class and Power in Canada* (Toronto: University of Toronto Press, 1985); Will Kymlicka, *Multicultural Citizenship: Liberal Theory of Minority Rights* (Oxford: Clarendon Press, 1995).

17 Howard Palmer, "Reluctant Hosts: Anglo-Canadian Views of Multiculturalism in the Twentieth Century," in Gerald Tulchinsky, ed., *Immigration in Canada: Historical Perspectives* (Toronto: Copp Clark Longman, 1994), 300.

18 Northrop Frye, *Mythologizing Canada: Essays on the Canadian Literary Imagination,* ed. Branko Gorjup (Ottawa: Legas, 1997); Frye, *Bush Garden.*

19 Raymond Williams, *Modern Tragedy* (Lancashire, England: Broadview Press, 2001).

20 Michel Foucault, *The Politics of Truth*, trans. Lysa Hochroth and Catherine
   Porter, Semiotext(e) Foreign Agent Series (Los Angeles: Semiotext(e), 2007).
21 John Finnis, *Natural Law and Natural Rights* (Oxford: Clarendon, 1980),
   16.
22 Berdyaev, *Destiny of Man*, 31–2.
23 Finnis, *Natural Law and Natural Rights*, 15fn. Here Finnis draws attention
   to Plato, *Republic* IX: 582a–e and III:408d–409e.
24 An example of this angst was on display in spring 2007 in the *Toronto
   Star*, Canada's largest-circulation and most liberal newspaper. In a series
   on multiculturalism, it found unease across the land primarily because
   newcomers from new sources were not adapting to some unspecified ideal
   of Canada and its values: "But the phenomenon of non-Western immigration has produced clouds on the Canadian multicultural horizon as well.
   The post-war immigrants originally addressed by the policy (mainly
   European, nominally Christian) have been replaced by a wide range of
   culturally and religiously diverse groups. The old assumption that integration – a sense of belonging to Canada – almost always occurs by the second generation no longer holds up. Breaking the silence that usually
   surrounds the subject, some analysts are asking whether it's time to rethink the policy, revamp it to reflect the new, 21st-century 'mosaic.' In no
   way at present, they say, does it encourage newcomers to move from immigrant 'them' to citizen 'us.' Nor does it stress that Canada holds certain
   non-negotiable values – the rule of law, sexual equality, freedom of expression and tolerance. If nothing else, they argue, *that* must be made explicit."
   Lynda Hurst, "Uneasy Mosaic: Multiculturalism Policy Falling Behind the
   Times," *Toronto Star*, 29 May 2007, www.thestar.com/News/article/
   218666 <29 May 2007>. One article claimed that immigration and the
   Charter of Rights have created fertile ground for conflict between "fundamental values of Canada" and a desire by newcomers, mainly non-
   Christian and non-European, for dominance in culture and law. It cited
   the attempt by some Muslims to apply Shari'a law in Canada and a few
   Muslims' seeming justification of wife killing for religious reasons: "True
   story: man kills wife, stabbing her in the neck 19 times with a steak knife,
   is convicted of first-degree murder and appeals on basis that she was un-
   faithful and, as a devout Muslim, he was protecting family honour. Nice
   try, and maybe elsewhere in the world Adi Abdul Humaid might have been
   acquitted. But the United Arab Emirate citizen made the mistake of mur-
   dering Aysar Abbas in Ottawa in 1999 and, ultimately, the Ontario Court
   of Appeal rejected his appeal."Linda Diebel, "When Rights Collide with
   Freedoms: Gender, Cultural, Religious: Looking for the Balance in a

Multicultural Society," *Toronto Star*, 28 May 2007, www.thestar.com/
printArticle/218355 <28 May 2007>.

25 Hurst, "Uneasy Mosaic."

26 Mary Stewart Van Leeuwen, *After Eden: Facing the Challenge of Gender Reconciliation* (Grand Rapids, MI: W.B. Eerdmans, 1993), 3.

CHAPTER EIGHT

1 Claudia Rosett, "A Tyrants Club: The U.N. Human Rights Commission Is Worse Than a Joke," *Wall Street Journal*, 22 Jan. 22, 2003, www.opinionjournal.com/columnists/cRosett/?id=110002944 <20 March 2013>.

2 For fuller discussion, see Innis, *Bilingualism and Biculturalism*; Foster, *Blackness and Modernity*. Also bear in mind the following point made by Will Kymlicka – that multiculturalism was effectively a policy without a plan or an outcome other than to save the Canadian federation. "What, then, is multiculturalism 'really' about? We cannot answer this question by referring to some canonical statement of its concepts or principles, for there is no such statement ... We now know that there was no well-developed theory underlying the original policy. It was introduced in haste, largely as a way of deflecting opposition to the apparent privileging of French and English that was implicit in the introduction of official bilingualism. Multiculturalism was introduced without any real idea of what it would mean, or any long-term strategy for its implementation ... To understand the meaning of multiculturalism, therefore, we need to look at what it does in *practice*." Will Kymlicka, *Finding Our Way: Rethinking Ethnocultural Relations in Canada* (Toronto: Oxford University Press:1998/2004). 40. In other words, multiculturalism is improvisation at the highest level – the image of tragedians at their wits' ends using whatever is at hand to get through the moment, simply hoping to arrive in a later moment of comedy when, magically, everything works well. In addition, because it was intended to unsettle the so-called societal cultures that were based on English and French nationalisms, multiculturalism in practice is discussion on how immigrants – people who arrive as individuals and not as nationalist representatives, can create a new state where in all their many natural differences and multiple diversities and cultures they can become citizens as persons embedded in a culture of their making.

3 Paul Ricoeur, *Lectures on Ideology and Utopia* (New York: Columbia University Press, 1916).

4 T.H. Green, *Lectures on the Principles of Political Obligation and Other Writings*, eds. Paul Harris and John Morrow (Cambridge: Cambridge University Press, 1986).

5 Benedict Anderson, *Imagined Communities* (London: Verso, 1991).

6 Martin Heidegger, *Being And Time*, trans. John Macquarrie and Edward Robinson (Oxford: Blackwell Publishers, 2000); Hegel, *Phenomenology of Spirit*; Taylor, *Sources of the Self*,

7 Sheila Greeve Davaney, *Historicism: The Once and Future Challenge for Theology (Guides to Theological Inquiry)* (Fortress Press, 2006), 41 (my emphasis).

8 Ibid., 38.

9 Jacques Maritain, *The Range of Reason* (New York: Scribner's, 1943), 54–5. Maritain had immense influence on Pierre Trudeau, the father of Canadian multiculturalism.

10 Jacques Maritain, "Man and the State," in Joseph W. Evans and Leo R. Ward, eds., *The Social and Political Philosophy of Jacques Maritain: Selected Readings*(New York: Scribner's, 1955), 136–7.

11 Ibid., 136–7.

12 Rex Martin, "T.H. Green on Rights and the Common Good," in William Sweet, ed., *Philosophical Theory and the Universal Declaration of Human Rights* (Ottawa: University of Ottawa Press, 2003), 76–7.

13 John Locke, *Two Treatises of Government*, ed. Peter Laslett (Cambridge: Cambridge University Press, 1998).

14 G.W.F. Hegel, *Lectures on the Philosophy of History*, trans. J. Sibree (London: George Bell, 1878).

15 This contradiction arises frequently. On 20 April 2007, under the headline "Tory: Hijab Incident 'Sad,'" the *Chronicle Herald* in Halifax wrote about a meeting of the Conservative federal government's caucus: "The chairman denounced the expulsion of hijab-clad Muslim girls from sport events in Quebec, calling it a sad over-reaction at a time Canadians should be celebrating the anniversary of the Charter of Rights and the minority freedoms it protects. Tory caucus chairman Rahim Jaffer broke his government's determined silence on the ouster of the girls from soccer and tae kwon do tournaments in Quebec in recent weeks ... He called the case of the five girls at last weekend's tae-kwon-do event especially said because it coincided with the 25th anniversary of the Charter of Rights and Freedoms. 'There seems to be a little bit of over-sensitivity against the hijab,' Jaffer said in an interview. 'We've seen this more and more over the last little while. And it is unfortunate that that sort of attitude is developing – especially when this is the week that we're celebrating the anniversary of the Charter. You have the ability to practice your religion freely and not be discriminated against on the basis of any characteristics here in Canada. Yet somehow that particular part of the Charter seems to be applied very

loosely in some cases.'" The Conservative government tends to do little to mark the Charter's anniversary (17 April).

16 Foster, *Where Race Does Not Matter*.

17 See, for, section 27 of the Charter of Rights and Freedoms: "This Charter shall be interpreted in a manner consistent with the preservation and enhancement of the multicultural heritage of Canadians." The Canadian Multicultural Act states that the federal government "recognize(s) and promote(s) the understanding that multiculturalism reflects the cultural and racial diversity of Canadian society and acknowledges the freedom of all members of Canadian society to preserve, enhance and share their cultural heritage." Perhaps my argument here is that if Canada tells itself often enough that it is multicultural, it will start to believe that it really is, and this belief will inform its behaviour, thereby creating a multicultural consciousness or spirit.

18 This is a vital issue not only to Canadians who consider themselves mainstream, but also to people who see themselves as authentically American, English, French, or any of Western culture and nationality. English-born Christopher Hitchens wrote in an American publication, *Vanity Fair*, of the ethnic changes that have overtaken parts of England – for example, London becoming "Londonistan" – within one generation, as Britain "move[d] from cricket and fish-and-chips to burkas and shoe-bombers." According to Hitchens, "They say that the past is another country, but let me tell you that it's much more unsettling to find that the present has become another country, too. In my lost youth I lived in Finsbury Park, a shabby area of North London, roughly between the old Arsenal football ground and the Seven Sisters Road. It was a working-class neighborhood, with a good number of Irish and Cypriot immigrants. Your food choices were the inevitable fish-and-chips, plus the curry joint, plus a strong pitch from the Greek and Turkish kebab sellers. There was never much 'bother,' as the British say, in Finsbury Park. Greeks and Turks might be fighting in Cyprus, but they never lifted a hand to one another in London. Many of the Irish had republican allegiances, but they didn't take that out on the local Protestants. And, even though both Cyprus and Ireland had all the grievances of partitioned former British colonies, it would have seemed inconceivable – unimaginable – that any of their sons would put a bomb on the bus their neighbors used. Returning to the old place after a long absence, I found that it was the scent of Algeria that now predominated along the main thoroughfare of Blackstock Road. This had had a good effect on the quality of the coffee and the spiciness of the grocery stores. But it felt odd, under the gray skies of London, to see women wearing the veil, and

even swathed in the chador or the all-enveloping burka. Many of these Algerians, Bangladeshis, and others are also refugees from conflict in their own country. Indeed, they have often been the losers in battles against Middle Eastern and Asian regimes which they regard as insufficiently Islamic. Quite unlike the Irish and the Cypriots, they bring these far-off quarrels along with them. And they also bring a religion which is not ashamed to speak of conquest and violence." Christopher Hitchens, "Multiculturalism: Londonistan Calling," *Vanity Fair*, June 2007, www. vanityfair.com/politics/features/2007/06/hitchens200706 <21 May 2007>. However, in an interview that appeared along with this article, Hitchens says that he disagrees with people who say that multiculturalism is destructive of British values. "No," he said, "I'm in favor of multiculturalism. I'm defending it against the hideous challenge from political Islam."

Another, and at times alternative, view to Hitchens's comes from Walter Laqueur. He compares the Europe of generations ago and the Europe of today in terms of what a visitor would encounter in a European city such as London: "Today, if our friend really wanted to see the future, a short walk or bus ride would do in order to get a preview of the shape of things to come. An excellent starting point would be Neukölln or Cottbusser Tor in Berlin, or Saint-Denis or Evry in the Paris *banlieues*. In some ways, moving about European cities has become much easier. There are fewer language difficulties; the argot of the outlying areas of major cities populated by immigrants, the *banlieues* (*verlan*), we are told by *Le Monde*, consists of 400 words. True, in Kreuzberg, a knowledge of Turkish could be more helpful than German. In London, if our visitor had a special interest in Southeast Asia, we would take him to Brent, in the north; if he was interested in things African, we would take a taxi to Peckham.

"Those parts offer much of interest, and the guidebooks recommend their gastronomic delights. The sounds of Cairo (minus the architecture) and the sights and smells of Karachi and Dacca can be found. A few of the quarters will strike the visitor as threatening (more perhaps in Paris than in London and Berlin), but many are charmingly exotic, the women in black in their *hijab*; the halal butchers, the kebab palaces, and the couscous eating places enriching the menus of the local restaurants, the Aladdin cafes and the Marhaba minimarkets. That is a far cry from the 1950s and 60s, when those areas were British or French or German working-class neighborhoods. The locals have mostly moved out. Such quarters are spreading, and within a generation they will cover a much greater area of the big cities of Europe.

"Great changes in the cities of Europe will occur within the next decades. Will they be one-sided, affecting only the natives and not the newcomers? Perhaps the Muslim women will opt for colors other than black, and perhaps the *hijab* will be reduced to something more symbolic. Perhaps mosque attendance will drop just as church attendance has in Western Europe ...

"Many of the immigrants today live in societies separate from those of their host countries. That is true in big cities and small. The new immigrants have no German or British or French friends. Their preachers tell them that their values and traditions are greatly superior to those of the infidels, and that any contact, even with neighbors, is undesirable. Their young people complain about being excluded, but their social and cultural separateness is quite often voluntary. Western European governments and societies are often criticized for not having done more to integrate the new citizens. But even if they had done much more, is it certain that integration would have succeeded?

"Europe as we once knew it is bound to change, probably out of recognition, for a number of reasons, partly demographic and cultural, but also political and social. Even if Europe should unite and solve the various domestic crises facing it, its predominant place in the world and predominant role in world affairs is a thing of the past. What kind of new Europe is likely to emerge as a successor to the old Continent? That, of course, is an open question, whose answer depends on events not only in Europe but also in other parts of the world." Walter Laqueur. "So Much for the New European Century," *Chronicle of Higher Education*, 11 May 2007, chronicle.com/temp/reprint.php?id=7fsyrdbskbvt8ghvo1pxbn18bz1f47jd <22 May 2007>.

19 Three good examples of this concern follows. The first is an article by pollster and social commentator Allan Gregg after Canadian federal elections in 2006 and 2008 that produced minority governments. In *Walrus* magazine, Gregg wrote about the polarization in Canadian politics, Parliament, and government as stemming from the country's ethnic ghettoes. Instead of producing unity and stability, they were generating fragmentation, disunity, and political dysfunction. Instead of its being a European "nation" because of its dominant European culture, Gregg saw Canada in danger of becoming a microcosm of the world – a multiculturalism without unity. "Canada, Britain, France, and Australia share a common dilemma. All are stable constitutional democracies that are based on the primacy of individual rights and all share secular-humanist leanings. Each recognizes the need for

immigration and is coping with growing visible-minority populations, and each is struggling in a post-nation-state world where well-defined national purposes are less certain. Without grand designs or defining national projects, new immigrants run the risk of arriving and going about their business with little sense of the roles they can play in their adopted homeland. With no national mythology to adhere to, they naturally retreat to the familiar, seeking out their own communities.

"Throughout Europe, nations known for their liberalism are now engaged in vigorous debate around one central question: what is more important to our national direction, inclusion under the umbrella of a unifying nationalism or the celebration of uniqueness and difference? Defenders of multiculturalism argue that these two options are not mutually exclusive and that both can be achieved by open, tolerant, and just societies. But in Britain, the decision to encourage uniqueness drove certain second-generation groups away from the mainstream and its values; in France, assimilationist policies have led to feelings of intense isolation.

"In Canada, we may live in a multicultural society, but the evidence suggests that fewer and fewer of us are living in multicultural neighbourhoods. Furthermore, the tradition of immigrants clustering in a community for one generation before the next generation moves on and 'melts' into mainstream culture seems to be breaking down. Large districts are evolving into areas dominated by individual ethnic groups that have chosen to live apart from those who do not share their ancestry. Meanwhile, most white Canadians would confess that the vast majority of their friends look a lot like they do and that they tend to stay within their own communities, rarely venturing into the ethnic enclaves that are burgeoning, especially in suburban Canada." Alan Gregg, "Identity Crisis: A Twentieth-Century Dream Becomes a Twenty-First Century Conundrum," *Walrus*, March 2006, www.walrus-magazine.com/articles/2006.03-society-identity-crisis/4/ <22 May 2007>.

A second and different view appeared in the *Globe and Mail* a few years later vis-à-vis the vibrancy of a cosmopolitan Muslim community in Calgary. "The city remains a haven for oilmen and cowboys, and is the political heartland of Prime Minister Stephen Harper's Conservatism. But Muslims here say their community now comprises about 65,000 Calgarians, most arriving within the span of two generations. As they've grown, Calgary Muslims have prided themselves on their unity. Other Islamic communities cleave by race, language and sect, but here, people from all corners of the globe pray together at a Sunni mosque in the city's southwest. The city's main mosque was surrounded by farmland when built 30 years ago. Today, its minaret looks out over a residential neighbourhood that has built up around it." Colin Freeze, "Amid Cowboys and Tory Blue, Muslims Thrive," *Globe and Mail*, 22 May 2007, www.theglobeandmail.com/servlet/story/ RTGAM.20070522.wcalgary22/BNStory/National/home <22 May 2007>.

A third example, countering Gregg's yearning for a centralizing mythology, came with French President Nicolas Sarkozy's announcement in May 2007 of his new government against the backdrop of the alienation that had produced rioting, mainly by non-white and Muslim youths. The Associated Press reported: "Rachida Dati, a woman with North African roots, was named justice minister in France's new cabinet today, an appointment rich with symbolism that the law will be colourblind in a country still coping with the fallout from riots across immigrant-heavy neighbourhoods two years ago. She was one of seven women that President Nicolas Sarkozy, himself of Hungarian immigrant background, appointed to his 15-member cabinet – making good on a campaign promise of gender balance after decades where women often played secondary roles or were outnumbered by men … Never before has a woman with family ties in France's former North African colonies been given such a high-ranking ministry, said Sarkozy spokesperson Franck Louvrier. Dati, a 41-year-old lawyer, was raised in a housing project in the winemaking Burgundy region. She is the second child in a Muslim family of 12 children from a mother with Moroccan roots and a father of Algerian background. 'I wasn't raised in a cultivated milieu,' Dati once said. Her appointment reached out to black and Arab immigrants and their French children who have scant regard for Sarkozy because of his tough stance on crime and immigration. As interior minister, he infuriated many when he described delinquents as 'scum' and said that crime-ridden poor neighbourhoods needed to be power-hosed clean. 'The message: if you're a woman, or have North African origins, or come from a disfavoured position in society, you can still make it in France,' said political analyst Dominique Moisi." Jamey Keaten, "Sarkozy Names Woman with North African Roots to Cabinet," *Toronto Star*, 18 May 2007, www.thestar.com/article/215727 <22 May 2007>. Notable about this announcement is that it shows that at least in France, a country not yet officially multicultural, it is now possible for immigrants to aspire to and hold two of the highest political offices in the land: president and justice minister.

20 G.W.F. Hegel, *Hegel on Tragedy*, ed. Anne Paolucci and Henry Paolucci (New York: Anchor Books, 1962), 123.

21 Ibid., 122.

22 Aristotle, *Politics*, trans. C.D.C. Reeve (Indianapolis, IN: Hackett, 1998).

23 Hegel, *Hegel on Tragedy*, 123.

CHAPTER NINE

1 Karl Marx, *The Eighteenth Brumaire of Louis Bonaparte* (1852).

2 Citizenship Act (R.S., 1985, c. C-29) laws-lois.justice.gc.ca/eng/acts/c-29/ <18 Nov. 2007>.

3 Plato, "Laws," in *The Collected Dialogues* (Princeton, NJ: Princeton University Press, 2005); Aristotle, *Politics* (www.bookshouldbefree.com/ book/politics-by-Aristotle <20 March 2013>); Thomas Hobbes, *On the Citizen*, ed. and trans. by Richard Tuck and Michael Silverthorne (Cambridge: Cambridge University Press, 1998); Derek Heater, *Citizenship: The Civic Ideal in World History, Politics and Education* (Manchester: Manchester University Press, 2004).

4 The Broadcast Act states: "The Canadian Broadcasting Corporation, as the national public broadcaster, should provide radio and television services incorporating a wide range of programming that informs, enlightens and entertains;
(m) the programming provided by the Corporation should
(i) be predominantly and distinctively Canadian,
(ii) reflect Canada and its regions to national and regional audiences, while serving the special needs of those regions,
(iii) actively contribute to the flow and exchange of cultural expression,
(iv) be in English and in French, reflecting the different needs and circumstances of each official language community, including the particular needs and circumstances of English and French linguistic minorities,
(v) strive to be of equivalent quality in English and in French,
(vi) contribute to shared national consciousness and identity,
(vii) be made available throughout Canada by the most appropriate and efficient means and as resources become available for the purpose, and
(viii) reflect the multicultural and multiracial nature of Canada."
www.crtc.gc.ca/eng/LEGAL/BROAD.htm <18 Nov. 2007>.

5 Laden and Owen, *Multiculturalism and Political Theory*, 34–5.

6 Canada, *Hansard: House of Commons Debates*, 1 May 1947, 2644–6.

7 Stephen Steinberg, *The Ethnic Myth: Race, Ethnicity, and Class in America* (Bostom: Beacon Press, 2001),

8 Ibid., 4.

9 Friedrich A. Hayek, *The Road to Serfdom* (1944; Chicago: University of Chicago Press, 1956), xiv.

10 Rawls, *A Theory of Justice*, 5–6.

11 Ibid.

12 Axworthy and Trudeau, *Towards a Just Society*; Kymlicka, *Multicultural Citizenship*; David Bennett, ed., *Multicultural States: Rethinking Difference and Identity* (London: Routledge, 1998); Trudeau, *The Essential Trudeau*.
13 Charles Taylor, "The Politics of Recognition."
14 Ibid., 27.
15 Jacques Maritain, *The Person and the Common Good*, trans. John J. Fitzgerald (1947; Notre Dame, IN: University of Notre Dame Press, 1966), 42.
16 Trudeau, *The Essential Trudeau*.
17 John W. Dafoe, *Canada: An American Nation* (New York: Columbia University Press, 1935); Frye, *Mythologizing Canada*; J.L. Granatstein et al., *Nation: Canada since Confederation* (Toronto: McGraw-Hill Ryerson, 1990).
18 Porter, *The Vertical Mosaic*; Jeffrey G. Reitz and Raymond Breton, *The Illusion of Difference: Realities of Ethnicity in Canada and the United States* (Ottawa: C.D. Howe Institute, 1994); Rick Helmes-Hayes and James Curtis, "Introduction," in Rick Helmes-Hayes and James Curtis, eds., *The Vertical Mosaic Revisited* (Toronto: University of Toronto Press, 1998); Reitz and Breton, *The Illusion of Difference*.

CHAPTER TEN

1 Jimmy Dean, "Big Bad John" (1961).
2 Hegel, *Phenomenology of Spirit*, 117.
3 Some of this "reality" of the state's desire for life and also its need to accommodate and control change by foreigners is visible in the aims and objective of Canada's Immigration Act:
   "The objectives of this Act with respect to immigration are
   (a) to permit Canada to pursue the maximum social, cultural and economic benefits of immigration;
   (b) to enrich and strengthen the social and cultural fabric of Canadian society, while respecting the federal and bilingual character of Canada;
   (c) to support the development of a strong and prosperous Canadian economy, in which the benefits of immigration are shared across all regions of Canada;
   (d) to see that families are reunited;
   (e) to promote the successful integration of permanent residents into Canada, while recognizing that integration involves mutual obligations for new immigrants and Canadian society;

(f) to support, by means of consistent standards and prompt processing, the attainment of immigration goals established by the Government of Canada in consultation with the provinces;

(g) to facilitate the entry of visitors, students and temporary workers for purposes such as trade, commerce, tourism, international understanding and cultural, educational and scientific activities;

(h) to protect the health and safety of Canadians and to maintain the security of Canadian society; and;

(i) to promote international justice and security by denying access to Canadian territory to foreign nationals who are criminals or security risks.

4 Hegel, *Phenomenology*, 117.

5 For fuller discussion, see Peter S. Li, *Destination Canada: Immigration Debates and Issues* (Toronto: Oxford University Press, 2003), 38–75.

6 Statistics Canada, *Projection of the Diversity of the Canadian Population 2006 to 2031*, report prepared by Éric Caron Malenfant, André Lebel, and Laurent Martel, cat. no. 91-551-X (March 2010), www.statcan.gc.ca/pub/91-551-x/91-551-x2010001-eng.pdf <20 July 2011>.

7 Statistics Canada, "Births," *Daily* (Ottawa), 12 April 2004, www.statscan/daily/English/040419/d040419b.hml <20 March 2013>.

8 Statistics Canada, *Population Projections for Canada, Provinces and Territories 2009 to 2036*, cat. no. 91-520-X (June 2010), www8.statcan.gc.ca/pub/91-520-x/91-520-x2010001-eng.pdf <20 July 2011>.

9 Statistics Canada, *Projection of the Diversity of the Canadian Population 2006 to 2031*.

10 Ibid.

11 Ibid.

12 William Arthur Deacon, *My Vision of Canada* (Toronto: Ontario Publishing, 1933); Freda Hawkins, *Canada and Immigration: Public Policy and Public Concern* (Montreal: McGill-Queen's University Press, 1972); Valerie Knowles, *Strangers at Our Gates: Canadian Immigration and Immigration Policy, 1540–1997* (Toronto: Dundurn, 1997).

13 Elinor Caplan, "Building Community in Multi-Ethnic Societies," Metropolis Conference Plenary, Washington, DC, 10 Dec. 1999 (Immigration and Citizenship Canada, 2001), www.cic.gc.ca/english/press/speech/met-e.html <20 March 2013>.

14 Kymlicka, *Finding Our Way*; Kymlicka. *Politics in the Vernacular*; Pico Iyer, *The Global Soul: Jet Lag, Shopping Malls, and the Search for Home* (New York: Vintage, 2000).

15 British citizens who were living in Canada before 1949 are still automatically Canadian citizens without requiring naturalization. This is a throwback to the days when a British subject – a British national or a white citizen from the other British dominions of Australia, New Zealand, and South Africa was automatically a Canadian citizen. See Hawkins, *Canada and Immigration*, for a fuller discussion.

16 Axworthy and Trudeau, *Towards a Just Society*; Trudeau, *The Essential Trudeau*.

17 "Canada Needs Its Immigrants," editorial, *Kitchener-Waterloo Record*, 19 March 2002.

18 Brent Jang, "Births Decline Again," *Globe and Mail*, 27 Sept. 2002.

19 Ibid.

20 Bruce Cheadle, "Canada's Population Growth Hit Record Low from 1996 to 2001," Canadian Press, 2 Dec. 2002, ca.news.yahoo.com/0203312/6/ktpi.html <20 March 2013>.

21 Daniel Girard, "The Picture, If We Don't Do Anything, Is Quite Distressing," *Toronto Star*, 20 July 2002.

22 Tonda MacCharles, "Boosting Birth Rate Not Option, PM Says: Aging Population Best Addressed with Immigration," *Toronto Star*, 17 July 2002.

23 Ibid. Chrétien had left office, but the government, even with different political stripes, has continued to follow his policies on immigration.

24 Elinor Caplan, "Trends In Global Migration Forum," *Notes for an Address by the Honourable Elinor Caplan, Minister of Citizenship and Immigration, to the Maytree Foundation* (Citizenship and Immigration Canada, 7 Sept. 2001), www.cic.ca/english/press/speech/maytree-e.html <20 March 2013>.

25 Diane Francis, "Why Size Doesn't Matter: We Don't Need More Immigrants to Support Us as We Get Older," *National Post*, 2 Sept. 2002, excerpted from Diane Francis, *Immigration: The Economic Case* (Toronto: Key Porter, 2002).

26 Ibid.

27 Ibid.

28 Ibid.

29 Ibid.

30 Martin Collacott, *Canada's Immigration Policy: The Need for Major Reform*, Public Policy Sources No. 64 (Vancouver: Fraser Institute, 2002).

31 Fraser Institute, "Canada's Current Immigration Levels Undermining Tolerance and Acceptance," media release, Vancouver, 22 Sept. 2002.

32 Ibid.

33 Ibid.

34 Ibid.
35 Daniel Stoffman, *Who Gets In? What's Wrong with Canada's Immigration Program – and How to Fix It* (Toronto: Macfarlane Walter & Ross, 2002).
36 Macfarlane Walter & Ross, media release, Oct. 2002.
37 Martin Loney, *The Pursuit of Division: Race, Gender, and Preferential Hiring in Canada* (Montreal/Kingston: McGill-Queen's University Press, 1998).
38 The literature includes Sedef Arat-Koc, "Good Enough to Work but Not Good Enough to Stay: Foreign Domestic Workers and the Law," in Elizabeth Comack, ed., *Locating Law: Race/Class/Gender Connections* (Halifax: Fernwood, 1999); Agnes Calliste, "Canada's Immigration Policy and Domestic Blacks from the Caribbean: The Second Domestic Scheme," in Elizabeth Cormack and Stephen Brickley, eds., *The Social Basis of Law*, 2nd ed. (Halifax: Garamond, 1991); Leo Driedger and Shiva S. Hall, eds., *Race and Racism: Canada's Challenge* (Montreal/Kingston: McGill-Queen's University Press, 2000); Frances Henry, Carol Tator, Winston Mattis, and Tim Rees, *The Colour of Democracy: Racism in Canadian Society* (Toronto: Harcourt Brace, 1995); Frances Henry and Carol Tator, *Racist Discourse in Canada's English Print Media* (Toronto: Canadian Race Relations Foundation, March 2000); Carl E. James, *Making It: Black Youth, Racism and Career Aspirations in a Big City* (Oakville, ON: Mosaic, 1990); Carl E. James, "Getting There and Staying There: Blacks' Employment Experience," in Paul Anisef and Paul Axelrod, eds., *Transitions: Schooling and Employment in Canada* (Toronto: Thompson, 1993); Peter S. Li, *Race and Ethnic Relations in Canada* (Toronto: Oxford University Press, 1990); Jeffrey G. Reitz, *Warmth of the Welcome: The Social Causes of Economic Success for Immigrants in Different Nations and Cities* (Boulder, CO: Westview, 1998).
39 Jeffrey G. Reitz, "Immigrant Skill Utilization in the Canadian Labour Market: Implications of Human Capital Research" (Toronto: Centre for Industrial Relations and Department of Sociology, University of Toronto, Oct. 2001).
40 Loney, *The Pursuit of Division*, 218.
41 Ibid., 217–18.
42 Ibid., xi.

CHAPTER ELEVEN

1 Tata Young, "Cinderella" (2004).
2 I explored the bifocality of knowing and its ability to explain multiculturalism as a real and yet an ethical order in *Blackness and Modernity*. I also

indicated in *Where Race Does Not Matter* how the ethical and supersensible ways of knowing drive our desires and can help us to dream of achieving the idyllic and utopian.

3 Austin, *Lectures on Jurisprudence*, 28.

4 Hegel, *Phenomenology of Spirit*, 475.

5 Vincent Massey, *Report: Royal Commission on National Development in the Arts, Letters and Sciences 1949–1951* (Ottawa, King's Printer, 1951),www.nlc-bnc.ca/2/5/h5-400-e.html, xxi. <20 March 2013>.

6 Ibid., 224.

7 Ibid., 227.

8 Desmond Morton, *A Short History of Canada* (Toronto: McClelland & Stewart Inc, 1997).

9 Kymlicka, *Finding Our Way*; Kymlicka, *Politics in the Vernacular*; Iyer, *The Global Soul*.

10 David Theo Goldberg, *Racist Culture: Philosophy and the Politics of Meaning* (Oxford: Blackwell, 1993), 7.

11 As quoted in Mark William Roche, *Tragedy and Comedy* (Albany: State University of New York Press, 1998), 187–8.

12 By "Western civilization" and "the West," I am referring not to geographical areas but to an idealized way of life that produced a specific living experience that observers usually associate with the benefits and good of modernity and with modern industrialized countries.

13 Hegel, *Hegel On Tragedy*, 76.

14 Ibid., 76.

15 Jean-Paul Sartre, *Being and Nothingness: An Essay on Phenomenological Ontology*, trans. Hazel E. Barnes (London: Methuen, 1957).

16 Trudeau, *The Essential Trudeau*, 144.

17 Ibid., 143.

18 Innis, *Biligualism and Biculturalism*.

19 René Lévesque, *My Québec* (Toronto: Totem, 1979).

20 Porter, *The Vertical Mosaic*.

21 Mark William Roche, *Tragedy and Comedy: A Systematic Study and a Critique of Hegel*. SUNY Series in Hegelian Studies (Albany: State of New York University Press, 1997), 56.

CHAPTER TWELVE

1 Dave Mathews Band, "Rapunzel," *Before These Crowded Streets* (1998).

2 Francis Bacon, *The Essays* (London: Penguin Books, 1985), 90

3 Ibid., 11.

4 Ibid., 20.

5 Richard H. Bell, *Rethinking Justice: Restoring our Humanity* (Lanham, MD: Lexington, 2007), 1–2.

6 Ibid., xi.

7 Note the discussion in many of the mainstream media in Canada, Britain, Australia, and elsewhere over whether states should "force" foreigners to be free. This was an issue of particular concern in Canada about 2006, when there was widespread debate over how Muslim women should express their freedom. Several writers argued that they should do so by uncovering themselves – discarding such pieces of clothing as the hijab, the burqua, and the nuque and revealing more of their bodies, joining the celebration that is part of the dominant notions of justice for women and equality of the sexes. Other suggested that forcing the women to dress in Western style would simply dehumanize them and make them radically inauthentic, to the point where there would be no justice in their lives.

8 Strauss, *On Tyranny*, 221.

9 Charles Taylor, *Modern Social Imaginaries* (Durham, NC: Duke University Press, 2004).

10 Strauss, *On Tyranny*.

11 Alexandre Kojève, "Tyranny and Wisdom," in Leo Struss, *On Tyranny – Revised and Enlarged by Leo Strauss* (Ithaca, NY: Cornell University Press, 1975)

12 Heater, *Citizenship*, 12.

13 Immanuel Kant, *Critique of Pure Reason*, trans. J.M.D. Meiklejohn (London: Everyman's Library, 1934).

14 Kojève, "Tyranny and Wisdom," 181.

15 Ibid., 181–2.

16 Ibid, 183.

17 Adelman, "Of Human Bondage."

18 Kojève, "Tyranny and Wisdom," 183.

19 Van Leeuwen, *After Eden*, 2. Cecil Foster, *Distorted Mirror: Canada's Racist Face* (Toronto: HarperCollins, 1991), looks in a more material way at multicultural Canada's reaction to this mirror distortion.

20 Anderson, *Imagined Communities*.

21 Northrop Frye, *Anatomy of Criticism: Four Essays* (Princeton, NJ: Princeton University Press, 1971), 141.

22 Terry Eagleton, *The Idea of Culture* (Oxford: Blackwell, 2000), 1–2.

23 Hayek, *The Road to Serfdom*, 34–5.

24 Berdyaev, *The Destiny of Man*, 75–6.

25 Taylor, *Modern Social Imaginaries*, 26.

26 Ibid., 28.

27 Ibid., 35.

28 Ibid., 36.

29 People of this mind might think about Robert Nozick's extensive quotation of P.J. Proudhon to make the case against a minimalist state – what I am calling the "comedy of existence" and what Taylor sees as a police state of sorts: "Proudhon has given us a description of the *state's* domestic 'inconveniences.' 'To be GOVERNED is to be watched, inspected, spied upon, directed, law-driven, numbered, regulated, enrolled, indoctrinated, preached at, controlled, checked, estimated, valued, censured, commanded, by creatures who have neither the right nor the wisdom nor the virtue to so do. To be GOVERENED is to be at every operation, at every transaction noted, registered, counted, taxed, stamped, measured, numbered, assessed, licensed, authorized, admonished, prevented, forbidden, reformed, corrected, punished. It is, under pretext of public utility, and in the name of the general interest, to be placed under contribution, drilled, fleeced, exploited, monopolized, extorted from, squeezed, hoaxed, robbed; then, at the slightest resistance, the first word of complaint, to be repressed, fined, vilified, harrassed, hunted down, abused, clubbed, disarmed, bound, choked, imprisoned, judged, condemned, shot, deported, sacrificed, sold, betrayed; and to crown all, mocked, ridiculed, derided, outraged, dishonored. That is government; that is its justice; that is its morality.'" P.J. Proudhon, *General Idea of the Revolution in the Nineteenth Century*, trans. John Beverly Robinson (London: Freedom Press, 1923)], 293–4, and trans. Benjamin Tucker in *Instead of a Book* (New York, 1893), 26, as quoted in Robert Nozick, *Anarchy, State, and Utopia* (New York: Basic Books, 1974), 11fn.

30 Taylor, *Modern Social Imaginaries*, 36.

31 J.M.S. Careless, *Canada: A Story of Challenge* (Toronto: Macmillan Canada, 1995).

32 Taylor, "Modernity and Difference"; Himani Bannerji, *The Dark Side of the Nation: Essays on Multiculturalism, Nationalism and Gender* (Toronto: Canadian Scholars' Press, 2000).

33 Joseph H. Carens, *Culture, Citizenship, and Community: A Contextual Exploration of Justice as Evenhandedness* (Oxford: Oxford University Press, 2000).

34 James Clifford, *The Predicament of Culture: Twentieth-Century Ethnography, Literature, and Art* (Cambridge, MA: Harvard University Press, 1988), 7.

35 Jacques Derrida, *On Cosmopolitanism and Forgiveness* (London: Routledge, 2001).

36 Foster, *Where Race Does Not Matter.*

37 Immanuel Kant, *Critique of Practical Reason*, trans. Lewis White Beck (Indianapolis, IN: Bobbs-Merrill, 1956).

38 Rawls, *A Theory of Justice.*

39 Ibid., 587.

40 Kant, *Critique of Practical Reason.*

41 Kymlicka, *Finding Our Way*; Carens, *Culture, Citizenship, and Community.*

42 Trudeau, *The Essential Trudeau*, 19–20. Even here we can see in Trudeau's thinking the kind of Kant–Rawls wish for a transcendental solution that goes beyond the everyday living condition. It gestures towards Rawls's "purity of heart" and Kant's desire for a universal law and not mere individual maxims to govern ethical relations. Indeed, the quotation here sounds similar to Kant's statement that "this holiness of will [i.e., Trudeau's perfect justice and Rawls's purity of heart] is, however, a practical ideal which must necessarily serve a model which all finite rational beings must strive towards even though they cannot reach it… The utmost that finite practical reason can accomplish is to make sure of the unending progress of its maxims towards this model and of the constancy of the finite rational being in making continuous progress" (Kant, *Critique of Practical Reason*, 33). While Rawls suggests that this pattern leads to an undesirable type of justice, Kant goes further and states that because there can never be apodictic certainty, all that remains is mere opinion, which "is very dangerous."

43 Anderson, *Imagined Communities.*

44 Leo Strauss, *Natural Rights and History* (Chicago: University of Chicago Press, 1953).

45 Trudeau, *The Essential Trudeau*, 59–60.

46 Ibid.

CHAPTER THIRTEEN

1 John Emerich Edward Dalberg-Acton, *Essays on Freedom and Power* (Boston: Beacon, 1949), 364.

2 Louis Hartz, *The Foundation of New Societies: Studies in the History of United States, Latin America, South Africa, Canada and Australia* (New York: Harcourt Brace World, 1964).

3 Trudeau, *The Essential Trudeau*, 4–5.

4 Ibid., 78–9.

5 Alan C. Cairns, *Citizen Plus: Aboriginal People and the Canadian State* (Vancouver: UBC Press, 2000).

6 Trudeau, *The Essential Trudeau*, 80.

7 Kymlicka, *Multicultural Citizenship*; Foster, *Where Race Does Not Matter* and *Blackness and Modernity*.

8 Hawkins, *Canada and Immigration*; Harold Martin Troper, *Only Farmers Need Apply: Official Canadian Government Encouragement of Immigration from the United States, 1896–1911* (Toronto: Griffin House, 1972); Taylor, "The Politics of Recognition"; Kymlicka, *Multicultural Citizenship*; Alan G. Green, "A Comparison of Canadian and U.S. Immigration Policy in the Twentieth Century," in Don Devoretz, ed., *Diminishing Returns: The Economics of Canada's Recent Immigration Policy* (Toronto: C.D. Howe Institute, 1995); Knowles, *Strangers at Our Gates*; Li, *Destination Canada*.

9 Rawls, *A Theory of Justice*, 9–10.

10 Hegel, *Phenomenology*.

11 Bissoondath, *Selling Illusion*; Cecil Foster, *A Place Called Heaven: The Meaning of Being Black In Canada* (Toronto: HarperCollins, 1996); Loney, *The Pursuit of Division*; Bannerji, *The Dark Side of the Nation*; Stoffman, *Who Gets In?*; Collacott, *Canada's Immigration Policy*.

12 Taylor, "The Politics of Recognition."

13 Foster, *A Place Called Heaven*; Cairns, *Citizen Plus*; Bannerji, *The Dark Side of the Nation*.

14 Citizenship and Immigration Canada, Planning and Research Strategic Policy, has prepared and published in Ottawa three studies: "Measuring Performance," *Special Studies: Strategic Research and Review* (March 1998), "The Economic Performance of Immigrants: Education Perspective," *IMDB Profile Series* (2000), and "Towards a More Balanced Geographical Distribution of Immigration," *Special Study: Strategic Research and Review* (May 2001); Informetrica, "Canada's Recent Immigrants: A Comparative Portrait Based on the 1996 Census," *Recent Immigrants in Metropolitan Areas* (Ottawa: Citizenship and Immigration Canada, Jan. 2001).

15 David Ley, "Myths and Meanings of Immigration and the Metropolis," *Canadian Geographer* 43, no. 1 (1999); Elizabeth Ruddick, "Trends in International Labour Flows to Canada," Statistics Canada Economic Conference 2000 (Ottawa: Citizenship and Immigration Canada, May 16, 2000); Alan Simmons, "Canadian Immigration Policy: An Analysis of Imagined Futures. A Paper Prepared for the Symposium on Immigration and Integration," Department of Sociology, University of Manitoba, Winnipeg, 25–27 Oct. 1996; Fraser Institute, "Canada's Current Immigration Levels Undermining Tolerance and Acceptance."

16 Alan B. Simmons and Dwaine E. Plaza, "Breaking through the Glass Ceiling: The Pursuit of University Training among African-Caribbean

Migrants and Their Children in Toronto," *Canadian Ethnic Studies* 30, no.3 (1998); Lisa Marie Jakubowski, "'Managing' Canadian Immigration: Racism, Ethnic Selectivity, and the Law," in *Locating Law*; Ninette Kelly and Michael Trebilcock, *The Making of the Mosaic: A History of Canadian Immigration Policy* (Toronto: University of Toronto Press, 1998).

17 Foster, *A Place Called Heaven*; Bannerji, *The Dark Side of the Nation*.

18 Kymlicka, *Multicultural Citizenship*; Kymlicka, *Politics in the Vernacular*; Carens, *Culture, Citizenship, and Community*.

19 Trudeau, *The Essential Trudeau*.

20 Ibid., 18–19.

21 Ibid., 179.

22 Ibid., 124–6.

23 Ibid., 143.

24 Ibid., 86.

25 Ibid., 181–2.

26 Bissoondath, *Selling Illusion*; Loney, *The Pursuit of Division*.

27 Trudeau, *The Essential Trudeau*, 144.

28 Bannerji, *The Dark Side of the Nation*, 7–8.

29 Ibid., 8.

30 Rawls, *A Theory of Justice*, 12.

31 Ibid., 587.

32 Ibid.

33 Ibid.

34 Kant, *Critique of Practical Reason*, 19.

35 Ibid. Kant reinforced the impracticality of such efforts to have actions flow out of an a priori reason: "Where one places his happiness is a question of the particular feeling of a pleasure or displeasure in each man, and even of the differences in needs occasioned by changes of feeling in one and the same man. Thus a subjectively necessary law (as a law of nature) is objectively a very contingent practical principle which can and must be very different in different men. It therefore cannot yield any [practical] law, because in the desire for happiness it is not the form (accordance with law) but only the material which is decisive; it is a question only of whether I may expect pleasure from obedience to the law, and, if so, how much" (ibid., 25). Again this creates a problem within Rawls's own theory, for he clearly states that the advantage and happiness that are the end result of this process are not what Rawls desires.

36 Strauss, *Natural Rights and History*; Leo Strauss, *The City and Man* (Chicago: Rand McNally, 1964).

37 This was a point that Jeremy Waldron argued against Will Kymlicka in their discussion on "The Practice of Law-Making and the Problem of

Difference" at the International Conference at Social and Political
Philosophy, University of Guelph, 13–14 November 2004.

38 Jean-Jacques Rousseau, *The Social Contract*, trans. Christopher Betts
(Oxford: Oxford University Press, 1994).

39 Rawls, *A Theory of Justice*, 13.

40 Ibid., 8.

41 Ibid.

CHAPTER FOURTEEN

1 Hegel, *Hegel on Tragedy*, 77.

2 Ibid., 78.

3 Ibid., 78.

4 Natan Sharansky with Shira Wolosky Weiss, *Defending Identity: Its
Indispensable Role in Protecting Democracy* (Philadelphia: Perseus Group,
2008), 8.

5 Hannah Arendt, *The Human Condition* (Chicago: University of Chicago
Press, 1958), 9.

6 Ibid., 177–8.

7 Hegel, *Hegel on Tragedy*, 367–88.

8 Brereton, *Principles of Tragedy*, 14.

9 Trudeau, *The Essential Trudeau*, 15.

10 Ibid., 17.

11 Ibid., 45.

12 Ibid., 17.

13 Ibid., 146.

14 Ibid., 144.

15 Ibid., 19.

16 Ibid., 173.

17 Ibid., 176.

18 Ibid., 179.

19 Ibid., 180.

20 Ibid., 177.

21 Books that look at this kind of unhappiness include Bissoondath, *Selling
Illusion*; Alvin J. Schmidt, *The Menace of Multiculturalism: Trojan Horse
of America* (Westport, CT: Praeger, 1997); Stanley A. Barrett, *Is God a
Racist? The Right Wing in Canada* (Toronto: University of Toronto Press,
1989); Collacott, *Canada's Immigration Policy*; Francis, *Immigration: The
Economic Case*; Granatstein, *Who Killed Canadian History?*; George
Grant, *Lament for a Nation: The Defeat of Canadian Nationalism*
(Toronto: Macmillan Canada, 1978); Loney, *The Pursuit of Division*.

22 Publications that present the state of unhappiness from a different point of view include Ken Alexander and Avis Glaze, *Towards Freedom: The African-Canadian Experience* (Toronto: Umbrella Press, 1996); Ian Angus, *A Border Within: National Identity, Cultural Plurality, and Wilderness* (Montreal/Kingston: McGill-Queen's University Press, 1997); Arat-Koc, "Good Enough to Work but Not Good Enough to Stay"; Constance Backhouse, *Colour-Coded: A Legal History of Racism in Canada, 1900–1950* (Toronto: University of Toronto Press, 1999); Cairns, *Citizen Plus*; Calliste, "Canada's Immigration Policy and Domestic Blacks from the Caribbean"; Tania Das Gupta, *Racism and Paid Work* (Toronto: Garamond, 1996); Henry, Tator, Mattis, and Rees, *The Colour of Democracy*; Henry and Tator, *Racist Discourse in Canada's English Print Media*; Vic Satzewich, *Racism and Social Inequality in Canada: Concepts, Controversies and Strategies of Resistance* (Toronto: Thompson, 1998).

23 Trudeau, *The Essential Trudeau*, 142.

24 Ibid., 144.

25 Ibid., 179.

26 Paul Franco, *Hegel's Philosophy of Freedom* (New Haven, CT: Yale University Press, 1999), 56.

27 Green, *Lectures on the Principles of Political Obligation*, 29.

28 Gadamer, *Truth and Method*, 102–3.

29 Jonathan Robinson, "Lord Haldane and the British North America Act," *University of Toronto Law Journal* 20 (1970).

30 C.B. Macpherson, *The Political Theory of Possessive Individualism: Hobbes to Locke* (Oxford: Oxford University Press, 2011).

31 Plato, *Republic*, m 619b.

CHAPTER FIFTEEN

1 Alighieri Dante. *The Divine Comedy of Dante Alighieri*, trans. Henry Wadsworth Longfellow (New York: National Library, 1909), Canto III.

2 The Citizenship Act (1947) says in the section "The Right to Citizenship," Persons who are citizens:

Subject to this Act, a person is a citizen if

(*a*) the person was born in Canada after February 14, 1977;

(*b*) the person was born outside Canada after February 14, 1977 and at the time of his birth one of his parents, other than a parent who adopted him, was a citizen;

(*c*) the person has been granted or acquired citizenship pursuant to section 5 or 11 and, in the case of a person who is fourteen years of age or over on the day that he is granted citizenship, he has taken the oath of citizenship;

($c.1$) the person has been granted citizenship under section 5.1;

(d) the person was a citizen immediately before February 15, 1977; or

(e) the person was entitled, immediately before February 15, 1977, to become a citizen under paragraph 5(1)(b) of the former Act."

Citizenship Act (RS, 1985, c. C-29), Department of Justice Canada, laws.justice.gc.ca/en/C-29/index.html <24 Oct. 2008>.

3 Ibid., section 6.

4 Immigration and Refugee Protection Act (2001, c. 27), Department of Justice Canada, laws.justice.gc.ca/en/ShowFullDoc/cs/I-2.5///en <24 Oct. 2008>.

5 Hegel. *Phenomenology*, 97.

6 Ibid., 97.

7 Ibid., 97.

8 Ibid., 98.

9 Ibid., 68–9.

10 Foster, *Blackness and Modernity*.

11 Hegel, *Phenomenology*, 101.

12 Ibid., 101.

13 Ibid., 135.

14 Ibid., 137.

15 Shklar, *Freedom and Independence*, 26–7.

16 United Nations, The Universal Declaration of Human Rights, www.un.org/Overview/rights.html.

17 Hegel, *Phenomenology of Spirit*, 27.

18 Strauss, *On Tyranny*, 190.

19 Ibid., 194.

20 Machiavelli, *The Prince*, 171.

21 Ibid., 173.

22 Ibid., 174.

23 Ibid., 184.

24 Hegel, *Phenomenology*, 126.

25 Hegel, *Lectures on the Philosophy of History*, 41.

26 Peter Hodgson, *G.W.F. Hegel: Theologian of the Spirit* (Minneapolis, MN: Fortress, 1997).

27 Ibid., 33.

28 Burbidge, *Hegel on Logic and Religion*.

29 Ibid., 112.

30 Ibid., 113. This Christian paradigm of reconciliation differs from the classical Hebraic paradigm – the mediator is also God. In the rebellion of Korach, Moses, as human servant of God, is the mediator – the intermediary for the vengeful, unbounded God, determined to employ, fairly

indiscriminately, collective punishment against society and the people who would be the victims of this punishment. In contrast, in Christianity it is God, embodied in the personhood of his Son, who serves as the mediator, a man-God rather than a man who can come face to face with God.

31 H.S. Harris explains: "For the Changeable Consciousness, God's becoming man is an *event*; but in order for the man to be truly God, the contradiction between finite mortality and infinite life must have been sublimated by the completion of the finite moment in death far away and long ago. God's human embodiment is now with the Unchangeable in its own place" *Hegel: Phenomenology and System* (Indianapolis: Hackett, 1995), 44.

32 Hegel, *Lectures on the Philosophy of History*, 336–7.

33 Hodgson, *G.W.F. Hegel*, 21–2.

34 Harris, *Hegel*, 44.

35 Burbidge, *Being and Will*, 126.

36 Ibid., 121–5.

37 Arthur J. Droge and James D. Tabor, *A Noble Death: Suicide and Martyrdom among Christians and Jews in Antiquity* (New York: HarperCollins, 1992).

38 Ibid., 199.

39 Burbidge, *Being and Will*, 121.

40 Ibid., 124.

41 Droge and Tabor, *A Noble Death*.

42 Hegel, *Lectures on the Philosophy of History*, 333.

43 Burbidge, *Being and Will*, 127 (my emphasis).

44 Ibid., 127.

45 Ibid., 129.

46 Harris, *Hegel*, 44.

47 Cone, *God of the Oppressed*.

48 Alexandre Kojève, *Introduction to the Reading of Hegel: Lectures on the Phenomenology of Spirit*, ed. Allan Bloom, trans. James H. Nichols, Jr (Ithaca, NY: Cornell University Press, 1969), 56.

49 Adelman, "Of Human Bondage."

50 Kojève, *Introduction to the Reading of Hegel*, 156–7.

Index

Abel, 429

aboriginal peoples: of Australia, 365; consciousness of, 114; displacement of, 109, 129, 146; in multiculturalism, 438n10; and Nature, 109. *See also* Native Americans; Native Canadians

academe, 270

Acadians, 151

accommodation, 11, 43, 55–7, 58, 403, 433; of Bad Johns, 65–6, 81–2, 83; in Canada, 37, 147–8, 151–2, 259, 260; under genuine multiculturalism, 12; of immigrants, 82, 166, 232; multiculturalization as, 189; by Muslims, 470n7; as postponement, 138–9; state employment as, 261; and tolerance, 189; in the United States, 151–2, 225–7. *See also under* Quebec

action, 91, 143, 314, 393, 408

Acton, John Dahlberg-Acton, 1st baron, 362

Adam, 171, 201–3, 288, 332; as Bad John or Prince Charming, 170, 277

Adelman, Howard, 392; on Adam and Eve, 201, 203; on human bondage, 98, 202; on the individual and society, 388–9, 391; on lordship and bondage, 202; on reconciliation, 393; on sex and love, 405, 426

Africa, 120, 414

African Americans, 86, 114, 218, 220, 228

ageing, 283–4, 289, 290, 360

agencies. *See* institutions

Alexander the Great, 340–1, 342, 355, 363

Algeria, 120

alienation, 212–13, 401, 416; of western Canada, 358

allophones, 322

American Revolution, 4

Americas: discovery and colonization, 107, 111, 114–15, 118–21, 129–30; genuine multiculturalism in, 200; in mythology, 246; as settler communities, 42–3, 341; the state in, 21, 111, 112

Amsterdam, 39

anarchy, 115, 116
Anderson, Benedict, 240, 343, 353
annexation, 127, 218, 364
Antigone, 5
Antigone, 69, 135
apologies, 146–7, 447n13
appearance, 408–9
Arendt, Hannah, 50, 376–7
aristocracy, 115
Aristotle: on individuals and the state, 3; on the reasonable man, 233; on socialization, 241, 255; on tragedy, 316; on tyrants and kings, 442n23
Armstrong, Chris, 167
arts, support for, 307–8, 383
assimilation, 6, 23, 33, 109, 260
audience, 196, 197
Austin, John, 149, 152, 450n4; on theory and practice, 171, 172, 182, 300, 449n2
Australia, 36, 185–6, 268, 365
authenticity, 7, 62, 154, 184, 334; in multiculturalism, 158, 213
authority, 52; the state as, 148

Baden-Wurttemberg, 39–40
Bad Johns, 64–7, 68–9, 72–4, 428; accommodation of, 65–6, 81–2, 83; Adam as prototype of, 170, 201, 202; in Barbados, 64, 74–6, 83, 86–7; death of, 87; deposed, 83; equality of, 60; as fear and feared, 72, 74; immigrants as, 70–1, 73, 121, 210, 229, 403; Lincoln as, 23–4; Prince Charming as, 57, 229; and religion, 86–7; as sceptics, 70, 280; socialization of, 83–5, 88–90, 249; in society, 335; and tragedy, 85, 193;

as unchangeable, 80; unnamed characters in story of, 43; and women, 83–6
Badman, 64
Bannerji, Himani, 350, 365
Barbados, 64, 74–7, 83, 86–7, 115
Basque country, 181
Baxter, David, 290
beauty, 203
belief, 421
Bell, Richard, 332
benevolence: absolute, 143
Berdyaev, Nikolai: on Christianity, 448n21; on freedom, 330; on good and evil, 188; on happiness, 172–3; on imagination, 346, 454n25; on tragedy, 42, 232; on the unhappy consciousness, 164
Berlin, 39
Berlin, Isaiah, 10, 53, 180
Bermuda, 115
Bernstein, J.M., 28
biculturalism, 161–2, 228, 237, 266, 300, 385; and language, 308, 318; in Massey Commission findings, 308, 309, 312; struggles in, 317–18, 357, 435n3
Bildung, 53, 67–8, 72, 100, 170–1, 392
bilingualism, 273, 311, 318, 385
Bill 101 (Quebec), 354
Billinghurst, Jane, 54–5
birth rate, 281, 283, 288–9, 291, 360
blackness, 144, 227–8, 280, 422
Blaine, James G., 218
Bradley, A.C., 379
Brereton, Geoffrey, 192, 379
Britain. *See* United Kingdom
British Empire, 120

British North America Act, 128. *See also* constitution (of Canada)

Broadcast Act, 464n4

Brown, Bad-Bad Leroy, 64

Brueggemann, Walter, 332

Brussels, 39

Burbidge, John, 392, 393, 415–16, 418–19, 420, 421–2

Butler, Judith, 440n23

Cain, 429

Calgary, 461n19

Callaghan, Morley, 441n13

Campbell, Joseph, 15, 24, 49, 50

Canada: accommodation in, 81–2; as being created, 185, 186–7, 235–6, 248, 308; as Christian, 247, 300–2, 304, 333–4, 344; as colonial, 151; colonization, 115; in comedy, 215, 255–6, 278; creation of, 116–17, 184, 185, 186–7, 210, 219, 233, 246–7, 311–12; death and rebirth, 423–4, 431–2; demographics, 280–1, 282–6, 288–92, 360; as ethical relationship, 393; as European, 131; founding myths, 318, 435n3; history, 140–1; intentions, 40; justice in, 387–8, 411; as liberal democracy, 187; as model of multiculturalism, 313; as postmodern state, 301; recognition in, 304–5, 308, 314; recognition of, 306, 319; as tolerant, 188; in tragedy, 241, 253–4, 277, 287, 303, 310, 388; as unhappy consciousness, 103, 186, 213, 238, 255, 287–8, 324, 349, 359, 360–1, 378, 423; as universal state, 387; US Civil War and, 217, 219; as "white man's country," 56.

See also biculturalism; bilingualism; official multiculturalism; Quebec

Canadian Broadcasting Corporation (CBC): mandate, 263, 464n4. *See also* CBC Radio

Canadian identity. *See* Canadianness; Massey-Lévesque Commission

Canadian literature: African-Canadian, 445n42

Canadian Multiculturalism Act, 259–60, 459n17

Canadianness, 344–5, 386, 398–9, 414, 427–8; v. Americanness, 128; as changeable, 106, 238; hyphenation, 158, 403; Nature and, 122–3; recognition of, 305–7, 310, 311; Pierre Trudeau on, 381

Caplan, Elinor, 291–2

Carens, Joseph, 350, 352

Caribbean, 120, 249–50; women in, 83–5

Castile, 20

categories, mixing of, 5, 8

categorization: based on difference, 7, 8–10

CBC Radio, 258–9, 260–4, 292, 373, 374–5, 377–8

Chabotto, Zuan (John Cabot), 114

change: as death, 277; externalization of, 393; immigration as, 30; as measurement of time, 61; as normal in life, 13, 99–100, 143, 224–5; social, 60–3, 100–1; and tragedy, 194, 215–16; and unhappy consciousness, 395

changeable, the, 412; death of, 423

character, 69–70

Charest, Jean, 451n22

Charter of Rights and Freedoms, 184, 266; anniversary of, 458n15; in the courts, 365, 450n14; multicultural-ism in, 459n17; purpose of, 286, 354, 383; rights protected by, 29, 267, 340, 370; Pierre Trudeau on, 357–8

Chechnya, 181

Chinese Canadians, 147

Chrétien, Jean, 291

Christian consciousness, 134, 164

Christianity: African-American, 114; in Canada, 284, 300–2; fundamen-talist, 247; and genuine multicul-turalism, 448n21; hope in, 421; living contradiction in, 113–14; and political cosmopolitanism, 340, 342–3; *poneria* in, 207; in Western civilization, 164, 247–8

Christian justice, 246, 301, 303, 413; in Canada, 247, 333; in Western society, 45, 334, 342

Christian mythology, 422; covenants in, 176–8, 179–80; in secular soci-ety, 45–6. *See* Abel; Adam; Cain; Eve; Fall, the; Jesus Christ

Cinderella, 50, 56

cities: diversity in, 283, 285, 286

citizens: becoming, 145–6; as produc-ers, 135; reasonable, 231, 233

citizenship, 5, 8–9, 34, 59–60, 89, 389; civic, 55, 339; as compromise, 231; cosmopolitan, 338–9, 339–40, 353; as covenant, 175; dual, 251; equality of, 167, 266, 271, 432–3; and freedom, 11, 243; in genuine multiculturalism, 26, 190; liberal, 65, 166, 232–3; rights and respon-sibilities of, 159, 259

Citizenship Act, 128, 259, 286, 340, 374, 398, 476n2

citizenship process, 281, 286, 347, 398–9, 467n15

civility, 346–7

civilization, 388; Western, 247, 469n12

civil rights, 167; in Canada, 221; in democracy, 244; after slavery, 159–60. *See also* civil rights movement

civil rights movement, 120, 150, 218, 219, 225

Civil War. *See* US Civil War

Clarke, George Elliott, 445n42

class, 437n4

Clifford, James, 351, 355

clothing, 251, 470n7

Collacott, Martin, 294–5

collectivity, 330, 414, 415

Colombo, Christoforo (Christopher Columbus), 114

colonialism, 21, 117–20, 120–1, 151, 250; in reverse, 121

colonization, 106–7, 111, 114–15, 117–21

comedy, 98–9, 192, 197–9, 375, 377, 378, 399; Canada as, 215, 255–6, 278; and conscience, 90; conver-sion to tragedy, 210, 216; conver-sion to utopia, 394, 395; democracy as, 412; emotion and, 203; and law, 256; of living, 92; multiculturalism as, 102, 150, 196, 270; recognition in, 304, 315; and scepticism, 415

Commission on the Future of Health Care in Canada, 290

common good, the: the individual and, 337; multiculturalism and,

239, 245, 355–6; the state and, 233; and tyranny, 331
Commonwealth, 120
compromise, 395
Cone, James, 50, 98, 114, 407, 422
Confederation, 116–17, 127, 128, 219, 311–12, 435n3
conformity: in Canada, 237–8, 287, 388; enforced, 23; by immigrants, 160–1; the individual and, 123–4; love and, 122; in multiculturalism, 152, 153
conscience, 77, 79–80, 81, 90, 369
consciousness, 133, 241, 388; Christian, 134, 164; and conscience, 90–1; double, 114; false, 98, 256; happy, 108; informed, 99. *See also* unhappy consciousness
constitution (of Canada), 191; multiculturalism in, 259; notwithstanding clause, 322, 359, 370; repatriation of, 184, 222, 286, 354, 358
contract theory, 149, 157–8
Cooper, Carolyn, 85
cosmopolitanism, 335, 337, 340–3, 351, 353, 355
courts, 175, 450n14
covenants, 256, 389, 390; biblical, 179–80, 451n18, 451n19; Canadian, 184; Christian, 176–7; v. social contracts, 150, 175–6
creativity, 346
credentials, foreign, 261, 262, 296
crime, 295
Criminal Code, 361
culture, 343, 345, 368–9; Canadian, 304, 305, 307–8, 310–11, 386, 387, 402; language and, 318; societal, 181–2, 264, 352, 387, 395

dancehall, 85
Dati, Rachida, 461n19
Davaney, Sheila Greeve, 241–2
death: of Bad Johns, 87; and change, 277; of the changeable, 413; in comedy, 210; as creative act, 419; fear of, 87, 303–4, 417; as forgiveness, 376; as metanoia, 376; physical, 50, 193–4; and reconciliation, 423–4; risking, 209; self-induced, 417–18, 419; social, 4, 60–1; spiritual, 417; of the state, 4–5, 13; steps in, 416–17, 418–19; in tragedy, 197; of the unchangeable, 113, 247–8, 416, 417, 421, 423
death wish, 229
Declaration of Independence, 179, 340
decolonization, 110
Delany, Martin, 189
democracy, 154–7, 181, 244, 249; as comedy, 412; conditions for, 115, 116; egalitarian, 338; individuals in, 243–4. *See also* liberal democracy; radical democracy
demographics, 156; Canadian, 280–1, 282–6, 288–92, 360; European, 39, 459n18; of the United States, 37–9
Derrida, Jacques, 351, 355, 440n23
desire, 53, 134, 416
despair, 192
deus ex machina, 377
Dewey, John, 195
dialectics, 241–2, 249, 414–15
dignity, 272–3
diremption, 30, 133, 134, 144, 146
Discourses (Machiavelli), 115, 411
discrimination, 29, 254, 296, 437n4
disobedience, 209

diversity: under biculturalism, 266; as
    difference, 335, 367; as end, 242;
    and inequality, 341; in liberal
    democracy, 264; in multicultural-
    ism, 112–13, 124–5, 407, 426;
    statistics on, 283, 284
Dollard, John, 57, 108, 110–11,
    444n21
Don, 64
Dosanjh, Ujjal, 261
drama, elements of, 100
dual citizenship, 251
dualism: human, 414. *See also*
    biculturalism
Du Bois, W.E.B., 227, 440n23
Durham Report, 285
Durkheim, Emile, 104, 134, 414

Eagleton, Terry, 345
Eden, 209, 246, 396, 419
11 September 2001, 42, 377
Eliot, T.S., 131–2
embrace, 201–2, 207, 211–12, 426–8,
    429–30
emigration, 291
emotion, 204
employment, 290
employment insurance, 290
enforcers, 75–6
England: nationalism in, 20. *See also*
    United Kingdom
English Canada. *See* biculturalism
English language, 185, 308
equality, 28, 29, 233, 235, 380
ethnic cleansing, 23
ethnic ghettoes, 26, 108, 252–3, 348,
    349
ethnic groups: disputes among, 58,
    385; unassimilated, 6
ethnicity, in Europe, 19–20

ethnic nationalism, 19–20, 371
ethnocentrism, 138, 268–9, 348
Europe: demographic change, 39,
    459n18; ethnicity in, 19–20, 111;
    immigration policy, 39–40; multi-
    culturalism in, 190, 195, 438n9
Eve, 201, 202–3, 277, 288, 332
evil, 418, 419–20, 423; death of, 421;
    and good, 41, 59, 92–3, 232,
    350–1

Fagundes, João Álvares, 115
fairy tales, 71–2
faith, 98, 236, 238, 392–3, 418, 421
Fall, the, 42, 419
false consciousness, 98, 256
Fanon, Frantz, 70, 108, 110, 440n23
fate, 100
Faulkner, William, 164
fear, 27; Bad Johns and, 72, 74, 75;
    and death, 87, 205–6; in the
    embrace, 427; and the state, 115,
    119; and tragedy, 171, 255
federalism, 220, 222; intergovern-
    mental conferences, 352, 358;
    under Pierre Trudeau, 266, 354,
    358, 369–70, 383
feminism, 211
fertility rate, 281, 283, 288–9, 291,
    360
50 Cent, 196
Finnis, John, 231, 233, 247
First Nations. *See* aboriginal peoples;
    Native Canadians
folk, the, 26, 33, 49, 51, 64
force, 368
forgiveness, 350, 376
Foster, Cecil: background and iden-
    tity, 32, 64, 249; as a Bad John,
    272; and CBC Radio, 258–9,

260–4, 271, 272, 276, 283, 287, 373, 374–5, 377–8

Foucault, Michel, 231

founding myths: of Canada, 318, 435n3; of genuine multiculturalism, 15

Fourier, Charles, 49

France, 20, 459n18, 461n19

Francis, Diane, 293–4

Franco, Paul, 163

fraternity, 6, 97–8, 104, 136, 443n3

freedom, 53, 134, 208–9, 316, 329–30, 378; absolute, 143, 147; v. conformity, 44, 74; desire for, 210–11, 269; as equality, 60; European, 108; justice as, 380; limits on, 148; in multiculturalism, 140, 144, 425; quest for, 200, 206–7, 413; represented by Prince Charming, 73; and slavery, 143, 147; spiritual, 89; and tyranny, 142–3, 148; universal, 211

Freeze, Colin, 461n19

French Canada. See biculturalism; Quebec

French language, 185, 308

French Revolution, 4

Frye, Northrop, 50, 122–3, 124–5, 229, 343–4

Fuhrer, Urs, 79

Gadamer, Hans-Georg, 53, 207, 391

Garden of Eden, 55, 209, 246

garrison mentality, 122–3, 124, 265

genocide, 21, 23, 109, 146

genuine multiculturalism, 12–14, 32–4, 92, 239, 269–70, 338, 396–7, 426–7; as blackness, 144; and Christianity, 448n21; as comedy, 18–19, 178, 270; diversity in, 124;

as ethical relationship, 157; as false consciousness, 19; founding myths of, 15; and freedom, 140, 144; as freedom, 425; goals of, 235; idealism of, 448n21; language of, 136, 139–42; and love, 141, 157; opposition to, 29, 30; as organic to the Americas, 21; as postmodern, 8; as pragmatism, 196, 200; as radical democracy, 22–3, 134, 153, 250, 395, 408; recognition in, 27; sharing in, 403–4; and slavery, 144; sovereignty in, 152; as tragedy, 18, 212, 431. See also multiculturalism; official multiculturalism

Germany, 459n18

Ghana, 120

globalism, 13

God, 50, 414, 419; death of, 134, 247–8, 421–2, 478n31; fear of, 417; the individual and, 224; reconciliation and, 421, 477n30; and the state, 80, 103–4, 134–6, 343

Goldberg, David, 313

Gone with the Wind, 223–4

good, 232; as changeable, 93; European male as prototype of, 71; and evil, 59, 92–3, 232, 350–1; God and, 80

Gough, Julian, 198

Graham, Ron, 25

Granatstein, J.L., 127, 445n42

Grant, Madison, 219

Greece, 190, 247–8, 414

Green, T.H., 239, 240, 244, 389

Gregg, Allan, 461n19

Gulliver's Travels, 41

Haitian Revolution, 4, 120, 220

Hamilton, Alexander, 437n8

Hansel and Gretel, 72

happiness: comedy of, 216; of individuals, 170; and multiculturalism, 103, 200; search for, 172–3, 192–3; and the state, 211; and transcendence, 378

Harper, Stephen, 146–7, 447n13

Harris, H.S., 417, 422, 478n31

Hayek, Friedrich, 139–40, 271, 345–6

health care, 289–90

Heater, Derek, 339

Hecate, 205

Hegel, G.W.F., 414–15, 440n23; on action, 314; on the Americas, 131, 246; on animal functions, 405, 406; on appearance, 408–9; on behaviour, 404–5; on bleeding hearts, 273, 368; as Christian philosopher, 414; on comedy, 315, 375; on consciousness, 241; critique of, 241–2; on culture, 368; on death, 303–4, 418; on discrimination, 254; on disorder, 249; on evil, 419; on fear, 277, 417; on freedom, 163; on God, 80, 104, 418; on happiness, 145, 173, 211, 323; on history, 197, 414; on immortality, 224–5, 323; on Jesus Christ, 417; on law, 172, 399–400; on liberalism, 273; on life, 98, 99; on lordship and bondage, 254–5; on loss, 141; on love, 78–9; on natural rights, 449n26; on nature, 278; on reason, 145, 299; on recognition, 145, 158, 315–16; on reconciliation, 407; on ritual, 113; on self-consciousness, 77–8; on socialization, 67–8; on spirit, 101, 182; on the state, 134, 135, 163, 338, 386, 413–14; on thinghood, 402–3; on tragedy, 255, 315, 322, 379; on truth, 405; on unhappiness, 382; on the unhappy consciousness, 111, 112, 368, 412–13; on Western civilization, 315–16

Heidegger, Martin, 158, 241

Herodotus, 193

Hiero or Tyrannicus, 330–3, 334, 376

High John, 64

historical materialism, 249

history, 203; under Christian covenant, 177; end of, 241–2; as search for happiness, 173

Hitchens, Christopher, 459n18

Hobbes, Thomas, 46, 67, 103–4, 182

Hodgson, Peter C., 414–15, 417

Holland, 20, 40, 115

homosexuality, 199–200, 205, 361

Hooks, Sidney, 189

hope, 192, 231, 316, 422, 423

Houston, Sam, 118

human bondage, 202

humanity, 67, 338, 423

humour, 197

Hurst, Lynda, 234

hyphenation, 403

idealism, 102, 316, 368, 392

identity, 254; as imaginary, 101–2. *See also* Canadianness

identity politics, 35, 56

ideology, 32, 238–9, 414

Ignatieff, Michael, 168, 178

imagination, 346

immigrants, 261–2; accommodation of, 82, 166, 232; as Adam or Eve, 288; as Bad Johns, 70–1, 73, 121, 210, 229, 403; and change, 30, 58, 168, 436n3; in comedy, 256, 431;

conformity and integration, 160–1, 227–8, 228–9, 234, 359, 391–2, 456n24; as cultural outsiders, 6; debate over, 251–2, 276; desires of, 9–11; equality of, 268; in false consciousness, 256; female, 70; as groups and as individuals, 371; illegal, 37, 38; language of, 137–8; in lordship-and-bondage relationship, 278, 280, 389–90; non-white, 71, 184–5; as Prince Charmings and Sweet Boys, 210, 288, 403; prophetic role of, 50; in Quebec, 320, 322; racialization of, 228, 282; rights of, 286; as sceptics, 280; socialization of, 239–40, 250–1, 345; subsequent generations, 166, 212, 234, 456n24; in tragedy, 256, 280, 423; as unhappy consciousnesses, 392; in the welfare state, 165–6

immigration: and biculturalism, 318; as change, 30; and citizenship, 121; debate over, 282, 292–7, 461n19; levels, 39, 291–2, 360; as solution to demographic crisis, 291; sources of, 360; statistics on, 284–5

Immigration Act, 262, 383, 447n13, 465n3

Immigration and Refugee Protection Act, 398–9

immigration policy, 219–20, 285–6, 291–2, 358, 371, 410; apologies for, 447n13; contradictions in, 370–1; in Europe, 40

immortality, 205–6, 224–5

improvisation, 457n2

Indian Act, 118

Indian subcontinent, 120

indigenous peoples. See Aboriginal peoples

individual, the: and collectivity, 330, 414, 415; and the common good, 337; in genuine multiculturalism, 408, 431–4; personhood, 3–4, 6–7; self-made, 166; in society, 91–2, 134, 335; and the state, 113, 136, 240–1, 242–3, 272, 329, 347, 348, 354

inequality, 166–7, 248, 341

infinity, 404

institutions, 264, 270–1, 271–2

interculturalism, 349–50

Inuit. See aboriginal peoples; Native Canadians

irony, 315; in comedy, 315; in tragedy, 255, 303, 323, 394

irrationality, 382

Islam, 247

Jackson Preece, Jennifer, 180

Jaffer, Rahim, 458n15

Jamaica, 64

James, C.L.R., 440n23

James, William, 79

Japanese Canadians, 147

Jay, John, 437n8

Jesus Christ, 247–8, 399, 417, 451n19

Jewish Canadians, 447n13

Jezebel, 66

Judaeo-Christian mythology, 45–6, 414. See also Adam; Christian mythology; Eve

Judaism, 247

jus soli, 281, 286

justice, 145, 173–6, 332, 378, 399; as arbitrary, 199; in Canada, 236, 247, 334, 373–4, 387–8, 411; Christian, 45, 301, 303; distributive, 178; as fairness, 352, 366, 369; as freedom, 380; liberal, 51;

and multiculturalism, 139, 145, 338; and reason, 383; and tragedy, 256, 378; and transcendence, 378. *See also* social justice

Just Society, 353, 361–2, 379

Kala Pani, 146, 464n4

Kant, Immanuel: on happiness, 173, 474n35; on the imagination, 353; on the individual, 429; and mediation, 350; on purity of heart, 352, 367–8; on reasoning, 367–8; on social order, 67; on universal law, 472n42; on utopia, 340

Kent, Tom, 128

Kerr, Walter, 197–8, 199

King, Martin Luther, Jr, 440n23

King, William Lyon Mackenzie, 265

knowing, ways of, 196, 299–300, 301, 403

knowledge, 69, 70, 101, 245–6

Kojève, Alexandre: on Canadian citizenship, 353, 358; on conformity, 347; on cosmopolitanism, 340–3, 355; debate with Strauss, 329–30, 334, 338–9, 349; on the individual, 355; on master-and-slave relationship, 342, 424–5; on the real, 431; on recognition, 336–7; on the state, 338

Kolbenschlag, Madonna, 85–6

Kore, 202, 205

Krabbe, Hugh, 61–2, 182

Kurdistan, 181

Kymlicka, Will: on the individual, 354; on liberal democracy, 264; on multiculturalism, 71, 352, 394–5, 457n2; on social mores, 165; on societal culture, 181–2; on tolerance, 164, 168

labour: as alienation, 416; forced, 129–30; meaningful, 391; sex as metaphor for, 406–7

Laforest, Guy, 162

language, 91, 336; and culture, 318; failure of, 246; and knowledge, 245–6; mother tongue, 51; in multiculturalism, 136–8; official, 185, 363; statistics on, 285. *See also* bilingualism

Laqueur, Walter, 459n18

Latin America, 120

Laurendeau–Dunton Commission, 144, 311, 312, 319, 401

law, 152, 230, 399–400, 404; in comedy, 256; in democracy, 411; disruption of, 374–5; natural, 177, 269, 399; as pragmatism, 335; reason in, 172; and the state, 148–9, 182–3

legends, 15

Lévesque, René, 322

Leviathan, 46, 67, 103–4

Levinas, Emmanuel, 245

liberal democracy, 14, 18, 49–50, 116, 148, 183; Canada as, 187; communitarian, 350; individual and society in, 65; and pluralism, 264; pluralism in, 180; tolerance in, 313

liberalism: bleeding-heart, 273; contradictions of, 254

Lincoln, Abraham, 23–4, 143, 155, 225

lineage, ancient, 441n13. *See also* old-timers

Liodakis, Nikolaos, 118

Lippmann, Walter, 437n8

literature, Canadian, 304, 310–11, 386, 387

Llewellyn, Karl N., 174
Locke, John, 46, 67, 246
London (England) 459n18
Loney, Martin, 296–7
lordship and bondage, 135–6, 150, 315–16, 386, 389; in Christian mythology, 177; freedom under, 143; of immigrants, 389–90; multiculturalism as, 213, 214; under pluralism, 267–8; as relationship, 79, 214; of the sovereign, 390
love, 3–4, 8, 78, 240–1, 405, 418, 429; as beauty, 203; biblical, 451n19; and immortality, 205; as mediator, 418, 421; in multiculturalism, 141, 157, 238, 384; need or desire for, 27, 133; Prince Charming and, 73; and recognition, 334; as recognition, 168; rejection of, 75; and sacrifice, 175; and sex, 203, 406; sharing as, 195; spiritual, 97; and the state, 119. See also embrace
Lugard, Frederick, 117
Lurie, Alison, 71–2

Machiavelli, Niccolò, 114–16; on colonization, 107; on the common good, 411; on death, 421; on fear, 166; on law, 411–12; on state formation and governance, 119; on survival, 27, 75; on tyranny, 332, 410–12
Mack the Knife, 64
MacLennan, Hugh, 285
Macpherson, C.B., 153, 393, 394, 395
Madison, James, 437n8
majority rule, 156, 362–3
Malthusianism, 117
Maritain, Jacques, 243–4, 273

marriage, 197
Marshall, T.H., 167, 340
Martin, Rex, 244
martyrdom, 417–18, 419
Marx, Karl, 134, 414
masks, 69–70
Massey-Lévesque Commission, 305–7, 308, 309, 310–11, 312, 318, 402
master–slave relationship, 316, 424–5; multiculturalism as, 214
material dialectics, 249
McCarthy, Thomas, 194
McGregor, David, 254
McMahon, Darren, 173, 192–3
Mead, George Herbert, 53, 97–8, 104, 196, 443n3
Meadows, Paul, 100–1
meaninglessness, 401–2
media, 270; on immigration, 234–5, 251–2
mediator, 350, 413, 416, 477n30; death of, 416; love as, 418, 421; the state as, 288
melancholia, 83, 153, 246
melting pot, 227–8
men, as storytellers, 55
meritocracy, 371
Merriam, C.E., Jr, 152
metanoia, 65, 376–7, 399, 416; of Bad John, 86; defined, 24, 86; and reconciliation, 423–4
Mexican–American War, 118
Milton, John, 207
minorities, 180; accommodation of, 260; ethnic, 228–9; recognition of, 385; visible, 184–5, 225, 284, 285
minorityism, 152
minority rights, 26, 183–4, 213, 267, 361, 363, 450n14
misrecognition, 23

Mitchell, Margaret, 223–4
mobility, 29, 370, 373
modernity, 8, 98, 101, 413; alienation in, 212–13; individual in, 329, 330
monarchy, 115
Moses, 477n30
multiculturalism: achievements of, 234; as American, 42–5; in Australia, 36; Canadian, 32, 103, 130–1, 235, 401–2 (see also official multiculturalism); as comedy, 150; as a common good, 239, 245; contract theory of, 157–8, 178–9, 213–14; criticism of, 26, 35, 103, 364–5, 384; egalitarian or hubless, 355–6, 370; in Europe, 190, 195, 438n9; hub-and-spoke, 355, 359, 370; as lordship and bondage, 213; models of, 354–5, 355–6, 359–60, 364; as path, 105; performance of, 189, 245; as pragmatism, 44, 219, 231; recognition in, 381–2; and sovereignty, 230; as tragedy, 152–3, 256–7; transcendent, 200; in the United Kingdom, 36; in the United States, 34–5. See also genuine multiculturalism; official multiculturalism
multiculturalization, 189
Muslims, 39, 40; in Canada, 253, 284, 456n24, 458n15; in Europe, 459n18, 461n19; women, 251, 470n7
myths: black women in, 441n17; function of, 15. See also Christian mythology; founding myths

Naipaul, V.S., 250
nationalism, 19–20, 362; ethnic, 19–20, 371

nation-state. See state, the
Native Americans, 118
Native Canadians: apology to, 146–7; in bicultural Canada, 318, 349; under colonialism, 118–19; displacement of, 129–30, 151, 252; in a Just Society, 361–2; living conditions of, 357; in multiculturalism, 359, 436n3; relationship to Canada, 211
Nature: in the Americas, 109; Bad Johns in, 80–1, 84, 88; Canadians and, 122–3
negotiation, 368, 369–70, 383; federal–provincial, 352, 358
Nelson, Hilde Lindemann, 101–2
neo-Hegelian argument, 77
Netherlands, 20, 40, 115
Nettleford, Rex, 85
Niebuhr, Reinhold, 50, 79–80, 98, 443n17
9/11, 42, 377
nobility, 232, 233, 386
non-recognition, 23
Nozick, Robert, 471n29

Obama, Barack, 38
October crisis, 353
Oedipus, 5, 247
official bilingualism, 273, 354, 363official multiculturalism: as Canadian, 31; creation of, 144–5, 150, 237, 312, 357; criticism of, 234–5, 350, 461n19; equality in, 380–1; ethnic fairs and rituals in, 112–13; as exportable, 394; failures of, 373; freedom in, 151, 380–1; v. genuine multiculturalism, 402; goals of, 106–7; as improvisation, 457n2; v. interculturalism, 349–50;

justice in, 145; legislation, 259–60, 459n17; narrative of, 51; as pragmatism, 219; purpose of, 125–6, 129, 183–4, 229, 230–1, 232, 437n4; radicalism of, 273; recognition in, 381–2; as tragedy, 238, 378; as unhappy consciousness, 349, 401–2

old-timers, 210–11, 276; beliefs of, 58; and change, 53, 425, 431–2; in comedy, 279–80, 287, 431–2; language of, 137–8, 140, 141; as Sleeping Beauties, 57; social death of, 278, 430; as stoics, 280; in tragedy, 256–7, 423

oligarchy, 115–16

Omi, Michael, 227–8

opportunity, 28, 380

Oracle of Delphi, 332

Orgad, Yoav, 39, 40

Organisation for Economic Development and Co-operation (OECD), 291

Orientalism, 265

Oslo, 39

Othello, 6

outsiders, 260

ownership, 56, 130, 348

Palmer, Howard, 228–9

Paradise Lost, 207

Parizeau, Jacques, 319–20

patriarchy, 406, 410, 441n17

patriotism, 51, 240, 348

Patterson, Orlando, 23

pensions, 290

people, the: in the Americas, 217; in democracy, 155–6; in multiculturalism, 250

perception, 403, 408–9, 421

performance, 196–7, 245

Pericles, 155

Persephone, 202

personalism, 273

personhood, 3–4, 6–7

Pichette, Yvon, 361

planning, 345–6

Plato: on death, 205–6, 406, 421; on history, 355; on the individual, 330; on love, 203, 205; on practicality, 233; on tyranny, 410; on utopia, 396

play, 207, 391, 430

pluralism, 190, 195, 238, 267–9; in Canada, 349; and inequality, 341; in liberal democracy, 264

points system, 285–6, 358

political correctness, 238

political rights, 167

Politics (Aristotle), 255, 442n23

Polynices, 69

poneria, 207, 208–10, 406, 427, 429–30

Popper, Karl, 242

Porter, John, 322

post-colonialism, 120–1

power: and authority, 52; and corruption, 362; diffusion of, 45, 154, 155; in genuine multiculturalism, 134

pragmatism, 249, 334; multiculturalism as, 44, 196, 200, 212, 219, 231

Prince, The (Machiavelli), 27, 107, 115

Prince Charming, 50, 55, 68–9, 72–3, 428; accommodation of, 56; Adam as prototype of, 170, 201; as a Bad John, 57; immigrant as, 210, 403; Lincoln as, 24; and Snow White, 54; and the state, 54, 55; as stoic,

70, 280; as symbol of love, 73; in
    tragedy, 193
procreation, 204, 206
Prometheus, 6, 209
Proudhon, P.J., 471n29
Proust, Marcel, 186
Prus, Robert, 196
Puerto Rico, 181
punishment, 399–401
purity of heart, 28, 351–2, 368,
    472n42

Quebec: accommodation in, 155,
    181, 220–1, 221–2, 223, 225, 233,
    334, 349, 451n21; biculturalism
    in, 435n3; disputes with Canada,
    319, 353, 385; immigrants in, 320,
    322; multiculturalism in, 180–1,
    252, 319, 322, 349–50, 363; rec-
    ognition of, 353; Pierre Trudeau
    in, 25
Quebec separatism, 144, 218, 221,
    317, 319–20, 321; argument
    against, 354; as negotiation, 369–
    70; referenda, 319–20, 321, 358

racialization, 66, 151, 227–8, 282,
    373, 437n4
racism, 138, 268–9, 300, 324, 348,
    438n9
radical democracy, 20–1, 187, 338;
    equality and, 243–4; genuine multi-
    culturalism as, 22–3, 134, 153,
    250, 395, 408
Rapunzel, 71
rationality, 299, 303; and action, 314;
    as comedy, 145; the folk as, 33; as
    gendered, 204; and justice, 139,
    383; and purity of heart, 367–8;
    rarity of, 34, 382

Rawls, John: on citizenship, 271; on
    the common good, 368; on happi-
    ness, 474n35; on justice, 50–1,
    352, 358, 361, 369, 371; on per-
    spective, 367; on persuasion, 366–
    7; on purity of heart, 351–2,
    472n42; on social behaviour, 52–3;
    on social contracts, 213; on the
    state, 149
reality, 334, 343, 431; in language,
    245–6; as social construction,
    345–6
reason. See rationality
rebellion of 1837–8, 127
rebirth, 376–7. See also metanoia
recognition, 53, 160–4, 273–6, 304–
    6, 393–4; choice as, 396; and citi-
    zenship, 6, 56; in comedy, 315;
    desire for, 9–11, 159–60; exter-
    nal, 275, 310–11, 319; of foreign
    credentials, 261, 262, 296; and
    identity, 28; internal, 243, 274,
    275–6, 313, 315, 317, 318, 319,
    321, 323, 336–7, 381, 385, 386,
    393–4; intersubjective, 308, 313,
    381, 383; justice and, 313–14;
    language of, 136; and love, 68,
    168, 334; in multiculturalism,
    12–13, 27, 158–9, 319, 381–2,
    408; objective, 313, 381, 385;
    politics of, 258, 273–4; of
    Quebec, 353; right to, 26; in
    tragedy, 315, 316, 323, 382–3,
    394; tragic, 275, 313
reconciliation, 392, 407, 414, 415–
    16, 421–4; Christian, 413, 477n30;
    as play, 430; in tragedy, 315, 382–3
redemption, 113, 176–8, 333
refugees, 390
Reitz, Jeffrey, 296

religion: Bad Johns and, 86–7; in Barbados, 76; in Canada, 247, 284, 285; and the state, 182; and tyranny, 411

reproduction, 204, 206

Republic (Plato), 396, 410

republicanism, 116

reservations, 21, 108, 151, 252

resurrection, 134, 413

revenge, 399–401

reversal, 383, 394

Ricœur, Paul, 238–9

rights, 156, 180; absolute, 26; charters of, 389; civil, 400; democratic, 55; natural, 158; political, 29, 340

ritual, 113

Robinson, Jonathan, 393

Roche, Mark William, 323

Romanow, Roy, 290

Romilly, Selwyn, 261

Roosevelt, Theodore, 118

Rorty, Richard, 185, 186

Rousseau, Jean-Jacques, 168, 369

Royal Commission on Aboriginal Peoples in Canada, 130

Royal Commission on Bilingualism and Biculturalism, 144, 311, 312, 319, 401

Royal Commission on National Developments in Arts, Letters and Science, 305–7, 308, 309, 310–11, 312, 318, 402

Rude Boy, 64

Sabine, George H., 182–3

Sacks, Jonathan, 175–6

sacrifice, 379, 390

safety net, 290

Said, Edward, 265

St Kitts, 115

St Laurent, Louis, 306

St Paul, 342

salt of the land, 403

Sarkozy, Nicolas, 461n19

Sarraut, Albert, 117

Sartre, Jean-Paul, 157, 245, 316

Satzewich, Vic, 118

scepticism, 139, 275; Bad Johns and, 70, 280; and comedy, 415; of immigrants, 280

Scotland, 181

Scott, Dred, 220

secularism, 302

segregation, 21

self, aspects of, 79

self-consciousness, 77–8

self-determination, 29, 151, 221

self-recognition. *See* recognition: internal

self-sacrifice, 67

separatism, 21, 144, 181. *See also* Quebec separatism

settler communities, 42–3, 107, 129–30, 341

sex, 405–7. *See also* embrace; *poneria*

Shakespeare, William, 396

Sharansky, Natan, 376

Shari'a law, 456n24

sharing, 194–6; of bodies, 404, 405, 407; as embrace, 429–30; in multiculturalism, 238, 403–4

Shepard, Walter J., 182–3

Shklar, Judith, 133, 406

Singh, Aakash, 330, 332

Sisyphus, 85

slavery, 129–30, 131, 133, 146; accommodation and, 56; and freedom, 143, 147; legacy of, 159–60; multiculturalism and, 139, 144 slaves: descendants of, 159–60

Sleeping Beauty, 56, 410; death and rebirth of, 50, 57, 428; v. Eve, 201; socialization by, 54; and the state, 54, 55

Smith, Adam, 99

Smith, Anthony, 19–20

Snow White. *See* Sleeping Beauty

social, the, 182

social construction, 345–6, 430; of justice, 175; negated by citizenship, 5; and power, 254

social contract, 150, 175–6, 213–14

social Darwinism, 117

social drama, 100–1

social imagination, 122–3, 334

socialization, 34, 179, 241, 243, 250–1; attitudes to, 214–15; of Bad Johns, 83–5, 88–90, 249; as bridge between tragedy and comedy, 378, 379; in Christian mythology, 177–8; in genuine multiculturalism, 12; and identity, 28; of immigrants, 239–40, 250–1, 390; limits of, 7; as tragedy, 390; by women, 54, 83–6, 201, 202

social justice, 28, 178, 248, 371; in Canada, 174, 260, 266; Christian basis of, 164; as love, 8; and official multiculturalism, 52; and tolerance, 189

social mobility, 56–7, 373

social order, 67

social stratification, 254–5; basis of, 176; in Canada, 151; and socialization, 179, 184; and social justice, 28

social welfare, 55

societal culture, 181–2, 264, 352, 387, 395

Socrates, 205–6, 215–16, 396, 406, 410

South Africa, 151, 223

sovereignty, 65, 217, 343, 388; absolute, 142; changeableness of the sovereign, 394; collective achievement of, 170; as culture, 182; in genuine multiculturalism, 152; in lordship and bondage, 390; and multiculturalism, 230; and rights, 26; of the state, 147–9, 217. *See also* federalism; state rights

Soviet Union, 151

spirit: non-transcendental, 77–9; phenomenology of, 101; of the times, 60, 62–3

Stagger Lee, 64

Stanfield, Robert, 266

state, the: absolute, 143; in the Americas, 111, 112; and change, 53, 168; death of, 4–5, 13; as ethical consciousness, 240; fear and, 119; and God, 80, 103–4, 134–6, 343; and happiness, 211; and the individual, 113, 136, 240–1, 242–3, 272, 329, 347, 348, 354; language of, 141–2; as lordship and bondage, 386; and love, 78, 114; as mediator, 288; minimalist, 471n29; postmodern, 351; rational, 382; rebirth of, 134; and religion, 413–14; sovereignty of, 147–9, 217; strong, 362; as time, 134; as unhappy consciousness, 52; universal, 330, 337, 341

state formation, 26, 65, 149, 163, 180–1, 249

state rights, 218, 220

Statistics Canada, 251, 280, 281, 284, 360

Steinberg, Stephen, 118, 268
Stoffman, Daniel, 295
stoicism, 139, 142, 275, 280, 339; of Prince Charmings and Sweet Boys, 70, 280; and tragedy, 415
stratification. *See* social stratification
Strauss, Leo: on·citizenship, 355; on conformity, 123–4; debate with Kojève, 329–30, 334, 338–9, 349; on the individual, 337; on individuals and the state, 229, 333, 347; on the state, 334; on theory and practice, 172; on tyranny, 334–5, 342, 409
subjecthood, 160, 162–3, 168, 274, 299
suicide, 417–18, 419
Supreme Court of Canada, 148, 221, 222, 267, 358, 450n14
Sweden, 20, 294
Sweet Boy, 69, 170; immigrant as, 288, 403; misrecognition of, 229; as stoic, 280; and tragedy, 193
symbolic interaction, 196
Symposium (Plato), 205–6, 406

Tamil Eelam, 181
Tasmania, 181
taxation, 290
Taylor, Charles: on authenticity, 62; biculturalism in, 393; on citizenship, 339; on civility, 346–7; on dignity, 272–3; on the good, 80; on instinct, 443n17; on language, 446n3; on loss, 141; on master–slave dialectics, 316; on the modern individual, 241; on modernity, 249; on multiculturalism, 97, 158–9, 318, 349, 359–60; on recognition, 97, 158–9, 160–3, 168, 315,

319, 382; on social imaginaries, 334
technology, 293, 295
temptresses, 55, 201
Ten Commandments, 179–80
terrorism, 41–2, 147, 148, 253, 295
theory and practice, 172, 300, 449n2
theyness, 241
thrownness, 158
Tillich, Paul, 203
time, 73, 134, 141; represented by Bad John and Prince Charming, 72, 74
Tocqueville, Alexis de, 447n4
tolerance, 90, 164–5, 187–9, 368; in liberal democracy, 313; in multiculturalism, 168, 184, 238
Toronto Hegelian school, 46, 388
Toronto Star, 456n24
Touraine, Alain, 195
tragedy, 58, 168–9, 192–4, 196–7, 230, 231–2, 303, 377, 452n2; Canada as, 241, 253–4, 303, 310, 388; conversion to comedy, 102, 178, 197–8, 210, 323–4, 378, 394, 395, 413; death in, 60–1; end of, 15; fear in, 255; good and evil in, 232; of the human condition, 170, 200, 231, 315, 378, 423; irony in, 323, 394; and justice, 378; multiculturalism as, 102, 105, 152–3, 212, 238, 256–7, 378, 431; privileging of, 198; as quest for freedom, 200; recognition in, 315, 316, 323, 382–3, 394; reversal in, 394; society as, 390; and stoicism, 415; thought and, 203; tyranny as, 412; and unhappiness, 215
tragic hero, 196, 197
transcendence, 378, 407

transmission, 195

Trudeau, Pierre Elliott: accomplishments and failures of, 25, 51, 272,
352, 353, 357, 358, 359, 366, 370,
371, 379, 380, 383–4, 386; on
biculturalism, 385; on
Canadianness, 353–4, 381; on the
Charter of Rights and Freedoms,
357–8; on equality, 207–8; on federalism, 126, 129, 383; on government record, 51; on immigration,
365; on individualism, 336; influences on, 52, 273, 361, 362; on justice, 174, 352–3, 361–2, 370, 380,
383, 384, 472n42; on language,
318, 363, 385; on multiculturalism,
44, 153, 265, 266, 336, 338, 355–
6, 359–60, 364, 365, 370, 379,
380–1; on Quebec, 127; on reason,
382; on rights, 362; on sharing,
194–5; on social contracts, 213; on
the state, 103, 337, 362; as tragic
figure, 25; on the US Civil War,
126–7, 129; on values, 384

truth, 404, 405

Tully, Patricia, 289

tyranny, 409–10; absolute, 142, 143;
benevolent, 148–9, 334–5, 354;
and the common good, 331; conditions for, 115; and freedom, 142–3;
limits on, 148; in multiculturalism,
332–3; as tragedy, 412

tyrants, 27, 51–2, 249, 331–2,
442n23; as unhappy consciousnesses, 52

unchangeable, the, 412; death of,
113, 247–8, 416, 417, 421, 423

unhappiness, 14, 215, 401–2

unhappy consciousness, 224, 368,
412–13; and change, 395; goal of,
112; Hegel on, 111, 112; immigrant as, 392; in modern society,
143; multiculturalism as, 349,
401–2; reconciliation in, 415–16;
society as, 390; the state as, 52;
tyrant as, 52. See also under
Canada

United Kingdom, 20, 36, 40, 185,
268, 459n18

United Nations, 44

United States: accommodation in,
151–2, 225–7; African Americans,
86, 114, 218, 220, 221; Bad Johns
in, 64; conflict with Mexico, 118;
creation of, 246–7; culture of,
437n8; demographic change in,
37–9, 40, 156; as European, 24;
immigration and immigrants, 147,
219, 228; master narrative, 185;
multiculturalism and pluralism in,
34–5, 267; relations with Canada,
127; rights in, 179; as tragedy, 215;
US South, 110–11; women in, 86

Universal Declaration of Human
Rights, 407

universities, 270

US Bill of Rights, 179

US Civil War, 24, 26, 120, 150, 181,
222–3; alternate history, 223; in
Canada, 219; as failure of
European model, 21; goals of, 23;
legacy of, 126–8, 129, 217–18,
220, 225, 227, 267, 312; lesson of,
149

US constitution, 179

usurpers, 55

utopia, 238, 340, 394, 395, 396